# THE PAPERS OF
# WOODROW WILSON

## VOLUME 26

SPONSORED BY THE WOODROW WILSON
FOUNDATION
AND PRINCETON UNIVERSITY

# THE PAPERS OF
# WOODROW
# WILSON

CONTENTS AND INDEX, VOLUMES 14–25

Volume 26 · 1902–1912

PRINCETON UNIVERSITY PRESS
PRINCETON, NEW JERSEY
1980

*Note to scholars*: Princeton University Press
subscribes to the Resolution on Permissions of
the Association of American University Presses,
defining what we regard as "fair use" of copyrighted works. This Resolution, intended to en-
courage scholarly use of university press publications and to avoid unnecessary applications
for permission, is obtainable from the Press or
from the A.A.U.P. central office. Note, however,
that the scholarly apparatus, transcripts of
shorthand, and the texts of Wilson documents
as they appear in this volume are copyrighted,
and the usual rules about the use of copyrighted materials apply.

Publication of this book has been aided by a
grant from the National Historical Publications
and Records Commission.

Printed in the United States of America
by Princeton University Press
Princeton, New Jersey

# CONTENTS

# EXPLANATORY NOTE

THE Table of Contents is divided into two sections: Wilson Materials and Collateral Materials. Together, they include, under established editorial headings and in alphabetical order, all the items printed in Volumes 14-25. Wilson's outgoing and incoming letters are listed in two alphabets, and collateral letters are listed in one alphabet by name of sender. Editorial Notes are listed separately under Collateral Materials. Wilson's public addresses, statements, reports and related materials, and writings are arranged chronologically, as are important subsections under main headings, such as New Jersey and Princeton University.

Illustrations and text illustrations are listed separately.

The index includes all persons, places, and subjects mentioned in the text and footnotes. All books, articles, pamphlets, and poems are indexed by author and title. Book titles and plays appear in italics; quotation marks are omitted for articles, editorials, and poems. Page references to footnotes which carry a comma between the page number and the "n" cite both text and footnote, thus: "162,n1." Absence of the comma indicates reference to the footnote only, thus: "286n3."

All entries consisting of page numbers only and which refer to concepts, issues, and opinions (such as democracy, the tariff, the money trust, leadership, and labor problems), are references to Wilson's speeches and writings. Page references that follow the symbol Δ in such entries refer to the opinions and comments of others who are identified. The present index supersedes the individual indexes of Volumes 14-25 in that it corrects errors and omissions discovered since their publication. *Subjects* are indexed selectively, not exhaustively; this is not intended to be a concordance to Wilson's writings.

The late M. Halsey Thomas indexed Volumes 14-23 and began the consolidation of these indexes. Phyllis L. Marchand indexed Volumes 24 and 25. The initial arrangement of the Table of Contents was done by Sylvia Elvin. The Table of Contents and major entries in the Index were checked against the volumes by Manfred Boemeke and Thomas J. Knock. The typescript was prepared by Karen F. Dennis and Muriel K. Godbout. David W. Hirst was general editor of this volume and gave his time and energies unstintingly to it.

**THE EDITOR**

*Princeton, New Jersey*
*September 24, 1979*

THE PAPERS OF
# WOODROW WILSON
VOLUME 26

# CONTENTS
## FOR VOLUMES 14–25

### WILSON MATERIALS

Anecdote about a classroom incident, April 23, 1904, **15,** 272

Appeals

Funds for the John Miller House, Princeton, N. J., Oct. 21, 1905, **16,** 197; Oct. 28, 1905, **16,** 208

Relief for Manchuria, Feb. 10, 1911, **22,** 416

Diaries, pocket notebooks, and engagement and record books

1902–1903: Sept. 1, 1902–Aug. 31, 1903, described, **14,** 122

1903: Jan. 1–Dec. 31, 1903, described, **14,** 308

1903–1904: Jan 1, 1903–Dec.31, 1904, described, **14,** 308

1903: April 30–June 30, 1903, described, **14,** 436

1903: July 10–Sept. 22, 1903, **14,** 521

1904: Jan. 1–Dec. 31, 1904, described, **15,** 114

1904, entries: Jan. 1, **15,** 115; Jan. 3, **15,** 117; Jan. 4, **15,** 117; Jan. 5, **15,** 118; Jan. 6, **15,** 119; Jan. 7, **15,** 119; Jan. 8, **15,** 119; Jan. 9, **15,** 120; Jan. 10, **15,** 120; Jan. 11, **15,** 121; Jan. 12, **15,** 121; Jan. 13, **15,** 126; Jan. 14, **15,** 131; Jan. 15, **15,** 131; Jan. 16, **15,** 134; Jan. 17, **15,** 134; Jan. 18, **15,** 135; Jan. 19, **15,** 135; Jan. 20, **15,** 136; Jan. 21, **15,** 137; Jan. 22, **15,** 137; Jan. 23, **15,** 139; Jan. 24, **15,** 140; Jan. 25, **15,** 140; Jan. 26, **15,** 140; Jan. 27, **15,** 141; Jan. 28, **15,** 142; Jan. 29, **15,** 146; Jan. 30, **15,** 151; Jan. 31, **15,** 152; Feb. 1, **15,** 153; Feb. 2, **15,** 154; Feb. 3, **15,** 155; Feb. 4, **15,** 156; Feb. 5, **15,** 159; Feb. 6, **15,** 161; Feb. 7, **15,** 162; Feb. 8, **15,** 164; Feb. 9, **15,** 164; Feb. 10, **15,** 165; Feb. 11, **15,** 165; Feb. 12, **15,** 166; Feb. 13, **15,** 167

1905: Jan. 1–Dec. 31, 1905 (2), described, **15,** 574

1906: Jan. 1–Dec. 31, 1906, described, **16,** 277

1907: Jan. 1–Dec. 31, 1907 (2), described, **16,** 542

Interviews

Impressions of a western tour of Princeton alumni groups, May 16, 1903, **14,** 459

Weaknesses in the college curriculum, June 11, 1905, **16,** 113

The effects of the Quadrangle Plan, Sept. 25, 1907, **17,** 399

Plans to continue promotion of the Quadrangle Plan, Oct. 18, 1907, **17,** 444

The financial situation in the East and football reforms, Nov. 8, 1907, **17,** 472

The Democratic nominee in 1908, Nov. 11, 1907, **17,** 489

Political and economic conditions, Nov. 24, 1907, **17,** 513

Woman suffrage and state feeding of children, March 3, 1908, **18,** 3

Upper class clubs, Oct. 17, 1908, **18,** 465

A national newspaper, March 19, 1909, **19,** 110

Misrepresentations of an address at St. Paul's School, Concord, N. H., June 9, 1909, **19,** 238

On seeking office, July 9, 1910, **20,** 567

The gubernatorial nomination, July 11, 1910, **20,** 572

The receptive candidate, July 20, 1910, **21,** 14

Alleged Wall Street connections, Sept. 16, 1910, **21,** 98

Publicity of campaign contributions and the control of corporations, Sept. 17, 1910, **21,** 120

Regulation of corporations, tariff reform, and conservation, Sept. 17, 1910, **21,** 125

Governmental supervision of corporations, Sept. 18, 1910, **21,** 134

No pledges, no promises, and the right of labor to organize, Sept. 28, 1910, **21,** 179

A candidate's principles, Oct. 2, 1910, **21,** 220

Political graft, Oct. 30, 1910, **21,** 477

Government for the people and party organization, Nov. 3, 1910, **21,** 522

Pitiless publicity as the cure for the ills of government, Nov. 10, 1910, **22,** 5

Servant of all classes and all interests, Nov. 10, 1910, **22,** 9

The new Democratic party and its opportunity, Dec. 18, 1910, **22,** 216

The senatorial contest, Dec. 21, 1910, **22,** 235

State regulation of corporations, Jan. 8, 1911, **22,** 312

Reform governor and practical politician, Jan. 17, 1911, **22,** 354

Party lines and progressivism, April 13, 1911, **22,** 554

The hour of opportunity for the Democratic party, April 30, 1911, **22,** 591

Trusting public opinion, May 5, 1911, **23,** 3

The presidency of the United States, May 9, 1911, **23,** 26

The presidency as a goal, May 13, 1911, **23,** 44

Oregon leading the way, May 18, 1911, **23,** 60

The Oregon system and progressive measures in New Jersey, May 20, 1911, **23,** 76

The governor as legislative leader, Aug. 19, 1911, **23,** 277

State responsibility *vs.* federal power, Aug. 26, 1911, **23,** 292

The Money Trust, Sept. 11, 1911, **23,** 312

The vital issues, Oct. 1, 1911, **23,** 366

Primary and election reform, Oct. 16, 1911, **23,** 454

Progressive Democracy and the issues, Dec. 24, 1911, **23,** 607

The major questions and the Governor's answers, Dec. 24, 1911, **23,** 614

Family life and general observations, Jan. 26, 1912, **24,** 74

Disclosure of campaign fund sources, April 30, 1912, **24,** 368

An alleged interview in the Governor's office, Jan. 22, 1912, **24,**
60; denial and protest, Jan. 23, 1912, **24,** 62

Conduct of the campaign, Oct. 22, 1912, **25,** 451

Letters and telegrams from Wilson to

Frank Frost Abbott, March 3, 1908, **18,** 5; April 6, 1908, **18,** 226

Charles Francis Adams, April 11, 1907, **17,** 104; Oct. 4, 1907, **17,**
417; Feb. 4, 1909, **19,** 23; May 29, 1909, **19,** 223; June 21, 1909,
**19,** 264

Edwin Plimpton Adams, July 17, 1907, **17,** 287

John Haslup Adams, June 21, 1912, **24,** 491

Cyrus Adler, Oct. 21, 1912, **25,** 450

Henry Mills Alden, Oct. 24, 1906, **16,** 471; Aug. 4, 1895, **17,** 620

Edwin Anderson Alderman, Jan. 29, 1903, **14,** 334; March 20,
1907, **17,** 86; June 6, 1912, **24,** 462

James Waddel Alexander, Dec. 24, 1902, **14,** 304; Dec. 31, 1903,
**15,** 113; Nov. 12, 1910, **22,** 30

Walter N. Alexander, Dec. 3, 1912, **25,** 580

Charles Dexter Allen, Sept. 26, 1910, **21,** 171

American Philosophical Society, secretary, March 21, 1905, **16,** 36

James Burrill Angell, May 17, 1907, **17,** 149

Robert Edwards Annin, Oct. 4, 1904, **15,** 504

Harry Howard Armstrong, Sept. 3, 1907, **17,** 370

Benjamin Palmer Axson, April 3, 1912, **24,** 285

Stockton Axson (full name: Isaac Stockton Keith Axson II), June
28, 1903, **14,** 498; July 31, 1908, **18,** 385

John Arthur Aylward, March 7, 1912, **24,** 226

John Hampden Chamberlayne Bagby, Dec. 8, 1903, **15,** 68

Warren Worth Bailey, March 29, 1911, **22,** 523; Aug. 7, 1911, **23,**
257

Baker, Christian S., Mrs., April 20, 1903, **14,** 417

Ray Stannard Baker, Feb. 8, 1911, **22,** 412; July 18, 1911, **23,** 217;
July 24, 1911, **23,** 226

Stephen Baker, Nov. 27, 1909, **19,** 535; Dec. 3, 1909, **19,** 545

James Mark Baldwin, Dec. 25, 1903, **15,** 108

Simeon Eben Baldwin, Nov. 9, 1910, **21,** 590

Daniel Moreau Barringer, Sept. 16, 1902, **14,** 131; Sept. 26, 1902,
**14,** 134; Feb. 19, 1904, **15,** 174; April 11, 1904, **15,** 242; Feb. 2,
1903, **15,** 581; Sept. 20, 1905, **16,** 187; Sept. 21, 1905, **16,** 187;
Feb. 16, 1909, **19,** 49; March 27, 1909, **19,** 125; April 3, 1909, **19,**
148; July 27, 1911, **23,** 232; Sept. 14, 1911, **23,** 327; Oct. 6, 1911,
**23,** 409; Dec. 28, 1911, **23,** 631; Jan. 4, 1912, **23,** 651

Bruce Barton, Sept. 7, 1911, **23,** 305

James Christy Bell, Nov. 16, 1909, **19,** 504

John Mirza Bennett, Jr., July 17, 1907, **17,** 287

Herman Bernstein, July 6, 1911, **23,** 191

Albert Jeremiah Beveridge, June 17, 1902, **19,** 758; Nov. 11, 1903, **19,** 759

Hiram Bingham, May 10, 1906, **16,** 388; March 15, 1905, **22,** 606; March 21, 1905, **22,** 607

Sarah Baxter Bird, April 13, 1904, **15,** 244

Charles Clarke Black, Jan. 11, 1907, **16,** 560 (2)

Anita McCormick Blaine, Nov. 8, 1909, **19,** 486; Nov. 30, 1912, **25,** 570

Betty Brese Blodget, Jan. 26, 1903, **14,** 333

Ernest Ludlow Bogart, May 5, 1909, **19,** 183

James W. Bones, Nov. 30, 1912, **25,** 569

Gutzon Borglum, Aug. 12, 1905, **16,** 178

Henry Eldridge Bourne, Sept. 27, 1900, **16,** 564

Jonathan Bourne, Jr., Nov. 13, 1910, **22,** 36

Herbert E. Bowen, Aug. 13, 1910, **21,** 53

Harry Laity Bowlby, Jan. 3, 1907, **16,** 546; Sept. 15, 1910, **21,** 90

Joseph McCarter Bowyer, May 23, 1908, **18,** 305

Thomas Duckett Boyd, Oct. 12, 1909, **19,** 411

Clarence Valentine Boyer, July 15, 1902, **14,** 13

John Joseph Bracken, Dec. 20, 1910, **22,** 230

Cyrus Fogg Brackett, April 10, 1908, **18,** 257

Gamaliel Bradford, Feb. 12, 1907, **17,** 32

William James Lee Bradley, Oct. 3, 1911, **23,** 381

Louis Dembitz Brandeis, Sept. 27, 1912, **25,** 272; Sept. 29, 1912, **25,** 286; Oct. 4, 1912, **25,** 339; Nov. 13, 1912, **25,** 545

Marcus Braun, Feb. 7, 1912, **24,** 135

Henry Skillman Breckinridge, Nov. 5, 1909, **19,** 483; Dec. 21, 1910, **22,** 236; March 30, 1911, **22,** 525

Robert Gunn Bremner, July 9, 1910, **20,** 570

Robert Bridges, July 17, 1902, **14,** 21; Nov. 6, 1902, **14,** 199; Dec. 8, 1902, **14,** 267; Dec. 15, 1902, **14,** 293; March 21, 1903, **14,** 397; March 30, 1903, **14,** 403; April 20, 1903, **14,** 417; Nov. 11, 1903, **15,** 50; March 31, 1904, **15,** 223; June 6, 1904, **15,** 360; June 9, 1904, **15,** 361; June 16, 1904, **15,** 383; July 13, 1904, **15,** 411; Oct. 25, 1904, **15,** 530; Dec. 9, 1904, **15,** 571; April 28, 1905, **16,** 86; May 24, 1906, **16,** 405; Sept. 9, 1906, **16,** 451; Feb. 11, 1907, **17,** 31; Oct. 4, 1907, **17,** 417; Oct. 25, 1907, **17,** 456; May 25, 1908, **18,** 308; May 27, 1908, **18,** 310; Dec. 15, 1908, **18,** 549; March 23, 1909, **19,** 117; March 23, 1909, **19,** 119; March 27, 1909, **19,** 123; April 5, 1909, **19,** 149; April 12, 1909, **19,** 158; May 10, 1909, **19,** 190; Aug. 19, 1909, **19,** 347; Aug. 21, 1909, **19,** 348; Nov. 16, 1909, **19,** 503; Oct. 17, 1910, **21,** 337; Nov. 10, 1910, **22,** 12; Jan. 2, 1911, **22,** 287; Jan. 14, 1911, **22,** 333; Feb. 8, 1911, **22,** 411; Jan. 24, 1912, **24,** 66; Jan. 27, 1912, **24,** 82; Jan. 31, 1912, **24,** 100

Howard Allen Bridgman, Oct. 22, 1909, **19,** 441

Calvin Easton Brodhead, Sept. 5, 1910, **21,** 84; Dec. 15, 1910, **22,** 199, Dec. 21, 1910, **22,** 238; Jan. 6, 1911, **22,** 308

*Brooklyn Daily Eagle*, editor, Sept. 11, 1912, **25,** 135

Herbert Bruce Brougham, Feb. 1, 1910, **20,** 69; Feb. 5, 1910, **20,** 79; May 9, 1910, **20, 425**

Robert Foligny Broussard, June 19, 1912, **24,** 488

William Garrott Brown, Nov. 7, 1911, **23,** 542

Jessie Bones Brower, Nov. 30, 1912, **25,** 569

Charles Wayland Bryan, July 31, 1912, **24,** 574

William Jennings Bryan, March 15, 1912, **24,** 249; April 3, 1912, **24,** 284; June 6, 1912, **24,** 462; June 22, 1912, **24,** 493; July 6, 1912, **24,** 542; July 8, 1912, **24,** 543; July 16, 1912, **24,** 553; Nov. 6, 1912, **25,** 526; Nov. 9, 1912, **25,** 532; Nov. 12, 1912, **25,** 540; Nov. 23, 1912, **25,** 559; Dec. 26, 1912, **25,** 624; Dec. 31, 1912, **25,** 648

Lewis T. Bryant, Sept. 20, 1911, **23,** 340

James Bryce, March 23, 1903, **14,** 397; Dec. 17, 1910, **22,** 211; Nov. 9, 1912, **25,** 533

Charles August David Burk, Oct. 14, 1907, **17,** 432

Nicholas Murray Butler, Jan. 30, 1903, **14,** 335; April 26, 1906, **16,** 375; May 14, 1906, **16,** 395; June 1, 1906, **16,** 413; Dec. 6, 1906, **16,** 495

Witter Bynner, June 20, 1911, **23,** 160

Richard Evelyn Byrd, Nov. 6, 1912, **25,** 528

John Lambert Cadwalader, Jan. 14, 1904, **15,** 127; Dec. 12, 1908, **18,** 541; Dec. 18, 1908, **18,** 557; March 6, 1909, **19,** 81; April 21, 1909, **19,** 170; June 2, 1910, **20,** 497

James Callaway, Oct. 30, 1907, **17,** 461

Cambridge University, registrar of, Aug. 27, 1902, **14,** 112

Arnold Guyot Cameron, Nov. 18, 1903, **15,** 52

Walter Chauncey Camp, Percy Haughton, and Howard Houston Henry, Feb. 1, 1910, **20,** 72

John Alexander Campbell, Oct. 4, 1909, **19,** 402

Edward Capps, March 25, 1907, **17,** 91; April 24, 1907, **17,** 116; April 29, 1907, **17,** 123; May 7, 1907, **17,** 139; Jan. 10, 1908, **17,** 596

Andrew Carnegie, Dec. 27, 1902, **14,** 306; April 17, 1903, **14,** 411; April 18, 1905, **16,** 67; March 27, 1907, **17,** 95; March 29, 1907, **17,** 98; April 30, 1907, **17,** 124; Nov. 2, 1907, **17,** 466; Jan. 12, 1908, **17,** 599; Aug. 4, 1908, **18,** 391; Aug. 7, 1908, **18,** 392; Dec. 26, 1908, **18,** 565; Dec. 28, 1909, **19,** 635; March 23, 1911, **22,** 515; Dec. 11, 1911, **23,** 592

Louise Whitfield Carnegie, Aug. 18, 1908, **18,** 405; Nov. 17, 1909, **19,** 507

William Henry Carpenter, Oct. 9, 1907, **17,** 427; Jan. 16, 1908, **17,** 605; Feb. 17, 1908, **17,** 616

Howard Carrow, Nov. 11, 1910, **22,** 25

David Laurance Chambers, Nov. 27, 1902, **14,** 224

James Julius Chambers, June 3, 1905, **16,** 110

Joseph Hodges Choate, Nov. 1, 1911, **23,** 520

Moses Edwin Clapp, Aug. 31, 1912, **25,** 64

Champ Clark, Nov. 7, 1912, **25,** 529; Dec. 3, 1912, **25,** 577

John Bates Clark, May 29, 1908, **18,** 311

Dumont Clarke, Jr., Feb. 11, 1907, **17,** 31

Grover Cleveland, March 5, 1906, **16,** 323; Sept. 26, 1907, **17,** 400

James Harlan Cleveland, July 22, 1904, **15,** 420

William Morrison Coates, Aug. 25, 1902, **14,** 106

Solomon Solis Cohen, Sept. 16, 1911, **23,** 329

Varnum Lansing Collins, Feb. 23, 1903, **14,** 364; Dec. 11, 1912, **25,** 586

R. D. Compton, June 30, 1905, **16,** 151; July 10, 1905, **16,** 153

Antoinette Cole Comstock, July 26, 1907, **17,** 295

Edwin Grant Conklin, Oct. 4, 1907, **17,** 416; Oct. 17, 1907, **17,** 438; Oct. 18, 1907, **17,** 445; Oct. 21, 1907, **17,** 447; Nov. 18, 1907, **17,** 507; March 3, 1908, **18,** 5; Oct. 10, 1908, **18,** 445; Feb. 18, 1909, **19,** 51; March 31, 1909, **19,** 135; Jan. 15, 1910, **20,** 15; Sept. 18, 1910, **21,** 136

Henry Groves Connor, Jan. 27, 1911, **22,** 383

Robert Digges Wimberly Connor, Feb. 20, 1906, **16,** 315

John Heman Converse, Jan. 14, 1904, **15,** 129; April 10, 1907, **17,** 102

Oscar Henry Cooper, Dec. 15, 1908, **18,** 548

Henry Bedinger Cornwall, May 11, 1904, **15,** 324; May 4, 1910, **20,** 409; June 4, 1910, **20,** 499

Francis L. Corrao, July 31, 1912, **24,** 575

John Kissig Cowen, Jan. 16, 1904, **15,** 133

Hardin Craig, Jan. 27, 1910, **20,** 60

Edwin Boone Craighead, Sept. 7, 1907, **17,** 375

Ralph Adams Cram, March 29, 1907, **17,** 97; May 15, 1907, **17,** 147; May 20, 1907, **17,** 152; May 24, 1907, **17,** 158; May 30, 1907, **17,** 168; June 3, 1907, **17,** 172; June 22, 1907, **17,** 220; Jan. 16, 1908, **17,** 604; April 7, 1908, **18,** 226; May 13, 1908, **18,** 295; Aug. 8, 1909, **19,** 333; Sept. 23, 1909, **19,** 388; Nov. 29, 1909, **19,** 537

Elijah Richardson Craven, Dec. 3, 1902, **14,** 254; May 27, 1903, **14,** 464

Homer Stillé Cummings, April 1, 1912, **24,** 272; Nov. 30, 1912, **25,** 570

Jabez Lamar Monroe Curry, July 15, 1902, **14,** 15

James L. Curtis, Nov. 30, 1912, **25,** 571

Cornelius Cuyler Cuyler, April 13, 1909, **19,** 162

Richard Heath Dabney, Oct. 31, 1902, **14,** 189; Nov. 10, 1902, **14,** 203; April 19, 1910, **20,** 371; Nov. 10, 1910, **22,** 13; Nov. 16, 1911, **23,** 551; Dec. 4, 1911, **23,** 563; Dec. 11, 1911, **23,** 591; Dec. 22, 1911, **23,** 604; Dec. 27, 1911, **23,** 631; Jan. 5, 1912, **23,** 653; Jan. 11, 1912, **24,** 29; Jan. 25, 1912, **24,** 71; Feb. 27, 1912, **24,** 217; March 20, 1912, **24,** 256; May 13, 1912, **24,** 398; Aug. 1, 1912, **24,** 578; Sept. 6, 1912, **25,** 112; Nov. 20, 1912, **25,** 553

*Daily Princetonian*, editor, Feb. 27, 1903, **14,** 379; Feb. 10, 1904, **15,** 164; Oct. 17, 1908, **18,** 466

Robert Shoemaker Dana, March 21, 1905, **16,** 35

Addie Worth Bagley Daniels, Nov. 9, 1912, **25,** 534

Josephus Daniels, June 13, 1911, **23,** 140; Jan. 23, 1912, **24,** 64; April 4, 1912, **24,** 288; April 29, 1912, **24,** 368; May 5, 1912, **24,** 385; May 7, 1912, **24,** 387 (2); May 13, 1912, **24,** 396; May 16, 1912, **24,** 402; June 5, 1912, **24,** 461; June 11, 1912, **24,** 471; June 15, 1912, **24,** 476; Dec. 11, 1912, **25,** 585

Winthrop More Daniels, July 20, 1902, **14,** 30; July 31, 1902, **14,** 44; Sept. 6, 1902, **14,** 124; June 12, 1903, **14,** 488; May 13, 1904, **15,** 330; July 4, 1904, **15,** 403; Oct. 1, 1904, **15,** 501; Oct. 5, 1904, **15,** 504; March 3, 1905, **16,** 19; March 13, 1905, **16,** 29; March 14, 1905, **16,** 30; March 27, 1905, **16,** 40 (2); April 27, 1905, **16,** 84; May 1, 1905, **16,** 88; May 9, 1905, **16,** 92; June 7, 1905, **16,** 111; June 17, 1905, **16,** 142; April 18, 1906, **16,** 372; April 26, 1906, **16,** 376; May 5, 1906, **16,** 385; March 3, 1909, **19,** 77; May 10, 1909, **19,** 190; Nov. 9, 1909, **19,** 488; Dec. 8, 1909, **19,** 560; Dec. 14, 1909, **19,** 604; April 5, 1910, **20,** 319; May 10, 1910, **20,** 430; July 9, 1910, **20,** 569; Sept. 28, 1910, **21,** 178; Oct. 17, 1910, **21,** 337; Nov. 11, 1910, **22,** 24

Landonia Randolph Dashiell, March 19, 1903, **14,** 396

John David Davis, March 18, 1910, **20,** 256

Emmett C. Davison, Feb. 7, 1912, **24,** 136

Harry B. Davison and Grace Walcott Davison, Oct. 24, 1912, **25,** 458

Frank Miles Day, Feb. 26, 1909, **19,** 68

Frank Miles Day and Brother, Dec. 18, 1908, **18,** 558; Jan. 26, 1909, **19,** 13; March 5, 1909, **19,** 80

Agostino De Biasi, Feb. 7, 1912, **24,** 135

William Henry Steele Demarest, Dec. 22, 1906, **16,** 538

Democratic Club of Philadelphia, Jan. 7, 1912, **24,** 6

Democratic Rallies, Nov. 2, 1912, **25,** 501

Democratic Voters, Aug. 15, 1912, **25,** 29; Nov. 4, 1912, **25,** 511

Democrats of New Jersey, May 24, 1912, **24,** 429

John Henry DeRidder, June 16, 1904, **15,** 383

John DeWitt, Jan. 27, 1910, **20,** 60

Joseph A. Di Silvestro, Feb. 4, 1912, **24,** 133

Thomas Dixon, Jr., Dec. 3, 1912, **25,** 578

William Edward Dodd, May 4, 1910, **20,** 408; Sept. 12, 1911, **23,** 317

Cleveland Hoadley Dodge, Dec. 14, 1902, **14,** 292; Jan. 29, 1903, **14,** 334; June 30, 1904, **15,** 400; June 15, 1905, **16,** 142; Oct. 24, 1905, **16,** 204; June 21, 1906, **16,** 429; Sept. 16, 1906, **16,** 453; Nov. 23, 1906, **16,** 491; Dec. 20, 1906, **16,** 536; Jan. 7, 1907, **16,** 550; Sept. 27, 1903, **16,** 566; Feb. 20, 1907, **17,** 47; March 30, 1907, **17,** 99; April 15, 1907, **17,** 109; July 1, 1907, **17,** 240; July 3, 1907, **17,** 245; Aug. 4, 1907, **17,** 334; June 18, 1908, **18,** 337;

Jan. 12, 1909, **18,** 610; Jan. 26, 1909, **19,** 12; Jan. 28, 1909, **19,** 15; April 30, 1909, **19,** 177; Sept. 22, 1909, **19,** 386; Oct. 1, 1909, **19,** 395; Oct. 26, 1909, **19,** 448; Oct. 28, 1909, **19,** 455; Nov. 15, 1909, **19,** 501; Dec. 23, 1909, **19,** 623; Dec. 27, 1909, **19,** 631; Jan. 2, 1910, **19,** 703; Jan. 14, 1910, **20,** 13; Feb. 7, 1910, **20,** 83; Feb. 18, 1910, **20,** 141; July 1, 1910, **20,** 553; July 11, 1910, **20,** 573; Sept. 19, 1910, **21,** 139; Oct. 11, 1910, **21,** 295; Nov. 12, 1910, **22,** 29; Dec. 21, 1910, **22,** 237; Jan. 27, 1911, **22,** 382; Feb. 18, 1911, **22,** 438; June 9, 1911, **23,** 139; June 15, 1911, **23,** 153; June 20, 1911, **23,** 160; June 23, 1911, **23,** 172; July 7, 1911, **23,** 193; July 16, 1911, **23,** 214; Oct. 24, 1911, **23,** 479; March 26, 1912, **24,** 266; May 16, 1912, **24,** 402; July 29, 1912, **24,** 573; Sept. 11, 1912, **25,** 135

Grace Parish Dodge, Dec. 26, 1902, **14,** 306

William Earl Dodge, March 15, 1903, **14,** 393

Davison McDowell Douglas, Nov. 15, 1912, **25,** 549

Theodore Dreiser, March 23, 1908, **18,** 68

Francis Ignatius Drobinski, Feb. 7, 1912, **24,** 134; March 4, 1912, **24,** 223

John Fairfield Dryden, June 16, 1910, **20,** 533; Feb. 10, 1911, **22,** 416

Henry Green Duffield, Feb. 26, 1906, **16,** 318; March 1, 1906, **16,** 322; Feb. 3, 1909, **19,** 20

William Butler Duncan, Nov. 11, 1903, **15,** 50

John Robertson Dunlap, April 1, 1908, **18,** 219

Louis Edelman, Sept. 20, 1909, **19,** 386

Editor of the *Brooklyn Daily Eagle*, Sept. 11, 1912, **25,** 135

Editor of the *Daily Princetonian*, Feb. 27, 1903, **14,** 379; Feb. 10, 1904, **15,** 164; Oct. 17, 1908, **18,** 466

Editor of the New York *Evening Post*, April 21, 1910, **20,** 378

Editor of the *New York Times*, Nov. 24, 1907, **17,** 521

Editor of the *Newark Evening News*, Nov. 5, 1911, **23,** 539

Editor of the *Princeton Alumni Weekly*, Nov. 21, 1908, **18,** 520

Editor of the *Springfield* (Mass.) *Republican*, July 6, 1909, **19,** 293

George Franklin Edmunds, June 2, 1903, **14,** 470

Louis Rinaldo Ehrich, June 18, 1909, **19,** 258

Charles William Eliot, Nov. 22, 1910, **22,** 78; Sept. 30, 1912, **25,** 286

Wade Edward Eller, March 21, 1912, **24,** 257

Edward Graham Elliott, July 15, 1902, **14,** 12; May 2, 1906, **16,** 382; July 17, 1907, **17,** 286; July 11, 1910, **20,** 575; Aug. 2, 1912, **24,** 584

Robert Erskine Ely, April 13, 1907, **17,** 107

Wilson Farrand, Jan. 4, 1910, **19,** 712

Zephaniah Charles Felt, Dec. 6, 1904, **15,** 552; April 26, 1910, **20,** 392; May 17, 1910, **20,** 459; Aug. 3, 1910, **21,** 36

Mabel Kingsbury Fentress, Nov. 26, 1907, **17,** 523

Henry Ferguson, Oct. 12, 1908, **18,** 450

Morris Patterson Ferris, Feb. 1, 1904, **15,** 153

John Wesley Fielder, Jr., Aug. 14, 1902, **14,** 84; Aug. 20, 1902, **14,** 96

Charles Bowdoin Fillebrown, Nov. 6, 1902, **14,** 200

Henry Burchard Fine, Dec. 9, 1907, **17,** 552; Nov. 23, 1912, **25,** 560

John Huston Finley, Aug. 8, 1902, **14,** 66; Sept. 6, 1902, **14,** 123

John Miller Turpin Finney, Nov. 8, 1911, **23,** 543

Carl Russell Fish, Dec. 28, 1909, **19,** 635

Harvey Edward Fisk, Nov. 11, 1908, **18,** 491; Jan. 12, 1909, **18,** 611

Robert Hunter Fitzhugh, March 19, 1906, **16,** 338

Henry Jones Ford, March 6, 1907, **17,** 62; May 5, 1908, **18,** 287; May 9, 1908, **18,** 294

Henry James Forman, April 10, 1908, **18,** 258

Raymond Blaine Fosdick, Aug. 21, 1912, **25,** 49

Eugene Noble Foss, Aug. 17, 1912, **25,** 42

David Paulson Foster and others, Oct. 29, 1910, **21,** 470

John Watson Foster, June 10, 1909, **19,** 239; Dec. 23, 1909, **19,** 622

John Fox, Dec. 10, 1910, **22,** 167

Abel McIver Fraser, Nov. 11, 1903, **15,** 49; Oct. 20, 1904, **15,** 522

George Corning Fraser, April 16, 1907, **17,** 110; June 15, 1907, **17,** 214

William Goodell Frost, Nov. 15, 1910, **22,** 48; Feb. 20, 1911, **22,** 440; Nov. 20, 1912, **25,** 552

Arthur Lincoln Frothingham, Jr., May 20, 1905, **16,** 103

Harry Augustus Garfield, June 11, 1903, **14,** 486; June 15, 1903, **14,** 491; July 29, 1903, **14,** 547; July 29, 1903, **14,** 548; Sept. 1, 1903, **14,** 556; Sept. 25, 1903, **15,** 5; Oct. 22, 1903, **15,** 25; Nov. 19, 1903, **15,** 54; Aug. 5, 1904, **15,** 433; April 28, 1906, **16,** 379; Sept. 3, 1906, **16,** 449; April 13, 1907, **17,** 108; June 28, 1907, **17,** 236; July 16, 1907, **17,** 284; Jan. 13, 1908, **17,** 600; April 10, 1908, **18,** 259; Sept. 14, 1908, **18,** 419; June 15, 1910, **20,** 531; Oct. 25, 1910, **21,** 421; Nov. 4, 1910, **21,** 559; Nov. 12, 1910, **22,** 30

John Work Garrett, Feb. 5, 1904, **15,** 158

Robert Garrett, June 29, 1904, **15,** 397; July 5, 1904, **15,** 404; March 3, 1905, **16,** 18; Feb. 13, 1907, **17,** 35; Feb. 28, 1907, **17,** 51; March 6, 1907, **17,** 62; April 13, 1907, **17,** 107; May 27, 1907, **17,** 159; Sept. 26, 1907, **17,** 400; April 19, 1909, **19,** 166; June 24, 1909, **19,** 268; July 9, 1909, **19,** 305; July 10, 1909, **19,** 306; Aug. 19, 1909, **19,** 347; Aug. 26, 1909, **19,** 353; Dec. 27, 1909, **19,** 633; Jan. 24, 1910, **20,** 48; March 16, 1910, **20,** 246; March 23, 1910, **20,** 288; July 9, 1910, **20,** 569; July 26, 1910, **21,** 25; Nov. 23, 1910, **22,** 84; Sept. 5, 1911, **23,** 302

William Jay Gaynor, March 11, 1912, **24,** 240

General Education Board, president and trustees of, March 6, 1907, **17,** 60

Gordon Hall Gerould, April 12, 1905, **16,** 52; April 25, 1905, **16,** 79

Anthony Geronimo, Aug. 16, 1912, **25,** 40

Franklin Henry Giddings, April 6, 1900, **14,** 559

Richard Watson Gilder, Aug. 6, 1902, **14,** 58; Oct. 31, 1902, **14,** 190

Newton Cloud Gillham, July 14, 1911, **23,** 200

Daniel Coit Gilman, July 15, 1902, **14,** 14; Oct. 10, 1902, **14,** 142; Oct. 18, 1902, **14,** 147; Nov. 3, 1902, **14,** 197; July 1, 1907, **17,** 240

Lawrence Gilman, July 17, 1911, **23,** 215

Thomas Mador Gilmore, Aug. 12, 1912, **25,** 21

Carter Glass, April 1, 1912, **24,** 273; Nov. 14, 1912, **25,** 547

Franklin Potts Glass, July 31, 1912, **24,** 576; Sept. 6, 1912, **25,** 113

Harold Godwin, Oct. 27, 1910, **21,** 444

Edward Field Goltra, Dec. 8, 1906, **16,** 504; July 21, 1910, **21,** 17; Dec. 15, 1910, **22,** 199

John Maxwell Gordon, Sept. 20, 1911, **23,** 339

Thomas Pryor Gore, Oct. 26, 1912, **25,** 460; Nov. 9, 1912, **25,** 534

Elgin Ralston Lovell Gould, Sept. 22, 1898, **22,** 606

Charles Henry Grasty, Sept. 16, 1910, **21,** 102; Nov. 10, 1911, **23,** 546; Feb. 14, 1912, **24,** 163; May 15, 1912, **24,** 401; Nov. 20, 1912, **25,** 554

Simon Gratz, Feb. 20, 1904, **15,** 175; Nov. 28, 1904, **15,** 544

Mary Livingston Potter Green, Aug. 14, 1902, **14,** 84

William Green, Oct. 13, 1912, **25,** 417

Jerome Davis Greene, May 14, 1906; **16,** 396; May 30, 1906, **16,** 412

Solomon Bulkley Griffin, Aug. 21, 1911, **23,** 284; Nov. 20, 1912, **25,** 554

Francis James Grimké, Nov. 30, 1912, **25,** 571

Edward W. Grogan, July 6, 1911, **23,** 191

Joseph Finch Guffey, March 21, 1908, **21,** 623

Curtis Guild, Dec. 3, 1912, **25,** 576

George Wilkins Guthrie, Nov. 6, 1912, **25,** 527

Arthur Twining Hadley, Oct. 1, 1902, **14,** 136; Dec. 9, 1909, **19,** 577; Dec. 23, 1909, **19,** 623; Jan. 1, 1910, **19,** 699; June 2, 1910, **20,** 497; Dec. 14, 1910, **22,** 187

William Bayard Hale, Feb. 10, 1911, **22,** 414; March 30, 1911, **22,** 526; April 30, 1912, **24,** 380

Granville Stanley Hall, Oct. 30, 1903, **15,** 581; June 10, 1909, **19,** 240

Charles Sumner Hamlin, Aug. 3, 1912, **24,** 585; Aug. 17, 1912, **25,** 42

Parker Douglas Handy, June 6, 1910, **20,** 501

Norman Hapgood, Oct. 21, 1912, **25,** 449; Nov. 20, 1912, **25,** 555

Henry Janeway Hardenbergh, Aug. 6, 1907, **17,** 339; Aug. 13, 1907, **17,** 344

John Ralph Hardin, Nov. 14, 1910, **22,** 37

John Maynard Harlan, June 23, 1910, **20,** 540

William Rainey Harper, Dec. 20, 1905, **16,** 273

Harper and Brothers, March 4, 1912, **24,** 223

Florence Jaffray Hurst Harriman, Nov. 6, 1912, **25,** 527

George Brinton McClellan Harvey, Feb. 3, 1906, **16,** 301; Dec. 16, 1906, **16,** 531; Jan. 7, 1907, **16,** 549; Jan. 11, 1907, **16,** 560; June 25, 1910, **20,** 541; July 7, 1910, **20,** 561; July 14, 1910, **20,** 576; July 16, 1910, **21,** 5; July 26, 1910, **21,** 24; Aug. 3, 1910, **21,** 35; Aug. 8, 1910, **21,** 40, 41; Aug. 9, 1910, **21,** 46; Aug. 23, 1910, **21,** 61; Sept. 10, 1910, **21,** 88; Sept. 21, 1910, **21,** 148; Oct. 5, 1910, **21,** 245; Oct. 11, 1910, **21,** 297; Oct. 17, 1910, **21,** 338; Oct. 26, 1910, **21,** 435; Nov. 10, 1910, **22,** 13; Nov. 15, 1910, **22,** 46; Dec. 25, 1910, **22,** 260; Jan. 11, 1911, **22,** 326; Feb. 17, 1911, **22,** 435; March 2, 1911, **22,** 467; June 6, 1911, **23,** 134; Dec. 21, 1911, **23,** 603; Dec. 27, 1911, **23,** 630; draft, Jan. 11, 1912, **24,** 30; Jan. 11, 1912, **24,** 31; Nov. 5, 1912, **25,** 515

Percy Duncan Haughton, June 23, 1910, **20,** 540

Alfred Hayes, Jr., May 23, 1910, **20,** 467

Isaac Minis Hays, Dec. 13, 1902, **14,** 285; Feb. 28, 1903, **14,** 381; April 8, 1903, **14,** 405

Azel Washburn Hazen, Feb. 24, 1905, **16,** 13; March 20, 1906, **16,** 338; Nov. 14, 1910, **22,** 37

James Calvin Hemphill, Jan. 26, 1906, **16,** 288; Nov. 7, 1910, **21,** 579

Robert Randolph Henderson, May 25, 1903, **14,** 463; April 6, 1904, **15,** 234; April 12, 1909, **19,** 159; June 13, 1909, **19,** 252; Nov. 17, 1910, **22,** 55

Bayard Henry, Nov. 25, 1900, **16,** 565; Aug. 6, 1907, **17,** 338

Robert Lee Henry, April 8, 1912, **24,** 305

Thomas Maxwell Henry, Feb. 23, 1909, **19,** 67; March 29, 1910, **20,** 303

James Curtis Hepburn, March 11, 1908, **18,** 13

Charles F. Herr, Oct. 13, 1911, **23,** 449

Waterman Thomas Hewett, Nov. 6, 1902, **14,** 200

Jenny Davidson Hibben, Aug. 31, 1902, **14,** 121; April 16, 1911, **22,** 573

John Grier Hibben, Nov. 12, 1902, **14,** 205; July 23, 1904, **15,** 420; Nov. 6, 1905, **16,** 213; June 4, 1906, **16,** 413; Jan. 26, 1907, **17,** 16; July 10, 1907, **17,** 268; July 16, 1907, **17,** 284; Jan. 15, 1909, **18,** 626; Feb. 10, 1910, **20,** 92; March 9, 1910, **20,** 223; Dec. 25, 1910, **22,** 259; Nov. 9, 1912, **25,** 534

John Grier Hibben and Jenny Davidson Hibben, Nov. 27, 1902, **14,** 224; Nov. 8, 1903, **15,** 47; Dec. 28, 1903, **15,** 110; Nov. 8, 1904, **15,** 532; Dec. 25, 1905, **16,** 275; Nov. 8, 1906, **16,** 484

Henry Lee Higginson, May 21, 1908, **18,** 303; Nov. 4, 1908, **18,** 482; May 19, 1909, **19,** 200; May 23, 1910, **20,** 467; Nov. 14, 1910, **22,** 38

Joseph Stanislaus Hoff, Sept. 16, 1910, **21,** 102; Feb. 10, 1911, **22,** 415

Peyton Harrison Hoge, Jan. 31, 1903, **14,** 336

Hamilton Holt, June 7, 1905, **16,** 110

Houghton, Mifflin and Company, May 21, 1908, **20,** 582; May 26, 1908, **20,** 583

Edward Mandell House, Oct. 18, 1911, **23,** 466; Oct. 24, 1911, **23,** 480; Dec. 4, 1911, **23,** 563; Dec. 22, 1911, **23,** 604; Dec. 26, 1911, **23,** 630; Jan. 4, 1912, **23,** 651; Jan. 27, 1912, **24,** 81; Feb. 6, 1912, **24,** 134; Feb. 14, 1912, **24,** 163; March 15, 1912, **24,** 248; April 26, 1912, **24,** 360; May 6, 1912, **24,** 385; May 30, 1912, **24,** 451; May 31, 1912, **24,** 451; June 9, 1912, **24,** 467; June 24, 1912, **24,** 498; July 17, 1912, **24,** 556; Aug. 22, 1912, **25,** 52; Sept. 11, 1912, **25,** 135; Sept. 21, 1912, **25,** 213; Sept. 24, 1912, **25,** 232; Nov. 7, 1912, **25,** 530; Nov. 30, 1912, **25,** 566; Dec. 3, 1912, **25,** 576

Morus B. Howard, Nov. 6, 1912, **25,** 528

Annie Josephine Wilson Howe, Aug. 2, 1906, **16,** 432

Edward Howe, Aug. 12, 1910, **21,** 51

George Howe III, July 6, 1912, **24,** 542; Dec. 3, 1912, **25,** 579

William Dean Howells, June 18, 1909, **19,** 259

Florence Stevens Hoyt, May 18, 1904, **15,** 337

James Alfred Hoyt, Jr., June 22, 1911, **23,** 171; June 30, 1911, **23,** 184

Robert Stephen Hudspeth, Oct. 21, 1912, **25,** 450; Nov. 12, 1912, **25,** 541

Mary Allen Hulbert, July 14, 1912, **24,** 550; July 21, 1912, **24,** 561; July 28, 1912, **24,** 572; Aug. 11, 1912, **25,** 20; Aug. 17, 1912, **25,** 45; Aug. 25, 1912, **25,** 55; Sept. 1, 1912, **25,** 66; Sept. 8, 1912, **25,** 116; Sept. 22, 1912, **25,** 220; Sept. 29, 1912, **25,** 284; Oct. 13, 1912, **25,** 416; Oct. 27, 1912, **25,** 461; Nov. 22, 1912, **25,** 556; Dec. 1, 1912, **25,** 573; Dec. 22, 1912, **25,** 615; *see also* Mary Allen Hulbert Peck

Harry Burns Hutchins, Jan. 15, 1910, **20,** 16

Harriet Hyde, Jan. 21, 1911, **22,** 361

James Hazen Hyde, March 16, 1903, **14,** 393

Andrew Clerk Imbrie, July 10, 1907, **17,** 270; July 15, 1907, **17,** 282; July 29, 1907, **17,** 297; March 26, 1909, **19,** 120

Indianapolis schoolchildren of the eighth grade, March 31, 1903, **14,** 403

Edward Ingle, Aug. 20, 1902, **14,** 96; March 22, 1904, **15,** 203; Dec. 11, 1911, **23,** 592

Italian-American Alliance, May 17, 1912, **24,** 404

W. M. Jackson, Jan. 13, 1903, **14,** 327

Melancthon Williams Jacobus, June 1, 1903, **14,** 468; June 27, 1907, **17,** 232; July 1, 1907, **17,** 241; July 6, 1907, **17,** 261; Sept. 20, 1907, **17,** 395; Oct. 23, 1907, **17,** 450; Nov. 6, 1907, **17,** 470; Jan. 11, 1908, **17,** 599; March 21, 1908, **18,** 63; June 1, 1908, **18,**

313; Sept. 25, 1908, **18,** 423; Nov. 11, 1908, **18,** 493; Nov. 16, 1908, **18,** 514; Dec. 19, 1908, **18,** 559; Jan. 4, 1909, **18,** 588; Jan. 11, 1909, **18,** 609; Jan. 15, 1909, **18,** 624; Jan. 23, 1909, **19,** 8; Feb. 9, 1909, **19,** 31; March 23, 1909, **19,** 116; March 27, 1909, **19,** 124; May 19, 1909, **19,** 201; Oct. 12, 1909, **19,** 411; Oct. 29, 1909, **19,** 458; Nov. 8, 1909, **19,** 487; Dec. 30, 1909, **19,** 657; Jan. 1, 1910, **19,** 697; Feb. 11, 1910, **20,** 119; March 19, 1910, **20,** 262; March 21, 1910, **20,** 271; April 2, 1910, **20,** 311; April 4, 1910, **20,** 314; April 6, 1910, **20,** 327; May 6, 1910, **20,** 412; May 9, 1910, **20,** 426; May 24, 1910, **20,** 469; Nov. 30, 1912, **25,** 567

Edmund Janes James, Dec. 17, 1907, **17,** 551

George Sibley Johns, Oct. 20, 1903, **15,** 20; April 1, 1910, **20,** 310

Charles William Leverett Johnson, April 7, 1903, **14,** 404

Robert Underwood Johnson, April 28, 1910, **20,** 399; Dec. 3, 1910, **22,** 126; Feb. 4, 1911, **22,** 406

Adrian Hoffman Joline, April 29, 1907, **17,** 124

Benjamin Franklin Jones, Jr., March 30, 1904, **15,** 220

David Benton Jones, Aug. 11, 1902, **14,** 74; March 20, 1904, **15,** 200; Sept. 26, 1907, **17,** 401; May 24, 1910, **20,** 470; May 30, 1910, **20,** 485; June 24, 1910, **20,** 541; June 27, 1910, **20,** 543; July 1, 1910, **20,** 552; July 14, 1910, **20,** 578; Sept. 25, 1910, **21,** 162

DeWitt Clinton Jones, Jr., Nov. 20, 1909, **19,** 528

Frank Johnston Jones, July 22, 1904, **15,** 419; Oct. 24, 1904, **15,** 530

Thomas Davies Jones, Dec. 27, 1909, **19,** 633; Dec. 28, 1909, **19,** 634; Jan. 1, 1910, **19,** 695; Jan. 14, 1910, **20,** 12; May 24, 1910, **20,** 469; May 30, 1910, **20,** 483; July 1, 1910, **20,** 552; Nov. 15, 1910, **22,** 48; Dec. 8, 1910, **22,** 154; Dec. 15, 1911, **23,** 594; Dec. 22, 1911, **23,** 603; Sept. 6, 1912, **25,** 114; Sept. 7, 1912, **25,** 115

Winifred Jones, Dec. 18, 1910, **22,** 223

Lindley Miller Keasbey, Feb. 15, 1911, **22,** 433

Henry Hopkins Kelsey, May 15, 1903, **14,** 458

Calvin Noyes Kendall, July 7, 1911, **23,** 192

John Hanson Kennard, Jr., Oct. 23, 1912, **25,** 457

Charles William Kent, Oct. 27, 1902, **14,** 188; Dec. 13, 1904, **15,** 574; July 25, 1905, **16,** 161; Aug. 2, 1905, **16,** 168; Oct. 14, 1905, **16,** 192; Jan. 14, 1911, **22,** 333

Frederick Paul Keppel, Dec. 15, 1903, **15,** 100

James Kerney, Aug. 2, 1910, **21,** 34

Edwin Silas Wells Kerr, April 30, 1909, **19,** 177

Daniel Kiefer, Dec. 26, 1910, **22,** 261

George Darius Kilborn, Oct. 6, 1912, **25,** 359

Wilson B. Killingbeck, Oct. 10, 1910, **21,** 288

Fannie Bayle King, Oct. 20, 1904, **15,** 522

James Hampton Kirkland, Dec. 9, 1897, **16,** 564; Oct. 25, 1907, **17,** 457

Joseph Rucker Lamar, Nov. 12, 1912, **25,** 542

Catherine Gansevoort Lansing, May 23, 1906, **16,** 404

Henry Hughart Laughlin, Jan. 16, 1904, **15,** 132

George William Lay, Aug. 12, 1907, **17,** 343

William Laurence Ledwith, July 29, 1902, **14,** 43

Ivy Ledbetter Lee, Oct. 31, 1902, **14,** 190

William Brewster Lee, Feb. 23, 1903, **14,** 364; Nov. 10, 1910, **22,** 14

Frederick H. Levey, Dec. 5, 1910, **22,** 136

William C. Liller, July 14, 1911, **23,** 200; Aug. 5, 1911, **23,** 254

Benjamin Barr Lindsey, Feb. 3, 1911, **22,** 405; March 30, 1911, **22,** 525; May 1, 1911, **22,** 599

Isaac Henry Lionberger, May 20, 1904, **15,** 341; March 8, 1910, **20,** 216; March 16, 1910, **20,** 247; April 28, 1910, **20,** 398; Oct. 23, 1911, **23,** 479

Martin Wiley Littleton, Nov. 30, 1912, **25,** 567

James Henry Lockhart, Jan. 14, 1904, **15,** 128

George Bryan Logan, Feb. 4, 1909, **19,** 24

Thomas Raynesford Lounsbury, Oct. 30, 1896, **14,** 558; Jan. 14, 1897, **14,** 559; July 16, 1902, **14,** 19; May 10, 1906, **16,** 388

Thomas Bell Love, Nov. 11, 1910, **22,** 25; Feb. 16, 1911, **22,** 434; April 24, 1911, **22,** 583; July 31, 1911, **23,** 242; Aug. 8, 1911, **23,** 258; Aug. 15, 1911, **23,** 267; Aug. 21, 1911, **23,** 286; Sept. 1, 1911, **23,** 302; Sept. 12, 1911, **23,** 316; Jan. 23, 1912, **24,** 64; May 5, 1912, **24,** 384; May 27, 1912, **24,** 446; Dec. 31, 1912, **25,** 648

Verner R. Lovell, Nov. 7, 1911, **23,** 658; Jan. 16, 1912, **24,** 44; Jan. 27, 1912, **24,** 82; Feb. 7, 1912, **24,** 137

Edgar Odell Lovett, March 21, 1905, **16,** 35; April 27, 1905, **16,** 80; March 11, 1907, **17,** 65; Jan. 14, 1908, **17,** 602, Aug. 11, 1908, **18,** 396

Seth Low, Oct. 28, 1902, **14,** 188

A. B. Lowe, Sept. 20, 1911, **23,** 339

Abbott Lawrence Lowell, Jan. 15, 1909, **18,** 627; Jan. 25, 1909, **19,** 11; Dec. 6, 1909, **19,** 556; Dec. 9, 1909, **19,** 578; Dec. 23, 1909, **19,** 623; Jan. 1, 1910, **19,** 699; Feb. 8, 1910, **20,** 88; March 23, 1910, **20,** 287; Sept. 20, 1910, **21,** 143; Nov. 12, 1912, **25,** 541

Hamilton Wright Mabie, Nov. 26, 1909, **19,** 533

William Gibbs McAdoo, Nov. 15, 1910, **22,** 51; Nov. 10, 1911, **23,** 547; Feb. 26, 1912, **24,** 217; Oct. 22, 1912, **25,** 452; Nov. 20, 1912, **25,** 552; Dec. 23, 1912, **25,** 617

Charles Williston McAlpin, Sept. 6, 1902, **14,** 125; Sept. 13, 1902, **14,** 130; March 14, 1903, **14,** 392; March 24, 1903, **14,** 398; May 27, 1903, **14,** 464; June 28, 1903, **14,** 497; July 31, 1903, **14,** 548; Dec. 16, 1903, **15,** 101; Feb. 29, 1904, **15,** 180; May 18, 1904, **15,** 339; Aug. 5, 1904, **15,** 434; Dec. 12, 1904, **15,** 571, 572; Feb. 6, 1905, **15,** 580; June 23, 1905, **16,** 146; Feb. 6, 1906, **16,** 304; March 2, 1906, **16,** 322; March 23, 1906, **16,** 343; July 19, 1906, **16,** 430; Jan. 11, 1907, **16,** 562; Jan. 26, 1907, **17,** 18; July 31,

1908, **18,** 385; Jan. 21, 1909 **19,** 5; Jan. 23, 1909, **19,** 7; Jan. 2, 1910, **19,** 703; Jan. 14, 1910, **20,** 12; Jan. 25, 1910, **20,** 52; July 20, 1910, **21,** 13; Oct. 29, 1910, **21,** 471; Jan. 3, 1911, **22,** 293; Jan. 19, 1911, **22,** 358; July 18, 1912, **24,** 557

George Meriwether McCampbell, Jr., Feb. 11, 1910, **20,** 120

Thomas Nesbitt McCarter, Jr., March 31, 1904, **15,** 225

Uzal Haggerty McCarter, March 31, 1904, **15,** 223

George Brinton McClellan, Jr., April 19, 1906, **16,** 373

Howard McClenahan, Nov. 19, 1908, **18,** 517

Alfred James Pollock McClure, June 1, 1903, **14,** 469

Charles Freeman Williams McClure, Feb. 24, 1904, **15,** 178; July 17, 1905, **16,** 155; Nov. 16, 1905, **16,** 223; Aug. 2, 1906, **16,** 431; Oct. 21, 1906, **16,** 469

Hugh S. McClure, April 9, 1910, **20,** 351

James Gore King McClure, Feb. 21, 1910, **20,** 151

William Frank McCombs, March 18, 1912, **24,** 253; July 24, 1912, **24,** 568; Nov. 5, 1912, **25,** 522; Nov. 30, 1912, **25,** 572

John James McCook and Charles Beatty Alexander, Dec. 9, 1905, **16,** 276

William Alexander MacCorkle, Jan. 31, 1901, **16,** 565

Cyrus Hall McCormick, Aug. 21, 1902, **14,** 98; Dec. 14, 1902, **14,** 291; Jan. 30, 1903, **14,** 335; Feb. 16, 1903, **14,** 360; May 1, 1903, **14,** 440; May 18, 1903, **14,** 463; Dec. 7, 1903, **15,** 67; April 8, 1905, **16,** 47; Oct. 11, 1905, **16,** 191; June 14, 1907, **17,** 212; Feb. 10, 1908, **17,** 615; March 20, 1908, **18,** 60; April 20, 1908, **18,** 274; June 1, 1908, **18,** 313; Dec. 14, 1908, **18,** 546; Dec. 21, 1908, **18,** 562; Jan. 25, 1909, **19,** 10; March 3, 1909, **19,** 75; April 12, 1909, **19,** 158; May 15, 1909, **19,** 196; Oct. 4, 1909, **19,** 400; Oct. 29, 1909, **19,** 460; Dec. 27, 1909, **19,** 631; March 21, 1910, **20,** 271; May 17, 1910, **20,** 458; May 24, 1910, **20,** 469; May 26, 1910, **20,** 472; July 14, 1910, **20,** 577; Nov. 4, 1910, **21,** 543; Nov. 12, 1910, **22,** 29; Feb. 4, 1911, **22,** 405; May 14, 1912, **24,** 400; July 11, 1912, **24,** 545; Nov. 7, 1912, **25,** 530

Harriet Hammond McCormick, March 20, 1908, **18,** 60; Feb. 16, 1909, **19,** 48

Nettie Fowler McCormick, May 8, 1908, **18,** 290

Henry Mitchell McCracken, Dec. 19, 1905, **16,** 272

Francis Charles Macdonald, Oct. 18, 1909, **19,** 422

Charles Howard McIlwain, April 10, 1905, **16,** 48; Sept. 15, 1905, **16,** 185; Sept. 10, 1906, **16,** 452

David L. MacKay, Oct. 11, 1910, **21,** 297; Oct. 17, 1910, **21,** 336

Alexander Jeffrey McKelway, Aug. 1, 1911, **23,** 244; Jan. 4, 1912, **23,** 651; Aug. 15, 1912, **25,** 30

St. Clair McKelway, March 11, 1906, **16,** 329; Dec. 5, 1910, **22,** 134

William Douglas Mackenzie, July 24, 1908, **18,** 376

Robert Morris McKinney, Oct. 26, 1908, **18,** 473

Thomas McKinsey, Dec. 21, 1910, **22,** 238

William Pierce Macksey, Dec. 17, 1910, **22,** 212; Jan. 13, 1911, **22,** 330

Malcolm MacLaren, June 13, 1908, **18,** 337; Nov. 19, 1908, **18,** 518

Andrew Cunningham McLaughlin, May 30, 1905, **16,** 106

John Van Antwerp MacMurray, Dec. 21, 1905, **16,** 570; Dec. 26, 1905, **16,** 571; March 9, 1907, **17,** 64; March 9, 1908, **18,** 12

Simon John McPherson, April 30, 1908, **18,** 278

Isaac Wayne MacVeagh, Sept. 22, 1910, **21,** 152; Nov. 14, 1910, **22,** 37; Dec. 16, 1910, **22,** 205

Hardin Mallard, June 28, 1911, **23,** 175

Theodore Marburg, Jan. 21, 1904, **15,** 136

Allan Marquand, Nov. 14, 1902, **14,** 206; Oct. 16, 1907, **17,** 436

Charles Henry Marshall, Dec. 26, 1902, **14,** 305; Jan. 29, 1904, **15,** 145; Dec. 4, 1909, **19,** 552; Dec. 30, 1909, **19,** 658

Thomas Riley Marshall, Nov. 5, 1912, **25,** 521

William Joseph Martin, July 19, 1912, **24,** 559

James Edgar Martine, Nov. 14, 1910, **22,** 36

Sir William Mather, Dec. 20, 1906, **16,** 536; April 15, 1907, **17,** 108; May 13, 1907, **17,** 140; June 18, 1907, **17,** 215; Aug. 7, 1907, **17,** 342; Sept. 18, 1907, **17,** 391; Nov. 1, 1907, **17,** 465

James Mathers, May 5, 1906, **16,** 386

Frank L. Mayes, March 21, 1912, **24,** 256

Mayor of Newark, Prosecutor of Pleas of Essex County, and the Sheriff of Essex County, Sept. 24, 1911, **23,** 357

Royal Meeker, Sept. 2, 1907, **17,** 369; July 1, 1912, **24,** 519; Dec. 3, 1912, **25,** 580

Wilton Merle-Smith, Dec. 3, 1909, **19,** 548

Ralph B. Merritt, Nov. 20, 1909, **19,** 524

S. D. Merton, April 20, 1910, **20,** 377

Louis E. Miller, Aug. 23, 1912, **25,** 53

Lucius Hopkins Miller, March 18, 1903, **14,** 396; March 26, 1903, **14,** 399; Aug. 3, 1907, **17,** 334; April 17, 1908, **18,** 273; Jan. 15, 1909, **18,** 625

Henry Oothout Milliken, March 9, 1905, **16,** 23

Henry Moffat, Nov. 20, 1909, **19,** 525

James Charles Monaghan, Sept. 4, 1912, **25,** 93

Andrew Jackson Montague, June 6, 1911, **23,** 134; Sept. 27, 1911, **23,** 361

John Bassett Moore, May 23, 1910, **20,** 467; Nov. 5, 1910, **21,** 559

Josephine Perry Morgan, Oct. 28, 1908, **18,** 475

John Pierpont Morgan, Oct. 22, 1909, **19,** 440; Nov. 4, 1909, **19,** 483

Henry Morgenthau, Jan. 13, 1912, **24,** 42

Benjamin Wistar Morris III, June 29, 1904, **15,** 398; July 30, 1904, **15,** 424; Aug. 22, 1904, **15,** 447; Aug. 25, 1904, **15,** 448; Sept. 2, 1904, **15,** 461; Sept. 15, 1904, **15,** 469; Oct. 1, 1904, **15,** 501; Oct. 29, 1904, **15,** 531; Nov. 17, 1904, **15,** 534; Dec. 13, 1904, **15,** 574;

Jan. 27, 1905, **15,** 580; July 18, 1905, **16,** 156; July 28, 1905, **16,** 163; Aug. 2, 1905, **16,** 169; Aug. 5, 1905, **16,** 171; Aug. 10, 1905, **16,** 175; Aug. 12, 1905, **16,** 178; Aug. 22, 1905, **16,** 181; Aug. 30, 1905, **16,** 185; Dec. 26, 1905, **16,** 275; Feb. 7, 1906, **16,** 305; March 9, 1906, **16,** 327; March 17, 1906, **16,** 335; March 22, 1906, **16,** 342; April 12, 1906, **16,** 357; April 17, 1906, **16,** 369; Feb. 12, 1907, **17,** 32; Feb. 14, 1907, **17,** 37

Roland Sletor Morris, June 16, 1910, **20,** 534; May 13, 1912, **24,** 397; June 5, 1912, **24,** 461

John R. Mott, March 15, 1905, **17,** 620; Oct. 25, 1905, **17,** 621; Nov. 1, 1905, **17,** 621; Nov. 21, 1905, **17,** 622; April 1, 1908, **18,** 218; May 1, 1908, **18,** 279; Jan. 25, 1910, **20,** 53

Charles Allen Munn, Nov. 11, 1908, **18,** 492

James Phinney Munroe, Jan. 1, 1903, **14,** 309

Hugo Münsterberg, March 18, 1903, **14,** 394; Sept. 15, 1904, **15,** 468

Hopson Owen Murfee, May 4, 1907, **17,** 131

Franklin Murphy, June 9, 1904, **15,** 362

Franklin Murphy, Jr., June 20, 1907, **17,** 217; Jan. 26, 1909, **19,** 13

Harold Griffith Murray, July 21, 1904, **15,** 418; Aug. 8, 1904, **15,** 435

William Starr Myers, May 5, 1906, **16,** 386; May 7, 1906, **16,** 386

Henry Beach Needham, July 10, 1911, **23,** 194; July 18, 1911, **23,** 217; Aug. 24, 1912, **25,** 54

New Jersey, voters of, Sept. 25, 1911, **23,** 358

New York *Evening Post,* editor, April 21, 1910, **20,** 378

*New York Times,* editor, Nov. 24, 1907, **17,** 521

Newark, Mayor of, Prosecutor of Pleas of Essex County, and the Sheriff of Essex County, Sept. 24, 1911, **23,** 357

*Newark Evening News,* editor, Nov. 5, 1911, **23,** 539

Francis Griffith Newlands, Jan. 23, 1912, **24,** 64; April 1, 1912, **24,** 272; April 2, 1912, **24,** 276; May 7, 1912, **24,** 388; May 10, 1912, **24,** 390; May 13, 1912, **24,** 399; May 20, 1912, **24,** 410; May 29, 1912, **24,** 450; July 5, 1912, **24,** 539

Edward Warren Ordway, Feb. 20, 1904, **15,** 175; May 7, 1904, **15,** 316

Daniel T. O'Regan, Sept. 6, 1912, **25,** 113

Arthur Herbert Osborn, July 17, 1907, **17,** 286

Henry Fairfield Osborn, Dec. 4, 1909, **19,** 551

Charles Grosvenor Osgood, Jr., April 8, 1905, **16,** 47; April 13, 1905, **16,** 53; Nov. 22, 1906, **16,** 489; Dec. 4, 1909, **19,** 553

Thomas Nelson Page, June 24, 1904, **15,** 393; Dec. 6, 1909, **19,** 556; Nov. 12, 1910, **22,** 30; Jan. 26, 1911, **22,** 377

Walter Hines Page, Feb. 24, 1905, **16,** 12; March 7, 1906, **16,** 324; March 18, 1910, **20,** 257; July 16, 1910, **21,** 5; Nov. 7, 1910, **21,** 579; Feb. 10, 1911, **22,** 413, 414; March 23, 1911, **22,** 515; June

7, 1911, **23,** 135; Aug. 21, 1911, **23,** 285; Oct. 10, 1911, **23,** 437; July 7, 1912, **24,** 543; July 17, 1912, **24,** 557; Nov. 6, 1912, **25,** 526; Dec. 23, 1912, **25,** 618

Alexander Mitchell Palmer, Nov. 11, 1910, **22,** 26; July 20, 1911, **23,** 221; Jan. 11, 1912, **24,** 29; April 11, 1912, **24,** 320; May 13, 1912, **24,** 396, 397; June 4, 1912, **24,** 453; June 5, 1912, **24,** 461

Stephen Squires Palmer, Aug. 17, 1907, **17,** 349; Aug. 31, 1907, **17,** 368; April 30, 1908, **18,** 277; Oct. 28, 1908, **18,** 475

Alfred L. Parker, July 24, 1910, **21,** 24

Fred Lewis Pattee, Nov. 1, 1906, **16,** 478

George Foster Peabody, March 26, 1912, **24,** 265; May 15, 1912, **24,** 401; June 13, 1912, **24,** 474; June 21, 1912, **24,** 491; Oct. 16, 1912, **25,** 422

Endicott Peabody, Oct. 13, 1905, **16,** 192

Mary Allen Hulbert Peck, Feb. 6, 1907, **17,** 29; Feb. 20, 1907, **17,** 48; March 27, 1907, **17,** 93; Jan. 25, 1908, **17,** 606; Sept. 30, 1908, **18,** 423; Oct. 12, 1908, **18,** 448; Oct. 19, 1908, **18,** 466; Oct. 25, 1908, **18,** 470; Nov. 2, 1908, **18,** 478; April 13, 1909, **19,** 160; April 28, 1909, **19,** 174; May 12, 1909, **19,** 191; May 25, 1909, **19,** 214; May 31, 1909, **19,** 224; June 4, 1909, **19,** 229; June 18, 1909, **19,** 258; June 19, 1909, **19,** 261; June 26, 1909, **19,** 270; July 3, 1909, **19,** 289; July 9, 1909, **19,** 304; July 11, 1909, **19,** 307; July 18, 1909, **19,** 311; July 25, 1909, **19,** 317; Aug. 1, 1909, **19,** 321; Aug. 8, 1909, **19,** 330; Aug. 22, 1909, **19,** 349; Aug. 29, 1909, **19,** 354; Sept. 5, 1909, **19,** 357; Sept. 12, 1909, **19,** 382; Sept. 19, 1909, **19,** 384; Sept. 26, 1909, **19,** 392; Sept. 29, 1909, **19,** 394; Oct. 24, 1909, **19,** 442; Oct. 25, 1909, **19,** 445; Jan. 2, 1910, **19,** 704; Feb. 8, 1910, **20,** 87; Feb. 12, 1910, **20,** 122; Feb. 14, 1910, **20,** 126; Feb. 18, 1910, **20,** 138; Feb. 20, 1910, **20,** 148; Feb. 25, 1910, **20,** 178; Feb. 28, 1910, **20,** 185; March 4, 1910, **20,** 210; March 16, 1910, **20,** 248; April 19, 1910, **20,** 370; May 2, 1910, **20,** 408; May 10, 1910, **20,** 429; May 26, 1910, **20,** 473; June 1, 1910, **20,** 491; June 5, 1910, **20,** 500; June 17, 1910, **20,** 535; July 11, 1910, **20,** 575; July 26, 1910, **21,** 26; Aug. 6, 1910, **21,** 38; Aug. 12, 1910, **21,** 50; Aug. 31, 1910, **21,** 64; Sept. 25, 1910, **21,** 163; Dec. 6, 1910, **22,** 139; Dec. 7, 1910, **22,** 141; Dec. 16, 1910, **22,** 204; Dec. 17, 1910, **22,** 209; Jan. 3, 1911, **22,** 292; Jan. 5, 1911, **22,** 294; Jan. 10, 1911, **22,** 323; Jan. 13, 1911, **22,** 329; Jan. 15, 1911, **22,** 333; Jan. 22, 1911, **22,** 362; Jan. 27, 1911, **22,** 382; Jan. 29, 1911, **22,** 391; Jan. 31, 1911, **22,** 396; Feb. 5, 1911, **22,** 407; Feb. 12, 1911, **22,** 424; Feb. 19, 1911, **22,** 438; Feb. 26, 1911, **22,** 453; March 5, 1911, **22,** 477; March 12, 1911, **22,** 500; March 19, 1911, **22,** 509; March 26, 1911, **22,** 517; April 2, 1911, **22,** 531; April 9, 1911, **22,** 543; April 16, 1911, **22,** 570; April 23, 1911, **22,** 581; April 30, 1911, **22,** 597; May 7, 1911, **23,** 11; May 13, 1911, **23,** 49; May 21, 1911, **23,** 80; June 25, 1911, **23,** 174; July 2, 1911, **23,** 184; July 5, 1911, **23,** 189; July 10,

1911, **23,** 193; July 16, 1911, **23,** 213; July 20, 1911, **23,** 220; July 24, 1911, **23,** 225; July 30, 1911, **23,** 239; Aug. 6, 1911, **23,** 256; Aug. 15, 1911, **23,** 267; Aug. 19, 1911, **23,** 283; Sept. 17, 1911, **23,** 329; Oct. 8, 1911, **23,** 424; Nov. 22, 1911, **23,** 559; Dec. 1, 1911, **23,** 560; Dec. 10, 1911, **23,** 590; Dec. 17, 1911, **23,** 596; Dec. 24, 1911, **23,** 606; Dec. 31, 1911, **23,** 633; Jan. 7, 1912, **24,** 5; Jan. 14, 1912, **24,** 43; Jan. 24, 1912, **24,** 65; Jan. 31, 1912, **24,** 98; Feb. 4, 1912, **24,** 132; Feb. 11, 1912, **24,** 150; Feb. 18, 1912, **24,** 177; Feb. 28, 1912, **24,** 218; March 10, 1912, **24,** 239; March 17, 1912, **24,** 249; April 1, 1912, **24,** 271; April 8, 1912, **24,** 305; April 13, 1912, **24,** 329; fragment, May 5, 1912, **24,** 385; May 11, 1912, **24,** 391; May 20, 1912, **24,** 409; May 26, 1912, **24,** 444; June 2, 1912, **24,** 451; June 9, 1912, **24,** 466; June 17, 1912, **24,** 481; June 23, 1912, **24,** 495; July 6, 1912, **24,** 541; *see also* Mary Allen Hulbert

George Walbridge Perkins, June 21, 1909, **19,** 263; Nov. 4, 1909, **19,** 482; April 21, 1910, **20,** 379

Bliss Perry, Dec. 3, 1902, **14,** 254; Oct. 24, 1904, **15,** 529; Aug. 9, 1905, **16,** 174

Ralph Barton Perry, March 4, 1905, **16,** 19; March 6, 1905, **16,** 21

Magnus Fraser Peterson, Nov. 30, 1912, **25,** 572

James Duval Phelan, May 3, 1912, **24,** 382

John Sanburn Phillips, June 7, 1911, **23,** 136

Nicholas L. Piotrowski, March 13, 1912, **24,** 242; July 15, 1912, **24,** 552; Dec. 11, 1912, **25,** 586

Pius X, Feb. 11, 1907, **17,** 32

Henry Cooper Pitney, Jr., Sept. 15, 1902, **14,** 131; Oct. 7, 1902, **14,** 142; Oct. 13, 1902, **14,** 144; Nov. 26, 1902, **14,** 222; Feb. 5, 1903, **14,** 349; Feb. 10, 1903, **14,** 355; June 20, 1903, **14,** 495; June 27, 1903, **14,** 497; June 30, 1903, **14,** 501; Nov. 9, 1903, **15,** 48

Chester Childs Platt, Sept. 6, 1912, **25,** 112

Dan Fellows Platt, July 23, 1910, **21,** 22; Aug. 3, 1910, **21,** 36; Aug. 22, 1910, **21,** 58; Sept. 21, 1910, **21,** 149; Oct. 26, 1910, **21,** 436; Nov. 24, 1910, **22,** 87; June 4, 1912, **24,** 454

Clarence Hamilton Poe, May 6, 1907, **17,** 138; March 13, 1911, **22,** 503; March 17, 1911, **22,** 509

John Prentiss Poe, April 30, 1908, **18,** 278

John Garland Pollard, June 14, 1911, **23,** 152; Sept. 11, 1911, **23,** 313; Dec. 22, 1911, **23,** 605; Jan. 27, 1912, **24,** 81

William Kelly Prentice, Jan. 10, 1907, **16,** 554

Robert Price, May 21, 1907, **17,** 153

*Princeton Alumni Weekly,* editor, Nov. 21, 1908, **18,** 520

Princeton University, Board of Trustees, Oct. 17, 1907, **17,** 443; Oct. 20, 1910, **21,** 362; Nov. 1, 1910, **21,** 492

Princeton University, Class of 1906, **16,** 420

Princeton University, secretaries of various classes, May 10, 1903, **14,** 455

Princeton University, various trustees, Jan. 4, 1910, **19,** 711

Henry Smith Pritchett, Feb. 8, 1906, **16,** 306; Jan. 4, 1907, **16,** 546; April 24, 1907, **17,** 115; May 21, 1907, **17,** 154; Nov. 19, 1907, **17,** 510; Nov. 27, 1907, **17,** 527; Dec. 6, 1907, **17,** 549; March 20, 1908, **18,** 61; April 10, 1908, **18,** 257; April 15, 1908, **18,** 272; April 6, 1909, **19,** 150; May 4, 1909, **19,** 182; May 8, 1909, **19,** 188; Oct. 23, 1909, **19,** 441; Oct. 29, 1909, **19,** 459; Aug. 6, 1910, **21,** 39; Sept. 24, 1910, **21,** 160; Nov. 1, 1910, **21,** 492; Nov. 11, 1910, **22,** 23; April 15, 1911, **22,** 569; May 25, 1911, **23,** 83; July 24, 1911, **23,** 226

Ralph Pulitzer, June 27, 1912, **24,** 501; July 17, 1912, **24,** 556; Nov. 9, 1912, **25,** 534

George Haven Putnam, March 17, 1897, **18,** 647

David Hunter McAlpin Pyle, Nov. 23, 1912, **25,** 560

Moses Taylor Pyne, Dec. 8, 1906, **16,** 503; Dec. 31, 1906, **16,** 541; Jan. 5, 1907, **16,** 547; Jan. 8, 1907, **16,** 552; Jan. 10, 1907, **16,** 553; Feb. 21, 1907, **17,** 48; Feb. 28, 1907, **17,** 51; April 24, 1907, **17,** 116; May 20, 1907, **17,** 152; Dec. 16, 1907, **17,** 560; Jan. 14, 1908, **17,** 602; Jan. 16, 1908, **17,** 604; May 5, 1908, **18,** 286; Nov. 16, 1908, **18,** 514; Jan. 28, 1909, **19,** 17; Feb. 16, 1909, **19,** 48; March 29, 1909, **19,** 126; May 19, 1909, **19,** 201; Oct. 12, 1909, **19,** 410; Oct. 16, 1909, **19,** 422; Nov. 26, 1909, **19,** 533; Nov. 29, 1909, **19,** 537; Dec. 3, 1909, **19,** 549; Dec. 21, 1909, **19,** 611; Dec. 22, 1909, **19,** 620; Dec. 25, 1909, **19,** 628; Dec. 28, 1909, **19,** 634; Dec. 30, 1909, **19,** 657; Jan. 8, 1910, **19,** 747

Adolphus Ragan, July 3, 1909, **19,** 292; July 20, 1910, **21,** 14

Walter Mead Rankin, March 16, 1909, **19,** 100

John Marshall Raymond, May 23, 1910, **20,** 467

George Lawrence Record, Oct. 11, 1910, **21,** 296; Oct. 24, 1910, **21,** 406; Nov. 10, 1910, **22,** 13; Jan. 27, 1911, **22,** 382

James Hay Reed, Jan. 13, 1904, **15,** 124

William Belden Reed, Jr., Aug. 31, 1907, **17,** 366; Sept. 6, 1907, **17,** 373

Louis Irving Reichner, July 20, 1907, **17,** 292

Edith Gittings Reid, July 12, 1902, **14,** 3; Oct. 22, 1902, **14,** 167; Nov. 2, 1902, **14,** 196; Dec. 11, 1902, **14,** 277; Feb. 3, 1903, **14,** 347; March 15, 1907, **17,** 72; May 2, 1910, **20,** 407; May 26, 1912, **24,** 445; Nov. 20, 1912, **25,** 551

Ira Remsen, Jan. 27, 1912, **24,** 82; Nov. 14, 1912, **25,** 547; Dec. 3, 1912, **25,** 578

James Ford Rhodes, May 10, 1910, **20,** 430; May 16, 1910, **20,** 457; May 28, 1910, **20,** 483; June 4, 1910, **20,** 499; Nov. 15, 1910, **22,** 49

Owen Willans Richardson, Aug. 15, 1906, **16,** 434; July 8, 1908, **18,** 354

Palmer Chamberlaine Ricketts, Jr., May 17, 1905, **16,** 102

William Henry Rideing, Feb. 4, 1911, **22,** 406

George Lockhart Rives, Dec. 11, 1912, **25,** 587

Morgan Poitiaux Robinson, Oct. 30, 1903, **15,** 32

James Slocum Rogers, Sept. 22, 1910, **21,** 153

Philip Ashton Rollins, March 19, 1910, **20,** 263

Henry Edward Rood, Oct. 24, 1906, **16,** 470

Theodore Roosevelt, Oct. 20, 1902, **14,** 148; Feb. 1, 1903, **14,** 337; Aug. 8, 1905, **16,** 172; Nov. 6, 1912, **25,** 526

Robert Kilburn Root, March 23, 1905, **16,** 37

Victor Rosewater, March 7, 1904, **15,** 182

Reginald Rowland, March 6, 1911, **22,** 480

Albertina Pyne Russell, April 19, 1909, **19,** 166

Archibald Douglas Russell, Feb. 13, 1907, **17,** 36

Henry Norris Russell, Aug. 27, 1902, **14,** 112

Julius Sachs, Dec. 9, 1902, **14,** 267

Clarence Sackett, Dec. 15, 1910, **22,** 200

Willard Saulsbury, April 22, 1912, **24,** 356; April 30, 1912, **24,** 379; May 29, 1912, **24,** 450; June 11, 1912, **24,** 471; Aug. 22, 1912, **25,** 52

Minot Judson Savage, Nov. 22, 1905, **16,** 230; Nov. 24, 1905, **16,** 232

Walter Hulme Sawyer, May 5, 1909, **19,** 184

John Sayles, Nov. 27, 1911, **23,** 559

Adolf Frederick Schauffler, Dec. 3, 1909, **19,** 547

William Gray Schauffler, June 29, 1911, **23,** 183

Jacob Gould Schurman, Nov. 12, 1910, **22,** 30

Austin Scott, Feb. 29, 1904, **15,** 180; May 11, 1904, **15,** 324; June 14, 1904, **15,** 378; June 18, 1904, **15,** 391

Charles Scribner, Aug. 14, 1902, **14,** 85; Dec. 24, 1902, **14,** 304; Sept. 22, 1908, **18,** 420; Sept. 25, 1909, **19,** 391; Sept. 20, 1910, **21,** 144

John Preston Searle, March 16, 1906, **16,** 335

John Franklin Shafroth, Oct. 23, 1911, **23,** 478

Thomas Berry Shannon, May 1, 1911, **22,** 598

Albert Shaw, Dec. 6, 1912, **25,** 581; Dec. 23, 1912, **25,** 617

Leslie Mortier Shaw, Aug. 11, 1906, **16,** 433

Edward Wright Sheldon, March 30, 1904, **15,** 219; March 27, 1907, **17,** 94; June 24, 1909, **19,** 266, 267; July 5, 1909, **19,** 293; July 10, 1909, **19,** 306; Aug. 26, 1909, **19,** 354; Oct. 12, 1909, **19,** 408; Oct. 19, 1909, **19,** 426; Oct. 22, 1909, **19,** 440; Oct. 28, 1909, **19,** 455; Nov. 4, 1909, **19,** 482; Dec. 27, 1909, **19,** 632; Dec. 30, 1909, **19,** 658; Feb. 4, 1910, **20,** 76; Feb. 11, 1910, **20,** 118; March 10, 1910, **20,** 226; March 21, 1910, **20,** 270; May 16, 1910, **20,** 456; May 30, 1910, **20,** 486; July 1, 1910, **20,** 554; July 11, 1910, **20,** 572; Nov. 10, 1910, **22,** 13

Robert W. Shultice, Nov. 27, 1910, **22,** 99

Edwin Sidney Simons, Nov. 15, 1909, **19,** 501

Albridge Clinton Smith, Jr., July 15, 1907, **17,** 283

Caroline W. Guppy Smith, Nov. 15, 1909, **19,** 503

Edgar Fahs Smith, Nov. 25, 1904, **15,** 539

Goldwin Smith, March 13, 1903, **14,** 391

Herbert Stearns Squier Smith, April 13, 1904, **15,** 246

James Smith, Jr., Nov. 9, 1910, **21,** 590

Samuel Archibald Smith, Nov. 20, 1909, **19,** 527

Thomas L. Snow, Sept. 16, 1904, **15,** 470; Oct. 20, 1904, **15,** 523

Emma C. Spenser, Jan. 19, 1903, **14,** 328

*Springfield* (Mass.) *Republican*, editor, July 6, 1909, **19,** 293

James Sprunt, Jan. 19, 1910, **20,** 31; June 7, 1912, **24,** 464; Aug. 1, 1912, **24,** 578

Frederick A. Steuert, Sept. 5, 1902, **14,** 122

Edwin Augustus Stevens, Jan. 2, 1907, **16,** 545; Jan. 11, 1907, **16,** 561

Bayard Stockton, Nov. 26, 1904, **15,** 544

Anson Phelps Stokes, Jr., Oct. 29, 1902, **14,** 189; Oct. 3, 1905, **16,** 190; April 30, 1907, **17,** 125; May 3, 1907, **17,** 129

Nathan Straus, Jan. 29, 1912, **24,** 95; Oct. 16, 1912, **25,** 422

Duane Reed Stuart, April 12, 1905, **16,** 51

G. McArthur Sullivan, Dec. 3, 1909, **19,** 550

George Hammond Sullivan, Nov. 4, 1910, **21,** 543

Jerry Bartholomew Sullivan, Nov. 20, 1912, **25,** 555

William Sulzer, Dec. 22, 1906, **16,** 539; Oct. 3, 1912, **25,** 329

Sun Yat-sen, Dec. 3, 1912, **25,** 576

William Howard Taft, Nov. 6, 1912, **25,** 526; Dec. 2, 1912, **25,** 574

Charles Andrew Talcott, May 25, 1909, **19,** 215; Nov. 9, 1910 **21,** 590; Feb. 28, 1911, **22,** 456

Arthur W. Tedcastle, Aug. 20, 1902, **14,** 95; April 10, 1906, **16,** 357; July 5, 1909, **19,** 292

Frank Thilly, Jan. 1, 1904, **15,** 114; Jan. 20, 1904, **15,** 136; Jan. 31, 1904, **15,** 152; Feb. 1, 1904, **15,** 152; Feb. 8, 1904, **15,** 163; March 11, 1904, **15,** 188; March 21, 1904, **15,** 202; April 13, 1904, **15,** 245; Aug. 12, 1904, **15,** 439; Aug. 25, 1904, **15,** 448; Nov. 18, 1904, **15,** 535; Nov. 30, 1908, **18,** 528

Augustus Thomas, Jan. 19, 1903, **14,** 329

Charles Spalding Thomas, Nov. 13, 1912, **25,** 545

Harvey Thomas, April 4, 1912, **24,** 289

Martha Carey Thomas, Jan. 5, 1903, **14,** 319

Henry Burling Thompson, June 22, 1907, **17,** 220; Sept. 17, 1907, **17,** 388; May 21, 1908, **18,** 303; Nov. 14, 1908, **18,** 510; Nov. 16, 1908, **18,** 515; Dec. 21, 1909, **19,** 612; Dec. 23, 1909, **19,** 624; March 9, 1910, **20,** 223; July 14, 1910, **20,** 578

Henry Dallas Thompson, April 3, 1912, **24,** 284

Samuel Huston Thompson, Aug. 1, 1912, **24,** 579

Samuel Huston Thompson, Jr., Sept. 21, 1910, **21,** 149; Feb. 3, 1911, **22,** 405; March 27, 1911, **22,** 521; March 29, 1911, **22,** 523; March 31, 1911, **22,** 527; April 18, 1911, **22,** 574; April 19, 1911, **22,** 577; Jan. 4, 1912, **23,** 650

Charles Franklin Thwing, Feb. 26, 1895, **23,** 657
Henry St. George Tucker, Dec. 31, 1910, **22,** 287; Nov. 29, 1911, **23,** 559
Joseph Patrick Tumulty, Nov. 25, 1912, **25,** 561; Nov. 30, 1912, **25,** 566; Dec. 3, 1912, **25,** 579; Dec. 11, 1912, **25,** 584 (2)
Frederick Jackson Turner, April 15, 1905, **16,** 58; June 17, 1907, **17,** 214
Horatio Whitridge Turner, Oct. 19, 1908, **18,** 468; Nov. 11, 1908, **18,** 493
Edna Henry Lee Turpin, June 28, 1909, **19,** 272; Aug. 23, 1909, **19,** 352
Oscar Wilder Underwood, July 3, 1912, **24,** 530; July 7, 1912, **24,** 542; July 19, 1912, **24,** 560; Dec. 17, 1912, **25,** 593
Unknown person, Nov. 6, 1910, **21,** 577; Aug. 15, 1911, **23,** 267
Samuel Untermyer, Nov. 12, 1912, **25,** 542
Irving Strong Upson, Oct. 23, 1902, **14,** 167
Frank Arthur Vanderlip, April 1, 1908, **18,** 219; Dec. 2, 1908, **18,** 529; Feb. 1, 1909, **19,** 18; Feb. 5, 1909, **19,** 29; June 18, 1909, **19,** 259; Dec. 14, 1909, **19,** 604; Dec. 20, 1909, **19,** 609
Henry van Dyke, July 5, 1907, **17,** 260; July 8, 1907, **17,** 263
Charles Richard Van Hise, Jan. 29, 1904, **15,** 145; Dec. 26, 1906, **16,** 539; Dec. 7, 1907, **17,** 551; Dec. 3, 1909, **19,** 550
Alexander Van Rensselaer, Jan. 13, 1904, **15,** 122
Claude Halstead Van Tyne, June 7, 1905, **16,** 111
Edwin Augustus Van Valkenburg, Sept. 25, 1910, **21,** 164; Oct. 4, 1910, **21,** 241
Various correspondents, Dec. 23, 1910, **22,** 252
Marion Jackson Verdery, Dec. 24, 1910, **22,** 257; April 12, 1911, **22,** 553
Ambrose White Vernon, Nov. 30, 1912, **25,** 568
Oswald Garrison Villard, Jan. 26, 1908, **17,** 609; Dec. 5, 1910, **22,** 135; Jan. 2, 1911, **22,** 288; Jan. 6, 1911, **22,** 308; Feb. 27, 1911, **22,** 454; Dec. 9, 1911, **23,** 589; Jan. 23, 1912, **24,** 63; Jan. 26, 1912, **24,** 73; Aug. 17, 1912, **25,** 41; Aug. 23, 1912, **25,** 52
Clyde Weber Votaw, Nov. 4, 1902, **14,** 198
Voters of America, Oct. 19, 1912, **25,** 432
Williamson Updike Vreeland, March 11, 1904, **15,** 189; March 10, 1905, **16,** 27; July 10, 1905, **16,** 154; Aug. 2, 1905, **16,** 167
John Milton Waldron, Nov. 14, 1912, **25,** 548
John Brisben Walker, Aug. 30, 1904, **15,** 460
Alexander Walters, Oct. 21, 1912, **25,** 448
Edward Joshua Ward, Nov. 13, 1912, **25,** 546
Catherine Carter Campbell Warren, May 6, 1910, **20,** 414
Salomé Machado Warren, Dec. 6, 1907, **17,** 548; Dec. 10, 1907, **17,** 554
Henry Watterson, Dec. 31, 1910, **22,** 286; June 15, 1911, **23,** 153; June 29, 1911, **23,** 182; July 14, 1911, **23,** 199; July 24, 1911, **23,** 226

Carolyn Wells, Oct. 24, 1912, **25,** 458

John Wesley Wescott, Sept. 18, 1910, **21,** 137; Sept. 22, 1910, **21,** 152; Dec. 16, 1910, **22,** 206; Jan. 2, 1911, **22,** 289; Jan. 30, 1911, **22,** 394; Feb. 10, 1911, **22,** 414; March 24, 1911, **22,** 516; March 27, 1911, **22,** 520; April 10, 1911, **22,** 548; Oct. 9, 1911, **23,** 425; Oct. 31, 1911, **23,** 518; Feb. 18, 1912, **24,** 179; May 29, 1912, **24,** 449; June 3, 1912, **24,** 452; June 6, 1912, **24,** 462; Sept. 14, 1912, **25,** 147; Sept. 19, 1912, **25,** 184

Andrew Fleming West, Aug. 20, 1906, **16,** 435; March 13, 1907, **17,** 66; May 6, 1907, **17,** 138; May 21, 1907, **17,** 154; May 23, 1907, **17,** 155; July 11, 1907, **17,** 280; July 23, 1908, **18,** 373; Nov. 9, 1908, **18,** 490; Jan. 26, 1909, **19,** 12; April 26, 1909, **19,** 172

Israel Losey White, June 15, 1910, **20,** 530

Edith M. Whitmore, Feb. 8, 1912, **24,** 140

James Howard Whitty, Dec. 16, 1909, **19,** 606

Whom It May Concern, Nov. 20, 1906, **16,** 487

Benjamin Lawton Wiggins, Oct. 4, 1902, **14,** 139; May 4, 1905, **16,** 90

William Royal Wilder, Sept. 21, 1910, **21,** 150; Jan. 19, 1911, **22,** 358

Harvey Washington Wiley, Nov. 9, 1912, **25,** 535

Louis Wiley, Nov. 23, 1905, **16,** 231; Dec. 20, 1907, **17,** 565; Sept. 5, 1912, **25,** 107; Sept. 7, 1912, **25,** 115

Walter Maurice Wilkins, Sept. 16, 1910, **21,** 102

George Fred Williams, Dec. 3, 1912, **25,** 578

James Thomas Williams, Jr., April 25, 1910, **20,** 390

John Rogers Williams, Aug. 15, 1904, **15,** 443; Sept. 2, 1904, **15,** 462; Aug. 5, 1905, **16,** 171

Edgar Williamson, Aug. 23, 1910, **21,** 59

Alfred McCalmont Wilson, Nov. 12, 1912, **25,** 541

Edwin Bird Wilson, July 24, 1911, **23,** 227; Aug. 17, 1912, **25,** 42

Ellen Axson Wilson
  July–August 1902
    July 13, **14,** 6; July 14, **14,** 9; July 15, **14,** 11; July 16, **14,** 17; July 17, **14,** 20; July 18, **14,** 24; July 19, **14,** 26; July 20, **14,** 29; July 21, **14,** 35; July 22, **14,** 38; July 23, **14,** 40; July 24, **14,** 41; Aug. 3, **14,** 48; Aug. 4, **14,** 51; Aug. 5, **14,** 52; Aug. 6, **14,** 56; Aug. 7, **14,** 60; Aug. 8, **14,** 64; Aug. 9, **14,** 67; Aug. 10, **14,** 70; Aug. 11, **14,** 73; Aug. 12, **14,** 76; Aug. 13, **14,** 79; Aug. 14, **14,** 83; Aug. 16, **14,** 89; Aug. 17, **14,** 89; Aug. 18, **14,** 91; Aug. 19, **14,** 93; Aug. 20, **14,** 94; Aug. 21, **14,** 97; Aug. 22, **14,** 100; Aug. 23, **14,** 103; Aug. 24, **14,** 104; Aug. 25, **14,** 105; Aug. 26, **14,** 108; Aug. 27, **14,** 110; Aug. 28, **14,** 116; Aug. 29, **14,** 117; Aug. 30, **14,** 118
  April–September 1903
    April 21, **14,** 418; April 22, **14,** 421; April 23, **14,** 422; April

24, **14,** 424; April 25, **14,** 426; April 27, **14,** 429; April 28, **14,** 431; April 29, **14,** 434; April 30, **14,** 437; May 1, **14,** 439; May 2, **14,** 447; May 4, **14,** 451; May 5, **14,** 453; Sept. 30, **15,** 8
March–May 1904
  March 21, **15,** 201; March 24, **15,** 207; March 28, **15,** 214; March 31, **15,** 221; April 4, **15,** 231; April 8, **15,** 237; April 12, **15,** 243; April 14, **15,** 246; April 17, **15,** 263; April 21, **15,** 269; April 26, **15,** 295; April 28, **15,** 300; May 3, **15,** 306; May 6, **15,** 311; May 9, **15,** 317; May 12, **15,** 324; May 12, **15,** 325; May 16, **15,** 335; May 19, **15,** 340; May 23, **15,** 344; May 27, **15,** 350
August–September 1906
  Aug. 21, **16,** 436; Aug. 22, **16,** 436; Aug. 23, **16,** 437; Aug. 24, **16,** 438; Aug. 25, **16,** 439; Aug. 26, **16,** 440; Aug. 27, **16,** 441; Aug. 28, **16,** 442; Aug. 29, **16,** 443; Aug. 30, **16,** 444; Aug. 31, **16,** 444; Sept. 1, **16,** 445; Sept. 2, **16,** 445; Sept. 3, **16,** 448; Sept. 4, **16,** 450
January 1907
  Jan. 2, **16,** 544; Jan. 4, **16,** 546; Jan. 12, **16,** 563; Jan. 14, **17,** 3; Jan. 22, **17,** 10; Jan. 26, **17,** 14; Jan. 27, **17,** 22; Jan. 30, **17,** 25
January–August 1908
  Jan. 26, **17,** 606; Feb. 4, **17,** 611; March 14, **23,** 657; June 20, **18,** 340; June 26, **18,** 343; July 1, **18,** 348; July 6, **18,** 351; July 8, **18,** 353; July 10, **18,** 356; July 13, **18,** 361; July 16, **18,** 364; July 20, **18,** 369; July 23, **18,** 373; July 27, **18,** 377; July 30, **18,** 381; Aug. 3, **18,** 387; Aug. 9, **18,** 393; Aug. 13, **18,** 398; Aug. 16, **18,** 399; Aug. 20, **18,** 405; Aug. 23, **18,** 409; Aug. 27, **18,** 412; Aug. 30, **18,** 414
February 1910–October 1912
  Feb. 14, 1910, **20,** 125; Feb. 17, 1910, **20,** 132; Feb. 20, 1910, **20,** 144; Feb. 25, 1910, **20,** 175; Feb. 28, 1910, **20,** 183; Nov. 19, 1911, **23,** 555; Oct. 6, 1912, **25,** 359
Jessie Woodrow Wilson, July 17, 1908, **18,** 367; Aug. 4, 1908, **18,** 391
Joseph R. Wilson, Jr., March 31, 1911 **23,** 657; Nov. 30, 1912, **25,** 568; Dec. 11, 1912, **25,** 585
William Lawrence Wilson, April 9, 1910, **20,** 351; April 13, 1910, **20,** 353
Felexiana Shepherd Baker Woodrow, Nov. 12, 1912, **25,** 540
James Woodrow, Jan. 30, 1903, **14,** 335
Hiram Woods, March 23, 1910, **20,** 285; May 28, 1910, **20,** 482; Nov. 20, 1912, **25,** 553
Lawrence Crane Woods, Sept. 16, 1907, **17,** 385; Oct. 25, 1907, **17,** 456; June 10, 1909, **19,** 239; June 23, 1909, **19,** 266; Oct. 4, 1909, **19,** 401; Jan. 25, 1910, **20,** 53; Feb. 5, 1910, **20,** 81; April 20, 1910, **20,** 376; April 26, 1910, **20,** 391; Oct. 27, 1910, **21,** 444
Neander Montgomery Woods, May 21, 1907, **17,** 154
Edward Henry Wright, Jr., Jan. 8, 1907, **16,** 551

Walter Augustus Wyckoff, May 12, 1903, **14,** 456

Isaac Chauncey Wyman, June 1, 1909, **19,** 225

Robert John Wynne, Aug. 12, 1906, **16,** 434

Frederic Yates, Oct. 6, 1906, **16,** 455; July 2, 1907, **17,** 242; Aug. 30, 1907, **17,** 365; June 1, 1908, **18,** 312; Sept. 5, 1908, **18,** 417; Sept. 25, 1908, **18,** 422; Sept. 9, 1910, **21,** 87; Dec. 14, 1910, **22,** 187

Frederic Yates and Emily Chapman Martin Yates, Oct. 22, 1906, **16,** 469; Nov. 6, 1906, **16,** 481

Charles Augustus Young, Dec. 8, 1892, **14,** 558

Letters and telegrams to Wilson from

Catharine Amory Palmer Abbe, Nov. 17, 1908, **18,** 516

Leon Abbett, Jr., Dec. 29, 1910, **22,** 281

Frank Frost Abbott, April 3, 1908, **18,** 225; Dec. 10, 1909, **19,** 591; Dec. 9, 1909, **19,** 592; Jan. 6, 1910, **19,** 736

Lyman Abbott, March 30, 1910, **20,** 306; April 8, 1910, **20,** 350

John William Abercrombie, Oct. 21, 1903, **15,** 25; March 29, 1904, **15,** 218; April 4, 1904, **15,** 234

Charles Francis Adams, Oct. 2, 1907, **17,** 409; Feb. 2, 1909, **19,** 20; Feb. 10, 1909, **19,** 32; June 19, 1909, **19,** 263

John Haslup Adams, June 21, 1912, **24,** 491

Penrhyn Stanley Adamson, Aug. 6, 1902, **14,** 59

Alvey Augustus Adee, March 15, 1904, **15,** 194

Walter Maxwell Adriance, March 23, 1907, **17,** 88

Edwin Anderson Alderman, Nov. 9, 1910, **21,** 595

Archibald Stevens Alexander, July 16, 1910, **21,** 6; July 22, 1910, **21,** 18; Sept. 16, 1910, **21,** 112; Oct. 20, 1910, **21,** 380

Caroline Bayard Stevens Alexander, Sept. 21, 1910, **21,** 150

Henry Eckert Alexander, Nov. 18, 1909, **19,** 522; March 28, 1910, **20,** 297; July 17, 1910, **21,** 8; July 18, 1910, **21,** 9; July 23, 1910, **21,** 22; July 27, 1910, **21,** 26; Aug. 1, 1910, **21,** 33; Aug. 5, 1910, **21,** 37; Aug. 16, 1910, **21,** 54; Aug. 19, 1910, **21,** 57; Aug. 23, 1910, **21,** 62; Sept. 23, 1910, **21,** 158; Sept. 25, 1910, **21,** 167; Sept. 29, 1910, **21,** 200; Oct. 1, 1910, **21,** 219; Oct. 2, 1910, **21,** 225; Oct. 4, 1910, **21,** 243; Dec. 20, 1910, **22,** 231; Aug. 10, 1911, **23,** 262

James Waddel Alexander, Dec. 29, 1903, **15,** 113; Jan. 4, 1904, **15,** 118; Sept. 8, 1904, **15,** 463; Dec. 28, 1909, **19,** 650

Lucien Hugh Alexander, Oct. 14, 1910, **21,** 328

Charles Dexter Allen, Sept. 25, 1910, **21,** 168

Hamilton Ford Allen, May 31, 1905, **16,** 106

Lamson Allen, Jan. 15, 1911, **22,** 335

Yorke Allen, Oct. 11, 1910, **21,** 300

William Outis Allison, Jan. 21, 1910, **20,** 44

Harlan Page Amen, Jan. 26, 1904, **15,** 141

Andrew Runni Anderson, April 14, 1905, **16,** 55

Benjamin McAlester Anderson, Jr., Oct. 15, 1912, **25,** 419

Patrick C. Anderson, March 19, 1912, **24,** 255

Charles McLean Andrews, Oct. 30, 1904, **15,** 532

Elisha Benjamin Andrews, July 5, 1912, **24,** 539

William S. Andrews, June 24, 1912, **24,** 500

Robert Edwards Annin, Oct. 3, 1904, **15,** 503

Henry Harbaugh Apple, Jan. 25, 1910, **20,** 55

Harry Howard Armstrong, Aug. 29, 1907, **17,** 364

Constantine Peter Arnold, April 22, 1910, **20,** 383

Olivia Goldthwaite Arrington, March 27, 1904, **15,** 213

Charles Duke Atkins, Nov. 27, 1908, **18,** 525; Dec. 9, 1908, **18,**
540; Dec. 12, 1908, **18,** 544

Joseph Smith Auerbach, Aug. 17, 1904, **15,** 446

Frank Rose Austin, Jan. 25, 1911, **22,** 375

Stockton Axson, Oct. 27, 1902, **14,** 187

John Arthur Aylward, Aug. 4, 1911, **23,** 253

Oliver B. Babcock, Sept. 11, 1902, **14,** 129

George Frederick Baer, Dec. 17, 1910, **22,** 215

Warren Worth Bailey, March 28, 1911, **22,** 522; Dec. 28, 1912, **25,**
640

Alfred Brittin Baker, Sept. 16, 1910, **21,** 117

Newton Diehl Baker, July 24, 1912, **24,** 568; Nov. 15, 1912, **25,**
549

Stephen Baker, Nov. 26, 1909, **19,** 534; Nov. 30, 1909, **19,** 538;
Dec. 4, 1909, **19,** 553

James Mark Baldwin, Aug. 18, 1903, **14,** 553; Dec. 22, 1903, **15,**
103; Dec. 23, 1903, **15,** 106; Dec. 24, 1903, **15,** 108; Dec. 26, 1903,
**15,** 109

Simeon Eben Baldwin, Sept. 17, 1910, **21,** 133; Nov. 10, 1910, **22,**
15

George Ballantine and Son, Oct. 13, 1906, **16,** 456

McKee Barclay, Aug. 11, 1911, **23,** 264; Aug. 14, 1911, **23,** 266

Edgar Starr Barney, May 30, 1909, **19,** 223

John Watson Barr, Jr., May 13, 1909, **19,** 196

Daniel Moreau Barringer, Nov. 9, 1910, **21,** 603; July 25, 1911, **23,**
227; Aug. 2, 1911, **23,** 245; Sept. 11, 1911, **23,** 314; Oct. 5, 1911,
**23,** 408; Dec. 22, 1911, **23,** 605

John William Basore, June 5, 1905, **16,** 110; June 8, 1905, **16,** 112

George Cullen Battle, Jan. 20, 1909, **19,** 4

Clarence Hughson Baxter, Sept. 22, 1910, **21,** 158

Edgeworth Bird Baxter, Nov. 5, 1910, **21,** 577

Sylvester Woodbridge Beach, Nov. 9, 1910, **21,** 597

Alexander Bell, Aug. 23, 1902, **14,** 111

Henry C. Bell, Jan. 9, 1912, **24,** 25

Blanche Wilder Bellamy, May 1, 1905, **16,** 89

Edward Webster Bemis, Nov. 9, 1910, **21,** 617

John Mirza Bennett, Jr., July 11, 1907, **17,** 280

Allan Benny, Jan. 30, 1911, **22,** 395

Albert Jeremiah Beveridge, June 12, 1902, **19,** 758

Hiram Bingham, June 17, 1905, **16,** 142

Charles Clarke Black, Jan. 12, 1907, **16,** 563; Dec. 10, 1910 **22,** 169

William Blackburn, Oct. 15, 1910, **21,** 335

Anita McCormick Blaine, Nov. 3, 1909, **19,** 481

De Witt Clinton Blair, Feb. 10, 1906, **16,** 312

Paul Lendrum Blakely, Dec. 14, 1907, **17,** 560

James Gillmor Blauvelt, Oct. 5, 1910, **21,** 260

Gilbert Ames Bliss, June 12, 1905, **16,** 136

Benjamin Boisseau Bobbitt, Oct. 13, 1910, **21,** 324

Ernest Ludlow Bogart, April 14, 1905, **16,** 55; May 1, 1909, **19,** 180

Edward William Bok, Sept. 16, 1910, **21,** 118; Nov. 10, 1910, **22,** 21

Harold Bolce, July 19, 1909, **19,** 314

Helen Woodrow Bones, Feb. 2, 1903, **14,** 346

Gutzon Borglum, Aug. 8, 1905, **16,** 173

Max Boucard, July 3, 1902, **14,** 30; Aug. 11, 1902, **14,** 124

Jonathan Bourne, Jr., Nov. 12, 1910, **22,** 34

Joseph McCarter Bowyer, May 22, 1908, **18,** 304

Cyrus Fogg Brackett, June 1, 1903, **14,** 469; April 8, 1908, **18,** 241; April 11, 1908, **18,** 261

Haven Darling Brackett, April 15, 1905, **16,** 59

Gamaliel Bradford, Feb. 6, 1907, **17,** 30; Dec. 5, 1910, **22,** 138

Louis Dembitz Brandeis, Aug. 1, 1912, **24,** 580; Sept. 28, 1912, **25,** 274; Sept. 30, 1912, **25,** 287; Nov. 6, 1912, **25,** 528

Henry Skillman Breckinridge, Nov. 7, 1909, **19,** 486; Dec. 17, 1910, **22,** 213; March 29, 1911, **22,** 523; April 16, 1912, **24,** 332; April 22, 1912, **24,** 357

Robert Gunn Bremner, July 5, 1910, **20,** 558; Sept. 17, 1910, **21,** 133; Sept. 22, 1910, **21,** 153

Robert Bridges, Nov. 5, 1902, **14,** 198; Nov. 20, 1906, **16,** 488; Oct. 22, 1907, **17,** 449; March 25, 1909, **19,** 119; March 26, 1909, **19,** 123; April 8, 1909, **19,** 154; May 13, 1909, **19,** 195; Aug. 20, 1909, **19,** 348; Nov. 22, 1909, **19,** 530; Oct. 11, 1910, **21,** 298; Nov. 9, 1910, **21,** 591; Jan. 13, 1911, **22,** 332

Samuel Russell Bridges, March 28, 1904, **15,** 216, 217

Henry Wilson Bridges, May 2, 1912, **24,** 381

Calvin Easton Brodhead, Sept. 2, 1910, **21,** 83; Nov. 10, 1910, **22,** 22; Dec. 14, 1910 **22,** 198; Dec. 16, 1910, **22,** 206; Dec. 20, 1910, **22,** 232; Jan. 4, 1911, **22,** 294

Sydney Brooks, July 10, 1912, **24,** 544

Walter Booth Brooks, Jr., Jan. 18, 1910, **20,** 27

Herbert Bruce Brougham, Jan. 31, 1910, **20,** 65; Feb. 4, 1910, **20,** 76; April 28, 1910, **20,** 401; Sept. 15, 1910, **21,** 97

Robert Foligny Broussard, June 19, 1912, **24,** 487, 488

Arthur Judson Brown, March 17, 1909, **19**, 109

Burt. E. Brown, Aug. 24, 1911, **23**, 291

Coleman Peace Brown, May 31, 1907, **17**, 169; Feb. 12, 1910, **20**, 123

Oren Britt Brown, Jan. 21, 1911, **22**, 361

William Garrott Brown, Aug. 13, 1902, **14**, 86; Oct. 30, 1911, **23**, 513; Nov. 10, 1911, **23**, 547

Webster E. Browning, April 12, 1906, **16**, 358

Philip Alexander Bruce, Dec. 23, 1910, **22**, 254

Charles Wayland Bryan, July 29, 1911, **23**, 237

Thomas Smith Bryan, April 18, 1911, **22**, 576

William Jennings Bryan, April 11, 1905, **16**, 50; Nov. 9, 1910, **21**, 600; Jan. 5, 1911, **22**, 307; March 1, 1911, **22**, 465; Aug. 20, 1911, **23**, 284; April 1, 1912, **24**, 273; June 21, 1912, **24**, 492; July 4, 1912, **24**, 537; July 22, 1912, **24**, 565; July 26, 1912, **24**, 571; Aug. 18, 1912, **25**, 46; Nov. 5, 1912, **25**, 522; Dec. 12, 1912, **25**, 587; Dec. 22, 1912, **25**, 616; Dec. 25, 1912, **25**, 622; Dec. 30, 1912, **25**, 645; Dec. 31, 1912, **25**, 648

William Swan Plumer Bryan, Sept. 29, 1910, **21**, 201

David Bryant, Nov. 8, 1910, **21**, 583

Lewis T. Bryant, Sept. 22, 1911, **23**, 352

James Bryce, Aug. 22, 1904, **15**, 447; Sept. 29, 1904, **15**, 500; Oct. 8, 1904, **15**, 506; March 16, 1907, **17**, 72; April 11, 1907, **17**, 105; June 30, 1907, **17**, 238; July 29, 1907, **17**, 307; Oct. 3, 1907, **17**, 414; Oct. 12, 1907, **17**, 431; Oct. 20, 1907, **17**, 446; Oct. 28, 1907, **17**, 460; Nov. 12, 1910, **22**, 33; Nov. 8, 1912, **25**, 531; Dec. 17, 1912, **25**, 606

John Calvin Bucher, Feb. 8, 1910, **20**, 88

Eckard Payson Budd, Nov. 8, 1911, **23**, 545

Huber Gray Buehler, Nov. 13, 1908, **18**, 509

Douglas Labaree Buffum, April 15, 1905, **16**, 60

Jacob L. Bunnell, Jan. 26, 1911, **22**, 378

Charles August David Burk, Oct. 12, 1907, **17**, 431

Samuel Henry Butcher, March 10, 1905, **16**, 28

Nicholas Murray Butler, Dec. 22, 1903, **15**, 105; Jan. 2, 1904, **15**, 116; April 25, 1906, **16**, 373; May 3, 1906, **16**, 383; May 15, 1906, **16**, 396; June 4, 1906, **16**, 414; Dec. 7, 1906, **16**, 496; April 26, 1907, **17**, 121

Pierce Butler, Oct. 28, 1909, **19**, 457; Nov. 6, 1909, **19**, 485; Nov. 12, 1909, **19**, 494

Richard Evelyn Byrd, Nov. 10, 1910, **22**, 20; June 18, 1912, **24**, 486; July 7, 1912, **24**, 543

John Lambert Cadwalader, Jan. 18, 1904, **15**, 135; July 7, 1904, **15**, 408; June 4, 1907, **17**, 174; March 12, 1908, **18**, 34; March 27, 1908, **18**, 217; May 25, 1908, **18**, 309; June 2, 1908, **18**, 317; Nov. 3, 1908, **18**, 481; Nov. 5, 1908, **18**, 483; Dec. 17, 1908, **18**, 554; Dec. 23, 1908, **18**, 565; Dec. 31, 1908, **18**, 568; Jan. 13, 1909,

**18,** 617; March 5, 1909, **19,** 80; June 1, 1910, **20,** 495; June 3, 1910, **20,** 498; Nov. 10, 1910, **22,** 17

Josiah Cleveland Cady, Feb. 11, 1911, **22,** 424

Donald Cameron, April 18, 1905, **16,** 67; May 20, 1905, **16,** 104

Edwin Camp, Oct. 27, 1910, **21,** 451

Sewall Frederick Camp, Jan. 25, 1910, **20,** 55

John Alexander Campbell, Oct. 5, 1909, **19,** 403

Edward Capps, April 20, 1907, **17,** 112; May 3, 1907, **17,** 130; June 4, 1907, **17,** 173; Jan. 8, 1908, **17,** 587; Jan. 13, 1908, **17,** 600; March 30, 1909, **19,** 132; Sept. 25, 1910, **21,** 166

Andrew Carnegie, April 14, 1905, **16,** 54; April 24, 1905, **16,** 78; March 21, 1911, **22,** 514

Jesse Benedict Carter, June 29, 1904, **15,** 398; July 31, 1905, **16,** 166; Aug. 24, 1905, **16,** 181

Alfred Thomas Carton, Jan. 19, 1909, **18,** 645

Hunsdon Cary, Sept. 16, 1910, **21,** 117

John Cawley, Oct. 25, 1906, **16,** 471

James Harmon Chadbourn, March 29, 1904, **15,** 217

Alexander Francis Chamberlain, Jan. 26, 1911, **22,** 379

George Earle Chamberlain, Dec. 12, 1910, **22,** 174

Benjamin Bright Chambers, Oct. 15, 1910, **21,** 336

David Laurance Chambers, Sept. 29, 1907, **17,** 407

John Hartford Chidester, April 18, 1910, **20,** 368

Richard Spencer Childs, July 10, 1909, **19,** 307; Oct. 14, 1909, **19,** 419 (2); Oct. 25, 1909, **19,** 446; Dec. 4, 1909, **19,** 553; Dec. 9, 1909, **19,** 579; Dec. 30, 1909, **19,** 661; Jan. 5, 1910, **19,** 729; Jan. 11, 1910, **19,** 756

Philip Hudson Churchman, March 23, 1904, **15,** 205

Champ Clark, July 2, 1912, **24,** 528

John Bates Clark, May 28, 1908, **18,** 310

John Hessin Clarke, April 13, 1908, **18,** 262

Philander Priestly Claxton, Jan. 4, 1909, **18,** 589

Frances Folsom Cleveland, Aug. 10, 1902, **14,** 72

Grover Cleveland, May 27, 1903, **14,** 465; March 25, 1906, **16,** 345; March 24, 1907, **17,** 89

Frank Irving Cobb, June 6, 1912, **24,** 463

Peyton Cochran, Nov. 29, 1910, **22,** 118

Peyton Cochran and Charles MaCauley East, Nov. 26, 1910, **22,** 96

Rudolph Isaac Coffee, Aug. 3, 1911, **23,** 249

Corpus Christi College, Oct. 29, 1907, **17,** 461

A. S. Colyar, June 23, 1911, **23,** 173

M. S. Commissariat, July 30, 1904, **15,** 426

John Haughton Coney, March 19, 1907, **17,** 85

Edwin Grant Conklin, Oct. 3, 1907, **17,** 416; Oct. 16, 1907, **17,** 437; Oct. 19, 1907, **17,** 446; Nov. 7, 1907, **17,** 471; Dec. 16, 1907, **17,** 561; Feb. 26, 1909, **19,** 69; March 30, 1909, **19,** 134; Jan. 14, 1910, **20,** 14; Jan. 16, 1910, **20,** 20; Sept. 16, 1910, **21,** 116

Cook Conkling, Jan. 30, 1911, **22,** 394

Robert Digges Wimberly Connor, Feb. 16, 1906, **16,** 314

John Heman Converse, Jan. 28, 1904, **15,** 144; Feb. 2, 1904, **15,** 155; June 14, 1904, **15,** 379

John W. Cornell, April 11, 1903, **14,** 405

Henry Bedinger Cornwall, May 12, 1904, **15,** 326; May 7, 1910, **20,** 422; June 6, 1910, **20,** 505

Francis L. Corrao, July 3, 1912, **24,** 536

Edward Samuel Corwin, June 3, 1905, **16,** 110

Hardin Craig, Jan. 25, 1910, **20,** 54

Sherman Montrose Craiger, Feb. 14, 1911, **22,** 428

Ralph Adams Cram, March 28, 1907, **17,** 96; March 30, 1907, **17,** 100; April 25, 1907, **17,** 118; May 13, 1907, **17,** 141; May 17, 1907, **17,** 150; May 18, 1907, **17,** 151; May 23, 1907, **17,** 156; May 28, 1907, **17,** 160; June 1, 1907, **17,** 169; June 4, 1907, **17,** 173; June 10, 1907, **17,** 207; Dec. 23, 1907, **17,** 566; Dec. 31, 1907, **17,** 585; March 11, 1908, **18,** 13; March 14, 1908, **18,** 52; March 31, 1908, **18,** 218; April 4, 1908, **18,** 225; April 8, 1908, **18,** 242; April 18, 1908, **18,** 273; April 30, 1908, **18,** 279; May 8, 1908, **18,** 291; May 14, 1908, **18,** 296; May 21, 1908, **18,** 304; June 1, 1908, **18,** 314; July 8, 1909, **19,** 303; Sept. 22, 1909, **19,** 387; Dec. 7, 1909, **19,** 558

Elijah Richardson Craven, Oct. 28, 1904, **15,** 530

Morris William Croll, April 24, 1905, **16,** 79

Fred J. Cross, Sept. 11, 1911, **23,** 315

Eugene Lee Crutchfield, Feb. 9, 1912, **24,** 147

Charles Allen Culberson, Nov. 7, 1910, **21,** 580

Juliet Clannon Cushing, Dec. 8, 1910, **22,** 156

Harry Madison Cutts, Nov. 4, 1909, **19,** 483

Cornelius Cuyler Cuyler, May 27, 1903, **14,** 465; July 14, 1904, **15,** 413; Oct. 11, 1904, **15,** 508; Nov. 14, 1905, **16,** 222; Nov. 17, 1905, **16,** 224

Theodore Ledyard Cuyler, Feb. 2, 1903, **14,** 346

Charles William Dabney, Feb. 26, 1903, **14,** 378

Richard Heath Dabney, July 20, 1902, **14,** 32; July 30, 1902, **14,** 44; Aug. 6, 1902, **14,** 58; Oct. 11, 1902, **14,** 143; Oct. 9, 1904, **15,** 507; Sept. 18, 1910, **21,** 138; Nov. 9, 1910, **21,** 597 (2); Jan. 25, 1912, **24,** 71; Jan. 26, 1912, **24,** 79; Jan. 29, 1912, **24,** 95; Dec. 19, 1912, **25,** 613

Robert Shoemaker Dana, March 15, 1905, **16,** 30

Josephus Daniels, Nov. 8, 1910, **21,** 585; Nov. 30, 1910, **22,** 121; Feb. 4, 1911, **22,** 406; June 9, 1911, **23,** 139; Jan. 19, 1912, **24,** 59; May 1, 1912, **24,** 380; May 6, 1912, **24,** 386; May 8, 1912, **24,** 388; May 10, 1912, **24,** 390; May 13, 1912, **24,** 399; May 17, 1912, **24,** 404; June 11, 1912, **24,** 471; Aug. 24, 1912, **25,** 55; Dec. 30, 1912, **25,** 647

Winthrop More Daniels, Dec. 4, 1903, **15,** 65; Jan. 12, 1904, **15,** 121; April 4, 1904, **15,** 233; Feb. 21, 1905, **16,** 7; Feb. 8, 1906, **16,**

306; May 4, 1906, **16,** 385; March 2, 1909, **19,** 73; March 31, 1909, **19,** 135; Dec. 6, 1909, **19,** 557; Dec. 10, 1909, **19,** 581; Dec. 6, 1909, **19,** 581; Dec. 20, 1909, **19,** 610; Dec. 21, 1909, **19,** 613; Feb. 2, 1910, **20,** 73; April 4, 1910, **20,** 317; July 18, 1910, **21,** 10; Sept. 27, 1910, **21,** 174; Oct. 13, 1910, **21,** 321

Charles Whitney Darrow, Aug. 20, 1907, **17,** 351

Edward Parker Davis, Feb. 16, 1909, **19,** 50; March 15, 1910, **20,** 243

Horatio Nelson Davis, Nov. 17, 1908, **18,** 516; Dec. 4, 1908, **18,** 532

John David Davis, July 6, 1904, **15,** 408; Dec. 31, 1908, **18,** 568; Jan. 6, 1910, **19,** 733; March 8, 1910, **20,** 216; March 15, 1910, **20,** 243; March 16, 1910, **20,** 252

John Davis Davis, Feb. 7, 1910, **20,** 83

John H. G. Davis, July 16, 1912, **24,** 553

Robert Davis, Oct. 26, 1910, **21,** 442; Nov. 11, 1910, **22,** 26

Emmett C. Davison, Feb. 1, 1912, **24,** 100

Edgar Dawson, Feb. 14, 1906, **16,** 313

Joseph Hill Dawson, March 19, 1907, **17,** 85

Frank Miles Day, Nov. 9, 1910, **21,** 618

Frank Miles Day and Brother, Nov. 14, 1908, **18,** 511; Jan. 20, 1909, **19,** 5

Joseph Albert Dear, Jr., Dec. 9, 1909, **19,** 599; Feb. 11, 1910, **20,** 121; July 8, 1910, **20,** 567; July 23, 1910, **21,** 23; Sept. 16, 1910, **21,** 116; Nov. 7, 1910, **21,** 580; Nov. 26, 1910, **22,** 97

Walter Moore Dear, Oct. 27, 1910, **21,** 450

Isabella Hammond Demarest, Aug. 3, 1911, **23,** 250

William Henry Steele Demarest, Nov. 9, 1910, **21,** 620

Alfred Lewis Dennis, Nov. 9, 1910, **21,** 592

Samuel Shepard Dennis, Nov. 10, 1910, **22,** 23

George Hutcheson Denny, Aug. 14, 1902, **14,** 87; Feb. 10, 1906, **16,** 313

Frances B. Denton, Dec. 26, 1911, **23,** 630; Dec. 30, 1911, **23,** 631

Francis Xavier Dercum, Dec. 17, 1908, **18,** 557

Edward Thomas Devine, July 5, 1904, **15,** 407

Martin Patrick Devlin, Dec. 3, 1910, **22,** 128

Arthur Granville Dewalt, March 30, 1910, **20,** 307; April 1, 1910, **20,** 311; April 12, 1910, **20,** 352; Sept. 16, 1910, **21,** 103

John DeWitt, Oct. 29, 1904, **15,** 531; Jan. 1, 1910, **19,** 701; Oct. 26, 1910, **21,** 442

Clinton Roy Dickinson, Sept. 25, 1910, **21,** 169

Bessie Louise Dickson, Nov. 8, 1910, **21,** 587

Thomas H. Dillow, Sept. 1, 1910, **21,** 82; Dec. 9, 1910, **22,** 163

Francis William Dinsmore, May 2, 1909, **19,** 181

William Frederick Dix, Oct. 1, 1909, **19,** 396; Oct. 27, 1909, **19,** 454

John Dixon, Jan. 7, 1910, **19,** 747

Thomas Dixon, Jr., Nov. 25, 1910, **22,** 96

William Edward Dodd, May 2, 1910, **20**, 408; Sept. 9, 1911, **23**, 311
Cleveland Hoadley Dodge, July 5, 1904, **15**, 407; June 14, 1906,
  **16**, 425; Oct. 15, 1906, **16**, 457; Nov. 22, 1906, **16**, 490; Dec. 19,
  1906, **16**, 534; Feb. 21, 1907, **17**, 49; March 6, 1907, **17**, 63;
  March 28, 1907, **17**, 95; May 28, 1907, **17**, 159; July 2, 1907, **17**,
  243; July 9, 1907, **17**, 265; Aug. 6, 1907, **17**, 341; Sept. 28, 1907,
  **17**, 405; Dec. 18, 1907, **17**, 563; Jan. 14, 1908, **17**, 603; June 10,
  1908, **18**, 335; June 19, 1908, **18**, 338; Sept. 30, 1908, **18**, 435;
  Dec. 13, 1908, **18**, 546; Jan. 13, 1909, **18**, 612; Jan. 27, 1909, **19**,
  14; March 16, 1909, **19**, 100; April 6, 1909, **19**, 151; Sept. 25,
  1909, **19**, 391; Oct. 27, 1909, **19**, 453; Nov. 12, 1909, **19**, 495;
  Dec. 21, 1909, **19**, 619; Dec. 28, 1909, **19**, 649; Jan. 3, 1910, **19**,
  707; Jan. 5, 1910, **19**, 727; Jan. 17, 1910, **20**, 20; Feb. 6, 1910, **20**,
  82; March 3, 1910, **20**, 208; June 30, 1910, **20**, 551; July 12,
  1910, **20**, 576; Sept. 16, 1910, **21**, 112; Sept. 18, 1910, **21**, 137;
  Oct. 10, 1910, **21**, 292; Oct. 21, 1910, **21**, 385; Nov. 9, 1910, **21**,
  591; Nov. 18, 1910, **22**, 72; Nov. 25, 1910, **22**, 94; Dec. 20, 1910,
  **22**, 232; Jan. 26, 1911, **22**, 377; Feb. 17, 1911, **22**, 436; May 15,
  1912, **24**, 402; Sept. 5, 1912, **25**, 109; Dec. 30, 1912, **25**, 646
Henry Nehemiah Dodge, Oct. 19, 1910, **21**, 354
William Earl Dodge, March 14, 1903, **14**, 392
Ralph Waldo Emerson Donges, Nov. 5, 1910, **21**, 577; Nov. 30,
  1910, **22**, 120
Thomas Marcus Donnelly, Oct. 27, 1910, **21**, 451
Joseph Dorsey, Sept. 22, 1910, **21**, 156
Lee Douglas, July 15, 1911, **23**, 211; July 31, 1911, **23**, 244
Edward Dowden, Dec. 16, 1902, **14**, 295
Julius Daniel Dreher, May 4, 1911, **22**, 604
Theodore Dreiser, March 20, 1908, **18**, 62
Francis Ignatius Drobinski, Feb. 2, 1912, **24**, 131; Feb. 29, 1912,
  **24**, 219
Garrett Droppers, June 23, 1912, **24**, 497; Aug. 21, 1912, **25**, 50
John Fairfield Dryden, Dec. 18, 1908, **18**, 558; Jan. 19, 1909, **18**,
  645; March 3, 1909, **19**, 78; June 15, 1910, **20**, 532
Edward Dickinson Duffield, June 22, 1909, **19**, 265; July 23, 1909,
  **19**, 316; Dec. 28, 1909, **19**, 651; Jan. 3, 1910, **19**, 708; March 9,
  1910, **20**, 226; March 15, 1910, **20**, 245
Henry Green Duffield, Feb. 4, 1909, **19**, 29; Dec. 13, 1910, **22**, 186
Francis Dundon, June 25, 1909, **19**, 269
Frederick A. Duneka, March 22, 1906, **16**, 343; Oct. 4, 1909, **19**,
  402; Nov. 10, 1910, **22**, 21
John Robertson Dunlap, March 18, 1908, **18**, 59
Maitland Dwight, Feb. 14, 1911, **22**, 430
Louis Dyer, April 11, 1903, **14**, 406; April 12, 1907, **17**, 105
John Henry Eastwood, Dec. 3, 1910, **22**, 129
Henry Morris Eaton, April 23, 1910, **20**, 385; April 27, 1910, **20**,
  397

Maurice Francis Egan, Oct. 20, 1902, **14,** 148

G. Fred Ege, Dec. 8, 1908, **18,** 534

William Simpson Elder, Nov. 10, 1910, **22,** 17

Charles William Eliot, Nov. 21, 1910, **22,** 78

Edward Graham Elliott, Jan. 12, 1909, **18,** 612; July 14, 1910, **20,** 580

Leroy J. Ellis, Nov. 10, 1909, **19,** 491; Nov. 29, 1910, **22,** 116; Dec. 21, 1910, **22,** 244

Matthias Cowell Ely, Nov. 3, 1910, **21,** 540; Nov. 23, 1910, **22,** 85

Richard Theodore Ely, July 3, 1912, **24,** 535

Robert Erskine Ely, Oct. 1, 1904, **15,** 501; March 25, 1907, **17,** 92

Ellen Woodrow Erwin, April 26, 1904, **15,** 299

Thomas St. Clair Evans, Aug. 27, 1902, **14,** 114; April 14, 1910, **20,** 357

Lewis Charles Everard, March 21, 1908, **18,** 68

Charles Apffel Eypper, Oct. 28, 1910, **21,** 464; Jan. 16, 1911, **22,** 344

Simon Faber, June 29, 1912, **24,** 511

Robert Alexander Falconer, Nov. 14, 1910, **22,** 45

Benjamin L. Farinholt, April 26, 1911, **22,** 587

Wilson Farrand, June 9, 1904, **15,** 362; June 17, 1904, **15,** 386; Dec. 14, 1908, **18,** 547; Jan. 6, 1910, **19,** 736

Thomas P. Fay, Oct. 11, 1910, **21,** 299

George G. Feigl, Jan. 25, 1911, **22,** 376

Joseph Fels, Dec. 29, 1910, **22,** 278

Zephaniah Charles Felt, Oct. 1, 1908, **18,** 435; April 21, 1910, **20,** 382; May 13, 1910, **20,** 453; July 18, 1910, **21,** 12

Henry Ferguson, Oct. 6, 1908, **18,** 436; Oct. 14, 1908, **18,** 450; May 27, 1909, **19,** 222

William T. Ferguson, July 22, 1910, **21,** 21; July 28, 1910, **21,** 28; Aug. 9, 1910, **21,** 47; Sept. 24, 1910, **21,** 162; Oct. 3, 1910, **21,** 238; Oct. 7, 1910, **21,** 275; Oct. 10, 1910, **21,** 292; Nov. 11, 1910, **22,** 28; Nov. 15, 1912, **25,** 549

Morris Patterson Ferris, Jan. 30, 1904, **15,** 151

James Fairman Fielder, Sept. 15, 1910, **21,** 97; Oct. 26, 1910, **21,** 442

John Wesley Fielder, Jr., July 12, 1902, **14,** 5; Sept. 5, 1902, **14,** 123

Robert Herndon Fife, April 18, 1905, **16,** 68; April 26, 1905, **16,** 80

Henry Burchard Fine, July 18, 1905, **16,** 156; July 19, 1905, **16,** 158; July 29, 1905, **16,** 163; Aug. 12, 1905, **16,** 178; May 19, 1906, **16,** 398; March 4, 1908, **18,** 7; April 1, 1909, **19,** 140, 141; Jan. 11, 1910, **19,** 753; Feb. 24, 1910, **20,** 173; July 10, 1910, **20,** 571; Sept. 16, 1910, **21,** 112

Henry Burchard Fine, Edward Capps, Edwin Grant Conklin, Winthrop More Daniels, Jan. 10, 1910, **20,** 114

John Huston Finley, Aug. 1, 1902, **14,** 62; June 8, 1903, **14,** 476; Nov. 29, 1905, **16,** 240; Dec. 6, 1907, **17,** 550

John Miller Turpin Finney, Nov. 7, 1911, **23,** 543

Charles Joel Fisk, Nov. 9, 1910, **21,** 614

Harvey Edward Fisk, Oct. 27, 1908, **18,** 474; Jan. 9, 1909, **18,** 608

John Joseph Fitzgerald, Nov. 10, 1910, **22,** 16

Robert Hunter Fitzhugh, March 15, 1906, **16,** 334; Nov. 23, 1906, **16,** 492; March 8, 1907, **17,** 63; March 4, 1908, **18,** 6; March 10, 1910, **20,** 227

David M. Flynn, Nov. 3, 1910, **21,** 541

Henry Jones Ford, Dec. 10, 1907, **17,** 555; May 6, 1908, **18,** 288; May 12, 1908, **18,** 294; Nov. 9, 1910, **21,** 606; Nov. 23, 1910, **22,** 84

Henry James Forman, April 14, 1908, **18,** 271

James Jackson Forstall, Nov. 23, 1907, **17,** 512

Franklin William Fort, Nov. 11, 1910, **22,** 27

John Franklin Fort, Nov. 9, 1910, **21,** 605 (2); Nov. 16, 1910, **22,** 53

Raymond Blaine Fosdick, Oct. 3, 1910, **21,** 238; Aug. 30, 1912, **25,** 64

Eugene Noble Foss, Nov. 9, 1910, **21,** 610

John Watson Foster, Feb. 20, 1909, **19,** 64; Dec. 21, 1909, **19,** 619; Nov. 9, 1910, **21,** 600

Solomon Foster, Dec. 13, 1910, **22,** 183; Dec. 25, 1910, **22,** 260

Robin William Cummins Francis, May 10, 1910, **20,** 431

George Corning Fraser, June 14, 1907, **17,** 213

Philip Hilton Fraser, Nov. 2, 1910, **21,** 519

David Ruddach Frazer, Oct. 23, 1903, **15,** 26; Oct. 20, 1910, **21,** 366

Hollis Burke Frissell, Jan. 16, 1909, **18,** 629; Dec. 6, 1910, **22,** 140

William Goodell Frost, Nov. 7, 1910, **21,** 579; Dec. 11, 1910, **22,** 172; Dec. 17, 1910, **22,** 214

Arthur Lincoln Frothingham, Jr., May 10, 1905, **16,** 93

Harry Augustus Garfield, June 13, 1903, **14,** 489; July 14, 1903, **14,** 544; Aug. 19, 1903, **14,** 554; June 26, 1907, **17,** 229; July 3, 1907, **17,** 246; April 10, 1908, **18,** 259; May 12, 1908, **18,** 294; June 10, 1910, **20,** 513; Nov. 4, 1910, **21,** 558; Nov. 9, 1910, **21,** 609

James Rudolph Garfield, Nov. 9, 1910, **21,** 609

Robert Garrett, July 4, 1904, **15,** 404; March 4, 1905, **16,** 20; Jan. 26, 1907, **17,** 19; March 2, 1907, **17,** 58; April 8, 1907, **17,** 102; April 10, 1907, **17,** 103; April 18, 1907, **17,** 111; April 25, 1907, **17,** 117; April 16, 1909, **19,** 165; April 21, 1909, **19,** 170; March 15, 1910, **20,** 244; March 22, 1910, **20,** 285; July 15, 1910, **21,** 3; Nov. 9, 1910, **21,** 622

Lindley Miller Garrison, Nov. 8, 1910, **21,** 587

Nelson Burr Gaskill, June 26, 1907, **17,** 230; Sept. 11, 1911, **23,** 313

Christian Frederick Gauss, April 15, 1905, **16,** 61; Sept. 16, 1910, **21,** 111

William Jay Gaynor, March 6, 1912, **24,** 224

William Cavanagh Gebhardt, Sept. 16, 1910, **21,** 110; Sept. 22, 1910, **21,** 156; Nov. 4, 1910, **21,** 558; Nov. 28, 1910, **22,** 101; Dec. 9, 1910, **22,** 162; Dec. 24, 1910, **22,** 257; Jan. 9, 1911, **22,** 321

Elmer Hendrickson Geran, Nov. 10, 1910, **22,** 18; Nov. 28, 1910, **22,** 100; Dec. 7, 1910, **22,** 145; Dec. 29, 1910, **22,** 280

Gordon Hall Gerould, April 15, 1905, **16,** 58; April 24, 1905, **16,** 79

Richard Watson Gilder, Aug. 2, 1902, **14,** 47

Raleigh Colston Gildersleeve, June 29, 1905, **16,** 150; July 8, 1905, **16,** 152; July 11, 1905, **16,** 154; July 25, 1905, **16,** 161; Aug. 11, 1905, **16,** 176; Aug. 24, 1905, **16,** 181; Aug. 23, 1905, **16,** 182; Sept. 1, 1905, **16,** 185; March 7, 1906, **16,** 324; May 9, 1906, **16,** 387

J. Robert Gillam, Feb. 23, 1912, **24,** 190

Newton Cloud Gillham, June 23, 1911, **23,** 172

Daniel Coit Gilman, Nov. 2, 1902, **14,** 197; June 28, 1907, **17,** 237

Washington Gladden, April 21, 1910, **20,** 380

Carter Glass, Nov. 7, 1912, **25,** 530; Dec. 14, 1912, **25,** 588; Dec. 18, 1912, **25,** 608; Dec. 29, 1912, **25,** 641

Franklin Potts Glass, Oct. 2, 1903, **15,** 11; March 14, 1904, **15,** 190; March 28, 1904, **15,** 216; Jan. 26, 1910, **20,** 58; Nov. 8, 1910, **21,** 588

Otis Allan Glazebrook, Sept. 15, 1910, **21,** 98

Robert Brodnax Glenn, Jan. 11, 1911, **22,** 327

Harold Godwin, Oct. 26, 1910, **21,** 442

Henry Mayer Goldfogle, Nov. 9, 1910, **21,** 618

Henry Cowper Gollan, Oct. 11, 1910, **22,** 14

Marie Louise Norris Gollan, Nov. 4, 1910, **21,** 556

Edward Field Goltra, April 27, 1904, **15,** 299; July 2, 1904, **15,** 403; Oct. 10, 1910, **21,** 294; Nov. 26, 1910, **22,** 97; Dec. 14, 1910, **22,** 197

Samuel Gompers, Oct. 20, 1910, **21,** 379; Dec. 16, 1912, **25,** 590

William Elliott Gonzales, March 16, 1911, **22,** 507; May 14, 1912, **24,** 400

Thomas Roseberry Good, Dec. 24, 1902, **14,** 305

Arthur Frederick Goodrich, Aug. 5, 1902, **14,** 63

Elliot Hersey Goodwin, Dec. 23, 1910, **22,** 256

Thomas Pryor Gore, Jan. 28, 1911, **22,** 387

John Franklin Goucher, June 5, 1908, **18,** 321

Elgin Ralston Lovell Gould, June 27, 1912, **24,** 503

John Young Graham, March 11, 1904, **15,** 189

Charles N. Grandison, Sept. 26, 1910, **21,** 171

Charles Travers Grant, July 9, 1907, **17,** 265

William Henry Grant, Dec. 19, 1908, **18,** 560; Dec. 2, 1909, **19,** 544

Charles Henry Grasty, Sept. 16, 1910, **21,** 102; Feb. 9, 1912, **24,** 146; July 1, 1912, **24,** 519; Sept. 9, 1912, **25,** 128

John Temple Graves, Sept. 24, 1912, **25,** 233

James Richard Gray, March 15, 1911, **22,** 506
James Albert Green, June 17, 1910, **20,** 536
William Green, Oct. 9, 1912, **25,** 399
Philip Barling Ben Greet, Nov. 13, 1910, **22,** 36
Julian Arthur Gregory, Dec. 21, 1910, **22,** 245
Moses J. Gries, March 28, 1908, **18,** 217
Edward Harrick Griffin, Nov. 8, 1910, **21,** 586
Solomon Bulkley Griffin, Aug. 2, 1911, **23,** 248
Rudolph Grossman, Nov. 25, 1908, **18,** 523; Dec. 16, 1908, **18,** 550
Alexander Barclay Guigon, Jan. 27, 1911, **22,** 383
Arthur Twining Hadley, Sept. 27, 1902, **14,** 135; Oct. 2, 1902, **14,** 138; June 10, 1902, **14,** 560; Nov. 24, 1908, **18,** 522; Dec. 8, 1909, **19,** 561; Dec. 11, 1909, **19,** 602; Dec. 24, 1909, **19,** 628; Dec. 28, 1909, **19,** 652; Dec. 31, 1909, **19,** 672; Jan. 3, 1910, **19,** 708; Feb. 10, 1910, **20,** 118; May 31, 1910, **20,** 487; Dec. 13, 1910, **22,** 184
Herbert Spencer Hadley, Sept. 2, 1912, **25,** 93
Susan Eliza Hall, Feb. 1, 1904, **15,** 154; Feb. 25, 1904, **15,** 178; April 8, 1904, **15,** 239
Abram Woodruff Halsey, Oct. 27, 1902, **14,** 186; March 22, 1904, **15,** 203; June 17, 1904, **15,** 386
Richard Townley Haines Halsey, June 10, 1904, **15,** 363; June 16, 1904, **15,** 385
James Alphonsus Hamill, Nov. 17, 1910, **22,** 72
Peter Joseph Hamilton, March 28, 1904, **15,** 217; April 9, 1904, **15,** 239
Charles Sumner Hamlin, July 18, 1912, **24,** 559; Aug. 1, 1912, **24,** 581
John Hays Hammond, May 27, 1907, **17,** 159
Albert Elmer Hancock, Feb. 8, 1910, **20,** 89
Lorin Andrew Handley, Aug. 3, 1911, **23,** 251
Norman Hapgood, Dec. 18, 1912, **25,** 609
Henry Janeway Hardenbergh, Aug. 26, 1907, **17,** 361
John Ralph Hardin, March 2, 1909, **19,** 75; Nov. 9, 1910, **21,** 610
John Maynard Harlan, June 11, 1910, **20,** 519; Oct. 5, 1910, **21,** 266; Oct. 21, 1910, **21,** 389
Samuel Allen Harlow, Sept. 16, 1910, **21,** 110
Judson Harmon, Nov. 10, 1910, **22,** 15
George McLean Harper, Dec. 28, 1903, **15,** 110; July 18, 1907, **17,** 289
George McLean Harper and Williamson Updike Vreeland, Oct. 26, 1903, **15,** 29
William Rainey Harper, Jan. 8, 1906, **16,** 280
Harper and Brothers, Oct. 4, 1902, **14,** 141; Nov. 23, 1903, **15,** 56; Feb. 2, 1904, **15,** 155; May 12, 1904, **15,** 327; May 11, 1905, **16,** 94; May 7, 1906, **16,** 387; May 11, 1906, **16,** 390; May 24, 1906, **16,** 404
J. Silas Harris, July 5, 1911, **23,** 190

Albert Bushnell Hart, May 12, 1910, **20,** 444

Archibald Clinton Harte, Sept. 18, 1903, **15,** 3

George Brinton McClellan Harvey, Feb. 8, 1906, **16,** 307; Dec. 17, 1906, **16,** 532; Jan. 10, 1907, **16,** 554; May 10, 1909, **19,** 191; Jan. 1, 1910, **19,** 700; July 7, 1910, **20,** 563; July 8, 1910, **20,** 564; July 21, 1910, **21,** 17; July 28, 1910, **21,** 27; Aug. 6, 1910, **21,** 40; Aug. 12, 1910, **21,** 52; Sept. 6, 1910, **21,** 85; Sept. 9, 1910, **21,** 87; Sept. 12, 1910, **21,** 89; Sept. 13, 1910, **21,** 90; Sept. 25, 1910, **21,** 166; Oct. 4, 1910, **21,** 243; Oct. 10, 1910, **21,** 292; Oct. 13, 1910, **21,** 320; Oct. 14, 1910, **21,** 327; Oct. 25, 1910, **21,** 433; Nov. 8, 1910, **21,** 585; Nov. 14, 1910, **22,** 38; Dec. 19, 1910, **22,** 227; March 1, 1911, **22,** 466; Jan. 4, 1912, **23,** 652; Jan. 16, 1912, **24,** 45; Nov. 4, 1912, **25,** 512

Charles Homer Haskins, June 10, 1907, **17,** 208

Harold Ripley Hastings, April 15, 1905, **16,** 60

Percy Duncan Haughton, June 22, 1910, **20,** 538

Percy Duncan Haughton and Howard Houston Henry, June 22, 1910, **20,** 539

Alfred Hayes, Jr., May 8, 1910, **20,** 424

Isaac Minis Hays, Feb. 27, 1903, **14,** 380

Azel Washburn Hazen, Jan. 16, 1903, **14,** 328; Sept. 16, 1910, **21,** 107

Job Elmer Hedges, June 15, 1909, **19,** 253

Charles G. Heifner, Dec. 18, 1911, **23,** 597

Henry John Heinz, Oct. 19, 1904, **15,** 521

Lynn Helm, Jan. 17, 1910, **20,** 21; Feb. 7, 1910, **20,** 86

Charles Robert Hemphill, Nov. 10, 1910, **22,** 21

James Calvin Hemphill, Jan. 22, 1906, **16,** 286; Nov. 3, 1910, **21,** 539

Robert Randolph Henderson, Oct. 10, 1908, **18,** 445; April 24, 1909, **19,** 172; Nov. 9, 1910, **21,** 599

Burton Jesse Hendrick, Sept. 5, 1911, **23,** 303; Sept. 7, 1911, **23,** 311

Charles Elvin Hendrickson, Jr., Dec. 10, 1909, **19,** 598

Charles O'Connor Hennessy, Dec. 1, 1910, **22,** 124

Alexander Henry, Sept. 23, 1904, **15,** 492

Bayard Henry, July 14, 1904, **15,** 417; Jan. 4, 1906, **16,** 277; Feb. 28, 1906, **16,** 321; July 29, 1907, **17,** 301; Aug. 16, 1907, **17,** 347; Jan. 8, 1910, **19,** 748

Howard Houston Henry, Dec. 11, 1909, **19,** 602; Jan. 2, 1910, **19,** 704; Jan. 25, 1910, **20,** 54; July 5, 1910, **20,** 559

Robert Lee Henry, Aug. 1, 1912, **24,** 581

Thomas Maxwell Henry, Feb. 22, 1909, **19,** 66

Jenny Davidson Hibben, Aug. 3, 1902, **14,** 50; July 5, 1903, **14,** 520; July 17, 1903, **14,** 545; July 26, 1903, **14,** 546; Aug. 9, 1903, **14,** 551; Aug. 16, 1903, **14,** 552; Aug. 21, 1903, **14,** 555; Aug. 30, 1903, **14,** 556; June 16, 1904, **15,** 384; June 28, 1904, **15,** 395; July 19, 1905, **16,** 158; Aug. 15, 1905, **16,** 180

John Grier Hibben, July 20, 1902, **14,** 34; March 10, 1903, **14,** 386; June 16, 1904, **15,** 384; July 11, 1904, **15,** 409; Aug. 13, 1904, **15,** 440; July 14, 1905, **16,** 155; Aug. 3, 1905, **16,** 170; Aug. 7, 1905, **16,** 172; July 8, 1907, **17,** 263; Jan. 15, 1909, **18,** 626; April 1, 1909, **19,** 143; May 27, 1909, **19,** 222; Oct. 27, 1909, **19,** 453; Feb. 9, 1910 **20,** 90; March 2, 1910, **20,** 208; Nov. 21, 1910, **22,** 77; Nov. 5, 1912, **25,** 522

John Grier Hibben and Jenny Davidson Hibben, June 8, 1904, **15,** 360

Henry Lee Higginson, May 21, 1909, **19,** 210; May 22, 1910, **20,** 465; Nov. 9, 1910, **21,** 612; Oct. 11, 1912, **25,** 414

Marion Phar Hilliard, March 25, 1905, **16,** 39

Mary Livingston Gilbert Hinsdale, Oct. 8, 1908, **18,** 440

Francis Wrigley Hirst, Dec. 20, 1910, **22,** 234

Samuel Colgate Hodge, Dec. 24, 1910, **22,** 259

Joseph Stanislaus Hoff, Sept. 15, 1910, **21,** 97

Hamilton Holt, Aug. 1, 1907, **17,** 333; Nov. 12, 1910, **22,** 32

John Allen Holt, July 6, 1907, **17,** 262

Franklin William Hooper, Feb. 12, 1910, **20,** 124

Rees P. Horrocks, July 27, 1911, **23,** 233

Houghton, Mifflin and Company, May 19, 1908, **20,** 582; May 23, 1908, **20,** 583

Edward Mandell House, Oct. 16, 1911, **23,** 458; Oct. 20, 1911, **23,** 470; Nov. 18, 1911, **23,** 552; Dec. 1, 1911, **23,** 560; Dec. 15, 1911, **23,** 595; Feb. 2, 1912, **24,** 131; Feb. 8, 1912, **24,** 140; March 6, 1912, **24,** 225; April 14, 1912, **24,** 332; June 7, 1912, **24,** 464; June 20, 1912, **24,** 489; July 31, 1912, **24,** 576; Aug. 21, 1912, **25,** 51; Sept. 2, 1912, **25,** 92; Sept. 19, 1912, **25,** 198; Sept. 21, 1912, **25,** 212; Nov. 22, 1912, **25,** 557; Nov. 25, 1912, **25,** 562; Nov. 28, 1912, **25,** 563; Dec. 6, 1912, **25,** 581

Morus B. Howard, Nov. 14, 1912, **25,** 548

Annie Josephine Wilson Howe, Sept. 8, 1904, **15,** 466; Dec. 13, 1906, **16,** 526; April 14, 1910, **20,** 358

George Howe III, May 28, 1903, **14,** 467; April 29, 1905, **16,** 86; Dec. 21, 1908, **18,** 561; Jan. 2, 1909, **18,** 588; Feb. 1, 1909, **19,** 19; Nov. 12, 1910, **22,** 33; March 25, 1911, **22,** 517; July 3, 1912, **24,** 535

Mark Antony De Wolfe Howe, Dec. 12, 1906, **16,** 505

Joseph Howell, Oct. 26, 1910, **21,** 443

William Bailey Howland, Nov. 9, 1910, **21,** 620

James Alfred Hoyt, Jr., Nov. 8, 1910, **21,** 588

Willard Evans Hoyt, June 27, 1908, **18,** 347

Robert Stephen Hudspeth, Nov. 9, 1910, **21,** 607; Jan. 9, 1911, **22,** 321

William Hughes, Sept. 20, 1910, **21,** 145; Sept. 30, 1910, **21,** 213; Nov. 9, 1910, **21,** 603; Nov. 10, 1910, **22,** 18; Dec. 9, 1910, **22,** 161

Lawrence Cameron Hull, Dec. 11, 1902, **14,** 278

Alexander Crombie Humphreys, June 27, 1912, **24,** 503

George Wylie Paul Hunt, Jan. 2, 1911, **22,** 291

Theodore Whitefield Hunt, June 26, 1907, **17,** 231; Oct. 8, 1907, **17,** 424; Feb. 2, 1910, **20,** 72; June 10, 1910, **20,** 514; Oct. 20, 1910, **21,** 377; Nov. 9, 1910, **21,** 602

Theodore Whitefield Hunt and Gordon Hall Gerould, Jan. 8, 1910, **19,** 748

Catherine Hunter, Nov. 10, 1908, **18,** 491

Fred Le Roy Hutson, April 14, 1905, **16,** 56

Andrew Clerk Imbrie, July 8, 1907, **17,** 264; July 13, 1907, **17,** 281; July 16, 1907, **17,** 285; July 25, 1907, **17,** 293; July 30, 1907, **17,** 308

Charles Henry Ingersoll, March 10, 1911, **22,** 499

Edward Ingle, Aug. 15, 1902, **14,** 89; Dec. 6, 1911, **23,** 583

William Mann Irvine, Nov. 10, 1910, **22,** 22

William Burhans Isham, Nov. 9, 1910, **21,** 602

Giles B. Jackson, Dec. 23, 1912, **25,** 619

W. M. Jackson, Jan. 10, 1903, **14,** 327

Melancthon Williams Jacobus, Feb. 28, 1905, **16,** 15; Aug. 29, 1905, **16,** 184; Dec. 20, 1905, **16,** 273; Nov. 4, 1906, **16,** 480; Nov. 9, 1906, **16,** 484; Dec. 13, 1906, **16,** 527; March 1, 1907, **17,** 57; July 2, 1907, **17,** 244; Sept. 29, 1907, **17,** 406; Oct. 8, 1907, **17,** 425; Oct. 14, 1907, **17,** 432; Oct. 16, 1907, **17,** 437; Oct. 25, 1907, **17,** 458; Nov. 5, 1907, **17,** 468; Nov. 11, 1907, **17,** 491; Dec. 29, 1907, **17,** 582; Jan. 1, 1908, **17,** 585; Jan. 10, 1908, **17,** 597; March 5, 1908, **18,** 8; May 31, 1908, **18,** 311; July 12, 1908, **18,** 359; Aug. 11, 1908, **18,** 397; Sept. 11, 1908, **18,** 418; Sept. 30, 1908, **18,** 434; Oct. 28, 1908, **18,** 476; Nov. 15, 1908, **18,** 512; Dec. 17, 1908, **18,** 555; Jan. 5, 1909, **18,** 591; Jan. 8, 1909, **18,** 593; Jan. 9, 1909, **18,** 606; Jan. 21, 1909, **19,** 6; Feb. 3, 1909, **19,** 21; March 20, 1909, **19,** 113; March 26, 1909, **19,** 121; April 12, 1909, **19,** 159; April 19, 1909, **19,** 167; May 18, 1909, **19,** 198; June 3, 1909, **19,** 228; July 15, 1909, **19,** 310; Oct. 8, 1909, **19,** 407; Oct. 15, 1909, **19,** 420; Oct. 28, 1909, **19,** 456; Nov. 5, 1909, **19,** 484; Dec. 28, 1909, **19,** 648; Dec. 31, 1909, **19,** 663; Jan. 6, 1910, **19,** 735; Jan. 13, 1910, **20,** 10; Feb. 10, 1910, **20,** 116; March 16, 1910, **20,** 251; March 22, 1910, **20,** 283; April 5, 1910, **20,** 320; May 4, 1910, **20,** 410; June 15, 1910, **20,** 531; July 16, 1910, **21,** 6; July 29, 1910, **21,** 30; Sept. 16, 1910, **21,** 109; Sept. 19, 1910, **21,** 142; Oct. 13, 1910, **21,** 321; Nov. 6, 1910, **21,** 578; Nov. 9, 1910, **21,** 594; Nov. 14, 1910, **22,** 44

John Franklin Jameson, Oct. 6, 1909, **19,** 405

Caesar Augustus Rodney Janvier, Feb. 12, 1910, **20,** 123; Nov. 8, 1910, **21,** 588

James Hopwood Jeans, March 20, 1909, **19,** 115

Ryerson W. Jennings, Dec. 30, 1910, **22,** 284

George Sibley Johns, July 3, 1907, **17,** 246; March 30, 1910, **20,** 306

Cone Johnson, Dec. 17, 1912, **25,** 603

Robert Underwood Johnson, Jan. 19, 1910, **20,** 31; Sept. 16, 1910, **21,** 109; Nov. 26, 1910, **22,** 98; July 3, 1912, **24,** 531

Roger Bruce Cash Johnson, April 15, 1905, **16,** 59

Tom Loftin Johnson, Nov. 18, 1907, **17,** 508

William E. Johnson, Dec. 17, 1908, **18,** 556

William Mindred Johnson, Nov. 10, 1910, **22,** 19

Adrian Hoffman Joline, Oct. 25, 1902, **14,** 186

Allan Dudley Jones, June 30, 1912, **24,** 514

Benjamin Franklin Jones, Jr., April 6, 1904, **15,** 235

Charles Hodge Jones, May 11, 1905, **16,** 95

David Benton Jones, Aug. 7, 1902, **14,** 64; Oct. 24, 1903, **15,** 28; March 15, 1904, **15,** 191; July 5, 1904, **15,** 405; May 15, 1907, **17,** 147; June 12, 1907, **17,** 210; Sept. 6, 1907, **17,** 374; Sept. 19, 1907, **17,** 392; Sept. 23, 1907, **17,** 397; Sept. 28, 1907, **17,** 404; Oct. 5, 1907, **17,** 419; Nov. 12, 1907, **17,** 495; June 12, 1908, **18,** 336; March 4, 1909, **19,** 79; Aug. 24, 1909, **19,** 352; Oct. 8, 1909, **19,** 407; Nov. 9, 1909, **19,** 490; Dec. 29, 1909, **19,** 656; Jan. 6, 1910, **19,** 734; March 12, 1910, **20,** 237; May 14, 1910, **20,** 455; May 19, 1910, **20,** 459; May 26, 1910, **20,** 474; June 28, 1910, **20,** 545; June 30, 1910, **20,** 550 (2); June 30, 1910, **20,** 551; July 1, 1910, **20,** 554; July 29, 1910, **21,** 29; Sept. 17, 1910, **21,** 132; Sept. 20, 1910, **21,** 144; Sept. 27, 1910, **21,** 173; Nov. 9, 1910, **21,** 593; Dec. 19, 1911, **23,** 599; July 13, 1912, **24,** 549

DeWitt Clinton Jones, Jr., Nov. 17, 1909, **19,** 507

Thomas Davies Jones, Dec. 22, 1909, **19,** 620; Dec. 30, 1909, **19,** 659; Dec. 31, 1909, **19,** 662; Jan. 13, 1910, **20,** 9; April 29, 1910, **20,** 403; May 27, 1910, **20,** 477; June 1, 1910, **20,** 493; June 29, 1910, **20,** 548; Nov. 9, 1910, **21,** 599; Dec. 1, 1910, **22,** 126; Dec. 19, 1911, **23,** 598; Sept. 2, 1912, **25,** 92; Sept. 10, 1912, **25,** 133

David Starr Jordan, Feb. 20, 1910, **20,** 151

Harry Pratt Judson, Sept. 20, 1910, **21,** 144

Francis Fisher Kane, July 1, 1904, **15,** 401; Nov. 14, 1909, **19,** 500; Oct. 6, 1910, **21,** 266; Nov. 9, 1910, **21,** 604; Dec. 22, 1910, **22,** 246; Feb. 16, 1911, **22,** 435; March 8, 1911, **22,** 486; July 19, 1911, **23,** 219; July 25, 1911, **23,** 229; Jan. 9, 1912, **24,** 26; June 23, 1912, **24,** 496; July 4, 1912, **24,** 537

Edward Lawrence Katzenbach, Sept. 17, 1910, **21,** 132

Frank Snowden Katzenbach, Jr., Sept. 15, 1910, **21,** 96

Welling Sickel Katzenbach, Aug. 12, 1907, **17,** 344; Aug. 17, 1907, **17,** 350

Lindley Miller Keasbey, Feb. 11, 1911, **22,** 422

Roy Dee Keehn, July 29, 1912, **24,** 574

William Williams Keen, Nov. 20, 1909, **19,** 529; Dec. 15, 1909, **19,** 605

John Kelman, July 18, 1902, **14,** 26

Frederick Wallace Kelsey, Dec. 7, 1910, **22,** 146

Calvin Noyes Kendall, July 17, 1911, **23**, 216

Charles William Kent, Nov. 9, 1907, **17**, 487; Nov. 26, 1907, **17**, 523; Jan. 10, 1911, **22**, 326

Henry Thompson Kent, Dec. 29, 1908, **18**, 567; Jan. 8, 1909, **18**, 593

Platt Kent, Feb. 27, 1909, **19**, 72

William Kent, Nov. 12, 1910, **22**, 31

Martin Jerome Keogh, June 21, 1904, **15**, 392; July 16, 1904, **15**, 417; May 16, 1907, **17**, 148

W. F. Keohan, Jan. 7, 1908, **17**, 586

John Worth Kern, Aug. 12, 1912, **25**, 22

James Kerney, July 30, 1910, **21**, 31; Dec. 15, 1910, **22**, 201

John Thompson Kerr, Nov. 9, 1910, **21**, 592

Daniel Kiefer, Dec. 24, 1910, **22**, 257; April 21, 1911, **22**, 578

Anthony Killgore, Dec. 9, 1910, **22**, 164

Wilson B. Killingbeck, Oct. 6, 1910, **21**, 267; Oct. 18, 1910, **21**, 351; Oct. 21, 1910, **21**, 386

Frederick Paul King, Feb. 9, 1909, **19**, 32

Darwin Pearl Kingsley, Nov. 9, 1910, **21**, 621

Eugene Francis Kinkead, Sept. 30, 1910, **21**, 213

Robert Bird Kirkland, June 19, 1912, **24**, 488

Burton Alva Konkle, Sept. 27, 1904, **15**, 494

Fernand Gustave Gaston Labori, Aug. 14, 1904, **15**, 443

Clara Schlee Laddey and Mary Loring Colvin, Jan. 2, 1911, **22**, 289

James Lafferty, Dec. 20, 1910, **22**, 233

Robert Marion La Follette, March 17, 1909, **19**, 108

George Mason La Monte, Nov. 9, 1910, **21**, 610; Nov. 22, 1910, **22**, 82; Dec. 12, 1910, **22**, 174; Jan. 6, 1911, **22**, 308

Franklin Knight Lane, Nov. 8, 1910, **21**, 586

John J. Lane, Dec. 7, 1910, **22**, 147

Adolph Lankering, Oct. 10, 1910, **21**, 295; Dec. 24, 1910, **22**, 258

Robert Lansing, Nov. 9, 1910, **21**, 607

John Holladay Latané, Nov. 9, 1910, **21**, 613

John E. Lathrop, Dec. 8, 1910, **22**, 159; Dec. 22, 1910, **22**, 247; Dec. 23, 1910, **22**, 255; Feb. 1, 1911, **22**, 404

James Laughlin, Jr., Feb. 15, 1904, **15**, 167; June 8, 1904, **15**, 361

Edgar R. Laverty, June 16, 1909, **19**, 255

David Lawrence, Nov. 9, 1910, **21**, 608

Luke Lea, July 13, 1912, **24**, 545

Edward E. Lee, Nov. 12, 1910, **22**, 31

John Jacob Lentz, April 2, 1910, **20**, 313; Dec. 19, 1910, **22**, 228

Frederick H. Levey, Dec. 1, 1910, **22**, 125

Leon Michel Levy, June 25, 1907, **17**, 222

Vivian Murchison Lewis, Nov. 9, 1910, **21**, 591

Charles Freeman Libby, Feb. 1, 1910, **20**, 71

William Libbey, July 21, 1902, **14**, 37

William C. Liller, April 25, 1910, **20,** 390; June 9, 1910, **20,** 512; Nov. 8, 1910, **21,** 587; Aug. 2, 1911, **23,** 245

Richard Vliet Lindabury, Sept. 19, 1910, **21,** 140; Oct. 7, 1910, **21,** 274; Oct. 20, 1910, **21,** 378; Oct. 21, 1910, **21,** 388; Oct. 27, 1910, **21,** 449

Benjamin Barr Lindsey, Dec. 28, 1910, **22,** 274; Jan. 28, 1911, **22,** 387; April 24, 1911, **22,** 584

Isaac Henry Lionberger, Feb. 13, 1910, **20,** 125; March 12, 1910, **20,** 238; April 24, 1910, **20,** 389; Oct. 16, 1911, **23,** 459; Nov. 13, 1911, **23,** 549

J. B. Lippincott Company, Sept. 26, 1902, **14,** 134

Job Herbert Lippincott, Dec. 4, 1909, **19,** 554; Sept. 20, 1910, **21,** 145; Oct. 7, 1910, **21,** 274; Dec. 1, 1910, **22,** 125

Thomas Littlehales, March 21, 1911, **22,** 513

Richard Ludwig Enno Littmann, Sept. 19, 1905, **16,** 186; Nov. 24, 1905, **16,** 233; Aug. 4, 1909, **19,** 327

James Henry Lockhart, Jan. 28, 1904, **15,** 144; July 1, 1904, **15,** 402; April 19, 1905, **16,** 69

George Bryan Logan, Jan. 29, 1909, **19,** 17

Frank Howard Lord, Aug. 1, 1902, **14,** 46

Frank E. Loughran, June 26, 1912, **24,** 500

Thomas Raynesford Lounsbury, June 24, 1902, **14,** 560

Thomas Bell Love, Nov. 8, 1910, **21,** 584; Dec. 1, 1910, **22,** 122; Dec. 19, 1910, **22,** 224; Feb. 7, 1911, **22,** 409; April 18, 1911, **22,** 576; July 26, 1911, **23,** 231; Aug. 5, 1911, **23,** 255; Aug. 9, 1911, **23,** 260, 261; Aug. 16, 1911, **23,** 267; Sept. 7, 1911, **23,** 308; Dec. 8, 1911, **23,** 589; Jan. 18, 1912, **24,** 50; Feb. 14, 1912, **24,** 163; March 14, 1912, **24,** 248; March 19, 1912, **24,** 254; Dec. 27, 1912, **25,** 624

Edgar Odell Lovett, Nov. 21, 1906, **16,** 488; March 13, 1907, **17,** 67; Jan. 3, 1908, **17,** 586; July 14, 1910, **20,** 580; Sept. 23, 1910, **21,** 159

A. B. Lowe, Sept. 23, 1911, **23,** 356

Abbott Lawrence Lowell, Feb. 15, 1903, **14,** 359; Jan. 15, 1909, **18,** 628; July 14, 1909, **19,** 310; Oct. 26, 1909, **19,** 448; Nov. 12, 1909, **19,** 495; Dec. 8, 1909, **19,** 562; Dec. 24, 1909, **19,** 627; Jan. 13, 1910, **20,** 11; Feb. 1, 1910, **20,** 72; Feb. 9, 1910, **20,** 91; March 21, 1910, **20,** 276; March 24, 1910, **20,** 289; May 23, 1910, **20,** 468; Sept. 16, 1910, **21,** 109; Nov. 9, 1912, **25,** 535

Arthur Crosby Ludington, Feb. 4, 1909, **19,** 25; April 11, 1909, **19,** 155; Feb. 4, 1910, **20,** 78

William Lustgarten, April 15, 1911, **22,** 570

Maurice F. Lyons, Aug. 21, 1912, **25,** 50

William Gibbs McAdoo, Sept. 16, 1910, **21,** 108; Oct. 5, 1910, **21,** 265; Oct. 11, 1910, **21,** 298; Nov. 15, 1910, **22,** 51; Dec. 8, 1911, **23,** 588; Dec. 20, 1911, **23,** 602; Jan. 10, 1912, **24,** 28; Jan. 18, 1912, **24,** 48; March 8, 1912, **24,** 237; March 27, 1912, **24,** 268;

April 1, 1912, **24,** 274; April 3, 1912, **24,** 286; April 8, 1912, **24,** 306; May 4, 1912, **24,** 384; May 16, 1912, **24,** 403; May 29, 1912, **24,** 450; June 6, 1912, **24,** 464; July 25, 1912, **24,** 570; Sept. 5, 1912, **25,** 111; Dec. 19, 1912, **25,** 611

Charles Williston McAlpin, Sept. 5, 1902, **14,** 122; Sept. 12, 1902, **14,** 130; Oct. 24, 1902, **14,** 167, 169; Feb. 27, 1903, **14,** 380; March 13, 1903, **14,** 391; June 29, 1903, **14,** 499; July 13, 1903, **14,** 543; July 17, 1903, **14,** 545; Aug. 3, 1903, **14,** 549; Nov. 19, 1903, **15,** 55; Dec. 17, 1903, **15,** 101; April 11, 1904, **15,** 242; Jan. 6, 1905, **15,** 576; March 10, 1905, **16,** 27; June 13, 1905, **16,** 137; June 21, 1905, **16,** 145; July 31, 1905, **16,** 167; Aug. 2, 1905, **16,** 169; Oct. 11, 1905, **16,** 192; Nov. 8, 1905, **16,** 214; Dec. 14, 1905, **16,** 266; Jan. 13, 1906, **16,** 282; March 22, 1906, **16,** 342; May 31, 1906, **16,** 412; Sept. 2, 1906, **16,** 446; Nov. 27, 1906, **16,** 492; Dec. 5, 1906, **16,** 495; Jan. 10, 1907, **16,** 556; Jan. 20, 1909, **19,** 3; July 19, 1910, **21,** 13; Aug. 10, 1910, **21,** 49; Oct. 28, 1910, **21,** 463; Nov. 3, 1910, **21,** 536; Dec. 23, 1910, **22,** 256

George Meriwether McCampbell, Jr., Feb. 10, 1910, **20,** 116

Robert Harris McCarter, Aug. 1, 1902, **14,** 46; Sept. 17, 1910, **21,** 131

Thomas Nesbitt McCarter, Nov. 22, 1910, **22,** 83

Thomas Nesbitt McCarter, Jr., Sept. 19, 1910, **21,** 139

Uzal Haggerty McCarter, April 14, 1904, **15,** 248; July 1, 1904, **15,** 402

George Brinton McClellan, April 18, 1906, **16,** 372; July 21, 1908, **18,** 372; Oct. 1, 1908, **18,** 436; April 21, 1909, **19,** 169; Nov. 9, 1910, **21,** 599

Howard McClenahan, June 17, 1906, **16,** 427

Alfred James Pollock McClure, Feb. 22, 1904, **15,** 176

Annie Dixon McClure, Nov. 5, 1909, **19,** 484

Hugh S. McClure, April 7, 1910, **20,** 349

James Gore King McClure, Sept. 10, 1909, **19,** 380; Jan. 26, 1910, **20,** 59

Samuel Sidney McClure, Nov. 23, 1910, **22,** 85

William Frank McCombs, Sept. 16, 1910, **21,** 108; Oct. 10, 1910, **21,** 294; Nov. 9, 1910, **21,** 607; April 22, 1911, **22,** 581; July 17, 1911, **23,** 215; July 28, 1911, **23,** 235; July 31, 1911, **23,** 242; Aug. 2, 1911, **23,** 247; Aug. 4, 1911, **23,** 252; Aug. 8, 1911, **23,** 259; Aug. 10, 1911, **23,** 261; Aug. 11, 1911, **23,** 263; Aug. 21, 1911, **23,** 287; Sept. 7, 1911, **23,** 309; Sept. 13, 1911, **23,** 324, 326; Sept. 20, 1911, **23,** 340; Sept. 21, 1911, **23,** 352; Sept. 23, 1911, **23,** 355; Sept. 26, 1911, **23,** 360; Dec. 30, 1911, **23,** 632; Aug. 13, 1912, **25,** 23; Aug. 19, 1912, **25,** 47; Nov. 5, 1912, **25,** 522; Nov. 30, 1912, **25,** 571; Dec. 23, 1912, **25,** 618

Walter Lee McCorkle, Dec. 4, 1908, **18,** 532; Dec. 21, 1908, **18,** 563; Sept. 16, 1910, **21,** 105

Cyrus Hall McCormick, Nov. 24, 1902, **14,** 210; Dec. 18, 1902, **14,**

297; Dec. 4, 1903, **15,** 64, 65; Oct. 7, 1904, **15,** 505; June 10, 1907, **17,** 206; April 16, 1908, **18,** 272; Dec. 12, 1908, **18,** 545; Dec. 17, 1908, **18,** 553, 554; Dec. 23, 1908, **18,** 564; March 2, 1909, **19,** 74; May 18, 1909, **19,** 199; Oct. 2, 1909, **19,** 397, 398; Oct. 18, 1909, **19,** 423; Oct. 27, 1909, **19,** 454; Dec. 1, 1909, **19,** 541; Dec. 11, 1909, **19,** 603; April 14, 1910, **20,** 353; April 15, 1910, **20,** 360; May 25, 1910, **20,** 471; July 18, 1910, **21,** 10; Sept. 19, 1910, **21,** 140; Nov. 2, 1910, **21,** 518, 519; Nov. 9, 1910, **21,** 594; Nov. 17, 1910, **22,** 71; Jan. 28, 1911, **22,** 388

Edith Rockefeller McCormick, Feb. 20, 1909, **19,** 65

Nettie Fowler McCormick, Nov. 4, 1910, **21,** 556

Vance Criswell McCormick, Feb. 6, 1911, **22,** 408

Henry Mitchell McCracken, Nov. 29, 1905, **16,** 238

Pirie MacDonald, Aug. 5, 1902, **14,** 56

Daniel John McGillicuddy, June 20, 1912, **24,** 490

Charles Howard McIlwain, April 13, 1905, **16,** 54; Dec. 9, 1910, **22,** 165

Norman Edward Mack, Oct. 30, 1909, **19,** 464; Sept. 16, 1910, **21,** 102

David L. MacKay, Oct. 8, 1910, **21,** 287; Oct. 13, 1910, **21,** 322

Alexander Jeffrey McKelway, Dec. 16, 1910, **22,** 206; Dec. 19, 1910, **22,** 226; July 28, 1911, **23,** 236; July 23, 1912, **24,** 566; Oct. 2, 1912, **25,** 310; Nov. 12, 1912, **25,** 543

St. Clair McKelway, March 15, 1904, **15,** 193; April 18, 1906, **16,** 372; Dec. 10, 1910, **22,** 170

William Douglas Mackenzie, July 10, 1908, **18,** 359

Ebenezer Mackey, Sept. 22, 1909, **19,** 387; Oct. 2, 1909, **19,** 399; Jan. 6, 1910, **19,** 738

Charles Follen McKim, Sept. 15, 1904, **15,** 469

Robert Morris McKinney, Oct. 23, 1908, **18,** 470

William Pierce Macksey, Dec. 20, 1910, **22,** 232

Samuel McLanahan, Feb. 8, 1910, **20,** 89

Malcolm MacLaren, June 18, 1908, **18,** 338

John Bach McMaster, Nov. 9, 1910, **21,** 609

John Van Antwerp MacMurray, Aug. 17, 1908, **18,** 403

Simon John McPherson, May 20, 1904, **15,** 343; April 24, 1908, **18,** 275; Jan. 5, 1910, **19,** 728

Donald Alexander MacRae, May 4, 1905, **16,** 90

Isaac Wayne MacVeagh, April 16, 1903, **14,** 410; Oct. 10, 1910, **21,** 293; Dec. 7, 1910, **22,** 143

John Gresham Machen, July 13, 1902, **14,** 8

David Magie, Jr., April 13, 1905, **16,** 54

William Francis Magie, Aug. 13, 1902, **14,** 81; Feb. 4, 1904, **15,** 157; Nov. 7, 1908, **18,** 489; Oct. 22, 1910, **21,** 406; Nov. 22, 1910, **22,** 79

William Jay Magie, Jan. 3, 1910, **19,** 707

Dudley Field Malone, Nov. 14, 1910, **22,** 45

Richard Irvine Manning, May 13, 1910, **20,** 453; May 21, 1910, **20,** 463

Theodore Marburg, Nov. 9, 1910, **21,** 614

Allan Marquand, Feb. 18, 1904, **15,** 173; April 4, 1910, **20,** 318

Erwin E. Marshall, Sept. 16, 1910, **21,** 106

Howard Marshall, Oct. 13, 1910, **21,** 324

Thomas Riley Marshall, Nov. 9, 1910, **21,** 603; Nov. 5, 1912, **25,** 521

William Joseph Martin, July 4, 1912, **24,** 538

James Edgar Martine, Nov. 16, 1910, **22,** 52; July 28, 1911, **23,** 234

Walter Taylor Marvin, May 8, 1905, **16,** 91

Franklin Marx, Sept. 8, 1910, **21,** 86

Victor Louis Mason, Nov. 8, 1910, **21,** 586

Frank Jewett Mather, Jr. April 18, 1910, **20,** 369

Sir William Mather, Nov. 19, 1906, **16,** 487; Dec. 3, 1906, **16,** 494; Jan. 25, 1907, **17,** 13; March 24, 1907, **17,** 90; April 30, 1907, **17,** 126; June 17, 1907, **17,** 214; June 30, 1907, **17,** 238; July 4, 1907, **17,** 359; Aug. 22, 1907, **17,** 358; Oct. 20, 1907, **17,** 447; Oct. 29, 1907, **17,** 460; Nov. 7, 1907, **17,** 471; Nov. 18, 1907, **17,** 509

Shailer Mathews, Oct. 23, 1907, **17,** 451

William Hunter Maxwell, Sept. 24, 1910, **21,** 161; Nov. 9, 1910, **21,** 617; Dec. 17, 1910, **22,** 214; Jan. 2, 1911, **22,** 290

William James Mayo, Nov. 23, 1909, **19,** 532

Edwin Doak Mead, June 22, 1912, **24,** 494; Aug. 10, 1912, **25,** 19

Royal Meeker, May 10, 1905, **16,** 94; June 30, 1912, **24,** 514

John Meigs, Jan. 16, 1906, **16,** 283

Colyer Meriwether, Feb. 4, 1906, **16,** 302

Wilton Merle-Smith, Nov. 30, 1909, **19,** 539

Daniel Merriman, July 18, 1908, **18,** 369

David Douglas Metcalfe, Nov. 16, 1909, **19,** 505

James Cowden Meyers, Sept. 16, 1910, **21,** 107

Lucius Hopkins Miller, May 19, 1906, **16,** 398; July 28, 1907, **17,** 296; Feb. 26, 1909, **19,** 71

Raleigh Colston Minor, Nov. 8, 1910, **21,** 585

Henry Collin Minton, Jan. 7, 1911, **22,** 311

Charles Wellman Mitchell, June 18, 1909, **19,** 260; Nov. 9, 1910, **21,** 599

Henry Moffat, Nov. 19, 1909, **19,** 523; Nov. 22, 1909, **19,** 531

John James Moment, April 2, 1906, **16,** 355

James Charles Monaghan, Aug. 30, 1912, **25,** 63

Andrew Jackson Montague, June 5, 1911, **23,** 133; Sept. 14, 1911, **23,** 327; Sept. 25, 1911, **23,** 359; Oct. 4, 1911, **23,** 390

John Alexander Montgomery, Sept. 16, 1910, **21,** 104

John Moody, Nov. 29, 1910, **22,** 114

Charles Sumner Moore, Dec. 13, 1911, **23,** 592; May 25, 1912, **24,** 444

John Bassett Moore, May 22, 1910, **20,** 464; Nov. 4, 1910, **21,** 557

Josephine Perry Morgan, Oct. 22, 1908, **18,** 469

Junius Spencer Morgan, Sept. 14, 1904, **15,** 467; Jan. 10, 1909, **18,** 609

Benjamin Wistar Morris III, Aug. 16, 1904, **15,** 444; Nov. 15, 1904, **15,** 533; Dec. 12, 1904, **15,** 573; Aug. 11, 1905, **16,** 177; Feb. 6, 1906, **16,** 305; Feb. 8, 1906, **16,** 308; March 15, 1906, **16,** 333; March 21, 1906, **16,** 339; May 21, 1906, **16,** 403

Roland Sletor Morris, Nov. 22, 1909, **19,** 531; Nov. 8, 1910, **21,** 584

William H. Morrow, Oct. 29, 1910, **21,** 476

Franklin Blake Morse, Feb. 29, 1904, **15,** 181

John R. Mott, Nov. 20, 1905, **17,** 621; May 5, 1908, **18,** 288; Jan. 21, 1910, **20,** 43; Jan. 27, 1910, **20,** 61

James Phinney Munroe, Oct. 14, 1909, **19,** 420

Hopson Owen Murfee, Aug. 6, 1902, **14,** 59; Oct. 19, 1903, **15,** 16; March 26, 1904, **15,** 213; March 31, 1904, **15,** 226; April 1, 1904, **15,** 226; April 21, 1905, **16,** 73; June 10, 1905, **16,** 113; Jan. 12, 1906, **16,** 281; Jan. 18, 1906, **16,** 284; March 12, 1906, **16,** 331; March 18, 1906, **16,** 337; March 31, 1906, **16,** 353; Nov. 16, 1910, **22,** 55

Edgar Gardner Murphy, Feb. 5, 1904, **15,** 159; Feb. 10, 1904, **15,** 165; Feb. 15, 1904, **15,** 168

Franklin Murphy, Sept. 30, 1910, **21,** 212

Franklin Murphy, Jr., June 7, 1907, **17,** 187; June 18, 1907, **17,** 216

Harold Griffith Murray, April 14, 1904, **15,** 249; July 25, 1904, **15,** 423; Aug. 4, 1904, **15,** 433; Feb. 5, 1906, **16,** 302; Feb. 8, 1906, **16,** 307; March 17, 1906, **16,** 336; March 20, 1906, **16,** 338; April 26, 1906, **16,** 376, 377; May 2, 1906, **16,** 383; May 10, 1906, **16,** 389; Jan. 9, 1907, **16,** 553; Feb. 18, 1907, **17,** 41

William Henry Murray, April 1, 1912, **24,** 275

Henry Beach Needham, July 8, 1911, **23,** 193

Fred Neher, Nov. 24, 1902, **14,** 211; Feb. 22, 1905, **16,** 10

Benjamin Franklin Nelson, Nov. 12, 1909, **19,** 494; Dec. 15, 1909, **19,** 605

Robert Jenkins Nevin, Dec. 4, 1903, **15,** 66

Francis Griffith Newlands, April 1, 1912, **24,** 275; April 3, 1912, **24,** 285; May 10, 1912, **24,** 390, 391; May 16, 1912, **24,** 403; June 6, 1912, **24,** 463; July 1, 1912, **24,** 520

Edwin A. Newman, Dec. 5, 1911, **23,** 566

Byron Rufus Newton, Aug. 7, 1911, **23,** 258

Richard Cole Newton, Dec. 8, 1910, **22,** 155

Edmund Favor Noel, Nov. 10, 1910, **22,** 16

Joseph M. Noonan, April 12, 1910, **20,** 352; Aug. 8, 1910, **21,** 42; Aug. 17, 1910, **21,** 54; Aug. 28, 1910, **21,** 63; Sept. 8, 1910, **21,** 85; Sept. 16, 1910, **21,** 108; Oct. 5, 1910, **21,** 265; Dec. 4, 1910, **22,** 133; Dec. 18, 1910, **22,** 223; Dec. 22, 1910, **22,** 245; Jan. 26, 1911, **22,** 377

Ernest Dressel North, Nov. 22, 1905, **16,** 231

George Tyler Northup, April 24, 1905, **16,** 79

James Richard Nugent, March 7, 1910, **20,** 215; Sept. 16, 1910, **21,** 106; Sept. 26, 1910, **21,** 173; Oct. 10, 1910, **21,** 290; Nov. 15, 1910, **22,** 49; Dec. 10, 1910, **22,** 171; Dec. 15, 1910, **22,** 203

Ellis Paxson Oberholtzer, July 6, 1907, **17,** 262

Patrick Henry O'Brien, June 17, 1912, **24,** 483

Joseph L. O'Connell, Oct. 3, 1910, **21** 239

Alexander Thomas Ormond, Dec. 31, 1909, **19,** 664; Feb. 8, 1910, **20,** 89; Nov. 9, 1910, **21,** 603

Arthur Herbert Osborn, July 9, 1907, **17,** 266

Henry Fairfield Osborn, Aug. 2, 1902, **14,** 54; Sept. 10, 1902, **14,** 126; March 15, 1904, **15,** 194; Sept. 17, 1907, **17,** 389

William Church Osborn, Sept. 18, 1903, **15,** 3; April 26, 1904, **15,** 298; April 28, 1904, **15,** 302; Sept. 26, 1904, **15,** 493; Sept. 22, 1910, **21,** 155; Sept. 26, 1910, **21,** 172

Edmund Burke Osborne, Jan. 24, 1911, **22,** 366

Harry Vliet Osborne, Dec. 13, 1910, **22,** 181; Dec. 30, 1910, **22,** 285; Jan. 7, 1911, **22,** 310

Thomas Mott Osborne, Sept. 10, 1912, **25,** 133

Charles Grosvenor Osgood, Jr., April 19, 1905, **16,** 70; Dec. 3, 1909, **19,** 550

Sir William Osler, Nov. 9, 1910, **21,** 618

Michael J. O'Toole, April 25, 1907, **17,** 121

Robert Latham Owen, Dec. 16, 1910, **22,** 208

William Alfred Packard, Oct. 11, 1905, **16,** 199; Oct. 25, 1905, **16,** 205; June 20, 1906, **16,** 429

Thomas Nelson Page, Nov. 9, 1910, **21,** 602

Walter Hines Page, Oct. 22, 1908, **18,** 469; Feb. 11, 1910, **20,** 121; Nov. 5, 1910, **21,** 576; Feb. 15, 1911, **22,** 433; July 16, 1911, **23,** 214; July 3, 1912, **24,** 530; Aug. 28, 1912, **25,** 62; Nov. 5, 1912, **25,** 515

Edwin William Pahlow, May 29, 1907, **17,** 164; June 20, 1907, **17,** 219; Aug. 14, 1909, **19,** 333; Aug. 22, 1909, **19,** 351

Alexander Mitchell Palmer, Nov. 9, 1910, **21,** 604; May 11, 1912, **24,** 392; July 25, 1912, **24,** 570

Stephen Squires Palmer, June 28, 1907, **17,** 237; July 23, 1907, **17,** 293; Aug. 13, 1907, **17,** 346; Aug. 19, 1907, **17,** 351; Aug. 27, 1907, **17,** 362; April 23, 1908, **18,** 274; Oct. 29, 1908, **18,** 476

George Frederick Parker, June 16, 1910, **20,** 534

Charles Henry Parkhurst, Nov. 9, 1910, **21,** 621

George Robert Parkin, March 24, 1903, **14,** 398

George William Patterson, Sept. 25, 1903, **15,** 5

Francis Landey Patton, Feb. 1, 1911, **22,** 404

Frederic John Paxon, July 16, 1902, **14,** 20

W. C. Payne, Nov. 9, 1910, **21,** 616

George Foster Peabody, Dec. 1, 1904, **15,** 550; June 12, 1912, **24,** 472; June 23, 1912, **24,** 497; Dec. 18, 1912, **25,** 608

Mary Allen Hulbert Peck, Feb. 25, 1907, **17,** 50; Feb. 10, 1910, **20,**

118; Feb. 15, 1910, **20,** 127; Feb. 18, 1910, **20,** 141; Feb. 22, 1910, **20,** 155; Feb. 25, 1910, **20,** 180; Aug. 10, 1910, **21,** 48; Nov. 27, 1910, **22,** 100; Jan. 13, 1911, **22,** 331; July 22, 1911, **23,** 222; July 30, 1911, **23,** 241; Aug. 12, 1911, **23,** 264; Jan. 5, 1912, **23,** 654; Jan. 15, 1912, **24,** 44; Jan. 19, 1912, **24,** 58; *see also* Mary Allen Hulbert

Thomas Jones Pence, June 10, 1912, **24,** 467; June 14, 1912, **24,** 475; July 15, 1912, **24,** 553

George Walbridge Perkins, Nov. 3, 1909, **19,** 479; Nov. 10, 1910, **22,** 19

Bliss Perry, July 20, 1902, **14,** 34; April 27, 1907, **17,** 122; Aug. 2, 1907, **17,** 333; Oct. 22, 1910, **21,** 406

Magnus Fraser Peterson, Aug. 17, 1908, **18,** 404; Nov. 9, 1910, **21,** 619

George Petrie, March 7, 1904, **15,** 182; April 7, 1904, **15,** 237

James Duval Phelan, April 20, 1912, **24,** 351; May 3, 1912, **24,** 384

David Graham Phillips, April 19, 1910, **20,** 372

John Sanburn Phillips, April 15, 1909, **19,** 163

William Wirt Phillips, June 25, 1907, **17,** 221; April 22, 1909, **19,** 170

Bowdre Phinizy, April 17, 1911, **22,** 573

Palmer Eddy Pierce, April 17, 1906, **16,** 369

Nicholas L. Piotrowski, March 11, 1912, **24,** 241

Lewis Eugene Pierson, March 2, 1908, **18,** 3

Henry Cooper Pitney, Jr., Nov. 29, 1902, **14,** 247; Feb. 3, 1903, **14,** 348; Feb. 6, 1903, **14,** 353; March 16, 1903, **14,** 394; June 22, 1903, **14,** 496; June 24, 1903, **14,** 496; June 29, 1903, **14,** 501; Nov. 4, 1903, **15,** 32

Mahlon Pitney, Nov. 11, 1910, **22,** 28

Dan Fellows Platt, Jan. 27, 1907, **17,** 23; July 18, 1910, **21,** 11; Aug. 18, 1910, **21,** 56; Sept. 19, 1910, **21,** 140; Sept. 26, 1910, **21,** 172; Nov. 23, 1910, **22,** 86

Marx Warley Platzek, March 2, 1906, **16,** 322

George Arthur Plimpton, Dec. 16, 1910, **22,** 209

Clarence Hamilton Poe, Feb. 17, 1911, **22,** 437; March 11, 1911, **22,** 499

Edgar Allan Poe, Nov. 9, 1910, **21,** 600

John Garland Pollard, June 8, 1911, **23,** 138; Aug. 24, 1911, **23,** 290; Dec. 19, 1911, **23,** 601; Jan. 18, 1912, **24,** 51

Frederick Pollock, Feb. 6, 1904, **15,** 162

Adolfo Gonzáles Posada, Feb. 10, 1903, **14,** 356

Joseph Hyde Pratt, March 26, 1911, **22,** 520

William Kelly Prentice, Nov. 23, 1906, **16,** 492; Oct. 3, 1907, **17,** 415

Jacob Cole Price, Jan. 10, 1911, **22,** 325

George Madison Priest, July 31, 1902, **14,** 45; March 6, 1910, **20,** 214

Princeton University Alumni, June 12, 1906, **16,** 424

Henry Smith Pritchett, Oct. 25, 1902, **14,** 186; Feb. 6, 1906, **16,** 304; June 9, 1906, **16,** 419; April 10, 1907, **17,** 103; Nov. 21, 1907, **17,** 511; Nov. 29, 1907, **17,** 545; Dec. 9, 1907, **17,** 554; March 11, 1908, **18,** 15; March 16, 1908, **18,** 52; April 2, 1908, **18,** 220; April 11, 1908, **18,** 260; May 6, 1908, **18,** 289; Feb. 18, 1909, **19,** 51; May 1, 1909, **19,** 180; May 5, 1909, **19,** 185; Oct. 21, 1909, **19,** 439; Nov. 3, 1909, **19,** 480; May 22, 1910, **20,** 464; Jan. 11, 1910, **20,** 584; July 22, 1910, **21,** 20; Sept. 23, 1910, **21,** 160; Nov. 3, 1910, **21,** 540; Nov. 9, 1910, **21,** 596; Dec. 3, 1910, **22,** 130; Dec. 7, 1910, **22,** 148; Dec. 29, 1910, **22,** 283; Jan. 24, 1911, **22,** 365; April 9, 1911, **22,** 548; May 29, 1911, **23,** 102

William Cooper Procter, June 7, 1909, **19,** 237; Oct. 8, 1909, **19,** 406; Oct. 13, 1909, **19,** 412; June 7, 1909, **20,** 105

A Progressive Republican, Oct. 17, 1910, **21,** 347

Joseph Pulitzer, Nov. 9, 1910, **21,** 595

Frederick K. Pulsifer, Nov. 29, 1910, **22,** 117

William Edmond Pulsifer, Feb. 27, 1903, **14,** 379

Edward Amos Purdy, June 18, 1912, **24,** 487

Moses Taylor Pyne, March 5, 1903, **14,** 382; June 13, 1903, **14,** 490; Dec. 24, 1903, **15,** 107; Dec. 29, 1903, **15,** 112; July 23, 1904, **15,** 422; July 26, 1904, **15,** 423; July 30, 1904, **15,** 424; Aug. 1, 1904, **15,** 432; Aug. 6, 1904, **15,** 434; Aug. 10, 1904, **15,** 436; Aug. 12, 1904, **15,** 440; April 18, 1905, **16,** 69; Aug. 11, 1905, **16,** 175; Aug. 25, 1905, **16,** 184; Jan. 5, 1906, **16,** 278; March 6, 1906, **16,** 323; May 2, 1906, **16,** 382; June 19, 1906, **16,** 428; Nov. 7, 1906, **16,** 482; May 21, 1907, **17,** 155; Dec. 6, 1907, **17,** 549; Dec. 17, 1907, **17,** 562; Dec. 24, 1907, **17,** 568; May 7, 1908, **18,** 290; Oct. 25, 1908, **18,** 472; Nov. 10, 1908, **18,** 490; Feb. 18, 1909, **19,** 52; March 30, 1909, **19,** 131, 132; July 27, 1909, **19,** 320; Oct. 14, 1909, **19,** 418; Oct. 18, 1909, **19,** 425; Nov. 30, 1909, **19,** 540; Dec. 1, 1909, **19,** 540; Dec. 9, 1909, **19,** 578; Dec. 20, 1909, **19,** 610; Dec. 24, 1909, **19,** 627; Dec. 29, 1909, **19,** 655; Jan. 10, 1910, **19,** 752; Jan. 19, 1910, **20,** 31; Oct. 19, 1910, **21,** 353; Nov. 10, 1910, **22,** 17

Moses Taylor Pyne and Archibald Douglas Russell, Jan. 13, 1908, **17,** 600

Arthur Hobson Quinn, Dec. 3, 1906, **16,** 495; Dec. 8, 1906, **16,** 504

Adolphus Ragan, June 26, 1909, **19,** 272

Charles Brewster Randolph, April 15, 1905, **16,** 61

Harrison Randolph, July 12, 1902, **14,** 5

Edwin Moore Rankin, April 17, 1905, **16,** 67

Emanuel Raphael, March 21, 1907, **17,** 88

Emanuel Raphael and James Everett McAshan, Jan. 10, 1907, **16,** 556

Hardwicke Drummond Rawnsley, July 5, 1912, **24,** 540

George Lansing Raymond, Dec. 20, 1907, **17,** 565

John Marshall Raymond and Andrew Fleming West, May 22, 1910, **20,** 464

Norman Bruce Ream, April 23, 1904, **15,** 271
George Lawrence Record, Oct. 5, 1910, **21,** 259; Oct. 17, 1910, **21,** 338; Nov. 9, 1910, **21,** 596
William Cox Redfield, Aug. 1, 1912, **24,** 579
James Hay Reed, June 3, 1904, **15,** 356; March 3, 1908, **18,** 6; March 30, 1908, **18,** 217
William Belden Reed, Jr., Aug. 27, 1907, **17,** 362; Sept. 3, 1907, **17,** 371
Louis Irving Reichner, July 17, 1907, **17,** 288; Feb. 22, 1911, **22,** 450
Edith Gittings Reid, Oct. 16, 1902, **14,** 146; Jan. 22, 1903, **14,** 330; Feb. 9, 1906, **16,** 308; March 5, 1907, **17,** 59; April 28, 1910, **20,** 402; Oct. 16, 1912, **25,** 422
Ira Remsen, Jan. 23, 1912, **24,** 65; Sept. 28, 1912, **25,** 282
James Burton Reynolds, Aug. 28, 1906, **16,** 442
Syngman Rhee, July 1, 1910, **20,** 556
James Ford Rhodes, June 1, 1910, **20,** 496; Nov. 11, 1910, **22,** 27
James Mauran Rhodes, Jr., June 11, 1907, **17,** 209
Ernest Cushing Richardson, April 28, 1906, **16,** 379; May 12, 1906, **16,** 390; May 12, 1906, **16,** 394; Oct. 27, 1906, **16,** 472
Evans Tulane Richardson, Sept. 26, 1912, **25,** 271
Owen Willans Richardson, June 24, 1908, **18,** 340
Charles Alexander Richmond, Feb. 1, 1909, **19,** 19; May 30, 1909, **19,** 223; Sept. 20, 1910, **21,** 146
William Henry Rideing, Dec. 7, 1906, **16,** 496; Dec. 18, 1906, **16,** 534; Dec. 21, 1906, **16,** 538
Adrian Riker, April 23, 1909, **19,** 171
William Henry Roberts, Feb. 4, 1907, **17,** 28; June 19, 1908, **18,** 339; Feb. 17, 1909, **19,** 51
Joseph Haswell Robinson, July 1, 1907, **17,** 241
William Courtland Robinson, April 21, 1910, **20,** 380
Charles Greene Rockwood, Jr., March 1, 1905, **16,** 17
John Augustus Roebling II, Oct. 27, 1910, **21,** 450
Philip Ashton Rollins, Jan. 28, 1910, **20,** 64
Theodore Roosevelt, Oct. 18, 1902, **14,** 147; Dec. 6, 1902, **14,** 265; Dec. 23, 1902, **14,** 303; Feb. 4, 1903, **14,** 348; Jan. 13, 1904, **15,** 127; Jan. 29, 1904, **15,** 147; Aug. 9, 1905, **16,** 175; Nov. 6, 1905, **16,** 213; Nov. 24, 1905, **16,** 233; Feb. 26, 1906, **16,** 319; Oct. 22, 1912, **25,** 453; Nov. 5, 1912, **25,** 521
Oren Root, April 3, 1905, **16,** 45
Robert Kilburn Root, April 19, 1905, **16,** 70
William Winston Roper, June 28, 1910, **20,** 547
Leo Stanton Rowe, Feb. 24, 1908, **17,** 619; Nov. 9, 1910, **21,** 614
Henry Norris Russell, April 6, 1905, **16,** 81
Lucius Thompson Russell, March 23, 1910, **20,** 288; Dec. 5, 1910, **22,** 137
Clarence Sackett, Dec. 17, 1910, **22,** 215
Margaret Olivia Slocum Sage, Nov. 13, 1908, **18,** 508

William W. St. John, Nov. 7, 1910, **21,** 581; Nov. 19, 1910, **22,** 76; Nov. 22, 1910, **22,** 81; Dec. 8, 1910, **22,** 155

Edward Seiler Salmon, Sept. 16, 1910, **21,** 105

Shosuke Sato, Dec. 6, 1910, **22,** 139

Willard Saulsbury, April 3, 1912, **24,** 285; April 13, 1912, **24,** 329; April 20, 1912, **24,** 353; May 2, 1912, **24,** 382; May 27, 1912, **24,** 447; June 10, 1912, **24,** 469

Walter Hulme Sawyer, May 3, 1909, **19,** 181

John Nevin Sayre, Nov. 21, 1909, **19,** 529

Adolf Frederick Schauffler, Dec. 1, 1909, **19,** 543

Rudolph Edward Schirmer, Nov. 9, 1910, **21,** 617

Carl Gustav Schulz, Dec. 1, 1909, **19,** 542

Jacob Gould Schurman, Nov. 9, 1910, **21,** 611; Jan. 31, 1911, **22,** 399

Charles Ernest Scott, Feb. 22, 1909, **19,** 65; April 30, 1909, **19,** 177

Hugh Lenox Scott, April 25, 1910, **20,** 391

William Berryman Scott, June 26, 1907, **17,** 231

Charles Scribner, Aug. 12, 1902, **14,** 79; Dec. 23, 1902, **14,** 303; March 24, 1905, **16,** 37; Sept. 24, 1909, **19,** 390; Sept. 16, 1910, **21,** 104; Nov. 15, 1910, **22,** 51

Charles Scribner's Sons, Nov. 17, 1908, **18,** 517

Edward Wallace Scudder, Sept. 27, 1910, **21,** 175; Dec. 20, 1910, **22,** 233

Wallace McIlvaine Scudder, Dec. 19, 1910, **22,** 225

Michael Welsh Scully, Sept. 17, 1910, **21,** 131

Thomas Joseph Scully, June 16, 1912, **24,** 481

Fred Loring Seely, Sept. 14, 1911, **23,** 328

Edmund Bayly Seymour, Jr., Sept. 14, 1907, **17,** 383; Sept. 23, 1907, **17,** 399

John Franklin Shafroth, Oct. 23, 1911, **23,** 478

Ashton Cokayne Shallenberger, Nov. 9, 1910, **21,** 622

Isaac Sharpless, March 21, 1908, **18,** 67

Albert Shaw, Dec. 15, 1909, **19,** 606; Oct. 11, 1910, **21,** 300

Joseph Bernard Shea, March 14, 1908, **18,** 51; March 23, 1909, **19,** 117; March 30, 1909, **19,** 131; Jan. 3, 1910, **19,** 707; Aug. 31, 1910, **21,** 81

Charles Monroe Sheldon, June 14, 1909, **19,** 252

Edward Wright Sheldon, Nov. 19, 1902, **14,** 206; March 24, 1907, **17,** 89; March 21, 1908, **18,** 64; Feb. 4, 1909, **19,** 27; June 25, 1909, **19,** 268; Oct. 11, 1909, **19,** 407; Oct. 13, 1909, **19,** 412; Oct. 20, 1909, **19,** 433; Oct. 24, 1909, **19,** 444; Oct. 27, 1909, **19,** 452; Dec. 28, 1909, **19,** 649; Dec. 29, 1909, **19,** 655; Jan. 9, 1910, **19,** 752; March 1, 1910, **20,** 190; March 9, 1910, **20,** 225; March 12, 1910, **20,** 237; March 22, 1910, **20,** 283; May 14, 1910, **20,** 454; May 27, 1910, **20,** 476; June 1, 1910, **20,** 493; June 25, 1910, **20,** 542; June 30, 1910, **20,** 551; July 6, 1910, **20,** 561; Nov. 9, 1910, **21,** 594; Dec. 9, 1910, **22,** 165

James Edward Shepard, Oct. 2, 1909, **19,** 399; Nov. 26, 1910, **22,** 98

Gwynn T. Shepperd, Feb. 1, 1906, **16,** 290

Henry Robinson Shipman, May 21, 1905, **16,** 104

Robert W. Shultice, Nov. 26, 1910, **22,** 99

George Sebastian Silzer, Nov. 8, 1910, **21,** 585; Dec. 21, 1910, **22,** 243; Jan. 7, 1911, **22,** 311; Jan. 12, 1911, **22,** 328

Evans Griffiths Slaughter, Dec. 15, 1910, **22,** 203

Charles F. Sleeper, Dec. 9, 1910, **22,** 164

William Milligan Sloane, Oct. 15, 1906, **16,** 457

Edwin Emery Slosson, May 23, 1910, **20,** 468

Albridge Clinton Smith, Jr., July 10, 1907, **17,** 273; April 28, 1910, **20,** 402

Goldwin Smith, March 10, 1903, **14,** 387

Henry Marston Smith, Jr., June 19, 1912, **24,** 489

Herbert Stearns Squier Smith, April 14, 1904, **15,** 247

Hoke Smith, March 6, 1911, **22,** 480

Howard Alexander Smith, May 1, 1905, **16,** 89

James Smith, Jr., Nov. 10, 1910, **22,** 15; Dec. 3, 1910, **22,** 132; Dec. 8, 1910, **22,** 154

John Walter Smith, Nov. 10, 1910, **22,** 15

Leon Rutherford Smith, June 17, 1912, **24,** 482

Samuel Archibald Smith, Nov. 17, 1909, **19,** 508

Charles Henry Smyth, Jr., June 8, 1905, **16,** 112

Thomas L. Snow, Sept. 13, 1904, **15,** 467; Oct. 16, 1904, **15,** 520

John Duncan Spaeth, April 19, 1905, **16,** 71

Edward Gleason Spaulding, March 3, 1910, **20,** 447

Robert Elliott Speer, Oct. 15, 1910, **21,** 334

Francis Speir, Jr., Sept. 20, 1907, **17,** 395

Charles Worthen Spencer, May 16, 1905, **16,** 101

Henry Russell Spencer, April 30, 1906, **16,** 380; March 20, 1907, **17,** 87

James Speyer, Nov. 16, 1908, **18,** 516

Traverse Alexander Spraggins, July 26, 1911, **23,** 232

James Cresap Sprigg, Aug. 27, 1910, **21,** 62

James Sprunt, April 2, 1904, **15,** 227

Edward Bushrod Stahlman, Jan. 25, 1911, **22,** 376

Edmund Clarence Stedman, April 12, 1903, **14,** 407

Alfred Anthony Stein, June 21, 1912, **24,** 493

Henry G. Steinson, Dec. 14, 1911, **23,** 594

Frederick A. Steuert, Aug. 27, 1902, **14,** 115

Edwin Augustus Stevens, Dec. 29, 1906, **16,** 539; Jan. 5, 1907, **16,** 548; Sept. 29, 1910, **21,** 198; Nov. 9, 1910, **21,** 601; Nov. 29, 1910, **22,** 113; Dec. 12, 1910, **22,** 173

George Black Stewart, Oct. 14, 1907, **17,** 433

John Aikman Stewart, Jan. 3, 1906, **16,** 277; Dec. 29, 1909, **19,** 656

Bayard Stockton, Sept. 17, 1910, **21,** 131

Anson Phelps Stokes, Jr., Oct. 2, 1905, **16,** 189; April 26, 1907, **17,** 122; May 1, 1907, **17,** 127; May 4, 1907, **17,** 136

Edward Casper Stokes, Nov. 1, 1910, **21,** 503

William Joel Stone, June 29, 1912, **24,** 507

George Butler Storer, Dec. 2, 1908, **18,** 530

Moorfield Storey, Oct. 21, 1910, **21,** 386; Dec. 31, 1912, **25,** 649

Daisy Allen Story, June 25, 1907, **17,** 224

Pleasant Alexander Stovall, March 25, 1911, **22,** 516; April 5, 1911, **22,** 543; July 29, 1911, **23,** 239; May 6, 1912, **24,** 387

Isidor Straus, Nov. 9, 1910, **21,** 613

Nathan Straus, July 21, 1910, **21,** 18; Oct. 7, 1912, **25,** 378

August C. Streitwolf, Jr., Dec. 21, 1910, **22,** 243; Aug. 12, 1911, **23,** 265

Josiah Strong, June 24, 1912, **24,** 498

Duane Reed Stuart, April 15, 1905, **16,** 60; May 15, 1905, **16,** 101

G. McArthur Sullivan, Nov. 20, 1909, **19,** 529

George Hammon Sullivan, Nov. 3, 1910, **21,** 541

Mark Anthony Sullivan, Nov. 10, 1910, **22,** 22

Roger Charles Sullivan, Nov. 8, 1910, **21,** 584

William Sulzer, Nov. 9, 1910, **21,** 616; Oct. 3, 1912, **25,** 329

William Gilbert van Tassel Sutphen, Feb. 14, 1910, **20,** 127

William Howard Taft, Nov. 5, 1912, **25,** 521

Motokichi Takahashi, Jan. 10, 1907, **16,** 557

Charles Andrew Talcott, Nov. 6, 1910, **21,** 578; Nov. 8, 1910, **21,** 583

John L. F. Talton, June 17, 1912, **24,** 484

Frank William Taussig, July 3, 1912, **24,** 536

James Monroe Taylor, Nov. 13, 1909, **19,** 499; Nov. 23, 1909, **19,** 532

Edward Nelson Teall, March 15, 1905, **16,** 30

John Conover Ten Eyck, June 26, 1907, **17,** 232

Harvey Waterman Thayer, June 8, 1905, **16,** 112

Frank Thilly, Feb. 4, 1904, **15,** 156; March 16, 1904, **15,** 197; March 18, 1904, **15,** 198; June 19, 1906, **16,** 428; Nov. 20, 1908, **18,** 519; Nov. 12, 1910, **22,** 35

Charles Spalding Thomas, Jan. 4, 1912, **23,** 652

Harvey Thomas, Jan. 6, 1911, **22,** 309

Norman Mattoon Thomas, June 11, 1908, **18,** 335

Alexander Marshall Thompson, Feb. 7, 1910, **20,** 85

Charles Willis Thompson, July 9, 1910, **20,** 570

Henry Burling Thompson, Dec. 21, 1905, **16,** 274; June 12, 1906, **16,** 424; April 15, 1907, **17,** 110; June 21, 1907, **17,** 219; July 10, 1907, **17,** 271; July 13, 1907, **17,** 281; Sept. 16, 1907, **17,** 386; Sept. 17, 1907, **17,** 391; Oct. 1, 1907, **17,** 409; Dec. 18, 1907, **17,** 564; May 4, 1908, **18,** 285; May 6, 1908, **18,** 290; May 20, 1908,

**18**, 301; July 28, 1908, **18**, 380; Nov. 6, 1908, **18**, 489; Nov. 12, 1908, **18**, 507; Feb. 24, 1909, **19**, 68; April 6, 1909, **19**, 152; Dec. 22, 1909, **19**, 620; Dec. 28, 1909, **19**, 649; Jan. 6, 1910, **19**, 731; Jan. 14, 1910, **20**, 13; Aug. 10, 1910, **21**, 49; Sept. 16, 1910, **21**, 104; Oct. 11, 1910, **21**, 299; Nov. 9, 1910, **21**, 593; Oct. 9, 1911, **23**, 436

Henry Dallas Thompson, July 21, 1905, **16**, 159; July 24, 1905, **16**, 160; July 26, 1905, **16**, 162; Aug. 5, 1909, **19**, 328; April 1, 1912, **24**, 274

James MacNaughton Thompson, July 31, 1902, **14**, 45; Aug. 8, 1902, **14**, 67; Aug. 21, 1902, **14**, 99

Samuel Huston Thompson, July 3, 1912, **24**, 534

Samuel Huston Thompson, Jr., Feb. 7, 1910, **20**, 84; Sept. 17, 1910, **21**, 130; Jan. 25, 1911, **22**, 375

Charles Franklin Thwing, Nov. 16, 1910, **22**, 53

John Lee Tildsley, Dec. 4, 1908, **18**, 533; Dec. 11, 1908, **18**, 541

Benjamin Ryan Tillman, June 18, 1912, **24**, 485

Frederick Todd, Dec. 1, 1910, **22**, 121; Dec. 13, 1910, **22**, 185

Edgar Bronson Tolman, March 30, 1907, **17**, 100

F. Tompkins, June 4, 1906, **16**, 415

Oliver Samuel Tonks, May 25, 1905, **16**, 106

Nancy Saunders Toy, May 26, 1910, **20**, 475

Ira Winthrop Travell, Aug. 9, 1902, **14**, 69

John Joseph Treacy, Dec. 9, 1910, **22**, 163

Lyman Hambright Treadway, Nov. 18, 1907, **17**, 507

Henry Inigo Triggs, Oct. 26, 1906, **16**, 472

William Monroe Trotter, Nov. 15, 1910, **22**, 50; July 18, 1912, **24**, 558

Augustus Trowbridge, Feb. 9, 1910, **20**, 91

Benjamin Franklin Trueblood, Sept. 19, 1908, **18**, 419

Henry St. George Tucker, Jan. 1, 1907, **16**, 542; Dec. 29, 1910, **22**, 282; June 8, 1912, **24**, 465; June 10, 1912, **24**, 469; Dec. 30, 1912, **25**, 647

Joseph Patrick Tumulty, Nov. 8, 1910, **21**, 589; Nov. 30, 1910, **22**, 118; Dec. 7, 1910, **22**, 145; Dec. 15, 1910, **22**, 200; Dec. 20, 1910, **22**, 233; Dec. 6, 1912, **25**, 581

Joseph Patrick Tumulty and Mark Anthony Sullivan, Oct. 25, 1910, **21**, 433

Edwin Litchfield Turnbull, June 12, 1912, **24**, 473

Frederick Jackson Turner, June 14, 1907, **17**, 213; Nov. 9, 1910, **21**, 602

Oscar Wilder Underwood, Nov. 25, 1910, **22**, 95; July 5, 1912, **24**, 540; July 10, 1912, **24**, 545; July 22, 1912, **24**, 565

Samuel Untermyer, July 3, 1912, **24**, 532; July 31, 1912, **24**, 577; Nov. 6, 1912, **25**, 528

Wilbur Marshall Urban, April 6, 1910, **20**, 335

William Simon U'Ren, Dec. 14, 1910, **22,** 197

Frank Arthur Vanderlip, Dec. 11, 1909, **19,** 601; Dec. 17, 1909, **19,** 607

Henry van Dyke, Aug. 14, 1904, **15,** 442; March 13, 1907, **17,** 67; March 13, 1907, **17,** 68; July 3, 1907, **17,** 246; July 5, 1907, **17,** 260

Paul van Dyke, March 7, 1910, **20,** 214; March 11, 1910 **20,** 235

Charles Richard Van Hise, July 16, 1912, **24,** 554

La Rue Van Hook, May 15, 1905, **16,** 101

Alexander Van Rensselaer, July 9, 1904, **15,** 409

Edwin Augustus Van Valkenburg, Sept. 29, 1910, **21,** 198

Francis Preston Venable, Nov. 10, 1910, **22,** 20

Marion Jackson Verdery, Dec. 15, 1910, **22,** 201; April 11, 1911, **22,** 552

Ambrose White Vernon, March 6, 1908, **18,** 10

Walker Whiting Vick, Sept. 16, 1910, **21,** 115; Nov. 9, 1910, **21,** 608

Jonas Viles, April 18, 1905, **16,** 68

Oswald Garrison Villard, Aug. 22, 1910, **21,** 58; Nov. 11, 1910, **22,** 26; Nov. 22, 1910, **22,** 83; Nov. 28, 1910, **22,** 101; Dec. 3, 1910, **22,** 127; Dec. 31, 1910, **22,** 287; Jan. 5, 1911, **22,** 307; Dec. 1, 1911, **23,** 560; Jan. 22, 1912, **24,** 59; Jan. 25, 1912, **24,** 72; Aug. 14, 1912, **25,** 26; Aug. 28, 1912, **25,** 60

Williamson Updike Vreeland, Oct. 26, 1903, **15,** 29; Dec. 8, 1909, **19,** 562; Sept. 22, 1910, **21,** 154

Eleanor Glasgow Voorhis, June 19, 1905, **16,** 143; June 25, 1905, **16,** 150

John Milton Waldron, Oct. 21, 1910, **21,** 387

John Brisben Walker, Sept. 3, 1904, **15,** 462

Robert Scott Walker, June 25, 1907, **17,** 225; Dec. 10, 1909, **19,** 597

Allan Bartholomew Walsh, Nov. 11, 1910, **22,** 29

Alexander Walters, Dec. 17, 1912, **25,** 606

John Wanamaker, Nov. 9, 1910, **21,** 601

Henry Burt Ware, Oct. 28, 1910, **21,** 463

Catherine Carter Campbell Warren, May 5, 1910, **20,** 412

Frederick Morris Warren, Feb. 12, 1904, **15,** 166

Salomé Machado Warren, Dec. 3, 1907, **17,** 546; Dec. 18, 1907, **17,** 565

Walter Hudson Watkins, June 24, 1908, **18,** 342; Aug. 13, 1908, **18,** 398; Sept. 23, 1908, **18,** 420; Oct. 16, 1908, **18,** 465

Henry Watterson, Dec. 7, 1910, **22,** 143; Dec. 9, 1910, **22,** 160; Dec. 13, 1910, **22,** 184; Dec. 17, 1910, **22,** 212; Dec. 28, 1910, **22,** 274; Jan. 29, 1911, **22,** 393; July 20, 1911, **23,** 221; Sept. 5, 1911, **23,** 303

William Henry Welch, April 17, 1910, **20,** 368; June 19, 1910, **20,** 538; Sept. 17, 1910, **21,** 129

Akos Weltnar and Cornelius Csongrávi, July 13, 1912, **24,** 548

John Wesley Wescott, Sept. 16, 1910, **21,** 103; Nov. 9, 1910, **21,** 604; Nov. 14, 1910, **22,** 42; Dec. 10, 1910, **22,** 169; Dec. 26, 1910, **22,** 261; Feb. 8, 1911, **22,** 413; Oct. 7, 1911, **23,** 424; Sept. 13, 1912, **25,** 146

Andrew Fleming West, July 17, 1902, **14,** 23; Oct. 4, 1902, **14,** 139; Nov. 29, 1902, **14,** 245; March 9, 1904, **15,** 184; Oct. 30, 1906, **16,** 478 (2); May 28, 1907, **17,** 160; July 10, 1907, **17,** 270; July 9, 1908, **18,** 355; Jan. 24, 1909, **19,** 8; Oct. 15, 1909, **19,** 421; Oct. 19, 1909, **19,** 426; Jan. 4, 1910, **19,** 712

John Howell Westcott, Oct. 19, 1903, **15,** 17; May 1, 1905, **16,** 88; Dec. 13, 1906, **16,** 528; Feb. 19, 1907, **17,** 46; May 29, 1907, **17,** 161; June 20, 1907, **17,** 218; Feb. 6, 1908, **17,** 613

Harry Clarkson Westervelt, Nov. 12, 1908, **18,** 507

Arthur Ledlie Wheeler, Dec. 16, 1908, **18,** 550; Dec. 22, 1908, **18,** 564

Benjamin Ide Wheeler, Nov. 16, 1910, **22,** 54

Israel Losey White, June 9, 1910, **20,** 512

Brand Whitlock, Nov. 9, 1910, **21,** 607

Edith M. Whitmore, Jan. 31, 1912, **24,** 100

George Franklin Fort Wilbur, Aug. 6, 1902, **14,** 63

Edward Seymour Wilde, Nov. 14, 1910, **22,** 41

William Royal Wilder, April 21, 1904, **15,** 270; Oct. 21, 1904, **15,** 528; Sept. 19, 1907, **17,** 393; Oct. 22, 1907, **17,** 448; Jan. 31, 1910, **20,** 65; March 8, 1910, **20,** 218; Sept. 17, 1910, **21,** 129; Jan. 21, 1911, **22,** 361

Louis Wiley, Sept. 6, 1912, **25,** 114

Walter Maurice Wilkins, May 6, 1910, **20,** 421; Sept. 15, 1910, **21,** 98

Day Allen Willey, July 14, 1902, **14,** 11

Charles Richard Williams, Nov. 16, 1910, **22,** 52

James Thomas Williams, Jr., April 19, 1910, **20,** 372

John Rogers Williams, Aug. 8, 1904, **15,** 436; Jan. 4, 1905, **15,** 575

John Sharp Williams, Nov. 4, 1910, **21,** 557; Nov. 24, 1910, **22,** 93; Dec. 14, 1910, **22,** 197; June 13, 1912, **24,** 474; June 20, 1912, **24,** 489

Linsly Rudd Williams, June 27, 1907, **17,** 234

Edgar Williamson, Aug. 18, 1910, **21,** 55; Sept. 16, 1910, **21,** 115

Westel Woodbury Willoughby, Dec. 17, 1907, **17,** 563

Frederick Newton Willson, July 4, 1907, **17,** 259

Edmund Beecher Wilson, April 12, 1907, **17,** 106; Oct. 22, 1907, **17,** 450

Edwin Bird Wilson, Aug. 14, 1912, **25,** 27

Ellen Axson Wilson

  July–August 1902

    July 12, **14,** 4; July 13, **14,** 7; July 14, **14,** 10; July 15, **14,** 15; July 16, **14,** 18; July 17, **14,** 22; July 18, **14,** 25; July 19, **14,**

27; July 20, **14**, 31; July 21, **14**, 36; July 22, **14**, 39; July 23, **14**, 41; July 24, **14**, 42; Aug. 3, **14**, 49; Aug. 5, **14**, 53; Aug. 5, **14**, 55; Aug. 7, **14**, 61; Aug. 8, **14**, 66, 67; Aug. 9, **14**, 68; Aug. 10, **14**, 71; Aug. 11, **14**, 75; Aug. 12, **14**, 77; Aug. 13, **14**, 80; Aug. 14, **14**, 85; Aug. 15, **14**, 87; Aug. 17, **14**, 90; Aug. 18, **14**, 92; Aug. 19, **14**, 94; Aug. 20, **14**, 96; Aug. 21, **14**, 99; Aug. 22, **14**, 101; Aug. 24, **14**, 105; Aug. 25, **14**, 106; Aug. 26, **14**, 109; Aug. 27, **14**, 113; Aug. 28, **14**, 117

April–September 1903
April 22, **14**, 422; April 23, **14**, 423; April 24, **14**, 425; April 26, **14**, 428; April 27, **14**, 430; April 28, **14**, 432; April 29, **14**, 435; April 30, **14**, 438; May 1, **14**, 440; May 4, **14**, 452; Sept. 29, **15**, 7

March 1904–June 1911
March 26, 1904, **15**, 208; April 3, 1904, **15**, 227; April 7, 1904, **15**, 235; April 10, 1904, **15**, 240; April 15, 1904, **15**, 250; April 17, 1904, **15**, 265; April 20, 1904, **15**, 268; April 24, 1904, **15**, 273; April 26, 1904, **15**, 297; May 1, 1904, **15**, 302; May 4, 1904, **15**, 308; May 7, 1904, **15**, 313; May 11, 1904, **15**, 320; May 15, 1904, **15**, 333; May 18, 1904, **15**, 337; May 23, 1904, **15**, 346; May 25, 1904, **15**, 348; May 29, 1904, **15**, 351; June 2, 1904, **15**, 355; June 5, 1904, **15**, 357; Feb. 17, 1910, **20**, 134, 137; Feb. 21, 1910, **20**, 152; Feb. 24, 1910, **20**, 172; Feb. 28, 1910, **20**, 188; Sept. 16, 1910, **21**, 101; May 6, 1911, **23**, 10; May 11, 1911, **23**, 30; May 15, 1911, **23**, 51; May 22, 1911, **23**, 81; June 1, 1911, **23**, 111; June 2, 1911, **23**, 127, 128

John Adams Wilson, March 9, 1907, **17**, 64; Sept. 24, 1910, **21**, 161
John Glover Wilson, March 9, 1903, **14**, 386
Joseph R. Wilson, Jr., May 9, 1904, **15**, 318; Dec. 20, 1906, **16**, 537; Sept. 7, 1907, **17**, 376; Nov. 5, 1908, **18**, 483; Jan. 24, 1910, **20**, 49; March 14, 1910, **20**, 239; Sept. 16, 1910, **21**, 114; Nov. 25, 1910, **22**, 95; Aug. 22, 1911, **23**, 288; Jan. 26, 1912, **24**, 78; Dec. 19, 1912, **25**, 612
Thomas Wilson, Nov. 11, 1909, **19**, 493
William Lawrence Wilson, July 22, 1910, **21**, 20; July 18, 1911, **23**, 218
Samuel Ross Winans, June 20, 1907, **17**, 218
Sarah Macdonald Winans, July 29, 1910, **21**, 30
Caleb Thomas Winchester, Nov. 12, 1910, **22**, 35
Erving Winslow, March 31, 1910, **20**, 309; April 2, 1910, **20**, 312
Henry Otto Wittpenn, Sept. 22, 1910, **21**, 155; Oct. 25, 1910, **21**, 434
Charles Wood, Oct. 15, 1907, **17**, 434; Jan. 5, 1910, **19**, 729; Jan. 10, 1910, **19**, 753
Josiah Townsend Woodhull, Jr., July 20, 1910, **21**, 16
Felexiana Shepherd Baker Woodrow, Nov. 10, 1912, **25**, 536
Herbert Hollingsworth Woodrow, Aug. 16, 1904, **15**, 444

Marion Woodville Woodrow, Nov. 7, 1910, **21,** 581

Charles Albert Woods, Sept. 17, 1910, **21,** 128

Edward Augustus Woods, June 18, 1904, **15,** 391

Gertrude Macrum Woods, Sept. 1, 1904, **15,** 461

Hiram Woods, Jan. 24, 1910, **20,** 50; March 20, 1910, **20,** 264; May 27, 1910, **20,** 478; Nov. 4, 1910, **21,** 555; Dec. 8, 1910, **22,** 158; Dec. 12, 1910, **22,** 175

Lawrence Crane Woods, May 23, 1906, **16,** 404; June 12, 1907, **17,** 211; Aug. 24, 1907, **17,** 360; Sept. 9, 1907, **17,** 378; Sept. 14, 1907, **17,** 384; Oct. 23, 1907, **17,** 452; Jan. 15, 1908, **17,** 603; Feb. 19, 1908, **17,** 616; June 5, 1909, **19,** 230; June 22, 1909, **19,** 264; Oct. 1, 1909, **19,** 396; Jan. 24, 1910, **20,** 50; April 23, 1910, **20,** 387; April 29, 1910, **20,** 404; Sept. 22, 1910, **21,** 157

Samuel Woolverton, Jan. 18, 1910, **20,** 27

Charles Baker Wright, Sept. 10, 1902, **14,** 125

Edward Henry Wright, Jr., Jan. 4, 1907, **16,** 547

Jacob Ridgway Wright, Sept. 16, 1904, **15,** 471

Julius Tutwiler Wright, June 24, 1904, **15,** 395; July 1, 1904, **15,** 402

James Edwards Wyckoff, May 18, 1908, **18,** 300

Walter Augustus Wyckoff, July 18, 1907, **17,** 291

John Allan Wyeth, Feb. 15, 1907, **17,** 40; March 9, 1907, **17,** 65; March 12, 1907, **17,** 66; March 24, 1907, **17,** 90; March 26, 1907, **17,** 93; June 18, 1907, **17,** 215; June 21, 1907, **17,** 220; Aug. 15, 1907, **17,** 347

John Joseph Wynne, Nov. 9, 1910, **21,** 612

Frederic Yates, Nov. 3, 1906, **16,** 479; Nov. 15, 1906, **16,** 485; Dec. 12, 1906, **16,** 506; Aug. 22, 1910, **21,** 59

George Green Yeomans, Nov. 9, 1910, **21,** 611

Charles Augustus Young, Dec. 9, 1904, **15,** 571; May 18, 1905, **16,** 103; Oct. 19, 1905, **16,** 194

John Wesley Young, July 6, 1905, **16,** 152

Franklin Zeiger, Dec. 21, 1908, **18,** 563; Jan. 4, 1909, **18,** 590; Jan. 13, 1909, **18,** 612

Harold Zeiss, June 27, 1907, **17,** 233

Charles Fishburn Zimmerman, July 13, 1904, **15,** 412

Memoranda

Edward Graham Elliott on a conversation with Wilson, Jan. 5, 1903, **14,** 320

Stockton Axson about Wilson's draft of an article, Aug. 29, 1904, **15,** 460

About his political prospects, Dec. 18, 1906, **16,** 534

On a conversation with Paul van Dyke, March 16, 1910, **20,** 249

John R. Mott on a conference with Wilson, March 31, **20,** 310

New Jersey: telegram and statement on senatorial candidacy, Oct. 2, 1906, **16,** 454; Oct. 15, 1906, **16,** 456

New Jersey: gubernatorial campaign

Statement on the nomination for Governor, July 15, 1910, **20,** 581

Speech in Trenton accepting the Democratic gubernatorial nomination, Sept. 15, 1910, **21,** 91

Report of remarks to the Democratic state convention in Trenton, Sept. 17, 1910, **21,** 118

Address opening the gubernatorial campaign in Jersey City, Sept. 28, 1910, **21,** 181

Campaign speech in Plainfield, Sept. 29, 1910, **21,** 193

Campaign speech in Newark, Sept. 30, 1910, **21,** 202

Campaign speech in Red Bank, Oct. 1, 1910, **21,** 213

Report of a campaign address in Long Branch, Oct. 3, 1910, **21,** 227

Campaign address in Trenton, Oct. 3, 1910, **21,** 229

Campaign speech in Woodbury, Oct. 5, 1910, **21,** 245

Report of a campaign address in Burlington, Oct. 7, 1910, **21,** 269

Report of a campaign speech in Bridgeton, Oct. 8, 1910, **21,** 276

Report of campaign speeches at Cape May Court House and Wildwood, Oct. 8, 1910, **21,** 281

Report of a campaign address in Paterson, Oct. 12, 1910, **21,** 301

Address to the Democratic Union in Caldwell, Oct. 12, 1910, **21,** 306

Report of remarks at Caldwell, Oct. 13, 1910, **21,** 309

Campaign address in Atlantic City, Oct. 13, 1910, **21,** 310

Report of speeches in Ocean County, Oct. 14, 1910, **21,** 325

Campaign address in Asbury Park, Oct. 15, 1910, **21,** 328

Remarks to the Democratic leaders of Mercer County in Trenton, Oct. 18, 1910, **21,** 349

Report of campaign speeches in Bound Brook and Somerville, Oct. 20, 1910, **21,** 354

Campaign address in Flemington, Oct. 20, 1910, **21,** 369

Report of a campaign speech in Flemington, Oct. 21, 1910, **21,** 381

Report of a campaign tour in Warren County, Oct. 21, 1910, **21,** 382

Report of a campaign speech in Phillipsburg, Oct. 22, 1910, **21,** 390

Campaign speech in Newton, Oct. 22, 1910, **21,** 396

Report of Wilson's itinerary for the last two weeks of the campaign, Oct. 24, 1910, **21,** 412

Report of campaign addresses in Camden, Oct. 25, 1910, **21,** 413

Campaign speech in Salem, Oct. 25, 1910, **21,** 423

Report of a campaign speech in New Brunswick, Oct. 26, 1910, **21,** 436

Report of three campaign addresses in Bergen County, Oct. 27, 1910, **21,** 446

Report of a campaign address in Hackensack, Oct. 28, 1910, **21,** 452

Campaign address in Elizabeth, Oct. 28, 1910, **21,** 454

Report of an after-dinner talk in Elizabeth, Oct. 29, 1910, **21,** 464

Report of a campaign address in Elizabethport, Oct. 29, 1910, **21,** 465

Report of three campaign addresses in Hudson County, Oct. 29, 1910, **21,** 471

Report of a campaign address in Bayonne, Nov. 1, 1910, **21,** 485

Campaign address in Passaic, Nov. 1, 1910, **21,** 493

Report of a campaign speech in Carlstadt, Nov. 2, 1910, **21,** 507

Campaign address in Montclair, Nov. 2, 1910, **21,** 508

Report of a campaign address in Orange, Nov. 3, 1910, **21,** 520

Report of campaign addresses in Madison, Dover, and Morristown, Nov. 3, 1910, **21,** 525

Campaign address in Morristown, Nov. 3, 1910, **21,** 527

Campaign address in Perth Amboy, Nov. 4, 1910, **21,** 543

Report of a campaign address in Carteret, Nov. 5, 1910, **21,** 560

Report of four campaign addresses in Essex County, Nov. 5, 1910, **21,** 561

Campaign address in Newark, Nov. 5, 1910, **21,** 564

Victory statement, Princeton, Nov. 9, 1910, **21,** 589

New Jersey: senatorial contest

Statement on the senatorship, Dec. 8, 1910, **22,** 153

Report of comments on the senatorial election, Dec. 20, 1910, **22,** 229

Proposed statement for the signature of Essex County assemblymen-elect, Dec. 21, 1910, **22,** 239

Reports of conferences with Democratic assemblymen-elect, Dec. 21, 1910, **22,** 239; Dec. 23, 1910, **22,** 253

Statement supporting James Edgar Martine, Dec. 23, 1910, **22,** 248

Comment on arrival in St. Louis about the selection of Martine, Dec. 27, 1910, **22,** 262

Reply to statement of James Smith, Jr., Dec. 28, 1910, **22,** 272

Address in Jersey City on behalf of Martine, Jan. 5, 1911, **22,** 295

Statements on Martine's election, Jan. 24, 1911, **22,** 365; Jan. 25, 1911, **22,** 367

New Jersey: Inaugural Address, Jan. 17, 1911, **22,** 345

New Jersey: legislative program and related materials

Announcement of Joseph Patrick Tumulty's appointment as Secretary to the Governor, Jan. 13, 1911, **22,** 328

Statement about the Hotel Martinique conference, Jan. 19, 1911, **22,** 357

Statement on the Geran election reform bill, Feb. 15, 1911, **22,** 430

Report of remarks at the annual dinner of the New Jersey Senate, New York, March 4, 1911, **22,** 474

Reports of conferences with Democratic assemblymen, March 7, 1911, **22,** 481; March 14, 1911, **22,** 504

Statement about an altercation with James Richard Nugent, March 20, 1911, **22,** 512

Remarks on the Senate's passage of the Geran bill, April 14, 1911, **22,** 569

Report of remarks about the commission government bill, April 18, 1911, **22,** 574

Statement on the work of the New Jersey legislative session of 1911, April 22, 1911, **22,** 578

Tour of state institutions: schedule, Aug. 23, 1911, **23,** 290; visits, Aug. 26, 1911, **23,** 300

Discussions at the Democratic state convention, Oct. 4, 1911, **23,** 384

Wilson-Pierce correspondence on the Republican grade-crossing plank, Oct. 23, 1911, **23,** 476

Report of an address on New Jersey harbor development and a cross-state canal, Trenton, Feb. 20, 1912, **24,** 183

Report of a conference with Democratic senators concerning the Fitzherbert scandal, March 13, 1912, **24,** 244; Senate vote on expulsion resolution, March 14, 1912, **24,** 245

Report of a statement on the Fitzherbert scandal, March 14, 1912, **24,** 247

Report of Republican criticism of Governor's vetoes, April 12, 1912, **24,** 324

Statement in reply to Republican attack on vetoes and absences from state, April 12, 1912, **24,** 324

Report of a conference with Atlantic City reformers about local graft, June 4, 1912, **24,** 452; statement, June 5, 1912, **24,** 458

Report of remarks about resigning the governorship, July 3, 1912, **24,** 528

Report of meeting with Oscar Wilder Underwood and comment on resigning governorship, July 17, 1912, **24,** 555

Report of intention to retain governorship, Aug. 2, 1912, **24,** 583

New Jersey: addresses and messages to the Legislature

Urging ratification of the Sixteenth Amendment, March 20, 1911, **22,** 511; Feb. 26, 1912, **24,** 216; special message to the Senate, April 4, 1911, **22,** 534

To the House of Assembly concerning public school administration and reform of city government, April 11, 1911, **22,** 549

Annual Message, Jan. 9, 1912, **24,** 18

Veto Messages

Salaries of fire department employees, March 17, 1911, **22,** 508

Appropriations by boroughs for fiftieth anniversary celebrations, March 30, 1911, **22,** 524

Establishing and regulating parks, March 31, 1911, **22,** 526

Care of wayward females, April 10, 1911, **22,** 548

Municipalities and public service franchises, March 25, 1912, **24,** 261

Establishing and maintaining county road systems, March 25, 1912, **24,** 263

Salary increases for public officials, March 25, 1912, **24,** 264

Licensing and regulating pool rooms, March 26, 1912, **24,** 266

Municipal regulation of sewage disposal, March 26, 1912, **24,** 267

Providing free transportation to the polls for voters, March 28, 1912, **24,** 268

Financing the draining or filling in of swamps by cities or boroughs, April 2, 1912, **24,** 276

Election of commissions to administer the employment of prisoners, April 2, 1912, **24,** 277

Election expenses, April 2, 1912, **24,** 278

Courts having criminal jurisdiction, April 2, 1912, **24,** 278

Franchises for trackless trolleys, April 2, 1912, **24,** 279

Congressional redistricting, April 2, 1912, **24,** 279

Commutation of prison terms, April 2, 1912, **24,** 280

Government of cities of the second class, April 2, 1912, **24,** 280

Sale of liquors, April 2, 1912, **24,** 281

Party nominating procedures, April 2, 1912, **24,** 282

Salaries of directors of boards of freeholders, April 2, 1912, **24,** 282

Public docks and shipping facilities, April 2, 1912, **24,** 282

Expenses of the legislature of New Jersey, April 2, 1912, **24,** 283

Elimination of grade crossings, April 11, 1912, **24,** 321

New Jersey: primary and legislative campaigns

Report of two addresses opening the Democratic primary campaign, Newark, Sept. 19, 1911, **23,** 330

Address in Jersey City, Sept. 21, 1911, **23,** 342

Report of speeches in Orange and Newark, Sept. 23, 1911, **23,** 353

Message to the voters of New Jersey about fraudulent voting in primaries, Sept. 25, 1911, **23,** 358

Statement on the Democratic primary election, Sept. 27, 1911, **23,** 361

Report of a speech opening the legislative campaign of 1911, Ocean City, Sept. 29, 1911, **23,** 364

Report of three speeches in Cape May County, Sept. 30, 1911, **23,** 364

Report of speeches at Toms River and Lakewood, Oct. 2, 1911, **23,** 380

Report of speeches in Salem County, Oct. 5, 1911, **23,** 391

Address in Woodbury, Oct. 5, 1911, **23,** 395

Meeting with David Baird, Oct. 6, 1911, **23,** 409

Report of two addresses in Camden, Oct. 7, 1911, **23,** 409

Address in Flemington, Oct. 7, 1911, **23,** 411

Address in Trenton, Oct. 9, 1911, **23**, 425

Report of speeches in New Brunswick and Perth Amboy, Oct. 11, 1911, **23**, 437

Report of speeches in Monmouth County: Asbury Park, Long Branch, Red Bank, and Freehold, Oct. 12, 1911, **23**, 442

Report of a speech in Princeton, Oct. 13, 1911, **23**, 447

Report of speeches in Hackensack and Ridgewood, Oct. 14, 1911, **23**, 449

Report of speeches in Morristown, Dover, and Madison, Oct. 16, 1911, **23**, 451

Report of a speech in Paterson, Oct. 17, 1911, **23**, 461

Report of two speeches in Sussex County, Oct. 18, 1911, **23**, 464

Report of a speech in Phillipsburg, Oct. 19, 1911, **23**, 466

Report of eight speeches in Union County, Oct. 20, 1911, **23**, 468

Report of a day's campaigning in Somerset County, Oct. 21, 1911, **23**, 470

Report of a speech at Glassboro, Nov. 1, 1911, **23**, 520

Report of an address in Atlantic City, Nov. 2, 1911, **23**, 522

Report of speeches in Pleasantville, Bridgeton, Vineland, and Millville, Nov. 3, 1911, **23**, 531

Report of a talk at the Soldier's Home in Kearny, Nov. 4, 1911, **23**, 534

Report of speeches in Jersey City, Hoboken, and Weehawken, Nov. 4, 1911, **23**, 535

Report of speeches in Burlington, Mount Holly, and Moorestown, Nov. 6, 1911, **23**, 539

Report of speeches in Bound Brook and North Plainfield, Nov. 7, 1911, **23**, 540

Statement on the election results, Nov. 8, 1911, **23**, 544

New Jersey: Thanksgiving Proclamation, Nov. 8, 1911, **23**, 545

Princeton University: Inaugural Address, "Princeton for the Nation's Service," Oct. 25, 1902, **14**, 170; oath of office, Nov. 1, 1902, **14**, 193; report of the ceremony, Nov. 1, 1902, **14**, 191

Princeton University: alumni addresses and related materials

Notes for an address, "The Future of the University," to the Chicago alumni, Nov. 26, 1902, **14**, 223; news item about engagements in Chicago, Nov. 28, 1902, **14**, 225; report of the address, Nov. 29, 1902, **14**, 226

Address to the alumni of New York, Dec. 9, 1902, **14**, 268; report, Dec. 13, 1902, **14**, 287

Report of an address in Baltimore to the Princeton Association of Maryland, Feb. 14, 1903, **14**, 358

Report of an address to the alumni of Harrisburg, Pa., Feb. 20, 1903, **14**, 362

Report of an address in Pittsburgh to the Princeton Club of Western Pennsylvania, March 8, 1903, **14**, 383

Report of an address to the alumni of the District of Columbia, March 28, 1903, **14**, 400

Report of an address to the alumni of Philadelphia, April 15, 1903, **14,** 408

Report of a lecture, "The National and University Life," to the Princeton Club of Philadelphia, April 18, 1903, **14,** 415

Report of an address to the Princeton Club of St. Louis, April 30, 1903, **14,** 436

Report of an address in St. Paul to the Princeton Alumni Association of the Northwest, May 2, 1903, **14,** 445

Report of arrival in Cincinnati to address the Western Association of Princeton Clubs, May 2, 1903, **14,** 446; report of meeting, May 3, 1903, **14,** 448; report of address, "The College, and Its Value to Society," May 3, 1903, **14,** 449

Report of an address to the Princeton Club of Newark, May 16, 1903, **14,** 459

Report of a speech at the annual alumni dinner in Princeton, June 10, 1903, **14,** 485

News item about a speaking engagement at the Princeton Club of Philadelphia, Dec. 12, 1903, **15,** 79; report, Dec. 19, 1903, **15,** 101

Report of a meeting with class secretaries, Feb. 6, 1904, **15,** 161

Report of a speech to the Princeton Alumni Association of Albany, Feb. 16, 1904, **15,** 168

Report of an address on patriotism to Princeton alumni in Syracuse, Feb. 17, 1904, **15,** 169

Address at an alumni luncheon on the revision of the course of study, Princeton, June 14, 1904, **15,** 379

Reference to a speech at a five-class reunion in New York, Nov. 19, 1904, **15,** 535

Report of a speech at an alumni dinner in East Orange, N. J., Nov. 26, 1904, **15,** 542

The Committee of Fifty and the tutorial system, Feb. 18, 1905, **16,** 3

Notes for an address at an alumni meeting in Pittsburgh, March 18, 1905, **16,** 31; report, March 19, 1905, **16,** 32

Report of an address at the University Club of Philadelphia, March 25, 1905, **16,** 38

Notes for an address to Detroit alumni on the reorganization of the undergraduate program, March 30, 1905, **16,** 42; report, March 31, 1905, **16,** 42

Report of a speech in Kansas City to the Western Association of Princeton Clubs, May 14, 1905, **16,** 100

Report of a speech to alumni in Princeton, June 14, 1905, **16,** 141

Notes for a speech to the Princeton Alumni Association of the Oranges, East Orange, Nov. 8, 1905, **16,** 214; report, Nov. 10, 1905, **16,** 215

Report of an address in Nashville to the Princeton Alumni Association of Tennessee, Nov. 29, 1905, **16,** 236

News item about an alumni affair in Brooklyn, Jan. 28, 1906, **16,** 289

Report of a speech to the alumni in Hartford, March 31, 1906, **16**, 352

Report of a talk in Boston on technical education to the Alumni Association of New England, May 4, 1906, **16**, 384

Report of remarks at a dinner in his honor given by alumni in Cleveland, May 19, 1906, **16**, 396

Report of an address in Cleveland to the Western Association of Princeton Clubs, May 26, 1906, **16**, 405

Report of addresses on Americanism and idealism in Chattanooga to the Princeton Alumni Association of Tennessee, Oct. 27, 1906, **16**, 474

Notes for an address to the Philadelphia alumni, Feb. 14, 1907, **17**, 38; reports, Feb. 15, 1907, **17**, 38, 39

Report of an address in Baltimore to the Princeton Alumni Association of Maryland, Feb. 19, 1907, **17**, 43

Report of an address, "The Hegemony of Princeton," to the alumni in Pittsburgh, April 3, 1907, **17**, 100

Notes for an address at the alumni luncheon in Princeton, June 11, 1907, **17**, 209

Report of an address in Memphis to the Princeton Alumni Association of Tennessee, Nov. 9, 1907, **17**, 480

Report of an address in Baltimore to the Princeton Alumni Association of Maryland, March 7, 1908, **18**, 10

Address to the Princeton Club of Chicago, March 12, 1908, **18**, 17

Address in Pittsburgh to the Western Association of Princeton Clubs, May 2, 1908, **18**, 280

Report of an address in Boston to the Princeton Alumni Association of New England, May 15, 1908, **18**, 297

Report of a speech at an alumni luncheon in Princeton, June 10, 1908, **18**, 334

Report of an address on making "generalized Americans" to the Princeton Club of Chicago, Feb. 14, 1909, **19**, 47

Report of an address to the Princeton Club of Philadelphia, March 20, 1909, **19**, 112

Report of an address on the problems of college life to the alumni in Newark, May 6, 1909, **19**, 186

Remarks on arrival in Louisville, May 22, 1909, **19**, 211

Report of an address in Louisville to the Western Association of Princeton Clubs, May 23, 1909, **19**, 212

Report of an address at an alumni luncheon in Princeton, June 16, 1909, **19**, 253

News item about remarks to the Princeton Club of Chicago, Nov. 3, 1909, **19**, 479

Report of addresses to New England alumni in Boston and Brookline, Mass., Nov. 13, 1909, **19**, 497

Notes for an address in Englewood to the Alumni Association of Northern New Jersey, Dec. 17, 1909, **19**, 608

Address in Baltimore to the Princeton Alumni Association of Maryland, March 11, 1910, **20**, 229

Address in Brooklyn to the Princeton Alumni Association of Long Island, March 21, 1910, **20**, 272

Address in Jersey City to the Princeton Alumni Association of Hudson County, March 25, 1910, **20**, 290

Abstract of an address in St. Louis to the Western Association of Princeton Clubs, March 26, 1910, **20**, 291

Address to the Princeton Club of New York, April 7, 1910, **20**, 337

Reports of an address in Pittsburgh to the Princeton Alumni Association of Western Pennsylvania, April 16, 1910, **20**, 363, 366, 373

Address to the Princeton Club of Chicago, May 12, 1910, **20**, 433

Abstract of an address at an alumni luncheon in Princeton, June 14, 1910, **20**, 528

Princeton University: campus addresses, meetings, reports, and related materials

Opening exercises, Sept. 18, 1902, **14**, 132; Sept. 24, 1903, **15**, 4; Sept. 23, 1904, **15**, 491; Sept. 22, 1905, **16**, 187; Sept. 20, 1907, **17**, 394; Sept. 25, 1908, **18**, 421; Sept. 24, 1909, **19**, 389; Sept. 22, 1910, **21**, 151

Philadelphian Society, Sept. 20, 1902, **14**, 133; report, Sept. 22, 1902, **14**, 133; Nov. 7, 1902, **14**, 201; Dec. 8, 1902, **14**, 265; March 27, 1903, **14**, 399; May 15, 1903, **14**, 457; Sept. 28, 1903, **15**, 7; Oct. 2, 1903, **15**, 10; March 18, 1904, **15**, 197; Sept. 26, 1904, **15**, 492; Sept. 29, 1904, **15**, 495; May 5, 1905, **16**, 91; Sept. 25, 1905, **16**, 188; Sept. 29, 1905, **16**, 189; Jan. 12, 1906, **16**, 280; April 26, 1906, **16**, 377; April 27, 1906, **16**, 378; Nov. 23, 1906, **16**, 490; May 9, 1907, **17**, 139; May 10, 1907, **17**, 140; Sept. 23, 1907, **17**, 396; Oct. 24, 1907, **17**, 454; report, Oct. 25, 1907, **17**, 455; May 28, 1908, **18**, 310; Nov. 20, 1908, **18**, 518; April 2, 1909, **19**, 147; March 18, 1910, **20**, 255; Sept. 26, 1910, **21**, 169; Sept. 28, 1910, **21**, 176; Dec. 9, 1910, **22**, 159

Notes for a talk at a vesper service, Sept. 21, 1902, **14**, 133

Reports of remarks at the annual mass meetings of the American Whig and Cliosophic Societies, Oct. 4, 1902, **14**, 138; Oct. 10, 1903, **15**, 15; news item, Oct. 27, 1905, **16**, 205

Report about the move to Prospect, Oct. 18, 1902, **14**, 147

Notes for a talk, "The Objects of Graduate Study," to the Graduate Club, Nov. 7, 1902, **14**, 202; report, Nov. 8, 1902, **14**, 203

First class in Constitutional Government after inauguration, Nov. 8, 1902, **14**, 203

News item about an address at a football banquet, Dec. 18, 1902, **14**, 297

Report of a speech of welcome to the Archaeological Institute of America, Princeton, March 1, 1903, 14, 382

*Daily Princetonian* banquets, March 11, 1903, **14**, 387; March 19,

1904, **15,** 199; March 23, 1905, **16,** 36; March 29, 1906, **16,** 345; April 11, 1908, **18,** 260; May 1, 1909, **19,** 178; April 30, 1910, **20,** 404; May 1, 1911, **22,** 600

Monday Night Club, May 26, 1903, **14,** 463; Nov. 13, 1905, **16,** 222; Jan. 25, 1909, **19,** 9

Baccalaureate sermons, June 10, 1903, **14,** 484; March 5, 1904, **15,** 182; June 12, 1904, **15,** 364; June 11, 1905, **16,** 119; June 9, 1907, **17,** 187; June 7, 1908, **18,** 323; June 13, 1909, **19,** 242; June 12, 1910, **20,** 520

Remarks about Henry Burchard Fine on his appointment as Dean of the University, June 13, 1903, **14,** 489

Attendance at a Princeton-Yale baseball game, June 13, 1903, **14,** 488

Announcement of a reception for freshmen by the St. Paul's Society, Sept. 30, 1903, **15,** 9; notes for a talk at, Sept. 30, 1903, **15,** 9

Plans for 1903–1904, Oct. 3, 1903, **15,** 13

Laying of the Cornerstone of Seventy-Nine Hall, Oct. 24, 1903, **15,** 27

Announcement about conducting religious services, Nov. 7, 1903, **15,** 47

Announcement of a reception at Prospect for the Class of 1907, Nov. 12, 1903, **15,** 51

Notes for an address of welcome to the American Philosophical Association, Dec. 29, 1903, **15,** 111

Announcements about conducting prayer meetings, Dec. 5, 1903, **15,** 67; April 7, 1906, **16,** 357

News item about the first Trask Lecture, Feb. 26, 1904, **15,** 179

Announcement about Rhodes scholarships, March 23, 1904, **15,** 204

News item about an address, "Leaders of Men," to the Fortnightly Club, March 24, 1904, **15,** 206

Remarks at the dedication of Seventy-Nine Hall, June 18, 1904, **15,** 387; June 18, 1904, **15,** 388

Report of an address at the 157th Commencement, June 18, 1904, **15,** 390

Address in Princeton to the Association of Colleges and Preparatory Schools of the Middle States and Maryland, Nov. 25, 1904, **15,** 540

News item about addresses of welcome to two educational organizations, Nov. 29, 1904, **15,** 545

Statement on the tutorial system, Feb. 18, 1905, **16,** 6

News item about a conference of the leaders of Christian work in the eastern states, Feb. 20, 1905, **16,** 7

Press Club banquets, April 17, 1905, **16,** 61; April 26, 1906, **16,** 374; April 23, 1907, **17,** 115; April 6, 1910, **20,** 326

Report of a testimonial dinner for Charles Augustus Young, May 18, 1905, **16,** 102

Report of an address at the 158th Commencement, June 14, 1905, **16,** 137

Notes for a talk to preceptors, Sept. 18, 1905, **16,** 185

Municipal Club, Oct. 27, 1905, **16,** 206; Sept. 27, 1907, **17,** 403; report, Sept. 28, 1907, **17,** 404; Dec. 3, 1908, **18,** 530

President Roosevelt entertained at Prospect before the Army-Navy football game, Dec. 4, 1905, **16,** 242

Announcement about the reformation of football, Dec. 18, 1905, **16,** 271

Notes for a talk at the opening of the Faculty Room in Nassau Hall, Nov. 2, 1906, **16,** 479; report, Nov. 10, 1906, **16,** 485

Report of the opening of Lake Carnegie, Dec. 8, 1906, **16,** 497

News release of an address to the Board of Trustees on the social reorganization of the university, June 10, 1907, **17,** 199

Notes for an address on the Quadrangle Plan to the Princeton University faculty, Oct. 7, 1907, **17,** 420; Dean West's abstract of the address, Oct. 7, 1907, **17,** 422

Report of addresses by Dean West, James Bryce, and Wilson at the dedication of the Mather Sundial, Nov. 1, 1907, **17,** 462

News report of an address to the Law Club, March 26, 1908, **18,** 216

Report of a testimonial dinner for Cyrus Fogg Brackett, May 19, 1908, **18,** 300

Report of an address, "The Claims and Character of the Christian Ministry," to the Ministerial Club, April 27, 1909, **19,** 173

Notes for an address on political reform to the graduate students, May 12, 1909, **19,** 194

Announcement of a testimonial dinner by the class of 1909, June 2, 1909, **19,** 226

Notes for an address, "The Problems of the University," at the senior dinner, June 10, 1909, **19,** 241

Remarks on accepting Campbell Hall, June 12, 1909, **19,** 241

Report of remarks on the opening of the Palmer Physical Laboratory, Oct. 27, 1909, **19,** 450

Notes for an address of welcome to the New Jersey Library Association, Oct. 27, 1909, **19,** 451

Notes for a talk at a Whig Hall smoker, Oct. 27, 1909, **19,** 452

Report of an address on ideals of study to the Graduate Students' Association, Nov. 10, 1909, **19,** 491

Report of welcome to the National Academy of Sciences, Nov. 17, 1909, **19,** 506

Remarks at a memorial service for Cornelius Cuyler Cuyler, Dec. 4, 1909, **19,** 551

Notes for a talk at the Senior Council dinner, Dec. 8, 1909, **19,** 560; report, Dec. 10, 1909, **19,** 579

Report of an address, "The Choosing of a Law School," to the Law Club, March 11, 1910, **20,** 228

Notes for a talk to a senior prayer meeting, April 3, 1910, **20,** 314

Notes for a talk, "The Power of Literary and Oratorical Form," at Whig Hall graduation, April 4, 1910, **20,** 315

Remarks to the Board of Trustees about the Wyman bequest, June 9, 1910, **20,** 507

Notes for an after-dinner speech, "Princeton Men," at the senior dinner, June 9, 1910, **20,** 511

Remarks at a ceremony honoring Moses Taylor Pyne, June 11, 1910, **20,** 518

Plans for resigning from Princeton and remarks on the coming gubernatorial campaign, Sept. 16, 1910, **21,** 101

Report of a talk to a student demonstration in his honor, Oct. 10, 1910, **21,** 289

Report of remarks to Princeton students about the gubernatorial victory, Nov. 10, 1910, **22,** 3

Report of a talk to the football team, Nov. 10, 1910, **22,** 4

Two reports of a farewell address to the senior class of Princeton University, Dec. 8, 1910, **22,** 149, 152

Princeton University: President's annual and special reports to the Board of Trustees: Aug. 31, 1902, **14,** 119; Oct. 21, 1902, **14,** 150; Dec. 10, 1903, **15,** 69; Oct. 7, 1904, **15,** 504; Dec. 8, 1904, **15,** 554; Dec. 14, 1905, **16,** 245; Dec. 13, 1906, **16,** 506; Dec. 13, 1906, **16,** 519; June 6, 1907, **17,** 176; Dec. 13, 1907, **17,** 555; Jan. 9, 1908, **17,** 590; Jan. 1, 1909, **18,** 569; Jan. 1, 1910, **19,** 674

Princeton University: Trustees' and Faculty Minutes, committee reports, resolutions, tributes, and related materials

Minutes of the Academic Faculty, Oct. 1, 1902, **14,** 137; Nov. 5, 1902, **14,** 199; Nov. 19, 1902, **14,** 207; Dec. 3, 1902, **14,** 258; Dec. 17, 1902, **14,** 296; April 8, 1903, **14,** 405

Report by the Finance Committee to the Board of Trustees, Oct. 14, 1902, **14,** 144

Minutes of the Board of Trustees, Oct. 21, 1902, **14,** 161; Oct. 25, 1902, **14,** 169; Oct. 21, 1903, **15,** 25; Dec. 10, 1903, **15,** 77; Oct. 21, 1904, **15,** 528; Dec. 8, 1904, **15,** 569; March 9, 1905, **16,** 27; June 12, 1905, **16,** 132; Oct. 21, 1905, **16,** 204; Dec. 14, 1905, **16,** 265; June 11, 1906, **16,** 422; Oct. 20, 1906, **16,** 468; Dec. 13, 1906, **16,** 526; March 14, 1907, **17,** 71; June 10, 1907, **17,** 198; Oct. 17, 1907, **17,** 441; Jan. 9, 1908, **17,** 594; April 9, 1908, **18,** 255; June 8, 1908, **18,** 333; Oct. 15, 1908, **18,** 458; Jan. 14, 1909, **18,** 623; April 8, 1909, **19,** 153; Oct. 21, 1909, **19,** 435; Jan. 13, 1910, **20,** 4; April 14, 1910, **20,** 356; June 9, 1910, **20,** 509; Oct. 20, 1910, **21,** 364

Minutes of the Faculty, Nov. 12, 1902, **14,** 205; Jan. 7, 1903, **14,** 326; Feb. 4, 1903, **14,** 349; June 3, 1903, **14,** 470; Oct. 7, 1903, **15,** 14; April 19, 1904, **15,** 293; April 17, 1905, **16,** 64; Dec. 18, 1905, **16,** 271; Sept. 26, 1907, **17,** 402; Sept. 30, 1907, **17,** 407; Oct. 7, 1907, **17,** 421; Oct. 14, 1907, **17,** 432; Oct. 21, 1907, **17,**

448; Nov. 4, 1907, **17,** 467; May 4, 1908, **18,** 285; June 5, 1908, **18,** 320; Dec. 2, 1912, **25,** 575

Memorandum on revision of the course of study, Nov. 20, 1902, **14,** 207

Tribute by the faculty to President Patton and an address of welcome and support to his successor, Dec. 3, 1902, **14,** 255

Minutes of the Science Faculty, Dec. 10, 1902, **14,** 277

Report to the Board of Trustees on the Mahlon Long Scholarship, June 8, 1903, **14,** 476

Memorandum on departmental organization, Nov. 20, 1903, **15,** 55

Reports of the Committee on the Curriculum to the Board of Trustees, June 5, 1903, **14,** 473; March 9, 1904, **15,** 183; June 13, 1904, **15,** 375; June 12, 1905, **16,** 128; Oct. 21, 1905, **16,** 198; June 11, 1906, **16,** 421; Oct. 20, 1906, **16,** 464; Jan. 13, 1909, **18,** 615

Resolution about the gift of a dormitory by the Class of 1879, March 10, 1904, **15,** 185

Report of the Committee on the Course of Study to the Faculty, April 16, 1904, **15,** 252

Tribute and farewell to Charles Augustus Young, Dec. 12, 1904, **15,** 572

Reports of the Committee on Honorary Degrees to the Board of Trustees, March 11, 1903, **14,** 388; March 8, 1905, **16,** 22; April 8, 1908, **18,** 228; Jan. 14, 1909, **18,** 622

Memorandum on the clubs at Princeton, Feb. 17, 1906, **16,** 314

A resolution about Andrew Fleming West, Oct. 20, 1906, **16,** 467

A resolution about Henry van Dyke, March 14, 1907, **17,** 70

To the Board of Trustees' Committee on the Graduate School, May 30, 1907, **17,** 164

Draft of an announcement about the Quadrangle Plan, Oct. 4, 1907, **17,** 418

Proposed announcement by the Trustees' Committee on the Supplementary Report of the President, Oct. 18, 1907, **17,** 426

Memorandum on the administrative reorganization of the University, Dec. 9, 1907, **17,** 552

Notes for remarks to the Board of Trustees about the proposed quadrangle system, Jan. 9, 1908, **17,** 589

Resolution on the death of Grover Cleveland, Oct. 14, 1908, **18,** 451

Resolution of gratitude to Stephen Squires Palmer, Oct. 14, 1908, **18,** 451

Memorandum describing the duties of the Dean of Scientific Studies, Nov. 3, 1908, **18,** 481

Proposed by-laws of the Board of Trustees, Jan. 13, 1909, **18,** 613

Three resolutions of thanks for donations to the University, Jan. 14, 1909, **18,** 623

Tribute to Junius Spencer Morgan, Jan. 23, 1909, **19,** 7

Inscription honoring Nathaniel Fitz Randolph, Jan. 26, 1909, **19,** 14

Drafts of a proposed by-law of the Board of Trustees, Feb. 4, 1909, **19, 27**; Feb. 4, 1909, **19,** 28

Resolution about Andrew Clerk Imbrie's appointment as Financial Secretary, April 8, 1909, **19,** 153

Proposed report for the Committee on the Curriculum, June 12, 1909, **19,** 242

Statement on undergraduate instruction, Aug. 7, 1909, **19,** 328

Minute from the Committee on Discipline, Dec. 8, 1909, **19,** 577

A proposed report to the Committee on the Curriculum about the organization of the teaching faculty, May 13, 1910, **20,** 445

Professional and personal affairs: news reports and announcements

Appointment as a vice-president of the Thomas Jefferson Memorial Association, Feb. 16, 1903, **14,** 360

Citations for honorary degrees: University of Pennsylvania, Feb. 28, 1903, **14,** 381; Brown University, June 17, 1903, **14,** 494; Harvard University, June 26, 1907, **17,** 225; Williams College, Oct. 7, 1908, **18,** 439

Inauguration of Francis Landey Patton as President of Princeton Theological Seminary, Oct. 15, 1903, **15,** 16

Appointment to the General Committee of the Japanese Relief Fund, March 11, 1905, **16,** 29

Election as vice-president of the American Academy of Political and Social Science, Feb. 10, 1906, **16,** 313

Return from vacation in England, Oct. 20, 1906, **16,** 463

Plans to sail for Bermuda, Jan. 11, 1907, **16,** 559

Return from Bermuda, Feb. 29, 1908, **17,** 619

Announcement of the marriage of Margaret Randolph Axson and Edward Graham Elliott, Sept. 3, 1910, **21,** 84

Description by Ellen Axson Wilson, July 28, 1912, **24,** 573

Public addresses, statements, reports and related materials

Report of an address, "Religion and Patriotism," at a student conference, Northfield, Mass., Aug. 23, 1902, **14,** 102

News item about Wilson's remarks at a dinner in New York in honor of the Crown Prince of Siam, Nov. 1, 1902, **14,** 195

Notes for an address to the New York Society of Mayflower Descendants, Nov. 21, 1902, **14,** 209; report, Nov. 22, 1902, **14,** 210

"The Relation of University Education to Commerce," the Commercial Club of Chicago, Nov. 29, 1902, **14,** 228; report, Nov. 30, 1902, **14,** 247

Notes for an address to the Presbyterian Union of New York, Dec. 1, 1902, **14,** 252; report, Dec. 2, 1902, **14,** 253

Report of an address to the Presbyterian Union of Baltimore, Dec. 5, 1902, **14,** 260

Report of an address, "The Meaning of a University Education," to the New Jersey High School Teachers' Association in Newark, Dec. 6, 1902, **14,** 261

Report of an address, "The Function of the University in the United States," at the Brooklyn Institute of Arts and Sciences, Dec. 12, 1902, **14,** 283

Report of an address, "The Relations of the University to Business," to a group of the New York State Bankers' Association, New York, Dec. 19, 1902, **14,** 298

Notes for an address, "The University and the Country," at the Lafayette Avenue Presbyterian Church, Brooklyn, Dec. 21, 1902, **14,** 299; report, Dec. 22, 1902, **14,** 300

Report of an address to the New England Society of Orange, East Orange, N. J., Dec. 23, 1902, **14,** 301

Notes for an address, "State Education: Its Relation to Political Life and Development," to the Twentieth Century Club of Boston, Dec. 29, 1902, **14,** 307; report, Jan. 3, 1903, **14,** 316

Report of an address, "What It Means to Be an American," to the Middlesex Women's Club, Lowell, Mass., Jan. 3, 1903, **14,** 314

Report of an address, "God Is Love," to the Trenton, Y.M.C.A., Feb. 9, 1903, **14,** 354

Report of an address, "The Meaning of a College Course," at the Peddie Institute, Feb. 13, 1903, **14,** 356

Address on patriotism to the Washington Association of New Jersey in Morristown, Feb. 23, 1903, **14,** 365

Report of an address on patriotism at the University of Michigan, April 22, 1903, **14,** 419

Report of a lecture, "What It Means to Be an American," in Minneapolis, April 26, 1903, **14,** 427

Report of a lecture, "The Expansion and Character of the United States," at the University Club of St. Louis, April 29, 1903, **14,** 433

Report of a talk to the Y.M.C.A. of Cincinnati, May 4, 1903, **14,** 450

Report of a lecture on patriotism at the Twentieth Century Club of Chicago, May 6, 1903, **14,** 454

Editorial about an address, "What It Means to Be an American," at the Mercersburg Academy, June 5, 1903, **14,** 471

Report of an address at the Lawrenceville School, June 6, 1903, **14,** 475

Report of an address, "Patriotism," at Brown University, June 17, 1903, **14,** 491

"John Wesley's Place in History," at Wesleyan University, June 30, 1903, **14,** 502; report, July 1, 1903, **14,** 515

Notes for a Fourth of July speech on board *R.M.S. Oceanic*, July 4, 1903, **14,** 520

"The Statesmanship of Letters," Pittsburgh, Nov. 5, 1903, **15,** 33; news report, Nov. 6, 1903, **15,** 46

Report of a Hill School Club Dinner in Princeton, Nov. 23, 1903, **15,** 57

Report of a speech, "The Land We Live In," to the St. Andrew's Society of New York, Dec. 1, 1903, **15,** 58

Report of an address, "Civic Patriotism," to the Board of Trade of Passaic, Dec. 3, 1903, **15,** 61

Report of a speech, "The Southerner in the North," to the Southern Society of New York, Dec. 10, 1903, **15,** 68

Notes for a religious address, "The Church and Society," at the Second Presbyterian Church of Philadelphia, Dec. 11, 1903, **15,** 78; report, Dec. 14, 1903, **15,** 98

"The College Course and Methods of Instruction," to the Schoolmasters' Association of New York and Vicinity, New York, Dec. 12, 1903, **15,** 79

Report of a talk on the nobility of service to the Philadelphia Y.M.C.A., Dec. 14, 1903, **15,** 99

Reports of an address, "Americanism," to the Outlook Club of Montclair, Jan. 23, 1904, **15,** 137; Jan. 28, 1904, **15,** 142

Reports of a speech in New York about British-American amity to the Pilgrims of the United States, Jan. 30, 1904, **15,** 147, 149

Report of a speech, "The University and the Church," to the Presbyterian Union of Albany, Feb. 16, 1904, **15,** 168

Notes for a talk on George Washington to the schoolchildren of Princeton, Feb. 19, 1904, **15,** 174

Report of a lecture at the Phillips Exeter Academy, Feb. 20, 1904, **15,** 175

Notes for an address, "The Young People and the Church," in Pittsburgh to the Pennsylvania Sunday School Association, Feb. 23, 1904, **15,** 177

Report of an address, "The Young People and the Church," to the Philadelphia County Sabbath School Association, Philadelphia, Feb. 27, 1904, **15,** 179

Report of an address, "University Men and the Country," to the University Club of Jersey City, March 16, 1904, **15,** 195

Announcement of Wilson's southern itinerary, April 2, 1904, **15,** 227

News item about the cancellation of a trip to the South, April 23, 1904, **15,** 272

News item about an introduction of President Cleveland, May 7, 1904, **15,** 313

Notes for an address on community cooperation to the Village Improvement Society of Princeton, May 8, 1904, **15,** 316; report, May 14, 1904, **15,** 330

Notes for a speech, "Business and Politics," in New York to the

American Institute of Bank Clerks, May 12, 1904, **15,** 328; report, May 13, 1904, **15,** 328

Notes for an address, "The Universities and the Law," in Cape May to the Pennsylvania State Bar Association, June 30, 1904, **15,** 400; report, June 30, 1904, **15,** 401

"The Variety and Unity of History," at the International Congress of Arts and Science of the Universal Exposition in St. Louis, Sept. 20, 1904, **15,** 472

Address commemorating the centennial of the assumption of the presidency of Union College by Eliphalet Nott, Sept. 29, 1904, **15,** 496

News item about fall engagements, Oct. 1, 1904, **15,** 500

Notes for an address on educational ideals to the Schoolmasters' Association of New York and Vicinity, New York, Oct. 8, 1904, **15,** 505

"The Young People and the Church," to the State Sabbath School Association Convention, Pittsburgh, Oct. 13, 1904, **15,** 510; report, Oct. 14, 1904, **15,** 519

Report of a lecture, "Americanism," for the Lecture Bureau of the Department of Education, New York, Nov. 20, 1904, **15,** 536

Report of an address about the South's political future to the Society of the Virginians of New York, Nov. 30, 1904, **15,** 545

Announcement of a lecture, "The University and the Nation," to the League for Political Education of New York, Dec. 3, 1904, **15,** 552

Report of an after-dinner speech, "George Washington," to the Sons of the Revolution, New York, Feb. 23, 1905, **16,** 11

Notes for an address, "The Individual and the Organization," to the People's Forum in New Rochelle, Feb. 26, 1905, **16,** 13; report, Feb. 27, 1905, **16,** 14

Report of an address, "The University and the Nation," to the Michigan Schoolmasters' Club in Ann Arbor, April 1, 1905, **16,** 44

Report of an address, "The University and the Nation," to the Presbyterian Union of Newark, April 11, 1905, **16,** 48

Notes for a speech on Benjamin Franklin to the American Philosophical Society, April 13, 1905, **16,** 53; report, April 15, 1905, **16,** 56

Report of an address, "The Profit of Belief," to the Trenton Y.M.C.A., April 17, 1905, **16,** 63

Report of an address at the Marion (Ala.) Military Institute, April 21, 1905, **16,** 71

Report of an address at the Dallas Academy, Selma, Ala., April 21, 1905, **16,** 72

Report of an address, "The University and the Nation," in Montgomery, April 22, 1905, **16,** 74

Remarks on arrival in Kansas City, May 12, 1905, **16,** 95

Report of talks at high schools in Kansas City, May 12, 1905, **16,** 98

Report of an address of welcome to the Pennsylvania Society of the Sons of the Revolution, Princeton, June 18, 1905, **16,** 143

Notes for an address at the dedication of Madison Hall, University of Virginia, Oct. 14, 1905, **16,** 193; report, Oct. 21, 1905, **16,** 195

Notes for an address, "The University and the Schools," to the Schoolmasters of Queens, Oct. 28, 1905, **16,** 207

Remarks at the opening exercises of the Institute of Musical Art, New York, Oct. 31, 1905, **16,** 208; report, Nov. 1, 1905, **16,** 210

Report of an address, "The University and the School," to the Barnard Club, Providence, Nov. 12, 1905, **16,** 219

Report of an address at the dedication of the Northeast Manual Training School of Philadelphia, Nov. 18, 1905, **16,** 225

Notes for an address, "Mediation of Youth in Christian Progress," to the Inter-Church Conference on Federation, New York, Nov. 19, 1905, **16,** 227; reports, Nov. 20, 1905, **16,** 228, 229

Report of a talk to the Y.M.C.A. at Princeton Theological Seminary, Nov. 23, 1905, **16,** 232

Announcement of a visit to Nashville, Nov. 27, 1905, **16,** 235

Report of a lecture, "Liberal Education," to the Nashville Teachers' Association, Nov. 30, 1905, **16,** 240

Report of a speech on education to the Wesleyan University Club, New York, Dec. 9, 1905, **16,** 243

News item about a talk, "University Ideals," to the Twentieth Century Club of Hartford, Dec. 12, 1905, **16,** 244

"The University and the Nation," at Swarthmore College, Dec. 15, 1905, **16,** 267

Report of an address in Trenton to the Association of History Teachers of the Middle States and Maryland, Jan. 8, 1906, **16,** 279

News item about a speech on patriotism, at the State Normal School, West Chester, Pa., Jan. 13, 1906, **16,** 282

Report of an address at a memorial service for William Rainey Harper, New York, Jan. 15, 1906, **16,** 282

Report of an address, "What it Means to Be an American," in Charleston, S. C., Jan. 19, 1906, **16,** 285

Address to the Lotos Club of New York, Feb. 3, 1906, **16,** 292

Report of an address, "The Relation of the University to Commerce," to the Commercial Club of Providence, Feb. 10, 1906, **16,** 309

Report of an address on George Washington to the University Club of Washington, Feb. 23, 1906, **16,** 315

Notes for an address, "The Young Man's Burden," to the North Carolina Society of New York, Feb. 27, 1906, **16,** 319; report, Feb. 28, 1906, **16,** 320

Report of a talk, "Liberal Training," to the Private Secondary School Association, Philadelphia, March 10, 1906, **16,** 327

Report of an address on patriotism at the People's Institute, Youngstown, Ohio, March 15, 1906, **16,** 332

Report of an address on Americanism at Oberlin College, March 22, 1906, **16,** 340

Report of a talk in New York to the alumni of the Lawrenceville School, March 25, 1906, **16,** 344

"The Minister and the Community," to the Conference of Christian Men of Eastern Colleges in Hartford, March 30, 1906, **16,** 346; report, March 31, 1906, **16,** 352

Report of an address on opportunity at the Rayen School, Youngstown, Ohio, April 1906, **16,** 354

News release of a speech on Thomas Jefferson at the Democratic Club Dinner, New York, April 13, 1906, **16,** 358; text, April 16, 1906, **16,** 362

Report of an address, "A Liberal Training," to the Essex County Teachers' Guild, Newark, May 1, 1906, **16,** 380

Cancellation of a proposed address at the inauguration of William H. Demarest as President of Rutgers College, June 16, 1906, **16,** 427

Report of an address on patriotism to the Southern Society of New York, Dec. 15, 1906, **16,** 529

Announcement of an address to the young people of St. Andrew's Presbyterian Church, Hamilton, Bermuda, Jan. 26, 1907, **17,** 22, notes, Jan. 27, 1907, **17,** 22

Notes for a sermon on duty at Christ Church, Warwick, Bermuda, Feb. 3, 1907, **17,** 27

Announcement of Wilson's lectures on "The Government of the United States," at Columbia University, Feb. 19, 1907, **17,** 45

Notes for an address, "Discretion," at the Hill School, Pottstown, Pa., Feb. 22, 1907, **17,** 49; news item, Feb. 26, 1907, **17,** 50

Reply to a toast, "John C. Calhoun," at the first annual meeting of the South Carolina Society of New York, March 18, 1907, **17,** 78

Report of an address at the dedication of the chapel of the First Presbyterian Church of Princeton, March 30, 1907, **17,** 98

Address on receiving the LL.D. degree at Harvard University, June 26, 1907, **17,** 226

Address, "The Author and Signers of the Declaration of Independence," at the Jamestown Exposition, July 4, 1907, **17,** 248; report, July 4, 1907, **17,** 247

Reports of addresses in Memphis: "Problems of the Future," to St. Mary's School and Memphis University School, Nov. 9, 1907, **17,** 474; to Memphis High School, Nov. 9, 1907, **17,** 475; "Ideals of Public Life," at the Goodwyn Institute, Nov. 9, 1907, **17,** 476

Arrival in Nashville, Nov. 11, 1907, **17,** 488

News report of an address, "False and True Conservatism," to the Watauga Club of Nashville, Nov. 12, 1907, **17,** 491

"The Ideals of Public Life," to the Cleveland Chamber of Commerce, Nov. 16, 1907, **17,** 497

Statement in the *New York Times* about business, Nov. 27, 1907, **17,** 524

Response to an address of welcome in New York to the Association of Colleges and Preparatory Schools of the Middle States and Maryland, Nov. 29, 1907, **17,** 528

"School and College," to the Association of Colleges and Preparatory Schools of the Middle States and Maryland in New York, Nov. 29, 1907, **17,** 529

Address on the uses of education to the Indiana State Teachers' Association in Indianapolis, Dec. 27, 1907, **17,** 569

News report of an address, "Ideals of Public Life," to the Contemporary Club of Indianapolis, Dec. 30, 1907, **17,** 582

Announcement of a lecture in the Princess Hotel, Bermuda, Feb. 15, 1908, **17,** 616

Report of talks on good citizenship to the Chicago Latin School and the University School for Boys, March 12, 1908, **18,** 16

"The Government and Business," to the Commercial Club of Chicago, March 14, 1908, **18,** 35

"The Training of Intellect," at a Yale Phi Beta Kappa dinner, March 18, 1908, **18,** 53

"The Government and Business," to the Traffic Club of Pittsburgh, April 3, 1908, **18,** 221

Press release of remarks, "Law or Personal Power," to the National Democratic Club of New York, April 13, 1908, **18,** 263; report, April 14, 1908, **18,** 269

Notes for an address, "Contribution of the Association to the Life of the Nation," at the Y.M.C.A. Jubilee, Chicago, April 27, 1908, **18,** 276; report, April 28, 1908, **18,** 276

Notes for a commencement address, "The College and the Country," at the Woman's College of Baltimore, June 3, 1908, **18,** 318; report, June 4, 1908, **18,** 318

Notes for an after-dinner speech on board *S.S. California*, June 27, 1908, **18,** 347; *S.S. Caledonia*, Sept. 11, 1908, **18,** 418

Statement on the death of Grover Cleveland, June 29, 1908, **18,** 348

"The Banker and the Nation," to the American Bankers' Association in Denver, Sept. 30, 1908, **18,** 424

Announcement of an address to the Men's League of the First Congregational Church, Pittsfield, Mass., Oct. 6, 1908, **18,** 436; report, Oct. 9, 1908, **18,** 440

Address at the inauguration of Harry Augustus Garfield as President of Williams College, Oct. 7, 1908, **18,** 437

Address at the seventy-fifth anniversary of Haverford College, Oct. 16, 1908, **18,** 459

Notes for a talk, "What Kind of Citizens Shall We Be?," at the Lawrenceville School, Nov. 4, 1908, **18,** 482

Report of address to the University Club of Jersey City, Nov. 6, 1908, **18,** 485

Report of an address on the relation between the college and the public school at Jersey City High School, Nov. 6, 1908, **18,** 487

"The Meaning of a College Education," Hotchkiss School, Lakeville, Conn., Nov. 12, 1908, **18,** 495

Speech on civic revival to the City History Club of New York, Nov. 14, 1908, **18,** 509

Report of an afternoon address, "Success and How to Attain It," to the Y.M.C.A. of Pittsburgh, Nov. 23, 1908, **18,** 520

Report of an evening address, "The Contribution of the Young Men's Christian Association to the Life of the Nation," to the Y.M.C.A. of Pittsburgh, Nov. 23, 1908, **18,** 521

Announcement of an address, "The Business Man and the Community," to the Toledo Chamber of Commerce, Nov. 27, 1908, **18,** 524; report, Nov. 28, 1908, **18,** 526; abstract, Nov. 27, 1908, **18,** 647

"Conservatism: True and False," to the Southern Society of New York, Dec. 9, 1908, **18,** 535

Report of an address, "The Business Man and the Nation," to the Wednesday Club of Newark, Dec. 17, 1908, **18,** 551

Notes for an address of welcome in Princeton to the Modern Language Association, Dec. 28, 1908, **18,** 566

"The Meaning of a Liberal Education," to the New York City High School Teachers Association, Jan. 9, 1909, **18,** 593

Report of an address on education to the Alumni Association of the Newark Academy, Jan. 16, 1909, **18,** 628

Address on Robert E. Lee at the University of North Carolina, Jan. 19, 1909, **18,** 631

News report of an address in New York to Williams College alumni, Feb. 6, 1909, **19,** 30

"Abraham Lincoln: A Man of the People," Chicago, Feb. 12, 1909, **19,** 33

Address on liberal education to the Presbyterian Union of Baltimore, Feb. 19, 1909, **19,** 52

Notes for an address in Philadelphia on Negro education, Feb. 26, 1909, **19,** 69

"Civic Problems," to the Civic League of St. Louis, March 9, 1909, **19,** 81; report, March 17, 1909, **19,** 101

News item about a speech to the Virginia Society of St. Louis, March 11, 1909, **19,** 97; report, March 17, 1909, **19,** 101

News report of an address, "The University's Part in Political

Life," to the University Extension Society, Philadelphia, March 13, 1909, **19,** 98

After-dinner remarks to the Friendly Sons of St. Patrick, New York, March 17, 1909, **19,** 102

News report of a speech, "Americanism," at Temple Rodeph Sholom of New York, March 19, 1909, **19,** 112

Report of an address, "What Ought a Man to Do?," at the Witherspoon Street Presbyterian Church of Princeton, April 3, 1909, **19,** 148

Notes for an address, "Political Reform," to the University Club of Detroit, April 16, 1909, **19,** 164

News item about an address, "The Schoolmaster," in Paterson, N. J., April 24, 1909, **19,** 171

News report of an address in New York at a dinner honoring George Brinton McClellan, Jr., April 28, 1909, **19,** 175

Address on John Witherspoon in Washington, May 20, 1909, **19,** 202

Address, "The Present Task of the Ministry," at the Hartford Theological Seminary, May 26, 1909, **19,** 215

Report of an address at the fifty-third anniversary of St. Paul's School in Concord, N. H., June 3, 1909, **19,** 226

Address at the inauguration of Charles Alexander Richmond as President of Union College, June 7, 1909, **19,** 231

Address, "The Spirit of Learning," to the Harvard University chapter of Phi Beta Kappa, July 1, 1909, **19,** 277

Address at the inauguration of Ernest Fox Nichols as President of Dartmouth College, Oct. 14, 1909, **19,** 413

Report of an address "The Democratic Opportunity," to the Democratic Club in Plainfield, N. J., Oct. 30, 1909, **19,** 461

Address, "The Ministry and the Individual," at McCormick Theological Seminary, Nov. 2, 1909, **19,** 471

Notes for a lecture, "Religion and Citizenship," Harvard Church, Brookline, Mass., Nov. 12, 1909, **19,** 496

Report of an address on Christian fraternity at the Phillips Exeter Academy, Nov. 13, 1909, **19,** 498

Address on political reform to the City Club of Philadelphia, Nov. 18, 1909, **19,** 509

Report of an address on public education to the Philadelphia Teachers' Association, Dec. 5, 1909, **19,** 554

Report of an address, "Our Flag and Our Day," in Summit, N. J., Dec. 10, 1909, **19,** 599

"The State and the Citizen's Relation to It," to the New Jersey State Teachers' Association in Atlantic City, Dec. 28, 1909, **19,** 635

"Position and Importance of the Arts Course as Distinct From the Professional and Semi-Professional Courses," to the Association of American Universities, Madison, Wis., Jan. 5, 1910, **19,** 713

Address at the inauguration of Henry Harbaugh Apple as President of Franklin and Marshall College, Jan. 7, 1910, **19,** 740

Reports of an address on statesmanship in banking to New York bankers, Jan. 18, 1910, **20,** 23, 25 (2), 26

Address to the Short Ballot Organization, New York, Jan. 21, 1910, **20,** 32

Notes for a talk on Bermuda in Penns Neck, N. J., March 9, 1910, **20,** 224

Report of an address, "Opportunity for Young Men in Politics," to the Contemporary Club of Philadelphia, March 15, 1910, **20,** 242

Address on Grover Cleveland to the National Democratic Club of New York, March 18, 1910, **20,** 257

Address to a Democratic Dollar Dinner in Elizabeth, March 29, 1910, **20,** 297

Report of a lecture at the First Presbyterian Church of Princeton, April 2, 1910, **20,** 312

"The Clergyman and the State," at the General Theological Seminary, April 6, 1910, **20,** 328

Statement on the death of Mark Twain, April 21, 1910, **20,** 378

Report of a speech in Ridgewood, N. J., April 23, 1910, **20,** 385

Abstract of an address to the Associated Press and the American Newspaper Publishers' Association, New York, April 28, 1910, **20,** 399

Address to the New Jersey Bankers' Association in Atlantic City, May 6, 1910, **20,** 414

Report of an address to the Lawyers' Club of Newark, May 21, 1910, **20,** 462

Address at the celebration of the centennial of the Lawrenceville School, June 11, 1910, **20,** 514

Announcement of a dedication address at the First Congregational Church in Old Lyme, Conn., June 18, 1910, **20,** 538

Report of an address, "The Function of the Country Church," in Old Lyme, July 16, 1910, **21,** 4

"The Lawyer and the Community," address to the American Bar Association, Chattanooga, Aug. 31, 1910, **21,** 64

Report of a speech to Die Wilde Gans Club of Jersey City, Sept. 21, 1910, **21,** 147

Remarks on arrival in Milwaukee, Nov. 17, 1910, **22,** 55

Report of a luncheon address in Milwaukee, Nov. 17, 1910, **22,** 57

Public lecture in Milwaukee, Nov. 17, 1910, **22,** 61

Report of a lecture on business and government, Chicago, Nov. 19, 1910, **22,** 74

Thanksgiving Day address, Har Sinai Temple of Trenton, Nov. 24, 1910, **22,** 87

Address to the Conference of Govenors, Frankfort, Ky., Nov. 29, 1910, **22,** 102

Report of a message to the Sons of Delaware of Philadelphia, Dec. 8, 1910, **22**, 148

Address to the Illinois Manufacturers' Association, Chicago, Dec. 12, 1910, **22**, 178; report, Dec. 13, 1910, **22**, 180

Address to the Southern Society of New York, Dec. 14, 1910, **22**, 188

Presidential address to the American Political Science Association, St. Louis, Dec. 27, 1910, **22**, 263

Report of a speech to the City Club of St. Louis, Dec. 29, 1910, **22**, 276

Report of a speech to the Princeton Club of St. Louis, Dec. 30, 1910, **22**, 283

Address at Temple B'nai Jeshurun of Newark, Jan. 8, 1911, **22**, 316

Report of an address on the direct primary principle in Newark, Jan. 16, 1911, **22**, 335

Report of a speech to the annual dinner of the Board of Trade of Jersey City, Jan. 20, 1911, **22**, 359

Address to the Board of Trade of Newark, Jan. 25, 1911, **22**, 367

Report of an address on civic awakening, Trenton, Jan. 27, 1911, **22**, 379

Report of an address to the Inter-Church Federation of New Jersey, Trenton, Jan. 28, 1911, **22**, 385

Report of a speech to the Kansas Society of New York, Jan. 29, 1911, **22**, 389

Address to the National Press Club, Washington, Jan. 31, 1911, **22**, 396

A tribute to Mark Anthony Sullivan, Feb. 1, 1911, **22**, 400

Report of a speech to the alumni of Stevens Institute, New York, Feb. 8, 1911, **22**, 410

Address on behalf of Berea College, New York, Feb. 10, 1911, **22**, 417

Report of an address to the Kentuckians of New York, Feb. 11, 1911, **22**, 421

Statement on a proposed increase in postal rates, Feb. 12, 1911, **22**, 427

Address to the Democratic Club of Philadelphia, Feb. 21, 1911, **22**, 441

Report of remarks to the New Jersey Consumers' League in Trenton, Feb. 25, 1911, **22**, 452

Report of remarks to the New Jersey Editorial Association, Trenton, Feb. 28, 1911, **22**, 455

Address to the West Hudson Board of Trade, Harrison, N. J., Feb. 28, 1911, **22**, 456

Address to the Board of Trade of Hoboken, March 2, 1911, **22**, 468

Report of an address to the Chamber of Commerce of Trenton, March 8, 1911, **22**, 482

Report of two speeches in Atlanta, March 10, 1911, **22,** 487

Address to the Southern Commercial Congress, Atlanta, March 10, 1911, **22,** 491

Report of a meeting with William Jennings Bryan in Princeton, March 13, 1911, **22,** 502

Remarks in Princeton to the New Jersey Conference of Charities and Correction, April 2, 1911, **22,** 528

Address to the Burlington County Democratic Club in Burlington, N. J., April 5, 1911, **22,** 535

Arrival in Indianapolis, April 13, 1911, **22,** 554

Address to the National Democratic League of Clubs in Indianapolis, April 13, 1911, **22,** 557

Report of remarks at the Free Synagogue of New York, April 25, 1911, **22,** 585

Report of remarks at a dinner in New York given in his honor by the New Jersey Senate, April 27, 1911, **22,** 588

Report of an address to the Board of Trade of Phillipsburg, N. J., April 28, 1911, **22,** 590

Reports of an address to the Pewter Platter Club of Norfolk, April 30, 1911, **22,** 592, 594

Report of a speech to the National Democratic Club of New York, May 3, 1911, **22,** 601

Report of two addresses on the new political epoch, Kansas City, May 6, 1911, **23,** 5, 9

Address on the Bible in Denver, May 7, 1911, **23,** 12

Report of remarks at a Bryn Mawr dinner in Denver, May 8, 1911, **23,** 21

Report of an address to the Denver Chamber of Commerce, May 9, 1911, **23,** 23

Report of a luncheon address to Princeton Alumni in Denver, May 10, 1911, **23,** 27

Report of an address to the Mile High Club of Denver, May 10, 1911, **23,** 28

Address to the Jefferson Club of Los Angeles, May 12, 1911, **23,** 32; report, May 13, 1911, **23,** 44

Remarks on arrival in California, May 13, 1911, **23,** 40

Report of a luncheon speech in Pasadena, May 13, 1911, **23,** 45

Report of an address to the City Club of Los Angeles, May 14, 1911, **23,** 50

Remarks during a busy day in San Francisco, May 16, 1911, **23,** 53

Report of an address to the Harvard, Yale, and Princeton Clubs in San Francisco, May 16, 1911, **23,** 55

Report of an address on corporations at Berkeley, May 17, 1911, **23,** 59

Remarks on arrival in Portland, May 19, 1911, **23,** 63

Report of an address to the Commercial Club of Portland, May 19, 1911, **23,** 65

Report of an address to the Press Club of Portland, May 19, 1911, **23,** 68

Address in Portland on reforms and responsible leadership, May 19, 1911, **23,** 69

Report of an address on problems of government, Portland, May 20, 1911, **23,** 73

Report of remarks in Seattle to Democratic leaders, May 21, 1911, **23,** 78

Report of a speech on commission government, Seattle, May 21, 1911, **23,** 79

Remarks during a visit in St. Paul and Minneapolis, May 25, 1911, **23,** 84

Report of a luncheon address to the Publicity Club of Minneapolis, May 25, 1911, **23,** 86

Report of an address to the Association of Commerce of St. Paul, May 25, 1911, **23,** 87

Report of an address at the University of Minnesota, May 25, 1911, **23,** 93

Report of a visit to the home of William Jennings Bryan and an address in Lincoln, Neb., May 27, 1911, **23,** 95, 96

Commencement address at the University of North Carolina, May 30, 1911, **23,** 104

An address in Raleigh, May 31, 1911, **23,** 110

Report of remarks at the laying of the cornerstone of the Y.M.C.A., Columbia, S. C., June 2, 1911, **23,** 113

Address in Columbia to the South Carolina Press Association, June 2, 1911, **23,** 114

Reports of remarks during a stop-off in Washington, June 4, 1911, **23,** 131; June 5, 1911, **23,** 128

Report of a speech on commission government in Bayonne, June 8, 1911, **23,** 136

Address on behalf of commission government in Trenton, June 13, 1911, **23,** 140

Reports of two addresses to reform Democrats in Harrisburg, Pa., June 16, 1911, **23,** 154, 156

Report of an address to the New Jersey Bar Association, Atlantic City, June 17, 1911, **23,** 158

Statement on Trenton's adoption of commission government, June 21, 1911, **23,** 161

Address on behalf of commission government in Hoboken, June 21, 1911, **23,** 161

Report of a statement concerning Alaska, June 28, 1911, **23,** 174

Remarks upon the defeat of commission government in Hoboken and New Brunswick, June 28, 1911, **23,** 176

Reports of an address in Newark to the Woodrow Wilson Democratic League of Essex County, June 29, 1911, **23,** 177, 178

Report of an address, in Stone Harbor at the opening of the Ocean Parkway, July 5, 1911, **23**, 185

Report of a Fourth of July address in Ocean Grove, July 5, 1911, **23**, 186

"The Lawyer in Politics," to the Kentucky Bar Association in Lexington, July 12, 1911, **23**, 194

Address in Jersey City on behalf of commission government, July 14, 1911, **23**, 201

Remarks about the adoption of commission government by Jersey City, July 19, 1911, **23**, 218

Report of a speech to Monmouth County Democrats in Asbury Park, July 19, 1911, **23**, 219

Report of an address in Passaic on behalf of commission government, July 21, 1911, **23**, 222

Report of a statement about the adoption of commission government by Passaic, July 27, 1911, **23**, 233

Report of a speech at the Warren County Farmers' picnic in Belvidere, Aug. 17, 1911, **23**, 270

Report of remarks and activities during a visit to Cape May County, Aug. 18, 1911, **23**, 272

Report of an address to farmers in Camden County, Aug. 18, 1911, **23**, 275

Report of comments after a tour of state penal and charitable institutions, Sept. 7, 1911, **23**, 304

Address at the dedication of the synagogue of the congregation Oheb Shalom of Newark, Sept. 7, 1911, **23**, 305

Report of a speech to the Hotel Men's Association of Atlantic City, Sept. 12, 1911, **23**, 315

Reports of remarks at the Governors' Conference at Spring Lake: welcome, Sept. 12, 1911, **23**, 317; on the initiative and referendum, Sept. 13, 1911, **23**, 319; on workmen's compensation, Sept. 13, 1911, **23**, 322

Report of a speech at the laying of the cornerstone of the high school, Woodbury, N. J., Sept. 28, 1911, **23**, 362

Address to a Sunday school rally in Trenton, Oct. 1, 1911, **23**, 372

Address on community centers in Madison, Wis., Oct. 25, 1911, **23**, 480

Luncheon address in Madison to the Democratic League of Wisconsin, Oct. 26, 1911, **23**, 488

"Life and the Bible," Dallas, Oct. 28, 1911, **23**, 494; report, Oct. 29, 1911, **23**, 510

Address at the Texas State Fair, Dallas, Oct. 28, 1911, **23**, 499

Remarks during a strenuous day in Dallas and Fort Worth, Oct. 29, 1911, **23**, 506

Report of an address in Fort Worth, Oct. 29, 1911, **23**, 511

Report of a speech in Little Rock, Oct. 31, 1911, **23**, 517

Remarks en route from Dallas to St. Louis on the Cannon Ball Express, Nov. 1, 1911, **23**, 519

Visits to the University of Virginia, Nov. 15, 1911, **23,** 549; Nov. 16, 1911, **23,** 550

Visits to Augusta and Savannah, Nov. 19, 1911, **23,** 552; Nov. 20, 1911, **23,** 555; Nov. 20, 1911, **23,** 557

Report of a memorial address to the Elks Lodge of Asbury Park, N. J., Dec. 4, 1911, **23,** 561

Report and statement about an application for a Carnegie pension, Dec. 5, 1911, **23,** 564, 565

Reports of a day's activities and an address on southern development in Baltimore, Dec. 6, 1911, **23,** 567, 569

Report of an address on behalf of commission government, Baltimore, Dec. 6, 1911, **23,** 572

Report of an address protesting Russian discrimination against American Jews, New York, Dec. 7, 1911, **23,** 583

Report of a speech to New Jersey mayors, Hoboken, Jan. 3, 1912, **23,** 634

Address on the tariff to the National Democratic Club of New York, Jan. 3, 1912, **23,** 637

Denial of break with Colonel Harvey, Jan. 6, 1912, **23,** 656

Unpublished statement about the Cleveland letter, Jan. 7, 1912, **24,** 3

Two unpublished statements about the Joline letter, Jan. 8, 1912, **24,** 8

Report of conferences in Washington and remarks to the National Press Club, Jan. 8, 1912, **24,** 7

Address in Washington at Jackson Day Dinner, Jan. 8, 1912, **24,** 9

Report of remarks to the National Press Club, Jan. 9, 1912, **24,** 16

Report of remarks at a New Jersey dinner in Washington, Jan. 9, 1912, **24,** 17

Address in New York to the National League of Commission Merchants, Jan. 11, 1912, **24,** 32

Report of an address to businessmen in Detroit, Jan. 18, 1912, **24,** 47

An unpublished statement about the Harvey affair, Jan. 18, 1912, **24,** 48

Reports of two political addresses in Detroit, Jan. 19, 1912, **24,** 51, 52

Report of two speeches in Ann Arbor, Jan. 19, 1912, **24,** 53

Report of remarks to the Newark Board of Trade, Jan. 25, 1912, **24,** 67

Report of an address to the Jersey City Board of Trade, Jan. 25, 1912, **24,** 68

Denial of Henry Watterson's role as fund-raiser, Jan. 27, 1912, **24,** 80

After-dinner address to real estate men in Boston, Jan. 27, 1912, **24,** 83

Report of an address to the City Club of Boston, Jan. 28, 1912, **24,** 92

Report of an address to the students and faculty of Harvard University, Jan. 28, 1912, **24,** 93

Report of a statement on the Watterson affair, Jan. 30, 1912, **24,** 97

Address to the General Assembly of Virginia and the City Council of Richmond, Feb. 1, 1912, **24,** 101

Report of an address to the student body of Richmond College, Feb. 2, 1912, **24,** 117

Report of a talk to the Senate of Virginia, Feb. 2, 1912, **24,** 119

Report of a talk to the Virginia House of Delegates, Feb. 2, 1912, **24,** 121

Address in Philadelphia to the Periodical Publishers' Association of America, Feb. 2, 1912, **24,** 122

Report of comments on the La Follette incident, Feb. 8, 1912, **24,** 137

Report of a political address in Allentown, Pa., Feb. 8, 1912, **24,** 138

Report of two addresses in Frankfort, Ky., Feb. 9, 1912, **24,** 141

Address to Chicago Democrats on Lincoln's Birthday, Feb. 12, 1912, **24,** 151

Report of a political speech in Concord, N. H., Feb. 16, 1912, **24,** 165

Address on civil service reform in New Haven, Feb. 16, 1912, **24,** 166

Report of after-dinner remarks to the Sussex Society of New York, Feb. 19, 1912, **24,** 179

Report of an address in Philadelphia to the Universal Peace Union, Feb. 19, 1912, **24,** 181

Report of remarks on arrival in Kansas City, Feb. 22, 1912, **24,** 185

Report of remarks on arrival in Topeka, Feb. 22, 1912, **24,** 187

Report of an address in Topeka to the Kansas Democratic Club, Feb. 23, 1912, **24,** 188

Report of remarks at a reception in Nashville, Feb. 24, 1912, **24,** 190

Address to the Wilson Club of Nashville, Feb. 24, 1912, **24,** 191

Address on behalf of the Nashville Y.M.C.A., Feb. 24, 1912, **24,** 206

Report of two addresses in Des Moines, March 2, 1912, **24,** 220

Report of activities in Des Moines, March 3, 1912, **24,** 222

Report of a meeting with Manuel Luis Quezon, March 5, 1912, **24,** 224

Address to the General Assembly of Maryland, March 7, 1912, **24,** 227

Report of an address to the Brooklyn League, March 10, 1912, **24,** 238

Report of an after-dinner address to the Friendly Sons of St. Patrick of Elizabeth, N. J., March 18, 1912, **24,** 251

Remarks to the Friendly Sons of St. Patrick of Montclair, March 18, 1912, **24**, 253

Remarks at a reception in Fond du Lac, Wis., March 23, 1912, **24**, 257

Report of a busy afternoon in Wisconsin, March 24, 1912, **24**, 258

Report of three addresses in Milwaukee, March 24, 1912, **24**, 259

Report of a conference in New York with New England Democrats, April 4, 1912, **24**, 286

Report of a conference in Washington with Democratic leaders, April 4, 1912, **24**, 287

Report of a busy day in Illinois, April 6, 1912, **24**, 290

Report of an address in Springfield, April 6, 1912, **24**, 292

Report of personal attacks by rivals during the Illinois tour, April 7, 1912, **24**, 299

Report of theft of Wilson's suitcase, April 8, 1912, **24**, 303

Report of an address in Syracuse on politics and business, April 9, 1912, **24**, 307

Reaction to the Illinois primary results, April 9, 1912, **24**, 308

Report of a speech to the University Club of Buffalo, April 10, 1912, **24**, 309

Report of a political address in Buffalo, April 10, 1912, **24**, 311

Remarks at a reception in Pittsburgh, April 11, 1912, **24**, 314

Report of an address in Pittsburgh, April 11, 1912, **24**, 316

Report of an address on tariff reform at a Jefferson Day Dinner in New York, April 14, 1912, **24**, 330

Report of remarks at a reception in Gainesville, Ga., April 17, 1912, **24**, 333

Report of a campaign address in Atlanta, April 17, 1912, **24**, 335

Reports of speeches in Georgia: Albany, April 18, 1912, **24**, 344; Waycross, April 18, 1912, **24**, 347

Report of an address in Jacksonville, April 19, 1912, **24**, 347

Report of an address in Savannah, April 20, 1912, **24**, 349

Report of remarks to college students in Macon, April 21, 1912, **24**, 354

Report of a campaign address in Macon, April 21, 1912, **24**, 355

Report of an address to the Woodrow Wilson Club of Paterson, N. J., April 24, 1912, **24**, 358

Report of a campaign address in Boston, April 27, 1912, **24**, 360

Report of a tour through Massachusetts, April 28, 1912, **24**, 367

Report of a campaign address in Baltimore, April 30, 1912, **24**, 370

Report of an address to the Methodist Social Union of New York, May 2, 1912, **24**, 381

Report of remarks to New Jersey Wilson men, Trenton, May 10, 1912, **24**, 389

Report of an address to the Reform Club of New York, May 12, 1912, **24**, 394

Report of an exchange on immigration with the Italian-American Alliance, May 17, 1912, **24,** 404

Report of an address to the Camden Democratic Club, May 19, 1912, **24,** 407

Report of remarks on laying the cornerstone of the German Hospital in Jersey City, May 20, 1912, **24,** 408

Report of a campaign address in Burlington, N. J., May 21, 1912, **24,** 410

Address at the annual banquet of the Economic Club of New York, May 23, 1912, **24,** 413

Campaign address in Jersey City, May 25, 1912, **24,** 434

Report of remarks to Princeton students, May 28, 1912, **24,** 448

Statement on the results of the New Jersey presidential primary, May 29, 1912, **24,** 449

Welcome to the American Medical Association, Atlantic City, June 4, 1912, **24,** 454

Statement on the Perth Amboy strike, June 15, 1912, **24,** 475

Remarks upon the breaking of the unit rule at the Democratic national convention, June 27, 1912, **24,** 501

Remarks on the balloting in Baltimore, June 28, 1912, **24,** 505

Remarks on William J. Stone's request that he withdraw, June 29, 1912, **24,** 509

No trading and stand fast, June 30, 1912, **24,** 512

Comments on the thirtieth ballot, July 1, 1912, **24,** 516

Family reactions and remarks on learning of his nomination, July 2, 1912, **24,** 522

Report about leaving Sea Girt to write acceptance speech, July 22, 1912, **24,** 562

Statement on immigration restriction, July 22, 1912, **24,** 563

Remarks to a delegation from the United Negro Democracy of New Jersey, July 31, 1912, **24,** 574

Report of conference with William Frank McCombs in New York, Aug. 4, 1912, **24,** 585

Speech accepting the Democratic presidential nomination in Sea Girt, Aug. 7, 1912, **25,** 3

Public letter soliciting campaign funds, Aug. 15, 1912, **25,** 29

Address at a farmers' picnic, Washington Park, N. J., Aug. 15, 1912, **25,** 31

Report of a Jersey Day address at Sea Girt, Aug. 17, 1912, **25,** 43

Remarks to Democratic women at Sea Girt, Aug. 17, 1912, **25,** 44

Report of a riotous affair near Hoboken, Aug. 20, 1912, **25,** 47

Reports of talk with Louis Dembitz Brandeis, Aug. 28, 1912, **25,** 56, 59

Report of a meeting with a delegation of colored men, Sept. 1, 1912, **25,** 65

Luncheon talk in Buffalo, Sept. 2, 1912, **25,** 67

Labor Day address in Buffalo, Sept. 2, 1912, **25,** 69

Evening address in Buffalo, Sept. 2, 1912, **25**, 80

Talk in New York to editors of foreign-language newspapers, Sept. 4, 1912, **25**, 94

Address at a workingmen's dinner in New York, Sept. 4, 1912, **25**, 98

Remarks to an Italian-American delegation at Sea Girt, Sept. 5, 1912, **25**, 107

Statement to the Democrats of New Jersey, Sept. 8, 1912, **25**, 116

Address to the New York Press Club, Sept. 9, 1912, **25**, 118

Address to Spanish War veterans in Atlantic City, Sept. 10, 1912, **25**, 129

Remarks to Democrats in Jersey City, Sept. 11, 1912, **25**, 136

Address on the tariff in Syracuse, Sept. 12, 1912, **25**, 137

Talk to state Democratic leaders in Syracuse, Sept. 12, 1912, **25**, 143

Remarks to newspapermen on the train, Sept. 12, 1912, **25**, 146

Remarks from the rear platform, Union City, Ind., Sept. 16, 1912, **25**, 148

Campaign address in Sioux City, Ia., Sept. 17, 1912, **25**, 148

Speech from a rear platform in Elk Point, S. D., Sept. 17, 1912, **25**, 156

Extracts from a speech in Sioux Falls, S. D., Sept. 17, 1912, **25**, 158

Remarks from a rear platform, Hawarden, S. D., Sept. 17, 1912, **25**, 161

A day in Sioux City, Ia., Sept. 18, 1912, **25**, 162

Talk to the Commercial Club of Minneapolis, Sept. 18, 1912, **25**, 164

Talk at the University of Minnesota, Sept. 18, 1912, **25**, 169

Address at the parade grounds in Minneapolis, Sept. 18, 1912, **25**, 172

Remarks from a rear platform, Michigan City, Ind., Sept. 19, 1912, **25**, 184

Rear Platform talk in Kalamazoo, Sept. 19, 1912, **25**, 185

Campaign address in Detroit, Sept. 19, 1912, **25**, 186

Speech to businessmen in Columbus, Sept. 20, 1912, **25**, 198

Campaign address in Columbus, Sept. 20, 1912, **25**, 203

Speech in Hoboken supporting William Hughes for senator, Sept. 21, 1912, **25**, 213

Campaign address in Scranton, Sept. 23, 1912, **25**, 221

Campaign speech in Hartford on new issues, Sept. 25, 1912, **25**, 234

Address in New Haven opening the Connecticut state campaign, Sept. 25, 1912, **25**, 245

Address to workingmen in Fall River, Mass., Sept. 26, 1912, **25**, 257

Report of a meeting with William Howard Taft, Sept. 26, 1912, **25**, 269

Voting in the primary election in Princeton, Sept. 28, 1912, **25,** 273

Tribute to William Frank McCombs, New York, Sept. 28, 1912, **25,** 274

Statement on the New York Democratic situation, Sept. 29, 1912, **25,** 283

Speech to the New Jersey state Democratic convention, Oct. 1, 1912, **25,** 304

Address on conservation in Indianapolis, Oct. 3, 1912, **25,** 312

Campaign address in Indianapolis proclaiming the New Freedom, Oct. 3, 1912, **25,** 321

Portion of an address in Kokomo, Ind., Oct. 4, 1912, **25,** 330

Speech to workingmen in Peru, Ind., Oct. 4, 1912, **25,** 332

Remarks to the Women's Democratic Club in Omaha, Oct. 5, 1912, **25,** 339

Nonpartisan talk to the Commercial Club of Omaha, Oct. 5, 1912, **25,** 340

Talk to Democratic workers in Lincoln, Oct. 5, 1912, **25,** 347

Campaign address in Lincoln, Oct. 5, 1912, **25,** 350

Address in Colorado Springs, Oct. 7, 1912, **25,** 362

Address in Denver calling for a "second emancipation," Oct. 7, 1912, **25,** 369

Campaign address in Topeka, Oct. 8, 1912, **25,** 378

Address in Kansas City, Oct. 8, 1912, **25,** 385

Remarks on the main issue of the campaign in Springfield, Ill., Oct. 9, 1912, **25,** 390

Speech in the Springfield Coliseum, Oct. 9, 1912, **25,** 393

Remarks in St. Louis to the Democratic Press Association of Missouri, Oct. 9, 1912, **25,** 395

Campaign address in Chicago, Oct. 10, 1912, **25,** 400

Campaign address in Cleveland, Oct. 11, 1912, **25,** 404

Message of sympathy to Roosevelt, Oct. 15, 1912, **25,** 418

Cancels future speeches, Oct. 15, 1912, **25,** 419

Extract from a speech in Georgetown, Del., Oct. 17, 1912, **25,** 424

Extract from a speech in Dover, Oct. 17, 1912, **25,** 424

Campaign address in Wilmington, Del., Oct. 17, 1912, **25,** 425

Campaign address at the Academy of Music in Brooklyn, Oct. 19, 1912, **25,** 435

Campaign address in Carnegie Hall, Oct. 19, 1912, **25,** 441

Report of accomplishments as a typist, Oct. 22, 1912, **25,** 452

An address in the First Presbyterian Church of Trenton, Oct. 23, 1912, **25,** 453

Draft of a statement about campaign contributions, Oct. 25, 1912, **25,** 459

Campaign address at West Chester, Pa., Oct. 28, 1912, **25,** 462

Campaign speech in Montclair, Oct. 29, 1912, **25,** 467

Campaign address in Cape May Court House, Oct. 30, 1912, **25,** 474

Campaign address in Wildwood, Oct. 30, 1912, **25,** 479
Campaign address in Burlington, Oct. 30, 1912, **25,** 485
Thomas E. Watson will not vote for Wilson, Oct. 30, 1912, **25,** 493
Campaign address in Madison Square Garden, Oct. 31, 1912, **25,** 493
Letter to Democratic rallies, Nov. 2, 1912, **25,** 501
Campaign speech in Long Branch, Nov. 2, 1912, **25,** 504
Report of an auto mishap, Nov. 4, 1912, **25,** 508
Report of a scalp wound, Nov. 4, 1912, **25,** 510
Letter to voters, Nov. 4, 1912, **25,** 511
Last speeches of the campaign in Passaic and Paterson, Nov. 5, 1912, **25,** 513
Voting in Princeton, Nov. 5, 1912, **25,** 517
Mrs. Wilson and the President-elect, Nov. 5, 1912, **25,** 518
Remarks on his victory to Princeton students and neighbors, Nov. 5, 1912, **25,** 520
President-elect declines further statements, Nov. 6, 1912, **25,** 523
Remarks at the dedication of Wilson Cottage at the State Home for Girls in Trenton, Nov. 12, 1912, **25,** 536
A Report about the purchase of his boyhood home, Nov. 12, 1912, **25,** 539
Remarks upon arriving in Bermuda, Nov. 18, 1912, **25,** 551
Objects to being photographed, Nov. 22, 1912, **25,** 556
Indigestion prevents visit to the Bermuda House of Assembly, Nov. 26, 1912, **25,** 562
Remarks to the Bermuda House of Assembly, Dec. 2, 1912, **25,** 575
Return from Bermuda, Dec. 16, 1912, **25,** 589
Statement of support for New Jersey progressive Democrats, Dec. 17, 1912, **25,** 590
Remarks upon returning from Bermuda, Dec. 17, 1912, **25,** 591
Address to the Southern Society of New York, Dec. 17, 1912, **25,** 593
Address at Mary Baldwin Seminary in Staunton, Va., Dec. 28, 1912, **25,** 626
Address at birthday banquet in Staunton, Dec. 28, 1912, **25,** 632
Salutation of an unfinished letter, Feb. 1, 1908, **17,** 611
Summer plans, June 18, 1904, **15,** 391; June 16, 1906, **16,** 427
Surgery and convalescence and general health, Jan. 7, 1905, **15,** 576; Jan. 7, 1905, **15,** 577; Jan. 21, 1905, **15,** 579; Feb. 18, 1905, **16,** 3; neuritis attack, Jan. 8, 1908, **17,** 587
Telephonic message to William Jennings Bryan, June 29, 1912, **24,** 508, 509
Writings
Preface to *The Proposed Graduate College of Princeton University* by Andrew Fleming West, Feb. 17, 1903, **14,** 361
Introduction to *The Handbook of Princeton*, Aug. 1, 1904, **15,** 427
Draft of an article on Princeton's new plan of study, Aug. 29, 1904, **15,** 450

The Preceptors, April 28, 1905, **16,** 84

A tribute to the Reverend Dr. John Hendrik de Vries, May 24, 1905, **16,** 105

The Princeton Preceptorial System, June 1, 1905, **16,** 107

New Plans for Princeton, June 24, 1905, **16,** 146

The Southern Colonist, March 1, 1907, **17,** 51

Grover Cleveland, Man of Integrity, March 17, 1907, **17,** 73

Education and Democracy, May 4, 1907, **17,** 131

Politics, 1857–1907, July 31, 1907, **17,** 309

The Personal Factor in Education, Aug. 1, 1907, **17,** 325

A Credo, Aug. 6, 1907, **17,** 335

Petition about the admission of automobiles to Bermuda, Feb. 1, 1908, **17,** 609

*Constitutional Government in the United States*, March 24, 1908, **18,** 69

    I    What is Constitutional Government?, March 24, 1908, **18,** 69

    II   The Place of the United States in Constitutional Development, March 24, 1908, **18,** 85

    III  The President of the United States, March 24, 1908, **18,** 104

    IV  The House of Representatives, March 24, 1908, **18,** 123

    V   The Senate, March 24, 1908, **18,** 142

    VI  The Courts, March 24, 1908, **18,** 162

    VII The States and the Federal Government, March 24, 1908, **18,** 182

    VIII Party Government in the United States, March 24, 1908, **18,** 199

A tribute to Charles William Eliot, Dec. 1, 1908, **18,** 528

Draft of a report about a Cleveland memorial, March 29, 1909, **19,** 126

My Ideal of the True University, July 6, 1909, **19,** 295

The Man Behind the Trust, Aug. 3, 1909, **19,** 324

What Is a College For?, Aug. 18, 1909, **19,** 334

The Tariff Make-Believe, Sept. 5, 1909, **19,** 359

Statement about the Bible, Oct. 8, 1909, **19,** 406

The Democratic Opportunity, Nov. 1, 1909, **19,** 465

Outline of an article on the reorganization of the University, Nov. 29, 1909, **19,** 536

The country and the colleges, Feb. 24, 1910, **20,** 157

Hide-and-Seek Politics, March 2, 1910, **20,** 192

Draft of a platform for the Democratic party of Pennsylvania, April 4, 1910, **20,** 315

To First Voters, June 6, 1910, **20,** 502

Life and Education, Aug. 1, 1910, **21,** 32

Platform of the New Jersey Democratic party: proposed, Aug. 9, 1910, **21,** 43; printed, Sept. 15, 1910, **21,** 94

New Jersey Democratic Platform of 1911, Oct. 3, 1911, **23,** 382

Outline of a Democratic platform, June 16, 1912, **24,** 476; planks, June 11, 1912, **24,** 470; June 16, 1912, **24,** 477
New Jersey Democratic platform of 1912, Oct. 1, 1912, **25,** 305

COLLATERAL MATERIALS

Robert Bridges, Poems
  The Pledge of Seventy-Nine, June 18, 1904, **15,** 389
  Cultural and Structural Entity, May 23, 1908, **18,** 307
Diaries
  Edward Mandell House, Sept. 24, 1912, **25,** 233; Sept. 28, 1912, **25,** 283; Sept. 30, 1912, **25,** 286; Oct. 12, 1912, **25,** 415; Oct. 15, 1912, **25,** 421; Oct. 16, 1912, **25,** 423; Oct. 20, 1912, **25,** 448; Nov. 2, 1912, **25,** 507; Nov. 8, 1912, **25,** 532; Nov. 16, 1912, **25,** 550; Dec. 18, 1912, **25,** 610; Dec. 19, 1912, **25,** 614; Dec. 23, 1912, **25,** 621
  William Starr Myers, Feb. 16, 1906, **16,** 314; Feb. 12, 1907, **17,** 35; March 2, 1907, **17,** 58; June 11, 1907, **17,** 209; Sept. 26, 1907, **17,** 403; Sept. 30, 1907, **17,** 408; Oct. 7, 1907, **17,** 424; Oct. 21, 1907, **17,** 448; Oct. 31, 1907, **17,** 462; April 14, 1908, **18,** 271; May 8, 1908, **18,** 293; May 20, 1908, **18,** 302
  Oswald Garrison Villard, Aug. 14, 1912, **25,** 24
  Mary Yates, July 31, 1908, **18,** 386
Editorial Notes
  The New Princeton Course of Study, April 25, 1904, **15,** 277
  Wilson at the Meeting of the Board of Trustees on January 13, 1910, **20,** 6
  Colonel Harvey's Plan for Wilson's Entry into Politics, Feb. 20, 1910, **20,** 146
  The Lawyers' Club Conference, July 8, 1910, **20,** 565
Editorials
  Charleston, S. C., *News and Courier*, on Southern conservatism, Jan. 22, 1906, **16,** 286
  *Daily Princetonian*, about the fence surrounding Prospect, Oct. 3, 1904, **15,** 503; Oct. 13, 1904, **15,** 509; on the Quadrangle Plan, Oct. 2, 1907, **17,** 411
  *Kansas City Star*, about Wilson, May 12, 1905, **16,** 97
  *The New York Times*, on the Graduate College fight at Princeton, Feb. 3, 1910, **20,** 74
  First Presbyterian Church of Princeton, Minutes of the Session, Feb. 3, 1906, **16,** 301
  George Brinton McClellan Harvey, speech proposing Wilson for the presidency, Feb. 3, 1906, **16,** 299
  Edmond Kelly, excerpt from *Twentieth Century Socialism*, Sept. 27, 1910, **21,** 175
Letters and Telegrams
  Frank Frost Abbott to Henry Burchard Fine, March 2, 1908, **18,** 8

Charles Beatty Alexander to the Board of Trustees of Princeton University, Feb. 6, 1906, **16,** 304

Joseph Smith Auerbach to Moses Taylor Pyne, June 29, 1904, **15,** 399

Stockton Axson to John Van Antwerp MacMurray, Dec. 14, 1905, **16,** 567; Dec. 16, 1905, **16,** 569

James Mark Baldwin to the Board of Trustees, Oct. 4, 1903, **15,** 13

James Mark Baldwin to Moses Taylor Pyne, Dec. 22, 1903, **15,** 104; Dec. 26, 1903, **15,** 109

James Edward Bathgate, Jr., to William Royal Wilder, Jan. 29, 1910, **20,** 67

Gutzon Borglum to Benjamin Wistar Morris III, Aug. 8, 1905, **16,** 173

Robert Bridges to Cornelius Cuyler Cuyler, Oct. 8, 1902, **14,** 149

Frank Obadiah Briggs to James Richard Nugent, Oct. 8, 1910, **21,** 291

John Stewart Bryan to Richard Heath Dabney, Jan. 26, 1912, **24,** 97

William Bull to Ellen Axson Wilson, May 5, 1904, **15,** 315

Henry Conrad Bunn to Cornelius Cuyler Cuyler, Oct. 18, 1904, **15,** 525

Howard Crosby Butler to Moses Taylor Pyne, Dec. 22, 1909, **19,** 621

John Lambert Cadwalader to Henry Wheeler de Forest, March 10, 1908, **18,** 35

John Lambert Cadwalader to Moses Taylor Pyne, Dec. 30, 1909, **19,** 661

Grover Cleveland to Moses Taylor Pyne, April 8, 1908, **18,** 229

Grover Cleveland to Edward Wright Sheldon, March 14, 1908, **18,** 66

Gilbert Fairchild Close to Arthur Twining Hadley, Nov. 26, 1908, **18,** 524

Gilbert Fairchild Close to Howard Houston Henry, July 7, 1910, **20,** 562

Gilbert Fairchild Close to Moses Taylor Pyne, Dec. 7, 1907, **17,** 552

Ralph Adams Cram to Edward Wright Sheldon, March 30, 1908, **18,** 250

Cornelius Cuyler Cuyler to the Board of Trustees of Princeton University, Oct. 21, 1904, **15,** 525

Winthrop More Daniels to John Grier Hibben, Aug. 9, 1907, **17,** 342

Winthrop More Daniels to Charles Worthen Spencer, Dec. 12, 1909, **19,** 615

Charles Whitney Darrow to the stockholders of Princeton University Press, Aug. 1, 1907, **17,** 352

John David Davis to Moses Taylor Pyne, Dec. 2, 1903, **15,** 60

Henry Wheeler de Forest to John Lambert Cadwalader, Dec. 22, 1908, **18,** 565

John DeWitt to John Grier Hibben, June 14, 1906, **16,** 425

John DeWitt to Moses Taylor Pyne, Jan. 22, 1910, **20,** 47; Jan. 27, 1910, **20,** 63

John Dixon to Andrew Fleming West, Jan. 24, 1910, **20,** 51; Feb. 11, 1910, **20,** 121

Cleveland Hoadley Dodge to Henry Burling Thompson, April 14, 1910, **20,** 359; Oct. 25, 1910, **21,** 435

Henry Green Duffield to James Mark Baldwin, Jan. 15, 1904, **15,** 132

Henry Green Duffield to Melancthon Williams Jacobus, Jan. 26, 1909, **19,** 22

Henry Burchard Fine to Henry Burling Thompson, Jan. 2, 1910, **19,** 705

Henry Burchard Fine to Cleveland Hoadley Dodge, March 1, 1910, **20,** 191

Henry Burchard Fine to Edward Wright Sheldon, Feb. 26, 1910, **20,** 182

David M. Flynn to James Kerney, Nov. 3, 1910, **21,** 542 (2)

George Corning Fraser to Henry Burchard Fine, March 18, 1907, **17,** 83

Arthur Lincoln Frothingham, Jr., to the Board of Trustees of Princeton University, May 10, 1905, **16,** 93

Robert Garrett to Archibald Douglas Russell, Jan. 26, 1907, **17,** 20

Raleigh Colston Gildersleeve to Moses Taylor Pyne, June 20, 1905, **16,** 144

Carter Glass to Henry Parker Willis, Dec. 29, 1912, **25,** 643

Samuel Gompers to the Executive Council of the American Federation of Labor, Dec. 21, 1912, **25,** 614

Henry Woodhull Green to Moses Taylor Pyne, Jan. 26, 1906, **16,** 289

Edward E. Grosscup to John James Gifford, May 23, 1912, **24,** 429

Arthur Twining Hadley to Abbott Lawrence Lowell, May 31, 1910, **20,** 487

Arthur Twining Hadley and others to Walter Chauncey Camp and others, Dec. 31, 1909, **19,** 672

Abram Woodruff Halsey to Ellen Axson Wilson, Oct. 8, 1912, **25,** 390

John Maynard Harlan to Edward Nash Hurley, July 4, 1910, **20,** 557

Harper and Brothers to Frederick A. Steuert, Aug. 26, 1902, **14,** 110

George McLean Harper to Wilson Farrand, Feb. 3, 1910, **20,** 73

George Brinton McClellan Harvey to Stockton Axson, Jan. 16, 1907, **17,** 9; Jan. 23, 1907, **17,** 12

George Brinton McClelland Harvey to the readers of *Harper's Weekly*, Jan. 20, 1912, **24,** 45

Bayard Henry to Moses Taylor Pyne, Jan. 2, 1906, **16,** 277

Bayard Henry to Henry Burling Thompson, July 13, 1907, **17,** 303

John Grier Hibben to Ellen Axson Wilson, Sept. 4, 1907, **17,** 372

Edward Mandell House to Charles Allen Culberson, Oct. 20, 1911, **23,** 470

Edward Nash Hurley to John Maynard Harlan, July 2, 1910, **20,** 556

Edward Nash Hurley to James Smith, Jr., July 5, 1910, **20,** 558

Melancthon Williams Jacobus to Cleveland Hoadley Dodge, Feb. 15, 1910, **20,** 128

Melancthon Williams Jacobus to Edward Wright Sheldon, Jan. 27, 1910, **20,** 61; March 8, 1910, **20,** 221; May 27, 1910, **20,** 481

Melancthon Williams Jacobus to Henry Burling Thompson, April 20, 1909, **19,** 168; June 28, 1909, **19,** 273; Dec. 23, 1909, **19,** 625; Jan. 3, 1910, **19,** 709; Jan. 22, 1910, **20,** 45

Charles William Leverett Johnson to Susannah Batcheller Johnson, Dec. 17, 1902, **14,** 296; April 16, 1903, **14,** 411

Adrian Hoffman Joline to the Editor of the *Princeton Alumni Weekly,* Oct. 9, 1907, **17,** 428

David Benton Jones to Henry van Dyke, July 10, 1907, **17,** 273

Thomas Davies Jones to Cleveland Hoadley Dodge, Feb. 18, 1910, **20,** 142

Thomas Davies Jones to Cyrus Hall McCormick, March 7, 1910, **20,** 219

Thomas Davies Jones to William Cooper Procter, Jan. 26, 1910, **20,** 97

W. Frank Kelly to Thomas Bell Love, Sept. 6, 1911, **23,** 309

John Worth Kern to Samuel Gompers, Aug. 10, 1912, **25,** 22

Francis Larkin, Jr., to Edward Wright Sheldon, April 11, 1908, **18,** 262

Thomas Bell Love to Walter Measday, March 28, 1912, **24,** 269

Abbott Lawrence Lowell to Arthur Twining Hadley, Jan. 13, 1910, **20,** 12; May 20, 1910, **20,** 487

Charles Williston McAlpin to Robert Garrett, Jan. 20, 1909, **19,** 4

Charles Williston McAlpin to G. McArthur Sullivan, Dec. 6, 1909, **19,** 557

Charles McCarthy to Charles Richard Van Hise, July 16, 1912, **24,** 554

William Frank McCombs to William Jennings Bryan, June 21, 1912, **24,** 492

John James McCook to the Board of Trustees of Princeton University, Feb. 5, 1906, **16,** 303

Cyrus Hall McCormick to Robert Bridges, March 26, 1909, **19,** 120, 123

Cyrus Hall McCormick to Henry Burchard Fine, March 24, 1909, **19,** 140

Cyrus Hall McCormick to Thomas Davies Jones, March 8, 1910, **20,** 220; April 26, 1910, **20,** 393; April 28, 1910, **20,** 403

Cyrus Hall McCormick to Edward Wright Sheldon, March 4, 1910, **20,** 211; March 8, 1910, **20,** 219; April 5, 1910, **20,** 321; May 11, 1910, **20,** 432; May 20, 1910, **20,** 460

McHugh to Walter Measday, Jan. 18, 1912, **24,** 49

Charles Howard McIlwain to Winthrop More Daniels, March 22, 1905, **16,** 41

Charles Follen McKim to Junius Spencer Morgan, Aug. 26, 1904, **15,** 449

Robert Fulton McMahon to the Editor of the New York *Sun*, March 21, 1910, **20,** 278

William Francis Magie to DeWitt Clinton Jones, Jr., Dec. 8, 1909, **19,** 576

William Jay Magie to Grover Cleveland, March 13, 1908, **18,** 64

William Jay Magie to Edward Wright Sheldon, Jan. 24, 1910, **20,** 51

Allan Marquand to the Board of Trustees of Princeton University, March 2, 1905, **16,** 17; Oct. 14, 1907, **17,** 433

Allan Marquand to Moses Taylor Pyne, Feb. 5, 1910, **20,** 81

James Edgar Martine to John Sharp Williams, Nov. 13, 1910, **22,** 94

Walter Measday to Edward Mandell House, Oct. 17, 1911, **23,** 463

Walter Measday to Thomas Bell Love, March 20, 1912, **24,** 256; March 30, 1912, **24,** 270

Junius Spencer Morgan to Henry Burling Thompson, Jan. 18, 1909, **18,** 630

Franklin Blake Morse to Charles Williston McAlpin, March 26, 1904, **15,** 212

Harold Griffith Murray to Cornelius Cuyler Cuyler, July 13, 1904, **15,** 414

Harold Griffith Murray to Cleveland Hoadley Dodge, June 5, 1906, **16,** 415; Oct. 17, 1906, **16,** 458; June 1, 1907, **17,** 170; Oct. 15, 1907, **17,** 435

Harold Griffith Murray to Andrew Clerk Imbrie, Sept. 12, 1907, **17,** 381

Alexander Thomas Ormond and others to the Board of Trustees of Princeton University, Oct. 21, 1905, **16,** 203

Francis Landey Patton to Cuyler, Morgan and Company, Aug. 2, 1902, **14,** 48

Francis Landey Patton to Moses Taylor Pyne, Aug. 2, 1902, **14,** 47

Henry Cooper Pitney, Jr., to the Members of the Washington Association of New Jersey, Nov. 10, 1903, **15,** 49

Henry Cooper Pitney, Jr., to Jonathan William Roberts, Nov. 14, 1903, **15,** 51

William Cooper Procter to Thomas Davies Jones, Feb. 6, 1910, **20,** 100

William Cooper Procter to Moses Taylor Pyne, Oct. 4, 1909, **19,** 403; Oct. 6, 1909, **19,** 406; Oct. 13, 1909, **19,** 413; Oct. 20, 1909,

**19,** 434; Oct. 25, 1909, **19,** 447; Jan. 12, 1910, **20,** 3; Jan. 22, 1910, **20,** 47; Jan. 30, 1910, **20,** 65; Feb. 8, 1910, **20,** 90; Oct. 25, 1909, **20,** 105; Jan. 12, 1910, **20,** 106; April 26, 1910, **20,** 396; May 13, 1910, **20,** 454; June 6, 1910, **20,** 506

William Cooper Procter to Andrew Fleming West, May 8, 1909, **19,** 189; Dec. 28, 1909, **19,** 652; May 8, 1909, **20,** 104; Feb. 23, 1910, **20,** 156; March 29, 1910, **20,** 303

Moses Taylor Pyne to James Mark Baldwin, Dec. 29, 1903, **15,** 112

Moses Taylor Pyne to Edward Capps, Dec. 7, 1909, **19,** 559

Moses Taylor Pyne to Ralph Adams Cram, May 18, 1909, **19,** 200

Moses Taylor Pyne to Wilson Farrand, Jan. 25, 1910, **20,** 56

Moses Taylor Pyne to Henry Woodhull Green, Jan. 18, 1910, **20,** 29

Moses Taylor Pyne to Bayard Henry, July 17, 1907, **17,** 306; April 20, 1910, **20,** 377

Moses Taylor Pyne to Andrew Clerk Imbrie, Oct. 23, 1907, **17,** 453

Moses Taylor Pyne to Cyrus Hall McCormick, Nov. 3, 1909, **19,** 481

Moses Taylor Pyne to William Cooper Procter, May 12, 1909, **19,** 194; Oct. 5, 1909, **19,** 404; Oct. 26, 1909, **19,** 449; Jan. 15, 1910, **20,** 17; May 10, 1910, **20,** 431; May 24, 1910, **20,** 470; Oct. 25, 1910, **21,** 434

Moses Taylor Pyne to Joseph Bernard Shea, Dec. 1, 1909, **19,** 544; Dec. 18, 1909, **19,** 608; Jan. 15, 1910, **20,** 19; May 19, 1910, **20,** 460; May 26, 1910, **20,** 476; May 31, 1910, **20,** 491

Moses Taylor Pyne to Edward Wright Sheldon, March 10, 1910, **20,** 228

Moses Taylor Pyne to Alexander Marshall Thompson, Feb. 16, 1910, **20,** 131

Moses Taylor Pyne to Andrew Fleming West, March 3, 1910, **20,** 210

Moses Taylor Pyne to Charles Wood, Jan. 18, 1910, **20,** 28

William Belden Reed, Jr., and John Douglas Kilpatrick to the Board of Trustees of Princeton University, May 15, 1903, **14,** 465

Ernest Cushing Richardson to Moses Taylor Pyne, Oct. 27, 1906, **16,** 473; March 20, 1910, **20,** 269

Jonathan William Roberts to the Members of the Washington Association of New Jersey, Nov. 14, 1903, **15,** 52

Jonathan William Roberts to Henry Cooper Pitney, Jr., Nov. 14, 1903, **15,** 51

Margaret Olivia Slocum Sage to John Lambert Cadwalader, June 3, 1910, **20,** 498

Joseph Bernard Shea to Moses Taylor Pyne, Jan. 17, 1910, **20,** 23; May 16, 1910, **20,** 458

Edward Wright Sheldon to John Lambert Cadwalader, Oct. 18, 1909, **19,** 434

Edward Wright Sheldon to Henry Green Duffield, Dec. 12, 1910, **22,** 177

Edward Wright Sheldon to Melancthon Williams Jacobus, Jan. 31, 1910, **20,** 68; March 10, 1910, **20,** 227

Edward Wright Sheldon to Francis Larkin, Jr., April 7, 1908, **18,** 227

Edward Wright Sheldon to Charles Williston McAlpin, April 13, 1908, **18,** 261

Edward Wright Sheldon to Cyrus Hall McCormick, Jan. 5, 1910, **19,** 730; May 8, 1910, **20,** 425; May 9, 1910, **20,** 427; May 11, 1910, **20,** 433; May 12, 1910, **20,** 445; May 27, 1910, **20,** 479

Edward Wright Sheldon to Moses Taylor Pyne, March 9, 1910, **20,** 224; March 11, 1910, **20,** 236; May 9, 1910, **20,** 428

Edward Wright Sheldon to Henry Burling Thompson, Feb. 17, 1910, **20,** 137; March 12, 1910, **20,** 238

Gwynn T. Shepperd to Henry St. George Tucker, Jan. 1, 1907, **16,** 543

William Milligan Sloane, Bayard Stockton, and Francis Larkin, Jr., to the Board of Trustees of Princeton University, Oct. 15, 1906, **16,** 458

William Milligan Sloane and others to Moses Taylor Pyne, Nov. 8, 1909, **19,** 488

William Milligan Sloane and Bayard Stockton to the Board of Trustees of Princeton University, June 8, 1910, **20,** 506

James Smith, Jr., to Edward Nash Hurley, June 28, 1910, **20,** 548; July 6, 1910, **20,** 561

Augustine Thomas Smythe to George Howe III, Nov. 9, 1910, **22,** 34

Charles Worthen Spencer to Winthrop More Daniels, Dec. 10, 1909, **19,** 613; Dec. 13, 1909, **19,** 616; Dec. 20, 1909, **19,** 617

Alfred Ernest Stearns to Charles Grosvenor Osgood, Nov. 15, 1906, **16,** 486

Frederick A. Steuert to Harper and Brothers, Aug. 25, 1902, **14,** 108

Josiah Strong to George Mason LaMonte, June 24, 1912, **24,** 498

Duane Reed Stuart to Andrew Fleming West, April 29, 1905, **16,** 87

Charles Willis Thompson to Reuben Adiel Bull, Dec. 12, 1912, **25,** 588

Charles Willis Thompson to Berenice Morrow Thompson, Oct. 6, 1912, **25,** 360; Oct. 6, 1912, **25,** 361

Henry Burling Thompson to Ralph Adams Cram, Jan. 4, 1910, **19,** 712

Henry Burling Thompson to Cleveland Hoadley Dodge, Feb. 18, 1907, **17,** 41; Sept. 10, 1907, **17,** 379; Oct. 2, 1907, **17,** 410; Oct. 15, 1907, **434;** Jan. 3, 1910, **19,** 711; Jan. 14, 1910, **20,** 14; March 16, 1910, **20,** 254; April 15, 1910, **20,** 361

Henry Burling Thompson to Melancthon Williams Jacobus, Oct.

26, 1908, **18,** 473; Nov. 27, 1908, **18,** 526; May 17, 1909, **19,** 197; June 17, 1909, **19,** 256; June 30, 1909, **19,** 276; July 27, 1909, **19,** 320; Jan. 6, 1910, **19,** 732

Henry Burling Thompson to Thomas Davies Jones, Feb. 7, 1910, **20,** 87; Feb. 26, 1910, **20,** 183

Henry Burling Thompson to Cyrus Hall McCormick, Oct. 9, 1908, **18,** 444

Henry Burling Thompson to Junius Spencer Morgan, Jan. 5, 1909, **18,** 592; Jan. 18, 1909, **18,** 630

Henry Burling Thompson to Harold Griffith Murray, July 16, 1907, **17,** 285

Henry Burling Thompson to Moses Taylor Pyne, July 30, 1907, **17,** 308; Dec. 31, 1909, **19,** 672; April 5, 1910, **20,** 324

Henry Burling Thompson to Edward Wright Sheldon, Jan. 7, 1909, **18,** 592; Jan. 15, 1910, **20,** 16; Feb. 15, 1910, **20,** 128; March 14, 1910, **20,** 241; May 31, 1910, **20,** 488, 489

James MacNaughton Thompson to Moses Taylor Pyne, July 30, 1904, **15,** 432

Henry St. George Tucker to Newton Diehl Baker, July 22, 1912, **24,** 569

Joseph Patrick Tumulty to James E. W. Cook, Jan. 18, 1911, **22,** 356

Joseph Patrick Tumulty to Henry Lee Higginson, Oct. 16, 1912, **25,** 423

Joseph Patrick Tumulty to Edward Mandell House, Dec. 17, 1912, **25,** 603

Henry van Dyke to Stockton Axson, March 5, 1907, **17,** 59

Henry van Dyke to Moses Taylor Pyne, Jan. 6, 1910, **19,** 739

Paul van Dyke to the Editor of the *Princeton Alumni Weekly*, Oct. 2, 1907, **17,** 413

Paul van Dyke to Moses Taylor Pyne, May 7, 1910, **20,** 422

Oswald Garrison Villard to Susan Walker Fitz Gerald, Aug. 14, 1912, **25,** 29

John Wesley Wescott to Joseph Patrick Tumulty, Feb. 22, 1911, **22,** 451

Andrew Fleming West to John Dixon, Jan. 25, 1910, **20,** 57

Andrew Fleming West to Matthew Corry Fleming, March 21, 1910, **20,** 277

Andrew Fleming West to William Cooper Procter, Oct. 5, 1909, **19,** 403

Andrew Fleming West to Moses Taylor Pyne, May 22, 1910, **20,** 465

Walter Lincoln Whittlesey to Winthrop More Daniels, May 3, 1906, **16,** 385

William Royal Wilder to Charles Williston McAlpin, June 12, 1904, **15,** 374

Louis Wiley to William Frank McCombs, Sept. 20, 1911, **23,** 352

Henry Parker Willis to Carter Glass, Dec. 31, 1912, **25,** 650

Ellen Axson Wilson to Richard Heath Dabney, Feb. 9, 1912, **24,** 147; March 13, 1912, **24,** 244

Ellen Axson Wilson to Robert Ewing, Jan. 12, 1912, **24,** 40

Ellen Axson Wilson to Anna Harris, March 11, 1905, **16,** 28; Dec. 1, 1906, **16,** 493; Feb. 12, 1907, **17,** 33; May 5, 1907, **17,** 137

Ellen Axson Wilson to John Grier Hibben, Feb. 10, 1912, **24,** 149

Ellen Axson Wilson to Florence Stevens Hoyt, June 27, 1906, **16,** 429

Ellen Axson Wilson to Mary Eloise Hoyt, Dec. 15, 1902, **14,** 293; June 12, 1906, **16,** 423

Ellen Axson Wilson to Charles Williston McAlpin, Jan. 3, 1905, **15,** 575

Ellen Axson Wilson to Mary Allen Hulbert Peck, Jan. 10, 1912, **24,** 27

Ellen Axson Wilson to Edith Kermit Carow Roosevelt, Oct. 15, 1912, **25,** 418

Ellen Axson Wilson to Nancy Saunders Toy, Sept. 23, 1912, **25,** 232

Ellen Axson Wilson to John Wesley Wescott, Feb. 23, 1912, **24,** 189

Ellen Axson Wilson to Frederic Yates, Dec. 20, 1910, **22,** 234

Frederic Yates to Ellen Axson Wilson, Sept. 2, 1908, **18,** 416

Charles Augustus Young to the Board of Trustees of Princeton University, Dec. 6, 1904, **15,** 553

John Wesley Young to the Board of Trustees of Princeton University, July 6, 1905, **16,** 152

News Reports

Columbia University's 150th anniversary celebration, Nov. 12, 1904, **15,** 533

Meeting of the trustees of the Carnegie Foundation, Nov. 17, 1905, **16,** 224

The vote of the Second Presbyterian Church of Princeton against merger with the First Church, Nov. 11, 1905, **16,** 218

Adrian Hoffman Joline's comments about Wilson's criticism of Bryan, Jan. 7, 1912, **24,** 5

Princeton University: reports of alumni affairs and campus activities

Shakespearean reading at Princeton University by Dr. Horace Howard Furness, Dec. 3, 1902, **14,** 259

Isham dinner in New York, Jan. 24, 1903, **14,** 330

American Rhodes Scholarships: conference in Philadelphia, Jan. 31, 1903, **14,** 336; examinations, April 23, 1904, **15,** 273

Mid-year examination failures, March 7, 1903, **14,** 383

Report of Andrew Fleming West's address to the Princeton Club of Albany, March 28, 1903, **14,** 400

The planning and construction of Lake Carnegie, Nov. 29, 1903, **15,** 57; Dec. 5, 1903, **15,** 66; Nov. 30, 1904, **15,** 549; Jan. 6, 1905, **15,** 575; Jan. 19, 1905, **15,** 578

Report about the plans for an alumni dormitory, April 16, 1904, **15,** 251

Honor system regulations, Jan. 29, 1904, **15,** 145; Feb. 6, 1904, **15,** 160

Campus improvements, Sept. 27, 1904, **15,** 493; May 10, 1905, **16,** 92

Seniors' demonstration about President's fence, Oct. 9, 1904, **15,** 507

Report about architectural plans for the alumni dormitory, Jan. 14, 1905, **15,** 577

The planning of McCosh Hall, March 4, 1905, **16,** 20; May 13, 1905, **16,** 100; May 20, 1905, **16,** 104; Nov. 4, 1905, **16,** 211; March 10, 1906, **16,** 329

New Faculty Room in Nassau Hall, Oct. 7, 1905, **16,** 190; Nov. 4, 1905, **16,** 212

Report about the progress of the Committee of Fifty, Feb. 3, 1906, **16,** 291

Naming of Patton Hall, March 10, 1906, **16,** 329

Addition to Blair Hall, April 7, 1906, **16,** 356

Furnishing the Tower Room of Seventy-Nine Hall, June 9, 1906, **16,** 419

Andrew Fleming West's invitation to the Presidency of the Massachusetts Institute of Technology, Oct. 20, 1906, **16,** 464

Henry van Dyke's resignation, March 4, 1907, **17,** 58

The gift of the Mather Sundial, March 20, 1907, **17,** 87

News report about a five-class reunion in New York, April 8, 1908, **18,** 228

Construction of a new Physical Laboratory, June 6, 1908, **18,** 322

Plans for the Sage Dormitory (Holder Hall), Nov. 25, 1908, **18,** 522

The Old North Tigers, Feb. 19, 1909, **19,** 63

Princeton University: Trustees' and Deans' reports, committee reports, resolutions, statements, and related materials

Report by Cornelius Cuyler Cuyler for the Committee on Grounds and Buildings to the President and Board of Trustees, Oct. 20, 1902, **14,** 149

Two resolutions by Grover Cleveland, Oct. 21, 1902, **14,** 162

Reports by Samuel Ross Winans to the Board of Trustees' Committee on Morals and Discipline, Oct. 21, 1902, **14,** 162; Dec. 11, 1902, **14,** 278; March 12, 1903, **14,** 389; June 8, 1903, **14,** 477

Memorandum by Henry van Dyke on sophomore English, Jan. 22, 1903, **14,** 329

Report by Moses Taylor Pyne to the Board of Trustees on the club situation, June 8, 1903, **14,** 479

Suggestion by John Howell Westcott for a classical curriculum, Oct. 19, 1903, **15,** 18

Plan by Winthrop More Daniels for a history and economics curriculum, Jan. 12, 1904, **15,** 122

Financial statement of Princeton University, 1903–1904, Aug. 10, 1904, **15,** 437

Committee on Finance to the Board of Trustees, Oct. 21, 1904, **15,** 525

Report by Archibald Douglas Russell for the Committee on Grounds and Buildings to the President and Board of Trustees, March 14, 1907, **17,** 71

A resolution regarding the entertainment of guest preachers and the conduct of Sunday Chapel services, June 10, 1907, **17,** 197

Plan by Andrew Clerk Imbrie for the organization of the Graduate Council, March 29, 1909, **19,** 128

Recommendations by Henry Burchard Fine on the Departments of Mathematics and Physics, March 31, 1909, **19,** 137

Proposed resolution of the Board of Trustees regarding Wilson's resignation, Oct. 19, 1910, **21,** 353

Petition by students in Wilson's course in jurisprudence, Oct. 21, 1910, **21,** 381

Minute of the Faculty on Wilson's resignation, Nov. 22, 1910, **22,** 79

Testimonial volume presented to Wilson by Princeton undergraduates, Jan. 9, 1911, **22,** 322

Henry Burchard Fine to the Board of Trustees' Committee on Morals and Discipline, Oct. 21, 1903, **15,** 20; Dec. 10, 1903, **15,** 75; March 10, 1904, **15,** 186; June 13, 1904, **15,** 376; Oct. 21, 1904, **15,** 523; March 9, 1905, **16,** 24; Oct. 21, 1905, **16,** 200; Dec. 14, 1905, **16,** 265; March 8, 1906, **16,** 325; Oct. 20, 1906, **16,** 466; March 14, 1907, **17,** 68; Oct. 17, 1907, **17,** 438; April 9, 1908, **18,** 243; Oct. 15, 1908, **18,** 457

Edward Graham Elliott, to the Board of Trustees' Committee on Morals and Discipline, April 14, 1910, **20,** 355

Special Committee on the Halls to the Board of Trustees, March 7, 1906, **16,** 325

Grover Cleveland for the Committee on the Graduate School to the Board of Trustees, June 10, 1907, **17,** 197

Report of the Trustees' Committee on upper-class clubs to the Board of Trustees and recommendations of the Alumni Committee on undergraduate social conditions, April 8, 1908, **18,** 229

Reports of the Committee of Fifty to the Board of Trustees, June 1, 1907, **17,** 170; Oct. 15, 1907, **17,** 435; June 1, 1908, **18,** 315; April 1, 1909, **19,** 144

Report of the Committee on the Graduate School to the Board of Trustees of Princeton University, April 9, 1908, **18,** 247

Report of the Special Committee of Five to the Board of Trustees, Feb. 10, 1910, **20,** 92

Report of the Trustees' Committee on the Graduate School to the Board of Trustees, April 14, 1910, **20,** 354

Andrew Fleming West to the Trustees' Committee on the Graduate School, May 13, 1907, **17,** 142

Memorandum by John Howell Westcott about the Classics Department Faculty, May 29, 1907, **17,** 161

Report of the Committee on Plan and Scope to the Committee of Fifty, Oct. 15, 1908, **18,** 452

Report of the Committee of Three to the Board of Trustees on the future of the Committee of Fifty, Jan. 13, 1909, **18,** 619

Reports to the President of the Faculty Committee on the Graduate School, Oct. 19, 1909, **19,** 426; supplementary report, Jan. 10, 1910, **19,** 754

Resolution on the Procter gift by the Class of 1894, Jan. 31, 1910, **20,** 67

Statement of Howard Crosby Butler, Oct. 19, 1909, **19,** 433; Feb. 10, 1910, **20,** 113

Memorandum by Edward Wright Sheldon and others of the proposed settlement of the Graduate School question, May 9, 1910, **20,** 428

Resolution of greetings and thanks to Wilson by the Plainfield Democratic Club, Nov. 9, 1909, **19,** 493

Reviews of *A History of the American People*:
Chicago *Dial* (Francis Wayland Shepardson), Dec. 1, 1902, **14,** 248; *Independent* (Charles McLean Andrews), Dec. 11, 1902, **14,** 280; *New York Times Saturday Review of Books and Art* (Augustus C. Buell), Dec. 13, 1902, **14,** 286; New York *Book Buyer* (George McLean Harper), Jan. 1903, **14,** 309; New York *Critic* (George Louis Beer), Feb. 1903, **14,** 338; New York *Nation* (William MacDonald), Feb. 5, 1903, **14,** 350; *Annals of the American Academy of Political and Social Science* (Claude Halstead Van Tyne), May 1903, **14,** 441; *American Historical Review* (Frederick Jackson Turner), July 1903, **14,** 516

Reviews of *Constitutional Government in the United States*: New York *Nation*, July 30, 1908, **18,** 384; New York *Outlook*, Oct. 10, 1908, **18,** 446; *Independent*, Oct. 29, 1908, **18,** 477

Second Presbyterian Church of Princeton, Minutes of the Session, May 24, 1905, **16,** 104; Oct. 27, 1905, **16,** 206; Nov. 25, 1905, **16,** 234

Statement by James Smith, Jr., on Wilson's view of the Senatorial situation, Dec. 9, 1910, **22,** 166

Henry van Dyke's article on the Quadrangle Plan, July 10, 1907, **17,** 276

Henry Watterson's statement on the Wilson-Harvey affair, Jan. 17, 1912, **24,** 45

Joseph Ruggles Wilson: death, Jan. 24, 1903, **14,** 330; report of the funeral services, Jan. 24, 1903, **14,** 331; tribute in the Columbia, S. C. *State*, Jan. 24, 1903, **14,** 331

# ILLUSTRATIONS

*Illustrations appear in center section of each volume*

Margaret Randolph Axson, **18**
James Mark Baldwin, **15**
Bermuda Hamilton Hotel, **17**
William Jennings Bryan, **24**
Howard Crosby Butler, **19**
Arnold Guyot Cameron, **15**
Edward Capps, **19**
Andrew Carnegie, **16**
Champ Clark, **24**
Edwin Grant Conklin, **19**
Convention Hall in Baltimore, **24**
Ralph Adams Cram, **19**
Winthrop More Daniels, **19**
Robert Davis, **21**
Joseph Albert Dear, Jr., **22**
John DeWitt, **20**
John Dixon, **20**
Cleveland Hoadley Dodge, **17, 20**
Walter Evans Edge, **22**
Map of the Lake District of England, **18**
Wilson Farrand, **20**
Harry Augustus Garfield, **15**
Robert Garrett, **20**
Elmer Hendrickson Geran, **22**
The Governor's Cottage in Sea Girt, **23**
Judson Harmon, **24**
George Brinton McClellan Harvey, **21**
William Randolph Hearst, **24**
Bayard Henry, **20**
Jenny Davidson Hibben, **15**
John Grier Hibben, **15, 19**
Melancthon Williams Jacobus, **17, 20**
Thomas Davies Jones, **20**
Samuel Kalisch, **22**
James Kerney, **21**
William Gibbs McAdoo, **24**
Charles Williston McAlpin, **15**
Cyrus Hall McCormick, **20**
James Edgar Martine, **22**

Mr. J. P. Morgan with the ladies of his party attending Wilson's inauguration, **14**
New Jersey State House in Trenton, **23**
Francis Griffith Newlands, **24**
James Richard Nugent, **21**
Henry Fairfield Osborn, **17**
Mary Allen Hulbert Peck, **19**
Princeton University:
　Fitz Randolph Gateway, erected 1905, **16**
　Guyot Hall near completion, 1909, **19**
　Holder Hall, with tower completed, **20**
　Lake Carnegie, **16**
　McCosh Hall, erected 1906, **17**
　Mather Sundial, **17**
　Faculty Room, Nassau Hall, **16**
　Palmer Physical Laboratory, shortly after completion, 1908, **18**
　Patton Hall, erected 1906, **16**
　Prospect, the residence of the President of Princeton, **14**; the entrance to, **14**
Henry Smith Pritchett, **22**
William Cooper Procter, **20**
Moses Taylor Pyne, **20**
George Lawrence Record, **21**
Theodore Roosevelt, **25**
Willard Saulsbury, **24**
Joseph Bernard Shea, **20**
Edward Wright Sheldon, **20**
James Smith, Jr., **21**
William Howard Taft, **25**
Frank Thilly, **15**
Henry Burling Thompson, **20**
Oscar Wilder Underwood, **24**
Paul van Dyke, **17**
Henry Watterson, **22**
John Wesley Wescott, **22**
Andrew Fleming West, **19, 20**
Ellen Axson Wilson:
　Portrait, **15, 18**
　Drawing by Frederic Yates, **16**
　With Eleanor Randolph Wilson, **18**
Jessie Woodrow Wilson, **17**
Margaret Wilson, **18**
Margaret Wilson and Jessie Woodrow Wilson, **18**
The Wilson house on Library Place, **14**
**Woodrow Wilson:**
　Two Purdy photographs taken in August 1902, **14**
　Academic procession entering Alexander Hall for the inauguration, **14**

On the day of his inauguration, **14**

Speaking from the steps of Nassau Hall after the inaugural ceremony, **14**

Breaking ground for Seventy-Nine Hall, **14**

Drawing in 1904, by George Timothy Tobin, **15**

Facsimile of a page of his diary for 1904, **15**

Facsimile of his letter to Ellen Axson Wilson, March 21, 1904, **15**

Oil painting by Frederic Yates, **16**

Drawing in 1906, by Frederic Yates, **16**

With James Bryce at the dedication of the Mather Sundial, **17**

With Mary Allen Hulbert Peck at Shoreby, Paget West, Bermuda, **17**

Portrait, **17, 19, 20, 21**

Drawing in 1908, by Frederic Yates, **18**

Letter to Ellen Axson Wilson, July 23, 1908, **18**

First page of his outline of the Phi Beta Kappa address at Harvard, **19**

With his family on the terrace at Prospect, **19**

With Vivian Murchison Lewis and John Franklin Fort, **21**

Reviewing the Inaugural Parade, **22**

At his desk in the New Jersey State House, **22;** at the window in his office, **24**

Bust by Blanche Nevin, 1911, **23**

With William Bayard Hale and Joseph Patrick Tumulty, in the Governor's office, **23**

With McKee Barclay and Frank Parker Stockbridge, **23**

In a Denver hotel, **23**

With the Rocky Mountain Princeton Club in Denver, **23**

In conference at Sea Girt, **23**

Commander-in-chief of the New Jersey National Guard at Camp Wilson, **23**

In action, **23**

With William Frank McCombs, **24**

Greeting visitors in Sea Girt, **24**

Oil painting by Seymour Thomas, **25**

Accepting the nomination at Sea Girt, **25**

With his family on the porch at Sea Girt, **25**

Reception at Sea Girt, **25**

Talking to school children in Minneapolis, **25**

New Jersey Day at Sea Girt, **25**

With Mrs. Wilson and Eleanor in Bermuda, **25**

Isaac Chauncey Wyman, **23**

Frederic Yates, **16**

# TEXT ILLUSTRATIONS

## Volume 14

Handwritten outline of his first report to the Board of Trustees, 120
The first page of the shorthand draft of his inaugural address, 172
The first page of Wilson's typed copy of his inaugural address, 173
"1910 That's All!" cartoon in the Princeton Tiger, March 1903, 384
The opening pages of a record of expenses of the European trip, 522

## Volume 15

A page of Wilson's notes for his address at the annual reception for
   Episcopalians in the freshman class, 11
The first page of Wilson's shorthand draft of his "begging letter" to
   Judge Reed, 125
The first page of a letter from Mrs. Wilson of May 1, 1904, 305
The first page of Wilson's shorthand draft of his baccalaureate ser-
   mon on June 12, 1904, 373

## Volume 16

Map of the University campus with proposed quads inked in by Wilson, 447
Draft of Wilson's resolution concerning Andrew Fleming West, 468

## Volume 17

First page of Wilson's shorthand draft of his report to the Board of
   Trustees, 178
First page of Wilson's typed draft of his report on the social coordi-
   nation of the University, 179
Shorthand draft of Wilson's unfinished letter of resignation, 444

## Volume 19

First page of Wilson's manuscript of "The Tariff Make-Believe," 360
Ormond's chart, 668

## Volume 20

Draft of Wilson's remarks to the Board of Trustees, 508
Letter of July 11, 1910, to Cleveland Hoadley Dodge, 574

## Volume 21

Outlines of Wilson's campaign speeches:
   Sept. 28, 1910, Jersey City, 182
   Sept. 29, 1910, Plainfield, 192

Sept. 30, 1910, Newark, 203
Oct. 5, 1910, Woodbury, 246
Oct. 6, 1910, Burlington, 270
Oct. 8, 1910, Wildwood, 282
Oct. 19, 1910, Somerville, 355
Oct. 20, 1910, Flemington, 368
Oct. 21, 1910, Phillipsburg, 391
Oct. 22, 1910, Newton, 397
Oct. 24, 1910, Camden, 414
Oct. 25, 1910, Salem, 422
Oct. 26, 1910, New Brunswick, 437
Oct. 27, 1910, Bergen County, 445
Oct. 28, 1910, Elizabeth II, 455
Oct. 28, 1910, Elizabeth I, 466
Oct. 29, 1910, Hoboken, 472
Oct. 31, 1910, Bayonne, 486
Nov. 1, 1910, Passaic, 494
Nov. 2, 1910, The Oranges, Montclair, 509
Nov. 3, 1910, Morristown, 528
Nov. 5, 1910, Glen Ridge, Bloomfield, East Orange, 562
Third page of the first draft of Wilson's letter to George Lawrence
Record, 410

## Volume 22

"He don't know where he's going, but he's on his way!" Cartoon in
The Baltimore *Sun*, Dec. 12, 1910, 176

# INDEX

A. *Mitchell Palmer: Politician* (Coben), 22:409n1,2; 23:156n3

Abbe, Catherine Amory Palmer (Mrs. Robert), 18:509-10,n1, 516

Abbe, Robert, M.D., 18:510n1

Abbett, Leon, 21:343n9; 22:173, 174n2, 281n1

Abbett, Leon, Jr., 22:281,n1

Abbot, Eleanor Hallowell (Mrs. Fordyce Coburn), 24:506n1

Abbot, Frank Frost, 17:161,n4, 173, 218, 587, 588, 596-97, 601, 614,n2; 18:5, 7, 8, 12, 225, 226, 575, 582; 19:11, 11n2, 393, 398, 425, 591-97, 736-38; 20:143, 175, 190, 484; 23:30, 31

Abbotsford, Roxburgh, Wilsons at, 14:524

Abbott, Jane Harrison (Mrs. Frank Frost), 18:8; 19:393, 737,n1

Abbott, Lawrence Fraser, 19:156, 307

Abbott, Lyman, 17:128; 19:444,n2; 20:306, 350,n1; 22:184

Abelard, Pierre, 20:64

Abercrombie, John William, 15:11,n1, 25, 189, 218-19, 234, 237

Aberdeen, Scotland, 15:273,n2; 16:528; 21:216

Aberdeen, University of, 15:273,n2

Abernethy, Lloyd M., 21:342n6

*Abner Daniel* (Harben), 14:72,n5

*Abraham Lincoln* (Oberholtzer), 17:262-n1

*Abraham Lincoln: The Tribute of a Century, 1809-1909* (ed. MacChesney), 19:46n

Abrams, Richard M., 25:414n1

*Abridgement of the Indian Affairs . . . Transacted in the Colony of New York, from the Year 1678 to the Year 1751* (Wraxall; ed. McIlwain), 16:42n1

academic costume, 14:143, 191

academic freedom, controversy at Roanoke College, 22:604n2

academic politics, 20:76n1

Academy of Music (Brooklyn, N. Y.), campaign address, 25:435-40

Ackerman, Ernest Robinson, 22:474, 588

Acton, John Emerich Edward Dalberg, 1st Baron, 14:295; 15:482-84, 485

Adam, James, 15:410

Adams (Mountain in Presidential Range), 14:111

Adams, Alva, 22:584,n2; 23:21; 25:645,-n1

Adams, Charles Francis II (1835-1915), 14:306n3; 15:292n; 17:104-105,n1,2, 274, 409-10, 417; 18:622, 625; 19:20, 23, 32-33, 223, 263, 264; 20:265n2; 24:83n1

Adams, Edwin Plimpton, 16:421,n6, 508; 17:287,n1, 408; 19:137, 138, 139, 677

Adams, Frank, 22:584,n1

Adams, Herbert Baxter, 16:309, 430

Adams, John, 14:315; 16:53; 17:249, 462; 19:209; 23:282

Adams, John Haslup, 24:491,n1

Adams, John Quincy, 16:144

Adams, Samuel, 17:250

Adams, William, 18:339,n3

Adams, William H., 22:584,n1

Adams County, Ohio, vote-selling scandal, 23:75n2

Adams Express, 15:424

Adams Hotel, Denver, 23:27, 28

Adamson, Penrhyn Stanley (Penrhyn Stanlaws), 14:59-60,n1

Addams, Jane, 18:590,n2; 22:157n1; 25:26, 546

Addicks, John Edward, 23:436,n2

Addison, Joseph, 14:503

Ade, George, 16:115; 23:553n2

Adee, Alvey Augustus, 15:194

Adelbert College, 16:131

Adler, Cyrus, 25:450,n1

Adler, Felix, 15:407, 408; 16:211,n2; 22:91,n5, 157n1

Admission to College by Certificate (West), 17:155, 160

Adriance, Harris Ely, 15:434,n4

Adriance, Helen Campbell (Mrs. Walter Maxwell), 17:89,n1

Adriance, Sarah Holmes (Mrs. Harris Ely), 15:434,n4

Adriance, Walter Maxwell, 16:421, 509; 17:88-89, 232, 408; 18:271, 294; 19:613

Adsit, Lynn Magruder, 15:57

Adult education, 25:183

*Adventure in Constructive Finance* (Glass), 25:547n, 641n1

*Advocate of Peace* (Boston), 18:420

*Aeneid* (Virgil), 15:118

Aeschylus, 19:594

Afro-American Industrial and Benefit Association, 21:275n1

Afro-American League, 21:21n1, 275n4

*Afro-American Ledger* (Baltimore), 21:47n1, 275n2

*After Forty Years* [of Princeton '86] *1886-1926*, 15:52n1

*After Twenty-Five Years: Class Record of* [Princeton] *1886*, 15:52n1

Agassiz, Alexander, 15:116

Agincourt, Battle of, 18:433
Agnew, A. G., 15:439
Agnew, James C., 23:343, 536n1
*Agricola* (Tacitus), 19:597
agriculture, 23:641-42, 646; 25:417, 618; W. H. Page, 25:516; *see also* farming and farmers
Ahaz, 17:463
Aiken, Sarah Elizabeth Noyes (Mrs. Charles Augustus), 14:36-37,n3
Aimone's Manufacturing Co., New York City, 14:10,n1, 17
Ainsworth, William Newman, 24:355,n2
Aitchison, Jane, 18:379,n8
Aitken, John William, 15:569, 572; 16:5, 500
Alabama, 23:319, 321, 341, 548; 24:576; Democrats, 23:513
Alabama, University of, 15:218, 227; 23: 328n3, 390
Alabama Educational Association, 16: 113; 22:55, 95
Alabama Polytechnic Institute, 18:579; 19:679
Alaska, 16:341; 19:479-80, 482; 23:76-77, 90; coal lands, 23:174-75,n1,2; public lands, 20:315-16; 21:546,n3; 25:355, 364, 397
*Alaska: A History of its Administration, Exploitation, and Industrial Development During its First Half Century Under the Rule of the United States* (Nichols), 23:175n2
Albany, Ga., 24:344
Albany, N. Y., 21:360; Fort Orange Club, 15:169; Madison Avenue Presbyterian Church, 19:20n1; Presbyterian Union, 15:168,n1; Princeton alumni, 14:400; 15:169; 16:418; Ten Eyck Hotel, 15:168; WW addresses, 15:168-69
*Albany Evening Journal*, 15:169n; 21: 252n6
Albert, Ernest, 19:318,n2
*Albert J. Beveridge: American Nationalist* (Braeman), 18:186n4
Albert J. Beveridge and the First National Child Labor Bill (Braeman), 18:186n4
Albertson, Charles Carroll, 14:114
Albion Hotel, Augusta, Ga., 23:552, 556
Albuquerque, N. M., 24:306
*Alcestis* (Euripides), 19:597
alcohol, 25:151; *see also* liquor; prohibition
Alden, Henry Mills, 16:299, 343, 470-71; 17:620,n4
Alderman, Edwin Anderson, 14:205n4, 334; 15:394,n4, 507-508,n1,2, 574; 16: 35-36,n1, 195; 17:86, 488n1; 18: 567; 19:109; 21:595-96; 22:140, 595, 596; 23:312, 328, 360, 390, 550; 24: 462-63
Aldrich, Chester Hardy, 23:98,n5
Aldrich, Nelson Wilmarth, 19:94n3, 191-

n1, 363,n1, 366,n4, 367, 601, 604, 607; 20:25, 26, 38, 39, 201, 385; 21:175, 215, n5, 243, 244, 249, 255, 272, 280, 456,n2, 457, 468, 475; 23:293-94,n3, 514, 542, 548, 605, 625, 643; 24:67, 273-74, 296, 420, 421; 25:33, 370, 380, 407, 437,n2
Aldrich plan, 23:293-94,n3, 312, 510, 542, 595, 617, 625, 643; 24:238,n2, 273-74, 581,n1, 582-83; 25:531, 564 Δ W. G. Brown, 23:513-15; D. M. Barringer, 23:605; W. J. Bryan, 23:632; Carter Glass, 25:642, 643
Aldrich-Vreeland Act of 1908, 19:94n3
Alexander, Alexander John Aitcheson, M.D., 14:97n3; 19:165
Alexander, Archibald (1855-1917), 21: 150n1
Alexander, Archibald Stevens (1880-1912), 16:563,n1; 17:10n2, 25,n6; 19: 165; 21:6-7,n1, 18-20, 112-14, 354; 23: 537; 25:66,n1
Alexander, Caroline Bayard Stevens, 21:150,n1,2; 22:530,n3; 23:290, 301, 588, 634; 24:514, 515
Alexander, Charles Beatty, 14:130,n1, 131; 16:276,n1, 277f, 304,n1, 424n1
Alexander, Claude Aitcheson, 14:97,n3
Alexander, Elizabeth Kirkwood (Mrs. Henry Eckert), 21:54,n2
Alexander, George, 14:253,n5; 23:44, 51
Alexander, Harriet Crocker (Mrs. Charles Beatty), 14:130; 16:322
Alexander, Henry Eckert, 19:522,n1; 20:297, 563, 564,n2; 21:8-9, 22-23, 24, 26, 27, 33-34, 40, 53n1, 54, 57-58, 62, 158-59, 164, 167-68, 200-201, 219, 225-26, 243-44, 275, 292; 22:231; 23: 160,n2, 215, 216, 262, 279n3; 24:393, 397
Alexander, Hooper, 23:236,n3,4, 244, 547
Alexander, James Waddel, 14:144, 168n1, 268,n2, 289, 290, 304-305, 490; 15:77, 113, 118, 184, 237, 238, 463-66, 546; 16:5, 276n1, 299,n1, 333n2; 18:493,n2, 494, 512; 19:17, 650-51, 703, 712; 20:8n, 130n1, 222, 321, 476; 22:30, 510
Alexander, John White, 18:469, 475, 622, 625; 19:23
Alexander, Lucien Hugh, 21:328,n1
Alexander, Samuel, M.D., 14:187, 195, 291
Alexander, Susan Mary Brown (Mrs. Henry Martyn), 16:322
Alexander, Walter N., 25:580,n1
Alexander and Green, New York law firm, 16:276n1
*Alexander Hamilton: An Essay on American Union* (Oliver), 20:339-40,n1
Alexandria Hotel, Los Angeles, 23:41-n4,5, 44, 49
Alexis, Tsarevich of Russia, 15:448,n3

Alger, Frederick Moulton, 16:43,n4
*Alice Through the Looking Glass*, 25: 235, 361
Alien and Sedition Laws, 25:40, 53, 108
All Souls College, Oxford, 17:464
Allen, Andrew Jackson, 19:708,n2
Allen, Anjenett Holcomb (Mrs. Charles Sterling), 17:29n1, 608, 612; 18:450,-n3, 481,n2; 19:192,n4, 193, 291, 312, 383, 395, 704; 20:141,n4, 172, 180, 188, 371, 493; 21:26; 22:100, 142, 295, 331, 334, 454, 501, 511, 520, 547, 572; 23:220, 221, 223, 241, 257, 265, 590, 655; 24:43-44, 329, 410; 25:45, 615,n1
Allen, Augustus Nichols, 18:309n1
Allen, Charles Dexter, 21:168,n1, 171
Allen, Charles Sterling, 17:29n1
Allen, Ethan (New York lawyer), 20: 139,n3; 22:39,n23
Allen, Frederick Hobbes, 24:28,n1
Allen, Hamilton Ford, 16:106-107, 130, 248, 421; 17:163,n13
Allen, John Mills, 21:423,n3; 25:642
Allen, Lamson, M.D., 22:335,n1
Allen (Secretary to J. P. Morgan), 19:483
Allen, William Harvey, 23:634n1
Allen, William Henry, 20:139n3; Mrs., 20:188
Allen, Yorke, 21:300-301,n1
Allen Academy, Chicago, 16:248
Allentown, Pa., 24:138-40
Allentown *Morning Call*, 24:137n, 140n
Allers, Henry H., M.D., 23:535,n2
Alliance of the Reformed Churches throughout the World Holding the Presbyterian System, 18:339; 19:51,n2
Allison, William Outis, 20:44-45,n1
Alloway, N. J., 23:392, 394
Alpha Portland Cement Co., 23:228n3
Alpnach, Switzerland, Wilsons at, 14: 539
Altland, Daniel Fickes, 22:581,n2
Alton Towers, 15:462
Alumni Press, *see* Princeton University Press
Alverstone, Richard Everard Webster, Viscount, 20:22,n6
Alyea, Garrabrant R., 22:87n2
Amalfi, EAW at, 15:235, 236, 240
Amalgamated Association of Street and Electric Railway Employes, 20:153-n10
*Amateur Spirit* (Perry), 15:529,n1,2
ambassadorial positions, W. J. Bryan, 25:623
Ambleside, Westmorland, 14:521; 16: 436, 439, 450, 480; 18:371, 379, 395, 406, 407, 415, 416
Amen, Harlan Page, 15:141,n1
Amen Corner, 22:453,n1
American Academy of Arts and Letters, 19:259, 556, 578, 602; 21:109,n2; 22: 27, 49
American Academy of Political and Social Science, 16:313

American Academy of Political and Social Science *Annals*, 14:445n; 18:576
American and Canadian Student Young Men's Christian Association Movement, 14:265-67
*American Architect*, 19:304,n1
American Association for the Advancement of Science, 18:575-76
American Bankers Association, 17:520; 18:3, 382, 385, 424, 434, 473; 19:95,n4; 20:38n4; 25:642; *Proceedings of the Thirty-Fourth Annual Convention*, 18:430n4, 434n
American Bar Association, 20:21-22, 66, 86, 572; 21:51, 64-81, 300n2, 386, 609; 25:311, 557,n4; *Report of Twenty-Third Annual Meeting . . .*, 21:81n
American Bible Society, 23:510-11
*American Citizenship* (Brewer), 14: 136,n1
*American College and University: A History* (Rudolph), 15:291n26
*American Commonwealth* (Bryce), 14:14
*American Constitution: The National Powers, the Rights of the States, the Liberties of the People* (Stimson), 18:446,n1
American Economic Association, 17:353; 22:262
American Epoch Series, 14:281
American Exchange National Bank, New York City, 16:533
American Express Co., 15:277, 310
American Federation of Catholic Societies, 25:63n3
American Federation of Labor, 18:186n4; 25:22n1, 22-23,n2, 614-15
*American Federationist*, 25:23n2
American flag, 25:106, 143, 377
American Historical Association, 22:27, 49; *Annual Report for 1898*, 14:443n2
*American Historical Review*, 14:519n; 18:575; 19:405n1; 25:150n4
American-Hungarian People's Voice (*Amerikai Magyar Népszava*), 24: 563,n1; 25:28, 275n3
American Indians, 25:162, 163
American Institute of Architects, 18:512
American Institute of Bank Clerks, New York Chapter, 15:272, 328
American Institute of Electrical Engineers, 18:577
American Institute of Sacred Literature, 14:198,n2
American Insurance Union, 22:229,n2
American Inter-Collegiate Football Rules Committee, 16:371,n4; 20: 487n1, 497, 539, 559
*American Journal of Archaeology*, 16: 187n1
*American Journal of Philology*, 17:114, 548n3; 18:575
*American Journal of Theology*, 18:575
American Library Association, 16:392
American Line, 16:179

*American Magazine*, **19**:164,n1,2,3; **22**: 412n1; **23**:136n1,2, 217; **24**:193n3

*American Mail: Enlarger of the Common Life* (Fuller), **22**:427n1

American Mechanics, **23**:363-64

American Medical Association, **24**:454-57; **25**:282n1

American Merchant Marine, **16**:539

American Mining Congress, Oregon chapter, **23**:64

American Morphological Society, **18**:575

American Museum of Natural History, **16**:550,n1

American Nation Series, **20**:583

American Newspaper Publishers' Association, **20**:59, 399, 402n1

American Peace Society, **18**:419-20n1; **20**:120n2

American Peace Society of Boston, **17**:92n2

American Philosophical Association, **15**:111-12, 114, 116

American Philosophical Society, **14**:285, 380, 381, 405, 470; **16**:36, 56-57; **18**:576; Franklin bicentennial 1906, **15**:539,n2

American Political Science Association, **19**:157; **22**:210,n4, 260, 262, 263

American Political Science Association *Proceedings*, **18**:576

*American Political Science Review*, **22**:272n

American Press Association, **21**:300

American Prison Association, **22**:207; **25**:311

American Red Cross, **22**:416

American Revolution, **14**:352, 445, 517; **15**:148, 149, 172; **16**:143; **17**:249, 462; **18**:98, 551; **19**:203; **21**:369, 482, 517-18; **22**:474, 476; **23**:94, 127, 186f, 435; **25**:596

American School of Classical Studies in Athens, **16**:247, 253, 254; **17**:556

American School of Classical Studies in Rome, **15**:399n1; **16**:166, 167, 247, 253, 510; **17**:556; **18**:575; **19**:551

American Smelting and Refining Co., **24**:475n1

American Society for the Excavation of Sardis, **17**:111,n1; *Publications*, 111,-n1

American Society for the Extension of University Teaching, **15**:494n4; **18**:525, 525n1, 540-41, 544; **19**:98-100, 108-109

American Society for Judicial Settlement of International Disputes, **21**:615,n1,2

American Society of Civil Engineers, **15**:579

American Sugar Refining Co., **19**:364n2; **20**:312n2

American Tobacco Company, **18**:7n1; **21**:206; **23**:118,n5, 361n2; **24**:394n1

American Wood Carving Company, **16**:387-88

Americanism defined, **16**:53

*Americans* (Münsterberg), **14**:76,n1

*America's Colonial Experiment* (Pratt), **17**:545n4

*America's* Cup races, **21**:38,n2

*Amerika*, S.S., **22**:274, 393

*Amerikaner* (Münsterberg), **14**:76,n1

Ames, James Barr (1846-1910), **22**:213

Amherst, Mass., Princeton alumni, **20**:320

Amherst College, **14**:403; **15**:234n; **16**:240; **17**:557; **18**:578; defeated by Princeton at football, Nov. 9, 1907, **17**:473,n4

Amiens, Wilsons in, **14**:535; Cathedral, **14**:535

Anacapri, EAW at, **15**:240

*Anatole France on Childhood* (Mantoux), **14**:440n2

Anchor Line, **16**:430n3, 450, 451, 453; **18**:340n1

*And Gladly Teach: Reminiscences* (Perry), **16**:180n

Anderson, Andrew Runni, **16**:55, 132, 252, 528; **17**:161-62,n1, 162, 408; **19**:676

Anderson, Anna E., **16**:234

Anderson, Arthur, **25**:55n1

Anderson, Benjamin McAlester, Jr., **25**:419-21n1

Anderson, Carrie, **16**:234

Anderson, Charles Palmerston, **18**:277,n1

Anderson, Charles W., **21**:47

Anderson, Donald F., **22**:427n1

Anderson, Harold MacDonald, **21**:508,n2

Anderson, James Reddie, **15**:359n4

Anderson, Mary, **14**:319-20

Anderson, Neal Larkin, **15**:12, 182,n2, 226

Anderson, Oscar E., Jr., **25**:150n4, 151-n6, 282n1

Anderson, Patrick C., **24**:255

Anderson, Robert M., **16**:301; **25**:536,n1

Anderson, Robert Patton, **14**:474; **15**:375

Anderson, William De La Roche, **23**:475-n1

Anderson, William Madison, **23**:511

Anderson Auction Company, New York City, **16**:379

Andover, N. J., **21**:413

Andover Theological Seminary, **18**:566-n1

Andrew, Abram Piatt, **16**:30,n1, 41, 372,n1

Andrew, Abram Piatt, Jr., **23**:293n3, 516, 548

Andrew, Saint, **15**:236

*Andrew Carnegie* (Wall), **16**:55n3, 305n4

Andrews, Charles McLean, **14**:280-83,-n1; **15**:532; **19**:405n2

Andrews, Edith R., **15**:231,n1, 238, 243, 266, 270, 295, 300

Andrews, Elisha Benjamin, **23**:98,n6; **24**:539-40

Andrews, William S., **24**:500,n1

Angell, James Burrill, **14**:418,n1, 419, 421; **17**:149-50; **19**:181, 185; **24**:54
Angell, James Rowland, **23**:31,n7
Angell, Sara Swope Caswell (Mrs. James Burrill), **14**:418, 421; **17**:150
Anglesea, N. J., **23**:274
Anglo-American School of Polite Unlearning (Crothers), **17**:534-35,n1
Anglo-Catholicism, **15**:201,n5
Ann Arbor, Michigan, **15**:444; **16**:60; **24**: 53-58; WW addresses, **14**:419-21; **16**:44-45; WW in, **14**:418, 425
*Ann Arbor Daily Argus*, **14**:421n; **16**:45n
Ann Arbor *Daily Times News*, **24**:58n
*Annals* (Tacitus), **19**:597
*Annals of the American Academy of Political and Social Science*, **14**:445n; **18**:576
Annapolis, *see* U. S. Naval Academy
Annapolis, Md., **15**:234
Anne, Queen, **14**:502, 503, 504
Annin, Jennie M. Bell (Mrs. Robert Edwards), **15**:503
Annin, Robert Edwards, **15**:503,n1, 504; **16**:215; **17**:378; **18**:18,n5; **19**:118,n2; **20**:211n1
*Annual Register*, **17**:16n3
Antaeus, **16**:216
Anthony, Alfred W., **16**:470n
anthracite coal strike of 1902, **22**:215n1
Anthracite Coal Trust, James C. McReynolds, **25**:557-58
Anti-Imperialist League, **20**:309n1
Anti-Saloon League, **22**:327n1
Anti-Saloon League of New Jersey, **22**:599n1
Antique Furniture Exchange, New York City, **14**:7,n7, 9
antitrust laws, platform plank, **24**:477-78; **25**:12, 287 Δ W. J. Bryan, **23**:235n3, 237; R. M. LaFollette, **25**:288; J. S. Williams, **24**:489; *see also* Sherman Antitrust Act
Apollo Belvidere (statue), **14**:79, 85, 97
*Apology* (Plato), **19**:597
Appel, John Wilberforce, **20**:56,n3
Apple, Henry Harbaugh, **19**:552,n4, 704, 740; **20**:55-56,n1
Applegate, Daniel H., **23**:447,n1
Applethwaite, Cumberland, **18**:409
Approaching National Peace and Arbitration Congress (Holt), **17**:92,n4
Appropriations Committee (U. S. Senate), anniversary of the Emancipation Proclamation, **24**:570, 571n1
Aqueduct, nr. Princeton, **15**:66, 578, 579
*Arabian Nights*, **25**:429
arbitration, labor, **23**:339n3, 357, 357n1
arbitration treaties, **22**:514, 514n1, 515; **23**:520
Arbuthnot, Wilson Shaw, **15**:248n1
Archaeological Institute of America, **14**:206, 382; **16**:253
Archer (Preceptor applicant), **16**:92,n2
Archer, Franklin Morse, **23**:592,n2
Architectural Development of [Prince-

ton] University (Cram), **18**:293,n1, 308n1
*Architectural Record*, **23**:350n2
architecture: no characteristic American form, **19**:639
*Archiv für lateinische Lexicographie und Grammatik*, **18**:575
*Arena* (Boston), **18**:575
Argonaut Hotel, San Francisco, **23**:53
Aristophanes, **19**:594, 597
Aristotle, **14**:208; **15**:441; **16**:354; **17**:577; **19**:232, 666, 724
Arizona, **22**:423, 433, 436, 438; **23**:40, 42; admission of, **23**:369; state constitution, **22**:291,n2, 592; Democratic party, **25**:271
*Arizona, the History of a Frontier State* (Wyllys), **22**:291n2
Arizona Statehood League, **22**:291n2
*Arizona Territory, 1863-1912* (Wagoner), **22**:291n2
Arkansas, **23**:233; Democrats, **23**:233-34; WW in, **23**:517-18
Arlington National Cemetery, **25**:574n3
Armanni (Alari), Dr., **15**:302,n2, 303, 304, 309, 314, 320
Armanni, Gabrielle, **15**:314
Armistead, George Daniel, **23**:231,n1, 268
Armour, George Allison, **15**:201,n6, 301, 351; **16**:472-74, 483; **18**:292, 355
Armour, Harriette Foote (Mrs. George Allison), **15**:201,n6, 301, 351
Armour, Jonathan Ogden, **14**:248
Armour Institute of Technology, **14**:248
Armstrong, Alvin H., **23**:99
Armstrong, Anne, **17**:15,n4
Armstrong, Charles Newton, **24**:311,n2
Armstrong, Harry Howard, **17**:364-65,-n1, 370-71
Armstrong, John Gassaway, **14**:388
Armstrong, Rebekah Sellers Purves (Mrs. William Park), **17**:16n4
Armstrong, William Metcalf, **17**:364
Armstrong, William Park, **17**:16n4
Army-Navy football game, Princeton, 1905, **16**:172-73, 175, 242-43
*Army and Navy Journal*, **24**:495
Arndt, Ernst Moritz, **19**:569
Arner, George Byron Louis, **18**:579; **19**:73,n1, 77, 315n2
Arnett, L. W., **24**:141
Arnold, Annie Brockway (Mrs. Constantine Peter), **20**:383,n3
Arnold, Constantine Peter, **20**:383-85,n1
Arnold, Frances Bunsen Trevenen, **16**: 493,n2; **18**:368,n8, 371, 376, 378-79, 410
Arnold, George, **24**:324,n1
Arnold, Harris A., M.D., **21**:239,n2
Arnold, Henry J., **23**:478,n1
Arnold, John P., M.D., **15**:9,n3
Arnold, Matthew, **14**:521,n2; **15**:371,n2; **16**:493, 493n2; **18**:368n8; **19**:573; **20**:187,n2
Arnold, Nezza Nevello, **23**:449,n1

Arnold, Thomas, **16**:493; **17**:327, 463; **18**:5n3, 365n6
Arnold, Thurman Wesley, **20**:383,n2
Arrington, Olivia Goldthwaite, **15**:213-14,n1
Arrington, Thomas Mann, **15**:214n1
Arthur, Ellen Lewis Herndon (Mrs. Chester Alan), **25**:513n1
Articles of Confederation, **14**:232; **18**:191; **19**:518
*As You Like It* (Shakespeare), **15**:340, 345
Asbury Park, N. J., **22**:50n3; **23**:219; casino, **23**:445; Coleman Hotel, **23**:262n3; Elks Lodge, **23**:561; Hippodrome, **21**:328; political meeting, **23**:270; Savoy Theatre, **23**:561; WW addresses, **23**:442-47, 561-62; WW campaign speech, **21**:328-34
Ashe, Samuel A'Court, **16**:187n1
Asheville, N. C., **23**:329, 513, 547
Ashland, Neb., **23**:96
Askew, Sarah Byrd, **20**:135,n5
*Assembly Herald*, Phil., **19**:178,n1
Assisi, **15**:240, 275, 338; EAW in, **15**:302, 303, 306, 308, 309, 310, 311, 313, 314, 320, 333, 335, 336, 337, 339, 346, 349; Basilica di San Francesco, **15**:275, 334, 338; Hotel Leone, **15**:302, 303, 308, 313, 320, 333, 337, 346
Associated Press, **16**:553; **17**:92; **19**:106, 111, 230,n1, 523; **20**:58, 390, 399, 401, 402n1; **21**:608, 608n1; **22**:197, 335; **25**:26, 46, 111, 544, 571
Association of American Universities, **15**:100,n3,4, 166,n2; **17**:511, 546n1; **18**:519,n2, 528; **19**:182, 448,n1, 550n4, 552, 634, 635, 713-27, 747; **20**:11n1; **22**:35, 81,n1
Association of American Universities, *Journal of Proceedings and Addresses of the Eleventh Annual Conference*, **19**:727n
Association of Colleges and Preparatory Schools of the Middle States and Maryland, **15**:540,n1, 542, 545; **16**:495, 504-505; **17**:154-55, 160, 528, 529, 533, 560; **18**:68; **20**:54; *Proceedings of Eighteenth Annual Convention . . .*, **15**:542,n; *Proceedings of the Twenty-first Annual Convention*, **17**:529, 545
Association of History Teachers of the Middle States and Maryland, **16**:279
Association of Locomotive Engineers, **25**:208
Association of State and National Food and Dairy Departments, **25**:282n1
Association of Teachers of Mathematics, **15**:545
Association to Prevent Corrupt Practices at Elections, **21**:155,n2
Astor Hotel, New York City, **15**:535; **18**:228, 560; **20**:32n1; **22**:250n2, 410, 585, 588, 601; **23**:559; **24**:32n1, 179, 391, 394, 413n1; **25**:274n1

*Astoria*, S.S., **16**:456
Athens, Archaeological Congress, **16**:93; Grove of Academus, **23**:86-87; Mars Hill, **20**:524-25
Atherton, Thomas Henry, **15**:471,n3; **16**:5
athletics, **18**:462; **19**:227, 252-53; intercollegiate, **20**:435-36; university, **18**:25-26, 58, 282
Atkins, Charles Duke, **18**:525,n1, 540-41, 544
Atkins, Gaius Glenn, **21**:4,n1
Atkins, V. B., **16**:73
Atlanta, **17**:484; **22**:206, 480; **23**:236, 328, 547, 594; **24**:566; Atlanta Auditorium, **22**:491n1; Atlanta Lecture Association, **14**:20n1; **15**:216, 217; campaign address, **24**:335-44; Capital City Club, **22**:488; Piedmont Hotel, **22**:489; WW in, **22**:487-98, 500, 502, 507; **23**:554; Young Men's Democratic League, **22**:488
*Atlanta Georgian*, **23**:236,n3, 328,n1
*Atlanta Georgian and News*, **21**:451n1
*Atlanta Journal*, **22**:491n, 506,n1,2; **24**:60n1, 335n. 344n, 347n, 356n
Atlantic City, N. J., **19**:387, 399; **20**:228; **21**:21, 29, 47, 551; **22**:49, 300, 309, 384; **23**:313, 315, 592, 634n1; **24**:444, 511; Apollo Theatre, **23**:522, 523; Chalfonte Hotel, **20**:222; corruption trials, **23**:592, 592n2; government, **23**:523f; graft cases, **24**:452-53,n1,2, 458-60,n2,4; Steeple Chase Pier theatre, **21**:310n1; Traymore Hotel, **23**:522; WW addresses, **19**:635-48; **20**:414-21; **23**:158-60, 522-31; to the American Medical Association, **24**:454-57; to Spanish War Veterans, **25**:129-34; WW campaign speech, **21**:310-20; WW in, **19**:634
Atlantic City Railroad, **23**:273
*Atlantic City Review*, **23**:531n; **24**:253, 289,n2
Atlantic Coast Line, **23**:558
Atlantic County, N. J., **21**:584n1; **22**:300n4, 309; **23**:382n2, 403, 432,n9, 522, 531, 532; government, **23**:523f
Atlantic Highlands, N. J., **24**:550, 561, 572
*Atlantic Monthly*, **14**:33, 54, 265,n1, 324; **15**:494; **16**:170, 180n2, 17:58n1, 122-23, 310, 325, 325n, 333, 534n1; **23**:133n1, 134,n1, 248, 248n1, 643n3; **25**:130n3
*Atlantic Reporter*, **23**:324n2
*Atlantic Review*, Atlantic City, **22**:309, 309n1
Atlantic Terra Cotta Co., **24**:475n1
Auburn Theological Seminary, **21**:367,n2
Auchincloss, Gordon, **25**:51n1
Auchincloss, Janet House (Mrs. Gordon), **25**:51n1, 611,n2
Auerbach, John Hone, **15**:400n1

Auerbach, Joseph Smith, **15**:399,n1, 446, 527
Auerbach, Katharine Hone (Mrs. Joseph Smith), **15**:446
Auger, Charles Louis, Jr., **19**:502n3
Augusta, Ga., **19**:33; **20**:142, 144; **23**:555, 557; **25**:542n2, 569, 592; Albion Hotel, **23**:552, 556; First Presbyterian Church, **14**:331-32; **23**:553, 555, 556; Grand Theater, **23**:554; Joseph T. Derry's School, **23**:557n2; Lightfoot baseball club, **23**:553,n5; St. Patrick's Church, **23**:554; WW in, **23**:552-55, 555-56
*Augusta Chronicle*, **23**:554, 555n, 556n
*Augusta* (Ga.) *Herald*, **22**:573, 573n1,2; **23**:553
Austen, Jane, **21**:225
Austin, Frank Rose, **22**:375,n1
Austin, William G., **23**:558
Austin, Texas, **23**:260, 261, 268, 595, 630, 631; Confederate Home, **23**:268
Austria, ambassadorship, **25**:610, 614,n1
Austrian Americans, **24**:406
*Autobiography of Benjamin Franklin*, **15**:477
*Autobiography of Benvenuto Cellini*, **15**:477
*Autocrat of the Breakfast-Table* (Holmes), **16**:226,n5; **17**:486
automobile: menace of reckless driving of, **16**:320
automobiles: criticized by WW, **21**:207, 209; **23**:626; opposed in Bermuda by WW, **17**:609-10
Avery, Samuel, **23**:97,n2, 98, 99, 100
Axson, Benjamin Palmer, first cousin of EAW, **14**:499; **23**:557,n1, 558; **24**:285,n1
Axson, Edward Stockton, nephew of EAW, **16**:86,n1, 88; **17**:34
Axson, Edward William, brother of EAW, **14**:4,n2, 438; **16**:86,n1, 88-89, 154n1; **17**:33,n1, 34, 137
Axson, Florence Choate Leach (Mrs. Edward William), **14**:4,n2; **16**:86,n1, 88-89; **17**:34
Axson, Isaac Stockton Keith, grandfather of EAW, **23**:557
Axson, Margaret Callaway (Mrs. Benjamin Palmer), **17**:461,n1
Axson, Margaret Randolph (Madge), sister of EAW, **14**:4,5n1, 7, 9, 12, 15, 17, 22, 35, 39, 53, 65, 68, 72, 74, 90, 95, 97, 98, 99, 101, 103, 108, 111, 435,n1, 438; **15**:7, 8, 9, 117, 134, 156n, 201, 230, 263, 270, 321, 325, 340, 351, 360, 396; **16**:28, 158, 187, 439,n1, 482, 527; **17**:12, 34; **18**:346n9, 347, 350, 353, 367, 368, 384, 390, 404, 409, 412, 472; **19**:225, 260, 313, 356, 384, 394, 442; **20**:59, 126, 134, 136,n11, 146, 176, 190, 424, 575,n1, 580; *see also*, Elliott, **Margaret Randolph Axson**
Axson, Stockton (*full name*: Isaac

Stockton Keith Axson II), brother of EAW, **14**:25,n2, 44, 95, 138, 139, 187-88, 326, 329, 395, 403, 418, 422, 423-24, 425, 426, 428, 430, 431, 432, 435, 437, 438, 439, 453, 498,n1; **15**:118, 136, 230, 232, 237, 263, 264, 267, 270, 288n, 306n1, 307, 308, 323,n5, 335, 355, 360, 396, 450n1, 460; **16**:28-29,n3, 154n1, 155,n1, 158, 180, 187, 469, 565n1, 567-70; **17**:9-10n1, 12, 34, 59-60, 222,n2, 224, 342-43, 408, 488n2, 606, 608; **18**:344, 347, 349, 350, 385-86, 404, **19**:384, 453; **20**:54, 81, 126, 134, 135, 146, 153, 176, 190, 580; **21**:52, 174, 243n2, 421, 558-59; **22**:142n1, 186, 187, 234; **23**:82, 83,n16, 112, 184; **25**:519
Ayers, Harriet Margaret Bower (Mrs. Stephen Beckwith), **25**:621,n1
Aylett, Lewis Dandridge, **24**:71,n4, 80, 96, 97
Aylward, John Arthur, **23**:253-54,n1, 259, 488n1; **24**:226
Ayres, John F., **23**:394

Babbitt, James Addison, M.D., **20**:539
Babcock, Oliver B., **14**:129
baby act (in tariff construction), **19**:368-69
Bacharach, Harry, **23**:432n9, 522n1, 524, 529n3; **24**:453
Backus, Harry F., **22**:253,n4, 481,n3
Backus, Truman Jay, **15**:540,n2, 542
Bacon, Alexander Samuel, **21**:421,n4, 467, 527; **24**:444
Bacon, Benjamin Wisner, **21**:4,n2
Bacon, Charles Reade, **21**:220,n1; **22**:50n2, 215,n1,2; **23**:30,n2; **24**:ix
Bacon, Mrs., **19**:192,n2
Bacon, Robert, **21**:615
Badley, John Haden, **18**:413,n1, 415
Baedeker, Karl, **14**:529; **16**:436
Baedeker handbooks, **15**:241, 266
Baer, George Frederick, **22**:215-16,n1
Bagby, John Hampden Chamberlayne, **15**:68,n1
Bagehot, Walter, **14**:13, 340; **16**:268; **17**:48, 94, 483; **18**:88, 95, 108; **19**:43,n3, 205; **22**:194,n4; **23**:282,n4; **24**:35,n4, 39; **25**:238n5, 634,n4
Bahrenburg, William H., **24**:32n2
Bailey, Elijah Prentiss, **23**:632
Bailey, Joseph Weldon, **22**:466,n2,3, 467; **25**:604,n1
Bailey, Thomas Andrew, **16**:559n3
Bailey, Warren Worth, **22**:409n1, 522,-n1, 523; **23**:257-58; **25**:640-41
Baillie, James Black, **15**:410,n7
Bainbridge, Helen, **23**:83,n17
Baird, David, **21**:219n2, 260, 278,n2, 305, 346, 378, 409, 420, 503; **22**:250,-n1, 300, 311n1; **23**:346, 354, 365n2, 392, 409; **24**:407, 431; **25**:39,n4
Baird, John Stuart, **14**:195

Baker, Alfred Brittin, **14**:453,n4; **15**:9; **21**:117,n1
Baker, Charles Dabney, **19**:502n3, 534, 535, 546
Baker, Christian S., Mrs., **14**:417,n1
Baker, Curtis Thompson, **22**:516,n2; **23**:275,n8
Baker, Frank L., **19**:552n3
Baker, Jacob Thompson, **21**:283,n2; **23**: 272,n3, 274; **25**:478,n6, 481, 482, 483, 484, 487, 491
Baker, John Stewart, **19**:535,n2,3
Baker, Newton Diehl, **23**:327,n3; **24**: 361,n1,2, 567, 568-69; **25**:405,n3, 406,n5, 549,n1, 616
Baker, Ray Stannard, **16**:154n1, 304n1; **19**:475n3; **20**:565n; **22**:142n1, 412n1,2; **23**:55n1, 136,n2, 217, 226; **24**:205n; **25**:x
Baker, Samuel, **16**:5
Baker, Stephen, **19**:534-36,n1, 538-39, 543, 545-46, 553
Baker, William Edgar, Jr., **19**:679
Baker's Hotel, Washington, N. J., **21**:383
Bakewell, Mary Ella, **24**:315,n3
Baldwin, C. H., Jr., **14**:331
Baldwin, James Mark, **14**:126,n1, 127, 128, 395, 395n1, 553, 556,n1; **15**:13-14, 25, 70, 71, 103-105, 106-10, 112, 113, 114, 115, 115n2, 116, 118,n1, 119, 121, 131, 132, 134, 163; **18**:352,n4
Baldwin, Oliver Perry, **23**:266
Baldwin, Simeon Eben, **21**:109,n3, 117, 133, 144, 386, 590, 596, 598, 615; **22**:15, 283, 453; **24**:496; **25**:245n2, 246
Baldwin Locomotive Works, **19**:743; **23**: 246
Balentine, Edward D., **22**:241, 242n2, 253, 281, 339; **23**:333, 353
Balfour, Arthur James, 1st Earl of Balfour, **14**:27,n2; **19**:191,n3
Balken, Edward Duff, **19**:165
Ball, Alwyn, III, **22**:323
Ball, John R., **24**:309-10
Ball, Thomas H., **24**:489
Ballagh, James Curtis, **17**:487,n2, 524
Balliet, Thomas Minard, **17**:529,n2
Ballinger, Richard Achilles, **21**:546n3; **25**:645
Ballinger-Pinchot controversy, **21**:546-n3; **22**:427n1; **23**:175n1
Balliol College, Oxford, **15**:96-97, 396,-n6, 441; **17**:277, 332, 557
ballot reform, **22**:351, 358
ballots, **21**:432-33
ballots, preferential, **23**:456
Baltimore, **19**:149, 484; **20**:402, 407; **22**:139, 201; **23**:218, 230, 264, 266, 543, 547, 563, 570, 574, 576, 578, 579, 582, 583, 592, 657; **24**:65; **25**:422; Arundel Club, **17**:43; **18**:10; as a seaport, **24**:87; charter revision, **23**:573,n1; City College, **18**:576; Civil Service League, **22**:158; Emerson Hotel, **23**:567; Fifth

Regiment Armory, **23**:568, 569; Franklin Street Presbyterian Church, **18**:494; Gilman School, **16**:308, 309n1, 509,n3, 510, 511; Lyric Theatre, **18**:318; **23**:567, 568, 572, 573; Maryland Week, **23**:266; Music Hall, **14**:260; noted convention site, **24**:28n4; Peabody Conservatory of Music, **18**:322n2; Presbyterian Union, **14**:260, 277n1; **19**:52-63; Princeton alumni, **17**:43; **19**:146; **20**:27-28, 50,n1, 229-35, 247, 254, 265, 268, 269, 285, 311; Roland Park, **20**:407; WW addresses, **14**:260-61, 358-59; **17**:43-45; **18**:10-11, 318-20; **19**:48-49, 52-63, 76,n5; **20**:27-28, 50,n1, 229-35, 247, 254, 265, 268, 269, 285, 311; **24**:370-79; Woodrow Wilson Democratic Association, **22**:523-24; WW in, **17**:72; **23**:266,n1, 567-83; Women's Good Government Committee, **23**:573,n1
*Baltimore American*, **18**:576; **23**:568n, 573n3; **24**:236n
Baltimore Convention, *see* Democratic National Convention of 1912
Baltimore County School for Boys, *see* Baltimore, *Gilman School*
Baltimore Hotel, Kansas City, **16**:95; **24**:185
*Baltimore News*, **18**:576; **19**:155
*Baltimore Sun*, **14**:261n; **17**:45n; **18**:11n, 320n; **21**:102, 525n, 539n2, 555,n1; **22**:158, 175; **23**:40n, 43, 96n, 266, 266n2, 568n1, 572n, 583n; **24**:26n1, 146, 163n1, 236n, 370n, 379n, 401, 486, 519,n1, 528n; **25**:48, 128-29, 554n1; *Evening Sun*, **24**:491,n1, 492, 493
Bancroft, Cecil Franklin Patch, **16**: 486,n4
Bancroft, Cecil Kittredge, **16**:486,n3
Bancroft, Edgar Addison, **14**:424,n1; **18**:562,n1
Bancroft, George, **14**:286, 379, 444
Bancroft, Hugh, **24**:85,n2
Bancroft, Margaret Healy (Mrs. Edgar Addison), **14**:424,n1
bankers, **20**:415n2
*Bankers Magazine*, **18**:576
Bankers Trust Co., New York City, **23**: 246
Bankhead, John Hollis, **23**:513n4; **24**: 400,n3, 471,n2, 522n1
banking, **23**:57n5; **25**:104-105
Banking and Currency Committee (House of Rep.), Carter Glass, **25**:588-89
banking and currency system, **16**:475-76; **17**:520; **23**:119, 156-57,n2, 560n2, 621; and big business, **24**:422; platform plank, **24**:479; reform, **23**:156-57,n2; **25**:14, 42, 167, 203, 234, 343, 354-55, 372, 380, 502, 580 Δ W. J. Bryan, **23**:235n3, 237, 238; Democratic

platform, **24:**581,n1; C. Glass, **25:**531, 547, 564, 588, 608, 641-44; C. S. Hamlin, **24:**581-83; E. M. House, **25:**564, 565; W. H. Page, **25:**516; Hoke Smith, **25:**563; H. P. Willis, **25:**641n1, 650
*Banking Reform* (Laughlin), **24:**581,n2
banks, branch, **23:**312
Bannard, Otto Tremont, **19:**499, 499n3, 500
Bannockburn, Battle of, **18:**350
Bannon Lodge, Thunderbolt, nr. Augusta, Ga., **23:**557
Baptists, **19:**558
Bar Harbor, Maine, **14:**92
Barbara, Saint, **15:**359
*Barbarossa*, S.S., **14:**468
Barber, Isaac, M.D., **21:**393n1
Barber, Thomas, M.D., **21:**393,n1
Barber, William A., **15:**546
Barbour Asphalt Co., **24:**475n1
Barclay, McKee, **23:**11,n1, 43, 60, 264, 266
Baring, Hugo, **19:**396,n2
Barkley, James Morrison, **16:**43,n3
Barnard, Frederick Augustus Porter, **17:**548
Barnard, Henry, **16:**219n1
Barnes, William, **21:**252,n6, 258, 259-n11; **22:**429
Barney, Edgar Starr, **19:**223,n1
Barnum and Bailey Circus, **15:**201,n3, 210
Barnwell, Charles H., **23:**563n2
Barr, Alfred Hamilton, **16:**42,n1
Barr, John Watson, Jr., **19:**123, 124, 131, 155, 158, 195,n1, 196, 212; **20:**238,n1, 247, 248, 252, 284, 285, 303, 305n3, 311, 320, 321, 324, 424, 461, 474, 481, 494, 531,n1, 534, 567; **21:**39,n1
Barret, LeRoy Carr, **17:**163,n11, 556; **19:**676
Barrie, Sir James Matthew, **14:**528n8
Barringer, Brandon, **23:**227,n2
Barringer, Daniel Moreau (1806-1873), **15:**581,n2
Barringer, Daniel Moreau (Princeton 1879), **14:**131-32, 134, 194,n4; **15:**64,n4, 67, 140, 174, 242; **16:**187, 336; **19:**49, 125, 148, 162; **21:**603; **23:**227-28, 232, 245-47, 314, 327, 408, 409, 605, 631, 651
Barringer, Daniel Moreau, Jr. (Princeton 1900), **23:**227,n2
Barringer, Elizabeth Wethered, **23:**227,n2
Barringer, John Paul, **23:**227,n2
Barringer, Lewin Bennett, **23:**227,n2
Barringer, Margaret Bennett (Mrs. Daniel Moreau), **15:**140; **19:**49,n3, 125; **23:**227,n1, 232
Barringer, Paul Brandon, M.D., **14:**130,-n1, 189,n2
Barringer, Richard Wethered, **23:**227,n2
Barringer, Sarah Drew, **23:**227,n2

Barry, Ralph Andrew, **16:**465, 512
Barsotti, Charles, **25:**28
Barstow, Cal., **23:**43, 44
Bartholdt, Richard, **21:**615,n4
Bartholomew, William T., **23:**268
Bartlett, Charles Lafayette, **24:**358n1
Bartlett, Frederick W., **23:**507,n5
Bartlett, H. C., **22:**173n1
Bartlett, Maitland Vance, **15:**120,n6
Barton, Bruce, **23:**305,n1
Baruch, Bernard Mannes, **25:**415,n1
*Baruch: The Public Years* (Baruch), **25:**415n1
Basel, Wilsons at, **14:**538
Basham, George L., **23:**517
Basking Ridge, N. J., **23:**475
Basler, Roy Prentice, **23:**407n9
Basore, John William, **16:**110, 112, 132, 252, 528; **17:**162,n2, 408; **18:**582
Bassett, John Spencer, **20:**583
*Batavia* (N. Y.) *Times*, **25:**112n1
Bates, John Lewis, **14:**515
Bathgate, James Edward, Jr., **20:**66,n4, 67; **22:**72,n2
Batten, Clayton, **23:**394
Battle, George Cullen, **19:**4-5,n1
*Battle Creek* (Michigan) *Enquirer*, **22:**238,n2
*Battle Creek* (Michigan) *Evening News*, **22:**238n3
*Battle Creek* (Michigan) *Journal*, **22:**238n
Battle of Princeton, **16:**143; **19:**127; **20:**74, 466
Baxter, Clarence Hughson, **21:**158,n1
Baxter, Edgeworth Bird, **19:**618,n1, 678; **21:**577,n1
Baxter, Walter, **20:**349,n4
Bay City, Mich., **24:**248n1
Bay Head, N. J., WW children at, **14:**50n4, 53
Baylor, Miss, **15:**230
Baylor University, **16:**252; **23:**511
Bayne, Howard Randolph, **15:**546
Bayonne, N. J., **21:**19; **23:**136, 137,n2, 295n5; Democratic Club, **21:**485, 487; First Baptist Church, **21:**487; First Methodist Church, **21:**487; St. Henry's R.C. Church, **21:**487; WW campaign speech, **21:**485-92; High School, **23:**136
Beach, Harlan Page, **18:**560,n2
Beach, Sylvester Woodbridge, **16:**301,n1; **17:**99n2; **21:**597,n1
Beach Haven, N. J., **21:**8
Beam, Jacob Newton, **14:**46,n3; **16:**421,n5, 510; **17:**408; **20:**451
Beam, John Cooke, **19:**679
Bean, Walton, **21:**342n5
Beard, Charles Austin, **16:**374n1; **19:**155, 156, 157, 307
*Beast* (Lindsey and O'Higgins), **22:**275,n2, 388, 538
Beatty, Annie, **14:**15-17, 18, 21, 28, 70
Beaty, Julian Bonar, **15:**120

*Beau Brummel* (Fitch), **15**:201
Beautiful Isle of Somewhere (Pounds-Fearis), **23**:379,n2
Beck, James Montgomery, **15**:146,n8, 150; **16**:11,n2
Beck, Will H., **25**:162, 163
Beckham, John Crepps Wickliffe, **24**:332n2
Beckwith, Harvey, **23**:64,n8, 66
Beckwith, John F. B., **22**:384,n7
Beddall, Marcus Melvin, **16**:58,n1
Bedford, Paul, **15**:471,n3
Bedinger, Maria Voorhees, **15**:8,n5
Bedminster, N. J., **23**:475
*Bee* (Washington), **21**:47n1
Beecher, Henry Ward, **14**:318, 372
Beechwood, Scarborough-on-Hudson, N. Y., **22**:187n2, 234
Beede's Post Office, Essex County, New York, **19**:277
beef trust, **16**:15n1; **20**:437; **25**:297
Beekman, Azariah M., **23**:475,n1, 541
Beekman, Daniel H., **23**:475,n3
Beer, George Louis, **14**:338-46
Beethoven, Ludwig van, **15**:153,n2; **17**:617
Begges, A. Elizabeth Wilson, aunt of WW, **17**:17,n11
Beggs, John Irvin, **22**:57,n2
*Beginners of a Nation* (Eggleston), **15**:484
Behrin, Nathan, **25**:xi,n1
Belair, Md., **23**:568
Belding, Don, **23**:657n
Beldon, Samuel W., **20**:31,n1
Belford, John Louis, **19**:314,n4
Belford, Samuel W., **24**:520,n3
Bell, Albert Thomas, **23**:316,n2
Bell, Alden, **24**:121,n1
Bell, Alexander, **14**:43n1, 94, 110, 111-12; **15**:413,n1
Bell, Henry C., **24**:25-26
Bell, Herbert, **16**:486,n1; **17**:243; **18**:406
Bell, James Christy, **19**:504-505,n1
Bell, John Cromwell, **20**:539
Bell, Lilian Lida, **14**:380n1
Bell, Robert Mowry, M.D., **19**:570, 576, 679; **20**:451
Bell, Samuel Dennis, **19**:502n3, 504,n2
Bell, Theodore Arlington, **22**:32n2; **23**:57,n4
Bell Buckle, Tenn., WW address, **16**:235
Bellagio, Italy, **17**:8; Grand Hotel, **14**:540; Villa Serbelloni, **14**:540; Wilsons at, **14**:539, 540
Bellamy, Blanche Wilder (Mrs. Frederick Putnam), **15**:166,n4; **16**:89-90,n1
Bellamy, Edward, **15**:166n4; **16**:89,n4
Bellamy, Frederick Putnam, **15**:166,n4
Bellamy, Paul, **16**:89,n3
Belleville, N. J., sewage disposal, **24**:267n1
Bellevue-Stratford Hotel, Philadelphia, **14**:380; **16**:56; **18**:550, 564; **21**:558;

**22**:148, 441n1, 487n2; **24**:163,n1, 177, 181
Bellini, Giovanni, **15**:359
Bellis, Lewis A., **23**:475,n2
Belloc, Hilaire, **17**:307
Bellows, Edward Clark, **23**:44,n11, 51
Belmont, August, **16**:532,n1, 534; **22**:160
Belmont Hotel, New York City, **19**:648; **20**:116, 119; **21**:321, 362n1; **22**:334
Beloit College, **16**:508
Belvidere, N. J., **21**:558; Allen's drug store, **21**:384; Court House, **21**:384; WW campaign speech, **21**:384
Belvidere Hotel (Baltimore), **24**:83
Bemis, Edward Webster, **21**:617-18,n1
Ben Greet players, *see* Greet, Sir Philip Barling Ben
Bender, Harold Herman, **19**:570, 576, 679
Benedetto da Rovessano, **15**:353
Benedict, Elias Cornelius, **14**:73,n1
Benedict, Sarah Hart (Mrs. Elias Cornelius), **14**:73
Benet, W. Christie, **23**:549
Bennet, William Stiles, **23**:584
Bennett, James Gordon (1841-1918), **22**:393,n1,2; **25**:34
Bennett, John Mirza, Jr., **17**:280,n1, 287
Bennett, Philo Sherman, **16**:50-51, 69, 199
Bennett, Reginald S., M.D., **23**:445; **24**:524-25
Bennett, William Stiles, **24**:180,n2
Benny, Allan, **22**:395,n1
Bensel, John Anderson, **25**:134,n3
Benson, Edwin North, **16**:336,n4
Benson, Edwin North, Jr., **16**:336,n4
Benton, Ark., **23**:517
Benton, Thomas Hart, **16**:53; **17**:313
benzoate of soda, **25**:150, 151,n6, 282,n1
Berea College, **21**:579; **22**:48-49,n2, 172, 214, 417-21, 425
*Berea Quarterly*, **22**:421n
Beresford-Hope, Alexander James Beresford, **15**:162
Bergen, Matthew, **16**:105
Bergen County, N. J., **21**:7, 11, 22, 41, 52, 141, 142, 149, 172-73, 436, 452, 507; **22**:86-87, 87n1,2, 124; **23**:386-87; **24**:266; WW campaign speeches, **21**:446-49, mentioned 412; **23**:449-51; **25**:582
Bergh, Albert Ellery, **14**:360n1
Bergner, Charles Henry, **14**:362
Berkeley, Cal., **23**:42, 54; Berkeley High School, **23**:60; WW in, **23**:55, 59-60
Berkeley, George, **14**:503; **19**:666
Berko, G. D., **25**:28
*Berkshire Evening Eagle* (Pittsfield), **18**:436n, 444n
Berkshire Hills, **19**:386
Berlin, **14**:245; **22**:604
Berlin, University of, **15**:444, 558; **16**:46, 248, 250, 257, 465, 507, 508; **17**:556;

**18:**575, 580; **19:**677, 678; Theodore Roosevelt Professorship, **21:**48,n4
Bermuda, **16:**535,n3, 536, 547,n1, 554, 559, 560; **17:**3-9, 10-12, 14-19, 22-23, 25-28, 29n1, 32, 34, 36, 50,n1, 428n2, 551, 565, 568, 598, 599, 600, 604, 605, 606-608, 609-10, 611-13, 615, 616, 619; **18:**67, 351, 376, 378,n5, 382, 383, 385, 436, 449, 471, 480, 517; **19:**161, 193, 229, 324n2, 383, 385; **20:**116,n2, 119, 122n1, 125-26, 126, 127, 132-34, 135, 138-42, 144, 145, 146,n4, 148n, 148-51, 155-56, 172-73, 175-77, 178-80, 182, 183-88, 191, 208, 210, 211, 214, 215, 216, 218, 223, 224, 225, 226, 257; **21:**164n1, 556, 591n1; **22:**14, 100, 139, 141, 142, 204, 205, 209, 292, 294-95, 323-25,n4,6, 329-30, 331-32, 396, 407-408, 440, 454, 500, 511, 517, 520, 533-34, 548, 569, 572; **23:**49, 80, 84, 330, 560, 596, 597,n1, 606; **24:**58-59, 239, 305, 550; **25:**45, 220,n1, 422, 523, 533, 540, 546, 560, 568, 573, 588, 616, 634; Agar's Island, **20:**187; Anchorage, **20:**187; Aquarium, **20:**188; automobiles opposed, **17:**609-10; Bay House, **20:**188; Clifton (house), **20:**179; Devonshire Church, **20:**224; Girls High School, **22:**331; Glencove, **22:**141, 142, 204, 210, 407; Government House, **20:**127, 132, 145, 150, 177, 179; **22:**408; Hamilton, **22:**331; Hamilton Hotel, **20:**125, 132-33, 138, 141, 148, 176, 178, 179, 185, 187, 210; Inwood (house), **20:**127,n7, 224n2; **22:**210,n3, 330n1; legislature, **17:**610n2; Old Homestead, Warwick, **20:**149; Paget, **20:**133, 139; **22:**407; Paget West, **23:**654; Saltkettle, **20:**126, 179; Saltkettle Ferry, **20:**138; **22:**141, 205, 364, 407, 454; Shoreby (house), **20:**126, 140, 156, 178-79, 179; **22:**210,n3, 407; Soncy, **20:**180; South Shore, **23:**225,n1; Verandah House, **20:**139, 150; Warwick parish, **20:**145; WW in, **17:**3-9, 10-12, 14-19, 22-23, 25-28, 29, 32, 34, 36, 428n2, 606-13, 615, 616, 619; **18:**3-5; **20:**125-26, 126, 127, 132-34, 138-42, 144-46, 148-51, 155-56, 172-73, 175-77, 178-80, 183-88, 208, 210-11; **25:**551-89; WW's remarks to House of Assembly, **25:**575; WW's remarks upon arriving on November 18, 1912, **25:**551; Yacht Club, **17:**4,n9; photo, *illustration section.* Vol. 25; *see also* Hamilton, Paget, Warwick
Bermuda Biological Station for Research, **20:**187,n1
*Bermuda Historical Quarterly*, **17:**28n1
Bermuda Natural History Society, **17:**616; **20:**187n1
*Bermudian*, S.S., **16:**563; **17:**8, 10, 15; **18:**351; **19:**161, 214; **20:**134, 139, 140, 178, 185, 210; **22:**407; **23:**606; **25:**589

Bernardsville, N. J., **21:**354; **23:**471
Bernstein, Herman, **23:**191,n1; **25:**55, 94n1, 97
Berrien, Andrew J., **21:**219,n3, 226
Berrien, E. D., **20:**539
Berry, George Andreas, M.B., **16:**444,n1, 445, 446
Berry, William H., **22:**409n2; **23:**75n1, 230,n8; **24:**538,n2; **25:**616
Beth, *see* Hibben, Elizabeth Grier
Bethany College, **18:**578
Beveridge, Albert Jeremiah, **18:**186n4; **19:**758-59, **21:**219,n5, 344n11; **22:**12,-n4; **23:**655; **25:**22,n2
Bible, **23:**11, 12-20, 373-80; **25:**457; 300th anniversary of translation into English, **23:**494, 510
*Bible: Its Origin and Nature* (Dods), **16:**400,n2
Bible Normal College, Springfield, Mass., **14:**459n3
*Bible Society Record*, **23:**499n1
Bickford, Dr., **16:**562
Bicknell, Frank Alfred, **19:**313,n1; **23:** 82,n10
Biddle, John Craig, **14:**408
Biddles of Philadelphia, **20:**179
big business, **21:**395, 549, 551; **22:**540; **23:**35, 157, 275, 284-85, 296, 298-99, 430, 442, 447-48, 467, 510, 626, 627; **24:**76, 299, 300-301, 422, 448-49; **25:**11, 152, 188, 199, 219, 245, 266, 267, 357, 358, 372, 391, 497; and government, **25:**123, 125, 178-79; and the Republican party, **25:**396-97 Δ W. F. McCombs, **23:**360, 437n2; T. B. Love, **24:**164, 165; *see also* business, monopoly
Bigelow, Samuel, Jr., **24:**510
Bill, Alfred Hoyt, **15:**544n1
Billard, Julius Benoit, **25:**378n2
Bill of Rights (English), **25:**639
bimetallism, **23:**652-53
Binder, Jacob W., **23:**326-27,n1,2
Bingham, Hiram, **16:**29, 30, 40, 131, 142-43, 250, 379-80, 388; **17:**208, 286, 557; **22:**606-607,n1
Binkerd, Robert Studebaker, **19:**155, 157, 307
*Biographical History of North Carolina from Colonial Times to the Present* (ed. Ashe), **16:**187n1
*Biological Bulletin*, **18:**576
Bipartizan Direct Primary League, **22:** 225
Birch, Helen Barr (Mrs. Thomas Howard), **22:**544,n1, 545
Birch, Thomas Howard, **22:**231,n1, 307, 501, 502, 535n1, 536, 544, 545; **25:**46, 485n1
Bird, Sarah Baxter (Mrs. William Edgeworth), **14:**347,n2; **15:**8,n3, 244-45
Birkhoff, George David, **19:**138n3, 677-78

Birmingham, Ala., **22:**206, 226
*Birmingham News*, **24:**576n2
Birrell, Augustine, **17:**227; **21:**51; **23:** 111,n3
Bishop, Joseph Bucklin, **14:**306n3
*Bishop's Move* (comedy by Hobbes and Carson), **14:**529,n10
Bismarck-Schönhausen, Otto Eduard Leopold von, **25:**320
*Bitter Cry of the Children* (Spargo), **22:**452n2
Bixby, William Keeney, **16:**504,n2
Black, Charles Clarke, **16:**541n2, 554, 560-61, 562, 563; **17:**10n1,2,3; **22:**169,- n1
Black, Charles Newbold, **23:**53,n2, 325
Black, Hugh, **16:**448,n4; **17:**125
*Black Patch War* (Miller), **18:**7n1
Blackall, Christopher R., **15:**492,n4
Blackburn, Joseph Clay Stiles, **24:** 227,n6,7
Blackburn, William, **21:**335,n1
blacklists, **22:**291n2
Blackstone, Sir William, **16:**298; **23:**197
Blackwell, O. I., **23:**272,n3
Blackwell, Robert Winthrop, **15:**131,n4
Blagden, Crawford, **20:**539
Blaikie, William Garden, **18:**339n2
Blaine, Anita McCormick (Mrs. Emmons), **19:**481,n1, 486-87; **25:**570
Blaine, Emmons, **19:**481n1
Blaine, James Gillespie, **14:**251; **19:** 481n1; **24:**125, 126, 193, 576; **25:**205
Blair, Albion Zelophehad, **23:**75n2
Blair, Clinton Ledyard, **15:**570, 573; **16:**5, 552,n2; **20:**129,n1,2, 141, 208, 208n4, 222, 227, 244, 246, 360, 361
Blair, DeWitt Clinton, **15:**437, 526; **16:**312,n1, 356, 552n2; **19:**674; **20:**130- n1
Blair, Francis Preston, Jr., **21:**335
Blair, James, **14:**311
Blair, John Insley, **16:**312n1, 356; **20:** 131n1
Blair Academy, Blairstown, N. J., **16:** 312; **21:**476,n2
Blair and Co., New York bankers, **15:** 325,n1, 336, 352, 355
Blair family, **21:**476
Blairstown, N. J., **21:**384
Blairstown Hotel, Blairstown, N. J., **21:**384
Blairstown Seminary, **21:**384
Blake, Aldrich, **23:**341,n2
Blakely, Paul Lendrum, **17:**560,n1
Blanchard, Newton Crain, **24:**483,n2
Blankenburg, Rudolph, **24:**126n4
Blanton, H. J., **25:**395n2
Blau, Julia Ellsworth (Mrs. Max Friedrich), **15:**155
Blau, Max Friedrich, **14:**146n5, 473; **15:** 155; **17:**408; **19:**570
Blauvelt, James Gillmor, **21:**256n9, 260-64,n1, 412

Blease, Coleman Livingston, **23:**173,n2
Bletchley, Bucks, Wilsons in, **14:**530
Blewett, Dennis Francis, **24:**257,n1, 258
*Blight of Seniority* (editorial, Bryan), **25:**648,n1
Bliss, F. R., Mrs., **14:**551
Bliss, Gilbert Ames, **16:**132, 136-37, 160, 162, 165, 258; **17:**408
Blodget, Betty Brese, **14:**333
Blodgett Mountain, Vermont, **14:**552
Bloomfield, N. J., sewage disposal, **24:** 267n1; WW campaign speech, **21:**563
Bloomington, Ill., **24:**291, 292
Bluck, Arthur William, **17:**26, 27n3
Bluck, Mary Everest Outerbridge (Mrs. Arthur William), **17:**26, 27n3
Bluck, Winifred, **17:**27,n3
Blue Valley School, Kansas City, Mo., **24:**484n1
Blumenthal, George, **16:**373,n1
B'nai B'rith, **15:**471; **25:**28
Boardman, Mabel Thorp, **22:**140,n3
Boatwright, Frederic William, **24:**118
Bobbitt, Benjamin Boisseau, **21:**299,n2, 324
Bobbs-Merrill Company, **18:**520n2
Boccaccio, Giovanni, **19:**703,n1
Böcklin, Arnold, **20:**181,n3
Bodenheim, G. A., **23:**519,n1
Bodleian Library, Oxford, **14:**532
Boettner, Frank A., **22:**241, 242n2, 253, 281, 339; **23:**333, 353
Bogart, Ernest Ludlow, **16:**55-56, 131, 250; **17:**408; **18:**271, 294; **19:**180, 183, 190, 315n2, 676
Bogart, John N., **25:**98n2
Böhm, Clara, **15:**117
Boisgilbert, Edmund, *pseud.* Ignatius Loyola Donnelly, **23:**q.v.
Bok, Edward William, **21:**118; **22:**21
Bolce, Harold, **19:**314,n1
Bolingbroke, Henry St. John, 1st Viscount, **14:**505
Bolivar, Simon, **16:**388n1
Bollschweiler, Albert E., **21:**547,n4
Bologna, Italy, **14:**246; EAW at, **15:**275
Bologna, University of, **16:**508
Bolterill, Samuel, **22:**546n5
Bolton, Tenn., **16:**250
Bombay University, **15:**427
Bonaparte, Charles Joseph, **16:**213,n2; **17:**228n1
Bonar Bridge, Ross and Cromarty, **18:** 392
Bonbright, William Prescott, **22:**202,n2
Bones, Helen Woodrow, first cousin of WW, **14:**346, 423, 431, 454; **20:**190,n5
Bones, James W., **25:**569
Bones, Jessie Woodrow, **25:**627n2
Bones, Marion McGraw, **25:**627n2; incorrectly identified at **14:**431,n3; *see* Erskine, Marion Brower
Bones, Marion Woodrow (Mrs. James W.), **23:**555,n9

*Bonfort's Wine and Spirit Circular*, **25**: 21,n1
Bonn, University of, **16**:249; **18**:575
Bonnat, Léon, **16**:437n1
Bonner, Walter Daniel, **16**:465, 512
*Book Buyer* (New York), **14**:313n
*Book Notes* (New York), **15**:238
books, WW on reading of, **14**:263
Boone, Iowa, high school, **16**:58
Booraem, John Van Liew, **22**:328,n3
Borah, William Edgar, **23**:132n1
Borden, Edward Payson, **16**:336,n5
Borden, Robert Laird, **21**:155,n3
Bordentown, N. J., Academy, WW talk, **14**:358n1
Borglum, Gutzon, **15**:27; **16**:173-74, 175, 177, 178; **18**:623, 625; **19**:23
*Boss Ruef's San Francisco . . .* (Bean), **21**:342n5
bosses, political, *see* political bosses
Boston, Mass., **14**:546; **18**:308; **19**:229, 290, 291, 304, 331, 333, 349, 350, 383; **20**:9n, 464, 465, 471, 496; **23**:258, 588, Back Bay Station, **20**:466; Boston City Club, **19**:420; **24**:92-93; Boston Public Library, **14**:44, 52, 70, 79; Boston Symphony Orchestra, **18**:303,n3,4, 482,n2,3; **19**:167, 167n3, 200-201, 200,n1, 210,n1; **20**:181; campaign addresses, **24**:83-92, 360-67; colonial days, **25**:596; Colonial Theatre, **14**:309, 316; Democratic City Committee, **23**:324,n1,2; Democratic rally, **23**:356; Keith's Theatre, **14**:70; Lowell Institute, **15**:447; Museum of Fine Arts, **15**:214n6; **16**:252; National Shawmut Bank, **23**:235; North Station, **14**:49; Princeton alumni, **20**:252, 410, 413, 466, 469; Parker House, **14**:398; Public Garden, **14**:39, 79; real estate, **24**:126-27; and the American Revolution, **25**:596; The Thorndike (hotel), **14**:51; Touraine Hotel, **20**:466,n4; trade, **24**:127; Twentieth Century Club, **14**:254, 307-308, 316-19; Union Club, **21**:40n1; University Club, **14**:309; **16**:384; **19**:483, 497; Vendome Hotel, **18**:297n1; **20**:466; WW addresses, **14**:316-19; **16**:384-85; **18**:295,n1, 297-300; **19**:497; WW at City Club, **24**:92-93; WW in, **14**:49, 51, 52, 57, 67, 70, 76, 79, 309, 316-19; **19**:383, 497; **21**:40, 40n1, 46, 51, 61
*Boston American*, **25**:288n1
Boston & Maine Railroad, **25**:414
Boston Common, **24**:418-19
*Boston Daily Advertiser*, **16**:385n
*Boston Daily Globe*, **24**:367n
*Boston Evening Transcript*, **14**:319n; **19**: 290, 323; **25**:269n
*Boston Herald*, **14**:25n2, 51; **18**:434,n2; **19**:497n; **24**:495, 559,n1, 585,n1; **25**:19-20, 562n1
*Boston Herald Traveler*, **25**:269n

*Boston Post*, **24**:78n, 95n, 367n
Boston Red Sox, **25**:390n3
Boston Suffrage League, **21**:21n1
*Boston Sunday Post*, **24**:368n
Boston Tech, *see* Massachusetts Institute of Technology
Boston University, **19**:676
Bostwick, Charles Byron, **15**:252; **17**: 382, 595; **18**:229, 241
Boswell, James, **16**:209
Bothe, Marion Bradley, **23**:381n
Bothwell (at De Vinne Press), **20**:277
Botsford, Alfred Clark, **15**:131,n3
Botticelli, Sandro, **15**:229, 317
Boucard, Max, **14**:30-31, 44, 124
Boulogne, **15**:384, 441
Bound Brook, N. J., **21**:361; **23**:475, 540; WW campaign speech, **21**:354-61
Bourbons, **23**:411
Bourne, Henry Eldridge, **16**:564; **19**: 333,n1
Bourne, Jonathan, Jr., **22**:34-35,n1, 36, 248, 334; **23**:132n1
Bourne, Randolph Silliman, **20**:350n2
Bowdoin College, **16**:257; **17**:369; **18**: 301n1; **22**:165n1
Bowen, Herbert E., **21**:53
Bowie, Walter Russell, **15**:200
Bowker, Lyman A., **14**:10,n2, 16
Bowlby, Harry Laity, **16**:546; **21**:90-91
Bowles, Frank, **14**:4,n5
Bowman, John Gabbert, **18**:258,n1; **19**: 182,n1
Boxer Rebellion of 1900, **18**:626n1; Boxer Indemnity, **18**:625,n1
Boxwood, Old Lyme, Conn., **16**:154n1, 155, 158; **18**:376
Boyd, Francis Darby, M.D., **16**:444,n2, 445
Boyd, James T., **24**:404
Boyd, John Yeomans, **16**:5
Boyd, Julian Parks, **14**:360n1
Boyd, Thomas Duckett, **19**:411-12,n1
Boyer, Clarence Valentine, **14**:13-14
Boyer, Joseph McCarter, **18**:304-305, 305-306
Boyle, Thomas A., **23**:354,n4
Bracken, John Joseph, **22**:253,n4; **23**: 333, 336, 337, 385, 388, 389-90
Bracken, John Joseph, Jr., **22**:231n
Brackett, Cyrus Fogg, M.D., **14**:159, 326, 395, 413, 469-70, 474; **15**:56, 74; **16**:64n1, 102, 103; **17**:146, 349,n1; **18**:64, 66, 67, 241, 248, 257, 258, 260-61, 272, 289, 300-301, 338, 571-72; **19**:451, 732
Brackett, Haven Darling, **16**:59,n1
Braddock, Edward, **14**:351, 352
Braddock Heights, Md., **23**:264, 266
Bradford, Ernest S., **19**:91n2
Bradford, Gamaliel (1831-1911), **17**:30-31, 32-33; **22**:138,n6
Bradford, Gamaliel (1863-1932), **22**: 138n6

Bradford, Helen Hubbard Ford (Mrs. Gamaliel), **22**:138n6
Bradley, Katharine Peck (Mrs. Mahlon), **20**:156,n3, 473,n1, 492-93, 500,n1, 535, 536; **23**:224,n7
Bradley, Mahlon, **20**:473, 500,n1, 536
Bradley, William James Lee, **22**:550n2; **23**:346, 354, 365,n2, 381, 400, 401, 417, 446, 474; **24**:432,n4
Bradley Polytechnic Institute, **16**:254
Braeman, John, **18**:186n4
Braga, Teófilo, **21**:439n1
Bragdon, Henry Wilkinson, **15**:52n1, 288n15; **16**:22n, 481n1; **17**:85n2; **19**:177n; **21**:103n
Bragg, Edward Stuyvesant, **24**:257,n2, 258, 259
Branchville, N. J., **21**:413
Brandeis, Louis Dembitz, **20**:136n8; **24**:580; **25**:56-58, 59-60, 272, 274,n1,2, 286, 287-304, 339, 545; congratulatory message, **25**:528; memo on LaFollette antitrust bill, **25**:295-304; suggestions on trusts, **25**:289-94; W. J. Bryan on, **25**:622, 646; H. L. Higginson on, **25**:414,n1, 423; E. M. House on, **25**:550, 558, 610-11; A. L. Lowell on, **25**:535, 541; A. J. McKelway on, **25**:544
*Brandeis: A Free Man's Life* (Mason), **20**:136n8; **25**:414n1,2
Brandeis and the New Haven-Boston & Maine Merger Battle Revisited (Abrams), **25**:414n1
*Brandeis Way: A Case Study in the Workings of Democracy* (Mason), **20**:136n8
brandy: gift to Hibbens, **15**:384
Branegan, Edward J., **23**:535
Branegan, Joseph M., **23**:536n1
Branin, Mark, **23**:534,n5
Brank, Rockwell Smith, **15**:155,n1, 201
Branson, Roswell H., **21**:154,n2
Brasenose College, Oxford, **15**:396,n5
Brattan, Joseph Yancey, **23**:568,n9
Braun, Marcus, **24**:135-36,n1
Braxton, Allen Caperton, **25**:632n1
Brayton Hotel, New York City, **21**:164n1
Breakers (hotel), Palm Beach, Fla., **15**:580
Breckinridge, Desha, **23**:183,n3
Breckinridge, Henry Skillman, **19**:483-84,n1,4, 486; **22**:213-14, 236-37, 412, 523-24, 525-26; **23**:112n2; **24**:146, 332-33, 357-58; **25**:23,n1
*Bremen*, S.S., **14**:542n18
Bremner, Robert Gunn, **20**:558,n1,2, 570; **21**:133, 153-54; **25**:511,n1, 513-14
Brensinger, George F., **23**:536n1
Brensinger, Joseph W., **23**:535,n2
Brett, Cornelius, **15**:195,n1
Brett, George Platt, **20**:155,n2, 185
Brett, Marie Louise Tostevin (Mrs. George Platt), **20**:155,n1, 185

Brewer, David Josiah, **14**:136,n1; **16**:227n2, 315
Brian, James, **20**:290
bribery, **19**:521; **21**:302, 393, 443; **22**:359
Brice, Calvin Stewart, **22**:113n2
*Bridge to France* (Hurley), **20**:519,n1,2
Bridges, Henry Wilson, **24**:381-82,n1
Bridges, Robert (Bob, Bobby, *pseud.* Droch), **14**:21-22, 149, 195, 198-99, 267, 293, 335, 360, 397, 403, 417; **15**:50, 223, 360, 361, 383, 388-89, 411, 530, 571; **16**:3, 134, 336, 339, 405, 451-52, 488; **17**:31, 351n2, 417-18, 449-50, 456; **18**:549; **19**:64, 117, 119, 120, 123, 123-24, 149, 154-55, 158-59, 190, 252, 347, 348-49, 390, 503-504, 530-31; **20**:213, 283; **21**:298, 337-38, 591; **22**:12, 287-88,n2, 332, 333, 361, 411-12; **24**:66-67, 82, 100; poem, Cultural and Structural Entity, **18**:307; WW requests withdrawal, **18**:308; WW letter of thanks, **18**:310
Bridges, Samuel Russell, **15**:216,n1, 217
Bridgeton, N. J., **23**:533n3; WW campaign speeches, **21**:276-81, mentioned, **21**:244, 322; **23**:531, 533-34
Bridgman, Henry H., **19**:199,n3
Bridgman, Howard Allen, **19**:441,n1, 475n3
Briery Close, Westmorland, **18**:394
Briggs, Charles Augustus, **14**:192
Briggs, Frank Obadiah, **16**:561n1; **21**:219n2, 244,n3, 249,n5, 290,n1, 291, 296, 330, 351; **22**:226; **24**:547; **25**:487
Briggs, LeBaron Russell, **15**:292n
Brigham, H. A., **14**:102
Bright, John, **17**:307,n5
Bright, John Albert, **17**:307,n5
Briner, Helen Bardwell, **16**:234
Brinley, Charles Augustus, **18**:544,n1
Bristow, Joseph Little, **23**:132n1
British Association for the Advancement of Science, **14**:82; **16**:157n7, 164; *Report of Seventy-Fifth Meeting*, **16**:157n7
British Iron and Steel Institute, **14**:544-n3
British Library Association, **16**:392
British Linen Company Bank, London, **14**:498, 528, 534, 548; **16**:165, 430; Londonderry, **18**:348
British North America Act, **18**:165
British Westinghouse Electric and Manufacturing Company, **18**:577
*Broadening Church: A Study of Theological Issues in the Presbyterian Church since 1869* (Loetscher), **15**:169n2
Brock, Louis M., **23**:535
Brockman, Fletcher Sims, **18**:291,n2
Brockson, Franklin, **25**:427,n5
Brodhead, Calvin Easton, **21**:83-84,n1, 84-85; **22**:22,n1, 198, 199, 206, 232-33, 238, 243-44, 294, 308, 309
Brodhead, William E., **21**:85n

Brodhead, William M., **22:**199n, 238n, 308n
Brokaw, Howard Crosby, **19:**165
Bronk, Mitchell, **21:**487
Bronson, Earl, **24:**221,n2
Brooke, Sir Charles Anthony Johnson, Rajah of Sarawak, **15:**209n2
Brookline, Mass., **19:**383,n6, 483; Harvard Church, **19:**483n2, 496, 497; WW address, **19:**483, 496, 497
Brooklyn, **19:**349, 354; **25:**419; Lafayette Avenue Presbyterian Church, **14:** 299-301; Princeton alumni, **20:**247, 272-76; University Club, **16:**289; WW addresses, **14:**283-85, 299-301; **16:** 289-90; **20:**272-76, 311, 320, 410; **25:**435-40; to delegation of Italian Americans from, **25:**107n1
*Brooklyn Daily Citizen*, **25:**435n1
*Brooklyn Daily Eagle*, **16:**331n1, 373n3; **20:**59,n3; **22:**134,n1, 170,n1, 226,n4; **23:**339,n1; **24:**238n4, 580; **25:**135-36n,n1, 440n, 522n
Brooklyn Institute of Arts and Sciences, **14:**283
Brooklyn League, **24:**238
*Brooklyn Times*, **20:**424n1; **24:**504
Brooks, James C., **16:**336,n2
Brooks, John Graham, **15:**408, 502; **22:**157n1
Brooks, John Milton, **14:**145,n7
Brooks, Robert Clarkson, **16:**306,n4
Brooks, Samuel Palmer, **23:**511
Brooks, Sydney, **23:**287n2; **24:**544
Brooks, Walter Booth, Jr., **16:**5; **20:**27-28,n1
Brougham, Herbert Bruce, **20:**65,n1, 69-71, 76-77, 79-80, 286, 401, 425; **21:**97-98; **22:**581,n1
Broughton, Leonard Gaston, M.D., **19:** 400,n5
Broughton-in-Furness, Lancs, **18:**369
Broussard, Robert Foligny, **24:**468, 487-88
Brower, Abraham Thew H., **14:**422n2, 423
Brower, Jessie Woodrow Bones (Mrs. Abraham Thew H.), first cousin of WW, **14:**422n2, 423, 428, 431, 438, 454; **25:**569-70
Brown, Alexander, **14:**353,n3; **15:**247
Brown, Alice Van Vechten, **14:**191
Brown, Allen Henry, **16:**23,n5
Brown, Arthur Judson, **19:**109-10,n1,3
Brown, Bruce Whiting, **20:**252,n2
Brown, Burt. E., **23:**291-92,n1
Brown, Charles F., **17:**164
Brown, Charles W., **22:**241, 253
Brown, Coleman Peace, **17:**169,n1, 384; **20:**123-24,n1, 212, 213, 221
Brown, Cyrus Billingslea, **23:**548,n1
Brown, Darius Alvin, **23:**9,n1
Brown, Edward Thomas, **23:**341,n5
Brown, Elliott Chipman, **16:**465, 512

Brown, Ernest William, **16:**157,n5, 489,n3
Brown, Francis, **16:**400,n5
Brown, George Dobbin, **16:**465, 511
Brown, George Stewart, **23:**568,n4
Brown, George Whitfield, Jr., **14:**544
Brown, Harrington, **23:**326,n5
Brown, Herman La Rue, **20:**136,n7,8,10
Brown, John, **14:**352-53; **20:**372n3; **22:** 604n2
Brown, Mrs., **16:**441
Brown, Mrs. (of Pittsfield), **19:**356,n1
Brown, Oliver Huff, **21:**324
Brown, Oren Britt, **14:**450,n1; **22:**361-62,n1
Brown, Roscoe Conkling Ensign, **19:** 156,n3
Brown, Susan Dod (Mrs. David), **14:**29, 71, 396,n2; **16:**134, 323n1
Brown, William Adams, **16:**448,n3
Brown, William Garrott, **14:**5n2, 56, 86-87, 206,n2; **23:**513-16,n1, 542-43, 547-49, 595-96, 604, 630
Brown, William H. C., **25:**620,n3
Brown Brothers & Co., **19:**73, 73n2
Brown Palace Hotel, Denver, **23:**11, 23, 27
Brown University, **14:**491, 494-95; **15:** 234n; **16:**213n1; **17:**329; **19:**558; **23:** 98,n7; Phi Beta Kappa, Rhode Island Alpha, **14:**491; Sayles Hall, **14:**49; WW honorary degree, **14:**494-95
Browne, Honor, **16:**437,n3, 438, 441
Browne, Thomas H., **24:**272,n3, 286
Browne (Yeoman of Troutbeck, Westmorland), **16:**438,n1
Brownell, Silas Brown, **19:**235,n1
Brownell, William Crary, **14:**454,n6; **25:**587,n2
Browning, Elizabeth Barrett, **14:**104; **15:**358
Browning, Oscar, **14:**356n2
Browning, Robert, **15:**35, 358; **16:**328; **18:**328n1, 638; **19:**41, 723
Browning, Webster E., **16:**358
Browning, William John, **23:**393, 394n3, 404, 409, 521
Brownlow, Louis, **24:**547
Brown's Hotel, London, **14:**535
Bruce, Elizabeth Tunstall Taylor Newton (Mrs. Philip Alexander), **22:**254,n4
Bruce, Philip Alexander, **14:**205n4, 353,-n3; **15:**395n3; **22:**254,n1
Bruce, William Cabell, **22:**384,n5
Bruère, Henry, **23:**634n1
Bruges, **15:**441
Brugmann, Karl, **14:**245,n2
Brush, Murray Peabody, **20:**264,n1
Brussels, **15:**440
Bryan, Alison Reid, **21:**201,n2
Bryan, Charles Wayland, **22:**519n4; **23:** 95,n3, 96, 98, 236n4, 237-39; **24:**565, 574-75
Bryan, D. L., **14:**331

Bryan, Frederick E., **20:**244, 256
Bryan, George, **20:**414,n1,2, 415, 419; **23:**563,n2; **24:**71, 79, 118
Bryan, John Pendleton Kennedy, **16:** 286,n1
Bryan, John Stewart, **23:**563,n2,3, 604; **24:**96, 97
Bryan, Mary Elizabeth Baird (Mrs. William Jennings), **23:**95,n4, 237,n1; **24:**462,n1,2, 465; **25:**286, 339n3, 507, 533, 540
Bryan, Nathan Philemon, **24:**273,n1, 287,n1
Bryan, Pendleton Taylor, **16:**5
Bryan, T. S., **14:**331
Bryan, Thomas Smith, **22:**576-77,n1; **23:**114,n2
Bryan, William Jennings, **14:**17n3, 250, 360n1, 445; **15:**506,n4, 550; **16:**43, 49, 50-51, 69, 311; **17:**30, 92n2, 124, 124n1, 461, 490, 516, 587; **18:**4, 6, 219-20, 269, 270, 351, 352, 386n3, 479-80, 479n1, 639-40; **19:**9, 10n2, 492; **20:**243, 349; **21:**21n1, 24n1, 86, 598, 600-601; **22:**115, 161, 217, 220, 221, 224-25, 231,n1, 255,n1, 284, 285, 285n3, 291n2, 307, 334, 409, 409n1, 435, 465-66n3, 466, 466n4, 501, 502, 502-503, 519n4, 522, 535, 535n1, 536, 540, 541, 543-44, 545, 553,n1, 553, 554, 557,n4, 571, 587; **23:**21, 32n5, 52,n3, 53n3, 76, 95, 98, 99, 100, 112, 112n2, 113n2, 130, 130n1, 131, 234n5, 235-36,n3, 237,n1, 237-38, 242, 242n2, 243n3, 284, 291, 436, 513, 515, 552, 593, 593n4, 602n1, 615, 631, 632, 651; **24:**26, 96, 185, 237, 249, 265, 364, 446, 450n1, 465, 472, 493, 494, 496, 497, 500, 503, 506, 508, 518, 520, 526, 531, 542, 543-44, 553, 588; **25:**46, 234, 271, 347,n3, 348, 350, 351, 361, 459,n1,3, 526, 532-33, 540, 559, 563, 564, 565, 587, 590, 610, 616-17,n2,4, 621, 624; advice on campaign, **24:**537, 565; Aldrich plan, **24:**273-74; appearance at Baltimore convention, **24:**512; attempt to unseat J. M. Guffey, **24:**7,n1; cabinet suggestions, **25:**622-23, 645-46, 648-49; congratulatory message, **25:** 522; E. M. House on, **24:**131, 140, 332; **25:**507, 550, 614; Joline letter, **24:**5,n2, 6, 8-9; W. F. McCombs on, **24:**547; E. D. Mead on, **25:**19,n2; New York's vote for Clark at Baltimore, **24:**512n1; G. F. Peabody on, **25:**608-609; prenomination funds, **24:**284; Secretary of State offer, **25:**616n2; shift to WW at Baltimore, **24:**510,n1; on tariff reform, **24:**330; on trusts, **24:**571; views on temporary chairman at Baltimore, **24:**462,n1, 492, 529-30; attitude of Virginia toward, **24:**486; WW support of in 1896, 1900, 1908, **23:**458, 463, 468, 470; WW votes for, **24:**298; WW's opinion of, **22:**501; **24:**10, 188, 189,n1,

291; photograph, **24:**illustration section
Bryan, William Swan Plumer, **21:**201,-n1; **22:**327,n2
Bryant, David, **21:**583
Bryant, Joseph Decatur, M.D., **15:**119,-n1; **23:**632,n3
Bryant, Lewis T., **23:**339n4, 340, 352
Bryant, William Henry, **23:**21,n8
Bryce, Elizabeth Marion Ashton, Lady Bryce, **15:**506; **17:**238, 431; **22:**211,n2; **25:**532n2
Bryce, James, Viscount Bryce, **14:**14, 397, 552; **15:**447, 500, 506; **16:**97, 527-28; **17:**72-73, 91, 105, 109, 127, 140-41, 215, 226n1, 228n1, 238, 301, 307-308, 338, 342, 347, 358, 360, 389, 392, 414-15, 431, 442-43, 446-47, 460, 462-65, 466, 469, 472, 497n1, 505, 508n1, 509-10,n3, 558; **18:**165, 447, 546; **19:**64, 157, 206, 240; **20:**22; **22:**33, 184, 211, 396n1, 483; **24:**507n1; **25:**531-32, 533, 606
Bryden, John Kerfoot, **16:**377
Bryn Mawr, Pa., **18:**467
Bryn Mawr College, **14:**6, 320; **16:**58-59, 79, 132, 255, 423,n1; **18:**395; **23:**21, 22; alumnae, **23:**21-22, 22n1
Buchanan, Frank, **23:**177,n4
Buchanan, James, **17:**310, 312, 315, 316, 317, 318; **23:**298,n7
Bucher, John Calvin, **20:**88
Buchtel College, **17:**550
Buckingham Palace Hotel, London, **14:** 529,n11, 548
Buckle, Henry Thomas, **14:**243
Buckler, William Hepburn, **17:**102, 108, 111,n1
Buckner, Garrett Davis, **19:**679
Buckner, Murrell L., **23:**507,n6
Buckner, Simon Bolivar, **23:**466, 470, 653
Budd, Eckard Payson, **23:**475,n4, 534, 545-46; **24:**44, 137
Buehler, Huber Gray, **18:**495,n1, 509
Buehler, Roberta Wolf (Mrs. Huber Gray), **18:**509,n1
Buell, Augustus C., **14:**286-87
Buell, Dora Phelps (Mrs. William J.), **23:**478,n1
Buenos Aires, Fourth International American Conference, **21:**557, 559
Buffalo, N. Y., **23:**559n1; **24:**309-10, 311-14; **25:**66; campaign speeches, 67-92
*Buffalo Evening Times*, **25:**92n
*Buffalo Express*, **24:**314n; **25:**69n, 79n, 92n
Buffalo Iron Co., Mannie, Tenn., **14:**3,n3
Buffon, Georges Louis Leclerc, Comte de, **19:**66,n2
Buffum, Douglas Labaree, **16:**60, 132, 256; **17:**233, 408; **19:**572, 576
Buley, Roscoe Carlyle, **16:**276n1
Bulkeley, Frances Hazen, **16:**13n; **22:**37n

Bull, Griffin William, **16**:537,n1; **20**:239,-n1

Bull, Lucy Morton Eggleston (Mrs. Griffin William), **20**:239,n1

Bull, Ole (Bornemann), **19**:317,n1

Bull, Reuben Adiel, **25**:588,n1

Bull, William, M.D., **15**:302,n4, 303, 304, 306, 309, 310, 313, 315-16, 322, 333, 344

Bull Hotel, Cambridge, England, **14**:3, 529, 530

Bull Moose party, *see* Progressive party

Bullitt, Alexander Scott, **19**:211,n1

Bullock, Catherine, **14**:438,n1

Bullock, Lady Amy Isabel Thomson, **25**:557,n5, 573

Bullock, Sir George Mackworth, **25**: 557,n5, 573

Bumsted, William H., **23**:203,n4

Buni, Andrew, **25**:619n1

Bunn, Henry Conrad, **14**:145,n3; **15**: 493,n1, 508, 509, 525; **16**:176, 324, 356; **17**:48,n3, 151, 153, 170, 207, 281, 282, 301, 362, 386, 387, 388, 389, 391, 510, 564, 567, 568; **18**:226, 227, 286, 291, 367

Bunnell, Jacob L., **22**:378,n1

Burd, George Brinton McClellan, **25**:80n2

Bureau of Mines and Mining, **25**:224

Bureau of Municipal Research, **23**:634n1

*Bureaucracy Convicts Itself: The Ballinger-Pinchot Controversy of 1910* (Mason), **21**:546n3

Burgan, J. A., **22**:173n1

Burgess, Frank Gelett, **25**:154,n7, 411

Burgess, John William, **21**:48,n4

Burgoyne, John, **14**:281

Burk, Charles August David, **17**:431,n1, 432

Burk, William F., **23**:428n7

Burke, Annie R., **16**:234

Burke, Edmund, **14**:14, 242, 322, 324, 443, 444, 503; **15**:148; **16**:284, 285; **18**:71, 77, 594, 601; **19**:726; **20**:196, 197; **24**:365; **25**:171

Burke, Eugene S., **22**:253,n2

Burke, John, **23**:320, 658,n2; **24**:82, 137, 565,n1; **25**:623,n1, 645

Burleigh, Edwin Chick, **25**:619n1

Burleigh, George William, **16**:5,n3, 134, 291, 416

Burleson, Albert Sidney, **22**:207,n5; **24**:287,n1, 467, 490, 571n1; **25**:421, 422, 550, 563, 565-66, 607, 610, 624, 626

Burlingame, Edward Livermore, **19**: 348,n1

Burlington, N. J., **21**:290n1; **22**:307, 502, 544, 545; **23**:539; **24**:410-13; Auditorium, **22**:535n1; WW campaign speech, **21**:269-74, mentioned, **21**:244; **25**:485-92

Burlington County, N. J., **21**:403; **22**:535; **23**:539-40; **25**:491-92; County Fair, **21**:269; Democratic Club, **22**:535n1

Burnett, Curtis R., **22**:367,n1; **24**:67,n1

Burns, Robert, **14**:503, 505; **18**:549,n2; **20**:181n1

Burns, William John, **24**:126n4, 452n2

Burns Detective Agency, **24**:452,n2, 453

Burr, Aaron, Jr., vice-president of the U.S., **14**:250, 439n1; **22**:218

Burrell, Edward Louis, **15**:101,n2

Burrows, Andrew, **17**:25,n1

Burt, (Maxwell) Struthers, **14**:490n3; **16**:465, 511, 553; **17**:165,n3, 384; **19**:430n1

Burton, Ernest DeWitt, **19**:544,n3, 545

Burton, Theodore Elijah, **17**:508n1, 509,n1

Bury, John Bagnell, **14**:295

Bush Hotel, Ecclefechan, **18**:361-62

Bushnell, Herbert, **16**:475

business, **22**:64f, 74-76, 106f, 178-81, 196, 222, 268f, 315, 389, 391, 397-98, 470, 585-86; **24**:76, 142-43, 156, 157, 158, 160, 200, 201, 228, 331-32, 342, 355-56; **25**:9, 13, 36, 57n1, 104, 152, 165, 173, 174-75, 191-92, 193-94, 196, 199-200, 210-11, 215, 343, 344-45, 357, 358, 402-403, 408-10, 427, 433, 438, 443, 444, 445, 463, 496, 502, 505, 524, 594, 601; confidence, **23**:443-45, 451; and government, **24**:108, 414-15, 420-21, 422-23, 424-25; legislators and, **24**:93; need for reform, **24**:111, 127; platform plank, **24**:470; politics and, **23**:122, 638-39; **24**:47, 375, 411; private control, **24**:11, 12; tariff, **24**:13; *see also* big business; competition; monopoly; small business

*Business History Review*, **25**:414n1

business opposition to WW, **23**:360

Bussell, Frederick William, **15**:396,n5, 410

Butcher, Rose Julia Trench (Mrs. Samuel Henry), **15**:296,n3

Butcher, Samuel, bishop of Meath, **15**:296

Butcher, Samuel Henry, **15**:296,n1, 421; **16**:28

Butler, Charles Henry, **20**:21,n2

Butler, Ed, **16**:216n3

Butler, Howard Crosby, **14**:97,n1, 267, 470, 473; **15**:375, 376n1; **16**:140n3, 186,n1, 198, 247, 263, 515; **17**:111n, 143, 408; **18**:291, 292, 295, 296, 304, 314; **19**:267, 305, 327, 426, 431, 433, 630, 653; **20**:107, 113-14, 318, 449

Butler, Howard Russell, **15**:57,n1, 549,-n1,2, 579; **16**:499

Butler, Nicholas Murray, **14**:69, 194, 261n2, 289,n2, 306n3, 335,n1,2, 546, 560; **15**:105-106, 116; **16**:224, 282, 283, 373-74, 375-76, 383, 395, 396, 413, 414-15, 495-96; **17**:3n2, 90, 106, 121; **19**:101, 156; **22**:209; **23**:632; **24**:148, 503, 504, 529; **25**:232

Butler, Pierce, **19**:457-58,n1, 485-86, 493, 494; **23**:85,n4
Butler, Samuel, **14**:503; **17**:13
Butler, Susanna Edwards Schuyler (Mrs. Nicholas Murray), **14**:335,n2
Butler, William Allen, **16**:500
Butler, Willis Howard, **14**:550,n3; **15**:161,n1, 162; **17**:125,n3, 127, 129
Butterfield, Mrs. and daughter (at Bermuda), **20**:187
Buttermere Hotel, Cumberland, **14**:523
Butterworth, J. C., **21**:584n1
Buttrick, Wallace, **17**:63,n1, 95
Butts, R. Freeman, **15**:292n27
Bynner, Witter, **23**:160,n1
Byrd, Harry Flood, **24**:71,n2; **25**:528n2
Byrd, Richard Evelyn, **22**:20,n1; **23**:359, 390; **24**:71, 101n2, 3, 118, 121, 398, 486, 543, 568, 569; **25**:528, 632n1
Byrne, Harry Stephenson, **23**:95,n1
Byron, George Gordon, 6th Baron Byron, **14**:503; **19**:573

Cabell, George W., **19**:352
Cabell, W. Carrington, **24**:525,n6
Cadman, Samuel Parkes, **14**:115
Cadwalader, John, Jr., **23**:229,n3
Cadwalader, John Lambert, **14**:306n3, 409; **15**:52n1, 127, 135, 184, 193, 207, 300,n2, 405, 406, 408-409, 526, 569, 572, 575; **16**:5, 39, 266, 303, 495; **17**:16, 174-75; **18**:8-9, 34, 35, 217, 302, 303, 309, 317, 481-82, 483, 541-44, 554-55, 557-58, 559, 565, 568, 617-18, 622, 622n1; **19**:80-81, 170, 175, 433, 434, 440, 490,n1, 661-62, 662; **20**:11, 15, 16, 31,n1, 183, 254, 425, 427, 428, 431, 433, 445, 454, 461, 470, 472, 476, 481, 483, 484, 486, 488, 489, 491, 493, 494, 495-96, 497, 498, 498n1, 502, 510, 511; **21**:353, 362n1, 364-66; **22**:17, 436
Cadwalader, Richard McCall, **14**:409
Cady, Addison Edgerton, **23**:97,n4
Cady, Josiah Cleveland, **22**:417n1, 424
Caesar, Julius, **16**:119, 221, 480; **17**:542
*Caesar's Column: A Story of the Twentieth Century* (Donnelly), **23**:246,n2,3
Caird, Edward, **15**:396,n6
Calais, Wilsons in, **14**:535
Calder, William Musgrave, **23**:584
Caldwell, N. J., birthplace of Grover Cleveland, **21**:309,n3; Democratic Union, **21**:306, 309; Essex Fells, **22**:413; Kingsley School, **21**:310; Monomonock Inn, **21**:306,n1; WW speeches, **21**:306-10
Caldwell, Benjamin Franklin, **25**:390n2
Caldwell, William, **23**:512,n4
*Caledonia*, S.S., **16**:427, 430,n3, 450, 451, 453, 455, 456, 463; **18**:344,n2, 408, 417, 418; **20**:349n3,4
Caledonian Hotel, Inverness, **18**:396
Calhoun, John Caldwell, **14**:519; **15**:45; **16**:53; **17**:78-83, 312; **19**:206; **22**:40n25; **25**:558n6

Calhoun, Patrick, **22**:39-40,n25; **25**:558,-n6
California, **21**:608n2; **22**:318, 519, 524; **23**:40, 41, 42, 43, 54, 56, 57, 101, 296, 601n1, 620; Democrats, **23**:251, 325-26; legislature, **23**:42, 252; Oriental immigration, **24**:351-53, 383,n1; presidential primary vote, **24**:383n1; Republicans, **23**:251, 473; statehood, **17**:311; Southern Pacific Railroad, **25**:240-41
*California*, S.S., **18**:340n1, 343, 347
California, University of, **15**:100n3; **16**:110, 250, 252, 489; **18**:579; **23**:59, 60; California Hall, **23**:60; Doe Library, **23**:60; Greek Theater, **23**:55, 59, 60; Press, **17**:352n2
*California Historical Society Quarterly*, **24**:383n1
*California Progressives* (Mowry), **22**:32n; **23**:43n9
Calkins, Gary Nathan, **16**:431,n1, 469
Callaway, James, **17**:461,n1
Calvin, Jean, **17**:52
Calvinism, **23**:497f
Cam, *see* Cameron, Henry Clay
Cambridge, England, Bull Hotel, **14**:3, 529, 530; WW on, **14**:3; Wilsons in, **14**:529-30
Cambridge, Mass., **22**:138,n3; preferential ballots, **23**:456; WW in, **19**:270, 273, 289, 291, 394, 408, 410, 411, 483
Cambridge, University of, **14**:112; **15**:409-10, 420, 421, 441; **16**:46, 81,n2, 83, 156-57, 157, 163, 164, 165, 198, 246-47, 434, 465, 507, 508, 509; **17**:241, 274, 304, 348,n1; **18**:254, 304, 314, 368n7, 578-79; **19**:128, 151; Cavendish Laboratory, **16**:508, 509; Christ's College, **15**:409-10; Emmanuel College, **15**:410; FitzWilliam Museum, **19**:739; Girton College, **14**:530; Jesus College, **14**:530; King's College, **15**:410; Newnham College, **14**:530; Observatory, **16**:83, 83n2; **18**:579; St. John's College, **14**:530; **15**:421; **19**:739
*Cambridge Modern History* (ed. Acton), **15**:482-84, 485
Camden, N. J., **20**:135; **21**:420, 426, 551; **22**:300; **23**:393, 400, 409-11, 412, 424, 425, 446, 518, 532; **24**:262, 407; Americus Club, **22**:514,n3,4; Broadway Theatre, **21**:421; **23**:411; Kaighn's Point, **23**:273; Line Ditch, **21**:416; post office, **23**:403; Princeton alumni, **19**:146; Pyne Poynt, **21**:416; registry lists, **21**:567; Temple Theatre, **21**:413, 416, 421; **23**:411; WW campaign speeches, **21**:413-21
Camden, Johnson Newlon, Jr., **25**:23,n2
Camden County, N. J., **21**:278n2, 417, 418, 577, 584n1; **22**:50; **23**:275,n1, 346, 349, 354, 364, 365,n2, 381, 403, 410-11, 417, 424, 432, 546; **25**:582
*Camden* (N. J.) *Courier*, **22**:249-50,n1

Camden *Daily Courier*, **23**:277n1, 533n2
Cameron, Anne Wood Finley (Mrs. Arnold Guyot), **15**:52n1
Cameron, Arnold Guyot, **15**:15, 52, 136, 207, 276, 294, 362-64, 385, 386, 464-66,n1; explanatory and biographical note, **15**:52-54
Cameron, Benehan, **23**:111n1
Cameron, Donald, **16**:67, 104, 132, 252, 528; **17**:117, 162,n3, 408; **19**:676
Cameron, George, Jr., **24**:465,n1
Cameron, Henry Clay (Cam), **14**:144-45; **15**:52n1, 364,n3, 464
Cameron, Mina Chollet (Mrs. Henry Clay, **15**:52n1, 464
Cameron, Sallie Mayo (Mrs. Benehan), **23**:111n1
Cameron, Simon, **21**:62,n1
Cammack (of Kansas City), **16**:98
Camp, Charles Wadsworth, **16**:569,n3
Camp, Edwin, **21**:451,n1
Camp, Joseph, **23**:273,n5
Camp, Sewall Frederick, **20**:55,n1
Camp, Walter [Chauncey], **19**:562,n1, 578, 672, 699, 704, 705; **20**:54, 72, 118, 487, 488, 539, 540, 547, 559, 560
campaign contributions and expenditures, **24**:364-65, 375; disclosure of, **23**:235n3; **24**:284, 305, 369; **25**:6, 15, 30, 64, 84, 120, 305, 307, 402, 459; Clapp Committee, **25**:109n1, 110n3,6; Public Service Corporation, **24**:412; Republican campaigns 1888, **24**:13; 1904, **25**:396n3; WW on own campaign, **24**:289 Δ C. R. Crane, **24**:554n2; W. J. Bryan, **24**:249; C. H. Dodge, **25**:109-11, 135; E. M. House, **25**:421; T. B. Love, **24**:254-55; C. H. McCormick, **25**:109,n2, 110,n4,6, 459,n1,3; Nathan Straus, **25**:378,n1, 422
*Campaign Contributions: Testimony before a Subcommittee of the Committee on Privileges and Elections*, **24**:554n2; **25**:109n2, 110n3
Campaign for Wilson (scrapbook), **25**:554,n1
*Campana*, S.S., **17**:447
Campbell, Henry Monroe, **16**:43,n4
Campbell, John Alexander, **14**:354; **16**:64,n2; **17**:388n3; **19**:402, 403; **22**:379, 380; **23**:140,n1
Campbell, Margaret Patterson (Mrs. Richard Crawford), **23**:21,n1, 22
Campbell, Milton Argyle, **19**:139n4, 679
Campbell, Richard Crawford, **23**:21,n1
Campbell, Thomas Mitchell, **22**:123,n2, 422,n2; **23**:509,n8; **25**:645
Campbell, William Irwin, **17**:99n2
Campbell, William Oliver, **16**:404,n3; **17**:211,n3
Campbell-Bannerman, Sir Henry, **17**:307,n2
Camp Wilson, **24**:509
Canada, **15**:500, 523; **18**:165; **21**:254;

**23**:422-23; **24**:330n2; **25**:253, 637; Conservative party, **22**:478n3; Liberal party, **22**:478n3; reciprocity with, **22**:478n3, 486, 592, 601; **23**:41, 90-91, 131-32,n1, 132n1, 369, 422, 442-43, 622
Canadian Express, **15**:424
cancer, **22**:11
Cann, George Turner, **23**:557,n4
canning industry, **25**:282n2
Cannon, Frank Jenne, **22**:584; **23**:21,n9
Cannon, Joseph Gurney, **16**:315, 316; **19**:99, 366,n3, 367, 604; **20**:258n1; **21**:215,n6, 221, 243, 244, 249, 249n2, 255, 280, 344,n12, 456, 457, 474, 564; **22**:226,n1; **23**:405; **24**:507n1, 567; **25**:370, 407
Canterbury, Archbishop of, **19**:109; Cathedral tower, **19**:538
Cape May, N. J., **22**:369; **23**:364; Lafayette Hotel, **23**:274; Schellenger's Landing, **23**:274
Cape May County, N. J., **21**:281, 283, 285, 286n4, 569, 584n1; **22**:203,n1, 516, 521; **23**:172, 272-75, 364-65; **25**:582; Democratic County Committee, **23**:272; politics, **25**:479-80, 482-84; speeches in, **25**:474-85
Cape May Court House, N. J., **23**:185, 273, 364; WW speech, **21**:281-87; **25**:474,n1
capital, search for, **23**:119-20
Capital Hotel, Frankfort, Ky., **24**:141
capitalists and capitalism, capitalistic system, **21**:268, 394-95, 401, 468; **22**:12
Capodimonte, EAW at, **15**:229
Capper, Arthur, **25**:621n2
Capps, Edward, **17**:46,n2, 91, 112-14, 116-17, 123-24, 130, 139, 161, 163, 173, 209, 218, 437n1, 555-56, 587, 596-97, 600-601; **18**:5, 582; **19**:10-11,n2,4, 132-34, 134n1, 141, 172, 398, 425, 429, 549, 559-60, 612, 621, 753-55; **20**:8n, 9n, 18, 19, 51, 58, 71n1, 93, 109, 114-15, 143, 144, 174, 190, 191, 210, 213, 269, 270, 319, 474, 484; **21**:166-67,n2; **23**:31
Capps, Grace Alexander (Mrs. Edward), **21**:167,n1
Capri, EAW at, **15**:240; Blue Grotto, **15**:240
Caproni, P. P. & Brother, Boston art dealers, **14**:10,n4, 71, 79, 97
*Captain Bill McDonald, Texas Ranger: A Story of Frontier Reform* (Paine), **25**:423n1
*Cardinal's Snuff Box* (Harland), **15**:349,n2
Carey, Rosa Nouchette, **14**:520n3
Carlisle, Cumberland, **18**:363, 367, 402; Cathedral, **18**:363; Crown and Mitre Hotel, **18**:363; WW in, **18**:361
Carlisle, George James Howard, 9th Earl of, **17**:106n3
Carlisle, John Griffin, **16**:534,n2

Carlisle, Pa., U.S. Indian Industrial School, **21**:53,n1
Carlstadt, N. J., WW campaign speech, **21**:507-508
Carlton Hotel, London, **15**:147
Carlyle, Alexander, **18**:362,n1
Carlyle, Thomas, **14**:340, 555; **17**:481-82, 504; **18**:76, 83n2, 133, 349, 362; **19**:82; **20**:384; **21**:513; **22**:62; **23**:379
Carmack, Edward Ward, **18**:485n2; **23**:289n2
Carmichael, Isaac W., **23**:380,n2
Carmichael, Otto, **25**:562,n1
Carnegie, Andrew, **14**:306-307, 411-15, 544; **15**:57, 58, 59, 67, 442, 443n1, 549, 579; **16**:4n2, 54, 67, 78, 139, 224, 336, 497-503; **17**:92n2, 95, 98, 103, 124, 150, 466-67, 546, 554, 599, 609; **18**:15, 61,n1,3, 220-21, 313,n3, 344, 349, 391, 392, 393, 398, 400, 401, 405, 509, 513, 513,n1, 565-66; **19**:19, 51,n1, 100-101, 150, 181, 182, 185, 480,n2, 507, 619, 622, 635,n1; **20**:584; **21**:615n2; **22**:23, 514-15, 514n4, 515; **23**:583, 592; **25**:152, 168, 193
Carnegie, Louise Whitfield (Mrs. Andrew), **16**:497, 500, 503; **17**:95, 98, 467,n2, 599n2; **18**:391,n1, 399, 401, 405; **19**:507,n1
Carnegie, Margaret, **17**:467,n2
Carnegie Corporation of New York, **16**:55n3
Carnegie Endowment for International Peace, **22**:514n1
Carnegie Foundation for the Advancement of Teaching, **16**:55n3, 67, 78n2, 224, 304-305,n2,3,4, 306, 306n1, 419, 429, 468, 469, 518; **17**:103, 104,149-50, 153, 154, 218, 470, 510-12, 527, 547, 548, 554,n1, 565, 601; **18**:15, 52-53, 61-62,n1,2, 220-21, 257, 258, 289, 480; **19**:76,n1, 150, 162, 181, 182, 229, 459-60,n1, 480, 507; **20**:31, 408, 409, 499, 584; **21**:492-93, 540, 540n1,2; **22**:23,n3, 23,n1, 53, 130-31,n1,2, 132, 365-66; **23**:564-65,n1, 565-66, 583,n1, 590, 592; **24**:505n1; *Second Annual Report . . .* , **17**:545,n1; pension for WW, **24**:72, 147-49, 244, 256, 270n1, 503,n2; *Fourth Annual Report . . .* , **19**:459-60,n1
Carnegie Hall, New York City, **22**:140, 412n2, 417n1, 514, 514n4, 515; **25**:448n1, 450; campaign address, **25**:441-47
Carnegie Institute of Pittsburgh, **14**:549; **15**:13, 46-47, 129n2; *The Eighth Celebration of Founder's Day Thursday November 5, 1903*, **15**:46
Carnegie Institution of Washington, **14**:412,n2; **16**:54, 82n2, 83, 489; **18**:579; **19**:405n1; Bureau of Historical Research, **16**:106n1
Carnegie Lake, *see* Princeton University, *Carnegie Lake*

Carnegie Teachers Pension Fund, *see* Carnegie Foundation for the Advancement of Teaching
Carnegie Trust for the Universities of Scotland, **16**:54,n2
Carnochan, John McDowell, M.D., **25**:509,n2
*Carolinas* (Rivers), **14**:342-43,n5
Carow, Emily, **16**:233,n1
Carpaccio, Vittore, **15**:359,n4
Carpenter, Emory W., **16**:321n1
Carpenter, George Rice, **19**:703n1
Carpenter, Jennie R., **16**:321n1
Carpenter, William Henry, **17**:427,n1,2, 605-606, 616
Carr, Edward Michael, **24**:221,n2
Carrington, John, **18**:229; **19**:254
*Carroccio, Il*, **24**:135n
Carroll, Beryl F., **24**:222,n3
Carroll, Charles, **17**:249
Carroll, Francis M., **24**:361n
Carroll, W. H., **17**:480n1
Carroll family of Carrollton, Md., **17**:618
Carrow, Howard, **21**:416; **22**:25,n1; **23**:158,n1, 364, 411
Carson, Murray, **14**:529,n10
Carstensen, Vernon, **17**:241n3
Carter, Charles David, **24**:287,n1
Carter, Ernest Trow, **14**:471n2
Carter, Jesse Benedict, **14**:138, 245, 326, 388, 394, 411, 434; **15**:183, 200, 294, 351, 375, 398-99,n1, 558; **16**:130, 166-67, 176, 180, 248, 421; **17**:162, 163,n12
Carter, Kate Benedict Freeman (Mrs. Jesse Benedict), **15**:351, 399; **16**:166, 167, 176
Cartmel Priory, Lancs, **18**:389
Carton, Alfred Thomas, **16**:382,n3; **18**:645,n1; **20**:437n1
Carton, Laurence Arthur, **16**:382,n1
Carton, Laurence Roberts, **16**:382,n2
Carver, Thomas Nixon, **16**:41,n6
Cary, Henry Francis, **19**:367n5
Cary, Hunsdon, **21**:117-18,n1
Cary, Lewis Robinson, **19**:612, 620, 624
*Casa Grande, Arizona, Times*, **25**:272n1
Case, Thomas, **17**:13,n2, 127, 360, 472
Casino Theatre, New York City, **25**:55n1
Caskey, Herbert K., **15**:99
Cassaboom, Joshua, **23**:533n3
Cassatt, Alexander Johnston, **16**:342,n1, 343; **22**:114, 115
Castle, William Richards, Jr., **19**:495,n1
Catchings, Thomas Clendinen, **22**:226,-n3
Catholic Church, *see* Roman Catholic Church
Catholic University of America, **14**:148; **15**:100n3
Catholic vote, **24**:565
Catlett, Charles, **25**:632,n2
Catok & Beller, **16**:387, 388
Cattell, James McKeen, **14**:21-22,n1,2,3
Catullus, Gaius Valerius, **19**:594, 597

Cauldwell, Thomas William, **19**:119,n2, 123

Cavour, Count Camillo Benso di, **25**:256

Cawley, John, **16**:471,n1

Cecil, John Howe, **14**:388

Cecil, Russell, **15**:345,n3

celibacy, clerical, **21**:319

Cellini, Benvenuto, **15**:477

Census Bureau, **25**:311, 316

*Central Government* (Traill), **14**:14

Central Railroad of Georgia, **14**:69,n3, 74, 499

Central Railroad Co., of New Jersey, **21**:343n9, 354; **22**:215n1

Central University of Kentucky, **19**:679

Centre College of Kentucky, **14**:401,n2; **15**:348n1, 356; **16**:247, 254

Century Association, New York City, **16**:531

*Century Cyclopedia of Names*, **18**:632,n1

*Century Magazine*, **14**:47n1, 54; **15**:353; **20**:31n1; **21**:322,n1

*Century of Education at Mercersburg, 1836-1936* (Klein), **14**:464n1

Cerberus, **22**:303,n5

Cesare da Sesto, **15**:229

Cha Fa Maha Vjiravudh, Crown Prince of Siam (afterward King Rama VI), **14**:195,n1

Chadbourn, Blanche King (Mrs. James Harmon), **15**:218,n2

Chadbourn, James Harmon, **15**:217-18,n1

Chaffee, Adna Romanza, **14**:290, 298,n1

Chafin, Eugene Wilder, **25**:390,n2

Chaldeans, **17**:463

Chalfonte Hotel, Atlantic City, N. J., **20**:222

Chalmers, Thomas, **16**:317; **24**:428

Chamberlain, Abiram, **14**:515

Chamberlain, Alexander Francis, **22**:379,n1

Chamberlain, George Earle, **22**:174-75,n1, 248; **23**:350,n5; **24**:273, 287,n1, 565,n1; **25**:492,n3

Chamberlain, Mary Hale (Mrs. William M.), **17**:146,n4

Chamberlain, Mellen, **14**:443,n3

Chamberlains (in Bermuda), **22**:210

Chamberlin, Rollin Thomas, **19**:544,n3

Chamberlin, Thomas Crowder, **19**:544,-n3

Chambers, Benjamin Bright, **21**:336,n1

Chambers, David Laurance, **14**:224-25,n1; **17**:222,n2, 224, 407,n1

Chambers, James Julius, **16**:110,n1

Chambersburg, Pa. *Public Opinion*, **14**:472n

Chandler, Arthur Dickinson, **22**:39,n7

Chandler, Janie Porter (Mrs. Samuel C.), **23**:10,n3, 81,n1

Chandler, Jefferson Paul, **23**:44,n10, 325-26

Chapel Hill, N. C., **15**:466-67; **16**:526, 527; **22**:406, 499, 507, 509, 517, 520;

24:535; WW in, **23**:104-10, 111n1, 112, 140

*Chapel Hymnal*, **19**:395

Chapin, Charles Sumner, **16**:219,n2

Chaplin, Maxwell, **22**:323

Chapman, Edward Mortimer, **21**:4,n3

Chapman, John Jay, **17**:431, 447

Chapman (station agent at Clifton, Mass.), **14**:65, 69

character: a by-product, **16**:228, 230, 311, 317; moral, **16**:327-28

Character of Sir Robert Peel (Bagehot), **23**:282n4; **25**:634,n4

*Characters and Events of Roman History, from Caesar to Nero* (Ferrero), **19**:262,n3

Charcos cable, **18**:346,n8

Charles II, **14**:343, 504

*Charles Eliot Norton, Apostle of Culture in a Democracy* (Vanderbilt), **15**:422n2

*Charles Evans Hughes: Politics and Reform in New York, 1905-1910* (Wesser), **19**:26n6

Charles River, **21**:518

Charleston, College of, **14**:5,n1, 86

Charleston, S. C., **16**:285-86; **17**:8; **23**:173; Hibernian Hall, **16**:285, 286; Saint Andrew's Society, **16**:533,n10; Villa Margherita, **16**:286; WW address, **16**:285-86

Charleston *News and Courier*, **16**:286, 286n, 286n1, 288n, 533; **23**:173n2

Charlotte, N. C., **24**:389

*Charlotte Daily Observer*, **24**:42n2

Charlottesville, Va., **16**:192; **23**:390,n1, 549; **24**:72n9, 80, 96, 121; Monticello, **22**:558; **25**:631

*Charlottesville Daily Progress*, **24**:72n9

Charlton, Walter Glasco, **23**:557,n7

Chartres, Cathedral, **15**:334; Wilsons at, **14**:537

Chase, Salmon Portland, **17**:314; **18**:176

Chase, Samuel, **25**:600,n3

Chateau des Grotteaux, **23**:154

Chateaubriand, François René de, Vicomte, **19**:573

Chatfield, Albert Hayden, **19**:423n1,2, 425, 454, 461

Chatham, William Pitt, 1st Earl of, **14**:281; **15**:148

Chatham County, Ga., **24**:387

Chatham Hotel, Paris, **14**:552, 555

Chattanooga, Tenn., Chattanooga Railways Co., **16**:476; Read House, **16**:476; WW address, **16**:474-77; WW in, **21**:64-81

*Chattanooga Times*, **16**:476n, 477

Chaucer, Geoffrey, **19**:751

Chautauqua, Chautauqua movement, **16**:253; **22**:327n1; **23**:82, 82n15, 212; **24**:346n1; **25**:649

Chavis, John, **15**:462n2

checks and balances, **24**:416, 417

Cherbourg, Wilsons at, **14**:542,n18

Cherry, Richard Robert, **17**:307,n4

Cheshire, England, **18**:402

Chester, England, Wilsons in, **14**:521

Chesterton, Gilbert Keith, **15**:506,n3; **19**:521,n7, 714; **20**:242; **22**:442,n4; **25**:202,n5

Chesterwood, Stockbridge, Mass., **19**: 152n1

Chew, Samuel Claggett, M.D., **19**:260,n2

Chicago, **18**:382, 546-47, 564; **19**:620, 634; **20**:216, 395, 548,n2; **21**:21, 344n11; **22**:154, 533; **23**:311, 360, 594, 598, 599; **24**:151, 302, 306, 587; **25**:400-404; Auditorium Hotel, **14**:247; Business Service Lecture League, **21**:163n1; **22**:74; Chicago Club, **14**:211, 248, 454; **18**:16; Chicago Latin School, **18**:16; Commercial Club, **14**:211, 226, 227, 228, 245n, 247; **18**:17, 35; Committee of Citizens, **21**:519; Committee of One Hundred, **18**:545, 546-47, 553-54; Congress Hotel, **14**:421; **18**:17, 276; **20**:432; Democrats, **23**:326; Fine Arts Building, **14**:454; 1871 fire, **23**:145; Industrial Club, **19**:10; Polish population, **24**:242; Princeton alumni, **14**: 211, 223, 225, 226-27, 447; **16**:405; **18**:16, 17, 18,n2, 23, 645-46; **19**:33-46, 47, 117, 118, 124, 131, 146, 155, 479; **20**:262, 351,n1,3, 433-43; Pullman strike of 1894, **15**:306, 313; Republican convention of 1860, **18**:110; Twentieth Century Club, **14**:448,n5, 451, 454; Unity Church, **23**:145n3; University Club, **14**:211, 226, 451; **18**:16, 645; **19**:47, 479; **20**:403, 455,n1; **21**:594; **22**:71; University School for Boys, **18**:16; WW addresses, **14**:225-45, 247-48, 454-55; **18**:16-34, 35-51, 272-73, 276-77; **19**:33-46, 47-48, 471-79, 479; **20**:351,n1,3, 360, 403, 433-43, 453, 520n1; WW in, **14**:421, 422-23, 428, 429, 448, 451, 453-54; **19**:461, 482, 483, 487, 735, 748; **20**:427, 429, 433, 454, 456, 460; **22**:178-81, 210, 223; **23**:657; WW's personal papers stolen, **24**:303; Young Men's Christian Association Hall, **22**:74,n1

Chicago, University of, **14**:157, 198n2, 225, 248; **15**:100n3, 234n; **16**:33, 159, 179,n1, 198, 248, 251, 253, 254, 257, 258, 259, 272n1, 282, 465, 511; **17**:91, 365, 371, 451, 555, 556, 587, 588,n6,7, 601; **18**:5n1, 8n1, 12, 225, 575, 580; **19**:138, 393, 424, 678, 679; **20**:75, 539; **23**:103, 311-12,n1,2; classics department, **17**:112-14,n1, 116-17, 124, 130; Oriental Educational Investigation, **19**:544,n3; University of Chicago Press, **17**:351n2, 356

Chicago and Alton Railroad Company, **17**:503n3

Chicago and North Western Railroad, **15**:505

Chicago Convention, *see* Republican National Convention

Chicago *Daily News*, **14**:226n

*Chicago Daily Tribune*, **14**:228n, 455n; **21**:344n11; **22**:76n, 181n; **24**:303n, 304n

*Chicago Evening Post*, **17**:497n; **18**:17n; **22**:388n1

Chicago *Inter Ocean*, **14**:248n, 274,n3; **18**:277n

*Chicago Record-Herald*, **19**:48n; **24**:274-n2, 292n

Chicora College, **22**:577n4

Chidester, John Hartford, **20**:368-69,n1

Chihuahua, Mexico, **23**:596, 634; **24**:218

Child, Clarence Griffin, **14**:95,n1

Child, Elizabeth Reynolds (Mrs. Clarence Griffin), **14**:95,n1

child labor, **18**:186-87,n4; **22**:11, 12,n4, 144, 152, 156-57n1,3, 206-208, 291n2, 452n2; **25**:30, 311; New Jersey, **25**:306, 308, 315

*Childe Harold* (Byron), **19**:573

children, **22**:594, 596; state feeding of, **18**:3-4

Childrens Bureau, **25**:311

Childs, Eleanor Stuart Patterson (Mrs. Harris Robbins, *pseud.* Eleanor Stuart), **18**:358n2

Childs, Richard Spencer, **19**:156, 157, 307, 419-20, 446-47, 553, 579, 661, 729-30; **22**:197n2, 257-58

Childs, Starling Winston, **22**:202,n2

Childs, William Hamlin, **19**:157,n6

China, **19**:109-10; **25**:576,n1; Christian education, **18**:560; **19**:109-10, 544; culture and society, **16**:121; government, **18**:87-88; Y.M.C.A. in, **23**:114

*China Collecting in America* (Earle), **14**:520,n1

China Dinner, New York City, Jan. 14, 1909, **18**:560,n3,4; **19**:478,n4

China Educational Committee, **19**:544

Chinese-American Treaty of 1903, **15**:143n2

Chinese Americans, **24**:241, 243, 351; immigration, **24**:382, 383,n1

*Chinese Honeymoon* (musical comedy), **14**:288n1

Chinese students and Boxer Indemnity, **19**:120-21,n2

Chinese Revolution (1911), **25**:576n1

Chippenham, Wilts, Wilsons in, **14**:533

Choate, Joseph Hodges, **14**:306n3; **15**: 147,n1; **20**:415; **21**:615n2; **23**:111, 520; **25**:587,n2,3

Choate, Rufus, **14**:262

Chopin, Frédéric François, **19**:34, 35

Christ Church, Oxford, **17**:119, 277

Christ Church, Warwick, Bermuda, **17**:28n1

Christ Church, Warwick, 1719-1969 (Law), **17**:28n1

Christian, Virginia, **25**:25,n4

Christian Church, **23**:373

Christian education, **15**:510-19

*Christian Point of View: Three Addresses* (Knox, McGiffert, Brown), **16**:400,n5

Christian Socialism, 14:555; 19:496; 20:333

Christianity, 24:209

Christie, Samuel M., 21:179,n1

Christ's College, Cambridge, 15:409-10

Christmas: Its Unfinished Business (Crothers), 25:130,n3

Chulalongkorn, King of Siam, 14:196n1

Church, Samuel Harden, 14:549,n1, 550

Church of Scotland, 19:202

church politics, 20:77n1

Churchill, Winston, (1871-1947) of New Hampshire, 19:419,n1, 446, 579

Churchill, Sir Winston (Leonard Spencer), 17:307

*Churchman*, New York, 20:335n

Churchman, Philip Hudson, 15:174,n2, 205-206,n1; 16:27,n1

Cicero, Marcus Tullius, 14:13, 208, 209; 18:575

Cincinnati, 19:404, 410, 413, 423, 436, 449; Grand Central Depot, 14:449; Grand Hotel, 14:449; Princeton alumni, 14:448-49, 450; 19:146; 20:252,n2; Queen City Club, 14:447, 449; WW addresses, 14:449-51; WW in, 14:439, 440n1, 446-47, 448-51; Y.M.C.A., 14:447, 448, 450-51, 452; Zoo, 14:449

Cincinnati, Hamilton and Dayton Railroad, 23:356-57

Cincinnati, University of, 15:419, 420, 530

Cincinnati *Commercial Tribune*, 14:450n, 451n

*Cincinnati Enquirer*, 14:449n; 22:255n1

*Cincinnati Times-Star*, 14:447n, 448n1,2

Cincinnati Traction Company, 14:449

circus, 15:201,n3, 210, 231; four-ring, 23:575

*Citizen in His Relation to the Industrial Situation* (Potter), 14:136,n1

citizenship, 19:496, 497

Citizens' League, 25:642

city government, 23:141, 573f; in U.S., 19:514f; 25:316-17

*Civic Problems: Address delivered March 9, 1909, at the Annual Meeting of the Civic League of St. Louis by Woodrow Wilson*, 19:97n

*Civic Victories: The Story of an Unfinished Revolution* (Childs), 22:197n2

civil procedure (N. J.), 25:307

Civil Service Commission (N. J.), 24:264-65

*Civil Service in Great Britain* (Eaton), 24:174n5

civil service reform, 22:78-79; 24:166-77

Civil War, 14:347, 445; 17:227, 309, 321; 18:101, 107, 184, 634; 21:227, 535; 22:444, 445, 604n2; 24:257,n2; 25:630-31

Clapp, Moses Edwin, 23:132n1; 24:473,-n5; 25:64-65, 109n1, 110n3,6

Clapp Committee, 25:109n1, 110n3,6, 396,n3, 459,n3

Clara d'Assisi, Saint, 15:338

*Clarence* (Mo.) *Courier*, 24:187n4

Clark, Champ (James Beauchamp), 21:608n2; 22:198,n2, 285n2, 478n3, 479, 486, 487, 544; 23:31n1, 61, 129, 156, 173,n3, 234n5, 243n2, 259, 291, 303, 315, 329, 341n1, 518,n2, 552, 584, 615; 24:26, 65n1, 165, 185, 188, 189, 265, 288, 290, 292, 380, 389, 451, 465, 468, 490, 503, 505, 511n1, 518, 523, 524, 530, 547, 555, 567; 25:272, 385n2, 386, 387, 388, 396, 529-30, 563, 577; Bryce's evaluation as Speaker of the House, 24:507,n1; campaign funds, 24:254,n1; California primary vote, 24:383n1; congratulatory note to WW, 24:528; Democratic National Convention, first ballot, 24:484n2; tenth ballot, 24:507,n1; thirtieth ballot, 24:516,n1; Georgia primary vote, 24:382n2; Houn' Dawg Song, 24:251,n1; Illinois, primary campaign in, 24:299, 308,n1; Kansas Democratic state convention, 24:248,n1; Kentucky conventions, 24:332,n1,2, 357, 358,n3; Louisiana, 24:482-83; Maryland primary vote, 24:387n1; Missouri, 24:187n3; Nebraska primary, 24:357,n2; Nevada, 24:391, 404, 520-21; New York, 24:497,n2, 500, 511n1; North Carolina, 24:399n1; Pennsylvania, 24:330n3, 397; temporary chairman controversy, 24:462n1, 492n1; Tennessee, 24:403n1; views on Canada, 24:330n2; Virginia, 24:486; Wisconsin primary, 24:285n1; portrait, 24:illustration section

Clark, George Rogers, 14:518; 16:144n3

Clark, George Roy, 23:86

Clark, Harry Newton, 17:557

Clark, J. William, 22:546n5

Clark, John (of Buffalo), 25:69n2

Clark, John Bates, 15:502,n5; 17:92n2, 546,n2; 18:310-11,n1, 311; 25:419-21,n3,4

Clark, Jonas Gilman, 19:240n3

Clark, Joseph, 15:519,n2

Clark, Kenneth Sherman, 16:24n2

Clark, W. A., 14:331

Clark, William (1770-1838), 16:143-44,n1,3,4

Clark, William Andrews, 22:278,n3

Clark College and Clark University, 15:100n3, 581n1; 16:59n1, 61n1; 19:240n3

Clarke, Courtlandt Charles, 15:247

Clarke, Dumont, 16:533, 534

Clarke, Dumont, Jr., 15:493; 17:31,n1, 32, 296

Clarke, James Paul, 23:517

Clarke, John Hessin, 18:262-63,n1; 25:404n2

Clarke, Thomas Shields, 18:308n1

Clarkson, James Sullivan, 23:247,n1, 252, 310

Clarksville, Tenn., 18:484

class structure, **24**:309-10; **25**:369
Classical Association of New England, **17**:114
Classical Association of the Middle States and Maryland, **17**:114
Classical Association of the Middle West and South, **17**:113,n3, 556; **19**:19,n4
*Classical Journal*, **17**:113; **18**:575
*Classical Philology*, **17**:112-14, 116-17, 123-24, 130, 139, 173, 556; **18**:575
*Classical Review*, **18**:575
Claxton, Philander Priestly, **18**:589-90,-n1
Clay, Henry, **16**:53; **17**:79, 311-12, 319; **24**:417; **25**:205, 242, 249
Clayton bill, **25**:614
Clearing House Committee, **24**:533; **25**:529
Cleburne, Texas, **23**:268, 509
Clemens, Jane (Jean) Lampton, **20**:133,n4, 139
Clemens, Samuel Langhorne, **14**:192, 194; **15**:334; **17**:607-608,n9, 610n2, 612; **20**:133,n3, 139, 188, 378,n1
Clemons, William Harry, **15**:375; **16**:38; **17**:290
Cleveland, Frances Folsom (Mrs. Grover), **14**:6,n5, 72-73, 84, 224, 546, 552; **15**:119, 120; **18**:346, 347; **19**:132; **20**:359, 500
Cleveland, Francis Grover, **14**:540,n17, 552,n3
Cleveland, Frederick Albert, **19**:509n1
Cleveland, Grace Matthews (Mrs. James Harlan), **15**:420
Cleveland, Grover, **14**:17n3, 73, 162, 168, 192n2, 194, 233, 236,n5, 251, 281, 282, 306n3, 311, 347, 352, 387, 391, 436, 447, 449, 465, 519; **15**:20, 103, 119, 120, 131, 135, 184, 232, 306, 308n3, 313, 319, 362, 390, 391, 572, 573, 575, 576; **16**:102, 136, 197, 198n3, 215, 276, 300, 323, 345, 422, 480n1, 485, 503, 535,n2, 536; **17**:12, 73-78, 89, 159, 197, 222, 394n5, 400, 442, 462, 484n3, 590n1, 600, 602; **18**:9n2, 64-67, 108, 119, 229, 248,n2, 249,n7, 259, 346,n6, 348, 355, 359, 360, 373, 391, 397, 418, 451, 494n1, 494, 513n2, 558-59, 569, 569-70, 574, 645; **19**:78, 126-28, 494, 516; **20**:77n1, 133, 215, 249-51, 255, 257-62, 278, 362,n4, 378,n1, 534n1; **21**:10, 86, 129, 160, 309-10, 345, 345n13, 621; **22**:11-12,n3, 39n21, 113n2, 218, 221, 226,n3,5, 416, 489, 514; **23**:302,n2, 515, 516, 594, 598, 632, 633n1,3, 653; **24**:6, 26, 61, 531; **25**:232, 445, 471, 514, 519, 544, 550; Blaine presidential campaign, **24**:576; graduate college controversy, **24**:3-4; tariff, **24**:540
Cleveland, James Harlan, **14**:448,n4, 451; **15**:420,n1; **22**:362,n2
Cleveland, Ohio, **17**:550-51; **23**:327, 327n3; **24**:567; **25**:406, 549; Central High School, **16**:397n1; Chamber of Commerce, **17**:497, 501, 507, 508, 508n1; **18**:217,n2, 262; **19**:725-26,n1; **23**:125-26,n9; *Annual* (1908), **17**:506n; East High School, **16**:397n1; Hollenden Hotel, **16**:397, 405; Princeton alumni, **16**:405-406; Temple, **18**:217-n1,3; University Club, **16**:396; University School, **16**:397n1, 510; WW addresses, **16**:396-97n1, 406-11; **17**:497-506; **25**:404-13
Cleveland, Ruth, **15**:119, 135, 308,n3
*Cleveland Leader*, **15**:5,n1; **16**:397n; **17**:508n1
Cleveland Monument Association and Cleveland Memorial Tower, **18**:513,-n2, 514-15, 558-59,n2, 645; **19**:78-79, 126-28, 131,n1, 131-32, 533n1, 537-38, 558-59, 609, 610, 612, 653; **20**:532-33,n1,2
*Cleveland Plain Dealer*, **16**:90n3; **25**:257n
Clifton, Mass., **14**:438; EAW vacation at, July 1902, **14**:4-43, *passim*; WW vacation at, Aug. 1902, **14**:48-98, *passim*
Clinton, N. J., **21**:383; library, **22**:480
Close, Gilbert Fairchild, **17**:7,n16, 401, 456, 552; **18**:374, 382, 389, 465, 524; **19**:419, 422, 557, 598, 712; **20**:134, 137, 144, 184, 562-63; **21**:13
Closter, N. J., **23**:250
Club of Famous Wits Rounds Out 50 Years (Baker), **19**:552,n3
Clucas, Edward Welch, **14**:388
coal mines, **23**:249,n2,3,4,5
coal strike of 1902, **14**:113,n1, 148
Coal Trust, James C. McReynolds, **25**:557-58
Coan, William James, **17**:440
Coates, William Morrison, **14**:106,n1
Coates House, Kansas City, Mo., **23**:3, 5; **24**:185
Cobb, Frank Irving, **24**:97,n1, 463; **25**:286
Cobb, Tyrus Raymond, **23**:553,n2, 554, 558
Coben, Stanley, **22**:409n1,2; **23**:156n3
Cochran, Garrett, **15**:215n4
Cochran, Peyton, **22**:96, 118
Cochran, Samuel, M.D., **19**:120,n1
Cockburn Hotel, Edinburgh, **14**:524
Cockermouth, Cumberland, **18**:374, 386
Cockran, William Bourke, **16**:322,n3
Coffee, Rudolph Isaac, **23**:249,n1
Coffin, Fulton Johnson, **14**:458,n2
Coffin, Henry Sloane, **17**:125
Coffin, Owen Vincent, **14**:515
Cohalan, Daniel Florence, **20**:402n1; **22**:602
Cohen, Lewis, **23**:81,n4
Cohen, Solomon Solis, M.D., **23**:329,n1
Coit, Dr., **17**:10,n1
Coit, Margaret L., **25**:415n1
Coke, Sir Edward, **19**:719; **21**:135
Coker, Francis William, **19**:678

Colby, Everett, **16**:215-17,n1, 218; **17**:24,n5; **21**:341, 352, 563; **22**:226n3, 366n2; **25**:428-29

Colby, Howard Augustus, **19**:165

Colby College, **16**:251, 509

cold storage warehouses, **22**:227-28, 260, 352-53, 438, 579,n5, 591

Cole, Charles Albert, **25**:332n2

Cole, Charles D'Urban Morris, **21**:527,n2

Cole, Chester Cicero, **16**:547,n1

Cole, Clarence Lee, **21**:310,n2, 315; **22**:309, 413,n1

Cole, Donald B., **25**:243n6, 426n4

Cole, George B., **21**:383

Coleman Hotel, Asbury Park, **23**:262n3

Coleridge, Ernest Hartley, **18**:368,n2, 369

Coleridge, Samuel Taylor, **14**:503; **18**:368, 368n2

Coletta, Paolo E., **23**:236n4

Colgate University, **16**:102, 131, 251

*Collected Works of Walter Bagehot* (ed. St. John-Stevas), **22**:194n4

*Collected Works of Abraham Lincoln* (ed. Basler), **23**:407n9

College: Two Points of View (*The Outlook*), **17**:307n1

college admission by certificate, **17**:155, 160

*College Charts Its Course: Historical Conceptions and Current Proposals* (Butts), **15**:292n27

college curriculum, shortening of, **14**:261,n2, 263-64, 272, 289,n2, 302, 318, 546n2

college education, **25**:276-79, 280, 281

Collège de France, **17**:556; **19**:739

College Democracy (G. S. Johns), **17**:247,n3

College for Women, Columbia, S. C., **22**:577,n4,5,6

College Men's League, **25**:274n1, 312

College of the City of New York, **16**:132, 249, 258; **25**:278n4; Townsend Harris Hall, **17**:528,n1

college politicians, **23**:93

college president, powers and duties of, at Princeton, **15**:393-95

college presidents, **19**:232f

College Reform—and Football (Shaw), **19**:597,n2

College Summer Conference, **14**:266

*College Widow* (Ade), **23**:553,n2, 554

colleges, U.S., **19**:334-47

collegiate Gothic architecture, **15**:577

Collier, Robert Joseph, **25**:449n1

Collier, Price, **19**:262,n3

*Collier's Weekly*, **16**:455n1; **19**:156,n3; **20**:147n, 541n1; **21**:40n1; **22**:73,n3, 182n1, 427n1; **25**:274n1, 449,n1

Collingwood Hotel, New York City, **21**:87; **22**:87, 141, 230; **25**:448, 507

Collins, Dennis Francis, **21**:296, 464, 465, 467; **24**:251, 252; **25**:582,n4

Collins, Gilbert, **21**:147,n2

Collins, John, **15**:215n4

Collins, Varnum Lansing, **14**:364, 439-n1; **16**:421,n4, 511; **17**:352n2, 408; **19**:576; **25**:575, 586

Collyer, Robert, **23**:145,n3

Colombia, **15**:60n1

*Colonel Edward M. House: The Texas Years 1858-1912* (Richardson), **25**:550n2

Colonial Dames: Virginia Society, **14**:396

colonialism (expansionism, imperialism), **14**:324, 325, 431,n2, 433-34; **20**:309,n2, 312

*Colonies* (Thwaites), **20**:582

Colorado, **21**:608n2; **22**:388,n1, 405, 519, 537; addresses in, **25**:362-77; Democrats, **23**:650; **25**:545-46,n1

Colorado, University of, **16**:254, 256

Colorado College, **17**:287

Colorado Equal Suffrage Association, **23**:478n1

Colorado Springs, Colo., **25**:362-68

Colquhon, Arthur Hugh Urquhart, **16**:266,n1

Colquitt, Oscar, Branch, **22**:423,n4; **23**:506,n2, 507,n6; **25**:625,n1

Columbia, *see* Missouri, University of

Columbia *Missouri Herald*, **15**:199n1

Columbia, S. C., **21**:201; **24**:400,n4; **25**:536, 539-40; Central National Bank, **22**:507; Charles H. Barnwell's School, **23**:563n2; Columbia Theatre, **23**:114,n1; First Baptist Church, **23**:113; First Presbyterian Church, **14**:331, WW in, **23**:112, 113-27, 129; Y.M.C.A., **22**:576-77, 577n6; **23**:113-14,n2

Columbia River, **21**:12

Columbia, S. C. *State*, **14**:331n, 333n; **22**:508n1; **23**:114n, 127n; **24**:528; **25**:539, 623,n4

Columbia (S. C.) Theological Seminary, **22**:21n3

Columbia University, **14**:157, 283, 398; **15**:100n3, 234n, 444n2, 447, 502n5; **16**:131, 157, 182, 196, 240, 249, 250, 251, 252, 258, 465, 488, 509, 511; **17**:90, 106, 109n1, 110,n1, 450, 561; **18**:577, 579; **19**:427, 480, 552n3, 676, 678; **20**:75, 78,n2, 108, 290, 450, 451; **22**:172n1; **23**:516n9; **25**:419n1; Blumenthal Lectures, **16**:373,n1, 375-76, 383, 395, 396, 413, 414-15, 495-96, 559,n1; **17**:3n2, 6,n12, 7, 11, 15, 26, 45-46,n1, 62,n1, 65,n1, 73,n1, 94, 121, 365-66, 427,n2, 605-606, 611-12, 616; **18**:477, 576; College of Physicians and Surgeons, **17**:235, 236n1; faculty compared with Princeton's, **14**:121, 127, 154; Faculty of Political Science, **16**:373,n1; football game with Princeton, Oct. 25, 1902, **14**:187,n1, 194; fraternities, **14**:480; Graduate Council, **18**:568, 620; Hamilton Hall,

Columbia University, (cont.)
  Morningside, **19:**539,n5; Installation of President Butler, April 19, 1902, **14:**191; Kaiser Wilhelm Professorship, **21:**49n4; Kennedy (J. S.) bequest, **19:**539,n5; newspaper publicity, **14:**490; 150th anniversary celebration, Oct. 31, 1904, **15:**533,n1; Phi Beta Kappa address 1906, **17:**104,n2, 410; **20:**265n2; School of Mines, **16:**247, 508; shortening of college curriculum for pre-professional students, **14:**261,-n2, 289,n2; Teachers College, **16:**282; **18:**612; **23:**103
Columbia University Press, **16:**374, 383; **17:**121, 352n2, 428n1
*Columbia University Quarterly*, **15:** 194,n1
*Columbian Magazine, or Monthly Miscellany*, **19:**607
Columbus, Christopher, **14:**442; **18:**89, 509
Columbus, Ohio, **23:**255; addresses in, **25:**198-212
Columbus *Ohio State Journal*, **25:**203n
Colvin, Mary Loring (Mrs. Fred H.), **22:**289-90,n1
Colwell, Percy Robert, **17:**222,n2
Colyar, A. S., **23:**173,n1
combinations in restraint of trade, **23:**621
Come Let Us Reason Together (editorial), **24:**399,n1
*Commentaries on the Gallic War* (Caesar), **16:**119, 221; **17:**542
commerce, *see* trade
Commercial Acetylene Co., **24:**245n1
Commercial Cable Company, **15:**147
Commercial Club of Chicago, **25:**570n2
Commercial Club of Davenport, Iowa, **24:**223n1
Commercial Club of Kansas City, **23:**9, 10n3
Commercial Club of Minneapolis, **25:** 164-69
Commercial Club of Omaha, **25:**340-47
Commissariat, M.S., **15:**426,n1
commission form of government for cities, **19:**91-92, 514, 521; **22:**551,n3, 574-75,n1,2,4,5, 581, 591; **23:**25-26, 40-41, 43, 78, 79, 91,n2, 92, 136-38,n1, 140-52, 161,n1, 161-71, 176-77, 178f, 201-11, 218,n1, 233,n1, 264, 271, 279, 299, 335, 344, 420, 427-28, 450-51, 512, 567, 572-83, 634; **24:**231, 480; **25:**164, 306 Δ R. S. Childs, **19:**729-30; **22:**197n2
*Commission Government in American Cities* (Bradford), **19:**91n2
Committee of Christian Education in China, **19:**544
Committee on Reference and Counsel, representing the Boards and Societies of Foreign Missions of all the Protes-
tant communions of the United States and Canada, **19:**109-10, 109n1,2
Commission on Uniform State Laws, **25:**311
common law, **24:**236
*Common Sense* (Paine), **14:**281
*Commoner* (Lincoln, Neb.), **22:**231,n3, 255n1, 285n2, 503,n3; **23:**130n1, 236n3,4, 237, 238; **24:**274n2; **25:**46n1, 649,n1
*Commonwealth*, S.S., **14:**398
community centers, **23:**480-88
commuters and commutation rates, **23:**450
Como, Italy, Wilsons at, **14:**539, 540
Como, Lake, **17:**8
competition, in business, **24:**12, 126, 193, 314, 349; **25:**10, 11, 13, 58, 74-75, 103, 122-23, 139-40, 152, 157, 158-59, 160, 167-68, 178, 180, 191-92, 193, 194, 196, 200, 201, 205-207, 227, 228, 245, 249-50, 266, 268, 272, 329, 342, 357, 367-68, 372-73, 383, 410, 434-35, 445, 447, 495, 496-97, 524 Δ B. M. Anderson, Jr., **25:**419-21; L. D. Brandeis, **25:**57, 289-94, 295-97; J. B. Clark, **25:**419-21; D. B. Jones, **24:**549
*Complete Poems of Edgar Allan Poe* (ed. Whitty), **19:**606,n2
Compromise of 1850, **17:**311, 312, 313, 320
Compton, R. D., **16:**151-52,n1, 153-54
Compton Wynyates, Warwickshire, **15:**446
Comstock, Antoinette Cole, **17:**295-96
*Conciliation with America* (Burke), **14:**14
Concord, N. H., **19:**229, 230, 238, 239; WW address, **19:**226-28; **24:**165-66
Concord, N. H., *Evening Monitor*, **19:** 228n; **24:**166n
Concord Publishing Company, **24:**549n1
Concordia Theological Seminary, St. Louis, **16:**257
Condit, Harry Hobart, **20:**76,n1
Cone, John Frederick, **20:**173n4
Coney, John Haughton, **14:**326, 395; **16:**130; **17:**85, 408; **18:**271, 293; **19:**615, 616
Confederate soldiers, **23:**268
Confederate States of America, **14:**238, 282, 311, 344, 347
*Confederate States of America, 1861-1865: A Financial and Industrial History of the South during the Civil War* (Schwab), **14:**344,n8
Confederate States government, **18:**601
Confederate veterans at University of N. C., **23:**109,n5
Confederation, **17:**506
Conference for Education in the South, **15:**159-60; *Proceedings . . . sixth Session*, **15:**159,n2
*Congregationalist and Christian World*

(Boston), **19**:441,n1,2, 475n3; **21**:5n, 31,n1

Congress, *see* United States Congress

Congress Hotel, Chicago, **18**:17, 276; **20**:432

Congress of Arts and Science, St. Louis, 1904, **15**:105-106, 116, 157, 433-34,n2,3, 468n3, 469, 472n1, 478, 491n; WW address, **15**:472-91; *see also* Louisiana Purchase Exposition, St. Louis, 1904; International Congress of Arts and Science, St. Louis, 1904

*Congress of Arts and Science, Universal Exposition, St. Louis, 1904* (ed. Rogers), **14**:395n1; **15**:491n

Congressional committees, **24**:13, *see also* names of individual committees, such as Appropriations Committee

Congressional investigations, **24**:423

*Congressional Record*, **16**:559n4; **18**:138-39, 434n5; **19**:363n1; **20**:38n5, 258n1, 312n2, 391; **21**:474; **22**:35n2; **23**:587n, 650n; **24**:16n, 40n, 284n2, 332n1, 428n, 457n; **25**:407

Coniston, Lancs, **18**:370

Conklin, Abram V., **17**:471,n1, 507

Conklin, Belle Adkinson (Mrs. Edwin Grant), **21**:117,n2

Conklin, Edwin Grant, **17**:416-17, 437-38, 445, 446, 447-48, 450, 471, 507, 561-62, 564, 604-605; **18**:5-6, 286, 290, 445, 575-76; **19**:11, 12, 14, 16, 17, 21, 29, 51, 69-70, 134n1, 134-35, 141-42, 172, 398, 425, 429, 612, 621, 682, 753-55; **20**:14, 15-16, 20, 58, 93, 109, 114-15, 143, 174, 187n1, 190, 191-92, 232, 474, 484; **21**:116-17, 136-37, 435,n2; **22**:436

Conklin, Maria Hull (Mrs. Abram V.), **17**:471,n2

Conkling, Cook, **22**:394-95,n1

Connecticut, **21**:598, 608n2; **22**:15; government, **24**:176; WW addresses in, **24**:166-77; **25**:234-57

Connecticut Civil Service Reform Association, **24**:166,n1

Connecticut State Peace Society, **20**:120n2

Connecticut Valley, Princeton alumni, **20**:320-21, 336

Connecticut Valley Historical Museum, **23**:285n

Connor, Henry Groves, **22**:383,n1

Connor, Robert Digges Wimberly, **16**:314,n1, 315

Conover, Helen Field (Mrs. Francis Stevens), **14**:36,n1

Conover, J. C., **16**:301

Conover, Juliana, **14**:37n1; **15**:152

Conover, Thornton, **14**:37n1, 97,n2

conscience, **23**:629

conservation, **21**:44, 88n3, 95, 126, 271, 402; **22**:111-12, 350, 371-72, 566-67, 594; **23**:25, 89, 107, 135, 298, 382-83; **24**:84, 90, 104-105, 124; **25**:5-6, 15-16, 176, 190, 234, 251-52, 312-21, 363-64, 397, 497, 502; East *vs* West, **25**:558; monopoly and, **25**:355, 370; New Jersey, **25**:308 Δ L. D. Brandeis, **25**:274; N. Hapgood, **25**:610; W. B. Heyburn, **22**:371n4; W. H. Page, **25**:516; J. Smith, Jr., **22**:205n2; E. C. Stokes, **21**:505

Conservation Congress, *see* National Conservation Congress

conservatism and conservatives, **23**:209-10; **25**:237

*Conservatism of the South* (Hemphill), **16**:286-88

Constitution, U.S., *see* United States Constitution

constitutional government, **18**:69-85; in the U.S., **18**:69-216

*Constitutional Government in the United States* (Wilson), **25**:617n1

*Constitutional History of England* (Maitland), **18**:356-57,n1

constitutions, **22**:102-103

Consumers' League of New Jersey, **22**:157, 157n1

Continental Congress, **19**:64, 203, 208-209, 506

Continental Hotel, Newark, N.J., **18**:551

contributions, *see* campaign contributions

*Control of Trusts: An Argument in Favor of Curbing the Power of Monopoly* (Clark), **25**:420,n3

Converse, John Heman, **15**:129-30,n1, 144, 155, 192,n1, 301n2, 379, 526; **16**:303, 336; **17**:102-103n1

Cook, Albert Stanburrough, **20**:65,n2

Cook, George W. B., **23**:517

Cook, James E. W., **22**:356,n1

Cooke, Henry Eleutheros, **15**:388n1

Cooke, Hereward Lester, **16**:465, 508; **17**:408

Cooke, Martin, **23**:634; **25**:213n2

*Cook's Excursion to Pompeii*, **15**:228,n1

Cooley, Alford Warriner, **16**:316,n5

Cooley, Clarissa Smith (Mrs. Francis B.), **20**:284,n1

Coolidge, Francis Lowell, **16**:384; **20**:410,n1

Coolidge, Louis Arthur, **16**:315,n1,318

Coolidge, Thomas Jefferson, **14**:306n3

Coombs, Henry, **23**:273

Coons, John Constine, **15**:471-72,n5

Coons, Joseph C., **15**:471-72

Cooper, Howard, **23**:424

Cooper, John H., **23**:536n1

Cooper, Oscar Henry, **18**:548-49,n1

Cooper Union (New York), **25**:183,n2

cooperatives, **23**:276

Cope, Walter, **14**:49,n3, 77-78, 83, 86, 94, 198,n1, 199; **15**:423, 424n1

Cope & Stewardson, architects, **16**:312, 312n3, 447; **17**:96-97; **18**:302,n1

Copley, John Singleton, **15**:213
Copley Plaza Hotel (Boston), **25**:270
Corbett, Joseph J., **23**:258,n2
Corbin, John, **17**:240,n2
Corkran, Sutton F., **16**:400n4
Cornelison, Isaac Amada, **19**:479
Cornell, Erza, **17**:124,n1
Cornell, John W., **14**:405-406
Cornell, Walter Stewart, M.D., **16**:225,n3
Cornell College, Iowa, **19**:677
Cornell Studies in Classical Philology, **17**:114
Cornell University, **15**:65, 100n3, 291n, 558; **16**:132, 159, 253, 257, 259, 272n1, 385n1, 398n1, 465, 511; **17**:124n1, 352n2, 557, 588; **18**:367, 519,n2, 579, 580; **19**:152, 453; **20**:75, 424, 539; **22**:359; fraternities, **14**:480
Cornill, Carl Heinrich, **16**:400,n4
Cornish, Johnston, **21**:383, 384; **22**:588,-n1; **23**:270, 271
Cornwall, Henry Bedinger, **14**:213,n3, 214, 218, 219, 220, 221, 258; **15**:293, 324, 326; **16**:92; **17**:408; **20**:409-10, 422, 426, 499, 505
Cornwall, Mary Hall Porter (Mrs. Henry Bedinger), **20**:426,n2
Cornwall, Richard Russell, **15**:324n
Cornwall, Sarah Jerusha, **20**:426,n1
Cornwell, George Gilbert, **18**:580; **19**:139,n4
*Corona* (Dodge yacht), **21**:38,n2; **24**:572
Corporation Act (N.J.), **25**:307
corporations, **17**:323-24, 325, 516, 522; **19**:324f; **20**:316, 437-38, 463; **21**:45; 60, 71f, 88n3, 93, 95-96, 99, 119, 122, 126, 134, 153, 165, 186-87, 204, 206, 207-10, 216, 222, 228, 233, 277, 304, 305, 326, 330, 331, 340-41, 345, 359, 371, 374-75, 407, 453-54, 469, 488, 489, 533, 568, 571; **22**:8, 63, 69-70, 75-76, 106, 107, 110, 217, 219, 220, 221, 222, 223, 312-16, 346-49, 351, 398, 485-86, 563, 586, 593; **23**:5-6, 8, 24, 25, 35-36, 51, 54, 59-60, 67, 78, 90, 91, 101, 108, 121, 126, 157, 159, 197, 198, 370, 382, 422, 434-35, 436, 448, 467, 512, 593n4, 613, 626, 627; **24**:144, 145, 196, 197-99, 301; **25**:11, 157, 159, 258-59, 382, 427, 496; campaign contributions, **25**:402; New Jersey, **25**:308, 358; Progressive platform, **25**:59n1 Δ C. W. Bryan, **23**:238; J. B. Clark, **25**:420; W. S. Elder, **22**:18; Jersey City Democratic Committee, **23**:203n3; R. V. Lindabury, **21**:140; W. G. McAdoo, **21**:298; T. N. McCarter, Jr., **21**:139; H. Marshall, **21**:325; J. Moody, **22**:114, 115; C. S. Moore, **23**:593n4; G. W. Perkins, **22**:19; **24**:346n2; Philadelphia *North American*, **23**:246n1; E. C. Stokes, **21**:503, 505; J. Smith, Jr., **22**:132-33; W. H. Taft, **23**:361n2;

F. Todd, **22**:121-22, 185; E. A. Van Valkenburg, **21**:199; G. W. Wickersham, **23**:361n3; and bribery in San Francisco, **21**:344n5
Corporations, Bureau of, **24**:412n3; **25**:294
Corpus Christi College, Oxford, **16**:472n2,3, 508; **17**:13,n1,2, 127, 461, 463, 465, 472, 558; Turnbull sundial, **16**:472n2; **17**:87-88, 127, 358, 359-60, 447n1, 461, 462, 463, 465, 509-10,n2, 558
Corrao, Francis L., **24**:536,n1, 575
correctional institutions, **24**:22, 567
Corrupt Practice Act of England, **24**:269
corrupt practices, **21**:195, 232, 256; **22**:455 Δ W. C. Osborn, **21**:155,n2, 172; Jersey City *Jersey Journal* editorial, **21**:244n1; New York State legislature, **21**:343n10; G. E. Chamberlain, **22**:175; non-partisan league, **22**:255-n2; G. L. Record, **22**:358,n4, 383n3
corrupt practices acts, **20**:316
corruption, **21**:231-32, 302, 479-80, 485; **22**:360; political, **23**:275
Corson, Hiram, **14**:389
Cortelyou, George Bruce, **24**:533
Corwin, Edward Samuel, **16**:110, 131, 250, 306, 376, 421; **17**:408; **18**:271, 294; **19**:619; **20**:430,n3, 583
Cory, William Earle, **17**:557
Cosey, Alfred B., **24**:556,n1
Cosgrove, John T., **22**:546n5
Cosmopolitan Club, **20**:556
*Cosmopolitan* magazine, **15**:450n1, 461n, 463, 463n1; **16**:375n1; **19**:314n1; **20**:372n1; **21**:342n7
cost of living, **25**:44, 139
cost of production, **24**:420
Cothran, Annie Wilson Howe (Mrs. Perrin Chiles), **22**:234,n1, 293, 517n4
Cothran, Perrin Chiles, **22**:234,n1
Coughlin, John William, M.D., **25**:257,n3
Coulomb, Harry R., **22**:310,n2,3
courts, **24**:278
Covington, Harry Franklin, **14**:329; **15**:65, 375; **18**:583; **19**:749n1
Covington, James Harry, **24**:287,n1
Cowan, Andrew, **23**:319,n2
Cowan, Henry, **15**:241
Cowen, John Kissig, **15**:77,n2,4, 78, 133-34,n1, 300,n2
Cowgill, James, **24**:186,n4
Cowles, Anna Roosevelt (Mrs. William Sheffield), **16**:243,n6
Cowles, William Sheffield, **16**:243,n6
Cowper, William, **14**:503
Cox, Albert Lyman, **23**:110,n2
Cox, Edwin P., **24**:119, 121, 122
Cox, Henry Bartholomew, **14**:190n; **16**:105n, 435n
Cox, Minnie M., **14**:359n1
Coxe, Alfred Conkling, **21**:298,n1
Coxe, George S., **22**:39,n14

Coyle, Robert Francis, **23**:13,n2
Cragsmoor Inn, Cragsmoor, Catskill, N. Y., **16**:152n1, 154
Craig, Hardin, **14**:46,n2, 224, 225, 474; **15**:137, 375; **16**:132, 254-55; **18**:583; **19**:749n1; **20**:54, 60-61
Craiger, Sherman Montrose, **22**:428-29
Craighead, Edwin Boone, **17**:375-76,n1
Craighead, Erwin, **16**:332
Craigie, Pearl Mary Teresa (*pseud.* John Oliver Hobbes), **14**:529n10
Cram, Elizabeth Carrington Read (Mrs. Ralph Adams), **17**:174,n4; **18**:14; **19**:333,n2, 349, 389
Cram, Ralph Adams, **17**:72n1, 96-97, 100, 118-21, 141-42, 147, 150-52, 152-53, 156-58, 158-59, 160, 168, 169-70, 172, 173-74, 207-208, 219, 220-21, 281, 301, 345, 346, 349, 386, 387, 388, 389, 550, 560-61, 562, 566-69, 568, 585, 604; **18**:8-9, 13-14, 52, 63, 64, 67, 218, 225-26, 226-27, 242, 247n1, 248, 249, 250, 250-54, 273-74, 279, 286, 291-93, 295-96, 296-97, 301, 302, 304, 308, 308,n1, 310, 314, 589; **19**:116, 135, 143, 172-73, 200, 303-304, 331, 333, 349, 350, 387, 388-89, 533,n1, 537-38, 540, 549, 558-59, 559, 622, 705-706, 712, 732; **20**:533; **21**:434; **22**:375
Cram, Goodhue & Ferguson, architects, **17**:72n1, 121n2; **18**:286, 302; **19**:544
Crampton, Guy Chester, **18**:5,n1, 579-80; **19**:70
Crane, Charles Richard, **24**:554,n2; **25**:558
Crane, Josephine Boardman (Mrs. Winthrop Murray), **23**:220,n1
Crane, Robert Treat, **19**:190,n1
Crane, Thomas Frederick, **14**:389
Crane, William N., **14**:253,n8
Crane, Winthrop Murray, **19**:109; **23**:223,n1; **24**:75,n3, 467,n1
Cranford, N. J., **23**:468, 477
Crater, David S., **25**:582,n3
Craven, Bruce, **24**:390,n2
Craven, D. Stewart, **23**:183, 394
Craven, Elijah Richardson, **14**:161, 254-55, 464; **15**:26,n2,3, 300,n3, 530-31; **16**:277, 278; **18**:9n3,4, 569
Craven, John V., **25**:462,n2
Cravens, William Ben, **24**:287,n1
Crawford, Caroline Rice (Mrs. Morris Barker), **18**:383n4
Crawford, Coe Isaac, **23**:132n1
Crawford, Frederick North, **18**:383n4
Crawford, Margaret, **18**:383
Crawford, Morris Barker, **18**:383,n4
Creamer, David Staley, **25**:645,n7
Creasey, Anna B., **14**:81,n2
Creasy, William Trenton, **25**:616,n1
Crebs, John Montgomery, **25**:393,n1
Credi, Lorenzo di, **15**:229
credit, **23**:157n2; **25**:167, 206, 215

Crédit Lyonnais, **14**:548, 549; **15**:324, 325, 336, 351-52
Creel, George, **23**:478,n1
Creelman, James, **22**:216
Creigh, Thomas, **20**:437n1
Creighton, Ga., **16**:86
Creighton, James Edwin, **15**:119,n1
Creighton University, **25**:360
Crenshaw, James Llewellyn, **19**:679
Cresse and St. Louis Exposition, **15**:443,n2
criminal law (N. J.), **25**:306
Crimmins, John Daniel, **22**:40,n28
*Crisis* (NAACP organ), **21**:276n3; **22**:50n3; **25**:26n4, 26, 66n
Crispin, Saint, **18**:434
Critchlow, Frank Linley, **15**:137,n1; **16**:132, 256; **17**:408; **19**:572, 576
*Critic* (New York), **14**:346n
*Critique of Pure Reason* (Kant), **19**:666
Crocker, Robert Stewart, **14**:388
Crocker, William Henry, **23**:57
Crockett, Davy, **23**:517
Crockett, John Wesley, **23**:233,n2, 517
Croes, John James Robertson, **15**:579; **16**:501,n2
Croker, Richard, **21**:342,n8; **22**:168n1, 312
Croll, Morris William, **16**:421,n2, 510; **17**:408
Croly, Herbert, **20**:350,n1,2; **21**:322
Cromwell, Oliver, **14**:146, 504; **17**:13; **21**:498
Crooks, James B., **23**:573n1
Crosby, Henry Lamar, **19**:677
Crosby, Howard, **18**:339,n2
Cross, Fred J., **23**:315,n1
Cross, J. J., **15**:66
Cross, Richard Kelso, **17**:59,n1, 72; **20**:402,n1
*Crossroads of Freedom: The 1912 Campaign Speeches of Woodrow Wilson* (Davidson), **25**:x, xin2
Crosthwaite, Cumberland, Wilsons at, **14**:523
Crothers, Austin Lane, **23**:266,n2, 568,-n2, 569
Crothers, Samuel McChord, **17**:534-35,n1; **18**:622, 625; **19**:23,n3, 325,n1; **20**:262; **25**:130,n3
*Crowded Years: The Reminiscences of William G. McAdoo* (McAdoo), **24**:524n3
Crown and Mitre Hotel, Carlisle, Cumberland, **18**:363; *see also* Carlisle, Cumberland
*Crown of Wild Olive* (Ruskin), **15**:365n1
Crozer, George Knowles, Jr., **19**:165
Crum, William Demos, M.D., **14**:359n1; **18**:386,n2; **25**:25,n2
Crummock Water, Cumberland, Wilsons at, **14**:523
*Crusader* (Baltimore), **21**:156n1
Crutchfield, Eugene Lee, **24**:147,n1
Csongravi, Cornelius, **24**:548-49,n1

Cuba, 15:41, 195; 25:623
Culberson, Charles Allen, 21:580,n1; 23:458n1,2, 466, 476, 499n1, 506, 507; 24:255, 273, 287,n1, 467; 25:563
Cumberland, England, Buttermere Hotel, 14:523; Keswick Hotel, 14:523,n3; Wilsons at, 14:523
Cumberland County, N. J., 21:277, 584n1; 22:531, 532; 23:531, 533,n3, 534; 25:582
Cumberland Gap, 14:518
Cummings, Homer Stillé, 24:272,n1, 286; 25:570
Cummins, Albert Baird, 21:219,n5, 251; 23:132n1; 24:494
Cuneo, Frank, 25:29
Cunniff, Michael Glen, 24:237,n1
Cunningham, Clarence, 21:546n3; 23:175n1
Cunningham, Yeates, 15:66
Cupid, 22:218
currency reform, see banking and currency system, reforms
currency, platform plank, 24:479, 581,n1
Current History, 22:519n4; 23:591n1
Current Literature, 24:140,n1
Current Municipal Legislation (Lapps, ed.), 23:573n1
Curry, George, 24:560,n2
Curry, Jabez Lamar Monroe, 14:15
Curti, Merle Eugene, 17:241n3
Curtin, Margaret Higgins, 14:52,n3, 70, 96
Curtis, Frank Grenville, 19:165
Curtis, George William, 24:167,n3
Curtis, James L., 25:571,n1
Curzon of Kedleston, George Nathaniel Curzon, 1st Baron and 1st Marquis, 15:97; 17:348n1
customs duties, 25:100
Cushing, Juliet Clannon (Mrs. George W. B.), 22:156-57,n1
Cutting, Churchill Hunter, 15:166,n2
Cutting, Elizabeth Brown, 15:165-66,n1; 16:89,n2
Cutting, Mary Dutton (Mrs. Churchill Hunter), 15:166,n3
Cutts, Harry Madison, 19:483
Cuyler, Cornelius Cuyler, 14:43n1, 67, 72, 77, 92, 94, 110-11, 144, 149-50, 198, 199, 293, 294, 306, 335, 360, 417, 465; 15:64,n2, 123, 128, 130, 131, 131n1, 137, 174, 193, 219, 271, 390, 413-14, 418, 423, 424, 426, 433, 434, 437, 440, 508-509, 509n2, 525, 528, 534, 570, 572, 573; 16:5, 69, 171, 208,n1,2, 210, 211, 222-23,n1, 224-25, 278, 279, 468, 488, 500; 17:170, 351n2, 568,n2; 18:242, 456; 19:64, 74, 77n3, 148, 155, 162, 308,n1, 323, 331, 333, 347n1, 389, 549, 551-52, 674-75; 21:617
Cuyler, Eleanor de Graff, 14:72, 294, 306; 15:131
Cuyler, May or Mary Townsend Nicoll

Lord (Mrs. Cornelius Cuyler), 16:223n1; 18:242; 19:331,n1
Cuyler, Theodore Ledyard, 14:300,n1, 346-47; 15:16
Cuyler, Morgan & Company, 14:48, 111, 117; 19:8

Dabney, Alice Saunders, 25:112n1
Dabney, Charles William, 14:378-79,n1; 15:419, 420, 530
Dabney, Lily Davis (Mrs. Richard Heath), 14:58, 70,n1, 74, 143, 189, 15:507
Dabney, Lucy Davis, 24:217n1
Dabney, Margaret Lavinia Morrison (Mrs. Robert Lewis), 14:378
Dabney, Richard Heath, 14:32-33, 44, 49, 51, 52, 58, 70, 74, 77, 79, 86, 143, 188, 189, 203-204; 15:507-508; 21:138, 597-99; 22:13; 23:550, 551-52, 563, 591,n2, 601,n1, 604, 631, 653-54; 24:29, 71-72,n9, 79-80, 95-96, 97,n2, 147-49, 217, 244, 256, 398, 578; 25:112, 553-54, 613-14
Dabney, Robert Lewis, 14:378,n2, 379
Dabney, Virginius, 14:70,n2
Daddow, Samuel Harries, 16:138
Dahlgren, Ulric, 14:126,n1, 128; 17:408, 561; 19:12, 14, 16, 17, 21, 29, 70
Daily Progress (Charlottesville, Va.), 23:550n
Dain, Nathaniel, 17:557
Dale, William Pratt, 19:211,n1
Dalhousie, James Andrew Broun Ramsay, Lord Dalhousie, 24:402
Dalhousie College, 16:253
Dallas, Texas, 22:576; 23:231, 255, 260, 261, 267, 269, 286, 308, 519, 589; 24:154; Church of the Incarnation (P. E.), 23:511; First Baptist Church, 23:506, 508, 510; Oriental Hotel, 23:506, 507, 508; Relk and Harris's band, 23:507; State Fair Coliseum, 23:506, 508, 509, 510; WW addresses, 23:494-99, 499-506; WW in, 23:506-10
Dallas Academy, Selma, Ala., 16:72-73
Dallas County Woodrow Wilson Club, 23:507
Dallas Home and State, 23:176n
Dallas Morning News, 23:499n, 506n, 510n, 511n, 512n; 24:50,n1
Dalrymple, Alfred N., 21:261,n3; 24:435,n4
Daly, Peter Francis, 22:294n2
Damrosch, Frank Heino, 16:208,n1,3, 209, 210,n, 211
Dana, Robert Shoemaker, M.D., 16:30-31, 35
Dance, George, 14:288n1
Daniels, Addie Worth Bagley (Mrs. Josephus), 21:585,n2; 22:121,n2, 406; 23:111n1, 139,n1, 140; 25:534-35, 585n2
Daniels, Frank Arthur, 23:139,n1; 25:585n2

Daniels, Joan Robertson (Mrs. Winthrop More), **14:**44, 124, 553
Daniels, Jonathan Worth, **23:**139,n1; **25:**585n2
Daniels, Josephus, **20:**566n; **21:**585n1; **22:**121, 406-407; **23:**111n1, 139-40, 140; **24:**59, 64, 288-89, 368, 380, 385, 386, 387-88, 388-89, 390, 396, 399, 402-403, 404, 461, 471-72, 476, 481n; **25:**55, 184n1, 550, 570, 578, 585, 610, 623, 647-48
Daniels, Josephus, Jr., **23:**139,n1; **25:** 585n2
Daniels, Robertson Balfour, **14:**124,n1; **16:**111n1
Daniels, Roger, **24:**383n1
Daniels, Winthrop More, **14:**30, 34, 44, 124, 297, 326, 327, 394, 456, 457, 488, 553; **15:**56, 65, 73, 120, 121, 233-34, 248n1, 291n, 330, 403-404,n4,5, 501, 504, **16:**7-8, 29-30, 40-41, 41-42, 84, 88, 92, 111, 142, 306, 372, 379,n1, 385, 386, 388; **17:**164, 208, 286, 290, 342-43, 402, 403, 408, 415, 416, 421, 424, 448, 467, 468; **18:**271, 293; **19:**70n1, 73, 77-78, 134n1, 135-36, 172, 180, 183, 184, 190, 429, 488-89, 557, 560, 581-91, 604-605, 610, 612, 613-14, 615, 616-19, 621, 753-55; **20:**9n, 18, 19, 58, 73, 78, 93, 109, 114-15, 143, 174, 190, 266n4, 317-18, 319-20, 371, 430, 484, 569; **21:**10-11, 174, 321, 337; **22:**25; **23:**310
Daniels, Worth Bagley, **23:**139,n1, 140,n1; **25:**585n2
Dante Alighieri, **17:**535, **19:**367n5, 574, 703,n1; **21:**217, 533; **23:**375, 498; **24:**212
Darrell, Miss, **19:**382-83,n3
Darrow, (Charles) Whitney, **17:**351,n1,2, 352-57; **19:**390
Dartmouth College, **16:**131, 189, 251, 252, 255, 489n5; **19:**408,n1, 409, 410, 413, 421, 422, 558, 678; **20:**539; **21:**21n1; *Inauguration of Ernest Fox Nichols . . . as President of Dartmouth College, October 14, 1909*, **19:**414,n2, 418n, 440n2; WW address, **19:**413-18
Dartmouth College case (Dartmouth College v. Woodward), **16:**298
Darwin, Charles, **18:**105, 106, 200; **19:**34, 35, 84, 85, 218; **23:**577
Darwinian theory, **24:**416
Dashiel, Paul J., **20:**539
Dashiell, Landonia Randolph, **14:**396
Daughters of the American Revolution, Cleveland (Ohio) branch, **16:**564
Davenport, Ia., **24:**222
David, King, **21:**319; **23:**15
*David Harum: A Story of American Life* (Westcott), **14:**72,n6; **22:**331,n5
Davidson, Daisy (later Mrs. Leonard Everett Ware), **15:**265,n4, 384,n1
Davidson, John, **14:**546,n3, 552; **22:** 573,n1

Davidson, John Wells, **25:**x, xin1
Davidson, Randall Thomas, **19:**109; **22:**514,n2
Davidson, William Newcomb, **14:**441,n4, 546,n1, 552, 553, 556; **15:**384n1
Davidson, William Stewart, **23:**343, 536n1; **24:**324,n3
Davidson College, **16:**509; **21:**201; **22:**327; **23:**563n2; **24:**538,n1
Davies, Joseph Edward, **23:**253,n2, 254, 259; **24:**553, 575, 584, 587
Davis, **14:**88
Davis, Charles Henry, **17:**16n3
Davis, Daniel Webster, **25:**620,n4,5
Davis, Edward Parker, M.D., **15:**140, 141, 388, 389; **19:**50, 148, 162; **20:**243; **23:**228,n4
Davis, Ellen-Duane Gillespie (Mrs. Edward Parker), **15:**140, 141
Davis, Henry Edgar, **20:**21,n4
Davis, Horatio Nelson, **18:**516-17,n1, 532-33
Davis, Jeff, **23:**517,n1
Davis, John David (Princeton 1872), **14:**168, 168n1, 290, 431, 432n1, 434, 439; **15:**60, 408, 527, 569, 572; **16:**5, 145, 146, 167, 266, 279,n1, 406; **17:**351n2; **18:**568; **19:**439, 698, 703, 711, 731, 733-34; **20:**135, 209,n6, 211, 216-18, 243-44, 245, 247, 252-53, 254, 256-57, 262, 321n1, 336; **22:**262
Davis, John Davis (Princeton 1879), **15:**390, 528; **20:**84,n1
Davis, John H. G., **24:**553
Davis, John Lionberger, **14:**430,n1; **17:** 351n2
Davis, John Warren, **23:**394
Davis, Kate Laura, **16:**234
Davis, Parke Hill, **19:**603,n2; **20:**539
Davis, Ralph, **14:**297
Davis, Robert, **19:**328n2; **20:**352n1, 564,n3, 565n; **21:**7, 18, 19, 26, 27, 43, 62, 63,n1, 85, 86, 90, 261, 341,n3, 345, 346, 347, 378, 388, 389, 409, 442, 503; **22:**26-27,n1, 73,n, 81, 81n1,2, 86n1, 87n2, 98n1, 118-19n1, 128, 133, 200, 201, 223-24, 245,n1,2; **23:**536n2
Davis, Westmoreland, **24:**71,n8
Davis, William F., **23:**535,n1
Davis, William H., **21:**416
Davis, William J., **21:**341,n3
Davis, William Vail Wilson, **18:**441
Davison, Emmett C., **24:**100,n1, 136
Davison, Grace Walcott, **25:**458
Davison, Harry B., **25:**458,n1
Davison, Henry Pomeroy, **23:**293n3
Davison, Woodrow Wilson, **25:**458,n2
Davisson, Clinton Joseph, **16:**199
Dawes, Anna Laurens, **19:**309,n2; **23:** 223,n6
Dawes, Henry Laurens, Jr., **23:**223,n2
Dawson, Edgar, **16:**306,n5, 313, 376,n2, 421, 509; **17:**233, 408, 524n1; **18:**271, 293; **19:**676
Dawson, Joseph Hill, **17:**85-86,n1

Dawson, William James, **17:**128,n6
Day, David Talbot, **17:**7,n14
Day, Frank Miles, **18:**291, 293, 302, 304, 380, 511-12, 514, 515, 522, 589; **20:**128,n1, 137, 495; **21:**618
Day, Frank Miles and Brother, architects, **18:**286, 380, 511-12, 557, 558, 565, 580
Day, Frank Miles, and the firm of Frank Miles Day and Brother, **19:**5,n1, 12-13, 68, 80, 538, 559, 611
Deal, N. J., **20:**541n1, 563, 564; **21:**27, 88, 89; **22:**181n1; **24:**98n2
Deane, John F., **18:**584
Dear, Joseph Albert, Jr., **19:**598,n3, 599; **20:**121, 567; **21:**23-24, 116, 580; **22:**98, 200, 357; **23:**201n1
Dear, Julia Allene Reid (Mrs. Joseph Albert, Jr.), **19:**599
Dear, Walter Moore, **21:**450-51,n1; **22:** 357
De Biasi, Agostino, **24:**135,n1
Debs, Eugene, Pennsylvania vote, **25:** 527n1; popular vote, **25:**518n1
Decatur, Stephen, **14:**250
Decatur, Texas, **23:**268
Decker, Sarah Chase Harris Platt (Mrs. Westbrook S.), **23:**21,n2, 22
Declaration of Independence, **14:**281; **16:**360, 397, 502; **17:**248-59; **18:**71, 74; **19:**203, 209, 272; **22:**540, 560; **23:**33, 34, 79, 210-11; **24:**130; **25:**103, 186, 236-37, 248
Declaration of Rights (English), **25:**639
declarations of independence, new, **23:**187, 188
*Decline and Fall of the Roman Empire* (Gibbon), **15:**473
Dederick, Louis Serle, **19:**679
*Deeds of Lewis; the Words of Wilson*, **21:**463
Defoe, Daniel, **14:**503
De Forest, Henry Wheeler, **17:**243,n1; **18:**34, 35, 217, 301-302, 309, 317, 380, 483,n1, 554-55, 557, 558, 565, 569
De Forest, Robert Weeks, **18:**483, **20:** 495, 497, 498n1; **22:**157n1
De Kalb, Ill., **24:**300
DeKay, Thomas, **23:**465
Delafield, Edward Coleman, **17:**221,n3
Delaware, **23:**436; **24:**356, 447; **25:**129, 419, 430, 431; Democrats, **23:**436n; **25:**425-26; Princeton alumni, **17:**110; **19:**152,n1; **20:**336,n1; Republicans, **23:**436,n2; WW speeches in, **25:**424-32
Delaware, Lackawanna & Western Railroad, **23:**339n3, 340, 352, 356
Delaware, University of, **16:**306n5, 313, 509
Delaware Bay, **23:**273
Delaware and Raritan Canal, **15:**58, 66, 549, 578, 579; **21:**403,n3
Delaware River, **15:**579; **24:**184
*Delineator* (New York), **18:**62,n1,2, 68,n1; **19:**303n

Della Robbia, Luca, **15:**353, 357
*Della Robbias in America* (Marquand), **17:**352n2
Delmonico's, New York City, **17:**66
DeLong, George Washington, **22:**393n2
Delphic Sibyl (Michelangelo fresco), **15:**298
demagogues, **21:**570; **23:**186
De Mange, Ralph Charles, **14:**384
Demarest, Isabella Hammond (Mrs. John Z.) **23:**250,n1
Demarest, William Henry Steele, **16:**335,n3, 427, 538-39; **18:**622, 625; **19:**23, 171; **21:**620,n1
democracy, **21:**268, 269; **22:**386, 420, 489, 604; **23:**623; **24:**202; **25:**99, 229, 237, 254, 375; and Abraham Lincoln, **24:**152; compared to monarchy, **25:**201-202
democracy, in college life, **21:**605
*Democracy in America* (de Tocqueville), **14:**14; **20:**329; **21:**512; **23:**127n10
Democracy in this State (editorial, Villard), **25:**25,n1
Democratic Club of Philadelphia, **24:**6
Democratic National Committee, **23:** 436, 531, 561n2, 566-67; **24:**5, 28n4, 29, 43, 492; **25:**30, 48, 63n1, 64,n1, 115n2, 543n2; McCombs's chairmanship, **25:**135-36,n1
Democratic National Convention of 1912 (Baltimore Convention), **23:**230, 231, 470, 552, 589, 593, 598, 616, 629; **24:**28n4, 65, 83, 450, 463, 465, 503, 505; **25:**3, 19, 22, 111, 127, 148, 347, 351, 603, 604, 647; Aldrich Plan, **24:**581,n1, 582-83; anti-Wilson tactics, **24:**515; ballots: first, **24:**483n2; tenth, **24:**507,n1; thirtieth, **24:**516,n1; fortythird, **24:**521,n5; invocation, **24:**473; platform planks, **24:**470, 472, 474, 476-77, 477-81, 496, 520, 567, 581n; temporary chairman, **24:**462, 491, 492, 500; unit rule, **24:**469, 501-502; Wilson demonstration, **24:**511-12; photograph, **24:**illustration section
Democratic party and Democrats, **15:**362n2, 472, 547-48, 550,n2,3,4, 551; **16:**12, 330, 358, 532, 533, 534n10; **17:**75-76, 77, 310-11, 318-19, 321, 586-87, 608, 609; **18:**264, 266, 269, 270, 280, 281, 372-73, 435, 480; **19:**461-64, 465-71, 492, 493; **20:**298, 299-300, 302, 303, 309, 313, 315-17, 349, 350, 351, 352, 390-91, 424, 454, 463, 467, 501, 503, 504, 534n2, 543-45, 562, 570; **21:**10, 21, 85, 144, 161, 183-85, 190-91, 193, 211, 212, 217, 223, 227, 237, 239, 255, 285, 294, 300, 335, 343n11, 344n12, 345n13, 373, 387, 396, 398, 427-28, 448, 474, 479, 501, 565-66, 586, 592, 595, 598, 605, 608n2, 613, 621, 622; **22:**3,n2, 6, 16, 17-18, 31, 32, 34, 44n3, 54, 61, 85, 94, 120, 125, 138, 167, 175, 181, 181n1, 189, 204,

207, 208, 213, 214, 215, 216, 217, 218, 219, 220, 221, 222, 223, 226, 229, 237, 250, 251, 255, 274-75, 277, 284-85, 291n2, 372, 376, 388, 409n1,2,3, 412n2, 423, 428-29, 441n3, 444, 465, 476, 478n3, 479, 480, 487, 488, 489, 491, 502, 534, 545, 554, 556, 557, 558, 559, 560, 561, 565, 567, 568, 569, 570, 573n2,5, 578, 584, 586, 587, 588, 591-92, 594, 595, 601; **23:**3-4, 7, 11, 32n5, 41, 44, 51, 53, 60-61, 64, 68, 70n2, 76, 77, 78-79, 89, 90, 91, 107, 108, 112,n2,3, 123, 128-31, 132, 154-57, 160n1, 166, 172, 183n3, 200n1, 200, 205, 213n2, 228, 235, 237-39, 249n1, 251, 253, 262, 278, 284, 287n2, 293, 300, 311, 328, 359, 361, 371, 383, 394, 412-24, 460, 463, 473-74, 489, 499n1, 504,n7, 509, 511, 515, 543, 548, 566, 573, 578, 593, 597, 602n1, 604, 615, 616, 623, 624, 630, 632, 649, 653; **24:**9, 10, 15, 110, 141, 142, 143, 144, 155, 159, 160, 162, 192, 195, 202-203, 259, 290, 359, 362-64, 365, 366, 372, 378, 411, 496, 497, 539; **25:**17, 29-30, 46, 47, 69, 71, 81, 89-90, 108, 125-28, 148, 155, 157, 185-86, 199, 202, 208, 213, 215, 230, 243, 245, 246, 247, 248, 250-51, 252-53, 254, 255, 266, 322, 325, 326, 327, 331, 332, 334, 351, 352, 366, 375-76, 379, 385, 386, 387-88, 389, 394, 398, 403-404, 408, 411, 413, 427, 428, 434, 435, 436, 440, 444, 445, 447, 463, 465-66, 467-70, 475-76, 479, 484, 496, 499-500, 504, 506, 512, 517, 603, 637-38; attracting youth, **25:**349; W. J. Bryan as leader, **24:**8-9, 10; business, **25:**408-10, 505; campaign of 1908, **18:**535, 639; compared to Progressive party (Brandeis), **25:**289-94; competition, **25:**74-75; control of state governments, **25:**503; different from other political groups, **25:**251; financial contributions, **25:**109n2, 110n5, 402; immigration, **25:**40, 53; importance of congressional elections, **25:**362-63; in Congress, **23:**566; **25:**260-62; Jefferson and Jackson, **24:**139; mining industry, **25:**399; monopoly, **25:**353, 372, 380, 383; National Convention of 1908 (Denver), **18:**258,n2, 271, 343,n1, 344, 349, 351, 352, 356, 380; Negroes, **25:**61, 607; number in House of Rep., **25:**503; platform, **25:**5, 17, 22, 36, 37; presidential term, **25:**565; Progressive party, **24:**499; **25:**43-44, 86; Social Service Bureau, **25:**310, 543,n2; tariff, **25:**243; trusts (Brandeis), **25:**289-94; U. S. Senate, **25:**524; J. R. Wilson, Jr., **25:**612; WW acceptance speech, **25:**3-18; WW message to Democratic rallies, **25:**501-504; WW remarks to Democratic women, **25:**44-45

Democratic party and Democrats in Arizona, **25:**271-72
Democratic party and Democrats in Arkansas, **23:**233-34
Democratic party and Democrats in California, **22:**31-32; **23:**251
Democratic party and Democrats in Colorado, **22:**599; **23:**650; **25:**545-46,n1
Democratic party and Democrats in Connecticut, **22:**15
Democratic party and Democrats in Delaware, **23:**436n1; **24:**356, 447; **25:**425-26
Democratic party and Democrats in Georgia, **23:**236; **24:**287-88; primary vote, **24:**381n2
Democratic party and Democrats in Illinois, **20:**544; **23:**326; **24:**308,n1, 357, 521,n5
Democratic party and Democrats in Indiana, **20:**544, 546; **25:**327-28, 333
Democratic party and Democrats in Iowa, **20:**544; **23:**310, 315; **25:**162-63
Democratic party and Democrats in Kansas, **23:**291; **24:**188-89, 191, 248,-n1, 357; **25:**621n2
Democratic party and Democrats in Kentucky, **24:**141, 146, 332-33,n1,2, 357
Democratic party and Democrats in Louisiana, **24:**468, 482-83
Democratic party and Democrats in Maine, **21:**119,n1, 123, 128, 136; **23:**341; **25:**51, 618-19,n1
Democratic party and Democrats in Maryland, **22:**158; **23:**218; **24:**371; **25:**129
Democratic party and Democrats in Massachusetts, **21:**598, **23:**235,n2, 258, 324
Democratic party and Democrats in Michigan, **23:**248, 263, 341; **24:**248,n1, 483-84
Democratic party and Democrats in Minnesota, **20:**544; **24:**487,n2
Democratic party and Democrats in Missouri, **24:**186-87,n3; **25:**93
Democratic party and Democrats in Nebraska, **23:**237; **24:**357,n2; **25:**339-40, 347,n1,2,3, 348-49
Democratic party and Democrats in Nevada, **24:**64n1, 391, 403-404, 520-21; **25:**359-60
Democratic party and Democrats in New Jersey, **16:**454-55,n1,3, 456-57, 471, 482, 539-41, 545, 547, 548-49, 549-50, 551-52, 554-55, 560-61n1, 561-62; **20:**297, 519-20, 540-41, 544, 545-46, 558-59, 562n1, 563-64,n1, 565n, 571, 577,n2, 577, 578, 578-79, 581; **21:**5, 6-7, 10, 11, 18, 19, 19,n7, 24n1, 39, 40n1, 43-46, 57, 63, 64, 82, 84, 86, 87-88, 89, 94-96, 100, 101, 103, 106, 112-14, 118-20, 125, 130, 131, 133, 134, 138, 139, 142, 145, 146, 158,

Democratic party and Democrats in New Jersey, (cont.)
159, 161, 164, 167-68, 168n2, 179, 181, 183, 184, 185, 189, 197, 198, 201, 202, 204, 214, 217, 219, 221, 223-24, 227, 236, 240, 247, 249, 260, 286, 287, 290n1, 295-96, 304, 311, 312-13, 314, 326, 332, 345-48, 352, 354, 356, 357, 362, 364, 369-70, 378, 380, 381, 383, 388, 395, 396-98, 404, 405, 409, 411, 413, 415, 417, 419, 420, 424, 429, 430, 431, 436, 448, 449, 451, 452, 457, 458, 461, 475, 495, 503, 504, 505, 510, 511-12, 514, 521, 523, 524, 529, 545, 547, 549, 552, 553, 563, 564, 566, 570, 572, 577, 581, 583, 584n1, 589, 603, 608n2, 610, 616; **22:**10, 15, 16, 22, 25, 27, 29, 41-42, 47-48, 49, 52, 72, 77, 81n1,2, 86,n1, 86-87, 113n1,2, 114-16, 124, 125-26, 128-29, 136,n1, 137n3, 142n1, 153, 155-56, 163, 170n1, 173,n1, 181n1, 199, 205n2, 206, 217, 221, 230, 236, 239, 240, 242n2, 245n2, 248-49, 250, 251, 253, 257, 278, 278n1, 281, 283, 284, 285, 294, 296-307, 308, 310, 321-22, 334, 337, 339, 340, 365, 366, 367, 378, 415n1, 455, 458, 460, 463, 466n4, 474, 475, 477, 481-82, 483, 505,n1, 512, 513n2, 517, 518, 532, 535, 536, 537n4, 545, 550n2, 561,n5, 582, 588, 589, 602; **23:**165, 177, 203n3, 219, 234,n1, 245n1, 255, 262n3, 265-66, 270-72, 276, 316, 330-39, 343-51, 353-54, 361, 362, 364, 365, 382-84, 384-90, 391-95, 396, 398, 399n4, 404, 406, 412-24, 428, 431, 439-40, 443, 447, 449, 452, 455, 462, 464, 465, 466, 467, 468, 469, 472, 475, 477, 518, 522n1, 532, 533, 533n1, 535, 536,n1,2, 538, 541, 542, 546, 627, 628, 629; **24:**17-18, 324, 372, 407, **429**, **436-44**, 449, 584; **25:**113n1, 216, 351, 467-68, 476, 477, 481-82, 484-85, 487-89, 511, 513-14, 579-80,n2; Democratic State Committee, **23:**234n1, 262n3, 265, 270, 271, 362, 396; Fitzherbert scandal, **24:**244-47,n1; Geran Act, **24:**429-34; Jersey City, **25:**136-37; legislative campaign of 1911, **23:**364-65, 380-81, 382-84, 391-95, 395-408, 544; platforms, 1910, **21:**43-46, 87-88,n3, 94-96, 139, 202, 204, 205, 275, 511, 512, 522, 525, 529, 552; 1911, **23:**382-84, 385-86; 1912, **25:**305-10; Overlords, **21:**266, 346, 347, 409, 503; senatorial race, **25:**116-18, 146-47,n1,2,3, 184n1; state convention of 1910, **23:**627, of 1911, **23:**384-90; Wilson Democrats, **23:**331; WW's intentions to keep party progressive, **25:**591-92; WW speech to convention in Trenton, **25:**304-305; WW statement to Democrats, **25:**590-91

Democratic party and Democrats in New Mexico, **24:**306

Democratic party and Democrats in New York, **20:**424, 546; **21:**608n2; **22:** 161,n1; **24:**497,n2, 500-501; **25:**24, 133-34,n1,2,3, 143-46, 233, 283-84, 378, 441, 499; Charles F. Murphy, **24:**507n1, 512,n1, 531, 532

Democratic party and Democrats in North Carolina, **23:**596, 604, 630; **24:**388, 471,n2

Democratic party and Democrats in North Dakota, **24:**82

Democratic party and Democrats in Ohio, **20:**544, 546; **22:**161,n1; **23:**327

Democratic party and Democrats in Oklahoma, **23:**506; **24:**190

Democratic party and Democrats in Pennsylvania, **20:**307-308, 315-17, 352,n1; **21:**103; **22:**408-409,n1,2,3, 522, 523; **23:**220, 221, 229-30,-n1,2,3,5,6, 249n2, 262; **24:**27, 138, 330n3, 392-94, 397, 453-54, 461, 538; **25:**462, 616,n1

Democratic party and Democrats in Tennessee, **23:**213n1,2,3, 218n2, 288-89,n2; **24:**78, 403,n1

Democratic party and Democrats in Texas, **22:**123, 409-10; **23:**231, 258, 259,n1,2, 260-61, 267-69, 302, 458, 470, 540, 589; **24:**225, 254, 384,n2, 515; **25:**603-606, 625-26

Democratic party and Democrats in Vermont, **25:**126

Democratic party and Democrats in Virginia, **22:**254,n2,3; **23:**311, 327, 328, 601,n1; **24:**398n1, 568; unit rule, **24:** 469, 486

Democratic party and Democrats in Washington state, **23:**598

Democratic party and Democrats in Western New York, **23:**559

Democratic party and Democrats in Wisconsin, **23:**253-54, 259-60, 488f; **24:** 257-58, 285,n1

Democratic platform of 1908, **23:**235n3

Democratic Politics and the Presidential Campaign of 1912 in Tennessee (Link), **18:**485n2; **22:**95,n1; **23:**213n2, 289n2; **24:**403n1

Democratic Press Association of Missouri, **25:**395n1

Democratic Society of Western New York, **23:**559

*Democratic Text-Book*, *1912*, **25:**115,n2, 150n4

Democrats, Progressive, **23:**607f

Democrats, Reform, **23:**154-57

Demosthenes, **22:**451

Deneen, Charles Samuel, **18:**277

Denègre, James Denis, **14:**445; **23:**85,-n4,5

Denison University, **16:**253

Denneberg, Mr. (of Baltimore *Evening Sun*), **24:**491

Dennett, Fred, **23:**175n1

Denney, James, **16:**23,n4

Dennis, Alfred Lewis, 18:400,n12; 21: 592-93
Dennis, Crowell Marsh, 19:679
Dennis, Dorothy, 18:400,n11
Dennis, Eliza Thomas (Mrs. Samuel Shepard), 18:400,n10; 22:23,n2
Dennis, James Shepard, 15:527
Dennis, James Shepard 2d, 18:400,n11
Dennis, Louis Monroe, 20:539
Dennis, Samuel Shepard, 18:400,n10; 22:23,n1
Denny, Collins, 23:511,n3
Denny, George Hutcheson, 14:87; 16: 313,n1; 23:327-28n2,3, 390
Denny, James O'Hara, 16:377
denominational colleges and Carnegie pensions, 18:52-53, 61,n2
Denton, Frances B., 23:630,n1, 631-32, 651; 25:562n2
Denver, 18:382, 385, 423, 424, 435, 436, 441, 448, 449, 470, 473; 21:130; 22:276n1,2, 519, 521, 525, 533, 537, 584-85, 599; 23:53n4, 310, 478, 652; Adams Hotel, 23:27, 28; 25:369-77; Bible Society, 23:11; Brown Palace Hotel, 23:11, 23, 27; Central Presbyterian Church, 23:13n2; Chamber of Commerce, 22:527; 23:23,n1, 24, 26; Denver Auditorium, 23:11, 12,n1, 27, 28; El Jebel Temple, 23:23; Mile-High Club, 22:523, 527; 23:27, 28; Presbyterian Church, 22:577; Princeton alumni, 15:552, 553; 19:146; 20:84,n4, 85; University Club, 23:27; WW addresses, 23:12-20, 21-22, 23-26, 27-30; 25:369-70; Woodrow Wilson Democratic Club, 23:478; WW in, 23:11-32
Denver Daily News, 23:22n
Denver Express, 22:584
Denver platform, 22:307, 465
Denver Post, 23:478n1
Denver Rocky Mountain News, 22: 388n1,584; 23:22n1, 26n, 27, 28n, 30n, 478n1; 25:368n, 369, 377n
De Pachman, Vladimir, 24:44n1
Depew, Chauncey Mitchell, 19:102,n1, 104; 22:429; 23:111
Dercum, Elizabeth Comly (Mrs. Francis Xavier), 18:577,n2
Dercum, Francis Xavier, M.D., 18:557,-n1; 23:82,n14,112
DeRidder, John Henry, 15:383,n1
DeRidder, John Howard, 15:383n1
De Ronde, Abram, 24:266,n3
Derr, Chester Burger, 19:165
Derr, Ralph, 19:165
Derry, Joseph T., 23:557n2; 25:542n2
Derwent Water, Cumberland, 18:394
De Schweinitz, George Edmund, M.D., 16:412n1
De Selincourt, Ernest, 18:365,n7, 370, 371, 380, 383, 388,n2, 394, 395, 396, 406
De Selincourt, Ethel Shawcross (Mrs. Ernest), 18:388,n2, 396, 406

De Selincourt, Oliver, 18:394, 396
De Selincourt, Theodora, 18:370
Descartes, René, 19:666
Deserted Village (Goldsmith), 15:310n4
Des Moines, Iowa, 22:533; 23:247, 247n1; 24:220-22, 302-303; city government, 19:91,n2, 93
Des Moines Leader, 21:251
Des Moines Register and Leader, 23: 341,n1; 24:222n, 223,n1
Detroit, Board of Commerce, 23:408n1; Detroit Club, 16:43; Jefferson Avenue Presbyterian Church, 16:42; University Club, 16:43; 19:164,n1; WW addresses, 16:42-43; 19:164,n1
Detroit, Mich., 24:47, 51-53, 302; 25: 186-98
Detroit Free Press, 16:43n; 25:198n, 470, 562n1
Detroit Journal, 25:188,n4, 562n1
Detroit News, 24:53n; 25:198n
Detroit Times, 22:229
Deutschen Patrioten (Arndt), 19:569
Development of Harvard University . . . 1869-1929 (ed. Morison), 15:292n28
Development of the Jury in England (McIlwain), 16:41
Dever, William Emmet, 24:151n3, 302,-n4
Devereux, William Kay, 23:387; 24:17
Devine, Edward Thomas, 15:407-408,n1; 22:157n1
Devlin, Martin Patrick, 21:141,n1, 153, 583n2; 22:128-29
De Vries, John Hendrik, 14:330; 16: 104-105,n2
Dewalt, Arthur Granville, 20:307-308, 311, 352; 21:103; 23:154, 230,n5
Dewey, Davis Rich, 19:405n2; 22:139
Dewey, George, 14:360,n1
Dewhurst, Frederic Eli, 14:552,n1
De Windt, Harry, 15:209,n2
Dewing, Henry Bronson, 18:579
DeWitt, Benjamin Parke, 17:571n3
DeWitt, John, 15:379n1, 531-32,n1; 16:16n1, 131, 199, 206,n1, 207, 234, 425-26; 17:198; 18:9, 421, 615; 19:439, 657, 698, 701-702, 703, 733; 20:9n, 47, 60, 63-64, 245, 247, 266,n4, 268, 269, 286, 361, 411, 413, 424, 509; 21:365, 366, 442; 24:559n1
DeWitt, John Riegel, 14:289,n3, 297
Dey, Robert, 24:307,n2
Dial (Chicago), 14:252n, 547,n2
Diary of Samuel Pepys, M.A., F.R.S., 18:471
Dias Creek (N. J.) Fishermen's Association, 23:273
Díaz, Porfirio, 17:159
Dicey, Albert Venn, 14:407; 18:165
Dicey, Elinor Mary Bonham-Carter (Mrs. Albert Venn), 14:407

Dick Brothers, bankers, **19:**175, 259, 308
Dickel, William L., **23:**274,n6
Dickens, Charles, **15:**334
Dickinson, A. G., **15:**546
Dickinson, Clinton Roy, **21:**169,n1
Dickinson, Goldsworthy Lowes, **16:**121,-n1
Dickinson, Jacob McGavock, **22:**478,n2, 500
Dickinson, Jonathan, **21:**169n1
Dickinson High School (Jersey City), **25:**214n4
Dicksee, Sir Francis Bernard, **14:**553
Dickson, Bessie Louise, **20:**144,n1; **21:**587,n1
Dickson, Leonard Eugene, **16:**179,n1
Dickson, William, **22:**546n5
*Dictionary of the Bible* . . . (ed. Hastings), **16:**400,n3
Diefenthaler, John V., **22:**242n2; **23:**354
*Die Waffen Nieder!*, **18:**400,n2
Diefenderfer, Robert Edward, **24:**287,n1
Dilke, Sir Charles, **14:**14
Dill, Lavinia H. Hibben (Mrs. James), **15:**207,n1
Dillard, James Hardy, **22:**140,n4
Dilling, George W., **23:**79,n1
Dillow, Thomas H., **21:**82-83; **22:**163-64
Dingley Tariff of 1897, **19:**361; **25:**503
Dinsmore, Francis William, **14:**388; **19:**181,n1
Dinsmore, Thomas H., **22:**389,n2
diphtheria, **15:**302, 303, 304, 305, 311, 316, 320, 323, 325, 334
*Diplomacy of the Russo-Japanese War* (White), **15:**150n3
direct election of U. S. Senators, **24:**480; **25:**6, 15, 237-39, 306
Direct Legislation League, **22:**247,n1
direct primaries, **19:**511; **21:**195, 204, 271, 272, 332; **22:**197, 335, 351; **23:**24, 369, 371; **24:**232, 480; **25:**236-37, 305, 306; platform plank, **24:**480 Δ J. M. Taylor, **19:**532-33; R. S. Childs, **19:**756; W. C. Gebhardt, **21:**157; G. E. Chamberlain, **22:**175; non-partisan league, **22:**255n2; W. B. Heyburn, **22:**371n4; J. G. Schuman, **22:**400,n2; W. F. McCombs, **23:**355
Direct Primary League, **22:**225n1
discipline, in education, **17:**537-40
discrimination, **25:**450; W. M. Trotter, **24:**558; O. G. Villard, **25:**53
Di Silvestro, Joseph A., **24:**133,n1; **25:**28
*Disruption of the Solid South* (Tindall), **19:**10n2
District of Columbia, Princeton alumni, **14:**303n1, 337, 400, 447
District of Columbia, *see* Washington, D. C.
*Divine Comedy* (Dante Alighieri), **19:**367n5; **23:**375
Dix, Edwin Asa, **15:**528,n3; **18:**228
Dix, John Alden, **21:**275n2, 322,n1, 598; **22:**45,n2, 161n1, 250n2, 285n2, 287,

289, 338,n3, 359,n2, 361, 407n2, 421, 453; **23:**340n3; **24:**330; **25:**133-34n3, 137n2, 283, 284n4
Dix, William Frederick, **19:**396-97,n1, 454-55
Dixon, Amzi Clarence, **14:**114
Dixon, John, **16:**145, 146, 167, 289; **17:**595; **19:**439, 712, 747; **20:**5, 8n, 9n, 11, 12, 13, 17, 29, 30, 48, 51, 57-58, 60, 82, 87, 97, 104, 121-22, 211, 217, 245, 247, 252, 254, 262, 284, 357, 361; **22:**380
Dixon, Thomas, Jr., **22:**96,n1; **25:**578, 579,n1,2
Dixon, Warren, **21:**63
Dixville Notch, N. H., The Balsams, **23:**248
Doane, George Herbert, **14:**90,n2
Doane, William Croswell, **14:**90,n3
Dr. Wilson's Plans at Princeton (*Review of Reviews*), **17:**333,n1
*Documents Illustrative of American History* (ed. Preston), **14:**353,n4, 518
Dod, Samuel Bayard, **14:**161, 255; **15:**527; **16:**145; **17:**152n1
Dodd, William Edward, **20:**408,n1, 408-409; **23:**311-12,n1, 317; **24:**205n
Dodge, Bayard, **14:**306,n2
Dodge, Cleveland Earl, **14:**306,n2
Dodge, Cleveland Earl, Jr., **16:**567n
Dodge, Cleveland Hoadley (Princeton 1879), **14:**194,n5, 265, 266, 292-93, 306n1, 334; **15:**192,n4, 301n2, 390, 400, 407, 509, 527, 569, 572, 573; **16:**4, 5, 21n1, 29, 69, 133, 136, 142, 192, 193, 195, 196, 204-205, 225, 266, 278, 291, 302, 303, 322, 325, 336, 339, 415-18, 425, 429, 431, 453-54, 458-63, 470-71, 490, 491, 526, 534-35, 536, 550-51, 552, 566-67; **17:**16, 19, 41-43, 47, 49, 51, 62, 63, 92n2, 95-96, 99-100, 109, 159, 170, 170-72, 219, 220, 243, 245-46, 265, 271, 272, 274, 281, 300, 334-35, 341, 379-81, 382,n1, 388, 405-406,n2, 410-11, 434-35, 435-36, 442, 563, 603; **18:**285, 290, 315-17, 335, 337-38, 338-39, 435, 472, 546, 555, 565, 610, 612; **19:**12, 14-16, 17, 21, 29, 74, 100-101, 109, 122, 144-47, 151, 152, 166, 177, 256, 269n1, 320, 386-87, 391, 395, 437, 439, 448, 453, 455-56, 480, 495, 501, 613, 619, 623, 624, 627, 631, 632, 633, 634, 649, 650, 655, 656, 657, 658, 673, 698, 699, 703, 707, 709, 710, 711, 727-28, 730, 732, 733; **20:**5, 6n, 11, 12, 13, 14-15, 16, 17, 20-21, 48 51, 52, 60, 82, 83, 87, 97, 104, 128-30, 137, 141, 142-44, 174, 182, 183, 190, 191-92, 208-209, 218, 241, 245, 254, 325, 359, 361-62, 460, 544, 551, 552, 553, 554, 561, 573, 576, 579; **21:**38, 112, 137-38, 139, 292, 295-96, 321, 385, 385n1, 435, 591-92; **22:**29, 72-73,n3, 94, 232, 237-38, 377, 382, 412, 436-37, 438; **23:**128, 128n1, 139,

153, 160, 172, 193, 214, 479, 601; **24**:209n, 266, 402, 572, 573; **25**:493n1, 646; campaign contributions, **25**:109-110,n2,3,5,6, 135, 459,n2,3
Dodge, Elizabeth Wainwright, **14**:306,n2
Dodge, Grace, **16**:195,n3
Dodge, Grace Parish (Mrs. Cleveland Hoadley), **14**:306,n1; **17**:246; **18**:546; **19**:152; **20**:21, 192, 359, 553, 576,n1; **21**:38,n1, 385,n3; **23**:128n1, 153, 172
Dodge, Henry Nehemiah, M.D., **21**:354,-n1
Dodge, Julia (Mrs. James Childs Rea), **23**:128,n1
Dodge, Julia Parish, **14**:306,n2
Dodge, Melissa Phelps (Mrs. William Earl; 1805-1883), **14**:393,n1
Dodge, Phyllis Boushall (Mrs. Cleveland Earl, Jr.), **16**:567n
Dodge, Sarah Hoadley (Mrs. William Earl; 1832-1903), **14**:306,n3; **16**:21n1, 195,n2, 490n1, 535, 536; **17**:39n1, 341,n1, 405; **18**:610,n1, 612
Dodge, William Earl (1805-1883), **14**:393n1
Dodge, William Earl (1832-1903), **14**:135, 136, 266, 306,n3, 388, 392-93, 398; **16**:566-67,n1; **22**:184
Dodge, William Earl (1858-1884; Princeton 1879), **14**:266
Dodge family, **17**:390
Dods, Marcus, **16**:400,n2
Dolliver, Jonathan Prentiss, **19**:191n1; **21**:219,n5
Donaghey, George Washington, **23**:233,-n2
Donatello, **15**:353, 357
Donges, Ralph Waldo Emerson, **21**:577,-n1; **22**:120-21
Donnelly, Charles, **23**:229,n2, 230
Donnelly, Frederick William, **22**:455,n1; **23**:387, 425,n2, 428n7, 435
Donnelly, Ignatius Loyola, **23**:246,n2
Donnelly, Thomas Frederick, **23**:637,n1
Donnelly, Thomas M., **22**:136n1; **23**:343, 536n1
Donnelly, Thomas Marcus, **21**:451-52,-n1; **24**:324,n3
Donohoe, Michael, **24**:287,n1
Dorf, Samuel S., **25**:29
Dorgan, John Thomas, **23**:97,n2
Dorr, Rheta Childe, **18**:62,n2, 68,n1
Dorsey, Joseph, **21**:156,n1
Doty, Paul, **23**:85,n4
Doubleday Page & Co., **14**:65; **22**:433,n1
Doughan, John E., **25**:245n3
Dougherty, Hugh, **22**:554,n1
Dougherty, Jeannie W., Mrs., **18**:377,n3
Douglas, Mr., **15**:462,n1
Douglas, Davison McDowell, **25**:549,n1
Douglas, Francis B., **24**:145, 146
Douglas, Lee, **23**:211-12,n1, 244, 288; **24**:192
Douglas, Stephen Arnold, **17**:312-13,

314, 315, 316, 320, 323; **18**:110; **19**:34; **21**:161; **24**:153; **25**:393
Dover, Del., **25**:424-25
Dover, Kent, Wilsons in, **14**:535
Dover, N. J., Baker Theatre, **21**:526; WW campaign speeches, **21**:526-27; **23**:451-53
Dowden, Edward, **14**:295
Dowden, Elizabeth Dickinson (Mrs. Edward), **14**:295
Dowling, Victor James, **25**:134,n2, 234, 286, 415
Downes, Steven, **15**:215n4
Downey, P. J., **23**:340, 340,n5
Downing's Foreign Express, **16**:542
Doyle, Michael Francis, **24**:565,n2
Draper, Andrew Sloan, **21**:620
Draper, Eben Sumner, **21**:612n1
Dred Scott decision, **17**:316, 318
Dreher, Julius Daniel, **22**:604,n1
Dreier, Margaret, **15**:166,n1
Dreiser, Theodore, **18**:62-63,n1, 68
Drew Theological Seminary, **21**:525-26
Dreyfus, Alfred, **15**:434n2
Drifton, Pa., **23**:219, 229
Drigg, Cumberland, **18**:371
Drobinski, Francis Ignatius, **24**:131, 132,n1, 134-35, 219, 223,n1, 383n1
Droppers, Garrett, **23**:242,n1; **24**:497,n1; **25**:50
Dropsie College (Philadelphia), **25**:450-n1
Dryburgh, Roxburgh, Wilsons at, **14**:524
Dryden, John Fairfield, **16**:455,n3, 561-n1; **18**:513n2, 514, 558-59, 645; **19**:78-79, 126-28, 131, 533n1; **20**:532-33; **22**:416
Drynock Farms, **24**:551, 561
Dublin, **18**:416
Dublin: National Gallery of Ireland, **15**:239n2
Dublin, University of, **17**:41
Du Bois, William Edward Burghardt, **21**:21n1, 47n1, 275n3, 292; **25**:60
Du Bose, F. G., **16**:73; Mrs., **16**:73
Dubose, McNeely, **17**:33
Dubose, Rose Anderson (Mrs. McNeely), **17**:33
Duccio di Buoninsegna, **15**:323
Duddon River and Valley, Lancs, **18**:371, 379, 385-86
Dudley, William Lofland, M.D., **20**:539
Duff, George Morgan, **17**:296, 396; **19**:71,n1
Duff, William M., **17**:361
Duffield, Edward Dickinson, **19**:265-66, 316-17, 651-52, 708-709; **20**:31,n1, 226, 245-46, 463
Duffield, George Barry, **16**:234; **18**:396,n4
Duffield, Helen Kennedy, **16**:234
Duffield, Florence Morell (Mrs. Henry Green), **16**:234
Duffield, Henry Green, **14**:145, 297; **15**:101, 106, 132, 177, 180, 321, 400,

Duffield, Henry Green, (*cont.*)
402, 403, 404, 424, 425, 535; **16**:3,n1, 162, 172, 234, 282, 318, 322, 431; **18**:490,n6; **19**:17, 20-21, 22-23, 29, 74, 482; **20**:54, 192, 378; **22**:165, 176, 187-87
Duffield, John Fletcher, M.D., **18**:396n4
Duffield, Margaret Cecil Wall (Mrs. John Fletcher), **16**:234; **18**:396n4
Duffield, Sarah E., **16**:234
Duffield, Sarah Elizabeth Green (Mrs. John Thomas), **16**:234
Dugan, Daniel Aloysius, **23**:354,n2
Dugan, Raymond Smith, **16**:199; **18**:578; **19**:139
Duke, Richard Thomas Walker, Jr., **23**:604,n1
Duke University (formerly Trinity College), **16**:255; **22**:489,n4; **24**:257,n1,3
Dulany, May, **20**:190
Dulin, Al, **22**:229,n3
Dullard, John Power, **21**:153,n1, 167
Dulles, Joseph Heatly, **14**:26, 36, 453,n5; **15**:117; **20**:152,n6
Dulles, William, Jr., **15**:248
Du Maurier, George Louis Palmella Busson, **18**:400,n4, 413
dummies, in corporations, **21**:122, 134
Du Mond, Frank Vincent, **18**:346,n10, 353-54, 357, 380, 382
Duncan, William Alexander, **24**:344,n1
Duncan, William Butler, **15**:50,n1, 60
Dundon, Francis, **19**:269
Duneka, Frederick A., **16**:343; **19**:402; **22**:21,n1
Dungan, Nelson T., **24**:517
Dunlap, John Robertson, **18**:59-60,n1, 219-20
Dunmail Raise, Westmorland, **18**:394-95, 415
Dunn (of Judd-Haven, Ont.), **15**:467
Dunn, Michael, **25**:514,n2
Dunne, Edward Fitzsimmons, **25**:623,n3
Dunne, Finley Peter, **14**:288n1
Dunning, Henry White, **15**:471,n3
Durand, Ella Sandys (Lady Durand), **16**:233n4
Durand, Sir Henry Mortimer, **15**:146,n2, 147, 149, 151; **16**:233n4
Dürer, Albrecht, **14**:245
Durham, England, Cathedral, **18**:363; Royal County Hotel, **14**:525,n4; EAW in, **16**:436; Wilsons at, **15**:525
Durham, N. C., National Religious Training School for the Colored People, **22**:98-99
Durham, Israel, **21**:342n6
Durkin, John, **23**:535
Durner, John G., **16**:234
Duryee, Joseph Rankin, **14**:475
Dutch Gallery (Van Wisselingh's, London), **16**:480
Dwight, Elsie Lenox Maitland (Mrs. Franklin Butler, I), **15**:248

Dwight, Franklin Butler, **15**:248
Dwight, Ill., **24**:292
Dwight, Maitland, **22**:150, 152, 323, 430, 430n1
Dwight, Richard Everett, **19**:165
Dwyer, John, **23**:230
Dye, Forrest R., **21**:62, 159
Dyer, Jessie Kennedy (Mrs. Harvey H.), **20**:49,n1
Dyer, Louis, **14**:406-407,n1; **17**:105-106
Dyer, Margaret Macmillan (Mrs. Louis), **14**:407
Dyer, Marion, **20**:49
*Dynamical Theory of Gases* (Jeans), **16**:157n1

Earl, Linton, **14**:164
Earle, Alice Morse, **14**:520n1
Earle (of Primos, Pa.), **20**:358
Easedale Tarn, Westmorland, **16**:443; **18**:368, 415
East, Charles MaCaulay, **22**:97
East Millstone, N. J., **23**:475
East Newark, N. J., **23**:535
East Orange, N. J., **23**:634n1; Berkeley Hall, **15**:542; **16**:215; Commonwealth Hall, **14**:301; **21**:563; Princeton alumni, **15**:503, 542; sewage disposal, **24**:267n1; WW addresses, **15**:542-44; **16**:214, 217-18; WW campaign speech, **21**:563; WW talk, **14**:301-303
*East Tennessee Historical Society's Proceedings*, **24**:403n1
*East Tennessee Historical Society's Publications*, **22**:95,n1; **23**:213n2
Easthampton, L. I., **19**:354
Eastman, Max, **24**:307,n4
Eastman College of Business, Poughkeepsie, **16**:310
Easton, F. C., Mrs., **19**:501n3, 503, 504, 505, 523, 527, 528, 546n1, 547, 577
Easton, Pa., **21**:393; WW in, **23**:468
Eastwood, John Henry, **22**:129-30,n1
Eaton, Dorman Bridgman, **24**:174,n4,5
Eaton, Edward Dwight, **14**:248
Eaton, Fred Laurine, **25**:148n2
Eaton, Frederick Heber, **22**:39,n12
Eaton, Henry Morris, **20**:385-87,n1, 397-98
Eberhart, Adolph Olson, **19**:605; **23**:85,-n1
Eberstadt (*formerly* Eberstaat), Ferdinand, **19**:502n3
Ebner, George, **23**:534,n4
Ecclefechan, Dumfriershire, Bush Hotel, **18**:361-62; WW in, **18**:361-62
Eckels, James Herron, **16**:534,n1
École des Beaux Arts (Paris), **25**:253
École des Hautes Études, **17**:556
Economic Club of New York, **24**:413,n1
*Economic History of Virginia in the Seventeenth Century* (Bruce), **14**:353,n3

economics, teaching of, **15**:65
*Economist* (London), **22**:209
Ecumenical Bearings of the Missionary Movement and the International Missionary Council (Latourette), **22**:385n2
ecumenical movement, **22**:385n2
Eddy, Henry Turner, **14**:171,n2
Edelman, Louis, **19**:386,n1
Edge, Camilla Sewall (Mrs. Walter Evans), **21**:606n1
Edge, Walter Evans, **21**:313,n3, 606n1; **22**:481, 546n5, 588,n1
Edgewater, Ill., WW at, **14**:421, 431, 454
Edinburgh, **15**:396, 442; **16**:446; **18**:344, 349, 350, 361, 393, 398, 399, 402; **21**:49; Castle, **14**:524; Cockburn Hotel, **14**:524; Conference of Congregationalists, **18**:357; Greyfriars Church, **14**:524; National Gallery, **18**:353; Royal Hotel, **16**:444, 452; Royal Infirmary, **16**:445, 446; St. George's Free Church, **14**:523; St. Giles Cathedral, **14**:524, 547; **18**:358; St. Mary's Cathedral, **18**:352-53; WW in, **16**:444, 445, 451,n2, 452, 454; **18**:351-54, 356-58; Wilsons in, **14**:523-24; World Missionary Conference, 1910, **22**:385,n2
Edinburgh, University of, **15**:421; **19**:138, 678
Edison, Thomas Alva, **14**:4; **21**:122, 520
Edmunds, George Franklin, **14**:470
Edmunds, Lewis, **15**:162
education, **20**:514f; **25**:17, 36-38, 76, 170, 171-72, 276-79, 280, 281
Education, Bureau of, **25**:311
education, state, **14**:307-308, 316-19
*Educational Innovators* (Stewart and McCann), **18**:414n1
*Educational Opportunity in China from Report of Committee on Reference and Counsel to Conference of Foreign Mission Boards . . .* , **19**:109,n2
Edward I, King of England, **18**:73
Edward VII, King of England, **17**:12; **21**:48
Edward the Confessor, King of England, **18**:73
Edwards, Charles Gordon, **23**:557,n4
Edwards, Edward Irving, **24**:68, 522-23; **25**:579-80,n2
Edwards, Elisha Jay, **23**:632,n1
Edwards, (Franklin) Boyd, **17**:296-97,n2
Edwards, Jonathan, **15**:111, 503n1; **17**:163
Edwards, Jonathan, Jr. (Princeton 1765), **15**:496n3
Edwards, William Hanford, **16**:336,n14, 338, 344; **25**:274n2
*Edwin A. Alderman: A Biography* (Malone), **14**:334n1; **15**:508n2
Eells, Stillman Witt, **22**:331,n1
Eells, Mrs. Stillman Witt, **25**:556,n2
Egan, Charles Michael, **22**:100, 133-34,n1, 481, 482,n4; **23**:343, 385, 386, 387, 388, 389, 536n1
Egan, Maurice Francis, **14**:148-49,n1
Ege, G. Fred, **18**:534-35,n1
Egenolf, Peter, **24**:251,n2, 252
Egerton, Hugh Edward, **14**:443,n3
Eggleston, Edward, **15**:484
eggs, cold storage, **21**:358
Egremont, Cumberland, **18**:374
Ehrich, Louis Rinaldo, **19**:258,n1
Ehrle, Franz, **14**:246
eight-hour day, **22**:291n2
*Eight Years with Wilson's Cabinet* (Houston), **23**:560n2
*Eighth Celebration of Founder's Day at the Carnegie Institute of Pittsburgh Thursday November 5, 1903*, **15**:46
Eisenberg, William Edward, **22**:604n2
Eisenhart, Luther Pfahler, **16**:64n1, 132, 160, 162, 258; **17**:408; **19**:138, 676-77; **22**:436
Elberon, N. J., **20**:541n1
Elder, Samuel James, **18**:297
Elder, William Simpson, **22**:17-18,n1
Elderkin, John, **16**:299n, 301n
election legislation: New Jersey, **24**:268-69, 282,n1
Election of 1896, **22**:307
Election of 1908, **17**:519, 521; **18**:479,n1
Election of 1912, **23**:132
election reform, **22**:383n3, 430-32; **24**:231-32, 290-91; Geran Act, **25**:113-14,n2, 309-10; relation to civil service reform, **24**:169-71; *see also* direct election of U. S. senators, direct primaries
elections, expenses and funds, **24**:249, 254, 278, 326; importance of voting, **24**:433; voting places (N. J.), **25**:307; *see also* primary system
elective studies (elective system), **15**:292n, 379, 459; **16**:381; **17**:104,n2, 530-31; **19**:606; **20**:230, 290
electric chair, **22**:238n1
*Elegy on the Death of a Mad Dog* (Goldsmith), **20**:190,n4
*Elektra* (opera by Richard Strauss), **20**:173,n4
Elena, Queen of Italy, **15**:297,n1
Elgin-Marcy Reciprocity Treaty of 1854, **22**:478n3
Eliot, Charles William, **14**:57, 92, 95, 515, 546; **15**:223n2, 284n, 408; **16**:170, 172, 176, 180, 281, 284, 331, 520n1; **17**:225-26, 228n1, 410, 547, 560,n3, 588; **18**:15, 297,n1, 519,n1, 528-29, 590,n2; **19**:157, 211n2, 252, 263, 290; **20**:290, 337-39, 556; **21**:615; **22**:78,n1, 78-79; **25**:286,n1
Elizabeth I, Queen of England, **17**:258; **18**:89, 90, 92, 93; **22**:190-91, 196
Elizabeth, N. J., **19**:508; **23**:468, 546; **24**:250, 493; Elk's Club, **21**:464; Proctor's Theatre, **21**:454; WW addresses, **20**:215,n2, 288-89, 297-303, 306, 307,

Elizabeth, N. J., (*cont.*)
349,n2, 350,n1; WW after dinner talk,
21:464-65; WW campaign speeches,
21:412, 454-62
*Elizabeth Daily Journal*, 24:252n
Elizabeth (N. J.) *Evening Times*,
20:289n1; 21:465n, 470n, 541, 583n1;
22:77n1, 117n1, 137,n1,3; 23:477;
24:475,n1
*Elizabeth Journal*, 23:477
Elizabethport, N. J., St. Patrick's Parish
Hall, 21:465n1, 467
Elk Point, S. D., 25:156-58
Elkins Act of 1903, 17:503n3
Elks Lodge, Asbury Park, 23:561
Eller, Adolphus Hill, 24:388,n1
Eller, Wade Edward, 24:257
Ellicott, Elizabeth Tabor King (Mrs.
William Miller), 23:568,n12
Ellicott, William Miller, 23:568,n12
Ellicott Club, 24:311,n1,3
Elliott, Edward Graham, 14:12, 18, 22,
88, 145, 320-25, 349, 471, 473; 15:6;
16:131, 250, 382; 17:286, 408; 18:271,
294, 612, 617,n4; 19:222,n1, 393,-
n1, 502n3, 504, 505, 507, 523, 524,
527, 528, 534, 535, 536, 538-39, 540,
543, 548, 577, 586, 590, 618, 651, 676;
20:319, 355-56, 485n1, 489, 490, 575,
580; 21:39-40, 51n3, 84, 87; 23:139;
24:584
Elliott, George Frank, 16:316,n3
Elliott, Margaret Randolph Axson (Mrs.
Edward Graham), Madge, sister of
EAW, 21:39-40, 48, 51n3, 84, 87;
24:77n8, 149,n3, 585n2
Elliott, Orrin Leslie, 22:131n3
Elliott (of Nashville), 23:288,n1
Ellis, Charles A., 19:210
Ellis, Leroy J., 19:464, 491-92; 22:22,n2,
116-17, 244,n1
Ellis, Lewis Ethan, 22:478n3
Ellison, E. D., 16:95
Ellyson, James Taylor, 24:119
Elmer, N. J., 23:391, 393, 394
Elmer, William, M.D., 14:78; Mrs., 14:78
Elsie (servant), 16:437
Elsing, William Thaddeus, 15:388, 389
Elson, Henry William, 16:387; 22:604n2
Ely, Anna Morris Anderson, 24:536,n1
Ely, Cambridgeshire, Cathedral, 14:526;
Lamb Hotel, 14:526; Wilsons at,
14:526
Ely, George Wells, 14:476, 500
Ely, Helena Rutherfurd, 14:520n2
Ely, Matthias C., 22:81n1, 85-86,n1, 98,
200, 201, 357
Ely, Matthias Cowell, 21:26,n4, 540
Ely, Richard Theodore, 14:430; 24:535-
36
Ely, Robert Erskine, 15:501-502; 17:92,-
n1, 98, 107
Emancipation Proclamation, 24:570,
571n1
Embury, Ayman II, 15:375

*Emergence of the American University*
(Veysey), 15:292n28
Emerson, Ralph Waldo, 15:223n2; 25:
602
Emerson Hotel, Baltimore, 23:567; 24:
500n1, 513
Emerson (Procter's secretary), 20:100
eminent domain, 16:321
Emmanuel College, Cambridge, 15:410;
16:509
Emmet, William Temple, 19:102,n1,2,
104
employers' liability, 22:291n2, 335,
357n4, 383n3, 455, 462f
*Emporia* (Kan.) *Gazette*, 14:239n6; 15:
171n4
*Endymion: A Poetic Romance* (Keats),
23:128,n2
*Enemy of the People* (Ibsen), 20:89
engineering, 22:411
*Engineering Magazine*, 18:59, 60n1
England, 22:604; 23:241; Bill of Rights,
18:83, 163, 164; city government, 23:
149, 166; Glorious Revolution, 19:207;
government, 18:89-90, 92, 96f; Liberal
Party, 18:401; Parliament, 18:73, 75,
76, 77, 89, 92, 108, 123f, 164, 201; Petition of Right, 18:83; politics, 21:439;
Privy Council, 18:165; Revolution of
1688, 18:75, 97; Whig party, 18:105-
106, 108, 115-16, 117, 123, 199-201,
203, 215
*England and the English from an
American Point of View* (Collier),
19:262,n3
Englewood, N. J., 21:141; Lyceum, 21:
141, 446; Princeton alumni, 19:608;
WW address, 19:608; WW campaign
speech, 21:446-49
English, Frank G., 23:275
English Citizen Series, 14:14
*English Constitution* (Bagehot), 14:13;
25:238n5
English language, 25:109
*Enjoyment of Living* (Eastman), 24:
307n4
Ennerdale, Cumberland, 18:374, 386
*Entirely New Cynic's Calendar of Re-
vised Wisdom 1905* (Mumford, Her-
ford, and Mizner), 16:33n6; 18:428,n3;
19:235,n2
Epicurus, 19:573
Epochs of American History, 20:582
Epochs of Philosophy series, 15:300,n4,
410, 441, 422n1,2
equal suffrage, 23:160
Equitable Life Assurance Society of the
United States, 16:276n1, 299,n1, 535,-
n2, 333n2; 17:78; 18:494n2; 20:534n1
*Equitable Life Assurance Society of the
United States, 1859-1964* (Buley), 16:
276n1
Erdman, Charles Rosenbury, 15:16;
20:556n2; 22:466,n1, 503n2

Erdman, Estelle Pardee (Mrs. Charles Rosenbury), 22:503n2
Ericksen, Anna C., 14:6,n4, 21, 23, 107; 15:326,n3
Erickson, Alfred William, 19:156,n1
Ericsson, Leif, 14:21
Erie, Pa., 21:161
Erie Railroad, 23:450n1
Erskine, Albert DeWolf, 14:431,n3
Erskine, Marion Brower (Mrs. Albert DeWolf), 14:431,n3
Erwin, Elizabeth Adams; Beth (Mrs. Hamilton), 14:109n1, 110
Erwin, Ellen Woodrow, 14:110,n3, 118,-n2; 15:299
Erwin, Hamilton, 14:109n1, 118,n1; 15:299,n2
Erwin, Hamilton, Jr., 14:109
Erwin, Mamie, 14:109,n1, 118
Erwin, Susan, 15:140,n2
Esk Valley, Cumberland, 18:389
*Essays on Government* (Lowell), 14:14
Essex County, Mass., Probate Court, 20:510
Essex County, N. J., 21:7, 89, 113, 161n2, 171, 341, 380, 412, 541n2, 561, 564, 585n1; 22:117, 156, 164, 200, 201, 205n2, 212n1, 225n1, 232, 239, 239n1, 240, 241, 242n2, 245, 253, 281, 285, 286, 297, 335, 336, 340, 343, 378, 537n4; 23:206n5, 331, 332n2, 334-35, 338-39, 349, 385, 386, 387, 388, 389-90, 403, 417-18, 433, 539, 544; 24:449n1; Democratic Party, 24:436; 25:137, 467, 566n1, 582; Direct Primary League, 22:245; Essex County Democratic Association, 23:449; Essex Eleven, 22:164; Lawyers Club, 19:651, 709n4; 20:226, 245-46, 462-63; primary election 1911, 23:361,n1; Prosecutor of Pleas, 23:357; Republican Party, 24:435; sample ballots, 23:355; sheriff, 23:357; Teachers Guild, 16:381; Woodrow Wilson Democratic League (Progressive Democratic League), 23:177, 178, 332n2, 338, 353, 354; 25:137, 467, 566n1, 582
Essex Fells (Caldwell), N. J., 22:413
Esthus, Raymond Arthur, 16:559n3
Ethel (servant of M.A.H. Peck), 20:181
*Ethiopia*, S.S., 18:345n4
Eton College, 16:344
*Etruria*, S. S., 14:546
Euripides, 19:594, 597
Europe, labor, 23:644
Eustis, William Corcoran, 25:640n1
Euterpean Quartette, 23:379n2
Evans, Britton D., M.D., 23:629
Evans, Frederick, Jr., 15:248n1
Evans, Lynden, 24:287,n1
Evans, Thomas St. Clair, 14:114-15; 20:357,n1
Evarts, William Maxwell, 24:227
Even, Louis M., 16:177,n1
Everard, Lewis Charles, 18:68,n1

Everett, Wash., 22:395
Everett House, New York City, 14:9
Ewing, Charles H., 23:273,n4
Ewing, Harriet Hoyt (Mrs. Robert, of Nashville), 16:235,n4; 17:495,n3; 23:303,n2
Ewing, Joseph Neff, 22:323
Ewing, Juliana Horatia Gatty (Mrs. Alexander Ewing), 16:451,n2
Ewing, Nathaniel, 15:168n1; 16:5, 377, 556,n2, 562; 17:101; 18:280,n1
Ewing, Robert, of Nashville, 16:235,n4; 17:495,n3; 23:288,n1, 303,n2; 24:40-42,n1,3
Ewing, Robert, Col. of New Orleans, 24:306, 468, 483
Exeter, N. H., 15:141, 175; WW addresses, 19:498-99
Exeter College, Oxford, 14:532
expansionism (colonialism, imperialism), 14:324, 325, 431,n2, 433-34; 15:171, 172, 175, 184, 330n3, 537
Experience of this Republic as to the Elective Franchise (MacCorkle), 16:565,n3
experts, 22:359-60
exports, 24:85, 125; *see also* foreign markets; trade
Exposition Music Hall (Pittsburgh), 24:316
Eypper, Charles Apffel, 21:464,n1; 22:344
*Ezra Cornell: An Address to the Students of Cornell University on Ezra Cornell Centennial Day, April Twenty-Sixth, 1907* (Carnegie), 17:124,n1

Faber, Simon, 24:511,n1
Fagan, Charles Aloysius, 24:315,n2
Fagan, Lawrence, 21:18, 23,n5, 26,n3
Fagan, Mark Matthew, 21:19,n2
Fagan, Michael J., 23:536n2
Fairbanks, Charles Warren, 14:297
Fairbanks, Frederick Cole, 14:297
Fairfield, Westmorland, 16:441
Fairmont Hotel, San Francisco, 23:53, 54
Falconer, Robert Alexander, 22:45,n1
Fales, Merton Sikes, 16:138
Fall River, Mass., 25:257-69, 285
*Farewell Address* (Washington), 23:292-93
Farinholt, Benjamin L., 22:587,n1
Farley, John Murphy, 14:298; 19:102n3
Farmer & Brindley, London sculptors, 17:125
Farmers' Loan & Trust Co., New York City, 15:192
farming and farmers, 23:570f, 641-42, 646; 25:31-34 Δ Walter Hines Page, 25:516; *see also* agriculture
Farmington, Conn., 19:169, 323
Farnam, Henry Walcott, 24:166n2
Farr, John, 19:64
Farr, Marcus Stults, 16:132, 259; 17:408; 19:70

Farrand, Margaret Washburne Walker (Mrs. Wilson), 20:57,n2
Farrand, Max, 21:309n2
Farrand, Samuel Ashbel, 18:547,n1, 629,n1
Farrand, Wilson, 15:52n1, 362-63, 386, 465; 17:598n2; 18:547-48, 555,n2; 19:118,n1, 119, 123, 155,n1, 195n1, 439, 711, 712, 736; 20:6n, 7n, 8n, 9n, 56-57, 63-64,n1, 73-74, 211, 217, 245, 247, 252, 254, 262, 284, 321, 476, 491; 21:152, 362n1, 365-66
Farrar, Edgar Howard, 25:557,n1
Farrar, Edgar Howard, Jr., 25:557n3
Farrar, Lucinda, 25:557n2
Farrelly, Stephen, 18:59; 22:602
Farrier, Benjamin E., 24:68,n2
Farwell, John Villiers, 18:49,n2, 272,n1, 277
Fassett, Jacob Sloat, 14:298,n1
Faunce, William Herbert Perry, 14:115, 491,n2, 494; 16:309; 17:125
Faust (Goethe), 19:571
Fay, James (New York antique dealer), 14:7,n7, 9, 12, 17, 20-21, 61, 65, 80
Fay, Thomas P., 21:299,n1
Fearis, John Sylvester, 23:379n2
Federal Commission bill: Robert M. LaFollette, 25:287, 293
Federal Council of the Churches of Christ in America, 16:227n2, 229n3; 23:511n2
federal incorporation, 23:617
federal power, 21:381
federal regulation, 22:107
federal reserve system, Carter Glass, 25:642, 644; Henry Parker Willis, 25:641n1
Federal Reserve System, Legislation, Organization and Operation (Willis), 25:641n1
Federalist Papers, 14:13; 15:44; 18:201, 23:577
Federalist party, 25:40, 53, 108
Federalist System (Bassett), 20:583
Feet of the Young Men (Kipling), 22:89,n3
Fehsenfeld, William Henry, 23:568,n10
Feigl, George G., 22:376,n1
Feitner, Thomas L., 18:59
Feke, Robert, 15:214n6
Fell, J. Ridgway, 23:428n7
Fels, Joseph, 22:278-80,n1
Fels Fund, 22:258n1, 278n1
Felt, Nora Belle Harker (Mrs. Zephaniah Charles), 20:382; 21:12,n1
Felt, Zephaniah Charles, 15:552-53,n1; 18:435; 20:382,n1, 392-93, 453, 458; 21:12, 38
Fentress, David, 17:473n2, 523; 23:218,n2
Fentress, Mabel Kingsbury (Mrs. David), 17:473n2, 523
Fenwick Point, Saybrook, Conn., 16:156

Ferguson, Henry, 18:436-37, 450-51; 19:222,n1, 226
Ferguson, William T., 21:21,n1, 28-29, 47, 162, 238-39, 275, 292; 22:28; 25:549-50
Fergusson, Harvey Butler, 22:563,n6; 24:287,n1
Ferrell, Thomas Merrill, 23:394,n3
Ferrero, Frances Lance, 19:262n3
Ferrero, Guglielmo, 19:262,n3
Ferris, Morris Patterson, 15:151,n1, 153
Ficklen, John Rose, 17:375,n3
Fiedler, Max, 19:200,n1
Field, James Alfred, 14:388
Fielder, James Fairman, 21:97, 442-43; 22:134, 157, 357; 23:137, 162,n4, 164, 167, 169, 387, 389, 537; 24:244
Fielder, John Wesley, Jr., 14:5-6, 16, 84-85, 88, 93, 96, 123; 15:208n2
Fielder, Phoebe Warren (Mrs. John Wesley), 15:207,n2,3
Fielding, Henry, 14:503
Fiesole, Italy, 15:304, 313, 315, 316, 336, 340, 348
Fife, Drummond, 24:439,n7
Fife, Robert Herndon, Jr., 16:68, 80
50th Anniversary of Dial Lodge, 19:117n2
Filene, Abraham Lincoln, 21:617,n2
Filene, Edward Albert, 21:617,n2; 23:588,n3; 24:92, 495
Filipinos, 14:464; see also Philippine Islands
Fillebrown, Charles Bowdoin, 14:200
Fillmore, Millard, 17:319
Finance Committee, see United States Congress, Senate
financial disclosure, see campaign contributions and expenditures, disclosure of
Finch, A. W., 18:335
Finch, Miss, 23:330
Fine, Henry Burchard, 14:26, 36, 82, 92, 137, 296, 297, 326, 394, 398n2, 486, 489, 497, 554,n1, 557; 15:4, 20-24, 56, 73, 75-77, 135, 154, 186, 188, 204, 247, 264, 273, 293, 312n1, 376-78, 391, 392, 434, 523-24, 554; 16:24-26, 145, 156-57, 158, 162, 163-65, 178-79, 180, 186, 200-203, 234, 265, 325-27, 382, 398, 414, 422, 423, 431, 434, 466-67, 482-83,n1,2, 491, 497, 556n1; 17:68-70, 83-85, 108, 110, 147-48, 274, 300, 398, 402, 408, 422, 438-40, 467, 552-53,n1, 564; 18:5, 7, 8, 225, 243-47, 354, 457, 473-74, 473n1, 476, 481n1, 513, 515, 528n1, 554, 589, 591n1, 592, 607, 609, 615, 617, 624, 626n1, 631; 19:6,n2, 7n2, 10, 11n2, 70n1, 134n1, 137-39, 140, 141-43, 160n1, 167, 168, 169, 172, 194, 197, 198, 228, 256, 257, 274-75, 276, 311, 429, 456, 457, 585, 621, 705-706, 753-55; 20:8n, 54, 57, 58, 93, 109, 114-15, 116, 129, 138, 143,

144, 148n, 173-75, 182, 189, 190, 191-92, 213, 266n3,4, 284, 317, 319, 461, 470, 474, 480, 484, 485n1, 571, 576; **21:**112, 385; **22:**430, 436, 528,n2; **23:**31, 139; **24:**528; **25:**547, 560, 578
Fine, John Burchard, **14:**297; **15:**103; **16:**272
Fine, Mary Ely Burchard (Mrs. Lambert Suydam), **16:**234
Fine, May Margaret, **14:**18n1; **24:**528,n2
Fine, Philena Fobes (Mrs. Henry Burchard), **14:**36, 56, 92, 101, 108; **15:**120, 139; **16:**165, 178, 179; **17:**549; **18:**7; **19:**140; **20:**152, 192, 571; **24:**528,n1
Fine, Susan Breese Packard, **15:**312,n1; **25:**560,n2
Finlay, William Wilson, **22:**140
Finley, Anna J., **14:**423,n1; **15:**119,n2
Finley, John Huston, **14:**62, 65, 66, 86, 123-24, 137, 290, 296, 297, 320, 326, 349, 388, 395, 424,n1,2, 476, 486, 487, 544,n2, 548; **15:**7, 9, 70-71, 119, 120n2, 308n3; **16:**121n1, 292n1, 240; **17:**528, 529, 550-51; **18:**571; **19:**156, 182, 184; **21:**137,n1; **25:**278,n4
Finley, Margaret Boyden, **15:**308,n3
Finley, Martha Ford (Mrs. John Huston), **14:**86, 424,n1
Finley, Robert Johnston, **16:**240,n1
Finley, William L., **25:**203n2
Finney, John Miller Turpin, M.D., **20:**48,n2, 130n1, 209,n3,4, 222,n1, 227, 244, 245, 246, 247, 288, 360, 361, 461, 474, 480, 481; **22:**158; **23:**543-44, 568; **24:**371
Fiore, F. A., **25:**28
*First Course in Physics* (Millikan and Gale), **18:**489,n1
*First Hundred Years of Roanoke College, 1842-1942* (Eisenberg), **22:**604n2
*First Presbyterian Church of Princeton: Two Centuries of History* (ed. Link), **16:**207n2
First Presbyterian Church of Trenton, **25:**453,n1
*First Republic in America: An Account of the Origin of this Nation* (Brown), **14:**353,n3
Firth, Joseph H., **21:**383
Firth of Forth, **18:**349
Fish, Carl Russell, **19:**635
Fish, Hamilton (1808-1893), **17:**314
Fish, Stuyvesant, **16:**96,n1
Fishburne, John Wood, **24:**462-63,n1
Fisher, Frederick, **15:**120,n4; **16:**104,n1, 105, 206, 234
Fisher, Hubert, **17:**474, 480
Fisher, Walter L., **23:**175n1
fishing laws (N. J.), **25:**474,n4
Fisk, Arthur L., **23:**64,n9
Fisk, Charles Joel, **21:**614,n1
Fisk, Harvey Edward, **18:**474, 489, 491-92, 611
Fisk, Harvey Edward, Jr., **18:**474,n2

Fisk, Pliny, **15:**527, 569, 573; **16:**5; **21:**614,n2
Fisk Teachers Agencies, **14:**429,n2
Fiske, John, **14:**343,n7, 547,n1, 551
Fitch, Clyde, author of *Beau Brummel*, **15:**201
Fite, Emerson David, **16:**306,n6
Fitzgerald, John Francis, **23:**258,n3; **24:**83n1, 92; **25:**508
Fitzgerald, John Joseph, **21:**327, 338; **22:**16,n1, 207n6; **24:**571; **25:**311
Fitzgerald, Mrs. (at Bermuda), **20:**138, 150, 177, 179; daughter, **20:**138, 177, 179
Fitz Gerald, Susan Walker (Mrs. Richard Y.), **25:**26,n5, 29,n1
Fitzherbert, Richard, **24:**244,n1, 245-47
Fitzhugh, George, **16:**335n1
Fitzhugh, Robert Hunter, **16:**334,n1, 336n1, 338, 492; **17:**63-64; **18:**6; **20:**227, **22:**587n1
Fitzpatrick, Edward A., **24:**554n1
Fitz Randolph, Nathaniel, **15:**468n1; **16:**213n1, 485; **20:**495, 498; tablet, **19:**5,n2, 8-9, 12, 13-14
Fitzsimmons, F. J., **17:**121
Fitzwilliam Museum, Cambridge, **14:**530; **19:**739
flag worship in U.S., **14:**319; **15:**171-72; **16:**30-31
Flanagan, Edith L., **16:**234
Flanzman, David, **22:**200
*Fledermaus*, **25:**55n1
Fleet, William Alexander, Jr., **17:**163,-n11, 557
Fleming, David, **15:**248
Fleming, Matthew Corry, **16:**5, **20:**277-78
Flemington, N. J., **21:**382; Court House, **21:**377n4, 381; Flemington Opera House, **21:**369,n1, 381; **23:**411,n1; WW campaign speeches, **21:**369-77, 377, **23:**411-24; WW in, **21:**558
Flenniken, D. R., **14:**331
Flexner, Abraham, **19:**77n1
Flinn, John William, **14:**331; **16:**87,n2
Flinn, Margaret Smyth, **14:**498,n2
Flint, George C., Co., New York City, **14:**10,n3, 17, 78, 80, 111
Flint v. Stone Tracy Co., **22:**511n2
Flood, Henry De La Warr, **23:**360,n3; **25:**632n1, 638,n5
Florence, Italy, **15:**240, 242, 275, 297, 298, 300, 304, 310, 311, 320, 322, 323, 324, 325, 333, 334, 336, 338, 339; Accademia delle Belle Arti, **15:**348; Bank of Italy, **15:**352; Boboli Gardens, **15:**352, 353; Cappelle Medicee, **15:**353; Certosa (Carthusian monastery), **15:**349, 353, convento di San Marco, **15:**347; Duomo, **15:**348; Galleria degli Uffizi, **15:**348, 349; Monte Morello, **15:**348; Palazzo e Galleria Pitti, **15:**348, 349, 353; Palazzo e museo del

Florence, Italy, (cont.)
  Bargello, **15**:353; Palazzo Medici-Riccardi, **15**:353; Palazzo Vecchio, **15**:348; Pensione Jennings-Riccioli, **15**:242, 306, 337, 338; Piazzale Michelangiolo, **15**:348; Protestant Cemetery, **15**:358; San Miniato al Monte, **15**:348, 353; Santa Maria del Carmine, **15**:357; Villa Trollope (pensione), **15**:338, 347, 348; EAW in, **15**:344, 346-59
Florida, **23**:320, 322, 558; **24**:257n1, 356, 386, 388; precampaign tour, **24**:347-48; presidential primary vote, **24**: 382,n1
Florida crackers, **21**:227
Florida tornado, **22**:274
Flüelen, Switzerland, Wilsons at, **14**:539
Flushing (Vlissingen), Holland, **15**:441
Flynn, David M., **21**:541-42,n1
Fogel, Philip Howard, **15**:410,n6, 441; **19**:677; **20**:153,n8, 446
Foley, Maggie, **14**:432; **15**:300,n1, 326, 339; sister, **15**:300, 326
Foley, Timothy, **23**:85,n4
Folk, Joseph Wingate, **16**:216,n3; **22**: 198,n2, 255n1, 275; **23**:61, 173, 235n3, 237, 259, 291, 310; **24**:26, 185; **25**:645
Fond du Lac, Wisc., **24**:258; WW's arrival, **24**:257-58
Fontainebleau, **15**:441
food preservatives, **25**:282n2; see also Pure Food and Drug Act
Foord, John, **18**:549,n3
football, **15**:102-103,n1; **19**:415, 556, 606; **22**:4-5; **23**:549-50, 554,n7; **24**:155; intercollegiate, **17**:473,n3,4,  476  Δ Army-Navy game, **16**:242; A Carnegie, **16**:500
football reform, **19**:556, 577-78, 623-24, 699, 700; **20**:12, 88, 562-63 Δ A. T. Hadley, **19**:628, 652, 672, 708; **20**:118, 487-88; A. T. Hadley and A. L. Lowell, **19**:561-62; P. D. Haughton, **20**:538-40; H. H. Houston, **19**:602-603, 704-705; **20**:54-55, 559-560; intercollegiate athletic association, **16**:369-71; A. L. Lowell, **19**:627, **20**:11, 72; H. M. MacCracken, **16**:238-40,n2,3; national football conference, **16**:271; W. W. Roper, **20**:547-48; A. Shaw, **19**:598n2; H. B. Thompson, **16**:274-75; R. S. Walker, **19**:597-98
Foote, Henry Stuart, **17**:314
For President—Woodrow Wilson! (editorial), **24**:450n1
Forbes, William Cameron, **25**:535-36
Ford, Albert, **17**:618
Ford, Cornelius, **22**:546n5; **23**:344-45, 387, 388, 536n1
Ford, Dorothy, **17**:617-18
Ford, Franklin, **17**:618
Ford, Bertha Batory (Mrs. Henry Jones), **17**:617; **23**:10
Ford, Henry Jones, **14**:14, 559; **16**:43n2,

97; **17**:62-63, 361, 378, 555, 563, 603, 616-18, 619; **18**:208n5, 259, 287, 288-89, 294-95, 576; **19**:157, 307, 615, 616; **20**:35,n3, 198, 569; **21**:606-607; **22**:84-85, 399,n1; **23**:10,n4, 183, 426-27,n6; **25**:110n3
Ford, Jeremiah Denis Matthias, **16**:172-n1
Ford, John Howard, **17**:618
Fordham University, **16**:240
Fordyce, Alexander Robert, Jr., **22**:225,-n2
foreign exchange, **25**:104-105
foreign languages, **25**:97, 109
foreign markets, **24**:125, 126, 236n8; **25**:16, 38, 101, 194
Foreign Missions Boards of the United States and Canada, **19**:544; Seventeenth Conference . . . , **19**:545n4
forests, U. S., **23**:298
Forman, Henry James, **18**:258-59,n1, 271-72
Fornes, Charles Vincent, **18**:59
Forsee, George H., **23**:9,n3
Forstall, James Jackson, **17**:512
Forsyth, Andrew Russell, **16**:157,n3, 163
Forsyth, William Holmes, **16**:5
Fort, Charlotte E. Stainsby (Mrs. John Franklin), **21**:606; **22**:54,n5
Fort, Franklin William, **14**:301; **22**:27,n1
Fort, John Franklin, **19**:186; **21**:219n2, 505, 584n1, 605-606; **22**:27n1, 53-54, 294n1, 402n3, 546n5; **23**:295n5, 318, 627; **24**:502
Fort Morgan, Colo. Herald, **23**:478n1
Fort Pitt Hotel (Pittsburgh), **24**:315
Fort Washington, Pa., **19**:705
Fort Worth, Texas, **23**:268; City Hall auditorium, **23**:512; First Congregational Church, **23**:511; First Presbyterian Church, **23**:512n4; WW address, **23**:511-12; WW in, **23**:506, 510
Fortnightly Review (London), **23**:287n2
Fortune, Timothy Thomas, **21**:275n4
Forward Step for the Democracy of Tomorrow (Thum), **23**:45n1
Foscolo, Ugo, **19**:573
Fosdick, Harry Emerson, **20**:188,n1
Fosdick, Raymond Blaine, **16**:138,n1; **19**:544,n3; **20**:188,n2; **21**:238,n1; **25**:49, 64
Foss, Cyrus David, **14**:114
Foss, Eugene Noble, **21**:598,n1, 610, 612n1; **22**:38, 74n2, 285n2, 335, 453; **23**:323; **24**:83n1, 92, 558; **25**:42,n1, 50, 51, 270, 535
Foss, George Edmund, **22**:74,n2
Foster, David Paulson, **21**:381-82,n1, 470-71
Foster, John Watson, **19**:64,n1, 109, 202, 239-40, 619-20, 622; **21**:600, 615n2
Foster, Martin David, **24**:287,n1
Foster, Mary Parke McFerson (Mrs.

John Watson), **19:**64,n6, 622; **21:**600,-n1
Foster, Solomon, **22:**183,n1, 260
Foster, Warren William, **18:**270,n1
Foster, William, Jr., **14:**215,n4, 216, 217, 218, 221, 474; **16:**11,n1, 198, 247; **17:**408
Foulke, William Dudley, **16:**316,n4; **21:**615,n6
Fountain, F. S., **16:**113
Fourth of July address, **23:**186-89
Fowler, Charles Newell, **21:**219,n5, 249,n2, 301, 383
Fox, Austen George, **14:**289; **22:**94
Fox, Charles James, **15:**148
Fox, John, **16:**362n1; **18:**59, 270; **22:**167-68,n1
Fox, John T., Mrs., **23:**249,n3
Fox How, Ambleside, Westmorland, **16:**493, 494n2; **18:**368, 379
Fra Angelico (Giovanni da Fiesole), **15:**250, 477
*Fragments of an Autobiography* (Moscheles), **18:**400,n5
France, **22:**514n4, 558; **25:**253; arbitration treaties, **23:**520; city government, **23:**166; government, **18:**83
France, Anatole, **14:**439,n2
Francesco d'Assisi, Saint, **15:**309, 334, 338
Francis, David Rowland, **20:**259,n2; **22:**198,n2
Francis, Robin William Cummins, **20:**431,n1
*Frank Leslie's Illustrated Newspaper*, **19:**513n4
Frankel, Lee Kaufer, **20:**136,n9,10
Frankfort, Ky., **22:**102, 113, 126, 127, 132, 135,n1, 138n1; WW campaign addresses, **24:**141-46; Conference of Governors, **21:**475-76, 605-606
Franklin, Benjamin, **14:**315; 405, 470, 507; **14:**477, 537, 539; **16:**53, 56-57, 226, 316, 341; **17:**249, 347; **19:**209, 744; **24:**211
Franklin, Fabian, **14:**15n; **19:**155, 158-59; **22:**32,n2
Franklin and Marshall College, **19:**552, 634, 678, 698, 704, 740; **20:**55-56,n2; WW address, **19:**740-47
*Franklin D. Roosevelt: The Apprenticeship* (Friedel), **22:**161n1
Franklin Furnace, N. J., **21:**413
Franks, Robert A., **16:**78, 224, 500
Fraser, Abel McIver, **15:**49,n1, 522; **22:**96,n2, 118; **25:**626n1
Fraser, George Corning, **15:**415,n2, 416; **17:**83-85,n1, 110-11, 213, 214, 382, 595; **18:**229, 241
Fraser, Philip Hilton, **21:**519-20
Fraternal Organizations of New Jersey, **21:**452n1
fraternities, **20:**399
Frazer, David Ruddach, **14:**161; **15:**26,-

n1; **16:**131, 199; **17:**594; **19:**703; **20:**30, 245; **21:**326n1, 366-67,n1
Frederick, Halsey Augustus, **20:**405,n1
Frederick, Herbert, **24:**139
free market, free trade, free enterprise, **24:**126, 156, 157, 193, 221; **25:**73-74, 100, 190, 191, 194-95, 199, 242, 248, 470,n5; *see also* trade freedom, **24:**112, 152-53; **25:**99-100, 106, 229
freedom of the will, **22:**530
Freehold, N. J., **22:**50n3; **23:**447; Armory Opera House, **21:**334,n4; WW campaign speeches, **21:**334; **23:**442-47
*Freehold* (N. J.) *Transcript*, **21:**218n, 334n
Freeholders, Boards of (N. J.), **24:**263, 282
Free-Soil Party, **17:**319-20
Freeman, James Edward, **14:**115
Freeman, Walter Jackson, M.D., **20:**429,n1
Freemasons, **23:**229
Freiburg i.B., University of, **16:**257
Frelinghuysen, Joseph Sherman, **21:**7,n5; **22:**474,n1, 532, 550n2; **23:**183
French (Bermuda bandmaster), **20:**139
French, Daniel Chester, **19:**152n1
French, Helen Wilson (Mrs. Thomas Rushmore), **15:**166,n2
French, John T., **23:**522n1, 529n3
French, Thomas Rushmore, M.D., **15:**166,n2
French, William Collins, **21:**421,n3
French, Lemon & Co., **15:**352,n1
French and Indian War, **14:**517
French Lick Springs, Ind., **20:**562n1
French Revolution, **15:**478; **18:**93; **19:**464, 471; **23:**435
Freneau, Philip, **16:**479n1
Freund, Katie, **16:**234
Freund, Louis W., **16:**104,n1, 105, 206, 234, 235
Freund, Wilhelmina, **16:**234
Frew, William Nimick, **15:**46
Frewen, Stephen, **20:**146,n4
Frick, Childs, **14:**544n4; **19:**165
Frick, Henry Clay, **14:**194, 544,n4; **16:**303, 336, 398, 490, 491; **25:**396n3
Friedel, Frank, **22:**161n1
Friedman, Milton, **15:**29n1
Friedrich der Grosse, **18:**90-91, 92
Friendly Sons of St. Patrick: Elizabeth, N. J., **24:**250, 251; Montclair, N. J., **24:**253
Friends, Society of, **20:**495, 498
Frissell, Hollis Burke, **15:**131,n2; **18:**629-30,n1; **22:**140,n1
*Frogs* (Aristophanes), **19:**594, 597
frontier, U. S., **15:**537; **22:**420
frontier thesis, **18:**100-101
Frost, Elliot Park, **19:**678
Frost, Lincoln, **23:**97,n2
Frost, William Goodell, **17:**226n1; **21:**579; **22:**48-49, 172, 214-15, 417,n1,

Frost, William Goodell, (*cont.*)
419, 421, 424, 425, 440-41; **25:**552-53
Frothingham, Arthur Lincoln, **17:**17,n4,-5,6
Frothingham, Arthur Lincoln, Jr., **14:**395, 441; **15:**183, 293, 294; **16:**93-94, 103, 130, 245, 246
Frothingham, Jessie Peabody (Mrs. Arthur Lincoln), **17:**17,n5
Froude, James Anthony, **14:**340; **18:**362,n2
Fruland, Ethel Wilson, **23:**227n
Fry, Wilfred W., **14:**354,n1
Fuess, Claude Moore, **18:**566n1
Fugitive Slave Law, **17:**311
Fuhrmann, Louis P., **23:**559n1
Fuller, Charles Humphrey, **24:**238,n3
Fuller, Henry Amzi, **15:**471,n3
Fuller, Inez C., **25:**x
Fuller, Wayne Edison, **22:**427n1
Fuller Construction Company, **17:**411
Furness, Horace Howard, **14:**381
Furness Abbey, nr. Barrow, Lancs, **18:**383; Wilsons at, **14:**521
Future (Arnold), **15:**371n2
Future of Democracy (Daniels), **21:**322,-n3

Gaboriau, Émile, **25:**458,n4
Gadsden, Edward Miles, **24:**336
Gailor, Thomas Frank, **17:**474
Gaines, Clement Carrington, **16:**292n1
Gainesville, Ga., **24:**333-35
Gaither, George Riggs, **23:**573,n2, 577
Gale, Henry Gordon, **18:**489n1
Galesburg, Ill., **24:**300
Galileo, **20:**188
Gallagher, Charles H., **23:**262n3
Gallagher, Charles Henry, **21:**27,n2, 34; **22:**133
Gallinger, Jacob Harold, **25:**543,n3
Galveston, Texas, **19:**520-21,n6; **23:**146, 309; city government, **17:**571,n3; **19:**91,n2; **20:**204-205; commission government, **23:**144, 163,n5, 512; Woodrow Wilson Club, **23:**308, 309
Gamaliel, **17:**394,n2
Gannon, Bernard M., **25:**582,n6, 584
Gansevoort, Henry Sanford, **16:**404
Garda, Lago di, **14:**246
Garden City, N. Y., **23:**214
Gardiner, James L., **22:**386
Gardner, John James, **25:**483,n11, 488
Gardner, Obadiah, **23:**341,n3; **24:**273, 467; **25:**618, 619
Garfield, Belle Hartford Mason (Mrs. Harry Augustus), **14:**548, 554, 557; **15:**55, 136, 301; **19:**230,n5; **21:**559, 609
Garfield, Harry Augustus, **14:**486-87,n1, 489-90, 491, 526, 544-45, 545, 547, 548-49, 553, 554-55, 556-57; **15:**5, 25-26, 26,n2, 54-55, 71, 136, 183, 200, 301, 330,n3, 433-34, 546; **16:**206n2, 379, 449-50; **17:**108, 110, 229, 237,

246, 262, 284-85, 307, 408, 497, 528, 550, 551, 555, 600, 607; **18:**229, 259-60, 271, 287, 293, 294, 347, 369, 382, 419, 423, 436, 437-39, 570, 571, 576; **19:**30-31, 230,n5, 260; **20:**513, 531; **21:**421, 558-59, 609, 609n1; **22:**14, 30-31; **23:**248, 249
Garfield, James Abram, **14:**238, 488n1; **15:**85-86, 546; **17:**329; **18:**119, 271; **21:**609n1; **25:**50
Garfield, James Rudolph, **16:**15n1; **21:**609-10,n1
Garibaldi, Giuseppi, **25:**256
Garmany, Jasper Jewett, M.D., **15:**471,-n2; **16:**500; **19:**100
Garner, James Wilford, **25:**617,n1
Garraty, John Arthur, **15:**65n2; **24:**346n2
Garrett, Alexander Charles, **23:**511,n4
Garrett, Alice Dickinson Whitridge (Mrs. Thomas Harrison), **14:**7n3, 147; **16:**18,n2
Garrett, Guy Harper, **20:**405,n1
Garrett, Horatio Whitridge, **14:**6,n3
Garrett, John Work (1820-1884), **14:**7n2
Garrett, John Work (Princeton 1895), **14:**147; **15:**158-59, 397,n1, 404, 411,n3, 526; **16:**18,n1, 20, 204, 205; **17:**58n1
Garrett, Katharine Barker Johnson (Mrs. Robert), **17:**117,n1; **19:**306; **20:**569
Garrett, Mary Elizabeth, **14:**6,n2
Garrett, Robert, **14:**123, 147; **15:**123, 158, 159, 192,n2, 300,n2, 339, 397, 404, 411,n3, 526, 570, 573; **16:**5, 19,n1,2, 20, 204, 205, 233, 266, 526; **17:**19, 19-21, 35-36, 51, 58, 58n1, 62, 102, 103, 107-108, 111,n1, 117-18, 159, 274, 300, 400, 459, 468, 596; **18:**311, 554, 622; **19:**3,n1, 4, 5, 49, 52, 165, 166, 170, 267, 268, 269, 305-306, 347, 353, 404, 418, 437, 439, 631, 632, 633, 634, 657, 735; **20:**27, 48, 130n1, 174, 182, 191, 209,n3, 222, 224, 244-45, 246-47, 285, 288, 354, 355, 361, 362, 402, 490, 569; **21:**3, 25-26, 622; **22:**84; **23:**302-303, 594; Baltimore Club, **17:**58, 62
Garrison, Charles Grant, **23:**275, 316
Garrison, Harry J., **22:**532,n4; **23:**533n3
Garrison, Lindley Miller, **20:**176,n2, 179; **21:**587,n1; **22:**40,n31, 210,n1
Garrison, Margaret Hildeburn (Mrs. Lindley Miller), **20:**179,n1; **22:**210,n1
Garrison, William Lloyd, **14:**351; **17:**609n1
Garwood, N. J., **23:**468
Gary, Elbert Henry, **23:**157,n1, 299,n8, 423; **24:**346,n2; **25:**160,n1, 381
Gary, Ind., **25:**354
Gaskill, Nelson Burr, **17:**230-31,n1; **22:**546n5; **23:**313,n1
Gaston, Wiliam Alexander, **23:**235,n2
Gates, Frederick Taylor, **17:**63,n2, 95; **19:**65,n3

Gates Robert Moores, **25**:612,n1
Gatewood, Willard Badgette, Jr., **18**: 387n1,2
Gaunt, George Washington French, **22**: 474,n1
Gauss, Christian [Frederick], **16**:61, 132, 256-57; **17**:408, 557; **19**:573-74, 574, 576; **21**:111
Gavegan, Edward James, **23**:263
Gawin, August M., **24**:260,n2
Gayley, Charles Mills, **23**:60
Gaynor, William Jay, **19**:499, 499n3; **20**:401, 402n1, 546; **21**:9n2, 144, 238; **22**:255n1; **23**:260,n7, 291; **24**:224-25, 240-41, 330
Gearin, John McDermeid, **16**:362n1, 558,n4
Gebhardt, William Cavanagh, **21**:110-11,n1, 156-57, 354, 558; **22**:101, 162, 257, 321, 357, 546n5; **23**:387, 417; **25**:147,n1,2
Geer, Curtis Manning, **14**:459n3
Geer, George Jarvis, Jr., **19**:165
General Education Board, **17**:51,n1, 60-62, 95-96, 99, 102; **18**:629,n4; **19**:185
General Electric Co., **22**:411n1
General Theological Seminary, **20**:328; **21**:105,n2
Genesee, Society of the, **16**:231; **17**:565
Geneva, Switzerland, Grand Hotel Beau Rivage, **14**:541; Wilsons at, **14**:540, 541
Geneva, University of, **16**:257
Genoa, **15**:275, 304, 309, 322, 333, 346, 348, 356, 357; **20**:359
Geohegan, Harry, **23**:46,n2
George, Henry, Jr. (1862-1916), **22**: 229,n4; **24**:395n2
George, Saint, **15**:359
George III, **14**:443
George, William James, **14**:297
Geo. Ballantine and Son, **16**:546
George C. Flint Co., New York City, **14**:10,n3, 17, 78, 80, 111
*George Harvey, 'A Passionate Patriot'* (Johnson), **16**:455n1, 534n10
*George W. Norris: The Making of a Progressive, 1861-1912* (Lowitt), **21**:344-n12
George Washington University, **19**:541
Georgetown, Del., **25**:424
Georgetown College (Ky.), **24**:146
Georgetown University, **23**:549
Georgia, **22**:543; **23**:341; **24**:237, 286, 287-88, 356, 384, 386, 388, 522,n1; **25**:493; Albany reception, **24**:344; Atlanta, **24**:335-44; Democratic primary vote, **24**:381,n2; Democrats, **23**:236; Gainesville reception, **24**:333-35; Judiciary, **20**:462; Legislature, **23**: 236,n3, 244; Macon reception, **24**: 354-56; Savannah speech, **24**:349-51; Waycross, **24**:347

Georgia Central Railroad, **14**:69,n3, 74; **23**:557
Geran, Elmer Hendrickson, **22**:18-19,n1, 100-101, 280-81, 309, 430, 470, 482, 505, 569n1
Geran Act, *see* New Jersey, Geran Election Reform bill and act
Gerard, James Watson, **25**:134,n2
German-American Alliance, **22**:258
German-American Alliance of New Jersey, **21**:295
German-Americans, **24**:57, 122, 252, 260-61, 409; **25**:47, 48-49, 108, 441; James Charles Monaghan on, **25**:63
*German Composition* (Thomas), **19**:570
German Hospital and Dispensary Association (Jersey City), **24**:408-409
German Influence on Religious Life and Thought in America During the Colonial Period (Hoskins), **16**:425,n2
German partisans and Carnegie Hall meeting, **23**:592n2
German Wallace College, **18**:579
Germany, **22**:514n4, 604; **21**:48; banking system, **23**:510; city government, **23**:166; cost of production request, **24**:420-21; government, **21**:405; industrial skills, **20**:420; industrial wages, **19**:362-63; report on wages in, **20**: 38,n5; **21**:468; steel trust, **25**:331-32; universities, **20**:273
Geronimo, Anthony, **25**:40-41,n1,2
Gerould, Gordon Hall, **16**:52, 58-79, 132, 255; **17**:408; **19**:748-52
Gerrans, Henry Tresawna, **14**:140,n2; **16**:165,n3
Gerry (English doctor in Florence), **15**: 347
*Gesetz und Verordnung* (Jellinek), **14**: 322, 324
Gettysburg, Battle of, **14**:250, 445; **22**:302
Gettysburg College (formerly Pennsylvania College), **16**:258, 510
Ghirlandio (Domenico di Tourmaso Bigordi), **15**:229
Gibbes, Wade Hampton, **25**:539
Gibbon, Edward, **14**:503; **15**:473; **20**:558
Gibboney, Stuart G., **24**:71, 79, 118
Gibbons, James Cardinal, **24**:473-74
Gibbs, **14**:88
Gibraltar, EAW at, **15**:210, 211, 212, 214, 221, 238, 268
Gibson, George Alexander, M.D., **16**: 445,n1
*Gibson Girl* (speedboat), **23**:274
Giddings, Franklin Henry, **14**:559-60; **18**:533
Giddings, Margaret, **14**:560n
Giessen, University of, **16**:465, 508
Gifford, John James, **23**:177,n1, 181-82; **24**:429,n1
Gifford Lectures, **14**:295,n2

*Gift* (pamphlet in Graduate College controversy), **20:**382n5
Gilbert, Hugh C., **24:**186,n1
Gilchrist, Albert Waller, **23:**320, 322
Gilder, Joseph B., **15:**232
Gilder, Richard Watson, **14:**47, 58, 190; **15:**232; **18:**525; **19:**100
Gildersleeve, Basil Lanneau, **14:**139; **16:**104; **17:**114, 588
Gildersleeve, Raleigh Colston, **16:**104, 144-45, 150-51, 152-53, 154, 161-62, 176, 181-83, 184, 185, 191, 212, 324, 387-88, 447; **17:**386, 388-89, 558
Gillam, J. Robert, **24:**190,n1
Gillespie, William, **14:**326,n4 **15:**14; **16:**132, 159, 160, 162, 258; **17:**408
Gillham, Newton Cloud, **23:**172-73,n1, 200-201; **24:**186,n2
Gilman, Arthur, **17:**123n1
Gilman, Daniel Coit, **14:**14-15,n2, 142-43, 147, 197-98; **15:**118; **17:**236, 240
Gilman, Elizabeth Dwight Woolsey (Mrs. Daniel Coit), **14:**15, 142, 198
Gilman, Lawrence, **23:**215,n1
Gilman School, Baltimore, **16:**308, 509,-n3, 510, 511
Gilmore, Clarence Edgar, **23:**268,n6
Gilmore, Thomas Mador, **25:**21,n1
Gimelson, Bruce, **16:**102n, 565n
Giorgione Il, **15:**349,n1
Giotto di Bondone, **15:**275, 311, 334, 340, 348, 354, 357
Girton College, Cambridge, **14:**530; **16:**163
Giuseppina Ruspoli, Principessa di Poggio Suasa, **15:**274,n4
glaciers, **19:**479-80, 482
Gladden, Washington, **16:**227n2
Gladner, Grover Cleveland, **24:**397,n2
Gladstone, N. J., **23:**475
Gladstone, William Ewart, **19:**34, 35; **20:**549; **22:**218; **25:**238n4
Glascow, William Anderson, Jr., **25:**557, 565, 622
Glasgow, **16:**432; **18:**313, 344, 349, 350, 351, 356, 391, 393, 408; city government, **19:**514-15; **20:**40-41, 203-204; **23:**149, 166, 579; **25:**223, 226, 259; Grand Hotel, **18:**345; St. Enoch Hotel, **16:**474; smoke pollution, **18:**350; WW in, **18:**348-49
Glasgow, Joseph Anderson, **22:**96,n2
Glasgow, University of, **16:**398n1, 465, 507
*Glasgow Herald*, **19:**514; **20:**41, 204; **23:**579
Glass, Carter, **23:**311; **24:**273, 287,n1; **25:**530-31, 547, 563, 564, 588-89, 608, 641-42,n1, 643-44, 650
Glass, Franklin Potts, **15:**6,n5, 11-13, 25, 190-91, 216, 239; **16:**75, 78, 168; **20:**58-59; **21:**588; **23:**341,n4; **24:**576; **25:**113
Glass, Franklin Purnell, **15:**7n5, 12-13,n3, 191; **16:**168,n5

Glass, John Purnell, **15:**7n5
Glass, Louise, **25:**113n2
Glassboro, N. J., WW campaign speech, **23:**520-21
Glastonbury, Somerset, Wilsons at, **14:**533; Glastonbury Abbey, **14:**533
Glazebrook, Otis Allen, **21:**98; **22:**126,n3, 136
Glencove, West Paget, Bermuda, **23:**596; **25:**220n1, 552,n1, 556, 573, 615
Glendale, Ohio, WW in, **14:**451, 452
Glen Gardner, N. J., **21:**383; **23:**290
Glen Ridge, N. J., **22:**242n2; Town Hall, **21:**563; WW campaign speech, **21:**563-64
Glenn, John Mark, **25:**310,n1
Glen, Robert Brodnax, **22:**327,n1
Glennon, John Joseph, **19:**102n1,3
Glenwood Springs, Colorado, **23:**23,n1
Globe-Wernicke Co., **15:**251-52,n1
Gloucester City, N. J., Washington Park, **23:**277n1
Gloucester County, N. J., **21:**245, 254; **22:**164, 233, 321; **23:**262n3, 362, 408, 546
*Gloucester County Democrat* (Woodbury, N. J.), **21:**259n; **23:**364n, 408n
Glynn, Martin Henry, **19:**26n3; **22:**400-n2; **25:**441,n2, 493n1, 649
Godbout, Muriel, **25:**xiii
Godfrey, Carlton, **23:**522n1, 529n3
Godkin, Edwin Lawrence, **14:**306n3
Godwin, Hannibal Lafayette, **24:**287,n1
Godwin, Harold, **21:**442,n1, 444
Godwin, Parke, **14:**192
Goethe, Johann Wolfgang von, **19:**571
*Golden Age* (Graham), **15:**510
Golden Bull (Hungary), **25:**256
Goldfogle, Henry Mayer, **21:**618,n1; **23:**584
Goldmark, Josephine Clara, **22:**157n1
Goldsborough, Phillips Lee, **23:**264n1, 573n1; **24:**227,n3
Goldsmith, Oliver, **14:**435,n2, 503; **15:**310n4; **20:**172, 190n4
Goldthwaite, Thomas, **15:**213
Gollan, Henry Cowper, **17:**26,n4, 613,n2; **18:**378,n5; **20:**127,n3, 132, 133, 138, 149, 151, 181, 184, 187, 187n1; **21:**556-57; **22:**14, 511,n1,2
Gollan, Marie Louise Norris (Mrs. Henry Cowper), **20:**127,n3, 132, 139, 181, 187; **21:**556-57; **22:**14,n1, 500,n3, 511n1,2
Goltra, Edward Field, **15:**299,n1, 403, 527; **16:**5, 504,n1; **21:**17, 294; **22:**97, 197-98, 199
Gompers, Samuel, **17:**92n2; **21:**322,n2, 379; **25:**22,n1, 22-23,n2, 590, 614-15
Gonzales, Ambrose Elliott, **25:**623,n4
Gonzales, Ambrosio José, **25:**623,n4
Gonzales, Narciso Gener, **25:**623,n4
Gonzales, William Elliott, **22:**507-508,-n1; **23:**114,n3, 173n2; **24:**237, 400, 528; **25:**539, 623,n4, 648

Gooch, Frank Austin, 14:41,n1, 52, 77
Gooch, Sarah Wyman (Mrs. Frank Austin), 14:41,n1
Good, Thomas Roseberry, 14:305
Good, William Pelton, 20:405,n1
Goodhue, Bertram Grosvenor, 17:174,n2; 18:279,n1, 291, 302
Goodhue, Helen Grosvenor Eldredge (Mrs. Charles Wells), 17:174,n2
Gooding, Mrs. (summer resident at Clifton, Mass.), 14:41
Goodnow, Frank Johnson, 19:157
Goodrich, Arthur (EAW friend of 1884-85), 14:62,n1, 69
Goodrich, Arthur Frederick (1878-1941), 14:62,n1, 63-64, 65
Goodrich, William Winton, 14:210,n1
good will, 23:307-308
Goodwillie, Mary C., 14:146,n1, 196
Goodwin, Clarence Norton, 24:302,n3
Goodwin, Elliot Hersey, 20:43n8; 22:78, 256,n1
Goodwin, R. Roy, 23:556,n3
Goodwin, Tyler, 23:513n4
Goodwin, William Watson, 17:588,n3
Gordon, George Angier, 14:115; 17:128,n3
Gordon, James Gay, Sr., 21:267; 24:393,n1
Gordon, James Waddell, 24:51,n1, 71,n7, 81
Gordon, John Brown, 20:415
Gordon, John Maxwell, 23:339,n1
Gordon, John P., 24:186,n4
Gordon, Sam, 23:628; 24:517
Gordon, Sloane, 21:300,n3
Gordon, William John, 14:521n1
Gordon, Reverend (of Chicago), 25:28
Gore, James Howard, 19:140,n1,2, 541, 557, 560, 603, 604, 610; 20:73
Gore, Thomas Pryor, 20:288-89,n5; 22:387,n1, 441, 441n3, 442; 23:112,n3; 24:65n1, 273, 395n2, 467, 468, 497, 571; 25:448, 460, 534, 562, 563, 564, 565
Gorham, N. H., 14:73, 79, 91; WW at, 14:93-121 passim
Gorman, Arthur Pue, 14:17n3; 21:345n13; 22:113n2, 282; 23:264,n1
Gothic architecture, Collegiate Gothic, 15:557; Tudor Gothic buildings at Princeton, 14:269; A. F. West on, 14:140; EAW on, 15:334, 335
Göttingen, University of, 16:258, 508; 17:557; 19:678
Götz von Berlichingen (Goethe), 19:571
Goucher, John Franklin, 18:321-22,n1
Goucher College (Woman's College of Balt.), 15:7-8n1, 118, 295, 296, 306, 308; 16:28n2, 423, 424n1, 470, 544; 18:278, 318-20, 321, 322n1,2; 20:16n3; Fensal Hall, 15:7
Gould, Elgin Ralston Lovell, 14:298; 15:502; 17:92n2; 22:606; 24:503

Gould, Lewis Ludlow, 22:123n3; 24:225-n1; 25:604n1
government, 24:200; 25:18, 81-82, 84, 88-89, 90, 102-103, 119-20, 122, 123, 126, 128, 137, 141-42, 143, 149, 152, 153, 154-55, 174, 185, 433; by the people, 24:170-71; business, big business, corporations and, 24:199, 414-15; 25:36, 123, 125, 157-58, 178-79; efficiency through civil service reform, 24:167-68; control of industry and labor, 25:103; cost of, 24:171-72; definition, purpose, 24:175, 204, 228; and human rights, 25:176-77; limitation of, 25:124; and monopoly, 25:73; Republican conception of, 25:353; tariff and, 25:9
Government by Commission Association, 23:136
government, separation of powers, 23:235n3
Governments and Parties of Continental Europe (Lowell), 14:14
Governor Hughes and the Albany Gang (Hendrick), 22:85n2
Gov. Wilson's Speech of Acceptance (article, Bryan), 25:46n1
governors, 22:108f; meeting in Frankfort, Ky., 21:475; power of, 23:320-22; 24:232-33
Governors' Conference, Frankfort and Louisville, Ky., Nov.-Dec. 1910, 22:54,n4, 94, 95, 102-113, 126-27, 131, 132, 133, 133n1, 134, 134n1, 135, 138,n1,4, 139, 141, 210; mentioned, 23:318,n1, 319n1; Proceedings of Third Meeting, 22:113n
Governors' Conference, Spring Lake, N. J., Sept., 12-16, 1911, 23:317-24; ment. 23:330, 440; Proceedings of the Fourth Meeting of the Governors, 23:319n, 322n, 324n
Governors' meeting, Baltimore, Dec. 1911, 23:567,n1, 569
Gozzoli, Benozzo, 15:353
grade crossings, see New Jersey, grade crossing elimination
Graduate College and the Quads (McMahon), 20:382n6
Grady, Thomas Francis, 19:102n1
graft, 20:416; 23:209, 635; honest and dishonest, 21:303,n3, 304, 342, 399-400, 419, 443, 479, 480, 481, 482, 483, 484, 485
Graft as an Expert Trade in Pittsburgh (Russell), 21:342n7
Graham, Benjamin, 15:137
Graham, Isabella Hummel (Mrs. John Young), 15:189
Graham, John Young, 15:189,n1, 218
Graham, Kenneth, 15:510
Graham, Mrs., 15:101,n1
Graham, Samuel Jordan, 24:315,n1
grain, 24:70, 85-86, 106, 125, 184, 193, 194

Grain Dealers' Association, **24:**185
Gramercy Park (N.Y.C.), **25:**94n1
*Grammar of Science* (Pearson), **19:** 666,n2
Granbery, William Langley, **16:**236,n1, 406, 476,n1; **17:**483,n2, 488, 492, 495; **23:**288,n1
Grand Army of the Republic, **16:**30-31, 35
Grand Ducal Observatory, Königstuhl-Heidelberg, **18:**578
Grand Hotel, Glasgow, **18:**345
Grandison, Charles N., **21:**171-72,n1
Grand Junction, Colo., preferential ballots, **23:**456
Grand Rapids, Michigan, **24:**58n2, 66; city government, **17:**571,n3; Democratic Club, **23:**341n2
*Grand Rapids News*, **24:**58n2
Granges, **22:**255
Grant, Charles Travers, **17:**265-66,n1
Grant, Frederick Dent, **16:**11,n4
Grant, Ulysses Simpson, **14:**311, 347; **16:**12n4, 221; **21:**367; **23:**516
Grant, William Henry, **18:**560-61,n1; **19:**544-45,n1
Grant Locomotive Works, Philadelphia, **15:**192
Granville, Ohio, high school, **16:**253
Grasmere, Westmorland, **16:**437, 440, 441, 449, 450; **18:**361, 383, 391, 393, 397, 399, 402, 405, 409, 414, 415, 422; **20:**424,n2; **21:**619; **25:**572; Moderate Reform Road, **18:**365,n6, 380; Radical Reform Road, **18:**411; Red Lion Inn, **18:**410; Rothay Hotel, **14:**523; **18:**364,n1, 370, 373, 375, 394, 396, 402, 413; St. Oswald's Church, **18:**393; WW in, **18:**364-68, 370, 373, 374, 376, 377, 381; Wilsons in, **14:**522, 523, 546
Grasty, Charles Henry, **21:**102,n1; **23:**546-47; **24:**146, 163, 401, 519-20; **25:**48, 128-29, 554,n1
Gratz, Simon, **15:**175-76, 544-45
Graustock, University of, **16:**257
Graves, John Temple, **25:**233,n1
Gray, George, **18:**280n2, 360, 512; **20:**336,n1
Gray, George R., **22:**54
Gray, James Gordon, **15:**274-75,n3
Gray, James Richard, **22:**506-507,n1; **24:**274,n1, 306, 384
Gray, John Clinton, **15:**169
Gray, Joseph Francis, **23:**557,n4
Gray, Thomas, **14:**503
Greacen, Edmund William, **23:**81-82,n6
Greacen, Ethol Booth (Mrs. Edmund William), **23:**82,n7
Greacen, Nanette, **23:**82,n8
*Great American Universities* (Slosson), **19:**7n3
Great Britain, **22:**514, 514n4; arbitration treaties, **23:**520; **25:**551; constitution, **23:**186; government, **23:**280,
281, 321, 579; House of Commons, **23:**579; Panama Canal tolls, **25:**606n1; *Parliamentary Debates*, **17:**348n1
*Great Britain* (Dilke), **14:**14
Grecian Archipelago, **20:**359
Greek Americans, **25:**29
Greek Revival architecture, W. F. Magie on, **14:**140
Greek tragedy, **23:**373
Greeley, Horace, **24:**116
Green, Andrew White, **16:**223,n2
Green, Anna Katharine, **25:**458,n3
Green, Charles Ewing, **14:**84n1
Green, Elmer Ewing, **15:**16
Green, Harrington, **20:**536,n2, 537
Green, Henry Woodhull, **14:**144, 168n1, 475, 500; **15:**116, 570, 572; **16:**266, 289, 500; **17:**594, 595,n2; **18:**246n4, 624; **19:**223, 437, 439, 712; **20:**5, 12, 13, 17, 29-30, 48, 60, 82, 87, 97, 104, 130n1, 357, 484, 514,n1; **21:**152
Green, James Albert, **20:**536-38,n1
Green, James Monroe, **14:**354,n2
Green, John Richard, **14:**141, 310, 340, 350, 516; **18:**89; **22:**190
Green, Joseph Coy, **20:**536,n2, 537
Green, Kate or Katheryne, **22:**364,n1
Green, Louise Coy (Mrs. James Albert), **20:**536,n3
Green, Mary Livingston Potter (Mrs. Charles Ewing), **14:**84
Green, Robert Morris, **20:**536,n2
Green, William, **25:**399-400, 417
Green Creek, N. J., Norbury's Landing, **23:**273
Greene, Clayton Wellington, **16:**203,n2
Greene, George Wellington, **24:**272,n4
Greene, Jerome Davis, **16:**396,n1, 412
Greene, Katherine Larned (Mrs. William Maxwell), **20:**132,n1, 138, 155
Greene, William Brenton, Jr., **17:**99n2
Greene, William Maxwell, **20:**132,n1, 138, 155
Greenock, Renfrew, Scotland, **18:**408, 417
Greensboro, N. C., **24:**386, 388-89, 390
Greensboro, Vt., **15:**403
Greensburg, Pa., Princeton alumni, **19:**146
Greenville, Del., **23:**436
Greenwood, Joseph Rudd, **16:**199
Greer, David Hummell, **16:**228,n1, 230; **22:**514,n3; **23:**584
Greet, Sir Philip Barling Ben, **15:**238,n1, 268, 340, 341; **20:**172,n2; **22:**36
Gregg, Curtis Hussey, **23:**249n5
Gregg, David, **14:**299,n1
Gregg, John Robert, **25:**xi
Gregg Publishing Co., **25:**xi
Gregg Shorthand, **24:**xi-xiii; **25:**xi
Gregory I, Saint (Gregory the Great), **15:**241, 338
Gregory, Charles Noble, **21:**615,n5
Gregory, Julian Arthur, **22:**225,n1, 245

Gregory, Thomas Watt, 23:268,n2
Grenoble, 15:444
Grenoble, University of, 16:256
Grey, Albert Henry George, 4th Earl Grey, 18:622, 625; 19:23
Grice, Mary Van Meter (Mrs. Edwin C.), 20:135,n6
Gries, Moses J., 18:217,n1
Griffin, Edward Herrick, 14:260; 21:586-87,n1; 23:248, 285
Griffin, Nathaniel Edward, 16:132, 255, 421; 17:233, 408
Griffin, Patrick R., 23:536n2
Griffin, Patrick Robert, 21:473,n1
Griffin, Solomon Bulkley, 23:248-49, 284; 25:554
Griffin, Thomas, 22:100, 280
Griffin, Thomas F. A., 22:574,n2,3, 575; 23:343, 536n1; 25:584,n7
Griggs, John W., 22:250,n2, 338
Griggs, John William, 15:146,n7; 21:276, 277, 280, 283, 301, 305, 357-58, 476
Grim, Webster, 22:409n2; 23:230,n8
Grimes, James Lee, 14:388
Grimké, Francis James, 25:571
Grindelwald, Switzerland, 16:178
Grinnell College, 16:16, 16n2,3,4
Griscom, Lloyd Carpenter, 15:150,n2,3; 21:252n6
Griswold, Benjamin Howell, Jr., 23:568,n7
Griswold, Florence, 18:346n9, 376, 387, 390, 390n5; 19:193n5, 307, 308, 313, 317, 355, 357; 20:541, 543; 23:81,n3
Griswold, Stephen M., 14:298
Griswold family of Connecticut, 19:308
Groesbeck, Ernest, 22:202-203,n3
Grogan, Edward Wesley, 23:191,n1
Groningen, University of, 16:82
Gronna, Asle Jorgenson, 23:132n1
Grosscup, Edward E., 22:321-22; 23:262n3, 316, 396, 471, 542; 24:429, 584; 25:579n2, 580, 582,n5
Grosscup, Peter Stenger, 17:503n3
Grossman, Rudolph, 18:523,n1, 550
Groton School, 16:192n1; 18:546, 546n2
*Grover Cleveland: A Study in Courage* (Nevins), 21:345n13
*Growth of American Foreign Policy: A History* (Leopold), 22:514n1
Grubb, Edward Burd, 22:231,n2, 545,-n3,4; 23:534
Grubb, Elizabeth Wadsworth Van Rensselaer (Mrs. Edward Burd I), 22:545,n4
Grubb, Violet Sopwith (Mrs. Edward Burd II), 22:545-46,n3
Gruby ware, 14:39
Gruening, Ernest, 23:175n2
Grunder, Garel A., 20:309n2, 312n2
Guadalupe-Hidalgo Treaty, 17:311
*Guardian* (Boston), 21:21n1, 47n1, 275n5; 24:556, 558n3
Guerin, Jules, 15:573,n1, 574
Guffey, James McClurg, 17:121; 21:623n1; 22:409n1,2, 522, 522n1; 23:154,n3, 229,n1; 24:7n1, 27
Guffey, Joseph Finch, 21:623,n1; 24:315,n1
Guggenheim, Daniel, 21:546n3; 25:190, 397
Guggenheimer, Untermyer & Marshall, 23:314n1; 24:534,n1
Guide, Mrs., 15:396,n2
Guigon, Alexander Barclay, 22:383-84,n1
Guild, Curtis, Jr., 17:228n1, 497n1, 499, 508n1; 25:576-77,n1
Guilde Internationale, Paris, 17:556
Guillaume (servant in Paris), 15:538, 542
Guinn, Walter, 21:52,n1
Gulf of Mexico, 23:419
Gulick, Alexander Reading, 15:549,n2; 16:500; 19:118,n5
Gunnison, Herbert Foster, 20:59,n3
Gurley, Boyd F., 22:584
Gustavus Adolphus College, St. Peter, Minn., 16:256
Gutekunst, Frederick (photographer), 15:141,n1
Guthrie, George Wilkins, 22:409n1, 441n3, 443; 23:154, 220, 229, 230; 25:527
Guttenberg, N. J., 21:464; 22:344
Guyot, Arnold Henry, 15:364,n2; 17:568,n1
Guy Fawkes' Day, 25:55
Guy's Cliff, Warwickshire, Wilsons at, 14:530
Gwinnet, Button, 17:249

Hack, Otto Anthony, 14:387
Hackensack, N. J., 21:11, 141; 23:634n1; Second Regiment Armory, 21:446, 452; Trinity Hall, 23:450; WW campaign speeches, 21:446-49, 452-54; 23:449-51
Hackett, Horatio Balch, 20:539
Hackettstown, N. J., 23:467; American House, 21:384; WW campaign speech, 21:383-84
Hadley, Agnes Lee, 25:93,n1
Hadley, Arthur Twining, 14:91,n3, 135-37, 138, 194, 294, 306n3, 560; 15:223n2; 16:281, 284, 331; 18:53,n1, 522, 524; 19:109, 110, 448,n2, 556,n1,2, 561-62, 577-78, 602, 623-24, 627, 628, 652, 672, 699, 708, 728n1; 20:11, 12, 54, 72, 88, 91, 118, 487-88, 497, 538, 547; 22:130, 184, 187
Hadley, Helen Harrison Morris (Mrs. Arthur Twining), 14:137, 138
Hadley, Herbert Spencer, 23:5n1, 10, 320; 24:494; 25:93
Hadow, Grace Eleanor, 18:394,n2, 395,-n3
Hadow, William Henry, 18:395,n3

Haeckel, Ernst, 19:314,n6
Haese, Henry F., 23:536n1
Hagemeyer, Arthur Herbert, 19:165, 708,n3
Haggard, Sir Henry Rider, 19:315n2
Hague, Frank, 24:436n5
Hague Conferences, 25:19
Hahn, Simon, 21:7,n3
Hale, Edward Everett, 15:502
Hale, Eugene, 20:385
Hale, Harriet Knowles Swinburne (Mrs. William Gardner), 14:454,n3
Hale, Henry Ewing, 16:301
Hale, William Bayard, 20:565n4; 22: 142n1, 414,n1, 414, 434, 438-39, 526; 23:200n1, 655n3; 24:28n2, 380,n1, 518n2; 25:609,n1
Hale, William Gardner, 14:454,n3; 17: 112,n1, 113, 130, 173, 588,n7
Hale, William Harlan, 22:414n, 526
Hall, Allen Garland, 23:211, 212
Hall, Arthur Cleveland, 14:457n4, 474, 488
Hall, Charles Cuthbert, 14:115, 550,n3; 16:282; 17:125
Hall, Charles Waite, 14:388
Hall, Edward Kimball, 20:539
Hall, Frank M., 23:97,n2
Hall, Granville Stanley, 14:554n1; 15: 116, 581-82,n1; 18:590,n2; 19:240,n1
Hall, Henry C., 25:362n2
Hall, James Knox Polk, 23:229,n5
Hall, John (Reverend), 25:454,n3, 455, 457
Hall, John Porter, 15:375
Hall, Luther Egbert, 24:483
Hall, Lyman, 17:249
Hall, Margaret Tannerhill Sprunt, 15:154n1, 178
Hall, Philip Louis, M.D., 23:97,n2
Hall, Susan Eliza, 15:154,n1, 178, 217-18, 239
Hall, Thomas Cuming, 15:139,n1, 140; 19:551,n1
Hall, William K., 14:253
Hall, William Maclay, Jr., 17:385,n1
Hall, William Thomas, 14:331
Halle, Saxony, 12:245
Halle, University of, 16:249, 250, 253; 17:161, 161n2, 556; 19:677
Halsey, Abram Woodruff, 14:47, 131,n2, 186-87, 194, 195, 397; 15:27, 203, 271, 386, 387, 389, 390, 571; 18:8-9, 63; 19:64, 109n3, 123,n1; 20:218; 25:390
Halsey, Charles Woodruff, 18:456
Halsey, Richard Townley Haines, 15: 52n1, 363-64,n1, 385, 464-65
Hamburg, N. J., 21:413
Hamer, Wesley, 25:361,n4
Hamill, Hugh, 14:475n1
Hamill, Hugh Henderson, 16:5
Hamill, James Alphonsus, 21:19,n4; 22:72,n1; 24:287,n1, 408, 434n2,3
Hamill, Samuel McClintock, 14:475n1

Hamilton, Alexander, 15:44, 537; 16:53, 206, 316; 18:98, 119, 122, 200, 201, 266, 538; 19:369, 370, 377, 378, 467; 20:229, 339-40,n1, 350; 22:444-45; 23:108, 293, 322; 24:225, 374; 25:84
Hamilton, Bermuda, 17:3, 14, 16, 18, 22, 25, 29; 25:551; Hamilton Hotel, 17: 3,n3, 4, 5, 6, 8, 606, 610n2; 18:4; 20: 125, 133, 138, 141, 148, 176, 178, 179, 185, 187, 210; St. Andrew's Presbyterian Church, 17:22,n1, 25
Hamilton, Dr., of Windermere, 18:382,-n2, 388,n1
Hamilton, Lord Frederick Spencer, 22:392,n1
Hamilton, Peter Joseph, 15:4, 217, 239, 395
Hamilton, Bermuda, Royal Gazette, 17:22n, 23n1, 28n2, 610n, 610n2, 616n; 18:3-5; 25:551n, 563n, 575n
Hamilton Club (Paterson, N. J.), 25:514
Hamilton College, 16:45-47n1, 239, 247, 257
Hamiltonian doctrine, 24:11
Hamlin, Alfred Dwight Forster, 16: 535,n5
Hamlin, Charles Sumner, 24:395n2, 559, 585; 25:42; banking reform, 24:581-83
Hammerstein, Oscar I, 20:173n4
Hammond, John Hays, 17:159,n1; 22: 478,n2
Hammond, Natalie Harris (Mrs. John Hays), 17:159
Hammond typewriter, 25:452,n2
Hampden-Sydney College, 16:132, 252
Hampton, N. J., 21:383
Hampton Normal and Agricultural Institute, 15:131,n2; 18:603, 629-30; 19:49,n2, 69; 22:140; 23:192, 192n3
Hancock, Albert Elmer, 20:89
Hancock, Elmer N., 23:557,n6
Hancock, John, 17:249
Hand, Robert Edmonds, 21:286,n4; 22: 476; 23:365,n1; 24:277n1; 25:477,n5, 480
Handbook of Princeton (Williams), 14: 490n4; 15:427-31, 436
Handbook for the Study of Roman History (Abbott), 18:575
Handley, Lorin Andrew, 23:44,n12, 251-52,n1
Handy, Parker Douglas, 17:352n2; 19:118,n4, 119, 175, 481; 20:22, 23, 208,n2, 218, 222, 227, 244, 246, 324, 361, 388, 392, 404, 476, 491, 501-502; 21:138
Haney, Bert Emory, 23:64,n5
Haney, Conrad, 21:176,n3,4
Hanley, Edward W., 22:161n1
Hanover, N. H., 15:571n2, 572; 16:194, 245; 18:570; 19:421; WW address, 19:413-18; WW in, 19:408,n1, 410
Hanson, Charles A., 22:61,n3
Hanson, Victor Henry, 24:576,n2

Hapgood, Norman, **19:**156; **22:**131n4; **25:**274,n1, 287, 449,n1, 555, 558, 609-10
Harbaugh, William H., **21:**148n1
Harben, William Nathaniel, **14:**72n5
Harcourt, Lewis, **17:**307,n3
Hardaway, Prof., **16:**73
Hardenbergh, Henry Janeway, **17:**141,-n2, 150-51, 153, 156-57, 158, 160, 168, 172-73, 173-74, 272, 293, 339-41, 344-46, 346, 349, 350, 351, 361-62, 368, 369, 387
Hardin, John Ralph, **21:**610; **22:**37, 86n1
Hardinge, Sir Charles, **15:**150n3
Hardy, Rufus, **24:**358, 444,n2
Hare, William Hobart, **18:**388n4
Harker's Hotel, York, England, **14:**525
Harlan, James Shanklin, **16:**5
Harlan, John Marshall (1833-1911), **19:**48n
Harlan, John Marshall (1899-1971), **19:**48n
Harlan, John Maynard, **19:**47,n1; **20:**519-20, 540-41, 548, 556-57, 558; **21:**266, 389; **22:**74,n2
Harlan, Richard Davenport, **14:**248
Harland, Henry, **15:**350n1
Harlow, Samuel Allen, **21:**110,n1
Harmon, Austin Morris, **17:**161,n3, 163, 556
Harmon, Judson, **16:**362n1; **20:**289,n3, 297, 504, 544, 546, 558, 562n1; **21:**9n2, 29, 71, 144, 275n2, 300,n3, 386, 596, 598; **22:**7, 15, 43, 133n1, 213-14,n3, 230, 255n1, 275, 285n2, 437,n2, 466,n3, 503,n3; **23:**31n1, 61, 135,n2, 173,n2, 234n5, 237, 238, 248, 255n2, 258, 259, 268, 289, 291, 311, 327,n1, 341, 359, 360, 391, 458, 513, 518, 520, 552, 568n1, 601, 615, 623, 652, 653; **24:**26, 65n1, 165, 185, 248,n1, 288, 299, 386, 472; **25:**203-204; campaign funds, **24:**254; Democratic National Convention, first ballot, **24:**483n2; tenth ballot, **24:**507n1; Georgia primary vote, **24:**381-n2; Maryland primary vote, **24:**387n1; Nebraska primary vote, **24:**358n2; Pennsylvania primary vote, **24:**330n3; Tennessee, **24:**78, 79, 403n1; portrait, **24:** illustration section
Harper, Belle Dunton Westcott (Mrs. George McLean), **14:**29, 53; **15:**340-41, 396; **16:**159; **17:**366; **18:**388
Harper, George McLean, **14:**29, 53, 297, 326, 327, 329, 395, 403; **15:**29-32, 52n1, 110-11, 340-41, 396, 403,n3; **16:**570; **17:**242,n1, 289-90, 366; **18:**388; **20:**73-74
Harper, George McLean, Jr., **14:**53,n1
Harper, Henry Sleeper, **22:**39,n8
Harper, Isabel Westcott, **14:**53,n1
Harper, Joseph Henry, **22:**38,n4
Harper, William Rainey, **14:**194, 198,

225, 248, 429,n3, 546; **16:**224, 273, 280, 282-83; **17:**601
Harper & Brothers, **14:**31,n2, 38, 88, 99, 108, 110, 115, 122, 141-42, 438,n3; **15:**56-57, 155, 327-28; **16:**94-95, 343, 387, 390, 404-405; **19:**402n2; **20:**583; **21:**51,n1; **22:**21n1, 38-39,n4,5,7,8, 46,n1, 48; **24:**223
*Harper's Bazar*, **16:**387n2
Harper's Ferry, Dunker Church, **14:** 352-53
*Harper's Magazine*, **14:**142, 350; **16:** 144n2, 343, 387n2, 470n1, 565; **17:**620,n3
*Harper's Weekly*, **14:**91, 108, 116, 142; **16:**149n, 302n2, 307n1, 387n2, 471n2; **17:**456,n3; **19:**513n4, 556,n1; **20:**147n, 303n, 349,n2, 544; **21:**28,n6; **22:** 38,n3,5, 39,n9, 439; **23:**215n1, 282n, 513, 603, 652,n1, 656; **24:**167n3; **25:**360n2; Harvey-Watterson-Wilson affair, **24:**30, 31, 40-42, 45-47,n1, 48-50, 50n1, 61
Harrigan, William, **21:**62,n2, 541n2
Harriman, Edward Henry, 1904 campaign contribution, **25:**396n3
Harriman, Florence Jaffray Hurst (Mrs. Jefferson Borden), **22:**324,n3; **23:**261,-n1, 588; **25:**44n1, 527
Harriman, Henry Ingraham, **16:**243
Harriman, Oliver, Jr., **15:**343n1
Harris, Anna, **16:**28-29,n1, 493-94; **17:** 33-35, 137-38; Lizzie, **17:**33; mother, **17:**137, 138
Harris, Anne Yeomans (Mrs. Walter Butler), **15:**155
Harris, Frank, **15:**162
Harris, George, **14:**194; **19:**602
Harris, J. Silas, **23:**190-91
Harris, Joel Chandler, **17:**488n1
Harris, Mr. (of New Jersey), **24:**179
Harris, Tracy Hyde, **14:**289; **19:**118,n6
Harris, Walter Butler, **14:**467,n2; **15:**14, 155, 398,n2; **16:**301; **17:**408
Harris, William C., **24:**556,n3
Harris, William Torrey, **15:**116
Harris (of Virginia), **23:**631,n2
Harrisburg, Pa., **20:**352; **23:**219, 220n3, 292, 293; **24:**274n1, 392; Board of Trade Auditorium, **23:**154,n1, 156; capitol building scandals, **23:**75,n1, 209; Casino Theatre, **23:**156; Central Democratic Club, **22:**408, 409n3; Harrisburg Club, **14:**362; Princeton alumni, **14:**362-64; WW addresses, **23:**154-57; WW speech, **14:**362-64
Harrisburg (Pa.) *Patriot*, **14:**364n
Harrison, Benjamin (1726[?]-1791), **17:**249
Harrison, Benjamin (1833-1901), **17:**76; **21:**431n6, 505; **24:**13n3
Harrison, Charles Custis, **14:**337,n2; **16:**224; **22:**130,n1
Harrison, Francis Burton, **23:**638n2

Harrison, James Henry, 15:252
Harrison, Mary St. Leger Kingsley (*pseud.* Lucas Malet), 14:529,n12
Harrison, N. J., 23:535, 634n1; West Hudson Board of Trade, 22:456
Harrison, Robert L., 15:546
Harrison, William Henry, 17:319
Harrity, William Francis, 22:487,n1
Harrod, J. A., 23:517
Hart, Albert Bushnell, 20:444-45; 25:311, 543
Hart, Hastings Hornell, 25:310-11,n5
Hart, Sir Robert, 19:109
Harte, Archibald Clinton, 15:3-4, 217, 226
Hartfelder, J. M., 23:558,n12
Hartford, Conn., 16:273; 17:244; 19:168, 169, 199, 323; campaign speech, 25:234-45; Hartford Club, 16:244, 353; Owl Club, 21:168,n3, 171; Princeton alumni, 20:284, 320-21,n1, 327, 335-36, 410; Twentieth Century Club, 16:244, 273-74,n1; University Club, 17:468, 470, 582,n2; WW addresses, 16:244, 346-53; 19:215-22; WW in, 15:350; 19:224, 228, 333, 350
Hartford College, Ky., 16:247
*Hartford Courant*, 16:244n, 352n, 353n; 17:244,n1, 261n1, 582n2
*Hartford Daily Times*, 24:177n; 25:245n
Hartford School of Religious Pedagogy, 14:458n3, 468-69
*Hartford Seminary Record*, 19:222n
Hartford Theological Seminary, 14:459-n3, 471,n2; 15:351n1,2; 16:184, 352, 353; 18:359, 376,n1, 397, 434, 512, 556; 19:199, 215,n1, 222n, 310-11,n1, 319, 473n1; 21:143; 25:568; *Hartford Theological Seminary, 1834-1934* (Greer), 14:459n3; *Services at the Inauguration of William Douglas Mackenzie . . .*, 15:351n2
*Hartford Times*, 17:244,n1, 261, 458,n2,3
Hartley, Frank, M.D., 18:622, 625; 19:23
Hartman Theater (Columbus, Ohio), 25:198n1
Hartridge, Walter Charlton, 23:557,n8
Hartzog, Henry Simms, 22:478,n2
*Harvard Crimson*, 14:388; 15:200
Harvard Democratic Club, 24:94
Harvard Graduates' Magazine, 16:520-n1; 17:226n, 228n,n1; 19:289n, 293, 407n1, 439,n1
*Harvard Lampoon*, 22:38n5
*Harvard Lectures on Greek Subjects* (Butcher), 16:28n1
*Harvard Monthly*, 18:529n
Harvard Studies in Classical Philology, 17:114
Harvard University, 14:157; 15:65, 100n3, 234n, 292n, 447; 16:20n1, 22n2, 41, 46, 89-90, 131, 135, 136, 137, 142, 145, 146, 170, 171, 172, 192, 249, 250, 251, 252, 253, 254, 255, 257, 258, 272n1, 306, 315, 396, 412, 489, 508, 510, 520; 17:59,n2, 106n2, 219n1, 225-29, 233, 236, 240, 244, 274, 286, 304, 409-10, 554, 556, 557, 587-88; 18:18, 27, 67, 230, 246, 297n1, 298, 307, 308, 519,n1, 546, 577, 578, 579, 607, 627; 19:6,n2, 10, 11n2,4, 56-57, 74,n3, 122, 133, 254, 263, 264n1, 266, 270, 272, 290, 294, 383, 394, 409, 410, 411, 448, 480, 556, 558, 602, 603, 606, 619, 623, 625n1, 652, 672, 677, 678, 679, 699, 700; 20:54, 72, 75, 187n1, 265n2, 290, 337-39, 436, 444, 475, 487, 539, 540, 547, 548, 556, 560; 21:167, 258, 259, 579,n1; 24:93; Corporation (President and Fellows), 18:618,n2, 627; 19:210; faculty compared with Princeton's, 14:121, 154; Graduate School of Applied Science (proposed), 19:74,n3; Graduate School of Business Administration, 19:74,n3; Harvard Union, 16:520,n1; 18:233, 234; Higginson Hall (Harvard Union), 14:128; Law School, 19:483; 22:213; Lawrence Scientific School, 19:74,n3; Lowell endowment, *see* Smith Professorship; Medical School, 19:627; Observatory, 16:488; overseers, 18:618,n3; Phi Beta Kappa, 16:396, 412; 19:11,n2, 277-89, 319; Princeton Fellowship, 19:619, 624, 627; residential colleges advocated, 17:105n2; senior societies, 14:480; Smith Professorship, 16:172,n1, 176; stadium, 23:28; WW at, 19:410, 411
Harvard Woodrow Wilson Club, 24:94, 360
Harvey, Alma Arabella Parker (Mrs. George Brinton McClellan), 20:147n, 541n1; 22:39,n10, 46, 260
Harvey, David, Jr., 22:173n1
Harvey, Dorothy, 22:39,n11, 46
Harvey, George Brinton McClellan, 14:290; 16:292n1, 299-301, 307, 329-30, 331, 338, 343, 455n1, 471n2, 531-33, 549-50, 554-55, 560; 17:9-10,n2, 12, 23; 18:258-59, 352; 19:191, 384, 402, 700; 20:146-48n, 177, 541,-n1, 544, 546, 561-62, 563-64, 565n, 568, 576-77, 577n2; 21:5, 6, 17, 24-25, 27-28, 35n1, 35, 37n1, 40-42,n1, 46, 52-53, 54, 61, 85, 87-90, 148, 166, 243, 245, 292-93, 297, 320, 327, 338, 433, 435, 585; 22:13, 38-41, 46-48, 72, 73,n3, 86n1, 143, 160, 181n1, 185, 214, 227-28, 237, 260, 274, 326-27, 393, 435,n1, 466,n3,4, 467,n1, 479, 516, 532,n6, 543, 571; 23:134, 222, 248, 513, 516, 548, 560n2, 603,n1, 630, 652, 656; 24:30, 31, 40-42, 45-57, 48-50, 59-64, 68, 71, 72-74, 77-78, 81,n1, 96, 400,n2; 25:512-13, 515, 564-65
Harvey, Henry, 17:138n1

Harvey, Penn, 17:137,n1
Harvey, Thomas William, M.D., 15: 248n1
Harvey-Watterson affair, 24:40-42,-n1,2,3, 45-47,n1, 48-50,n1, 59-63, 64, 71, 72-74, 77-78, 79, 80-81,n1, 97n2, 118, 237
Haskell, Paul T., 23:557
Haskins, Charles Homer, 17:164, 208, 214
Haskins, Frederick Jennings, 24:16,n1
Hastings, Gen. (at Bermuda), 20:176,n1; Mrs., 20:139, 176, 180, 187; daughter, 20:187
Hastings, Harold Ripley, 16:60, 132, 252-53, 528; 17:162,n4, 162, 408; 19: 676
Hastings, James, 16:400,n3
Hatcher, John Bell, 14:223,n3
Hatfield, Edwin, 18:339n2
Hatfield House, Herts, 14:233
Haughton, Percy Duncan, 19:562,n2, 578, 602, 627, 699, 704, 705; 20:72, 118, 487, 488, 538-40, 547, 548, 559, 560, 562-63
Haussling, Jacob, 21:564,n2; 22:242n2
Havemeyer, Horace, 20:312n2
Haverford, Pa., Poplar Grove, 23:246
Haverford College, 16:239, 465, 511; 18:67, 420, 449, 459, 466, 466-67; 20:89, 539; alumni, 14:106; WW address, 18:459-66
*Haverford College Bulletin*, 18:465n
Havron, John, Jr., 18:580
Hawaiian Islands, 24:352
Hawarden, S. D., 25:161
Hawes, Gene R., 17:352n2
Hawes Water, Westmorland, 18:389
Hawks, Francis Lister, 14:342-43,n6
Hawthorne, Nathaniel, 14:71
Hay, John, 16:297, 344; 17:159; 18:121
Hay, Marion E., 23:323
Hay-Bunau-Varilla Treaty, 15:60n1
Hayden Company, 16:153
Hayes, Alfred, 18:364,n3
Hayes, Alfred, Jr., 18:364,n2, 367; 20: 424-25, 467
Hayes, Christine Grace Robertson (Mrs. Alfred, Jr.), 18:364,n3
Hayes, Mary Miles Van Valzah (Mrs. Alfred), 18:365,n3
Hayes, Rutherford Birchard, 23:303n1
Hayes, William Van Valzah, M.D., 14:423,n2, 424
Hayne, Robert Young, 14:251, 282; 15: 45; 18:101
Haynes, James C., 25:164n2
Hays, Isaac Minis, 14:285, 380, 381, 405
Hay-Pauncefote Treaty, 25:606n1
Hazeltine, Mayo William, 18:272n1
Hazeltine, Orre, 16:355
Hazen, Azel Washburn, 14:328, 515n2; 16:13, 338; 21:107; 22:37
Hazen, Mary Butler Thompson (Mrs.

Azel Washburn), 14:328; 16:13; 21: 107,n1
Hazen, Maynard Thompson, 14:328
Heald, Charles Mercer, 24:312n3
*Health of a Nation: Harvey W. Wiley and the Fight for Pure Food* (Anderson), 25:282n1
Heard, Elizabeth Burt (Mrs. William Augustus), 18:417,n2
Heard, William Augustus, 18:417,n2
*Hearings before the Committee on Investigation of United States Steel Corporation*, 23:299n8
Hearst, William Randolph, 16:372,n2; 18:373n3; 19:499, 499n3; 20:401, 402n1; 21:85n1; 23:263, 329, 584, 590,n1, 632; 24:244,n1, 225,n2, 268, 270, 290, 292, 298, 299, 301, 384, 518, 520, 531, 563, 574n2; 25:51, 233,n2, 362; Democratic party, 24:363-64; portrait, 24: illustration section
Hearst Newspapers, 24:383n1, 574,n1; 25:50-51, 233, 360n2, 361n4
Hearst-Made War News (Russell), 25: 360n2
Heath, D. C. & Co., 14:356
Hebrews, 22:317, 320
Hebron Academy, Hebron, Maine, 16:251
Hedges, Job Elmer, 14:290, 291; 15:60,n5; 19:170,n2, 253; 20:50, 211, 373,n1; 24:179, 180; 25:284
Heermance, Radcliffe, 19:679
Hefford, Robert Rodman, 24:312n4
Heflin, James Thomas, 22:28,n1
Hegel, Georg Wilhelm Friedrich, 14: 104,n1, 547n2,3; 18:430
*Hegel's Logic: An Essay in Interpretation* (Hibben), 14:104,n1, 547,n2
Heidelberg, University of, 15:558; 16:247, 250, 257, 509; 18:578; 19:677
Heifner, Charles G., 23:76-77,n1, 78, 79, 597-98
Heine, Heinrich, 15:118
Heinz, Henry John, 15:126, 520, 521-22
Helen (guest at Tedcastle's), 14:4
Helm, Lynn, 20:21,n1, 66, 71, 86; 23:44, 51, 325, 326
Helm, Nathan Wilbur, 14:91,n2; 21: 320,n2
Helmolt, Hans Ferdinand, 14:339,n3
Helping to Make a President (Inglis), 16:455n1; 20:147n, 541n1; 22:181n1
Hemans, Lawton Thomas, 24:484,n3
Hemphill, Charles Robert, 22:21,n1
Hemphill, Emma Muller (Mrs. Charles Robert), 22:21,n2
Hemphill, James Calvin, 16:286n1, 286-88, 533, 534; 21:539n1, 579; 24: 40,n2
Henderson, George, 19:159,n1,2, 172
Henderson, Louisa Patterson (Mrs. Robert Randolph), 19:172,n1

Henderson, Rebecca Magruder (Mrs. George), **14**:463,n1
Henderson, Robert Randolph, **14**:380, 463; **15**:234, 360n2, 361; **18**:445-46; **19**:159, 172, 190, 195, 252; **20**:50; **21**:555-56,n2, 599-600; **22**:55; **24**:82,n2
Henderson, Walter T., **23**:507,n5
Hendrick, Burton Jesse, **22**:81n1, 85, 85,n4, 142n1, 504n1; **23**:303-304,n1,3, 311
Hendrickson, Charles Elvin, Jr., **19**: 598-99,n1; **21**:346,n15
Hendrickson, George Lincoln, **17**:113,n2, 588,n6
Hendrix, Eugene Russell, **14**:515,n2; **23**:511,n2
Hendrix, Joseph Clifford, **14**:200,n2
Heney, Francis Joseph, **21**:342,n5; **22**: 412n2
Henneman, John Bell, **15**:167,n1
Hennessey, James, **21**:412; **23**:536n2; **25**:581, 584
Hennessy, Charles O' Connor, **22**:124,n1; **23**:386; **25**:566n1
Henney, William Franklin, **16**:352, 353,n1; **20**:320,n2
Hennings, Robert E., **24**:383n1
Henry V of England, **18**:433-34
Henry VII of England, **17**:87
Henry, Alexander, **15**:126,n1, 492; **16**: 188,n2
Henry, Howard Houston, **19**:602-603,n1, 623, 628, 699, 704-705; **20**:54-55, 72, 118, 487, 488, 539-40, 559-60, 562-63
Henry, James Addison, **16**:145, 278
Henry, (James) Bayard, **14**:16,n4, 78, 144, 161, 169, 463; **15**:175, 417, 426, 435, 437, 509, 527, 528, 569, 570, 572, 575; **16**:5, 175, 266, 277-78, 278, 321, 336, 448, 526, 565; **17**:19, 126, 282, 300, 301-307, 308, 309, 338-39, 340, 341, 381, 405, 441, 594; **18**:360, 515; **19**:101, 122, 303, 439, 603n1, 711, 712, 748; **20**:14, 15, 63, 124, 222, 324, 353, 357, 362, 377-78, 395, 484, 489; **21**:152, 362n1, 366
Henry, Jane Irwin Robeson (Mrs. James Bayard), **17**:307; **19**:101,n2
Henry, Joseph, **19**:451; **20**:485n1
Henry, Robert Lee, **23**:508,n7; **24**:165n3, 284,n2, 287,n1, 305, 361n1, 369, 434n3, 467, 581; **25**:563, 564, 626
Henry, Thomas Maxwell, **19**:66-67,n1, 67-68; **20**:303
Henry bill, **24**:369
Henry R. Worthington Co., of Kearny, N. J., **23**:535n2
Hepburn, James Curtis, M.D., **14**:191; **16**:23,n2, 29; **18**:13,n1
Hepburn Act of 1906, **17**:520,n5, 584n1
Heppenheimer, William C., **21**:473
Herbert, Sir Michael Henry, **14**:388
Herford, Oliver (Brooke), **16**:33n6; **18**: 428,n2,3; **19**:235,n2

Hering, Rudolph, **18**:63,n1, 64, 248; Hering and Fuller, hydraulic and sanitary experts, New York, **18**:64n1
Hermann, Joseph A., **21**:560
*Hermann und Dorothea* (Goethe), **19**:571
Hermitage Hotel (Nashville), **24**:190, 191n1
Herndon (Englishman), **18**:400
hernia, **15**:571n1, 574, 576, 577
Herodotus, **17**:463; **19**:597
Herr, Charles F., **23**:449,n1
Herrmann, Jesse, **19**:174
Hertford, Richard Seymour-Conway, 4th Marquis of, **14**:528n9
Hessellius, Gustavus, **15**:66n2
Hewett, Waterman Thomas, **14**:200-201,n1,3
Hewett-Thayer, Harvey Waterman, **19**:570, 571, 576
Hewitt, Abram Stevens, **14**:113,n2
Hexateuch (Hastings, ed.), **16**:400,n3
Heyburn, Weldon Brinton, **22**:368,n2, 371,n4, 372
Hibben, Elizabeth Grier (Beth; afterward Mrs. Richard Maxwell Scoon), **14**:34, 97, 546, 551, 552, 553, 555; **15**:146,n3, 203, 265, 300, 301, 312, 384, 396, 397, 410, 421; **16**:275; **17**:269, 284
Hibben, Jenny Davidson (Mrs. John Grier), **14**:8, 34, 50-51, 57, 86, 93, 95, 104, 106, 111, 118, 121-22, 224, 387, 418, 425, 428, 441, 499, 520-21, 545-47, 551-53, 555-56; **15**:47, 110, 117, 118, 119, 120, 131, 134, 135, 137, 140, 146, 152, 153, 154, 161, 162, 163, 164, 201, 207, 232, 265, 270, 300,n4, 301, 307, 317, 320, 323, 336, 352, 360, 384-85, 395-97, 410, 420, 421, 491n3, 532-33; **16**:155, 158-59, 171, 180, 213, 275, 412, 484, 544; **17**:14, 269, 284, 333, 372; **19**:290; **20**:223; **22**:573; **23**:425
Hibben, John Grier, **14**:8, 34, 50-51, 57, 86, 93, 95, 98, 104, 111, 118, 121, 205, 224, 297, 326, 330, 386-87, 395, 418, 425, 428, 435, 440, 441, 468-69, 499, 520, 546, 547, 551, 552, 553, 555, 556; **15**:25, 47, 104, 107, 109, 110, 112, 116, 117, 118, 119, 120, 131, 134, 135, 140, 146, 152,n1, 153, 161, 162, 163, 167, 201, 203, 207, 232, 245, 265, 270, 300,n4, 301, 307, 323, 336, 360, 384, 385, 396-97, 409-10, 420-22, 440-42, 491n3, 529, 532-33; **16**:37, 155, 158, 170-71, 172, 180, 213, 275, 398, 412, 413-14,n1,4, 422, 424, 425-26, 429, 431, 459, 484, 485, 544; **17**:14, 16-18, 147-48, 263-64, 268-69, 284, 333, 342-43, 372-73, 379, 380, 382, 399, 402, 403, 410; **18**:340, 357, 383,n5, 417,-n1, 456, 543, 626-27,n1; **19**:134n1, 143-44, 172, 222, 433, 453-54, 621, 669, 670, 673; **20**:81, 90-91, 92, 93, 98,

208, 209n1, 223, 265-66,n3, 266, 267-68, 286, 466; **22:**77, 259, 426; **23:**31, 139, 425, 479; **24:**43, 149-50, 274, 284,n1, 391; **25:**520n1, 522, 534
Hicks, John, **16:**358,n2
Hicks, Robert Drew, **15:**201n4
Hidden, Isabel McKee (Mrs. William Henry), **14:**25,n1, 41
Higbee, Enoch A., **22:**310,n4
Higgins, James Henry, **23:**235,n1; **25:** 623,n2
Higgins, Thomas F., **25:**257n2
Higginson, Henry Lee, **16:**135,n7, 142, 145, 146, 192, 520n1; **18:**303,n1, 482; **19:**166-67,n3, 200-201, 210, 619; **20:**465, 467-68; **21:**612; **22:**38; **25:**414-15, 423
Higginson, Thomas Wentworth, **17:** 122,n3
*High Court of Parliament and its Supremacy* (McIlwain), **16:**42n1; **22:** 165,n2
*Higher Realism of Woodrow Wilson and other Essays* (Link), **18:**485n2
Highland Park College (Des Moines, Iowa), **24:**222
Hightmans, Mrs., **14:**66
Hightstown, N. J., **25:**508-10; WW talk, **14:**356-57
*Highway of Fate* (Carey), **14:**520,n3
Hilfers, Henry F., **21:**82,n1
Hill, Albert Ross, **18:**490,n1; **19:**97
Hill, David Bennett, **14:**17n3; **17:**461,n2; **22:**113n2
Hill, David Jayne, **21:**615
Hill School, Pottstown, Pa., **14:**142, 144, 399; **15:**57; **16:**248, 283n1,2, 539n2; **17:**48, 50; *Hill School News*, **17:**50n
Hillery, Thomas J., **21:**340n2, 408
Hilliard, Edward Hobbs, **15:**199, 200
Hilliard, Marion Phar, **15:**202n2; **16:**39-40,n1
Hillis, Newell Dwight, **17:**78n1
Hillside Grammar School (Montclair, N. J.), **25:**467n1
Hillyer, George, **22:**488,n2; **24:**335,n1,2, 336
Hinchliffe, John, **15:**61; **22:**312,n2; **24:**358, 389; **25:**514,n2, 582
Hinners, William Henry, **22:**87n2
Hinsdale, James Henry, **18:**440n1
Hinsdale, Mary Livingston Gilbert (Mrs. James Henry), **18:**440,n1, 449
Hinton, Charles Howard, **18:**376,n1; **20:**146,n5
Hirst, David Wayne, **20:**541n1
Hirst, Francis Wrigley, **22:**209, 234
Hiss Company, **16:**153, 182, 183, 185, 388
*Histoire de France depuis les origines jusqu'à la Révolution* (ed. Lavisse), **14:**339
history, the nature and writing of, **15:**472-91

*History and Description of Roman Political Institutions* (Abbott), **18:**575
History Association of the Middle States, **14:**267
*History of Argiculture and Prices in England from the Years after the Oxford Parliament* (Rogers), **14:**558
*History of American Presidential Elections, 1789-1968* (Schlesinger and Israel), **25:**57n1
*History of Merwick* (Jones), **19:**755n2
*History of North Carolina* (Hawks), **14:**342-43,n6
*History of Rome* (Mommsen), **15:**485
*History of Sir Richard Calmady* (Malet), **14:**529,n12
*History of South Carolina in the Revolution, 1775-1780* (McCrady), **14:**353,n2
*History of South Carolina in the Revolution, 1780-1783* (McCrady), **14:**353,n2
*History of South Carolina under the Proprietary Government, 1670-1719* (McCrady), **14:**353,n2, 518
*History of South Carolina under the Royal Government, 1719-1776* (McCrady), **14:**353,n2
*History of Tammany Hall* (Myers), **21:**343n10
*History of the American People* (Wilson), **24:**132,n3, 133-34, 135-36, 219, 223,n1, 226, 241-43, 260, 269,n1, 351,n2, 383n1, 405; **25:**57, 60, 639
History of the [Carnegie] Lake (Butler), **15:**57,n1
*History of the Dividing Line, and Other Tracts* (ed. Wynne), **17:**620,n2
*History of the Ecumenical Movement, 1517-1948* (eds. Rouse and Neill), **22:**385n2
*History of the English People* (Green), **14:**141
*History of the French Revolution* (Carlyle), **18:**83n2
*History of the People of the United States* (McMaster), **14:**310, 441
*History of the Presbyterian Church in South Carolina since 1850* (eds. Jones and Mills), **22:**577n4
*History of the United States* (Smith), **14:**249
*History of the United States for Grammar Schools* (Thwaites and Kendall), **20:**583,n1
*History of the United States from the Compromise of 1850* (Rhodes), **14:**282
*History of the United States of America* (Elson), **16:**387,n1; **22:**604n2
*History of the United States since the Civil War* (Oberholtzer), **17:**262,n3
*History of the University of Virginia, 1819-1919* (Bruce), **14:**205n4; **15:**395-n3
*History of Tom Jones, a Foundling* (Fielding), **14:**503

*History of University Reform from 1800 A.D. to the Present Time . . .* (Tillyard), 17:348n1

Hitchcock, Clara Adelaide Young (Mrs. Hiram Augustus), 16:194,n1

Hitchcock, Gilbert Monell, 25:340n2

Hitchcock, Hiram Augustus, 16:194n1

Hoar, George Frisbie, 14:360n1; 15:103; 20:309,n2

Hobart College, 17:115,n3; 18:579; 19:499, 678

Hobbes, John Oliver (*pseud.* Pearl Mary Teresa Craigie), 14:529,n10

Hobbes, Thomas, 19:666

Hobbs, Edward Henry, 15:226,n3

Hoboken, N. J., 21:18, 19, 43, 112, 412; 23:163, 164, 168, 178n1, 179, 180n2, 634n1; Board of Trade, 22:468; Castle Point, 23:634; commission government, 23:161-71, 176,n1; Commission Government League, 23:161n1; Democratic City Committee, 23:162n3; German Club, 22:468n1; Home Trust Company, 16:78; Naegeli's Hotel, 21:295; Public School No. 9, 23:537; St. Mary's Hall, 21:473; 23:161n1; WW addresses, 21:473-76; 23:161-71; 25:213-20

Hoboken *Observer* (afterwards *Hudson Observer*), 21:18,n1, 19, 20, 23,n5, 26, 113, 449, 541, 582; 22:77n1, 81n1, 86, 96,n1, 113n2, 129, 360n, 415n2

Hodge, Archibald Alexander, 15:59,n2

Hodge, Charles, 14:368; 23:105

Hodge, Edward Blanchard, Jr., M.D., 15:409n1

Hodge, G. Woolsey, 16:143

Hodge, Gretchen Greene (Mrs. Edward Blanchard, Jr.), 15:409n1

Hodge, Samuel Colgate, 22:259,n1

Hodgehead, Beverly, 23:59

Hodges, Earle William, 23:233,n2, 517

Hodges, George, 17:128,n1

Hodges, George Hartshorne, 25:621n2

Hodges, LeRoy, 22:498n

Hoff, Joseph, 23:467,n1

Hoff, Joseph Stanislaus, 21:97,n1, 102-103, 120, 219; 22:415,n1,2

Hoffman, Beatrice Amanda Pope (Mrs. Harry Leslie), 19:313,n2

Hoffman, Harry Leslie, 19:313,n1

Hofmann, William J., 23:64,n9

Hogan, Joseph Francis Aloysius, 17:535,n2

Hoge, Moses Drury, 14:378,n5, 379

Hoge, Peyton Harrison, 14:336

Hogg, James Stephen, 23:458n1, 499,n2

*Hohenzollern*, S.S., 15:202n1, 208, 214, 263, 264

Hohenzollerns, 22:399

Holder, Christopher, 20:495, 498

Holland, 15:441

Holland, John W., 15:325,n2

Holland, William M., 23:507,n5

Holland House, New York City, 19:422, 499; 20:3, 7n

Hollands, Edmund Howard, 16:465

Hollenden Hotel, Cleveland, 16:397, 405

Holley, Alfred T., 22:173n1; 24:17,n1

Hollis, Daniel Walker, 16:87n2; 22:577n4

Hollis, Henry French, 24:472,n1, 473

Holly Beach (N. J.) Yacht Club, 23:272, 274, 275

Holmes (interior decorator in Philadelphia), 14:19, 23, 94

Holmes, Miss (friend of Mrs. Peck), 19:161,n4

Holmes, Oliver Wendell, (1804-94), 16:226,n5; 17:486, 506; 25:145, 320

Holmes, Oliver Wendell (1841-1935), 15:116

Holmes, Sherlock, 16:216; 23:614

Holmes, William F., 24:237n2

Holsapple, Ralph Tilden, 19:502n3

Holt, Edwin Bissell, 14:77

Holt, Hamilton, 16:110-11; 17:92,n4, 333; 22:32,n1

Holt, Henry Winston, 22:96,n2

Holt, John Allen, 17:262,n1

Holt, Orren T., 23:268,n3

Holy Cross College (Worcester, Mass.), 24:367

home rule, 25:307

Homer, 17:463, 535; 22:218

Homer, Charles Christopher, Sr., 23:568,n8

*Honor* (steam yacht), 20:359

honor system, 16:281, 284, 337

Hook, Edward B., 23:554,n6

Hooper, Ben Walter, 23:289n2; 24:206n2,3,4

Hooper, Franklin William, 20:124,n1

Hooper, J. F., 16:73

Hope, Walter Ewing, 15:252

Hope, N. J., 21:384

*Hope Loring* (Bell), 14:380,n1

Hopkins, Harvey Sylvester, 21:396,n2

Hopkins, Henry, 17:229,n2, 237

Hopkins, Herbert Webb, 14:405

Hopkins, Johns, 24:213, 214

Hopkins, Mark, M.D., 15:86, 17:229n2, 328, 329-30

Hopkins, Miss, 14:432

Horace (Quintus Horatius Flaccus), 19:594, 597

Hornbeck's Hall, Sussex, N. J. 23:465

Hornblower, William Butler, 15:527, 546

Hornbrook, Cal., 23:60

Horrocks, Rees P., 23:233-34,n1

Horton, Robert Forman, 19:21-22,n1, 31

Hosford, Hester Eloise, 24:523,n2

hosiery, 21:215-16

Hoskins, John Preston, 14:137,n3, 146-n5, 326; 15:293; 16:425,n1,2; 17:408; 19:570, 576, 625-26,n1

Hosmer, George E., 23:478,n1

Hotchkiss School, 18:495, 509

Hot Springs, Va., **23**:133, 224, 241, 265, 283, 330; **25**:573

Hotel Men's Association, **23**:315

Houdon, Jean Antoine, **15**:213

Hough, Perry B., M.D., **16**:544,n3

Houghton, Herbert Pierrepont, **17**: 163,n11, 557

Houghton, Mifflin & Co., **14**:65; **17**:334; **20**:582-83

Houn' Dawg song, **24**:251,n1

House, Edward Mandell, **22**:466,n1,3, 467; **23**:458,n1, 463, 466, 470, 480, 552, 560, 563, 595-96, 604, 630, 631, 651; **24**:81, 131, 134, 140-41, 163, 225,n1, 248, 332, 360, 385-86, 451, 464-65, 467, 489-90, 498, 509n1, 556, 576-77; **25**:51-52, 92, 111n3, 135, 198, 212-13, 232, 233-34, 283, 286, 415, 448,n1, 507-508, 530, 532, 562, 566-67, 576, 581, 603, 621-22, 623; cabinet suggestions, **25**:550,n1,2, 557-59, 563-66, 610-11, 614; on campaign curtailment, **25**:421-22; William J. McDonald, **25**:423-24,n1

House, Janet: *see* Auchincloss, Janet House

House, Loulie Hunter (Mrs. Edward Mandell), **24**:498n1

*House Called Morven: Its Role in American History, 1701-1954* (Bill), **15**: 544n1

House of Representatives *see* United States Congress, House of Representatives

*Housekeeper* (New York), **23**:305n1

Houston, David Franklin, **23**:560,n1,2, 563

Houston, Texas, **23**:268

How the Senate Stands (editorial), **25**: 585,n1

How Woodrow Wilson Won His Nomination (Stockbridge), **22**:519n4; **23**:591n1

Howard, Morus B., **25**:528,n1, 548-49

Howard, Thelma, **25**:528,n2, 548

Howard University, **25**:571n1

Howe, Annie Josephine Wilson (Mrs. George, Jr.), sister of WW, **14**:7,n8, 49, 57, 76, 117, 196, 197, 199, 294, 346, 405, 429, 435, 467, 468n3, 498; **15**:9,n2, 116, 117, 134, 136, 137, 466-67; **16**:87, 423, 432-33, 526; **17**:377; **19**:385,n1; **20**:49, 137, 189, 240, 358; **22**:293, 517,n4; **24**:149,n2

Howe, Annie Wilson, niece of WW (later Mrs. Perrin Chiles Cothran), **14**:196, 198, 199, 293-94; **15**:466; **16**:87, 423; **19**:385,n2; **20**:189, 358; **22**:234,n1, 293, 517,n4

Howe, Arthur Millidge, **16**:372,n1

Howe, Charles M., **15**:61

Howe, Edward, **14**:49,n1; **15**:120,n5, 549; **20**:136,n12; **21**:51-52; **25**:110n3

Howe, Frederick Clemson, **17**:550,n1; **22**:412n2

Howe, George, Jr., M.D., **15**:303,n6

Howe, George III, nephew of WW, **14**:7n8, 245, 428-29, 467-68, 498n2; **16**:86-87, 527; **18**:561-62, 588; **19**:19; **20**:358,n2; **22**:33-34, 517, 520; **23**:111n1; **24**:535, 542; **25**:579

Howe, George Allaire, **15**:248; **16**:377

Howe, Harland Bradley, **25**:157,n1

Howe, James Wilson, nephew of WW, **14**:468,n4; **20**:358,n1

Howe, Leavitt, **14**:102,n1

Howe, Margaret Smyth Flinn (Mrs. George III), **14**:498,n2; **16**:87,n1; **18**:562,n4, 588; **19**:19,n3; **22**:34,n1, 517n2; **23**:112,n5

Howe, Mark Antony De Wolfe, **16**:505; **18**:388n1

Howe (of Tennessee), **23**:212,n5

Howe, Rosalie Cumming (Mrs. Leavitt), **15**:102,n1

Howe, Virginia (Mrs. James W.), **20**: 358,n1

Howe, William Henry, **23**:377,n1

Howell, Burt L., **23**:273,n5, 377,n1

Howell, Clark, **21**:327,n1

Howell, George Coes, **15**:209,n1

Howell, George Samuel, **15**:209,n1

Howell, Joseph, **21**:433-44,n1

Howell, Mary Alice Streit (Mrs. George Coes), **15**:209,n1

Howells, William Dean, **14**:192, 306n3; **15**:356; **17**:122,n1; **19**:259

Howison, George Holmes, **15**:117,n2

Howland, Henry Elias, **14**:289

Howland, William Bailey, **21**:620-21

Hoyt, Florence Stevens, first cousin of EAW, **14**:38n1, 294; **15**:8,n3, 117, 304, 337; **16**:423, 429-30, 546; **17**:373,n1

Hoyt, Franklin S., **20**:582,n2, 583

Hoyt, James Alfred, Jr., **21**:588-89,n1; **23**:171, 184

Hoyt, Margaret Bliss, first cousin of EAW, **15**:8n6

Hoyt, Mary Eloise (Minnie), first cousin of EAW, **14**:17n1, 38n1, 50n4, 97,n4, 101, 102, 105, 106, 108, 109, 111, 293; **15**:211,n5, 228, 230, 233, 241, 268, 274, 297, 304, 309, 310, 313, 314, 315, 320, 322, 333, 335, 336, 337, 338, 346, 347, 352, 354, 355, 357; **16**:423-24, 429,n1; **17**:373,n1; **24**:523

Hoyt, Thomas Alexander, maternal uncle of EAW, **14**:105,n1

Hoyt, Willard Evans, **18**:347-48,n1

Hoyt, William Dana, first cousin of EAW, **14**:38,n1, 39

Hoyt, William Dana, Jr., **14**:295n; **16**:424n, 430

Hoyt, William Dearing, M.D., uncle of EAW, **14**:116,n1, 435,n2

Hoyts of Rome, Ga., **16**:493

Hubard, Robert Thruston, III, **15**:167,n1

Hubbard, Oliver H., **16**:197,n4, 208

Huckin, Charles, **17**:354,n1, 355

*Hudibras* (Butler), **17**:13
Hudson, Virginia Tyler, **22**:354
Hudson & Manhattan Railroad Co., **23**:258n1
Hudson County, N. J., **21**:7, 19, 37n1, 63,n1, 90, 97, 113, 147, 172, 173, 275, 297, 341, 346n15, 380, 412, 415, 449, 464, 540, 584n1; **22**:26, 73,n3, 81n1, 98n1, 100-101,n1, 119, 120, 133, 134, 135,n1, 137, 145, 200, 201, 245n2, 249, 258, 280, 304, 344, 352, 353, 367, 404; **23**:164, 206n5, 343, 345, 385, 387, 388, 403, 432, 535, 536n2, 537, **24**: 408, 434, 459; **25**:113,n1, 136-37, 582; Democratic organization, **20**:352n1, 577n2; Democratic party, **24**:436,n5; Princeton alumni, **19**:155n1, 598, 599; **20**:290; sheriff, **23**:208,n6; Square Deal Democratic Association, **21**:452n1; WW campaign speeches, **21**:471-76
Hudson County Democratic Association, **25**:136n1
Hudson County University Club, **15**:195
Hudson County Water Co., **23**:294-95n4,5,6, 295n6
Hudson County Water Co. *vs.* McCarter, Attorney General of the State of New Jersey, **23**:295n5
Hudson Engineering & Contracting Co., **15**:579
Hudson-Fulton Celebration: Naval Pageant, **19**:394,n5
*Hudson Observer* (Hoboken), **22**:77n1, 81n1, 86, 96,n1, 113n2, 129, 360n, 415n2
Hudspeth, Robert Stephen, **20**:563,n2, 565n; **21**:607; **22**:119, 321-22; **23**: 245n1, 255; **24**:18, 571; **25**:450, 541-42, 582; and Negroes, **25**:608
Hughes, **14**:544
Hughes, Charles Evans, **16**:220n3, 276-n1, 455n3; **17**:92n2, 247-48, 490, 513, 515-16,n1, 521; **19**:25,n4,6, 109, 499,-n2, 561, 756,n1; **21**:146, 195, 341,n4, 598, 621; **22**:85, 85n2, 140, 184; **23**:281, 627, 628; **24**:494
Hughes, Charles James, Jr., **22**:388n1, 584,n3; **25**:545n1
Hughes, Gerald, **22**:584,n3
Hughes, Thomas, **17**:327
Hughes, William, **21**:57,n2, 145, 153-54, 213, 302, 603; **22**:18, 161, 173n1; **23**:310n2, 344; **24**:287,n1, 358; **25**:31n1, 33, 37, 63, 147,n1,3, 184n1, 217-18, 311, 467, 468, 475, 477-78, 480, 481, 487, 511, 514, 582; primary vote, **25**:236n3; WW speech supporting, **25**:213-20
Hughitt, Marvin, **14**:233,n4
*Hugo Münsterberg: His Life and Work* (Münsterberg), **14**:395n1
Hulbert, Allen Schoolcraft, **17**:29n1, 607,n7, 612; **18**:450,n4, 471-72, 481,n2; **19**:162,n5, 174, 175, 191,n1,

259-60, 308, 349, 445, 704; **20**:141,n4, 156, 180, 181, 188, 371, 493; **21**:26; **22**:142, 295, 334, 454, 501, 511, 520, 547, 572; **23**:221, 265, 267, 590, 655; **24**:6, 44, 151, 329; **25**:461, 573, 616
Hulbert, Mary Allen, **24**:550-52, 561-62, 572; **25**:20-21, 45-46, 55-56, 66-67, 116, 220-21, 284-85, 416, 461, 556-57, 573-74, 615-16; *see also* Peck, Mary Allen Hulbert
Hulbert, Thomas Harbach, **17**:29n1; **23**:655
Hulett, George Augustus, **16**:130, 247; **17**:408; **19**:677
Hull, Lawrence Cameron, **14**:278
Hulsizer, Abraham Chalmers, **21**:369,n2
Hulsizer, William Richey, **17**:557
human resources, **25**:313, 314-15, 319, 330
human rights, **25**:176-77, 224; Progressive party and, **25**:388
Hume, David, **14**:503; **19**:666
Hume, Thomas, **16**:195,n1
Humphrey, Theodore Friend, **15**:425,n4; **16**:460; **20**:68,n2
Humphreys, Alexander Crombie, **14**: 290, 291, 381; **16**:224; **22**:39,n24; **24**:503-504,n1
Humphreys, Mary Prince (Mrs. Willard Cunningham), **15**:491,n3; **16**:426
Humphreys, Willard Cunningham, **14**:137,n2, 145, 200, 473; **15**:492n3; **16**:426
Hun, Caroline Gale (Mrs. Edward Reynolds), **18**:419,n2
Hun, John Gale, **14**:474; **16**:160, 162; **18**:419n2, 578; **19**:138, 139
*Hungarian American*, **24**:135n1
Hungarian Americans, **24**:135-36, 226, 241, 269n1, 406, 548, 563-64,n1; **25**:28, 275-76
Hungary, **25**:256
Hungary, Golden Bull, **18**:72-73
Hunt, Fanny Waugh (Mrs. William Holman I), **15**:358,n2,3
Hunt, George Wylie Paul, **22**:291,n1,2
Hunt, Marion Edith Waugh (Mrs. William Holman II), **15**:358n3
Hunt, Theodore Whitefield, **15**:56, 73; **16**:38, 70; **17**:231, 402, 403, 408, 424-25; **19**:70n1, 748-52; **20**:54, 72-73, 514; **21**:377-78, 602
Hunt, William Holman, **15**:358,n1
Hunter, Catherine, **18**:491,n1
Hunterdon County, N. J., **21**:354, 369n2, 381, 382; **23**:411-12; **24**:23; **25**:582
*Hunterdon County Democrat* (Flemington, N. J.), **21**:377n; **22**:162, 164n1; **23**:424n
Huntington, **16**:323
Huntington, James Otis Sargent, **14**: 550,n3; **15**:201,n4,5; **17**:125, 127, 129
Huntington, W. Va., **23**:202
Huntingtons (of Princeton), **23**:52,n5

Huntley, David P., **19:**359n1
Hurley, Edward Nash, **20:**519-20,n1, 541, 548, 556-57, 558, 561, 564
Hutchins, Harry Burns, **19:**186n1; **20:** 16,n1
Hutchinson, C. X., **21:**487
Hutchinson, Kan., **24:**248n1
Hutchinson, Paul, **21:**393
Hutson, Fred LeRoy, **15:**375; **16:**56, 132, 253, 528; **17:**163,n10, 557
Hutton, Eleanor Varnum Mitchell (Mrs. Laurence), **14:**106; **15:**351
Hutton, Laurence, **14:**90; **15:**351, 491,n2, 556-57
Huxley, Thomas Henry, **15:**35
Hyde, Harriet, **22:**361,n1
Hyde, James Hazen, **14:**389, 393-94; **16:**276n1
Hyde, Walter Woodburn, **16:**465; **17:**163
Hyde Park (London), **25:**173
Hyer, Robert Stewart, **23:**511
Hyperion Theater (New Haven), **25:** 245n1

Ibsen, Henrik, **20:**89
*Idylls of the King* (Tennyson), **23:**459,n1
*If Wilson only Could and Would*, **21:**335n2
Iles, Ivory Victor, **17:**557; **18:**294
*Iliad* (Homer), **17:**535
Illinois, **22:**279; **24:**357; delegation at Baltimore convention, **24:**521, 521n5; Democratic party, **20:**544; Democrats, **23:**326; legislature, **21:**343n11; Negroes, **25:**607; pre-convention tour, **24:**292-304; preferential primary vote, **24:**308,n1; Republicans, **23:**311; WW addresses, **25:**390-95, 400-404
Illinois, University of, **15:**442n2; **19:**180, 676
Illinois Central Railroad, **16:**96
Illinois College, **17:**555
Illinois Manufacturers Association, **21:**266, 389; **22:**71,n2, 178-81, 210
Imbrie, Andrew Clerk, **15:**249, 251, 413, 414, 415, 416, 433, 435; **16:**5; **17:**170,n1, 236, 264-65, 270, 281, 282-83, 285, 293, 297-301, 308, 362, 367, 381-83, 399n1, 410n1, 424, 431, 453-54, 595; **18:**236, 285, 456, 584, 615, 624; **19:**3, 3n1, 4, 5, 15, 120-21, 153, 160, 228, 273, 439, 611, 672, 698, 703; **20:**245, 254, 410, 466,n1, 469, 497; **25:**646
*Imitation of Christ* (Thomas à Kempis), **15:**110
*Immigrant City: Lawrence, Massachusetts* (Cole), **25:**243n6, 426n4
immigration, **24:**252, 258, 260, 351, 405-407, 563-64; **25:**40, 53-54, 59-60, 76, 94, 95-97, 105, 108, 182-83, 212, 256-57, 400-401 441-42, 450, Δ Edwin Bird Wilson **25:**27; orientals, **24:**382, 383,n1; platform plank, **24:**481

immortality, **23:**561-62
Imperial Hotel, New York City, **15:**471
Imperialism (Bryan), **23:**284,n1
imperialism (colonialism, expansionism), **14:**324, 325, 431,n2, 433-34; **15:**171, 172, 175, 184, 330n3, 537; **16:**297-98
inauguration plans, **25:**571, 572, 640,n1 Δ William T. Ferguson, **25:**550; Giles B. Jackson, **25:**620
*In Bohemia with du Maurier . . .* (Moscheles), **18:**400,n5
*In His Steps* (Sheldon), **19:**253n1
*In Many Moods* (Williams), **22:**52,n2
*In the Days of McKinley* (Leech), **22:**371n5
income tax, **16:**529, 530-31,n3; **22:**94, 144, 326,n1, 409, 434, 465, 511-12,n1,2,3,4, 534-35,n2, 591; **23:**235n3
income tax amendment, **24:**216-17
*Independence of the Executive* (Cleveland), **14:**236,n5
*Independent* (New York), **14:**11, 283; **16:**109n, 266-67; **17:**92,n4, 333, 456,-n1; **18:**477-78, 576; **19:**6,n3,4, 122,n4; **22:**32,n3; **23:**481n1; **25:**420,n4
Indiana, **21:**608n2; **22:**570, 571; **25:**22n2, 148, 350, 354, 607; delegation at Baltimore convention, **24:**527n8; Democratic party, **20:**544, 546; **25:**327-28; Princeton alumni, **14:**447; WW addresses, **25:**28,184, 312-38
*Indiana Magazine of History*, **18:**186n4
Indiana State Teacher's Association, **17:**407,n2, 569
Indiana University, **16:**250
Indianapolis, **20:**313, 390; **22:**523, 533, 571; **23:**192, 192n3, 216, 217, 245; Contemporary Club, **17:**407,n3, 582; Irvington Athenaeum, **17:**583; Murat Temple, **22:**557n1; Propylaeum, **17:** 582, 584; Tomlinson Hall, **17:**569n1; University Club, **22:**554; WW addresses, **17:**569-82, 582-84; **25:**312-29; WW in, **22:**554-56; WW letter to 8th grade schoolchildren, **14:**403-404
*Indianapolis News*, **14:**17n3; **22:**52n1, 466n3, 525, 554n, 556n, 557n3, 568n; **24:**254,n1; **25:**321n, 329n
*Industrial History of the Negro Race in the United States*, **25:**620-21,n5
Industrial Relations, Commission on, Alexander J. McKelway and, **25:**311
Industrial Workers of the World, **25:**243n6, 426n4
industry, **25:**75, 103, 175, 176-77, 343 Δ Louis D. Brandeis, **25:**57
*Inferno* (Dante), **21:**533; **23:**375, 498; **24:**212
inflation, **25:**9-10
Ingersoll, Charles Henry, **22:**499,n1
Ingersoll, Robert H., **23:**522n1, 529n3; **24:**458,n1
Ingham, Mrs. (at Bermuda), **20:**188

Ingle, Edward, **14**:89, 96; **15**:203; **23**:583, 592

Inglis, William Otto, **16**:455n1; **20**:147n, 148n, 541n1; **21**:40n1, 53, 54, 62, 293; **22**:39,n9, 73,n3, 181n1, 228,n2, 260; **24**:72

inheritance tax (N. J.), **25**:310

initiative, referendum and recall, **17**:461,n3; **19**:512, 730; **21**:142, 149, 269, 352; **22**:175, 208, 246-47, 255n2,3, 258, 279, 280, 291n2, 315, 355, 376, 412n2, 448-49, 521, 578, 592, 594, 597; **23**:8, 26, 32n5, 37, 42, 43, 62, 67, 71, 72, 75, 77, 92, 101, 102, 132, 203, 219, 239, 243n3, 244, 282, 302, 319, 320, 321, 322, 327, 355, 359-60, 361-62, 369, 371, 440, 459, 551, 581, 591n2, 601n1, 619, 620, 625; **24**:220-21, 234, 235, 263, 339, 350; **25**:155, 186-87, 239-40, 240-41; platform plank, **24**:480-81; recall of judges, **23**:33,n3, 39, 40, 41, 41-42, 42-43, 44, 62, 73, 76, 132, 322, 341, 360, 362, 369-70, 539, 551-52, 601n1, 619 △ L. D. Brandeis, **25**:293; W. J. Bryan, **24**:565; New York *World*, **24**:96

Institute of Electrical Engineers of Great Britain, **18**:577

Institute of Musical Art, New York City, **16**:208-11,n1,3; **22**:91n5

*Institute of Musical Art 1905-1926* (Damrosch), **16**:210n

institution defined, **22**:103

Insular Cases of 1901, **17**:544n4

insurance frauds, **17**:78n2, 103-104, 515-16

insurance investigation of 1905, **16**:220, 276, 320, 333,n2

insurance scandals in New York state, **21**:341,n4, 392, 393, 418

Insurgency in Philadelphia, 1905 (Abernathy), **21**:342n6

Insurgent Club, **22**:412,n2

insurgents, **21**:306, 457-58; **23**:89, 90, 91; **25**:85, 86, 121, 323, 472; Republican, **24**:142, 155, 177, 221

integrated schools, **23**:309, 316

intellectual classes, ignorance of, **23**:442

Inter-Church Conference on Federation, New York, 1905, **16**:227-30,n2; mentioned, **17**:621-22n1

Inter-Church Federation, **22**:259; of New Jersey, **22**:385

Intercollegiate Athletic Association, **16**:272n1, 369; Rules Committee, **17**:473,n3

Intercollegiate [Football] Rules Committee, **16**:272,n1, 371,n3; **19**:562,n3, 704

"interests," **22**:75, 255n1, 258, 261, 275, 278, 297, 298, 299, 300, 302, 303, 337, 341, 342, 375, 388, 429, 468-69, 495, 513, 540; **23**:238, 359, 548, 605n1, 620, 639; *see also* Wall Street

interlocking directorates, **23**:228n3, 448, 504n6

intermediate state, **22**:368,n3

International Association of Machinists, **21**:335n1

International Brotherhood of Maintenance of Way Employees, **23**:340n1

International Catholic Truth Society, **21**:542

International Congress of Arts and Science, St. Louis, 1904, **14**:394,n1; *see also* Congress of Arts and Science, St. Louis, 1904

International Congress of Chambers of Commerce of the World, **25**:270

International Harvester Co., **14**:292n1; **15**:65,n2; **23**:5n1, 120,n6,7, 314,n2; **24**:412n3, 549; **25**:110, 115, 133, 381n6

International Southern Observatory, **16**:489

International Traction Co., **20**:542, 561

international trade, **25**:16-17

Interparliamentary Union for the Promotion of International Arbitration, **21**:615n4

Interstate Commerce Act, Louis D. Brandeis, **25**:297, 300

Interstate Commerce Commission, **17**:584,n1; **25**:208, 209, 227, 274

interstate commerce regulation, **20**:316; **22**:313, 316

Interstate Livestock Fair Association, **25**:148n2, 162, 282

*Introduction to Philosophy* (Paulsen), **19**:666,n2

invention, **25**:199, 201, 209, 227, 249, 254, 383-84

Inverness, **18**:392, 393, 396, 398; Caledonian Hotel, **18**:396

Inwood, Paget East, Bermuda, **17**:50,n1

*Iolanthe* (Gilbert and Sullivan), **22**:298

Iowa, **22**:519; **23**:341; **25**:161, 429, 439, 555; campaign funds, **24**:254n1; Democratic party and Democrats, **20**:544; **23**:310, 315; **25**:162-63; pre-convention campaign, **24**:220-23; Republican party, **25**:246-47; State Teachers' Associations, **23**:247; WW address in Sioux City, **25**:148-56

Iowa, University of, **16**:258

Iowa College, *see* Grinnell College

Iowa State College, **16**:251; **18**:577

Iowa Wesleyan University, **16**:257

*Iphigenie auf Tauris* (Goethe), **19**:571

Iredell, Samuel, **24**:501

Ireland, self-government, **21**:439

Irish Americans, **24**:57, 122, 252, 260-61, 409; **25**:400-401

Iron Brigade, **24**:257n2

Iron Mountain Railroad, **23**:517, 519

Iroquois Club (Chicago), **24**:151,n1

Irvine, Camille Hart (Mrs. William Mann), **22**:22,n2

Irvine, William Mann, **14**:464n1; **22**:22,n1

Irving, Sir Henry, **14**:528n8; **23**:608

Irwin, Agnes, **14**:191

Irwin, Frank, **18**:579
*Is Woodrow Wilson A Bigot?* (Monaghan), **25**:63n1
Is Woodrow Wilson Bryanizing? (New York *World*), **23**:242n3, 246n1
Isaac, Paul E., **18**:485n2; **23**:289n2
Isham, William Burhans, Jr., **14**:47, 330; **15**:27, 131,n2; **17**:31; **19**:64; **21**:602; **22**:519; Isham Dinner, **17**:31,n2
Ishpeming, Michigan, **16**:250
Isle of the Dead (painting by Böcklin), **20**:181,n3
Isle of Death (Rachmaninoff), **20**:181
Israel, Fred L., **25**:57n1
*Israel Zangwill* (Wohlgelernter), **25**:105n5
Italian-American Alliance, **24**:404-407
Italian-American Association of Connecticut, **25**:41n1
Italian Americans, **24**:133-34, 135, 226, 241, 269,n1, 404-407, 536, 575; **25**:28, 40-41, 57, 59-60, 107-109,n1, 400
Italian Columbus Society, **24**:536n1
Italy, **25**:256, 610; city government, **23**:166; Wilsons in, **14**:539-40
Ives, William D., **23**:536n1

J. P. Morgan & Co., **18**:494n3; **23**:120,n7, 151n1, 228n3, 246n1,4, 293n3, 504n6, 514, 632; **24**:78, 412n3, 533, 567n2; *see also* Morgan, John Pierpont, Sr. and Jr.
Jackson, Mich., **24**:58n2
Jackson, Andrew, **14**:251-52, 311, 312, 344, 420, 517, 518; **15**:148, 551; **16**:53, 359; **17**:12, 74, 319; **18**:107, 109, 115, 174, 184, 446; **19**:272; **20**:34; **21**:512; **22**:18, 215, 318,n2, 559; **23**:556; **24**:10, 139, 539
Jackson, Arthur Phelps, **23**:333-34,n5
Jackson, Giles B., **25**:619-21n1,5
Jackson, Nellie, **15**:213
Jackson, Philip Nye, **16**:5
Jackson, Thomas Jonathan (Stonewall), **17**:231
Jackson, W. J., **14**:327
Jackson, Wm. H. & Co., **15**:449
Jackson, William Schuyler, **25**:649,n5
Jackson *Patriot*, **24**:58n2
Jacksonville, Fla., **24**:347-48
Jacksonville, Ill., **24**:291, 292
Jacksonville *Florida Times-Union*, **24**:348n
Jacobi, Abraham, **24**:454n1
Jacobs, Zillah Young (Mrs. Robert P.), **15**:348n1
Jacobus, Clara Cooley (Mrs. Melancthon Williams), **16**:184,n1, 215n2; **17**:57, 395; **18**:423, 607, 610; **19**:168,n2, 197; **20**:284,n1
Jacobus, Melancthon Williams, **14**:458, 468-69, 471; **15**:531,n1; **16**:15-16, 131, 184, 199, 244, 273-74, 279, 353, 421, 442, 465, 480, 484, 526, 527-28; **17**:19, 57, 198, 232-33, 241, 244-45, 261, 274,

300, 395, 406, 419,n1, 425, 427n1, 432, 437, 450-51, 458-59, 468-69, 470-71, 491, 496, 582, 585, 595, 597-98, 599; **18**:8-9, 63, 311-12, 313-14, 359-60, 397, 418, 423, 434, 473-74, 476, 493-94, 512, 514, 555-56, 559-60, 588-89, 591, 593, 606-609, 609-10, 615, 624-25; **19**:6-7, 8, 21-23, 31-32, 113-15, 116-17, 121-22, 124-25, 159-60, 167-69, 197-99, 201-202, 228-29, 256-57, 273-76, 276-77, 293,n2, 310-11, 320-21, 350, 407, 418, 420-21, 436, 437, 439, 456-57, 458-59, 484, 487-88, 541, 625-26, 631, 632, 633, 634, 648, 657-58, 663-64, 697-98, 709-10, 711, 727, 728, 731, 732-33, 734, 735-36; **20**:4-5, 6n, 7n, 8n, 9n, 10-11, 45-46, 61-63, 68-69, 116, 119-20, 128-30, 143, 174, 190, 191, 192, 221-22, 224, 227-28, 245, 246, 251-52, 254, 271-72, 283-84, 311-12, 314, 320-21, 325, 327-28, 354, 355, 356, 362, 410-12, 412-13, 426, 469, 481, 491, 576, 579; **21**:6, 30-31, 109, 142-43, 321, 362n1, 578, 594; **22**:-44, 436; **23**:31, 594; **25**:567-68
Jacobus, Porter Ogden, **16**:214-15,n2
Jacobus de Varaigne (*Jacopo da Varagine*, Richardson), **16**:393,n2
Jagels, Claus Henry Carl, **22**:468,n2; **23**:634,n2, 635
Jagger, Albert, **14**:388
Jamaica earthquake of Jan. 14, 1907, **17**:6-7,n13, 11-12, 16n3
James II of England, **14**:504
James, Charles C., **23**:536n1
James, Edmund Janes, **14**:248; **17**:552,n1
James, Louis Norwood, **14**:191
James, Ollie Murray, **24**:332,n1, 462n1, 570; **25**:3,n1
James, Peter H., **22**:352n3, 481,n3; **23**:344, 536n1
James, Thomas Lemuel, **23**:632,n2
James, William, **14**:295,n2,3; **19**:666,n2
James, William T., **17**:26,n2; Mrs., **17**:26
Jamesburg, N. J., **23**:290, 300, 302
Jameson, John Franklin, **19**:405, 417,n4
Jameson Raid, **20**:475
Jamestown Exposition, Norfolk, Virginia, 1907, **16**:290,n1, 505, 538, 542-44; **17**:7, 51, 56, 247-59; **22**:593,n1
Jamison, Albert Leland, **19**:253n1
Jamison, Albert Woodward, **19**:165
Jamison, Herbert Brotherson, **19**:165
Jamison, Robert, **25**:164n1
Janvier, Câesar Augustus Rodney, **14**:114, 550,n3; **20**:123,n1; **21**:588
Janvier, Ernest Paxton, **19**:174
Japan, American missionaries straw vote for President, **25**:390; Japanese views on death, **25**:278
Japanese Americans, **24**:351; immigration, **24**:382, 383,n1
Japanese labor controversy, **16**:558-59n3
Japanese Relief Fund, **16**:29

Jay Treaty of 1794, **14**:250
Jean Marie (servant in Paris), **14**:538, 542
Jeans, Sir James Hopwood, **16**:64n1, 156,n1, 157, 158, 162, 163-64, 165, 180, 198, 246-47; **17**:408; **19**:115-16, 137, 138, 139, 675, 677
Jefferson, Joseph, **20**:133,n5; **23**:147
Jefferson, Matthew, **22**:516,n1, 521
Jefferson, N. H., **23**:287
Jefferson, Thomas, **14**:131,n3, 251, 344, 360, 360n1, 519; **15**:79, 507; **16**:53, 144, 322, 330, 358-69, 372, 373n3; **17**:74, 75, 249, 250-51, 252, 258, 462; **18**:59, 112, 119, 269, 270, 293, 539; **19**:272, 377; **20**:179; **21**:510; **22**:18, 280, 530n6, 540, 545, 558-59, 570, 592; **23**:33, 34, 216n2, 282, 412-13, 623; **24**:120, 139, 225, 228, 330, 331, 341, 336; **25**:19, 20, 89-90, 94, 126, 222, 248, 250, 387, 389, 410, 413, 432, 631-32, 640
Jefferson Hotel (Richmond), **24**:96, 118
Jefferson Hotel (St. Louis), **25**:395n1
Jefferson Medical College, **18**:557n1; **19**:50, 50,n2, 74,n1, 75-76, 77n1, 162, 163
*Jeffersonian Democracy* (Indianapolis), **20**:505n
*Jeffersonian Image in the American Mind* (Peterson), **14**:360n1
Jeffery, Oscar Wilde, **20**:68,n3
Jeffries, L. G., **16**:73
Jekyl Island Club, Brunswick, Ga., **19**:75
Jelke, Ferdinand, **14**:450
Jellinek, Georg, **14**:321-22, 324, 325
Jena, University of, **16**:249, 254, 257, 511
Jenkins, Charles Rush, **24**:355,n3
Jenkins, Paul Burrill, **16**:101
Jennings, John Gundry, **16**:377
Jennings, Ryerson W., **22**:284-85,n1,2
Jerome, William Travers, **14**:210,n1; **15**:179; **16**:206,n3
Jersey Central Railroad, **21**:343n9, 354; **24**:510
Jersey City, N. J., **21**:8, 19, 23, 42-43, 173, 241, 341; **22**:98,n2, 118n1, 119, 229n1, 233, 286, 295, 508; **23**:146, 147, 164, 165, 201-11n3,5, 218, 218,n1, 232, 447, 537, 634n1; **24**:434-44; **25**:136-37, 214n4; Board of Trade, **19**:598; **22**:359; **24**:68-70; Bumsted Act of 1871, **23**:203-204,n4; Carteret Club, **20**:290; Columbian Club, **22**:400n1; Commission Government League, **23**:201n1; Democratic City Committee, **23**:203n3; Die Wilde Gans Club, **21**:147; German Hospital, **24**:408; government, **19**:730; Grand View Hall, **21**:191n1; High School, **23**:201n1; Jersey City Club, **22**:359; Jersey City High School, **18**:487; Pennsylvania Railroad Station, **19**:620, 627, 628,

630; Princeton alumni, **20**:247, 256, 284, 290; St. John's Hall, **21**:492n1; St. Patrick's Hall, **21**:191n1; **22**:295-96,n1; **23**:342,n1, 535, 537; St. Peter's Hall, **21**:181; University Club, **18**:485, 487; University Club of Hudson County, **15**:195; WW addresses, **15**:195-97; **18**:485-89, 534-35; **20**:290-91, 311; **21**:181-91, 310, 412, 492n1; **23**:201-11, 342-51
Jersey City *Evening Journal*, **15**:197n; **18**:5n1, 489n
*Jersey City Herald*, **21**:94n
*Jersey Journal* (Jersey City), **20**:291n, 567, 577n2; **21**:23-24n1, 42,n1, 191n1, 218n, 228n, 243,n1, 244n1, 256,n8, 265,n1, 293, 451n1, 476n, 492n, 541, 582; **22**:77,n1, 97, 211,n6, 245n2, 307n, 329n, 465n, 474n, 569n1; **23**:171n, 203n3, 208n6, 211n, 218n, 351n, 538n; **24**:70n, 409n, 444n
Jersey justice, **23**:43
*Jerseyman's Journal: Fifty Years of American Business and Politics* (Edge), **22**:546n5
Jesse, Richard Henry, **15**:156,n2, 189
Jessie (English girl), **15**:349
Jesup, Morris Ketchum, **14**:290, 298, 393; **15**:422,n1, 527; **16**:416
Jesus Christ, **23**:494f, 571
*Jesus Christ and the Civilization of To-Day* (Leighton), **17**:116n3
Jesus College, Cambridge, **14**:530
Jewish Americans, **24**:58, 122, 252, 260-61; **25**:28, 63, 577n3; in Russia, **23**:191,n2, 329
*Jewish Exponent* (Philadelphia), **23**:329n
Jewish Territorialist Organization, **25**:105n5
Jews, **15**:471; **23**:259, 583-87; in Bermuda, **24**:59
Jèze, Gaston, **14**:30
*Joan of Arc* (Clemens), **15**:334
Jobe, John R., **23**:517
John A. Roebling's Sons Co., **23**:109n4
*John D. Rockefeller: The Heroic Age of American Enterprise* (Nevins), **23**:118n4
John (King of England 1199-1216), **18**:70, 104; **23**:15
John Wilson Bishop Company, builders, **16**:156,n1; **18**:285,n3
Johns, George Sibley, **15**:20,n1; **17**:246-47; **20**:306-307, 310-11
Johns Hopkins Press, **17**:352n2
Johns Hopkins University, **14**:9, 14, 15n2, 157, 197, 337, 410, 553,n1; **15**:14, 70, 100n3, 104-105, 106, 112, 114, 136; **16**:18, 20, 31, 33, 97, 132, 198, 252, 255, 256, 258, 465, 509, 510, 511; **17**:102, 511, 527, 546n1, 548,-n1, 554, 555, 556, 557, 563, 588; **18**:288, 575, 576, 578; **19**:427, 678, 679; **20**:108, 192, 345; **21**:587n1, 613n1,

617; **22**:139, 523; **23**:22, 248, 567, 583; **24**:361,n2; **25**:457n1, 547, 552n2; Glee Club, **16**:316; **24**:147; Phi Beta Kappa chapter, **20**:402,n1
Johnson, Alba Boardman, **16**:336,n7
Johnson, Andrew, **25**:513n1
Johnson, Arthur Menzies, **16**:15n1
Johnson, Asher K., **24**:397,n1
Johnson, Charles F., **25**:618, 619n1
Johnson, Charles William Leverett, **14**:296,n1, 404-405, 411
Johnson, Cone, **23**:509,n9; **25**:603-605, 645
Johnson, Eliza McCardle (Mrs. Andrew), **25**:513,n1
Johnson, Enoch L., **23**:432n9
Johnson, Frederick Foote, **18**:388n4
Johnson, Henry Sibley, **16**:406
Johnson, Henry Underwood, **24**:531n1
Johnson, Hiram Warren, **21**:608n2; **22**:32n2; **23**:43,n9, 55n1
Johnson, James A. Courvoisier, **22**:87,-n1,2, 589,n2
Johnson, John Albert, **18**:269, 270; **23**:4,n1, 85, 86n1,6, 248,n4
Johnson, John Gilmore, **24**:571,n1
Johnson, John Graver, **20**:31,n1
Johnson, Joseph Travis, **24**:287,n1
Johnson, M. B., **25**:548
Johnson, Robert Underwood, **20**:31, 399; **21**:109,n1, 322,n1; **22**:98, 126-27, 406; **24**:531
Johnson, Roger Bruce Cash, **15**:163,n1; **16**:59, 131, 249; **17**:408; **19**:666,n1, 669
Johnson, Samuel, LL.D., **14**:503; **16**:209; **20**:384; **21**:253
Johnson, Susannah Batcheller, **14**:296, 411
Johnson, Tom Loftin, **17**:507-508,n1, 508-509; **22**:161n1, 466n3, 557n4, 571; **25**:406n5
Johnson, Tristam Burges, **20**:43n8
Johnson, William E., **18**:556,n1
Johnson, William Mindred, **14**:290; **21**:7,n6; **22**:19-20,n1
Johnson, Willis Fletcher, **16**:455n1, 534n10
Johnston, Charles, **23**:215,n2, 277
Johnston, James Marion, **14**:400,n1
Johnston, Joseph Forney, **23**:513,n5
Johnstown, Pa., **22**:523
*Johnstown Democrat*, **22**:522n1
Joliet, Ill., **24**:291, 292
Joline, Adrian Hoffman, **14**:186, 290; **16**:5, 141, 533; **17**:124,n1, 428-31; **19**:254; **20**:209,n5, 238, 248, 284, 303,n1, 311, 324, 325, 382, 416,n4, 481, 531n1; **21**:39,n1; **23**:602,n1, 632; **24**:5,n1,2, 7n5, 8, 148; **25**:232
Joline, John Forsyth, Jr., **17**:124n1
Joline letter, **24**:5,n1,2, 7,n5, 8-9, 28
Joline, Mary Larkin (Mrs. Adrian Hoffman), **14**:186, 186n2

Jones, Adam Leroy, **16**:131, 249; **17**:163, 408; **19**:676; **20**:446
Jones, Allan Dudley, **24**:514,n1
Jones, Benjamin Franklin, Jr., **15**:220-21, 235, 527; **16**:5, 336, 383
Jones, Charles F., **16**:557n2
Jones, Charles Hodge, **16**:95; **17**:161,n2; **19**:677
Jones, Charles Octavius, **23**:556,n4
Jones, Clarence Trimingham, **20**:127,n6; **22**:330n1
Jones, David Benton, **14**:64, 74-75, 211, 230, 248, 421,n1, 423, 424, 440, 448, 451,n1, 454,n7; **15**:28-29, 184, 191-93, 200, 405-406, 526, 569, 572; **16**:5, 131, 279, 406, 526; **17**:19, 39n1, 147-48, 175,n3, 206, 207, 210-11, 273-75, 300, 374-75, 392-93, 397-98, 401-402, 404-405, 419, 425, 435, 468, 495-97, 598, 598n2; **18**:255, 311, 333, 336, 360, 418, 423, 434,n1, 482, 623,n1; **19**:79, 352-53, 407, 451, 490, 631, 632, 633, 656, 658, 662, 709, 734-35; **20**:211, 216, 237, 252, 266, 266n4, 269, 278, 321, 455,n4, 459-60, 470, 473, 474, 483, 485-86, 541, 542n1, 543-45, 545-47, 548, 549, 550, 551, 552, 553, 554-55, 557, 561, 571, 578, 579; **21**:10, 29, 132, 144, 162-63, 173-74, 385, 389, 593-94; **22**:71, 126, 223n1; **23**:599-601; **24**:549-50; **25**:109-10,n2,5
Jones, DeWitt Clinton, Jr., **19**:507,n1, 528-29, 576-77
Jones, DeWitt Clinton III, **19**:502,n3, 507, 508
Jones, F. D., **22**:577n4
Jones, Francis, **17**:50n1
Jones, Frank Johnston, **15**:419,n1, 530
Jones, Frederick Robertson, **16**:306,n1
Jones, George H., **23**:536n1
Jones, Henry Arthur, **15**:396n3
Jones, Herbert, **15**:405,n1
Jones, Herbert Gresford, **18**:415,n2
Jones, John Fisher, **16**:494n1
Jones, John Sparhawk, **14**:435,n3; **15**:306,n3; **17**:125, 127, 129-30
Jones, John William, **16**:197,n5
Jones, Leonard Chester, **19**:755n2
Jones, Louise Lightbourn Trimingham (Mrs. Eugenius), **20**:127,n5, 224,n2; **22**:330,n1
Jones, Margaret Cropper (Mrs. William), **18**:415,n3
Jones, Mary McMasters (Mrs. Benjamin Franklin), **15**:235
Jones, Raymond Watson, **18**:579
Jones, Thomas Davies, **14**:423, 424, 448, 451n1, 454,n7; **15**:406, 526; **17**:39n1, 397; **18**:9n4, 360, 397, 418, 423, 434, 476,n1, 623,n1; **19**:79,n1, 169, 257, 424, 451, 609, 620, 631, 632, 633-34, 657, 659-61, 662, 695-97, 698, 699, 709, 735, 736; **20**:5, 8n, 9-10, 11, 12-13, 16, 17, 20-21, 46-48, 51, 60, 65, 68, 82,

Jones, Thomas Davies, (*cont.*)
83, 87, 92-104, 116, 128, 129, 142-44, 174, 183, 190, 213, 219-21, 223, 238, 245, 246, 252, 254, 262, 264, 265-66n3, 283, 284, 321, 324, 325, 360, 362, 393-95, 403, 403-404, 455n4, 458n1, 469, 473, 477-78, 483-85, 493-95, 541,-n1, 544, 545, 547, 548, 548-50, 550, 551, 552, 552-53, 554, 555, 556, 557, 571, 579; 21:163, 321, 362n1, 385, 599; 22:48, 126, 154, 223,n2; 23:594, 598-99, 600, 603-604; 25:92, 109n2, 110,n5, 114, 115, 133
Jones, Walter, 20:192,n1
Jones, William Atkinson, 22:282,n2; 23:311, 601; 24:287,n1; 25:623; Philippines, 24:560,n1, 566
Jones, William Larimer, 16:336,n12
Jones, Winifred, 22:223,n1
Jones & Laughlin Steel Co., Pittsburgh, 15:361
Jordan, David Starr, 15:116; 20:151,n1; 22:130-31,n3
Jordan, William Chester, 24:xi
*Journal of American History,* 16:412n1
*Journal of an Expedition Across Venezuela and Colombia 1906-1907* (Bingham), 16:388n1
*Journal of Experimental Zoölogy,* 18:576
*Journal of Morphology,* 18:576
*Journal of the Rev. John Wesley,* 14:421,n3, 512
*Journal of Southern History,* 23:513n4
journalism, 20:400-401
Jowett, Benjamin, 14:407,n5
joy-rides, 19:325; 21:207; 23:626
Joyce, Robert Michael, 23:97,n2
Joyner, James Yadkin, 19:400,n4
Juarez, Mex., 24:218
Judd, Charles Hubbard, 23:103
Judd Haven, Ont., 15:411, 418, 419, 420, 424, 433, 434, 435, 439, 447, 448, 460, 461, 462, 467, 470, 491n3, 520, 523
judges, recall of, 24:235-36; 25:240-41
judicial system, 25:240, 251, 293 Δ L. D. Brandeis, 25:291
Judson, Frederick Newton, 25:448,n3
Judson, Harry Pratt, 14:248; 18:8,n1; 21:144-45,n1; 23:31,n8
Judson College, Marion, Ala., 16:73
Juilliard School of Music, New York City, 16:210n1
Junkin, Jessie McElroy, 23:657
Jupiter, 15:354
jurisprudence, 21:577
Jusserand, Elise Richards (Madame Jean Adrien Antoine Jules), 16:233n4
Jusserand, Jean Adrien Antoine Jules, 16:233n4; 17:226n1, 228n1; 21:615n2
justice, 23:307; 25:261, 264-65
Justice, Department of; Louis D. Brandeis, 25:294
Justice, Edwin Judson, 24:388,n1
Justinian, 15:195

Juvenal (Decimus Junius Juvenalis), 14:209

Kalamazoo, Mich., 25:185-86
Kalisch, Samuel, 23:432n9; 24:453, 459
Kallen, Horace Meyer, 15:3n2, 375
Kane, Francis Fisher, 15:401-402,n1; 19:500,n1, 605; 20:534,n2; 21:266-67, 604-605; 22:246-47, 409n1, 435, 441,n2, 486-87, 487n3; 23:219-20; 229-30; 24:6n1, 26-27, 496, 537-38
Kansas, 22:389-91; 23:100; 24:191, 248,n1, 357; address in, 25:378-85; Democratic Club, 23:291; politics, 25:621,n2, 622; pre-convention trip, 24:187-89; Republicans, 23:291
Kansas, University of, 17:557; 24:191,n1
*Kansas: A History of the Jayhawk State* (Zornow), 25:621n2
Kansas City, Kansas, 24:191
Kansas City, Mo., 22:519n4, 533; 23:172, 190-91, 511; 24:185; Central High School, 16:98; Coates House, 23:3, 5; Commercial Club, 23:9, 10n3; Country Club (at Westport), 16:97, 100; 23:9; Hotel Baltimore, 16:95; Knife and Fork Club, 23:4, 5, 31n; Manual Training High School, 16:98; 23:9; Prosso Preparatory School, 16:97,n3; University Club, 16:95, 97, 101; Westport High School, 16:98; WW addresses, 16:47, 95-100, 100-101; 25:385-90; WW in, 23:3-10, 11, 31n1
*Kansas City Star* (Mo.), 16:98n, 100n, 101n; 23:5n, 262, 262n2; 24:185, 187n, 191n1
*Kansas City Times* (Mo.), 16:97n; 23:10n; 25:390
Kansas-Nebraska Bill, 17:316, 320
Kansas Society of New York, 22:389
Kant, Immanuel, 19:666
Kapteyn, Jacobus Cornelis, 16:82,n3
Kaskaskia, Ill., 14:518
Katzenbach, Augusta Mushbach (Mrs. Frank Snowden, Jr.), 21:27,n4
Katzenbach, Edward Lawrence, 14:456-57, n2; 21:27,n3, 132
Katzenbach, Frank Snowden, Jr., 21:23,n3, 24,n2, 27,n2,3, 33-34, 34n1, 35-n1, 37,n1,2, 40, 52, 54, 90, 96, 101, 103, 103n1, 104, 106, 120, 121, 137, 141, 174, 213, 229n1, 295, 329,n3, 330, 331, 354, 409, 421, 584n1; 22:47, 77n1, 415n2, 535n1, 540, 545; 23:219
Katzenbach, Welling Sickel, 17:344, 350
Kean, John, 15:61; 21:90,n1, 200,n1, 219n2, 244, 249,n4, 260, 330, 346, 503; 22:113, 137n1, 153, 155, 199, 226, 240, 248, 250, 367; 23:392, 447
Kearns, Michael H., 23:272,n3, 275
Kearny, N. J., Disabled Soldiers' Home, 22:231n2; 23:534-35
Keasbey, Lindley Miller, 22:422-23,n1, 433

Keating, Edward, 23:478,n1
Keats, John, 14:503; 23:128,n2
Keehn, Roy Dee, 24:574,n1,2
Keeley Institute, 24:286n2
Keen, William Williams, M.D., 19:529,n1, 605-606
Keene Valley (N. Y.), 18:352; Country Club, 17:295-96
Keener, John Henry, 15:252; 16:30,n2
Kellen, William Vail, 14:491,n1
Keller, Gottfried, 19:569
Kelley, Florence, 22:157n1, 452,n3
Kellogg, George Dwight, 16:132, 253, 528; 17:162,n5, 408
Kellogg, Oliver Dimon, 16:160, 165
Kelly, Edmond, 21:174,n2, 175, 179
Kelly, George Armstrong, 16:377
Kelly, James J., 23:208,n6, 536n2
Kelly, W. Frank, 23:308-309, 316
Kelman, John, 14:26,n1
Kelsey, Clarence Hill, 22:40,n26
Kelsey, Frederick Wallace, 22:146-47,n1
Kelsey, Henry Hopkins, 14:458,n1
Kelso, John Bolton, 16:306,n7
Kelvin, William Thomson, 1st Baron, 16:157,n4, 163
Kendall, Calvin Noyes, 20:582, 583n1; 23:192,n1,3, 216-17, 226, 363
Kende, Geza, 24:563,n1, 564; 25:275-76,n3
Kenilworth Castle, Warwickshire, Wilsons at, 14:530, 531
Kennard, John Hanson, Jr., 25:457,n1,2, 458
Kennedy, Anderson Ross, 20:50n1
Kennedy, Arthur March, 16:86n1
Kennedy, Charles Rann, 15:340-41,n1
Kennedy, Charles William, 16:465, 511; 18:579
Kennedy, Edith Wynne Matthison (Mrs. Charles Rann), 15:340-41,n1
Kennedy, George H., 25:80,n3
Kennedy, John Stewart, 17:109,n1; 19:539,n4,5
Kennedy, Joseph Leland, nephew of WW, 20:50,n2
Kennedy, Marion Williamson Wilson (Mrs. Anderson Ross), sister of WW, 20:49, 50n1
Kennedy, William Blake, nephew of WW, 20:50,n3
Kenny, Edward, 21:346,n15; 22:136n1, 357, 481,n1, 482; 23:177, 345, 535
Kent, Charles William, 14:188; 15:574; 16:161, 168, 192-93, 281, 284; 17:487-88, 523-24; 22:326, 333
Kent, Eleanor A. Smith (Mrs. Charles William), 14:188
Kent, Frank Richardson, 21:525,n1
Kent, Henry T., 19:97
Kent, Henry Thompson, 18:567,n1, 568, 593
Kent, Platt, 19:72-73,n1

Kent, William, 22:31-32,n1; 25:618
Kentucky, 23:194, 199, 202, 213, 220, 231; 24:141-46, 332,n1,2,3, 333, 357-58,n3; 25:23; night riders, 18:6,n1, 483,n1; WW in, 22:210; 25:23
Kentucky, settlement of, 14:518
Kentucky, State University of, 19:679
Kentucky and Kentuckians, 22:421-22, 524
Kentucky Bar Association, 23:194
Kentucky General Assembly, 24:141
Kentwell Hall, 15:446
Kenyon, William Squire, 23:132n1
Kenyon College, 19:679
Keogh, Martin Jerome, 15:392-93, 417; 16:14n1; 17:148-49
Keohan, W. F., 17:586-87,n1
Keppel, Frederick Paul, 15:100,n1; 17:121,n1
Kern, Araminta Cooper (Mrs. John Worth), 22:571,n1
Kern, John Worth, 18:385,n3; 21:587; 22:571n1; 24:165,n3; 25:22, 321n2, 327,n4
Kerney, James, 20:565,n1; 21:23,n4, 31, 34-35, 35n1, 142n1, 542, 583n2; 22:86n1, 113n2, 142n1, 200, 201, 357, 357n2,4, 383n3, 503n2, 546n5; 23:192n3; 25:582, 584
Kerr, Edwin Silas Wells, 19:177,n1
Kerr, John Henry, 15:535
Kerr, John Thompson, 21:592,n1
Kerr, Wilbur Franklin, 14:145,n2
Keswick, Cumberland, 18:361, 364, 374, 386, 391, 394, 395; Keswick Hotel, 14:523,n3; Wilsons at, 14:522-23
Ketchum, Alexander Phoenix, 14:253
Keuffel, Willy Gottfried, 23:161,n2
Keyser, Robert Brent, 23:568,n5
Keystoners (independent Pennsylvania ticket), 23:230,n7
Kidd, Benjamin, 18:443,n1
Kidder, Peabody & Co., 21:40n1
Kiefer, Daniel, 22:257-58,n1, 261, 576
Kilborn, George Darius, 25:359,n1
Kilbourne, James, 25:198n2
Kilburn, Frederick D., 14:298
Kill van Kull, 23:295n5
Killgore, Anthony, 22:164,n1
Killingbeck, Wilson B., 21:267-69,n1, 288, 351-53, 386, 584n1
Kilpatrick, John Douglas, 14:465-67
Kimball, Arthur Lalanne, 20:265,n2, 268
Kin Beyond Sea (Gladstone), 25:238n4
Kindred, John Joseph, 24:287,n1
King, Benjamin Mandeville, 24:239,n2
King, Fannie Bayle (Mrs. William Wayt), 15:522,n1
King, Frederick Paul, 15:252; 19:32,n1
King, Henry Churchill, 16:56,n1; 17:128
King, William Rufus, 25:645,n3
King, William Wayt, 15:522n1
King Fisher College, Okla., 18:579

King's College, Cambridge, **15**:410; **16**:83n2

Kingsley, Charles, **14**:555

Kingsley, Darwin Pearl, **21**:621-22,n1

Kingston, Jamaica, earthquake of Jan. 14, 1907, **17**:6-7,n13, 11-12, 16n3

Kingston, N. J., **15**:549, 575, 578

Kinkead, Eugene F., **23**:310,n2, 343n3

Kinkead, Eugene Francis, **20**:563,n2, 565n, 577n2; **21**:17, 19, 213, 249n3, 341; **22**:228,n1; **23**:310,n2, 343n3, 404, 438, 447, 539; **24**:287,n1, 408

Kinley, David, **19**:180,n1

Kinney, Thomas, **15**:156n2, 186-87

Kipling, Rudyard, **15**:537; **16**:180; **20**:135,n4; **22**:89,n3; **23**:104, 398,n3; **24**:181, 446; **25**:316

Kirk, Harris Elliott, **18**:494, 512; **20**:152-53,n4

Kirk, John Foster, **14**:135n1

Kirkland, James Hampton, **16**:564; **17**:457, 492; **23**:103

Kirkland, Robert Bird, **24**:488,n1

Kirkman, Christina, **18**:406,n1, 410, 411

Kirkman, William Wright, **18**:406n1

Kirkstone, Westmorland, **15**:438, 441; **18**:381, 409

Kirkstone Pass, Westmorland, Wilsons at, **14**:521

Kishinev (Bessarabia) pogrom (1903), **15**:471

Kiskiminetas Springs School, Saltsburg, Pa., **16**:251

Kitchener, Sir Frederick Walter, **19**:383,n4,5; **20**:132,n2, 145, 150-51, 179, 180, 187n3; **22**:324,n4, 331n2; **23**:655,n2; **24**:239,n1

Kitchener, Horatio Herbert, 1st Earl Kitchener of Khartoum, **19**:383n4; **20**:132n2, 145, 150, 156

Kitchin, Claude, **16**:320; **24**:67, 287,n1

Kitchin, William Walton, **23**:320,n1

Kittredge, George Lyman, **17**:226n1

*Kleider machen Leute* (Keller), **19**:569

Klein, Charles, **20**:153n9

Klein, Harry Martin John, **14**:464n1

Kleinert, Abram, **17**:24,n4, 25

Kluckhohn, Charles Louis, **23**:85,n2, 87

Knapp, Emily Hale Perkins (Mrs. Howard Hoyt), **23**:82,n12

Knapp, Howard Hoyt, **23**:82,n11

Kneisel String Quartet, **15**:153,n1,2

Knickerbocker Club, New York City, **24**:31

Knickerbocker Hotel, New York City, **18**:269, 270; **24**:286

Knickerbocker Trust Company, New York City, **17**:96n1

Knights of Columbus, **25**:63n1,2, 452, 493

Know-Nothing Party, **17**:320, 321

Knox, Andrew, **21**:172,n1

Knox, Anne Eliza McCosh, Lady Knox, **19**:192,n3; **20**:139, 155

Knox, George William, **16**:400,n5

Knox, Sir James, **19**:192,n3; **20**:139, 155, 181

Knox, John, **14**:524

Knox, Philander Chase, **21**:615,n3; **22**:478n3

Knox & Reed, lawyers, Pittsburgh, **17**:4n6

Koehler, Henry, **24**:186,n2

Koelble, Alphonse G., **22**:514n4

Kohn, August, **22**:507; **23**:114,n2

Kokomo, Ind., **25**:330-32

*König Albert*, S.S., **15**:333, 350

Konkle, Burton Alva, **15**:494,n1

Korea, **20**:556n1

Koren, William, **16**:132; **17**:408; **19**:572, 574, 576

Kosciusko, Thaddeus, **24**:260

Kosek, John, **25**:28

Kossuth, Louis, **24**:511

Kramer, C. C., **23**:519

Krespach, Frank L., **14**:68,n1, 76; **15**:321,n2

*Kroonland*, S.S., **19**:306

Ku Klux Klan, **14**:250, 312, 445

Kuehnle, Louis, **22**:300,n4, 309, 310, 311n1; **23**:432n9, 522n1, 592n2; **24**:458n1,2

Kuhn, Loeb & Co., **23**:293n3

Kulm, Mt., Switzerland, Wilsons at, **14**:538

*Kurfürst*, S.S., **19**:328,n1

Küsel, G. C. (Philadelphia dentist), **14**:38,n2, 39

La Barre, George, **23**:428n7

La Barre, George B., **21**:54,n3, 167

Labor, Bureau of, A. J. McKelway, **25**:311

labor and labor unions, **14**:363; **16**:13-15; **19**:245, 309-10; **21**:5, 45, 60-61, 63, 83-84, 88-89, 113, 114, 179-80, 254-55, 280, 287-88, 297-98, 336-37, 350, 392, 394, 395, 401, 425-26, 467, 468-69, 487-89, 491, 527, 553-54, 560, 567, 570; **22**:12, 179, 221, 222, 565; **23**:25, 309, 339, 344-45; **24**:89, 90-92, 124, 301; **25**:70-72, 75, 103, 160, 194-95, 208-209, 214, 223, 226, 252, 262-64, 268, 318, 334-35, 382, 498; New Jersey laws, **25**:306, 308; platform plank, **24**:481; trusts and, **25**:504-505; wages, **25**:268 Δ Arizona Constitution and, **22**:291n2; W. Blackburn, **21**:335; R. G. Bremner, **21**:133, 153-54; W. J. Bryan, **23**:25; T. H. Dillon, **22**:163; F. Dundon, **19**:269-70; W. R. Hearst, **21**:85; S. C. Hodge, **22**:259; J. W. Kern, **25**:23; R. V. Lindabury, **21**:449; W. F. McCombs, **23**:263; D. L. MacKay, **21**:322-23; W. MacVeagh, **22**:144; D. F. Platt, **21**:141; Progressive Voters of Labor, **21**:335n2, 463,n2; H. B. Ware, **21**:463; *see also* prison labor

labor reform, **25**:13-14, 177-78; New Jersey, **25**:315
*Labor Standard* (Orange, N. J.), **21**:55n1, 61n
Labori, Fernand Gustave Gaston, **15**:434,n2,3, 436, 443, 504
labyrinths, **23**:142
La Cava, EAW at, **15**:235
Lackawanna Railroad, **23**:339n3, 340, 352, 356
Lacy, Eric Russell, **18**:485n2; **23**:298n2
Laddey, Clara Schlee (Mrs. Victor H. G.), **22**:289-90,n1
*Lady Rose's Daughter* (Ward), **15**:97,n5
La Farge, John, ̧306n3
Lafayette Hotel (Buffalo), **25**:67n1
Lafayette, Marie Joseph Paul Yves Roch Gilbert du Motier, Marquis de, **16**:144
Lafayette, N. J., **21**:413
Lafayette College, **16**:240; **19**:679; **21**:393
Lafayette Hotel, Cape May, N. J., **23**:274
Laffan, William Mackay, **16**:532,n3, 534; **17**:41, 65, 66, 90, 93, 93,n1, 215, 335n1, 347; **18**:259, 271
Laffan Press, **22**:160
Laffan Syndicate, **19**:522
Lafferty, James, **22**:233,n1
La Follette, Belle Case (Mrs. Robert Marion), **22**:412n2
La Follette, Fola, **22**:412n2
La Follette, Robert Marion, **19**:108-109, 191n1, 363n1; **20**:38n5; **21**:343n11; **22**:18, 32, 234, 412n2, 461, 485; **23**:132n1, 234n5, 415, 540; **24**:29, 126n4, 137,n2, 193,n3, 444, 546, 554n2; **25**:57, 247, 276, 287, 293, 323-34, 379-80, 412, 429, 436, 472, 475-76
La Follette antitrust bill, **25**:288, 289, 295-304
La Follette Federal Commission bill, **25**:287, 293
La Follette-Stanley antitrust bills, **25**:287, 290, 291, 292
*La Follette's Autobiography*, **24**:193n3; **25**:323,n3
La Forte, Robert Sherman, **25**:621n2
*Laird's Luck and Other Fireside Tales* (Quiller-Couch), **14**:526,n5
Lake District, **16**:451, 463, 469, 481; **18**:4, 349, 355, 357, 359, 385, 389, 393, 394, 397, 405, 407; Wilsons at, **14**:521-23, 546, 550
Lake Forest, Ill., **14**:211; **20**:403
Lake Forest College, **15**:441n3; **16**:132, 255
Lake Mohonk Conference on International Arbitration, **25**:19,n2
Lake Placid Club, **17**:347
Lakewood, N. J., **18**:66; **23**:380, 467n1, 513,n2, 514; WW campaign speech, **21**:325-26
Lakow, Samuel, **16**:388; **17**:37
Lakowka, A. F., **25**:28
Lamar, Joseph Rucker, **25**:542,n1,2,3

Lamar, Lucius Quintus Cincinnatus, **17**:347
Lamar, Philip, **25**:542,n2,3
Lamb, Charles, **17**:360
Lamb Hotel, Ely, Cambridgeshire, **14**:526
Lambert, John S., **18**:373n3
Lambeth, William A., M.D., **20**:539
La Monte, George Mason, **21**:131, 361, 610; **22**:82-83, 174, 308-309, 481,n3; **23**:475, 476,n5, 541; **24**:498-500; Mrs., **21**:361
La Monte, Isabel, **23**:541
*Lamp: A Review and Record of Current Literature*, **15**:223,n1, 238; **16**:121n1
Lancaster, Pa., **20**:56; WW addresses, **19**:552, 634, 740-47
Lanciani, Rodolfo Amadeo, **14**:247,n4
Landers, George Marcellus, **17**:582,n3
Landis, Kenesaw Mountain, **17**:503n3, 583
Landon, Francis Griswold, **15**:127,n1,2
Lane, Franklin Knight, **21**:586,n1; **25**:558
Lane, John, **18**:362
Lane, John J., **22**:147,n1
Lang, John Marshall, **15**:273,n2
Langdales, Westmorland, **18**:394, 410
Lanham, Samuel Willis Tucker, **23**:458n1
Lankering, Adolph, **21**:295,n1; **22**:258
Lansing, Catherine Gansevoort (Mrs. Abraham), **16**:404,n1
Lansing, Robert, **21**:607,n1
Lapps, John A., **23**:573n1
Larchmont, N. Y., **25**:233, 234
Larkin, Francis, **14**:186,n2
Larkin, Francis, Jr., **14**:186,n3; **16**:458; **18**:227,n1, 261-62; **19**:488; **20**:506,n1
Larkin, Ida Rahm (Mrs. John), **15**:146,n4
Larkin, John, **15**:146,n4
Larkin, William, Jr., **20**:31,n2
Larkin, William P., **25**:63,n2
La Salle Hotel (Chicago), **24**:162n
Latané, John Holladay, **21**:613,n1
Lathrop, John E., **22**:159,n1, 175, 237, 247-48, 255, 255n3, 292,n1, 404, 524; Mrs., **22**:404
Lathrop, Julia, **25**:544
*Latin Sight Reader* (Howe), **18**:562,n5
Latourette, Kenneth Scott, **22**:385n2
Latourette, Sarah M., **16**:234
Latourette, William, **15**:385,n
Lauchheimer, Sylvan Hayes, **23**:568,n5
Laughlin, Henry Hughart, **15**:132-33,n1
Laughlin, James, Jr., **15**:77,n1,3, 132, 167-69, 361, 527; **16**:336
Laughlin, James B., **16**:336
Laughlin, James Laurence, **14**:241,n7, 248; **24**:581,n2, 582
Laughlin, Sidney Ford Page (Mrs. James, Jr.), **15**:132, 133
Laurence, Lt. P.R.B., **25**:573,n4
Laurier, Sir Wilfrid, **22**:478n3; **24**:329-30,n1, 379, 382

La Vake, Myron E., **14**:94,n1, 97
Laverty, Edgar R., **19**:255,n1; **21**:323
Lavisse, Ernest, **14**:339,n3
law, **22**:263f; **25**:197, 319
Law, Edward, **19**:125,n2
Law, Esther K., **17**:28n1
law, study of, **20**:229
law and legal profession, **21**:64-81
*Law of the Federal and State Constitutions of the United States* (Stimson), **18**:446,n1
law schools, WW on, **20**:229
Lawrence, David, **21**:608,n1; **25**:46,n2, 361,n4
Lawrence, Frank Richard, **16**:292n1,2
Lawrence, Kans., **23**:291; **24**:191
Lawrence, L. I., **18**:483
Lawrence, Mass., **25**:243,n6, 249, 335-36, 409, 426,n4, 430
Lawrence, R. V., **22**:173n1
Lawrence, William Watson, **15**:248
Lawrenceville School, **14**:475; **15**:233, 343; **16**:255, 344; **17**:160; **18**:275-76, 278, 482-83, 609; **21**:84; *The Lawrence*, **18**:483n1; WW address, **20**:514-18
laws, uniformity of, **22**:111
*Laws of New Jersey*, **21**:340n1; **22**:157n3, 546n5, 550n2, 569n1, 575n5, 579,-n3,4,5,6,7; **23**:245, 295n5; **25**:474n4
Lawton, Alexander Robert, **23**:557,n4
Lawton, Alexander Rudolf, **23**:557,n4
*Lawyer in Politics* (Wilson), **23**:199n
lawyers and the legal profession, **20**:462-63; **21**:64-81; **23**:125f, 158, 194-99
Lay, George William, **17**:343-44
Layden, Thomas R., **23**:333-34,n5
L. Castelvecchi and Co., New York City, **14**:10,n4
Lea, Luke, **21**:343n11; **23**:212,n3, 244, 289n2; **24**:206n4, 273, 468, 545-48
Lea, Mary Louise Warner (Mrs. Luke), **23**:212,n4, 244
*Leaders of Reform: Progressive Republicans in Kansas, 1900-16* (La Forte), **25**:621n2
leadership, **22**:109f; **23**:72, 279, 282
League of Nations, **17**:512n1
Leahy, Walter T., **19**:266,n1
Learned, Florence J., **21**:48,n1; **23**:49,n2
Leary, Russel Woodward, **15**:324, 378,n2
Leary, William Matthew, Jr., **16**:89n1
Leavitt, Harry D., **22**:53,n2, 574n1
Lebanon, N. J., **21**:383
*Lectures on Moral Philosophy* (Witherspoon), **17**:352n2
Leda, **15**:354
Ledwith, William Laurence, **14**:43-44,n1
Lee, Alice Ives (Mrs. William Brewster), **14**:364
Lee, Blair, **23**:264,n1, 266n2, 567; **24**:371
Lee, Edward E., **22**:31,n1
Lee, Edward W., **23**:428n7
Lee, Edwin H., **15**:22,n3
Lee, Henry (Light Horse Harry, Princeton 1773), **17**:249; **18**:633; **19**:208

Lee, Ivy Ledbetter, **14**:190,n1, 490n3; **16**:460
Lee, Jubal Early, **23**:507,n5
Lee, Robert Edward, **14**:47n1, 58, 311; **18**:6, 561, 631-45; **19**:53; **20**:439
Lee, Robert Emmett, **24**:287,n1
Lee, William Brewster (Chang), **14**:195, 364; **15**:411,n4; **19**:252; **22**:14
Lee House, Phillipsburg, N. J., **21**:385
Leech, Margaret, **22**:371n5
Le Fevre, Eva Frederica, **23**:21,n10
Lefferts, Harry I., **23**:536n1
*Legal Opinions on Swann Bequest*, **20**:47
legal profession, *see* lawyers and
Legarda, Benito, **24**:224,n2
legislative committees, **21**:473-74
legislative process, **24**:229
legislative reform, **23**:101
legislatures, **23**:91, 92
Lehigh University, **16**:132, 198, 239, 257; **24**:139
Lehigh Valley Co., **24**:475n1
Lehigh Valley Railroad, **21**:403,n3, 499; **23**:450n1
Lehmann, Frederick William, **25**:448,n2
Leicester Hospital, Warwick, Wilsons at, **14**:531
*Leiden des jungen Werthers* (Goethe), **19**:571, 573
Leigh, Frederick Tollington, **22**:39,n6
Leigh (Princeton tradesman), **14**:76
Leighton, Joseph Alexander, **17**:115
Leighton, Victoria Elizabeth Paul (Mrs. Joseph Alexander), **17**:115,n1
Leipzig, **14**:245
Leipzig, University of, **15**:444; **16**:247, 248, 251, 252, 256, 257, 509; **18**:577; **19**:678, 679
Leipziger, Henry Marcus, **15**:536
Leland Stanford Jr. University, **22**:130
*Length of the College Course* (West), **14**:446n2
Lenroot, Irvine Luther, **25**:288,n2
Lentz, John Jacob, **20**:313,n1; **22**:228-29,n1
Leonard, Col. (at Bermuda), **20**:145,n3; Mrs., **20**:139, 149
Leonard, William Day, **16**:243
Leopardi, Giacomo, Conte, **19**:573
Leopold, Richard William, **22**:514n1
Lester, John Calvin, **23**:9,n2
Lethbridge, Edgar E., **16**:548,n1; **21**: 346,n14
*Letter to the Sheriffs of Bristol* (Burke), **14**:14
*Letters* (Pliny the Younger), **19**:597
*Letters from a Chinese Official: Being an Eastern View of Western Civilization* (Dickinson), **16**:121n1
*Letters from John Chinaman* (Dickinson), **16**:121n1
*Letters of Grover Cleveland, 1850-1908* (ed. Nevins), **21**:345n13; **22**:226n3
*Letters of the Presidents of the United States of America: Reproduced from the Collection of Don Belding*, **23**:657n

Leupp, Francis Ellington, **19**:154-55
Levey, Frederick H., **22**:125-26,n1, 136
Levy, Leon Michel, **17**:222-24,n1
Lewis, Edwin Seelye, **15**:155, 294; Mrs. I, **15**:155
Lewis, Griffith Walker, **21**:313n3; **22**:474,n1
Lewis, James Hamilton, **22**:557,n2
Lewis, Loran Ludowick, Jr., **24**:311,n2
Lewis, Lucius Allen, **15**:343n1
Lewis, Robert Ellsworth, **24**:206,n5, 208, 210
Lewis, Vivian Murchison, **21**:7,n4, 20, 43, 62, 90, 114,n2, 158, 217, 219,n1, 226n1, 229, 230, 244, 249, 250, 265, 274, 293, 301, 311, 312, 313, 324, 329, 331, 335n2, 352, 370, 380, 390, 392, 393, 416, 443, 446-47, 452, 463, 485, 487, 495, 511, 520, 521, 526, 529, 549, 584n1, 586, 591; **22**:3, 9, 19, 27, 309; **23**:279,n2,3, 426n4, 628
Lewis, William Henry, **25**:557,n4
Lewis and Clark Centennial Exposition, Portland, Oregon, 1905, **16**:150,n1
Lewis and Clark Expedition, **16**:143-44,n3
Lewisburg (West Virginia) University School, **16**:252
Lexington, Ky., **23**:213; Opera House, **23**:194; WW address, **23**:194-99; WW in, **23**:183
Lexington, Mass., **25**:31
*Lexington* (Va.) *Gazette*, **23**:328n2
Lexington (Ky.) *Herald*, **23**:183n3
Lexow, Clarence, **19**:86,n1
*Liars* (play by H. A. Jones), **15**:396n3
Libbey, Edward Drummond, **18**:530,n2
Libbey, William, **14**:37, 82, 127, 326; **15**:390; **16**:97n2, 485, 498; **17**:143, 387, 388, 409; **21**:229n1, 234; **22**:415n2
Libby, Charles Freeman, **20**:21, 22, 71, 86
Libby, Orin Grant, **14**:231,n3
liberal education, **23**:484-85
liberal education versus manual training, **18**:597-99
liberals, **22**:594, 596
liberty, **14**:321-22; **22**:443-44; **24**:128, 153; **25**:124, 145, 250, 262, 408
*Liberty, Equality, Fraternity* (Stephen), **14**:13
*Liberty* (magazine), **17**:30n1
Liberty Corners, N. J., **23**:475
Liberty Party, **17**:319
Library of Congress, **21**:293
*Library of Southern Literature*, **17**:487,-n1,2, 523-24n1
Lick Observatory, **18**:578
*Life* magazine, **22**:38n5; **23**:177n2
*Life and Labors of Bishop Hare: Apostle to the Sioux* (Howe), **18**:388n1
*Life and Opinions of Tristram Shandy* (Sterne), **14**:503
*Life and Times of Thomas Smith, 1745-1809* (Kon **15**:494,n3
*Life and Times of William Howard Taft* (Pringle), **24**:412n3

*Life of Cicero* (Trollope), **14**:13
*Life of Daniel Coit Gilman* (Franklin), **14**:15n
*Life of Gladstone* (Morely), **24**:506
*Life of Johann Wolfgang Goethe* (Sime), **19**:571
*Life of William Ewart Gladstone* (Morley), **15**:116, 117, 119
*Life of Woodrow Wilson* (Daniels), **20**:566n
Liller, William C., **20**:390-91,n1, 512; **22**:554; **23**:200, 245, 254-55, 259,n3,4
Lilley, Alexander Spinning, **23**:53,n2, 325
*Lin McLean* (Wister), **14**:453,n3
Linbarger, W., **22**:173n1
Lincoln, Abraham, **14**:238, 311, 347, 427; **15**:134, 272; **16**:53; **17**:74, 459, 462, 551; **18**:107, 110, 176, 545, 546n2, 546-47, 602, 646; **19**:30, 47, 53-54, 55, 57, 59-60, 61, 63, 113, 205-206; **20**:365, 367, 375, 384, 389, 399; **21**:62n2, 161-62, 180, 196, 275n2, 292, 329, 330, 404,n4, 418, 425; **22**:4, 280, 419, 421, 429; **23**:23, 24, 216n2, 367, 397-98, 407,n9, 445-46, 466, 488; **24**:75, 151, 152, 153, 261, 292-93, 294, 299, 300, 311, 499, 519; **25**:64, 389, 392, 393, 394-95, 505, 512; WW centennial address, **19**:33-46
Lincoln, Robert Todd, **14**:192, 194
Lincoln, Thomas (1853-1871), **21**:162,n1
Lincoln, Ill., **24**:292
Lincoln, Lincs, Castle, **14**:526; Cathedral, **14**:526; White Hart (hotel), **14**:526; EAW in, **16**:439; Wilsons in, **14**:525-26
Lincoln, Neb., **21**:622; **22**:519n4, 587; **23**:81, 97, 100n1, 237, 284; Burlington Depot, **23**:96; Commercial Club, **23**:95, 96, 97, 98, 99; Fairview, **23**:95, 98, 100; Lincoln hotel, **23**:96, 97, 99; WW in, **23**:95-102, 131; WW addresses, **25**:347-59
*Lincoln Daily Star*, **25**:349n, 359n
Lincoln Protective League, **24**:299n1
Lind, John, **22**:395,n2
Lind, Norman, **22**:395n4
Lindabury, Richard Vliet, **19**:456,n2; **20**:31,n1, 563,n2, 565n; **21**:35n1, 140, 274, 354, 356, 378-79, 388, 449; **22**:181n1, 225
Lindbergh, Charles Augustus (1860-1924), **23**:605n1
Lindell Hotel (Lincoln, Neb.), **25**:347n1
Lindsay, Samuel McCune, **22**:207n4
Lindsey, Benjamin Barr, **19**:419-20,n4, 661; **22**:274-76,n1,2, 291n2, 387-88n1, 405, 525, 537, 584-85, 599; **23**:310,n4, 324-25, 478
Lines Composed a Few Miles above Tintern Abbey (Wordsworth), **16**:378,n2; **17**:192-93,n1
Link, Arthur Stanley, **16**:207n2, 480n1; **17**:124n1; **18**:485n2; **20**:362n4, 564n3, 566n; **21**:91n1; **22**:95,n1, 123n2,

Link, Arthur Stanley, (*cont.*)
    262n2, 282n1, 436n1, 447n5, 512n1,
    575n2, 579n3,4; **23:**213n2, 262n3,
    267n1, 289n2, 432n9, 513n4, 544n1,
    583n1, 591n1, 602n1, 603n1; **24:**5n2,
    9n1, 42n2, 225n1,2, 248n1, 308n1,
    332n2, 398n1, 400n2, 403n1, 501n1,
    524n3; **25:**23n2, 25n1, 96n2, 143n1,
    284n4, 493n1, 520n1, 566n1, 579n2,
    587n3, 632n1
Lionberger, Isaac Henry, **15:**341-43;
    **20:**125, 216, 238, 247-48, 304, 305,
    305n4, 306, 322, 389-90, 398-99;
    **23:**459-60, 479, 549
Lionberger, John Shepley, **20:**125,n1,
    216
Lionberger, Louise Shepley (Mrs. Isaac
    Henry), **19:**734,n1; **20:**216,n1
Lipper, Arthur, **22:**39,n17
Lippi, Fra Lippo, **15:**229, 335
Lippincott, J. B., Company, **14:**134-35;
    **16:**501n5
Lippincott, James Dundas, **16:**5
Lippincott, Job, **25:**582
Lippincott, Job Herbert, **19:**554; **21:**
    145-46, 274-75; **22:**125
Lippmann, Walter, **20:**350n2
Lipscomb, Andrew Adgate, **14:**360n1
Lipscomb, Guy Fleming, **19:**679
liquor, **25:**21n3, 151; *see also* prohibition
liquor interests, **20:**565n
*Literary Associations of the English
    Lakes* (Rawnsley), **16:**451,n1
*Literary Digest,* **17:**560,n2, 566
*Littèll's Living Age,* **14:**440,n2
Little, Henry Stafford, **15:**300,n2,
    339,n1; **18:**574
Little Presidential Primary (*World's
    Work*), **23:**234,n5
Little Rock, Ark., Woodrow Wilson Club,
    **23:**233, 517; WW speech, **23:**517-18
Littlecote, Wilts, **15:**446
Littlehales, Thomas, **22:**513,n1
Littleton, Martin Wiley, **14:**210,n1;
    **22:**192,n3; **25:**566,n1
Littmann, Richard Ludwig Enno, **15:**
    121,n2, 134, 376n1; **16:**186-87,n1,
    233-34; **19:**165,n1, 166, 170, 266-67,
    268, 269, 305, 306, 327-28, 347n1, 353
Livermore, John Robert McDowell,
    **25:**467,n2
Liverpool, **18:**416; Wilsons in, **14:**521
Liverpool, University of, **16:**157
Livezey, William Edmund, **20:**309n2,
    312n2
*Living Age,* **14:**440,n2
Livingston, William Smith, Mrs., **16:**
    18,n3
Livy (Titus Livius Carus), **14:**287; **19:**597
Lizzie (caretaker at Dodge Lodge),
    **21:**385
Lloyd, Ernest W., **23:**365
Lloyd, Francis Vernon, **17:**384
Lloyd, James Tilghman, **23:**566,n2
Lobb, Mary Beatrice Jackson (Mrs.

Reginald Popham), **20:**184,n1, 185-86,
    188; **22:**325,n6
Lobb, Mrs. (mother of R. P. Lobb), **20:**186
Lobb, Reginald Popham, **20:**184n1, 185-
    86, 187, 188; **22:**325,n6
lobbying and lobbyists, **22:**355, 541-42;
    **23:**8; **24:**199, 229, 421, 440; *see also*
    special interests
Lobingier, Charles Sumner, **22:**279,n4
*Local Government* (Chalmers), **14:**14
local option, **21:**354; **22:**599; **23:**207, 623
Lochner, Louis Paul, **20:**556n2
Locke, John, **19:**666
Lockerbie, Dumfriesshire, **18:**361
Lockhart, Charles, **15:**129n1
Lockhart, Florence Dilworth (Mrs.
    James Henry), **16:**69,n1
Lockhart, James Henry, **15:**128,n1, 144,
    402, 526, 570, 573; **16:**5, 69-70, 336
Lockwood, Thomas Brown, **24:**311,n2
Locomotive Engineers, Association of,
    **25:**208
Locust Dale Academy, Virginia, **16:**252
Lodge, Henry Cabot, **14:**8, 352;
    **21:**275n2; **24:**467,n2
Lodge, James Thornton, **23:**511
Lodge, Sir Oliver (Joseph), **19:**729,n1
Loeb, James, **16:**210n1, 211
Loeb, William (1866-1937), **16:**243
Loetscher, Christian, **16:**426
Loetscher, Frederick William, **16:**104,-
    n1, 426,n3
Loetscher, Lefferts Augustine, **15:**169n2
log-rolling in Congress, **19:**372
Logan, George Bryan, **19:**17,n1, 24-25
Logan, George Bryan, Jr., **19:**17, 25n2
Logan, Joseph C., **24:**566
Logue, William Augustin, **22:**413,n3,
    415
London, **14:**246; **15:**385, 396; **18:**344;
    **22:**604; Albert Hall, **22:**514; Bishop of,
    **19:**109; British Linen Company Bank,
    **15:**355; Brown's Hotel, **14:**535; Buck-
    ingham Palace Hotel, **14:**529,n11, 548;
    Carlton Hotel, **15:**147; Comedy
    Theatre, **14:**527n7; Dorchester House,
    **21:**592; Duke of York's Theatre,
    **14:**528n8; Dutch Gallery (Van Wisse-
    lingh's), **16:**480; Garrick Theatre,
    **14:**529n10; Hotel Portland, **14:**550;
    Hotel Thackeray, **16:**436,n2, 438, 444;
    Liverpool Street Station, **14:**529; Lord
    Mayor, **19:**109, 534; National Portrait
    Gallery, **14:**527, 534; Royal Academy
    exhibition, **14:**527, 552; Tate Gallery,
    **14:**552, 555; The Temple, **14:**552;
    Temple Church, **14:**527; Wallace Col-
    lection, **14:**528,n9; Westminster Ab-
    bey, **14:**552; **15:**396; EAW at, **16:**445,
    449; Wilsons in, **14:**526-29, 534, 548,
    552
London, University of, **16:**465, 507;
    **18:**368n7
*London and Its Environs: Handbook for
    Travellers* (Baedeker), **16:**436

London & North Western Railway, **16**:444

London *Times*, **15**:148, 162n1; **16**:506,n2; **18**:410,n2; **19**:111

*London Tribune*, **16**:460

Lone Starry Hours (music of, used for Class Ode of '79), **15**:388n1

Long, Augustus White, **14**:225,n2, 474; **15**:375; **16**:132, 255; **17**:408

Long, John Davis, **17**:228n1

Long, Mahlon, **14**:476

Long Branch, N. J., **21**:218n7, 227; **25**:504-507, 511; Lyceum, **23**:446; Ocean Park Casino, **21**:228n1; WW campaign speeches, **21**:227-28; **23**: 442-47

*Long Branch* (N. J.) *Record*, **21**:299n2; **22**:300

Long Island, Princeton alumni, **20**:272-76

*Long Night* (Weyman), **15**:115,n1

Longmans, Green & Co., **20**:582

Longview, Texas, WW in, **23**:519

Loomis, Elmer Howard, **14**:221,n8, 277, 326, 327; **17**:408

Loomis, Francis Butler, **21**:615,n7

Loos, Isaac Althaus, **14**:559

LoPezzi, Annie, **25**:426n4

Lord, Daniel Minor, **14**:552n2

Lord, Frank Howard, **14**:46-47

Lord, J. Walter (*formerly* John Walterhouse Lord), **20**:264,n1

Lord, May or Mary Townsend Nicoll (Mrs. James Brown), **16**:223n1

Lord, Miss (daughter of Daniel Minor Lord), **14**:551,n2

Lord, William Rogers, **14**:551,n1

Lorenz, Adolf, M.D., **14**:298,n1

Lorimer, George Claude, **15**:60,n4

Lorimer, William, **21**:343-44,n11; **24**: 291,n1, 299n1

Lorimer-Lincoln League, **24**:299,n1

Los Angeles, **20**:86; **22**:519n4, 533; **23**:37, 251; Alexandria Hotel, **23**:41n4,5, 44, 49, 51; Annandale Country Club, **23**:51; Bar Association, **20**:86; City Club, **23**:41, 44, 50-51; Hamburger's restaurant, **23**:32n1; Jefferson Club, **23**:32,n1, 41n4, 45; LaGrande Station, **23**:44; New Jersey Society, **23**:41,n5, 44, 46, 51; Princeton alumni, **19**:146; Princeton Club, **23**:41,n4, 44, 60; Temple Auditorium, **23**:50; WW addresses, **23**:27, 32-48, 50-51, 52; Woodrow Wilson Club, **23**:251, 251n1

Los Angeles County, Cal., Democratic County Convention, **23**:251

*Los Angeles Examiner*, **23**:40n, 45, 45n, 51n

*Los Angeles Times*, **23**:44n, 50n1

Lotos Club, New York City, **16**:292,n1, 301, 532, 533

Loubet, Émile François, **15**:273,n1, 297, 353

Loudenslager, Henry Clay, **23**:393

Loudenslager, William B., **23**:522n1, 523, 529n3

Loughran, Frank E., **23**:259,n6; **24**:500-501,n1, 510

Loughrigg Cottage, Rydal, Ambleside, Westmorland, **16**:430; **18**:368n4, 370, 371,n7, 376, 379, 380, 407, 415, 416

Loughrigg Fell, **18**:342

Louis XIV, **18**:87

Louisiana, **23**:596; **24**:468, 482-83

Louisiana Purchase, **14**:433, 519; **16**:364; **17**:311

Louisiana Purchase Exposition (or Universal Exposition), St. Louis, 1904, **14**:395n1, 434,n1, 437, 439; **15**:60,n1, 105-106, 318, 443, 463, 472n1; *see also* International Congress of Arts and Science, St. Louis, 1904

Louisiana State University, **19**:412

Louisville, Ky., **19**:196, 484; **20**:238; **22**:102, 113, 138,n1; **23**:154, 199, 221, 303; **24**:358; Churchill Downs, **19**:212; Country Club, **19**:212; Fidelity Trust Co., **19**:123; Louisville High School, **19**:196,n2; Princeton alumni, **14**:447; **19**:155, 196, 212-14; Seelbach Hotel, **19**:211, 212; WW address, **19**:212-14; WW in, **19**:211, 212

Louisville & Nashville Railroad, **18**:465

Louisville *Courier-Journal*, **16**:533n2; **19**:211n, 214; **20**:541n1, 544; **23**:199,-n1, 303n1; **24**:146n

*Louisville Times*, **24**:358n3

Lounsbury, Thomas Raynesford, **14**:19-20,n1, 329, 558-59, 560; **16**:388-89

Louvre, **14**:536

love and charity, **22**:528-29

Love, Alfred Henry, **24**:182,n1

Love, Sarah Jane Rodgers (Mrs. Thomas Calvin), **24**:446,n1

Love, Thomas Bell, **21**:584,n1; **22**:25, 122-23, 224-25, 409-10, 422-23, 433, 434, 576, 583-84; **23**:231, 242, 255-56, 258, 260-61, 267-69, 286, 302, 308-309, 316, 507, 512, 589; **24**:50, 64, 163-65, 248, 254-55, 256, 269-71, 384, 446, 464, 467; **25**:624-26, 648

*Love Letters of Thomas Carlyle and Jane Welsh* (ed. Carlyle), **18**:362,n1

Loveen, Michael, **22**:253,n4

Lovejoy, Owen Reed, **22**:157

Lovelace, Richard, **23**:110,n6

Lovell, Verner R., **23**:658; **24**:82, 137

Lovett, Adelaide, **20**:581,n1

Lovett, Edgar Odell, **14**:277, 326, 394; **15**:14, 17, 213, 508n1; **16**:35-36, 80, 81, 194, 284, 331, 332, 337, 488-89, 557n3; **17**:65-66, 67, 88, 146, 408, 448-49, 586, 602; **18**:396-97, 416, 570, 571; **19**:558; **20**:580-81; **21**:159

Lovett, Henry Malcolm, **20**:581,n1

Lovett, Mary Ellen Hale (Mrs. Edgar Odell), **18**:397; **20**:581,n1

Low, George Clark, **22**:375,n2; **23**:467n1

Low, Seth, **14**:69, 188; **17**:92n2; **19**:26n2, 109; **22**:172,n1, 214, 417n1, 424
Low Wood Inn, nr. Grasmere Cumberland, **18**:409
Lowe, A. B., **23**:339-40,n1, 340, 340n3, 356
Lowell, Abbott Lawrence, **14**:14, 31, 359; **15**:292n; **16**:384; **18**:607n3, 622, 625, 627; **19**:11, 23, 32-33,n1, 210,n2, 254, 260, 263, 270, 274,n1, 290, 310, 383, 407,n1, 416, 448, 495-96, 556,n1, 561, 562, 577, 578, 602, 619, 622-23, 623, 627, 628, 649, 652, 672, 699, 699-700, 704, 708; **20**:11, 12, 72, 75, 88, 91, 118, 276-77, 287-88, 289, 468, 475, 487-88, 497, 538, 548; **21**:109, 143, 580n1; **23**:133,n2, 134; **24**:77; **25**:535-36, 541
Lowell, Anna Parker Lowell (Mrs. Abbott Lawrence), **14**:359; **19**:270, 290
Lowell, James Russell, **16**:172, 174; **22**:335
Lowell, Josephine Shaw, **22**:157n1
Lowell, Mass., **25**:268; Middlesex Women's Club, **14**:314; WW address, **14**:314-16
*Lowell* (Mass.) *Sun*, **14**:316
Lowitt, Richard W., **21**:344n12
Lowrie, James Walter, **16**:23,n6
Lowry, Edward George, **25**:27,n2
Loyalists of the American Revolution, **14**:312
Lucas, Edward Verrall, **18**:411,n3
Lucerne County, Pa., **21**:211
Lucian, **19**:597
Lucretius Carus, Titus, **14**:208; **18**:582
Ludington, Arthur Crosby, **19**:25-26,n1,2,3,4, 155-58, 307; **20**:78,n1; **22**:400n2
Ludington, Katharine, **18**:390,n1; **20**:78,n3
Ludlow, James Meeker, **24**:514,n2
Luigi Amedeo, Duke of Abruzzi, Prince of Savoy, **17**:226n1, 228n1
Lukeman, Joseph P., **14**:368n1, 378n4, 394, 495n1, 496, 497
Luongo, Frederico, **24**:404, 406
*Luria, A Tragedy* (Browning), **18**:328n1; **19**:41,n2
Lusk, James W., **23**:85,n4
Lustgarten, William, **22**:570,n1
Luther College, Decorah, Iowa, **16**:257
Luzern (Lucerne), Tivoli Hotel, **14**:539,n16; Wilsons at, **14**:538, 539, 540, 541
Lycidas (Milton), **14**:381
Lyme and Old Lyme, Conn., **16**:153,n1, 154,n1, 155, 156, 158, 160,n1, 161, 163, 167, 168, 169, 171, 172, 174, 175, 178, 181; **18**:346,n9, 351, 354, 367, 381, 384, 387, 393, 412, 413, 422; **19**:193, 262, 270, 304, 307, 308, 309, 311, 312, 317, 321, 330, 333, 348, 349, 352, 353, 354, 357-58, 359n1, 382, 384, 385, 388; **20**:501, 538, 541,n1, 543,

552, 553, 554, 561, 562, 567, 569, 572, 573, 575,n1, 577, 578, 581; **21**:4, 5, 13, 14, 15, 17, 22, 24, 25, 26, 34, 35, 36, 38, 39, 40, 41, 46, 50, 51, 53, 58, 59, 84, 87, 88, 107, 143, 225; **22**:534; **23**:81, 111, 127, 128, 134, 139, 153, 172, 174, 184; Boxwood, **18**:354n1; First Congregational Church, **20**:538,n1; **21**:84; Lyme artists' exhibition, **19**:355-56, 357; Princeton alumni, **20**:320
Lynch, Frederick Bicknell, **23**:85,n3
Lynett, Edward James, **25**:221n2
Lynn, Mass., **20**:465
Lynton, Devon, **15**:410
Lyon, Adrian, **22**:294,n1,2, 308
Lyon, Charles Edward, **14**:146n5; **16**:198
Lyons, Maurice F., **24**:509n1; **25**:50
Lyons, University of, **17**:556
Lyric Theatre (Allentown), **24**:138, 140
Lyric Theatre (Baltimore), **24**:370f as, **19**:597

Mabie, Hamilton Wright, **15**:216,n3; **17**:123n4; **18**:525,n5; **19**:533-34,n1; **22**:172,n1
Mabie, Jeannette Trivett (Mrs. Hamilton Wright), **19**:533,n4
McAdoo, Sarah Fleming, **24**:217n1
McAdoo, William Gibbs, **21**:108, 265, 298; **22**:51, 188,n1; **23**:135n3, 247, 258n1, 285, 303,n2, 470, 547, 561, 584n2, 588, 602-603; **24**:18, 28, 48, 71, 217, 237, 268, 274, 286, 306,n2, 384, 386, 400, 403, 450, 472, 473, 524n3, 568, 588; **25**:24, 60, 62, 92, 109n1, 110, 111-12,n2, 134, 135n1, 184n1, 283, 288, 421, 423, 448, 452-53, 507, 532, 550, 552, 611-12, 617-18; acceptance of vice chairmanship of national committee, **24**:570; Bryan on, **25**:623, 645; photograph, **24**: illustration section
MacAlister, James, **17**:510,n1
McAllister, Albert R., **23**:533n3
McAlpin, Charles Williston, **14**:5,n2, 122-23, 125, 130-31, 167-69, 380, 391-92, 398, 464, 490, 497-98, 499-500, 543-44, 545, 548, 549-50; **15**:15, 55, 101, 180, 212, 242-43, 339-40, 374, 434, 441, 570, 571, 573, 575, 576, 580; **16**:5, 15, 27, 137, 145, 146, 167, 169-70, 192, 214-15, 266-67, 273, 282, 304, 308, 322, 342, 343, 389, 412, 430-31, 446, 448, 474, 488, 492-93, 495, 504, 556, 562; **17**:18-19, 221, 459n1, 596; **18**:259, 261-62, 340, 382, 385, 631; **19**:3, 3n2, 4, 5, 195n1, 407, 412, 557-58, 626, 659, 703; **20**:12, 13, 17, 52, 96, 102, 430, 471, 476, 486, 493, 496, 497; **21**:13, 13-14, 49-50, 463, 471, 536-39; **22**:256, 293, 358; **24**:557; **25**:560n1
McAlpin, David Hunter, M.D., **22**:256,n1
McAlpin, Henry, **23**:558,n9

McAlpin, Sara Carter Pyle (Mrs. Charles Williston), **14:**5,n2, 498, 500, 549, 550; **15:**441; **16:**430, 448,n1; **18:**385; **21:**13,-n3; **22:**293,n1; **24:**557,n2
McAneny, George, **21:**617-18
McArthur, John E., **23:**536n1
MacArthur, Robert Stuart, **14:**298,n1
McAshan, James Everett, **16:**556-57,n1
McAteer, James Joseph, **23:**535
Macaulay, Thomas Babington, 1st Baron Macaulay, **15:**473
Macauley, Charles Raymond, **25:**55, 118n1
McBee, Silas, **16:**228
*Macbeth* (Shakespeare), **20:**559,n3
Macbeth, William, **16:**506
McBride, Andrew Francis, M.D., **19:**171,n3; **21:**302; **25:**514n2
McCabe, David Aloysius, **19:**615,n1, 678
McCall, John Augustine, **16:**333n2
McCampbell, George Meriwether, Jr., **20:**116-17, 120-21, 134-35,n1
McCann, William Phillip, **18:**414n1
McCardle, Eliza, *see* Johnson, Eliza McCardle
McCarter, Robert Harris, **14:**46; **15:**390, 573; **19:**119,n3; **20:**22, 31,n1; **21:**131-32; **23:**295n5
McCarter, Thomas Nesbitt, **14:**544,n5; **22:**83-84,n1, 359; **23:**346, 354; **24:**432,n3
McCarter, Thomas Nesbitt, Jr., **15:**225,n1, 527; **21:**27,n1, 139
McCarter, Uzal Haggerty, **15:**223,n1, 248, 402, 527, 569; **16:**5
McCarthy, Charles, **24:**554,n1; **25:**287
*McCarthy of Wisconsin* (Fitzpatrick), **24:**554n1
MacCauley, Clay, **16:**384
McCay, Leroy Wiley, **14:**213,n3, 214, 215, 216, 218, 219, 221, 326, 395; **15:**126; **17:**155, 408; **18:**301
MacChesney, Nathan William, **19:**46n
McClellan, George Brinton (1826-1885), **21:**86
McClellan, George Brinton, Jr. (1865-1940), **15:**533; **16:**23, 322, 362n1, 372, 372n2, 373; **18:**372-73,n1, 436, 574; **19:**169, 170, 175-77; **20:**402n1; **21:**137, 599
McClellan, Georgiana Louise Heckscher (Mrs. George Brinton, Jr.), **18:**373; **19:**170,n1
McClenahan, Bessie Lee (Mrs. Howard), **15:**120,n3, 152
McClenahan, Howard, **14:**326; **15:**152; **16:**64n1, 427-28, 464; **17:**394,n5, 402, 403, 408; **18:**341, 477, 489, 492, 517-18, 518n1, 572-74; **19:**450
McClintock, Andrew Hamilton, **15:**471,-n3
McClintock, Euphemia, **22:**577,n5
McClung, Thomas Lee, **19:**448,n2, 561
McClure, Alexander Kelly, **14:**194

McClure, Alfred James Pollock, **14:**469; **15:**176-77, 388n1
McClure, Alfred James, Jr., **14:**469; **15:**176,n1,4
McClure, Annie Dixon (Mrs. James Gore King), **19:**484-85,n1
McClure, Charles Freeman Williams, **14:**126,n1, 127, 128, 326, 395; **15:**178, 294, 295, 411; **16:**155-56, 223, 431-32, 469; **17:**106, 387, 408, 409, 437, 561, 564, 605; **18:**286; **19:**70, 402n2
McClure, Hugh S., **20:**349,n1, 351
McClure, James Gore King, **16:**412,n1; **17:**125; **19:**380-81,n1, 481, 485; **20:**59,n1, 151
McClure, Jay Cooke, **14:**469; **15:**176,n1,4
McClure, Louise Foster Cutter (Mrs. Alfred James Pollock), **14:**469,n2; **15:**176,n2
McClure, Samuel Sidney, **14:**97,n1; **22:**85,n1
*McClure's Magazine*, **14:**527n7; **15:**306-n4; **22:**81n1, 85, 85n1,2, 142n1, 504n1; **23:**75n2, 303,n1,3
McCollum, Augustus R., **23:**268,n7
McComas, Henry Clay, **19:**678
McCombs, William Frank, **21:**108, 294-95, 607; **22:**518n3, 519n4, 581; **23:**135,n3, 184, 213, 215-16, 218, 233, 233,n4, 235-36, 242-43, 247-48, 252,-n2, 253, 259-60, 261, 263, 287, 289, 309-10,n3, 324-27, 340-41, 352, 355-56, 360-61, 437,n2, 470, 561, 589, 596, 601, 602, 604, 632-33; **24:**7,n3, 42, 81, 253, 286-87, 289n1, 357, 369, 382, 383n1, 384, 464, 464-65, 467, 468, 472, 490, 492, 500n1, 507n2, 509n1, 523, 524n3, 527n8, 531, 553, 568, 570, 586, 587, 588; **25:**23, 47, 60, 64, 92, 135,n1, 198, 212-13, 233, 234, 286, 415, 421, 423, 507, 524, 525, 550, 562, 571, 572, 610, 618-19, 623n1, 642; ambassador-ship, **25:**610-11, 614,n1; Clapp com-mittee, **25:**109,n1, 110,n6, 459n3; congratulatory message, **25:**522; health, **25:**50; New York politics, **25:**283; Senator Lea's views on, **24:**546-48; WW tribute, **25:**274-81; photo-graph, **24:**illustration section
McCook, John James, **14:**253, 290, 396,-n1; **15:**184, 185, 527; **16:**131, 199, 276,n1, 277f, 303, 304n1, 424n1
McCord, Alvin Carr, **18:**17,n1, 20
McCorkle, Walter Lee, **18:**532,n1, 563; **21:**105,n1; **22:**413-14,n1, 433, 518n3, 519n4; **25:**593n1
MacCorkle, William Alexander, **16:**565,n1
McCormick, Cyrus (Princeton 1912), **18:**423, 547, 554, 562
McCormick, Cyrus Hall, Sr. (1809-1884), **14:**98, 110, 115, 122, 517; **19:**380,n2, 401
McCormick, Cyrus Hall, Jr. (1859-1936;

McCormick, Cyrus Hall, Jr., (cont.)
  Princeton, 1879), **14:**98-99, 108, 115,
  122, 144, 195, 210-11, 225, 227, 248,
  291-92, 297-98, 335, 360, 421, 422,
  423, 424, 429, 435, 440, 453, 465;
  **15:**64-65, 67, 390, 405, 505, 569, 573;
  **16:**5, 47-48, 191; **17:**206-207, 212, 615;
  **18:**16, 60-61, 272-73, 274, 423, 434,
  444-45, 545, 546-47, 553-54, 562, 564,
  624; **19:**10-11, 64, 65n1, 74-75, 75-77,
  119, 120, 124, 140, 140n2, 155, 158,
  159, 162, 163, 195, 196-97, 199, 256,
  257, 267, 268, 293n2, 388,n1, 397-99,
  400-401, 404, 418, 423-25, 439, 454,
  456, 460-61, 481n1, 481-82, 541, 557,
  560, 603, 609, 620, 631-32, 632, 633,
  634, 657, 662, 697, 698, 727, 728, 730-
  31, 733, 735, 748; **20:**8n, 73, 130n2,
  174, 191, 192, 211-14, 216, 217, 219-
  21, 222, 224, 236, 241, 245, 246, 252,
  253, 254, 262, 263, 270, 271-72 283,
  321-24, 353-54, 354-55, 357, 360, 361,
  362, 377, 393-95, 396-97, 403, 425,
  427-28, 431, 432, 433, 445, 454,
  455,n1,2,3,4, 456, 458, 460-61, 469,
  471, 472-73, 477, 479-81, 483, 485,
  493, 494, 501, 544, 545, 548, 550, 551,
  553, 554, 555, 556, 557, 577-78; **21:**10,
  140, 152, 321, 353, 362n1, 385, 518-19,
  543, 594-95; **22:**29, 71, 388, 405-406,
  436; **23:**314,n2, 594; **24:**400, 545;
  **25:**135, 530; campaign contributions,
  **25:**109,n2, 110,n4,6, 459,n1,3; photograph, **20:**illustration section
McCormick, Edith Rockefeller (Mrs.
  Harold Fowler), **14:**453,n1; **19:**65,n1
McCormick, Harold Fowler, **14:**453,n1;
  **19:**165; **25:**110n4
McCormick, Harriet Hammond (Mrs.
  Cyrus Hall, Jr.), **14:**99, 292, 335, 424,
  453; **18:**60, 547, 562; **19:**48,n1, 74, 75,
  77
McCormick, [Nancy] Nettie Maria
  Fowler (Mrs. Cyrus Hall, Sr.), **14:**335;
  **18:**287, 290-91; **21:**541,n2, 543, 556;
  **25:**110n4
McCormick, Stanley Robert, **15:**573
McCormick, Vance Criswell, **22:**408-409,
  409n1; **23:**155, 220, 230
McCormick family, **16:**18n4; **21:**492
McCormick Harvesting Machine Co.,
  **14:**292n1; **15:**65,n1,2, 67
McCormick Theological Seminary, **16:**
  248; **19:**380,n2, 401, 471, 479, 485
*McCormick Theological Seminary His-
  torical Celebration* . . . , **19:**479n
McCosh, Andrew James, M.D., **15:**134,-
  n1, 571n1, 572, 577
McCosh, Isabella Guthrie (Mrs. James),
  **14:**106, 552
McCosh, James, **14:**46, 186,n1, 347, 408,
  415, 482; **15:**111, 134n1, 185n1, 271,
  284n, 462n2, 499, 503n2, 529n6;
  **16:**264, 500, 501; **17:**230, 328, 330-31,
394-95, 581,n6; **18:**257, 339, 339n2,
  608; **19:**193n3, 506; **24:**255
McCosh, James (of Merksworth, Dalry,
  Ayrshire), **19:**193n3
MacCracken, Henry Mitchell, **16:**238,n1,
  272, 292n1
McCrady, Edward, **14:**353,n2, 518
McCran, Thomas Francis, **22:**575n2;
  **24:**325,n4; **25:**513,n1
McCrea, James, **18:**40
McCreary, James Bennett, **24:**141, 145,
  146
McCurdy, Richard Aldrich, **16:**333n2
McCutcheon, Samuel St. John, **22:**550n2
McDermit, Frank M., **21:**263n4; **22:**
  147,n2, 235-36,n1
McDermott, Edward John, **24:**145
McDermott, Malcolm Mallette, **24:**94,n1
MacDonald, Francis Charles, **16:**132,
  255; **17:**290,n1, 408; **19:**422-23,n1;
  **20:**172,n1
MacDonald, Gordon, **18:**490,n5
MacDonald, James, **19:**238,n4
McDonald, John F., **23:**258
MacDonald, Pirie, photographer, **14:**40,-
  n2, 43, 56, 76, 88, 97, 101
MacDonald, William, **14:**350-53
McDonald, William Jesse (Bill), **25:**423-
  24,n1, 448, 507, 508, 509, 518, 525-26,
  532
McDowell, William Fraser, **17:**128,n4
McElroy, Katharine Louise, **14:**92
McElroy, Louise Robinson Booker (Mrs.
  Robert McNutt), **14:**92, 95; **20:**137
McElroy, Robert McNutt, **14:**92, 95;
  **15:**200; **16:**92; **19:**615, 616; **20:**137
McEnerney, Garret William, **23:**56,n3
McEwan, William Leonard, **14:**452,n2;
  **15:**214,n1, 339; **17:**125, 127, 130
McFane, James Augustine, **19:**264n1,
  266; **21:**90,n4
MacFarland, Grenville S., **25:**288,n1
MacFarland, Henry Brown Floyd, **19:**
  64,n5, 400
MacFarlane, James Rieman, **15:**569,
  572-73; **16:**5; **17:**211,n4, 385; **18:**334,n1
McGaffey, Amasa B., **24:**306,n1
McGiffert, Arthur Cushman, **16:**400,n5
McGill, Alexander Taggart, Jr., **21:**
  343n9
McGill University, **16:**465, 508-509; **19:**
  138
McGillicuddy, Daniel John, **24:**287,n1,
  467, 490; **25:**618, 619n1
McGinnis, Peter James, **25:**513,n1
McGovern, Francis Edward, **22:**57, 61,
  64; **23:**320, 322, 480n1
McGovern, John Joseph, **23:**169,n9
McGowan, Michael J., Jr., **22:**253,n5,6,
  367,n1
McGrath, James J., **22:**136n1, 367,n2;
  **23:**345
McGraw, John Thomas, **25:**649,n4
McGregor, Duncan, **23:**480n1

Machen, John Gresham, 14:8-9
McHenry, John Geiser, 24:287,n1
machine politics, 20:36, 193, 195f;
    22:593, 594, 602, 603; 23:8, 34-37, 284,
    303, 361, 364, 366, 459, 522, 544n1,
    546-47, 567, 575, 577, 578, 620;
    24:110, 168-70, 232, 431, 480; 25:79,
    117, 236, 244, 267, 347 Δ I. H. Lion-
    berger, 23:459; A. J. Montague,
    23:359; J. Garland Pollard, 23:601,
    602n1
McHugh (code name), 24:49-50,n1
McIlhany, Hugh Milton, Jr., 16:195,n4
McIlvaine, Anne, 21:53,n2, 54n1, 62
McIlvaine, William Brown, 15:569; 16:5;
    17:598n2; 19:118, 118n1, 123, 124,
    609, 631, 632, 633, 657, 662; 20:11,
    211, 216, 217, 245, 252, 253, 321, 485,
    545, 548, 550, 551, 553, 554, 556, 557,
    579; 21:10; 23:594
McIlwain, Charles Howard, 16:41, 41-
    42,n1, 48, 131, 185, 251, 452n1;
    17:408; 18:271; 19:619; 20:86; 22:165-
    66,n1
McIlwain, Mary Irwin (Mrs. Charles
    Howard), 16:452,n1
MacInnes, Charles Ranald, 16:160, 163,
    198; 18:578; 19:138, 139
McIntire, Michael F., 21:22,n1, 23
Mack, Norman Edward, 19:464-65; 21:
    101, 102; 23:566; 24:5, 497, 515;
    25:67n1
McKaig, Ida A., 16:234
MacKay, David L., 21:287-88, 297-98,
    322-23, 336-37
McKay, Douglas, 14:331
McKay Metallic Fastening Machine,
    25:296
McKelway, Alexander Jeffrey, 22:206-
    208,n1, 226; 23:236, 244, 651; 24:566;
    25:30, 310-12, 543-45
McKelway, St. Clair, 14:253; 15:166,
    193-94; 16:372,n3; 22:134-35, 170;
    25:454,n2, 455, 457
McKelway, Virginia Brooks Thompson
    (Mrs. St. Clair), 15:166
McKenney, Frederic Duncan, 16:5
McKenny, Luke, 21:335n2, 463
McKenzie, Alexander, 14:114
MacKenzie, Ian Douglas, 17:491,n1
Mackenzie, John M., 15:579
Mackenzie, W. A., 15:579
Mackenzie, William Adams, Jr., 24:
    308,n5
Mackenzie, William Douglas, 15:350,-
    n1,2; 16:274n2, 352; 17:125, 491,n1;
    18:9,n5, 63, 359, 376, 397, 494, 512;
    19:168,n3, 361,n4, 736
Mackey, Ebenezer, 19:387-88,n1, 399,
    738-39
McKim, Charles Follen, 15:449-50,n1,
    467,n1, 468, 469-70
McKim, Mead and White, 15:450n1, 467,
    468; 16:182

McKinley, William, 14:344, 352; 15:
    148-49; 21:506; 23:379n2; 24:193,
    257,n2; 25:205
McKinley Tariff, 1890, 19:361
McKinney, Glenn Ford, 18:456
McKinney, Robert Morris, 18:470,n1,
    473
McKinsey, Thomas, 22:238,n1,3
Macksey, William Pierce, 22:212,n1,
    232, 241, 253, 330, 330n1; 23:333, 353
Macksey Commission, 24:458,n2
McLanahan, Allen, 20:89,n3
McLanahan, James Craig, 20:89,n2
McLanahan, John Davison, 20:89,n4
McLanahan, Samuel, Sr., 16:207,n3;
    20:89-90
McLanahan, Samuel, Jr., 20:89,n4
McLanahan, Stewart Kennedy, 20:89,n4
MacLaren, Donald Campbell, 14:82,n5
MacLaren, Elizabeth Higgons (Mrs.
    Donald Campbell), 14:82,n5
MacLaren, Malcolm, 18:337,n1, 338,
    517,n2,3, 518,n1, 577
McLauchlan, William Henry, 15:126,-
    n3,4
McLaughlin, Andrew Cunningham,
    16:106,n1, 111-12
McLaughlin, Annie M., 14:21,n1; 15:
    326,n3
McLean, Andrew, 25:435n1
Maclean, John, Jr., 14:301n2; 15:284n,
    557
Maclean, John (Princeton 1816), 15:
    284n, 557
McLean, John Roll, 22:255n1
McLean, William Pinkney, 23:512,n2
McLeod, Archibald Angus, 14:6n4, 72-73
McLeod, Archibald Angus, Jr., 14:6n4,
    73
McLeod, Elizabeth Atkins (Mrs. Arch-
    ibald Angus, Sr.), 14:5,n4,6, 72-73,
    84-85
MacLeod, Norman M., 20:556n2
Macloskie, George, 14:126,n1, 127, 128;
    16:419, 421, 506-507,n1, 518; 19:
    261,n1
Macloskie, Lila Mansfield Smith Camp-
    bell (Mrs. George II), 19:261n1
Macloskie, Mary Dunn (Mrs. George I),
    19:261,n2
McLoughlin, Robert W., 24:35,n3
McMahon, John, 23:536n2
McMahon, Robert Fulton, letter to N. Y.
    Sun, 20:278-82, 311, 314, 320, 382,n3,
    383,n6, 424; W. M. Daniels on, 21:11
McMaster, George Hunter, 25:519,n2
McMaster, John Bach, 14:280, 286, 310,
    441, 442; 17:263,n2,3; 21:609,n1
McMaster, S. B., 14:331
McMillan, Charles, 15:294, 295; 17:408
Macmillan Company, 19:7n3
MacMurray, John Van Antwerp, 15:
    143n2; 16:567-70,n1, 570-71; 17:64;
    18:12,n1,2,3,4, 403-404

MacNair, Theodor Monroe, **23**:46,n4
McNary, William Sarsfield, **24**:361,n1
McNeill, Israel C., **17**:475
MacNeish, Harris Franklin, **18**:580; **19**:679
Macon, Ga., **24**:354-56
Macon, Ga., *Daily Telegraph*, **17**:461-n1,3; **24**:355n
McPheeters, Thomas Shanks, **18**:567,n2
McPherson, James Rhoderic, **22**:41,n3, 42
McPherson, Oscar Harmon, **19**:73n3
McPherson, Simon John, **14**:114, 161, 475; **15**:184, 233-34, 278n1,2, 343-44,n2,3, 396,n1; **16**:15,n1, 289; **17**:596; **18**:246n6, 255, 275-76, 278, 458, 591,n1, 609, 624; **19**:6,n7, 8, 438, 439, 711, 712, 728; **20**:9n
MacRae, Donald Alexander, **16**:90, 132, 253, 528; **17**:162,n6, 408; **19**:676
McRae, Milton Alexander, **24**:47,n1
MacSherry, Solomon Hillen, **16**:167,n3
Macrane, Silas Marcus, **14**:338n2
McReynolds, James Clark, **25**:550,n1, 557-58, 611
MacVeagh, Franklin, **19**:601,n1; **20**:25, 26, 38,n4, 201; **22**:396n1
MacVeagh, (Isaac) Wayne, **14**:194, 410-11; **19**:396,n4; **21**:152, 293-94, 320,n1; **22**:37, 39, 143-44, 205; **24**:400n2
McVicker's Theater (Chicago), **25**:282n2
McWilliams, Sherrell Norton, **24**:311,n2
Madden, Walter, M.D., **21**:23,n2, 219, 226, 232; **23**:426,n5
Madison, James, **14**:185, 414, 519; **16**:53, 144, 193, 197, 206, 501; **17**:222, 249, 462, 487, 523,n1; **18**:98, 112, 122; **19**:208, 272; **22**:218, 532n6; **23**:322; **24**:225
Madison, N. J., WW campaign speech, **21**:525-26; **23**:451-53
Madison, Wisc., **16**:161,n2; **19**:448, 620, 634, 657, 698, 703, 704, 705, 708, 747; **20**:11,n1; **23**:242n1, 253, 657; **24**:154; WW in, **14**:430, 435; **18**:17; **19**:550, 552, 706, 713; WW address, **19**:713-27; Madison Club, **23**:254,n5
Madison Square Garden (New York City), **25**:418n1, 493,n1
Madison *Wisconsin State Journal*, **24**:226n
Madonna della Cintola (Tuscan altarpiece, 1484, School of Bontifigli), **15**:173,n1
Magdalen College, Oxford, **14**:140; **17**:277, 557
Magdalen Tower, Oxford, **15**:445; **19**:538, 559
Magee, John D., **25**:487,n2
Magie, David, Jr., **14**:245; **15**:173,n2, 228, 265, 375; **16**:54, 131, 253, 528; **17**:46, 162,n7
Magie, Mary Blanchard Hodge (Mrs. William Francis), **14**:82, 140, 440,n2

Magie, William Francis, **14**:23, 81-82, 137, 140, 199, 259, 326, 395,n1; **15**:52n1, 157-58, 164, 273, 285n, 293, 294, 295, 340, 528; **16**:102, 159, 203, 301; **17**:287, 343, 408; **18**:301, 337, 338, 354, 355, 489-90, 528n1; **19**:228,n1, 576, 621; **20**:236; **21**:406; **22**:79
Magie, William Jay, **14**:82, 191, 193, 290; **15**:572, 575; **16**:276; **17**:441, 600, 602; **18**:45, 64-67, 246n4; **19**:439, 456,n1, 630-31, 657, 703, 707-708; **20**:17,n2, 30, 51-52n1, 61-62, 68, 210-n4, 245, 362, 455, 476,n2; **22**:426,n4
Magna Carta, **18**:49, 70, 71, 72, 73, 75, 83, 109, 163, 164, 168; **21**:328, 438; **23**:15; **25**:256
Mahaffie, Charles Delahunt, **18**:579
Mahan, Alfred Thayer, **14**:306n3; **15**:408
Mahool, John Barry, **23**:573n1
Main, John Hanson Thomas, **16**:16,-n2,3,4
Maine, **20**:505; **22**:535, 556; **25**:51, 52; Democrats, **21**:119,n1, 123, 128, 136; **23**:341; **25**:618-19,n1; Republican party, **25**:619n1
Maine, Sir Henry James Sumner, **14**:280, 324, 463,n2; **15**:131, 494; **17**:58; **18**:103,n3
Maine, University of, **16**:257
Maitland, Frederic William, **18**:356-57,n1
Major, Elliott Woolfolk, **22**:198,n2; **24**:186,n4
*Making Woodrow Wilson President* (McCombs), **24**:509n1, 524n3
Malet, Lucas (*pseud.* Mary St. Leger Kingsley Harrison), **14**:529,n12
Mallard, Hardin, **23**:175-76,n1
Mallock, William Hurrell, **22**:404,n1
Mallory, H.S.D., **16**:73
Malone, Dudley Field, **22**:45-46,n1; **23**:177, 326n2, 347, 356, 447, 475, 523, 523-24; **24**:17, 58,n1, 74, 92, 118, 297, 301, 303, 304, 312, 361n, 529, 572, 573; **25**:63, 64, 270, 272,n4, 507, 519, 589
Malone, Dumas, **14**:334n1; **15**:508n2
Malone, James Henry, **17**:474
Malone, Maud, **25**:438,n3,4
Maltbie, Milo Roy, **21**:617,n3
Man and Religion Forward Movement, **23**:511,n1
Manasquan, N. J., **24**:527
*Manchester Guardian*, **17**:472n
Manchester school of economics, **14**:555
Manchuria, opening of trade with, **15**:143,n2
Manchurian relief, **22**:416-17
Manhattan Club, **24**:31n1, 42n3, 50n1, 59, 60n1
Manhattan Hotel, New York City, **17**:31n1; **19**:425
Manhattan Hotel, Trenton, **23**:184
Manhattan Opera Company, **20**:173n4,5
manifest destiny, **21**:317

Manitoba, University of, **16**:159, 160; **18**:578

Mann, Parker, **23**:424-25

Mann, William Hodges, **24**:101n2,3, 119, 121, 122; **25**:632n1

Mannie, Tenn., **14**:3,n3

Manning, James, **14**:495,n1

Manning, Richard Irvine, **20**:453-54,n1, 463

Mansell, Elizabeth V. H., **25**:536,n1, 537

Mansfield, Richard, **14**:527n7; **15**:201

Mantoloking, N. J., **20**:571

Mantoux, Paul, **14**:440n2

Manuel II, King of Portugal, **21**:439n1

*Manufacturers' Record*, **14**:89,n1, 96

manufacturing, **24**:124, 184, 194

Mara, Hugh, **21**:487

Marble Faun (statue by Praxiteles), **15**:276

Marblehead, Mass., **20**:465; WW at, **14**:65

Marburg, Fannie Grainger (Mrs. Theodore), **18**:394,n1, 409, 410

Marburg, Theodore, **15**:136,n1; **18**:394,n1, 409, 410; **21**:614-15,n1

Marburg, University of, **16**:257

Marbury, William Luke, **24**:371

March, Herman William, **16**:199

Marcosson, Isaac F., **23**:366-72

Marelli, Henry, **21**:301

Marietta, Ohio, **25**:580n1

Marine Biological Laboratory, Woods Hole, Mass., **18**:575

Marion, Ala., WW address, **16**:71-72

Marion (Ala.) Military Institute, **15**:213, 226, 227; **16**:71-72, 256, 353-54; *Institute Bulletin*, **16**:72n1, 73n1, 113n1

Marjory (English girl), **15**:345

Markham, Edwin, **15**:223n2

Markham, Va., **15**:466, 467

Markley, Paul Hamilton, M.D., **22**:356, 356n5; **23**:381,n2

Marquand, Allan, **14**:147, 206, 326, 395; **15**:136, 173, 301, 441; **16**:17-18,n4; **17**:309, 352n2, 408, 433-34, 436, 441; **18**:12; **20**:81, 318-19, 448-50

Marquand, Eleanor Cross (Mrs. Allan), **15**:136, 301, 339, 441; **20**:81,n2; **22**:426,n5

Marsh, Frank Burr, **16**:306,n3, 376,n6

Marsh & Burke (Princeton druggists), **14**:51,n2

Marshall, Charles Henry, **14**:305-306,n1; **15**:145; **19**:552,n1, 658

Marshall, Edward, **21**:477

Marshall, Erwin E., **21**:106,n1, 167

Marshall, F. A., **22**:39,n16

Marshall, Howard, **21**:324-25,n1

Marshall, James William, **22**:385,n1

Marshall, John, **14**:373-74, 519; **16**:53; **18**:173, 174, 179; **19**:272, 744; **24**:416-17

Marshall, Lois Kimsey (Mrs. Thomas Riley), **22**:571,n2

Marshall, Mrs., **18**:412

Marshall, Thomas Riley, **20**:289,n4, 546; **21**:587, 603; **22**:554, 557, 571; **23**:235n3, 237; **24**:237, 483n2, 484, 527,-n8, 534, 565; **25**:22, 327,n4, 521

Marshall, Texas, **23**:519, 520; Baptist Church, **23**:519; Trinity Church (P. E.), **23**:519

Martial (Marcus Valerius Martialis), **17**:464n2

Martin, Chalmers, **15**:390

Martin, Edward Sandford, **22**:38,n5

Martin, John Andrew, **20**:312,n2

Martin, Lewis J., **22**:378,n2

Martin, Mr. & Mrs. (of Chicago), **14**:454,n4

Martin, Luther, **25**:600

Martin, Patrick Henry, **24**:258,n1

Martin, Paul, **19**:550

Martin, Thomas Francis, **22**:136n1, 504-n1; **23**:343-44, 387, 536n1; **25**:563

Martin, Thomas Staples, **22**:282,n1,2; **23**:133n1, 311, 388, 389, 390,n1; **24**:51, 72n9, 163, 398n1, 568; **25**:563, 590, 638n5

Martin, William Joseph, **24**:538-39,n1, 559-60

Martin, William Parmenter, **21**:313n3

Martin, Winfred Robert, **16**:353,n2, 384

Martine, James Edgar, **16**:555n1, 561n1; **17**:23,n3; **19**:492,n4; **21**:263,n4, 581-83,n2; **22**:36-37, 47, 52, 73,n3, 77n1, 81n1, 83, 86, 86n1, 87n2, 93-94, 100, 101, 113, 115-16, 124, 128, 133-34, 135, 136, 136n1, 137n3, 142n1, 145, 146, 147,n2, 153, 155, 160,n1, 162, 163, 164, 170n1, 173-74n1, 175, 185, 198, 200, 205n2, 228, 230, 231,n3, 233, 235, 236, 238n1, 239, 240, 241, 242,n2, 243, 244n1, 245n2, 248, 251-52, 253, 263, 273, 278, 280, 281, 286n2, 303, 304,n6, 311,n1, 321, 330n1, 339, 340, 341, 344, 365,n1, 367, 378, 382, 387, 437, 524, 525, 535n1, 541, 544, 545n2, 552; **23**:107,n3, 129, 234, 255, 343n2, 344, 381, 537; **24**:255, 273, 287,n1, 408, 411, 430-31; **25**:44

Martini, Simone, **15**:334

Martinique Hotel, New York City, **22**:328n1, 357, 357n4

Marvel, David Thomas, **14**:485; **15**:103

Marvin, Walter Taylor, **16**:91-92, 131, 249; **17**:17,n7, 408; **20**:446

Mary Baldwin Seminary, **25**:626,n1

Maryland, **21**:600; **22**:16; **23**:582; **24**:370-79; **25**:129; Democratic banquet, **22**:177; Democratic State Convention, **23**:264n1; presidential primary vote, **24**:387,n1; Princeton alumni, **17**:43; **18**:10; **20**:27-28, 229-35, 268, 269; Republicans, **23**:264n1, 573,n2; State Board of Trade, **23**:264, 266; WW's address to the General Assembly,

Maryland, (*cont.*)
24:227-36; Woodrow Wilson Democratic Association, 23:218n1
Maryland, University of, 16:510; 18:278
Maryland Bar Association, 15:234
Maryland Hotel, Pasadena, Cal., 23:45, 51
Maryland Week Celebration and Horticultural Exhibition, Baltimore, December 1911, 23:569,n1
Marx, Franklin, 21:86,n1
Masaccio (Tommaso Guidi), 15:357-58
Mason, Alpheus Thomas, 20:136n8; 21:546n3; 25:200n4, 414n1,2
Mason, Charlotte Maria Shaw, 18:368,n9
Mason, George (1725-1792), 14:518; 24:115, 339
Mason, Victor Louis, 21:586,n1
Mason City, Ill., 24:292
Massachusetts, 21:598, 608n2, 612; 22:556; 23:101, 323; 25:26, 535; Bill of Rights, 18:80; Constitution, 21:500; Democratic State Committee, 23:258; Democrats, *see* Democratic party and Democrats in Massachusetts; Princeton alumni, 20:262; Savings Bank Life Insurance system, 20:136,n8,10; WW addresses in, 24:360-67; 25:257-69; tobacco trust, 25:296; United Shoe Machinery Company, 25:297; woman suffrage, 25:42n1
Massachusetts Bay, 19:350
Massachusetts Institute of Technology, 14:186; 16:464, 478,n1, 478, 480n1, 482,n1; 18:579; 19:673; 20:8n-9n, 28, 76n1; 22:139
Massachusetts Reform Club, 19:420
Massachusetts Single Tax League, 14:200,n3
Massey, John Edward, 22:338-39n4
Masson, Thomas Lansing, 23:177,n2
*Master of Manhattan: The Life of Richard Croker* (Stoddard), 21:342n8
Mastro-Valerio, A., 25:28
Matawan, N. J., WW at, 15:300, 301
*Materials for a Life of Jacopo da Varagine* (Richardson), 16:393,n2
Mather, Emma Watson (Lady Mather), 16:494; 17:109, 127, 141, 215, 307, 342, 359, 392, 466, 510
Mather, Frank Jewett, Jr., 20:318-19,n1, 369-70, 449, 450
Mather, Sir William, 15:243n1, 417, 504; 16:23,n1, 454,n3, 472n2,3, 487, 494, 536-37; 17:13, 87-88, 90-91, 105, 108-109, 126-27, 140-41, 214, 215, 238-39, 301, 307, 338, 342, 358, 359-60, 391-92, 414, 442, 447, 460, 462, 463, 465-66, 471-72, 509-10,n2, 558; 18:368; 21:49
Mathers, James, 16:386, 405

Mathew, Charles Massy, 20:145,n4, 148-49, 155, 181
Mathew, Janet Knox (Mrs. Charles Massy), 19:192n3; 20:145,n4, 148-49, 155, 176, 179, 181
Mathews, Charles Engley, 16:198; 19:572, 576
Mathews, John Mabry, 19:678
Mathews, Shailer, 17:451,n1
Mathis, John Cass, 14:226
Mathis, Thomas Alfred, 23:467,n1
Matter, John, 16:24n2
Mathews, John A., 23:386, 386-87, 387-88
Matthews, John Joseph, 22:357, 481,n3, 575n5
Matthews, Paul Clement, 14:448,n3, 452
Matthews, Thomas E., 23:288,n1; 24:191n2
Matthews, William Robinson and Matthews Construction Company, 14:6,n6, 21, 24, 35-36; 15:449, 450, 470, 525; 16:153, 161, 182, 183, 184, 212, 329; 18:286,n4
Matthison, Edith Wynne, 15:340-41,n1
Mauck, Edward E., 23:116,n3, 609,n1; 25:333,n3
Maxwell, William Hunter, 21:161,n1, 617; 22:214,n1, 290
Maxwell House, Nashville, 16:235, 236
Mayes, Frank L., 24:256,n1
*Mayflower* (the ship), 14:210
Mayflower Descendants: New York Society, 14:209-10
Maynard, Joseph Adolphus, 23:324,n1
Mayo, William James, M.D., 19:532,n1
*Mayor Who Mastered New York: The Life & Opinions of William J. Gaynor* (Thomas), 19:500n3
Mazarin, Mariette, 20:173,n5
Mead, Edwin Doak, 24:494,n1, 25:19-20,n1,3,4
Mead, Lucia Ames, 17:92,n4
Meaning of Education Missed (*Literary Digest*), 17:560,n2
Measday, Walter, 23:215-16,n1, 463, 506, 568; 24:49-50, 118, 163, 186, 222,n1, 256, 269, 270-71, 303, 304, 390n1, 529; 25:125, 362, 518, 519
measles, 15:231, 265, 266, 268, 300, 308, 312, 326, 336, 339
meat packers, investigation of, 24:89,n3, 143, 196-97, 373; 25:140
meat trust, 20:301-302
Medford, Ore., 23:63
*Medical Education in the United States and Canada* (Flexner), 19:77n1, 162
Medici family, 15:353
*Medieval and the True Modern Spirit in Education* (Osborn), 14:54,n1
Meeker, Royal, 16:92, 94, 131, 251, 421; 17:369, 408; 18:271, 294, 577; 19:183, 615, 616; 20:418; 24:514-15, 519; 25:580

Meeker, Stephen J., 23:354,n5
Meigs, John, 14:142,n1, 144; 15:57; 16: 283,n1
Meigs, Marion Butler (Mrs. John), 16:283
Meinken, Charles Gledhill, 19:73n3
*Meistersinger von Nürnberg* (Wagner opera), 14:245
Meldrim, Peter W., 22:543n2
Melick, Tunis, 23:475
Mellier, Walter G., 16:95-96
Mellin's Food, 23:172,n2
Melrose, Roxburgh, Wilsons at, 14:524
Melvin, Frederick J., 25:474n2
*Memoirs of William Jennings Bryan*, 24:426n1
Memphis, Tenn., Country Club, 17:473, 474; Gayoso Hotel, 17:473, 474; Goodwyn Institute, 17:473, 476; High School, 17:475; University School, 17:474-75, 481; Princeton alumni, 17:480; St. Mary's School, 17:474; WW addresses, 17:474-87; WW in, 17: 472-87 *passim*
Memphis *Commercial Appeal*, 17:480n; 25:612n1
*Memphis News Scimitar*, 17:473n
*Menace*, 25:649,n4
Mendelson, Jack, 25:518, 519
Mendelssohn-Bartholdy, Felix, 15:153-n2; 18:400n5; 19:34, 35
Mercantile Trust Co., New York City, 23:246
Mercer, Edward C., 19:71,n2
Mercer, Jesse, 24:347
Mercer County, N. J., 19:71-72; 21:25n2, 34, 37n1,2, 39, 40, 90, 97, 104, 168, 219, 229, 349, 584n1; 22:29; 23:262n3, 425-26,n4, 427, 432, 435; 25:492, 582; ballots, 19:510; Country Club, 24:555; Democratic Committee, 21:97, 102, 103; Democratic League, 21:351n1
Mercer University, 24:354
Mercersburg Academy, 14:464,n1, 471,-n1; 22:22n1
Merchant Marine, 22:205n2, 371n4; 23:622, 642; 24:33-34, 70, 86, 106, 125, 184, 194, 236n8; 25:6, 15-16, 24-25, 34, 38, 105, 341-42; W. J. Bryan on, 25:46; O. G. Villard on, 25:27, 41
*Merchant of Venice* (Shakespeare), 15:238,n1
Meredith, Charles Vivian, 23:311,n3
Meredith, William Farragut, 15:251-52
Meredith, Wyndham Robertson, 24:71,-n5
merit system in appointments, 20:316
Meriwether, Colyer, 16:302,n1
Merle-Smith, Wilton, 14:114; 16:29; 19:539-40, 548-49
Merriam, Charles Edward, 19:25,n5; 23:311,n2
Merriman, 18:369,n1
Merritt, Ralph B., 19:524-25

*Merry Countess* (Unger), 25:55,n1
*Merry Wives of Windsor* (Shakespeare), 15:397n4
Merton, Seth D., 20:377,n1
Merton College, Oxford, 18:388,n2
Messer, Loring Wilbur, 18:272,n2
Metcalf, Henrietta McCrea (Mrs. Willard Leroy), 18:390,n7
Metcalf, John Calvin, 24:118,n1
Metcalf, Victor Howard, 16:559n3
Metcalf, Willard Leroy, 18:390,n7
Metcalfe, David, 15:180
Metcalfe, David Douglas, 19:505-506,n1; 20:252,n1
Metcalfe, James Stetson, 24:126n4
Methodist Episcopal Church, 24:381
Methodist Episcopal Church, South, 23:511n2
Methodist Social Union of New York, 24:356n1, 381
Methodists, 23:556
*Methods of Ethics* (Sidgwick), 19:666
Metropolitan Club, New York City, 20:9-10, 100, 129
Metropolitan Life Insurance Company, Industrial department, 20:136,n9
Metropolitan Museum of Art, 15:181
Mexican War, 14:445
Mexico, 23:590, 596, 634; 24:218
Meyer, Charles A., 23:465
Meyer, Charles Anthony, 22:253,n1, 378, 481,n3
Meyer, Charlotte English Seaman (Mrs. Henry Coddington), 17:609,n11
Meyer, Edward, 20:84n2
Meyer, Henry Coddington, 17:609,n11, 610
Meyer, Margaret Theodora, 16:163,n1
Meyers, James Cowden, 21:107-108,n1
Miami University, Oxford, Ohio, 15:163; 16:41, 59, 131, 249, 251
*Michael. A Pastoral Poem* (Wordsworth), 18:415,n4
Michaud, Régis, 17:556; 19:572, 576
Michelangelo Buonarroti, 15:250, 274, 276, 353, 358
Michelet, Jules, 20:558
Michener, Albert Oswald, 16:225
Michigan, 23:247, 263; 24:248,n1; delegation to Democratic National Convention, 24:483-84; Democrats, 23: 248, 263; Republicans, 23:263; WW addresses, 25:185-98
Michigan, University of, 15:100n3, 444n1; 16:60, 87-88, 92n1, 106n1, 130, 131, 132, 247, 250, 254, 256, 257, 376, 465, 489, 508, 510, 511; 19:181-82, 184-85, 185n1, 189; 20:16n1; 24:54; Student Lecture Association, 16:44,n1; WW lecture, 14:419-21, 421, 425
Michigan City, Ind., 25:184
Michigan Schoolmasters' Club, 16:44,n1
Middle Ages, 18:638; 19:743; 23:94

Middle West, **20**:385, 579; insurgents in, **21**:457-58

middlemen, **23**:489-90

Middlesex County, N. J., **21**:354, 412, 436, 560; **22**:145, 200, 201, 229n1, 294, 308; **23**:438; **25**:582; Democratic County Committee, **23**:265-66

Middlesex Women's Club, Lowell, Mass., **14**:314

Middletown, Conn., **18**:383; **19**:475n3; **25**:234; North or First Congregational Church, **14**:515,n1; WW address, **14**:502-15

*Middletown* (Conn.) *Tribune*, **14**:515n

*Midsummer Night's Dream* (Shake-speare), **15**:340

Mierow, Charles Christopher, **16**:138; **19**:678

Milan, **15**:275, 314

Milbank, Albert Goodsell, **15**:570, 573; **16**:5

Milburn, John George, **24**:413,n2

Miles, George Washington, **14**:203, 205n4; **15**:508,n2

Miles, Lee, **23**:517

Miles, Louis Wardlaw, M.D., **16**:421,n3, 510; **17**:408

Milford, Pa., **22**:144n3

militarism, **24**:494-95

Mill, John Stuart, **14**:242, 323; **19**:666

Miller, Adolph Caspar, **23**:59

Miller, Charles Ransom, **16**:533,n7, 534

Miller, Dickinson Sergeant, **24**:503n2, 504

Miller, Hugh, **20**:262,n1

Miller, James Roberts, **14**:387-88

Miller, John, **16**:198n1

Miller, John Eschelman, **23**:97,n2

Miller, John G., **18**:7n1

Miller, Louis E., **24**:28,n3; **25**:28, 53-54

Miller, Lucius Hopkins, **14**:293,n2, 334, 396, 396n3, 399; **16**:130, 248, 398-403; **17**:296-97, 334, 408; **18**:273, 625-26; **19**:17,n2, 25n1, 71-72, 120

Miller, Mae Coffeen (Mrs. Lucius Hop-kins), **17**:334

Miller, Margaret, **16**:197, 198n1, 208

Miller, Mary Ridgly Talbot (Mrs. Pitser), **17**:523,n1

Miller, Milton Armington, **23**:64,n6

Miller, Mortimer Craig, **16**:377

Miller, Polk, **22**:191,n2

Miller, Thomas Noble, **18**:400,n8, 401

Miller, William & Sons Co., **20**:580

Millikan, Robert Andrews, **18**:489n1

Milliken, Henry Oothout, **16**:23,n1

Mills, Alada Thurston Paddock (Mrs. Albert Leopold), **16**:243

Mills, Albert Leopold, **14**:290; **16**:243

Mills, Andrew, Jr., **17**:103, 107,n1

Mills, Edward Kirkpatrick, **22**:546n5

Mills, W. H., **22**:577n4

Millstone River, **15**:66, 576, 578, 579

Millville, N. J., **23**:533n3; WW speech, **23**:531, 534

Milner, Alfred, 1st Viscount Milner, **15**:97

Milner, William L., **18**:537,n1, 530

Milod, James K., **21**:564,n1

Milton, George Fort, **24**:403

Milton, John, **14**:381n1; **16**:103,n1; **17**:535; **19**:751; **20**:384

Milton, Mass., WW at, **19**:270,n2, 290, 293

Milwaukee, Wisc., **22**:55-71; **24**:270; City Club, **21**:163n1; **22**:56, 57; Lecture Service League, **22**:61; Pabst Theatre, **21**:163n1; Press Club, **22**:56; Schlitz Palm Garden, **22**:56, 57; Schlitz Thea-ter, **22**:58, 61; University Club, **22**:56; WW speeches, **24**:259-61

*Milwaukee Journal*, **22**:56n, 61n, 71n; **24**:243n, 258n, 259n, 261n, 285,n2, 546

Milwee, Rufus Franklin, **23**:517

Mines, Department of, **25**:399

minimum wage, **25**:72

mining industry, **25**:224, 399-400, 417

Ministerial Responsibility and the Con-stitution (Lowell), **23**:133,n2

ministers and society, **20**:330f

Minneapolis, Minn., **20**:156, 535; **22**:519n4; Commercial Club, **23**:93, 95; Minneapolis Club, **23**:83, 84; Ply-mouth Church, **14**:427; Princeton alumni, **19**:146; Publicity Club, **23**:86, 112; West Hotel, **23**:86; WW addresses, **14**:129-30, 427-28; **25**:164-69, 173-84; WW in, photo, **25**:illustration section

Minneapolis and St. Paul, WW ad-dresses, **23**:86-95; WW in, **23**:83, 84-95

Minneapolis, S.S., **14**:246

*Minneapolis Morning Tribune*, **23**:87n

Minneapolis *Sunday Tribune*, **14**:428n

Minnesota, delegation to Democratic National Convention, **24**:487,n2; Democratic party, **20**:544; WW ad-dresses in, **25**:164-84; WW on, **23**:86

Minnesota, University of, **15**:100; **16**:258; **19**:457-58, 485-86, 493-95, 532, 542-43, 605, 679; **20**:54, 60-61, 357,n3, 539; **23**:82, 93; WW speech, **25**:169-72

Minnesota Railroad and Warehouse Commission, **22**:122n2

Minnesota rate case, **22**:122,n2, 313-14

Minor, John Barbee, **18**:31,n7; **21**:585n1

Minor, Raleigh Colston, **21**:585,n1

Minton, Henry Collin, **14**:192; **22**:311,n1

Mirr, Roman B., **25**:28

Miss Fine's School, Princeton, **24**:528

Miss Porter's School, Farmington, Conn., **19**:323,n4

missionaries, **25**:405

Mississippi, **22**:16; **24**:237

Mississippi, University of, *Bulletin*, **15**:180n

Mississippi River, **25**:16, 397

Mississippi River Valley, **20**:546; **24**:107

*Mississippi Valley Historical Review*, **16**:15n1

Missouri, **22**:519, 544; **23**:320; **25**:93, 530; Democrats, **24**:186-87,n3; WW addresses, **24**:185-86; **25**:385-90, 395-99

Missouri, University of, **15**:134, 152, 156-67,n1,2,3,4, 163, 198-99,n1, 202, 557; **16**:41, 68-69, 88,n2, 132, 160n6, 165, 258; **18**:490; **19**:677

Missouri Compromise, **14**:445; **17**:311, 313, 316, 317; **18**:184

Missouri Historical Society, **16**:144n3

Missouri, Kansas & Texas Railway Company, **17**:124,n1; **23**:506,n1

*Mr. Baruch* (Coit), **25**:415n1

Mitchell, Charles Wellman, M.D., **15**:361; **19**:252, 260; **21**:599; **23**:568; **24**:82

Mitchell, Clarence Blair, **17**:352n2

Mitchell, John, **14**:113n1,2; **25**:399,n2

Mitchell, John Hipple, **25**:645,n6

Mitchell, Roscoe, **25**:360,n2, 361, 588

Mitchell, Samuel Chiles, **22**:140; **25**:539

Mitchell, Silas Weir, M.D., **14**:306n3; **15**:232, 408

Mitre Hotel, Oxford, **14**:531, 532

Mizner, Addison, **16**:33n6; **18**:428n3; **19**:237n2

mob rule, **23**:437, 440-41

Mobile, Ala., University Military School, **15**:325n1, 402-403

*Mobile Register*, Mobile, Ala., **16**:332

Mobus, Frank, **21**:131

*Modern Battles of Trenton* (Sackett), **20**:566n5; **21**:343n9; **23**:295n5

*Modern German Prose* (Nichol), **19**:569

Modern Language Association of America, **18**:566,n1

Modern Views of the Bible and of Religion (Miller), **18**:273,n2

Moffat, Henry, M.D., **19**:523-24,n1, 525-27, 531

Moffat, James David, **16**:106,n1

Moffat, Stanley Matthews, **19**:502n3, 523, 524, 526, 527, 531

Moffet, Samuel Erasmus, **15**:550n2

Moffett, William Walter, **22**:604n2

Moger, Allen Wesley, **24**:398n1; **25**:632n1

Mohonk Arbitration Conferences, **25**:19,n2

Mohr, George C., **23**:536n1

Moline, Ill., **24**:300

*Molly Make-Believe* (Abbott), **24**:506,n1

Moment, John James, **16**:355-56

Mommsen, Theodor, **15**:485-86

Monaghan, James Charles, **25**:63-64,n1, 93

Monaghan, Thomas M., **25**:425,n3

monarchy in America, **22**:541; **25**:228

*Monetary History of the United States* (Friedman and Schwartz), **15**:29n1

Monetary Commission, *see* National Monetary Commission

monetary reform, W. G. Brown, **23**:513-14; *see also* money trust

money trust (money control, money monopoly, money power, money question), **22**:489,n3; **23**:119f, 157, 157n2, 293-94, 312, 447, 504, 504n6, 625; **24**:196, 204, 274,n2, 345, 368, 373, 577n1; **25**:12-13, 542 Δ D. M. Barringer, **23**:228, 246, 314; W. G. Brown, **23**:513-16, 605; Democratic platform, **24**:581n1; C. A. Lindbergh, **23**:605n1; T. B. Love, **24**:164,n2, 165; W. F. McCombs, **23**:325, 340; Philadelphia *North American*, **23**:246,n1; S. Untermyer, **23**:605n1; **24**:532, 577-78n1; **25**:528-29; New York *World*, **23**:243n3; *see also* monopoly

Monk of Siberia, **18**:32

Monmouth County, N. J., **21**:227, 324; **22**:200, 229n1, 309; **25**:581, 582; Democratic Committee, **23**:219; WW addresses, **23**:442-47

monopoly, **18**:47; **24**:14, 69, 144, 145, 160, 193, 196, 201, 331, 395, 470; **25**:5, 8, 12, 58, 73, 74-75, 88, 103, 123, 133, 139, 152-53, 159, 160, 167-68, 178-80, 182, 191, 193, 194-95, 196, 199, 200-201, 202, 204, 206, 207, 208, 209, 215, 226-27, 228, 229, 245, 254-55, 304, 307, 323, 324, 329, 331-32, 344, 352-53, 354, 355, 357, 358, 364-65, 367-68, 370, 371-74, 379-85, 386-87, 388, 392, 395, 398, 408, 410, 413, 433, 434, 438, 439, 443, 445, 447, 466, 472, 496-97, 502 Δ B. M. Anderson, Jr., **25**:419-21; L. D. Brandeis, **25**:57, 289-94, 294, 295-97; J. B. Clark, **25**:419-21; D. B. Jones, **24**:549; T. Roosevelt, **25**:389; *see also* trusts

Monroe, James, **14**:518, 519; **16**:144

*Monroe County* (Mo.) *Appeal*, **25**:395n2

*Monsieur Beaucaire* (Tarkington), **14**:527,n7

Montague, Andrew Jackson, **23**:133, 134, 311, 327-28, 359-60, 361-62, 390-91, 601; **24**:71

Montague, Robert Lynch, **24**:71,n3

Montana, **22**:278

Montclair, N. J., **24**:250, 253; Hillside Grammar School, **21**:508; High School, **21**:310; Outlook Club, **15**:137, 142; Princeton alumni, **19**:155n1; **20**:76n1, 265,n3; sewage disposal, **24**:267n1; WW addresses, **15**:137-39, 142-43; **21**:508-18; **25**:467-73

*Montclair* (N. J.) *Times*, **15**:139n; **21**:169n1

Monte Carlo, **22**:393

Monteagle, Tenn., **18**:484; Monteagle Assembly, **23**:211-12, 244

Montesquieu, Charles de Secondat, Baron de La Brède et de, **14**:13; **16**:284; **18**:106, 108

Montfort, Simon de, Earl of Leicester, **18**:73

Montgomery, John Alexander, **21**:104,n1

Montgomery, William Andrew, **23**:64,n9

Montgomery, Ala., Girls' High School, 16:74; No Name Club, 15:213,n3; WW address, 16:74-78
*Montgomery* (Ala.) *Advertiser,* 15:25; 16:73n, 78n; 22:96
Monticello (Jefferson's home), 25:631
Monticello, Iowa, 23:315
Moody, Dwight Lyman, 15:93; 19:475-76,n2,3
Moody, John, 22:114-16,n1
Moody, William Revell, 14:114
Moore, Addison Webster, 15:117,n1
Moore, Alfred Austin, 16:132, 257; 17:408; 19:572, 576
Moore, Charles Sumner, 23:592-93,n1; 24:444
Moore, Eliakim Hastings, 16:159,n2
Moore, Ernest Carroll, 23:103
Moore, John Bassett, 20:464,n1, 467; 21:557-58,n1,2, 559
Moore, Margaret Malona Tillman (Mrs. Charles Sumner), 23:592-93n1
Moore, Robert Lee, 16:465, 511
Moore, Walter William, 19:380n2
Moore's Hill College, Indiana, 16:511
Moorestown, N. J., 23:539
moral responsibility, 20:329
Moravians, 21:384
More, Paul Elmer, 20:380,n2
Morehead, John Alfred, 22:604n2
Morehouse, Frederic Cook, 22:57,n1
Morey, Charles Rufus, 16:421,n1, 510; 17:408; 20:318, 449
Morgan, George, 14:439n1
Morgan, George Campbell, 14:114, 115
Morgan, J. P. & Co., *see* J. P. Morgan & Co.
Morgan, John Pierpont (1837-1913), 14:192, 194; 16:303; 17:16,n1,2, 96n1, 519,n4, 520; 19:433, 434, 440-41, 444, 482, 483; 20:25-26, 562n1; 21:35n1; 22:39n21, 255n1; 25:396n3; and J. P. Morgan & Co., 18:494n3; 23:120,n7, 151n1, 228n3, 246n1,4, 293n3, 504n6, 514, 632; 24:78, 412n3, 533, 567n2
Morgan, John Pierpont (1867-1943), 24:533
Morgan, Josephine Perry (Mrs. Junius Spencer), 14:73, 74, 89, 118; 15:165, 321; 18:469, 475
Morgan, Junius Spencer, 14:74, 77, 89, 90, 92, 95, 111, 118, 326; 15:165, 184, 449, 467-68, 470; 16:390,n1, 391, 394, 470n2, 473-74; 17:16,n1, 382, 408, 595; 18:229, 241, 592, 609, 624, 630-31; 19:3,n2, 5, 6, 7-8, 8, 676; 21:48
Morgenthau, Henry (1856-1946), 23:588n2; 24:42,n1, 527, 587; ambassadorship, 25:610
Moriarty, James, 16:216
Morison, Elting Elmore, 19:364n2; 21:252n6
Morison, Samuel Eliot, 15:292n28; 16:520n1
Morley, John, Viscount Morley of Black-

burn, 14:341; 15:116, 117, 242,n1, 504; 18:399, 401
Morley, John, 21:619; 24:506
Morningside College, 25:162
Morris, Benjamin Wistar III, 14:267,n2, 293, 335, 417; 15:27, 398,n1, 415,n5, 419, 423, 424, 432, 444-46, 447, 449, 461-62, 469, 501, 531, 533, 534-35, 573, 574, 577, 580; 16:156, 163, 169, 171-72, 173, 175, 177, 178, 181, 185, 275, 305, 305-306, 308, 327, 333, 335-36, 339-40, 342, 357, 369, 403, 447; 17:32, 37, 550, 560, 561, 562, 566-68, 585, 604
Morris, Charles Satchell, 25:620,n2
Morris, Du Bois Schanck, 14:399
Morris, Robert, 17:249
Morris, Roland Sletor, 14:475; 19:531,n1; 20:534,n1; 21:584, 604; 22:285, 409n1, 435, 450; 24:397, 454, 461
Morris, Walter E., 23:536n1
Morris Canal, 21:403,n3, 499
Morris County, N. J., 21:412, 525; 22:201, 229n1, 253; 23:452; 25:582
Morris Plains, N. J., 23:290; State Hospital, 23:290, 304, 629
Morrison, Andrew J., 16:225, 226
Morrison, Frank, 25:614,n1, 615
Morrissey, Patrick Henry, 23:357,n2
Morristown, N. J., Friday Evening Club, 18:420; WW speeches, 21:527-36; 23:451-53; Lyceum Theatre, 21:527,n1
Morristown School, Morristown, N. J., 14:353-54, 356, 497, 501
Morrow, Emerson Boyd, 16:160, 163, 198
Morrow, Mary Wilhelmina Wychoff (Mrs. William H.), 21:477,n3
Morrow, William H., 21:383, 476-77,n1; 22:550n2
Morse, Franklin Blake, 15:181,n1, 212-13
Morse, Sarah Virginia Center (Mrs. William Horace), 15:181, 212, 213
Morse, Virginia Center, 15:212
Morse, William Horace, 15:181,n2, 212
Morse, William Otis, 15:181, 212; 19:73n3
Mortal Man Inn, Troutbeck, Westmorland, 18:381
Morton, Levi Parsons, 15:237
Moscheles, Felix, 18:400
Mosely, Sir Alfred, 18:590,n2
Moses, 20:152; statue by Michelangelo, 15:276
Mott, John Livingstone, 19:453,n1
Mott, John R., 14:266; 16:228-30; 17:128, 296,n2, 620-22; 18:218-19, 279-80, 288; 19:109, 151-53,n2,3, 177, 453, 456,n1, 501, 703, 707; 20:43-44, 52, 53, 61, 141,n1, 209,n7, 310; 22:159, 385n2; 24:208, 209
Mt. Bethel, N. J., 23:475
Mt. Holly, N. J., 23:405, 475; Court House, 23:539, 540; Fair, 23:409
Mount Rydal, England, 24:524

Mountjoy, Clifford Arnold, **22**:384,n6
Moville, Donegal, **18**:344, 346
Mowbray, Hilda (Mrs. Louis Leon), **20**:188,n5
Mowbray, Louis Leon, **20**:187-88,n5
Mowry, George Edwin, **19**:191n1; **21**:148n1, 344n12; **22**:32n; **23**:43n9
Moyn's Park, **15**:446
*Much Ado About Nothing* (Shakespeare), **15**:340
Münsterberg, Hugo, **14**:65,n1, 69, 76-77, 86, 344, 394, 395n1; **15**:468
Münsterberg, Margaret, **14**:395n1
Muhlenberg College, **24**:139
Muir, Ramsay, **18**:544,n2
Mulford, Elisha, **14**:14
Muller, J. S., **14**:331
Muller, Thornwell, **14**:331
Muller, W. R., **14**:331
Mulry, Thomas M., **25**:493n1
Mumford, Ethel Watts, **16**:33n6; **18**:428n3; **19**:237n2
*Mummy Monarch* (Princeton Triangle Club Show, 1907), **17**:64n1, 100,n1
Munich, **14**:246
Munich, University of, **15**:444; **16**:254, 511; **17**:556; **18**:578
Municipal Corruption (Ford), **16**:43n2; **20**:35n3
minicipal government, **23**:573f
Munn, Ann Elder (Mrs. Henry Norcross), **18**:490,n2, 492, 623
Munn, Charles Allen, **16**:173,n1, 243,n5; **18**:490,n1,2,3, 491, 492-93, 623; **19**:119,n1, 123
Munn, Orson Desaix (1824-1907), **16**:173n1; **18**:490,n3, 492
Munn, Orson Desaix (1883-1958), **18**:491n2
Munro, David Binning, **14**:140,n1
Munro, Wilfrid Harold, **14**:135n1
Munroe, James Phinney, **14**:309, 317; **19**:420,n1
Munsey, Frank Andrew, **19**:155; **25**:544
*Munsey's Magazine*, **23**:360,n1, 372n, 655,n1
Murch, Herbert Spencer, **16**:465, 511
Murfee, Hopson Owen, **14**:59; **15**:3-4,n1,2, 16-17, 182-83, 213, 226-27; **16**:73, 113, 281, 284-85, 331, 337, 353-54; **17**:131; **22**:55
Murfee, Mary McQueen Smith (Mrs. Hopson Owen), **15**:227; **16**:73, 113
Murphy, Charles Francis, **19**:500n3; **22**:161n1, 602, 603; **24**:7,n4, 497,n2, 500, 507n1, 512,n1, 531, 532; **25**:111,n2, 112n3, 129, 133-34, 135n1, 233, 283, 284n3,4
Murphy, Edgar Gardner, **15**:159-60,n1, 165, 168; **22**:157n1
Murphy, Franklin, **14**:161-62, 169, 191, 194; **15**:16, 362; **21**:90,n2, 212, 219n2, 346, 409, 503, 504; **23**:295n5, 392
Murphy, Franklin, Jr., **17**:187,n1, 216-17, 595; **18**:229, 241; **19**:13,n1, 32

Murphy, Fred Towsley, M.D., **19**:627,n1
Murphy, James, **23**:146,n4, 150
Murphy, William D., **16**:11,n3
Murray, Charles Edward, **23**:30,n6
Murray, George Gilbert Aimé, **17**:105,n2
Murray, George Richards, **14**:297
Murray, Harold Griffith, **14**:490n3; **15**:249, 251, 413-16, 418-19, 423, 433, 435-36; **16**:291, 302-303, 307-308, 308, 336, 338, 376-77, 389, 403, 415-18, 458-63, 504, 547, 552, 553; **17**:41, 170-72, 285, 381-83, 435-36; **18**:315-17, 456; **19**:15, 144-47; **20**:543,n2, 573
Murray, John P., **23**:183
Murray, Mary Henrietta Howard (Lady Murray), **17**:105
Murray, William Francis, **24**:287,n1, 358
Murray, William Henry, **24**:275,n1
Murray Hill Hotel, New York City, **16**:238
Muskoka, Ont., **15**:467; *see also* Judd Haven, Ont.
Muskoka Lakes, Ontario: The Bluff, The Woodington, **17**:334
Muskogee, Okla., **23**:506
Mussey, Henry Raymond, **16**:376,n1
Mutual Life Insurance Company of New York, **16**:333n2; **19**:396-97, 454-55,n1; **21**:26, 51, 152,n2, 294; **22**:39n12; **25**:195,n6
*My People of the Plains* (Talbot), **14**:453n3
*My Relations with Carlyle* (Froude), **18**:362n2
Myers, George William, **17**:529,n2
Myers, Gustavus, **21**:343n10
Myers, Henry Lee, **24**:285, 287,n1, 468
Myers, Paul Forrest, **25**:273,n1
Myers, William Starr, **16**:37n, 71, 308-309,n1, 317, 385, 386, 421, 509; **17**:233, 408, 437,n1; **18**:294, 294n1; **19**:613; diary quoted, **17**:35, 58, 209, 403, 408-409, 424, 448, 462; **18**:271, 293-94, 303
Mylod, James P., **22**:241, 242, 242n2, 253, 286,n2, 339; **23**:353, 354
*My Life and Work* (Walters), **25**:449n

Nab Scar, nr. Rydal, Westmorland, **18**:389
Naegeli's Hotel, Hoboken, N.J., **21**:295
Nahant, Mass., **14**:7, 8, 58; **19**:304, 333, 349, 388; WW at, **14**:49, 70, 74
Nall, James O., **18**:7n1, 485n1
Name the Strongest Candidate! (Baltimore *Sun*), **24**:519n1
Nantucket, **24**:451, 482, 495, 561, 572; **25**:45
Naples, convent, **15**:298; EAW at, **15**:221, 227, 229f, 235, 240, 246, 268, 270, 276, 298
Napoléon I, **15**:441
*Napoleon: The Last Phase* (Rosebery), **23**:292,n1

Narcissus, **22:**218

Narragansett Hotel, Providence, R. I., **16:**309

*Narrative and Critical History of America* (ed. Winsor), **14:**342,n5, 443n3; **15:**482

Narrative of the Graduate College of Princeton University from its Proposal in 1896 until its Dedication in 1913 (West), **16:**414n2, 480n1; **17:**138n1; **18:**67n2, 626n1; **19:**125n1; **20:**6,n3, 7n, 8n

Nashville, Tenn., **18:**342, 398-99, 420, 421, 465, 467, 483, 484; **23:**211, 212, 244, 288; **24:**403n1; **25:**585, 613; The Hermitage, **17:**495; Maxwell House, **16:**235, 236; Moore Memorial Presbyterian Church, **16:**538n1; Watauga Club, **17:**488,n1, 489, 490, 491; Watkins Hall, **16:**235, 240; WW addresses, **16:**235-38; **17:**491-95; **24:**190, 191, 206-16; WW in, **16:**481; **17:**488-90, 491-95; **21:**114

*Nashville* (Tenn.) *Banner*, **16:**235n, 238n, 242n; **17:**376-77, 488, 489n, 489;**18:**483, 484; **20:**240; **22:**376n1; **24:**42n3, 191n, 216n; **25:**24

Nashville Teacher's Association, **16:**235, 240, 241

*Nashville Tennessean*, **17:**377, 490; **18:**485n2; **23:**288; **24:**205n, 206n3, 216n

Nashville Woodrow Wilson Club, **23:**288

Nassau Club of Princeton, **15:**141-42,n2; **17:**381, 383; **18:**303

Nassau Fjord, Alaska, **19:**480, 482

Nassau Hall (Princeton), **25:**520n1

Nassau Inn (Princeton), **24:**448n2

*Nassau Literary Magazine*, **17:**353

*Nassovia* (asteroid), **18:**578

Nast, Thomas, **19:**90-91, 513,n4; **20:**40, 331; **22:**59; **23:**574-75

*Nation* (London), **22:**144n1

*Nation* (Mulford), **14:**14

*Nation* (New York), **14:**350n1, 353n; **15:**494; **18:**384, 575; **20:**408,n2, 453; **21:**322,n3; **22:**205

*Nation in the Making: The Philippines and the United States, 1899-1921* (Stanley), **24:**224n3, 560n1,4

National Academy of Sciences, **18:**576; **19:**506, 507

National Afro-American Council, **21:** 21n1, 275n3

National American Woman Suffrage Association, **25:**29n1

National Arbitration and Peace Congress, New York City, April 1907, **17:**92,n2, 98, 107; *Proceedings*, **17:** 92n2

National Arts Club (New York City), **25:**94n1

National Association for the Advancement of Colored People, **21:**275n1,3; **22:**50n3

National Banking Act, **24:**577

national banks, C. S. Hamlin, **24:**582; A. P. Pujo, **24:**577n1; S. Untermyer, **24:**577

National Child Labor Committee, **18:**186n4; **22:**157, 157n1, 206,n1,4, 226; **23:**651

National Citizens' Committee, **23:**520, 584, 584n2

National Citizens League of Chicago, **24:**581,n3

National Civic Federation, **22:**172n1

National Civil Service Association, **22:**201

National Civil Service Reform League, **22:**78-79, 256; **23:**70n2

National Collegiate Athletic Association, **16:**272n1, 371n5

National Colored Democratic League, **21:**275n3; **25:**448n1, 571,n1

National Conference of Charities and Corrections, **22:**207; **24:**566

National Conservation Congress, **25:** 62,n1,3; **25:**312-21

National Consumers' League, **22:**157n1, 452,n1,3

National Democratic Club, **24:**330

National Democratic Committee, *see* Democratic National Committee

National Democratic League of Clubs, **20:**313, 390, 501n5, 512; **22:**554, 557n1

National Educational Association, **14:**546n; **22:**207

National Federation of Churches, **16:** 227n2

National Gallery of Ireland, Dublin, **15:**239n2

National Independent Democratic League, **22:**428,n2

National Independent Political League of Colored Voters, **21:**21n1, 47,n1, 275n2,4,5, 387, 616; **22:**50; **24:**556; **25:**619

National Institute of Arts and Letters, **14:**329; **21:**109,n2

National Intercollegiate Football Conference, **16:**272n1

National League of Commission Merchants, **24:**32-40

National Liberal Immigration League, **22:**89,n4; **25:**96,n2

National Monetary Commission, **24:** 581-82; **25:**380,n5, 531, 642

*National Monthly* (Buffalo), **19:**464,n1, 471n; **20:**309,n3; **25:**272,n4

National Municipal League, **18:**468n2; **19:**157, 420n5; **23:**70n2

*National Municipal Review*, **23:**573n1

National Negro Educational Congress, Kansas City, **23:**190-91,n1

National Negro Woodrow Wilson League, **25:**619,n1

National Press Club, **24:**16-17

National Progressive Democratic League, **23:**259n3

National Religious Training School and Chautauqua for the Colored Race, Durham, N. C., **19**:400,n2,4

National Reserve Association of the United States, **23**:293n3

National Society of Scottish Artists, **18**:353

National Women's Democratic League, **25**:339,n4

Natural Bridge, Va., **23**:328n2

natural resources, **25**:176, 312-21

naturalization, **25**:53, 54

*Nature Similes in Catullus* (Howe), **18**:562,n5

Naughton, Bevie, **16**:234

navigable streams, **23**:298

Navigation Acts, **14**:342-43, 352, 443; **15**:148

Naylor, Lawrence Plummer, Jr., **19**:502n3, 508

Nebraska, **23**:100, 101, 609; **24**:357,n2, 547; **25**:356, 358; Democratic Party, **25**:347-50; Democratic State Convention, **23**:237; WW addresses, **23**:95-102; **25**:339-59; WW in, **23**:116, 131

Nebraska, Semi-Centennial of territorial organization, **15**:182

Nebraska, University of, **15**:100,n5; **23**:96, 98

*Nebraska State Journal* (Lincoln), **23**:102n

Nebraska State Teachers' Association, **21**:600-601, 622

Nebraska Weslyan University, **16**:465, 512

Needham, Henry Beach, **23**:193, 194, 217, 292; **25**:54

Negro-American Political League, **21**:21n1, 275n1

Negro Democratic Governor Woodrow Wilson for President Club, **24**:484

Negro Educational Convention, Denver, **23**:232

*Negro and the Intelligence and Property Franchise* (MacCorkle), **16**:565,n2

*Negro in Virginia Politics, 1902-1965* (Buni), **25**:619n1

Negroes, **15**:32, 59, 462; **18**:386; **19**:10n2, 69, 386, 399-400, 529, 550, 557-58; **21**:21,n1, 28-29, 47,n1, 106, 156, 161, 162, 171-72, 183, 206, 238-39, 255, 275-76, 292, 333, 335n2, 387, 390, 392, 423, 583, 616; **22**:31, 50, 50n3, 214, 290,n1; **23**:190-91, 232, 316, 628, 629; **24**:484-85, 553, 556, 558,n2, 570, 574; **25**:25-26, 41, 448-49, 450, 548, 549-50, 571 Δ G. B. Jackson, **25**:619-21; O. G. Villard, **25**:25-26, 53, 60-61; J. M. Waldron, **25**:65-66; A. Walters, **25**:607

Nehemiah, **20**:152

Neher, Fred, **14**:145, 211-22, 277, 395, 473; **15**:56, 74, 164, 290n, 324, 340; **16**:10-11; **17**:408

Neher, John Henry, **16**:11

Neill, Charles Patrick, **23**:249n2

Neill, Stephen Charles, **22**:385n2

Nelms, Richard Runnells, **23**:507,n5

Nelson, Benjamin Franklin, **19**:494-95, 605

Nelson, Knute, **23**:132n1

Nelson, Richard Henry, **14**:114

Nelson, W. R., **16**:73

Nelson, William Rockhill, **23**:262,n2

*Nelson W. Aldrich: A Leader in American Politics* (Stephenson), **23**:293n3

Neptune Heights, N. J., Scotty's Cafe, **23**:234n1

Nero, **17**:483; **19**:43

Netherlands, **15**:441; Princeton A.B. recognized for admission to universities in, **15**:194

Netlich, Joseph, **25**:xin1

Nettleship, Henry, **17**:463,n1

netsukes (Japanese ivory carvings), **15**:181,n2,3, 212-13

Neumann, Leon J., **16**:177,n1

Nevada, **24**:64n1, 391, 399, 403-404, 410, 450; **25**:359-60; delegation to Baltimore convention, **24**:520-21

Neville of Kensington, **22**:143,n1

Nevin, Martha J., **15**:66

Nevin, Robert Jenkins, **15**:66,n1

Nevins, Allan, **21**:345n13; **22**:226n3; **23**:118n4

New Brunswick, N. J., **15**:579; **22**:144; **23**:178n1, 179, 265, 634n1; commission government, **23**:176,n1; Opera House, **21**:438; WW campaign speeches, **21**:436-41; **23**:437-42

New Brunswick Presbytery, **16**:105n2; **19**:208

*New Brunswick* (N. J.) *Times*, **21**:541

New Castle, Del., **23**:112

New England, character, **19**:350; Democrats, **23**:235, 324; Princeton Alumni, **14**:360,n1; **16**:357, 384-85; **18**:295,n1, 297-300,n1, 411; **19**:483, 497; **20**:262,n1

*New England and the North in Early Southern Life* (Ingle), **14**:89,n1

New England Arbitration and Peace Conference, Hartford, 1910, **20**:120,n2

New England College Presidents, **21**:558

*New England Magazine*, **18**:575

New England Society in the City of New York, *Ninety-Fifth Anniversary Celebration*, **19**:758,n1

New England Society of Orange, N. J., **14**:301

New England Suffrage League, **21**:275n5

*New Englands True Interest . . .* (Stoughton), **22**:89,n2

New Freedom (article, Wilson), **25**:640-41

*New Freedom* (Wilson; ed. Hale), **22**:414n1; **25**:609n1

*New Freedom* (Link), *see Wilson: The New Freedom*

New Hampshire, **23**:101; Republicans, **23**:473, 474; WW address, **24**:165-66
New Haven, Conn., **19**:562; **25**:271; Chamber of Commerce, **18**:522, 524; WW in, **18**:53; WW addresses, **24**:166-77; **25**:245-57

*New Haven Evening Register*, **25**:257n
New Haven Railroad, L. D. Brandeis, **25**:414,n1
New Idea Republicans, **25**:86, 121, 322, 379, 428-29
*New International Encyclopedia*, **18**:579

## NEW JERSEY

**22**:365f, 393, 466n4, 537, 538-39, 556, 562, 589, 602; **23**:101, 170, 176, 190, 500; **24**:103, 113, 377, 444, 445, 493, 502, 546, 569; **25**:69-70, 80, 87, 333, 334, 337, 348, 351, 355, 410, 429, 463, 480-83, 500, 635, 636, 638, 639; administrative reorganization, **21**:94-95; Agricultural Experiment Station, **22**:144,n2; annual appropriation for Princeton scholarships requested, **17**:594-95; **18**:255-56; *Annual Returns of the General Election of 1911*, **23**:544n1; automobile laws, **21**:45, 96, 305; **22**:591; automobile use, **23**:383; ballots, **21**:262-63, 339, 407-408, 531-32, 567, 571; **23**:336; Banking Commissioner, **23**:628; benevolent and correctional institutions, **23**:382; Board of Education, **22**:550n2; Board of Equalization of Taxes, **22**:322,n1; board of guardians, **25**:39; Board of Health (local), **22**:510; Board of Health (state), **22**:579n5; Board of Pardons, **22**:28; Board of Park Commissioners, **22**:527; Board of Public Utility Commissioners, **22**:579n4; boss system, bosses, **21**:303n2, 340, 346, 408, 411, 417, 420, 443, 458-59, 504, 506, 571; **25**:189-90, 437; Bureau of Roads, **22**:144; campaign contributions, expenses, **21**:31; **25**:567; Cape May County, **25**:480; canals, **21**:225, 359, 403; Charities and Corrections Department, **23**:304n1; child labor, **25**:311; city charters, **23**:634, 635; city government reform, **22**:549, 551-52; Civil Service, **21**:45, 96, 505, 532, 567; **24**:168-69, 264; Civil Service Commission, **22**:457, 569; coal combine scandals, **21**:343,n9, 345, 504; cold storage bill, **21**:324; cold storage warehouses, **22**:227-28, 260, 352-53, 438, 579n5, 591; commission government for cities, **19**:729; **22**:551,n3, 574-75, 581, 591; *see also* Walsh Act; Commissioner of Charities and Correction, **24**:22; Commissioner of Insurance, **24**:11; Commissioner of Roads, **21**:234; **24**:264; commissions, multiplicity of, **24**:172; commuters, **21**:446, 449, 453, 516; Congressional District reapportionment, **23**:386, 387; conservation, **21**:44, 88n3, 95, 126, 402, 505; **23**:383; Constitution, **19**:203, 513; **21**:250; **22**:338, 504n1, 548; **23**:624; corporations, **25**:358-59; corrupt practices bill and act, **21**:45, 83n3, 96, 111, 126, 272, 313-14,

326, 332, 339-40, 359, 408, 420, 499, 504, 511, 567; **22**:481, 547,n6, 579,n3, 581; **23**:78, 349, 365, 401, 418, 419, 431, 446, 531; **25**:486; County Board of Elections Law, **21**:340n1, 408; County Board of Taxation Law, **21**:264, 340n1; county clerks, **21**:264; Court of Chancery, **18**:45; **20**:427, 428, 432, 472, 480, 511,n4; **23**:295n5; Court of Errors and Appeals, **22**:54; **23**:295n5, 316, 324; delegation to the Baltimore convention, **24**:517, 524; Democratic party, *see* Democratic party and Democrats in New Jersey; Democratic State Auxiliary Committee, **19**:554,n1,2,3; Democratic State Committee, **20**:215n1,2; determinate sentences for criminal offenses, **22**:579,n6; direct nominations, **21**:45, 96, 100; direct primaries, **21**:31, 111, 126, 127, 258,n10, 261-62, 307, 359, 420, 496-97, 505, 511, 521, 567, 582; employers' liability, **21**:31, 45, 95, 195, 256-67,n9, 280-81, 305, 307, 340, 408, 469-70, 489-90, 490-91, 497, 521, 553, 554, 561, 567; **22**:291n2, 347, 462f, 481, 546n5, 579,n1; **23**:109, 322, 345, 353, 402; *see also* New Jersey: Workingmen's Compensation Act; Education Board, **23**:183; Education Commissioner, **23**:102-104, 192n3, 216-17, 226; Egan public utility rate making bill, **22**:481; eight-hour law, **21**:45, 95; election frauds and corruption, **21**:345, 403; **23**:358-59; election laws, **21**:326; **22**:357n4; *see also* Geran election reform bill; election of 1910, **22**:3-4; election process, **24**:231-32; electoral reform, **21**:307; factory and workshop inspection, regulations, **21**:521; **23**:384; Finance Board, **23**:146; finances, **23**:384; fire department employees, **22**:508; Fish and Game Commission, **23**:273; fishing law, **25**:474,n4; Forestry Commission Act, **21**:505; free trade, **25**:242; gas companies, **21**:312, 340, 341; **23**:420; Geran Election Reform bill and Act, **21**:340n1; **22**:430-32, 447n5, 455, 456-57f, 470-72, 481-82, 483-84, 484-85, 504,n1, 512, 513n2, 518,n1, 536-37, 537n4, 561,n5, 571, 579,n2, 581, 590; **23**:219, 233, 332n2, 344, 348, 358, 385, 386, 410, 430, 432, 454, 455, 457, 629; **24**:60, 328, 429-34; **25**:113-14,n2, 306, 309; provisions and analysis, **22**:569,n1

*New Jersey, cont.*

*Governor and governments,* **19:**328, 513; **21:**503-504, 573, 574; **23:**168; Governor's mansion, **21:**606,n1; Governor's secretary, **21:**606-607; **22:**328-29; grade crossing elimination, **23:**383-84, 468-69, 476-78; **24:**24, 321-23,n1, 324, 325, 326,n6; grand juries, **21:**418, 531; **23:**382,n2; Great Channel, **23:**185; Hahn Investigating Committee, **21:**7,n3; harbor development, **24:**183; Hillery Maximum Tax Act, **21:**340n2, 408; Home for Feeble Minded Children, Vineland, **23:**290, 300; Home for Feeble Minded Women, Vineland, **23:**290, 300; horse racing and betting, **21:**343n9; incorporation laws, **21:**45, 88n3; **23:**382; indeterminate sentences for criminal offenses, **22:**591; inheritance taxes, **25:**310; Inland Lakes Act, **21:**505; inland waterway, **21:**316, 324, 327; **22:**538-39, 591; judiciary and judicial system, **23:**168, 383; **24:**24, 460; labor, **25:**223-24, 315; Labor Commissioner, **23:**339,n4, 356; *Laws of New Jersey,* **22:**157n3, 546n5, 550n2, 569n1, 575n5, 579n3,4,5,6,7; **23:**206,n5, 245, 295n5, 467n2; **24:**136n, 281n, 325n6, 326n8,9, 431n2

*Legislature,* **16:**502; **19:**203, 292, 512-13; **21:**229, 230, 231, 234, 251, 303, 339, 343n9, 346, 347-48, 358, 360-61, 370, 375, 388, 475, 504, 523, 534, 548, 564, 573, 574, 581, 582, 605, 606; **22:**155, 157, 162, 166-67, 171, 175, 182, 205n2, 206, 212, 226n1, 235, 240, 241, 242n2, 244, 249, 251, 252, 278, 279, 301, 303n5, 304, 311, 321, 328n1, 333, 339, 340, 343, 352, 353, 357n2, 365, 367, 382n1, 383n3, 396, 410, 430, 431, 432, 434, 436n1, 438, 454, 455, 459-60, 471, 476, 477, 481-82, 483, 484, 485, 504, 505, 508n2, 511, 531, 534, 547, 549, 550n2, 552n, 569, 571-72, 578-79, 581f, 583n4, 589, 590, 591, 597, 598, 602, 603; **23:**26, 43, 67, 68, 69, 74, 78, 79, 123-24, 164, 203, 257, 274, 280-81, 286, 295n5, 302, 304, 305, 305n2, 324,n1, 330, 333, 335, 337, 343, 348, 353, 364, 380, 381, 384, 400, 417, 427, 430, 439-40, 446, 450, 452, 453, 454, 467, 533, 627, 629, 635; **24:**18-25, 24, 136, 191, 216-17, 229-30, 261-65, 263, 266, 267,n1, 268-69, 271, 276-77, 277-78, 278, 279, 279-80, 280, 281,n1, 281-82, 282, 282-83, 283-84, 321-23, 324, 326, 327,n10, 430-34, 440-41; **25:**305-10, 486, 574; Acts of the 135th Legislature, **22:**452,n4; *Assembly,* **21:**313, 324, 372; **22:**232, 233, 239,n1, 240, 241, 242n2, 243, 253, 280, 301, 308, 352n3, 477, 481-82, 483, 504-505, 508, 518,n1, 534, 538, 539, 546n5, 569n1, 575,n2, 583, 591; **23:**343, 344, 353-54, 383, 388, 544,n1, 545; Committee on Labor and Industries, **22:**546n5; election of speaker, **25:**566, 581-84; Fitzherbert scandal, **24:**244,n1, 245-47; Leavitt-Walsh bill, **22:**575n5; *Minutes . . . ,*

*New Jersey, cont.*

**21:**8n3; **22:**508n, 525n, 546n5, 548n, 552n, 575n2; **24:**25n, 217n, 234n, 235n5, 264n, 265n, 266n, 267n, 280n, 281n, 282n, 283n, 284n, 323n; rules of order of Senate and General Assembly, **23:**383; *Senate,* **21:**324, 504; **22:**352n3, 474, 477, 482, 511n1,3, 531,n3, 534, 536, 538, 549, 550n2, 561,n5, 569n1, 574-75, 582, 583, 588-89; **23:**346, 446, 544,n1, 545; Committee on Corporations, **22:**546n5; *Journal . . . ,* **22:**244n1, 527n, 535n, 546n5, 552n4; **24:**263n, 269n, 277n, 278n, 279n, 280n, 325n5; *Report of Senate Committee to Investigate the Methods and Practices, Expenses and Disbursements of the Public Schools,* **22:**549n,1,2; Limited Franchise Act, **21:**506; liquor laws and home rule, **21:**45, 57, 63; lobbyists, **23:**427; machine government, **21:**418; *Manual of the Legislature,* **21:**369n3; **23:**392n2

*Mayors,* **23:**634,n1; messenger boy bill, **22:**452,n4; mother of corporations, **21:**100, 134, 204; **23:**296; National Guard, **23:**213,n1, 234n1, 241, 367; Camp Wilson, 225, 256; chaplains, 240; natural resources, **21:**44, 88n3, 95, 505; Negroes, **25:**607; Non-pecuniary Profit Act, **18:**558; Ocean Highway, **21:**324; Ocean Parkway, **23:**185; patronage, **22:**262n2, 513,n2, 518; personal registration, **21:**263; petit jury reform, **21:**505; Pierce bill, **21:**325; political machine, **24:**110; **24:**169; politics and politicians, **23:**5, 6, 115-16, 347f, 461-63, 472-73, 627; popular election of U. S. Senators, **21:**31, 263, 339, 348; Potable Water Acts, **21:**505; primary elections and reforms, **21:**123, 262, 339, 407, 408, 505, 533,n3; **22:**357n4, 358, 383n3, 456f, 459f; **25:**467; *see also* Geran Election Reform bill and act; Prosecutor of the Pleas, **23:**431; public health laws, **25:**308-309; public school reform, **22:**549, 550n2, 579,n8, 581, 591; Public Service Commission, **21:**44, 88, 93, 95, 119, 196, 204, 207-208; **22:**11; Public Service Corporation of New Jersey, **15:**226n1; **22:**359, 462,n2; **23:**346-47, 354, 434, 438, 439; **24:**412, 432; **25:**358-59, 431, 486; public service corporations, **21:**44, 88n3, 207n2, 228; **23:**420; **25:**431; Public Service Electric & Gas Company, **17:**24; public service franchises, **24:**261-63, 262; Public Utilities bill and Act of 1911, **22:**11, 310, 357n4, 447-48, 455, 460f, 485, 547,n6, 579,n4, 581, 590; **23:**8-9, 78, 354, 420, 433-35, 438, 439; Public Utilities Commission, **21:**31, 42-43, 111, 207n2, 226, 233, 247, 263-64, 305, 311, 312, 316, 324, 325, 331, 339, 369n3, 407, 440, 495-96, 505, 561, 567, 571; **22:**448, 581, 590; **23:**78, 310, 383-84, 402, 420, 433-35, 437, 438, 439, 450,n1, 469, 477; **24:**25, 234n1, 321-23, 326n6, 431; **25:**308, 309, 431; Public Utilities Law (old), **21:**207-208,n2; **22:**84n2, 349-

*New Jersey, cont.*
50; race-track scandals, **21:**343,n9, 345, 504; railroads, **21:**42-43, 63, 311-12, 340,n2, 402-403, 449,n1, 453, 571; **22:**538-39; **25:**336; Railroad Commission, **19:**513,n2,3; **21:**207,n2, 505; railroad tax acts, **21:**504; railway full crew bill, **23:**384; rate-making power, **21:**307, 311-12, 324-25, 332; Register of Deeds, **21:**264; registration laws, **21:**325; representative government, **24:**318, 319; Republican party, *see* Republican party and Republicans in New Jersey
*Road Commissioner*, **22:**415,n1; Robbins bill, **21:**325; sample ballot return scandal, **23:**403, 417, 433; Sanitation laws, **21:**567; School fund, **21:**44,n1, 95; School system, **23:**78, 84; Second Regiment, New Jersey National Guard, **22:**230; senatorial contest, **25:**116-18, 146-47,n1,2,3, 184n1, 213-20, 236,n3, 238, 345-46; Sheriffs, **21:**521; **23:**382,n2; ship canal, **21:**225; Simpson Corrupt Practices bill and Act, **22:**481, 547,n6, 579,n3, 581; special interests, **24:**337-38; State Board of Assessors, **21:**264; State Board of Riparian Commissioners, **21:**264; state government, **23:**280; State Home for Delinquent Boys, Jamesburg, **23:**290, 302; State Home for Soldiers, Sailors or Marines and Their Wives, Vineland, **23:**290, 300; State Hospital for the Insane, Morris Plains, **23:**290, 304, 629; State House, **22:**230; **23:**366-67, 628; State House Commission, **21:**606; **22:**510; State Reformatory, Rahway,

*New Jersey, cont.*
**23:**290, 305; State Reformatory for Women, Glen Gardner, **23:**290; State Treasury, **21:**521; State Village for Epileptics, Skillman, **23:**290; State Water Supply Commission, **21:**276, 277, 280; stock-watering act, **21:**505; Supreme Court, **23:**324n2; taxation and tax system, **21:**44, 95, 100, 257, 304, 375, 567, 568; **23:**382, 421; **24:**21, 172; Tenure of Office Act, **23:**206,n5; transportation, **22:**538; trolleys, **21:**226, 312, 340, 341; treasurer election controversy, **25:**579,-n2; Tuberculosis Sanitarium, Glen Gardner, **23:**290; U. S. senatorship, **21:**200-201, 263, 505, 581-83; vote buying, **21:**167-68; voter registration, **25:**328; Walsh Act (Commission Government), **23:**162n3, 202, 211, 344, 420, 450, 580-81; water rights, **21:**44, 88n3, 95; **23:**382-83; watersheds and water supply, **21:**316, 341, 359, 402, 498-99, 516, 521, 567; Water Works Board, **23:**146; Weights and Measures Act, **22:**579,n7, 591; WW intention to remain resident, **25:**591-92, 596-97; WW's message to N. J. Democrats, **24:**429-34; WW's remarks in Trenton to his supporters, **24:**389-90; WW statement on results of presidential primary, **24:**449; WW to retain governorship, **24:**583-84; Women's Christian-Temperance Union, **23:**250; Workingmen's Compensation Act, **22:**546,n5, 579,n1, 581, 590; **23:**323-24, 345; *see also* New Jersey: employers' liability

*End of New Jersey entry; see also*
WILSON, WOODROW, GOVERNOR

New Jersey Alumni Federation, **19:**155,n1
New Jersey Bankers' Association, **20:**414-21; *Proceedings of Seventh Annual Convention . . .*, **20:**421n
New Jersey Car Advertising Co., **21:**341n3
New Jersey Central Railroad, **23:**450n1
New Jersey Charities Aid Society, **23:**290
New Jersey Child Labor Committee, **22:**156,n1,2, 157, 157n1
New Jersey Civic Federation, **19:**729, 730
New Jersey Conference of Charities and Correction, **22:**528; *Proceedings*, **22:**531n
New Jersey Consumers' League, **22:**452
New Jersey Editorial Association, **22:**455
New Jersey Federation of Labor, **22:**546n5
New Jersey Harbor Commission, **24:**183
New Jersey Herald and Sussex County

Democrat (Newton, N. J.), **21:**405n; **22:**378n1,2
New Jersey High School Teachers' Association, **14:**69,n1
New Jersey Historical Society, **21:**502n, 518n, 536n, 576n
New Jersey Library Association, **19:**451
*New Jersey Progressivism before Wilson* (Noble), **19:**513n2; **21:**207,n2, 219n1, 256,n9,10, 340n1, 533,n3
New Jersey Society of Los Angeles, **23:**44
New Jersey Society of Pennsylvania, **22:**226n1
New Jersey State Bar Association, **22:**50; **23:**158
New Jersey State Conference of Charities and Correction, *Proceedings of Ninth Annual Meeting . . . at Canada, Feb. 1910*, **20:**135n2
New Jersey State Federation of Labor, **21:**55,n2, 56n1, 57, 59, 60, 82, 83, 256n9
New Jersey State Home for Girls (Trenton), **25:**536n1, 537

New Jersey State Teachers' Association, **19**:387-88, 399,n1, 634, 635, 738-39; *Annual Report . . . 1909*, **19**:648n
New Jersey Tuberculosis Sanitarium, **22**:356
New Jersey Woman Suffrage Association, **22**:289-90
*New Letters of Thomas Carlyle* (ed. Carlyle), **18**:362,n1
New London, Conn., **18**:387; **20**:541n1
New Mexico, **22**:563n6; **24**:306
New Nationalism, **21**:322, 322n1, 337, 381; **22**:9
New Orleans, La., **25**:557n1; Benjamin Morgan Palmer, leading figure of, **25**:457
New Orleans *Daily States*, **24**:468
New Plans for Princeton (WW), **16**:146-49; mentioned, **17**:456,n3
New Providence Academy, Virginia, **16**:509
*New Republic*, **20**:350n2
New Rochelle, N. Y., Peoples Forum, **15**:392, 417; **16**:13; **17**:148-49; **21**:322-23, 335n2; WW address, **16**:13-15
New Willard Hotel, Washington, D. C., **14**:400; **24**:16
New York Academy of Sciences, **18**:579
*New York Age*, **21**:239n1, 275n3; **24**:558n2
*New York American*, **18**:373n3; **20**:402-n1, 561,n1, 563, 564, 564n1; **22**:223n; **23**:252,n1; **24**:132n, 135n, 219n, 223n; **25**:233,n1, 360n2, 449n2, 559
New York *Christian Advocate*, **24**:381n
New York City, **18**:422, 424; **19**:445; **20**:84; **23**:95, 194, 589, 590, 602; **24**:241; Amen Corner, **22**:453, 453n1; Astor Hotel, **15**:535; **18**:228, 560; **20**:32n1; **22**:250n2, 410, 585, 588, 601; **23**:559; Bankers, **19**:601, 607; Bankers Trust Company, **23**:246; Barnard Club, **15**:166; Belmont Hotel, **19**:648; **20**:116, 119; **21**:321, 362n1; **22**:334; Board of Education, **16**:256; Brayton Hotel, **21**:164n1; Brick Presbyterian Church, **14**:267,n1; **15**:50; **19**:331, 333, 347n1; **21**:579,n2; Broadway Tabernacle, **16**:228, 230; Burns Society, **18**:549,n2; Café Savarin, **15**:131; Carnegie Hall, **16**:227, 227n2, 228, 231, 233; **17**:92, 93n2; **20**:181; **21**:320,n3; **22**:140, 214, 412n2, 417n1, 514, 514n4, 515; **23**:583, 584, 592n2; Central Park, **19**:635,n1; Century Association, **16**:531; **17**:390; **19**:561; **22**:209; Church of the Messiah, **16**:231n1; **23**:145n3; Citizens Union, **19**:25,n2; city charter, **20**:42, 206-207; City Club, **19**:155, 156, 156n3, 307, 419; **21**:617; City History Club, **18**:509-10, 516; College of the City of New York, **14**:486, 544n2; **15**:7, 9,n4, 70; **16**:132, 249, 258; **18**:571;

**19**:182, 184; **23**:260; Collingwood Hotel, **21**:87; **22**:87, 141, 230; Colony Club, **23**:588,n1; Cooper Union, **15**:536; Delmonico's, **14**:210; **15**:58, 147, 149, 150; **16**:11; **17**:66; **19**:30, 102n1; **20**:147n; Democratic National Convention, **24**:500-501; Department of Education, **15**:536; DeWitt Clinton High School, **18**:534, 541; editorial policy of newspapers, **23**:509-10; Equitable Building, **16**:535; **20**:565n; Everett House, **14**:9; Fifth Avenue Hotel, **14**:238; Fifth Avenue Presbyterian Church, **18**:339; **19**:51; Fire Department, **18**:510; Free Synagogue, **22**:585; Friendly Sons of St. Patrick, **18**:59; **19**:102,n1; *The 125th Anniversary Dinner . . .* , **19**:102n1, 108n; Friends School, **16**:305n3; Garden Theatre, **20**:172; German American Citizen's League, **22**:514n4; government, **19**:86; Grand Central Station, **19**:214, 223, 307; harbor facilities, **24**:184; Henry Street Settlement, **22**:207n4, 452n3; High School Teachers Association, **18**:533, 541, 593; Holland House, **19**:422, 449; **20**:3, 7n; Hudson Terminal, **21**:449; Imperial Hotel, **15**:471; Institute of Musical Art, **16**:208-11,n1,3; **19**:551,n2; Insurgents' Club, **22**:455; Juilliard School of Music, **16**:210n1; Kansas Society, **22**:389, 392; Kentuckians of New York, **22**:421; Knickerbocker Club, **14**:306n3; **17**:417n1; Knickerbocker Hotel, **18**:269, 270; Lawyers' Club, **20**:565n; **21**:5n1, 356,n1; League for Political Education, **15**:501-502, 552; Lenox Mansion, **16**:211; Lotos Club, **16**:292,n1, 301, 532, 533; **19**:579; Madison Square Garden, **15**:202n3; **21**:510; Madison Square Presbyterian Church, **21**:621n1; Manhattan Club, **23**:603, 603n1; Manhattan Hotel, **17**:31n1; **19**:425; Manhattan Opera House, **20**:173n4; Marble Collegiate Church, **19**:544, 545; Martinique Hotel, **22**:328n1, 357, 357n4; Mercantile Trust Co., **23**:246; Metropolitan Club, **14**:196; **20**:9-10, 100, 129; Metropolitan Museum of Art, **15**:181; Murray Hill Hotel, **16**:238; National City Bank, **19**:29, 308; **23**:293n3; National Democratic Club, **16**:322, 323n1, 358, 362n1, 372n2, 373; **18**:59,n3, 219-20, 263, 269; **20**:257-62; **22**:167, 167n1, 208, 601; **23**:637; *Annual Dinner on the Birthday of Grover Cleveland* (1910), **20**:262n; *Annual Dinner on Jefferson Day . . . (1906)*, **16**:319n; Princeton Alumni, **17**:381; **19**:146, 158, 159, 175-77; **20**:84, 85, 247, 269, 310, 324, 328, 382n4,5; Nineteenth Century Club, **22**:606;

New York City, (cont.)
Normal College (now Hunter College), **19**:676; North Carolina Society, **16**:320, 324; **19**:10n2; Pennsylvania Station, **23**:193; People's Institute, **16**:332n1; Plaza Hotel, **18**:509; **22**:421, 425; Presbyterian Hospital, **15**:571n1, 576, 577, 579; **16**:3; Presbyterian Union, **14**:252; Princeton Club, **14**:46-47,n1,2, 291; **19**:651; **20**:64,n2, 263,n1, 337-48, 466; provinciality of, **20**:24, 25, 26; **23**:46-47; public opinion, **23**:87; Purcell's restaurant, **15**:201; Ritz-Carlton Hotel, **22**:474, 477; robbery of poor, **21**:483, 484; Round Table Club, **14**:306,n3, 381n1, 397; **15**:145,n2, 159, 237; **17**:417,n1; **19**:23,n4, 33, 500n2, 552, 658; St. Denis Hotel, **15**:79n1, 328, 500, 505; St. Nicholas Collegiate Reformed Church, **18**:339; St. Nicholas Society, **23**:47,n5; Savoy Hotel, **14**:253; **16**:243; Schoolmasters' Association of New York and Vicinity, **15**:79, 468, 500, 505-506,n1,2,3,4; *Eleventh Annual Report, 1903-1904*, **15**:98n; sightseeing buses, **21**:207; Society of the Virginians, **15**:545; South Carolina Society, **17**:78n1; Southern Society, **15**:68; **17**:215-16, 220n1, 347, 587; **18**:532, 535, 540n, 563, 567,n3; *Year Book for 1909-10*, **18**:540n; **19**:272n1; **21**:105n1, 265, 298,n1; **22**:51, 51,n1, 188-96; *Year Book for 1911-12*, 196n; **22**:188-96, 202-203,n4, 210; street railways, **21**:343n10; Tammany Hall, **16**:43, 218, 323n1; **18**:60n3; **19**:86n1, 512; **20**:402n1; **21**:303n2, 342n8, 344n12, 523; **22**:161n1, 602; **23**:259; Temple Rodeph Shalom, **18**:523; **19**:112; Thursday Evening Club, **19**:552,n3; Trinity Church, **15**:551n4; Tweed Ring, **19**:90-91, 513-14; **23**:574-75; United Colored Democracy, **22**:31; U. S. financial resources in, **22**:603-604; U. S. Sub-Treasury, **15**:551; University Club, **14**:489, 491; **15**:146, 237, 534, 571; **16**:143, 301; **17**:264-65, 456; **18**:59; **19**:119,n4, 619, 700; **21**:473; **22**:287,n1, 294, 333, 334, 391, 607; **23**:603, 652; Waldorf-Astoria Hotel, **14**:288, 298; **15**:68, 545; **16**:320, 344, 362n1, 369, 529; **17**:65, 78n1, 215; **18**:532; **19**:175, 601; **20**:66, 402n1, 556; **21**:265, 621; **22**:51, 274, 389, 392, 453n1; Webster Hotel, **19**:229n3; Wesleyan alumni, **16**:243; Williams College alumni, **19**:30-31; WW addresses, **14**:268-76, 287-91, 298; **15**:326, 328-29, 536-39; **16**:11-12, 227-29, 243-44, 319-20, 344, 529-31; **17**:528-45; **19**:30-31, 102-108, 112, 175-77; **20**:23-27, 32-43, 44-45, 58-59, 64, 249,n1, 257-62, 263,n1, 328-35, 337-48, 357, 382n4,5, 392, 399-401; **24**:394-95, 413-28; WW on, **22**:489; WW unrecognized on trip, **24**:585-87

New York Clearing House, **24**:533, 534
New York Educational Council, **15**:201,-n2
*New York Evening Journal*, **21**:85n1; **24**:225n2
*New York Evening Mail*, **20**:116
New York *Evening Post*, **14**:547,n2; **15**:146n, 291n25, 403,n4,5, 501,n2, 502; **16**:229n, 454, 455n, 457; **17**:35, 409,n1, 609n1; **18**:576; **19**:154; **20**:24n, 141, 153n2, 266,n4, 378-79,n1,2, 380,n1,2, 382n6, 408, 566n; **21**:81,n1, 85, 168,n2, 274n, 320, 322n1, 377n, 381n, 385n1, 454n, 508n, 541, 555n, 618; **22**:32, 83, 86n1, 102n1, 181n1, 289, 308, 358n, 421n, 432n, 439; **23**:30,n1,3, 130n1, 206, 636n, 652n; **24**:45n, 63n, 73n1, 134n, 439,n7, 538,-n1; **25**:25n1,3, 26, 27n2, 106n, 111n2, 156n, 161n, 169n, 501n, 521n, 531n1; William Sulzer, **25**:361
New York *Evening Sun*, **16**:532,n5, 533n3,4; **17**:445, 453; **24**:62n; WW misquoted, **24**:62-63
New York *Evening Telegram*, **19**:256n1; **21**:323
New York *Evening World*, **22**:181n1, 235-36n
New York Giants (baseball team), **25**:390n3
New York *Globe and Commercial Advertiser*, **22**:356n; **24**:585,n1
*New York Herald*, **15**:149-50, 150n, 150n3, 507n; **16**:12n, 110n1,2, 119n, 211, 244n; **18**:466n1; **19**:111, 111n, 112n; **20**:66,n2, 69, 69,n1, 71, 76,n1, 117, 286; **22**:41,n2, 50n3, 393; **23**:606n2; **25**:588n2
*New York Herald*, Paris edition, **14**:539; **18**:352; **21**:166
New York *Independent*, **24**:383n1
*New York Journal*, **25**:233, 360n3
New York *Journal of Commerce*, **25**:531n1
New York Juvenile Asylum, **25**:310n2
New York Law School, **21**:147,n3
New York Life Insurance Company, **16**:333n2
New York, New Haven and Hartford Railroad, **24**:176,n7; **25**:414
New York Observatory and Nautical Museum, **16**:488
New York Peace Society, **17**:92n2
New York Polyclinic Medical School and Hospital, **17**:40, 41
*New York Press*, **21**:180; **23**:53n3
New York School of Philanthropy, **15**:407, 408n1
*New York Social Register*, **19**:390
New York state, **21**:598; **24**:548; **25**:24, 143, 283, 326, 419, 594-95, 599-600; anti-racetrack legislation, **21**:393; beet sugar manufacturers, **21**:343n10;

Commissioner of Labor, **23:**340, 340-n3; Court of Appeals, **23:**324n1; dairy interests, **21:**343n10; delegation at Democratic National Convention, **24:**497n2, 507n1, 508, 512,n1, 520; Democratic Party *see* Democratic Party & Democrats in New York; free trade, **25:**242; government, **23:**164; gubernatorial race, **25:**112, 133-34,n3, 286, 441-47; Hughes nomination in 1906, **23:**628; Insurance scandals, **21:**341,n4, 392, 393, 399, 418; legislature, **21:**343n10; **22:**602, 603; Armstrong Insurance Investigating Committee, **16:**220, 276, 320, 333,n2; *Report of the Joint Committee . . . to Investigate Corrupt Practices in Connection with Legislation and the Affairs of Insurance Companies . . .*, **21:**343n10; Nathan Straus, **25:**378, 422; national banks, **24:**577; Negroes, **25:**607; Politics and government, **19:**25-26,n1,2,3,4,5,6; **23:**473; Primary Law (Hinman-Green bill), 499-500,n2; Public Service Commission, **23:**281; race track interests, **21:**343n10; reformers, **21:**360; Republican Party *see* Republican Party & Republicans in New York; Senate, Lexow Investigation, **19:**86,-n1; street railway companies, **21:**343n10; Superintendent of Insurance, **21:**343n10; WW addresses, **24:**307-14; WW in, **24:**304-14; workmen's compensation act, **22:**564,n7; *see also* New York City

New York Press Club, **25:**118-26, 534
New York *Review of Reviews*, **25:**617n1
New York Southern Society *see* Southern Society of New York
New State Bankers' Association, **14:**292, 298-99; **15:**383; **18:**424; **20:**23-27
New York State Museum, **16:**259
New York Stock Exchange, **17:**96n1; **22:**582; **24:**582; **25:**529; Panic of 1907, **24:**533
New York *Sun,* **14:**63, 546; **15:**549n; **16:**30,n1,2, 532; **17:**41, 65; **18:**259, 576; **19:**522; **20:**116, 278-82, 307, 307,n2, 311, 382n6, 402n1; **21:**225-26, 287, 299, 335n2, 493n; **22:**160, 283n1,2, 311n1, 391n; **23:**30,n5, 53n4, 565n, 565n1, 602n1; **24:**5,n2, 100n, 140n, 244, 504n3, 579, 580; **25:**544, 559
New York, Susquehanna & Western Railroad, **23:**450n1
*New York Times,* **14:**25n2, 113n2, 253, 285n, 297, 360n; **15:**58n, 60n, 69n, 143n2, 149n, 215n2, 291n25, 329n, 539n; **16:**50n3, 229n, 231n1, 239n3, 283n, 292n2, 320n, 344n, 495n1, 531n, 532, 533n6; **17:**16n3, 78, 83n, 124n, 248n, 460n1, 473n4, 513-23, 524-27, 565n1; **18:**271n1, 373n3; **19:**31n, 255, 269, 552n3, 728n1; **20:**26, 38n, 65, 69n2, 69, 76,n1, 153n10, 306, 382,n5,

402n1, 570, 572; **21:**98, 101n, 124n3, 362n1, 485n, 519; **22:**24n1, 121, 122n1, 131n4, 168n, 186, 240, 243n, 261, 337-38,n1,2,3, 422n, 479, 514n4, 524, 524n1, 581n1, 604n; **23:**30, 30n4, 112n3, 192n1, 227-28,n3, 232, 246, 246n1, 252,n2, 287, 287n1,2, 325, 352, 355-56, 408n1, 437n2, 504n6, 568n1, 587n, 605n1, 606n2, 626, 629n, 650; **24:**47n, 81n, 81n1, 135n, 248n1, 269n1, 287n, 308n, 502n, 507n, 519n, 528n, 530n, 564n, 589n; **25:**44n, 49n, 58n, 106n, 107, 114, 118n, 143n, 146n, 271n, 284n, 286n1, 329n, 360n1, 381n6, 419n, 419n2, 420, 425n, 447n, 457n, 459n1, 493,n, 493n1, 521n, 522n, 526, 527n2, 566n3, 593n1, 617n3, 619n1, 632n; Carnegie pension, 503n2, 504; Graduate school controversy, **20:**69-71, 81,n1, 117, 131, 132, 213, 215, 250, 265, 286; WW letters to H. B. Brougham, 69-71, 79-80; editorial on controversy, 74-76; M. T. Pyne reply to editorial, 81,n1
*New York Times Annual Financial Review*, **22:**121-22, 186, 312, 313, 316n
*New York Times Saturday Review of Books and Art*, **14:**287n
New York *Tribune,* **14:**210n, 299n; **15:**64n, 549, 552n; **16:**15n, 229n, 290n; **17:**31n1, 587n1; **18:**510n; **19:**521; **20:**27n; **22:**77n1, 454; **25:**128n, 519
New York University, **15:**201; **16:**39, 238-40; **20:**187n1; Law Alumni, **20:**65
New York *World,* **15:**550,n2,4; **16:**110n; **20:**25n, 402n1, 566n7; **21:**5,n1, 85, 134-36, 148; **22:**10, 12n, 181n1, 421n, 454n, 455, 546n5; **23:**132n, 215, 242,n3, 246n1, 252, 261, 614n; **24:**7n, 60n1, 96, 97, 98n2, 225n, 238n, 239n2, 332n, 395n, 450,n1, 463, 475, 492n, 501, 511n, 512n1, 514n; **25:**55, 98n3, 128n, 286, 435n, 459n3, 493n, 501n, 520n, 521n, 522n, 534, 557, 562n1, 579, 603n
New York Zoölogical Garden, **19:**63
Newark, N. J., **19:**652n2, 708; **21:**146, 171; **22:**171, 199, 229n1, 242n2, 278n1, 280, 286, 333, 334, 343; **23:**206n5, 342, 403, 588n4, 594; fraudulent ballots, **23:**348, 353; Board of Trade, **22:**373; City Hall, **19:**729; Commission government, **23:**178n1; Congregation Oheb Shalom, **23:**305,n1; Continental Hotel, **14:**262; **18:**551; D.L.&W.R.R. depot, **22:**285; Elliot Street School, **16:**381; Essex Club, **20:**462; Essex County Lawyers' Club, **20:**226, 245-46, 462-63; First Presbyterian Church, **16:**380-81; First Troop Armory, **23:**330, 331; Government, **19:**730; Harburger's Hall, **23:**330; Hebrew Benevolent and Orphan Asylum Society, **22:**183,n2, 316,n1; Ironbound District, **23:**330,n1; Jewish Community Coun-

Newark, N. J., (cont.)
  cil, **22**:321n; Krueger Auditorium,
  **21**:202n1, 564n1; **22**:285; **23**:177, 178,
  354,n1; lawlessness, **23**:357; Lawyers'
  Club, **19**:651, 709,n4; mayor, **23**:357;
  New Auditorium, **14**:459; **22**:285,
  285n1, 335; **23**:449; Newark Academy
  Alumni Association, **18**:547, 628;
  Presbyterian Union, **16**:48,n1; Presbytery, **21**:367; Princeton alumni,
  **14**:459; **19**:155n1, 186-88, 652; Roseville Presbyterian Church, **16**:48;
  Temple B'nai Jeshurun, **22**:183, 316;
  Wednesday Club, **18**:548, 551; WW
  addresses, **14**:261-65, 459-62; **16**:48-
  50, 380-82; **18**:547-48, 628-29;
  **19**:186-88; **20**:462-63; **21**:202-12, 412,
  564-76; **23**:353-54; voter registration,
  **25**:328,n6
*Newark Advertiser*, **16**:455n1; **22**:300,n3
Newark Board of Trade, **24**:67-68
Newark District Telegraph Co., **23**:
  324n2
*Newark Evening News*, **14**:303n, 462n;
  **16**:50n, 218n, 382n, 460, 561n2;
  **17**:10n2,4, 171; **18**:552n, 629n;
  **19**:172n, 188n, 464n, 601n, 608n1;
  **20**:385n, 463n, 513n1, 565n, 566n8,
  568, 569n, 581n; **21**:5, 6, 40n1, 53,
  56,n1, 125, 128, 175n1,3, 176, 212n,
  219n1, 288n, 290n1, 306n, 310n,
  340n1, 361n, 388, 388-89, 396n, 413n,
  433n, 449,n1, 450, 492n1, 505, 521n,
  541, 541n2, 561, 582; **22**:4n, 73,n3, 77,
  81n1,2, 87n2, 93n, 113n1, 133n1,
  136n1, 142n, 167n, 180n, 181n1,
  203n1, 205, 226n1, 230n, 234n1,
  236n2, 242n2, 245, 250n2, 272, 274n,
  284n, 344n, 357, 365, 371n4, 374n,
  399n, 404n, 417, 432n, 465n, 474n,
  513n, 514n2, 537n4, 542n, 543,n3,
  546n5, 569n, 579n, 586n, 589n, 591n;
  **23**:112n2, 138n, 160n, 161n1, 175n,
  177n, 182n, 186n, 189n, 219, 222,
  233n, 262n3, 272n, 308n, 310,n2,
  316n, 319n, 322n, 324n, 339n, 354,
  359n, 365n, 381n, 384n, 388, 390n,
  395n, 408n, 411n, 442n, 447n, 451n,
  453n, 454, 458, 463n, 466, 468, 469n,
  476, 476n, 477, 478n, 494n, 506, 518n,
  520n, 521, 534n, 535n, 539, 541, 544n,
  544n1, 545n, 562n, 566; **24**:17n, 18n,
  63n, 68n, 98n, 181n, 185n, 224n,
  244n1, 245n, 247n, 253n, 267n1,
  304n1, 360n, 390, 407n, 412n, 434n,
  449n, 453n, 460n, 476n; **25**:492n,
  511n, 536n1, 540, 579, 592n, 640n1
*Newark Evening Star*, **21**:17,n1, 541;
  **22**:300,n3
Newark *Morning Star*, **22**:300,n3,
  311,n1, 357, 357n1, 383,n2
Newark Principals' Association, **16**:381
*Newark Star*, **19**:492
*Newark Sunday Call*, **22**:37n, 42n2

Newberry, Harriet Josephine Barnes
  (Mrs. Truman Hardy), **16**:243
Newberry, Truman Hardy, **16**:43,n4, 243
Newbold, William Romaine, **14**:337n2
Newcomb, Simon, **14**:395n1
Newhouse, S. M., **24**:121
Newlands, Edith McAllister, **24**:275,n1
Newlands, Francis Griffith, **24**:64,n1,
  272-73, 275, 276, 285, 287,n1, 388,
  390-91, 399, 403-404, 410, 450, 463,
  520, 539; **25**:293; portrait, **24**:illustra-
  tion section
Newman, Edwin A., **23**:566-67,n1
Newman, Harry Ellsworth, **22**:145,n1;
  **23**:380-81,n1, 513,n3
Newman, John Henry, **15**:38; **16**:281
Newman College, Cambridge, **14**:530
Newport News (Va.) *Daily Record*,
  **24**:514n
Newspapers, **24**:16-17, 120; **25**:94-97,
  146, 396; national and local, **19**:105-
  106, 110-11, 149, 154-55; *see also*
  under individual newspapers, such as
  *New York Times*
Newton, Byron Rufus, **23**:235n1, 258,n1,
  325, 326, 547
Newton, Sir Isaac, **16**:247; **16**:247;
  **18**:105, 106, 107, 115, 141, 200; **19**:35,
  83-84, 85, 98
Newton, Richard Cole, M.D., **22**:155-
  56,n1, 286
Newton, Sir Isaac and the Newtonian
  Universe, **23**:577
Newton, N. J., High School, **23**:465;
  Newton Public School, **21**:396; WW
  campaign speeches, **21**:396-405, 413;
  **23**:464-66; Woodrow Wilson Club,
  **21**:396n2
Newtonian theory, **24**:416
*New-Yorker Staats-Zeitung*, **25**:441n1
Niagara Movement, **21**:21n1
Niblack, William Caldwell, **24**:254,n2,
  304
Niccolls, Samuel Jack, **19**:97
Nichol, **19**:569
Nicholas II, Tsar of Russia, **15**:150n3
Nichols, Ernest Fox, **19**:408n1, 422,
  439-40,n2, 441
Nichols, Hugh Llewellyn, **23**:135n2
Nichols, Isaac T., **21**:277; **22**:431,n1,
  511n1, 531-32, 532, 571; **25**:474,n3
Nichols, Jeannette Paddock, **23**:175n2
Nicholson, Octavius Henry Lothian,
  **20**:187,n3
Nicoll, De Lancey, **15**:399,n2, 446, 527
Nieman, Lucius William, **24**:285,n2,
  546,n2
night riders in Kentucky and Tennessee,
  **18**:6,n1, 483,n1, 485n1
Nike, **22**:218
Nixon, George Stuart, **24**:520,n2
Nixon, Horace Franklin, **22**:520,n2
Nixon, Lewis, **25**:649,n6
Nixon, Paul, **17**:163,n11, 557

Nobel Prize, **18**:400,n2
Noble, Ransom Elwood, Jr., **19**:513n2; **21**:207,n2, 219n1, 256n9,10, 340n1, 533,n3
Noel, Edmund Favor, **22**:16,n1
Nöldeke, Theodor, **19**:328,n3
nominating conventions, **18**:109f
nonpartisan voting, **23**:276
Noonan, Joseph M., **20**:352-53,n1; **21**:42n1, 42-43, 54-55, 56, 58, 63-64, 85-86, 108, 265-66; **22**:133-34, 223-24, 245-46, 377
Norcross Bros., **15**:449
Norfolk, Va., **24**:569; **25**:620,n2, 647,n2; Commission Form of Government League, **22**:254n2; Democratic Club, **22**:254,n2; Pewter Platter Club, **22**:254,n5, 591,n1, 592, 593, 596, 597; WW addresses, **17**:247-59; WW interview, **22**:591-92; Woodrow Wilson Club, **22**:99; Woodrow Wilson Presidential Club, **22**:99, 254,n2
*Norfolk* (Va.) *Landmark*, **22**:591, 592n, 597n
Norfolk (Va.) *Ledger-Dispatch*, **22**:99n1, 254n2
Norfolk *Virginian-Pilot*, **22**:594n
Norfolk & Western Railroad, **19**:464
Norris, Edwin Lee, **25**:645,n2
Norris, Edwin Mark, **14**:490,n2; **17**:48,-n1,2, 351n2, 378, 456n1; **19**:625n1; **20**:134, 304,n2, 466,n2
Norris, Frederick Albert, **15**:376n1
Norris, George Washington, **22**:441, 441n3; **23**:230,n6
Norris, George William, **21**:344n12
Norris, James Nelson, **20**:148; Mrs., 127,n4, 138, 139, 148, 181
North, Ernest Dressel, **16**:231,n1; Mrs., 231
*North American Review*, **16**:387n2, 533,-n9; **17**:259n2, 456,n5; **18**:259, 271,n1; **19**:191, 193, 359, 380; **20**:148n, 180, 207n; **21**:557,n2; **22**:467,n1, 479, 509, 532, 532n6; **25**:238n4
North Carolina, **22**:327, 437, 499; **23**:320; **24**:59, 237, 257, 380, 385, 386, 388, 396, 399, 471,n2, 476; **25**:129; Democrats, *see* Democratic Party and Democrats in North Carolina State Democratic Convention, **24**:464n1
North Carolina, University of, **14**:467,-n2; **16**:255, 435, 509; **18**:311, 561,n1, 562, 588, 631; **19**:678; **22**:20n1,2, 406, 517, 520; **23**:104-10; *Record*, **18**:645n; WW address, **18**:631-45
North Carolina Society of New York, **16**:320, 324
North Carolina State Literary and Historical Association, **17**:138, 139n2
North Carolina Teachers' Assembly, **16**:314, 315
North Dakota, **23**:320; **24**:44, 82
Northeast Harbor, Maine, **14**:73, 84; **15**:417, 426, 434, 436, 440; Kimball House, **15**:426; WW at, **14**:89-90, 91, 93, 95
North German Lloyd steamship line, **15**:202n1, 229; **19**:328n1
North Philadelphia, **23**:275
North Plainfield, N. J., **23**:475, 540, 541
North River tunnel (1904), **15**:195,n3
Northampton, Mass., **23**:541
Northcliffe, Alfred Charles William Harmsworth, Viscount, **21**:482,n1, 484
Northfield Student Conference, **14**:8-9,n2, 26, 102-103, 114,n2; **17**:296
Northrop, Cyrus, **14**:427,n1; **19**:485,n1, 494, 532, 542
Northup, George Tyler, **16**:79, 132, 257, 421; **17**:233, 408; **19**:574, 576; **20**:451,n2
Northwest Territory, **18**:184; Ordinance of 1787, **17**:311
Northwestern University, **14**:248; **16**:179, 198, 259; **18**:575 **19**:676, 679
Norton, Charles A., **23**:272,n3
Norton, Charles Dyer, **21**:124,n2,3, 132
Norton, Charles Eliot, **15**:421,n2; **17**:122,n1
Norton, Robert L., **24**:74-78
Norvell (of Tennessee), **23**:288
Norway, **18**:416
Notman, William Robson, **14**:248; **17**:125,n4, 127, 129
Nott, Eliphalet, **15**:496,n1, 497, 498, 499, 500; **17**:328, 329
Nowrey, Joseph E., **21**:421,n2; **22**:413,n2
Noyes, La Verne W., **22**:180,n1
Nugent, James Richard, **20**:215,n1, 563,n2, 565; **21**:106-107, 141, 142, 173, 243, 261, 290-91, 290n1, 292, 296, 345, 347, 361, 367, 378, 388, 389, 409, 503, 577,n1; **22**:49-50, 73,n3, 145, 171-72, 181n1, 201, 203, 203n1, 436,n1, 512-13, 513n2, 518, 548,n1, 575n2, 603; **23**:177, 219, 234,n1, 262,n3, 270, 271, 332n2, 361, 361n, 449n3, 544n1; **24**:63,n1, 449n1; **25**:566n1, 579n2, 581, 582, 583
nullification, **22**:68
Numsen, George N., **24**:371
Nuremberg, **14**:245
Nyon, Switzerland, Wilsons at, **14**:541

Oakes, William, **23**:272
Oakland, N. J., **21**:43
Oberholtzer, Ellis Paxson, **17**:262,n1
Oberlin, Ohio, WW address, **16**:340-41
Oberlin College, **16**:56, 131, 250, 340; **17**:550; **20**:539; WW address, **16**:340-41; *Oberlin Review*, **16**:342n
Obermann (Arnold), **19**:573
O'Brien, Morgan J., **24**:510
O'Brien, Patrick Henry, **24**:483-84,n1
O'Brien, Philadelphia Jack (Joseph Francis Aloysius Hogan), **17**:535,n2

O'Brien, Thomas Dillon, **23**:85,n4; **25**:172n1

O'Callaghon, Peter J., **24**:302, 304

Ocean City, N. J., **23**:364

Ocean County, N. J., **22**:145; **23**:380, 467, 467n1; WW speeches, **21**:325-27

Ocean Grove, N. J., Auditorium, **23**:186; WW address, **23**:186-89

Ocean Grove Campmeeting Association, **24**:17,n2

*Oceana*, S.S., **20**:122, 126; **22**:332

*Oceanic*, R.M.S., **14**:520; **15**:441

Ochs, Adolph Simon, **16**:532,n6, 534; **23**:356

O'Connell, Denis Joseph, **14**:246

O'Connell, Joseph L., **21**:239-41

O'Conner, Annie, **18**:407-408

O'Connor, Frank A., **23**:354,n3

O'Connor, James L., **24**:260,n1

*Odes* (Catullus), **19**:597

*Odes* (Horace), **19**:597

O'Donnell, Thomas Jefferson, **23**:21,n3

*Odyssey* (Homer), **15**:296

*Oesterreichisch-Ungarische Zeitung*, **24**:135n1

Officer, Harvey, **15**:9,n1

Ogden, Robert Curtis, **14**:253; **15**:159,n3; **18**:590,n2

Ogden, Rollo, **20**:380,n2

Ogdensburg, N. J., **21**:413

O'Gorman, James Aloysius, **22**:161n1, 601, 602, 603; **23**:584; **24**:9n2, 74, 273, 304, 330, 462, 468, 490, 520, 529, 553; **25**:133, 134, 184n1

O'Higgins, Harvey Jerrold, **22**:275n2

Ohio, **21**:598, 608n2; **22**:213, 214, 217, 229, 230, 255n1, 437, 524; **24**:78, 130; **25**:379, 405; Adams County bribery, **23**:432; Democratic party, *see* Democratic party and Democrats in Ohio; high school fraternities, **20**:537; legislature, **20**:537; Negroes, **25**:607; State Constitutional Convention, **23**:620; WW addresses, **25**:198-212, 404-13

Ohio Press Bureau, **23**:327,n1

Ohio State University, **16**:259, 376, 510, 512; **17**:87

Ohio University, **17**:557

Ohio Wesleyan University, **18**:575

Ohl, Frederick, murder of, **15**:215n4

oil trust, **23**:361n2

O'Keefe, Patrick, **23**:507,n3

Oklahoma, **22**:247, 441, 442, 524n2; Democrats, **23**:506; **24**:190

old age pensions, **22**:143

Old-Fashioned Democrat letter to *Indianapolis News*, May 1, 1902: text, **12**:356-58; mentioned, **14**:16,n3

Old Lyme, Conn., *see* Lyme, Conn.

Old Nassau (song), **24**:527

*Old New England School: A History of Phillips Academy* (Fuess), **18**:566n1

Old Orchard, Maine, **14**:7

Old Point Comfort, Va., **22**:119

*Old Virginia and Her Neighbors* (Fiske), **14**:343,n7, 547,n1, 551

Olden, Frank G., **14**:145,n2

Olden, Susan W., **17**:145,n2

Oldham, Hugh, **17**:87

Oliver, Frederick Scott, **20**:339-40,n1

Oliver, George Tener, **17**:616-17

Oliver, Marion Rathbone (Mrs. Robert Shaw), **16**:233,n2

Oliver, Robert Shaw, **16**:233,n2

Olmsted, Frederick Law, **14**:306n3

Olney, Richard, **17**:159; **24**:83n1, 93

Olney, Warren, Jr., **23**:59

Omaha, Neb., **18**:639; **23**:237; **25**:349,n4, 360; Commercial Club, **25**:340-47; Omaha Club, **23**:95; Princeton alumni, **14**:447; **19**:146; WW in, **23**:95-96, 97; WW address, **25**:339-47

*Omaha Bee*, **15**:182n1; **18**:639; **20**:243; **23**:99n9

O'Malley, Edward Richard, **19**:102n1

On Being Something in the Ministry (WW), **19**:178,n1

O'Neal, Emmet, **23**:319-22

O'Neill, Frank R., **15**:20,n2,3

Onondaga Hotel (Syracuse, N. Y.), **24**:307; **25**:143n1

*Open Road. A Little Book for Wayfarers* (Lucas), **18**:411,n3

Opper, Frederick Burr, **25**:360,n3

Optional Third Class Law for cities, **22**:197,n2

Orange, N. J., **22**:147; ballots returned, **23**:348; Columbus Hall, **21**:520; **23**:354; Essex County Country Club, **23**:354; Princeton alumni, **15**:503,n1,2; **16**:214, 215-18; **17**:273,n2, 383; **19**:155n1, 316, 651,n1; **20**:76n1; sewage disposal, **24**:267n1; WW speeches, **21**:520-21; **23**:353-54

Oranges, N. J., **21**:171, 412

oratory, Southern, **14**:345

Orbison, John Harris, M.D., **15**:388n1

Ordway, Edward Warren, **15**:175,n1, 316

O'Regan, Daniel T., **25**:113-14,n1

Oregon, **21**:608n2; **22**:159, 175, 197, 247, 248n2, 255n2, 278, 334, 351, 352, 355, 357, 357n4, 433, 442, 458, 466, 521, 578; **23**:40, 61, 77, 132, 147, 302, 551, 591, 601n1; **24**:175-76; **25**:492, 541, 645; Advocates of Better Government, **23**:73; legislature, **23**:66, 67, 68, 71, 72, 74, 147, 350; Oregon system, **23**:63-64, 73, 74, 77, 282, 369, 619; primary law, **21**:141,n2; Republicans, **23**:350; scenery, **23**:70

Oregon, University of, **16**:465, 511; **17**:213; **23**:77

Oregon City, Ore., **23**:60

Order of Foresters of America, **21**:452n1

Oriel College, Oxford, **17**:127, 463

Oriental Education Commission (Fosdick), **19**:544n3

Oriental Education Commission, University of Chicago, **19**:544,n3
Oriental immigration, **24**:351-53, 382, 383,n1, 384
orientation, in education, **17**:536-37
*Origin of Species* (Darwin), **19**:218
*Original Journals of the Lewis and Clark Expedition, 1804-1806* . . . (ed. Thwaites), **16**:144n3
*Origins of the New South, 1877-1913* (Woodward), **19**:10n2
Ormond, Alexander Thomas, **14**:258, 326, 395, 395n1; **15**:56, 65, 73, 117, 135, 136, 163; **16**:59, 97n2, 203; **17**:17,n9, 242,n2, 302, 408; **19**:664-72; **20**:89, 446; **21**:603-604; **25**:575
Orris, Samuel Stanhope, **17**:117
Orth, Samuel Peter, **17**:550-51,n2
*Orthodoxy* (Chesterton), **19**:521,n7, 714; **22**:442,n4
Osborn, Alexander Perry, **14**:128,n2; **15**:194,n2
Osborn, Arthur Herbert, **17**:266-67,n1, 286
Osborn, Chase Salmon, **24**:51
Osborn, Edwin Curtis, **16**:92
Osborn, Henry Fairfield, **14**:54-55, 56, 73-74, 90, 126-29; **15**:3n1, 194, 468,-n2,3; **17**:110,n1, 389-91, 395, 397, 397-98, 400, 402, 406, 598,n2; **19**:551-52
Osborn, Henry Fairfield, Jr., **14**:128,n2
Osborn, Lucretia Thatcher Perry (Mrs. Henry Fairfield), **14**:73; **19**:552,n2
Osborn, William Church, **15**:3,n1, 298-99, 302, 493, 569, 573; **16**:5; **21**:172; **22**:359,n2, 361
Osborn, William Henry, **24**:286,n2, 306, 386, 388, 396
Osborne, Edmund Burke, **22**:366,n1; **23**:183
Osborne, Harry Vliet, **21**:520; **22**:157, 181, 181n1, 225, 229n1, 245, 285-86, 310-11, 312, 357; **23**:177, 333, 337, 361, 387, 388, 539, 544n1
Osborne, John E., **25**:645,n1
Osborne, Thomas Mott, **21**:47; **25**:133-34, 234, 553,n2
Osborne, William W., **23**:557,n4
*Oscar Hammerstein's Manhattan Opera Company* (Cone), **20**:173n4,5
Osgood, Charles Grosvenor, Jr., **16**:47, 53, 70, 132, 255-56, 486-87, 489-90; **17**:408; **18**:582; **19**:550, 553; **20**:76n2
Osgood, Herbert Levi, **14**:443
Osgood, Isabella Sheldon Owen (Mrs. Charles Grosvenor), **15**:351; **18**:415,-n1; **19**:550,n1, 553; **20**:76n2
Osler, Grace Linzee Revere Gross (Lady Osler), **18**:409
Osler, Sir William, M.D., **18**:409; **21**:618,n1
Ossining, N. Y., **21**:38
Ostrogorski, Moisei Yakovlevich, **16**:97

O'Toole, Michael J., **17**:121
Ottley, Robert Lawrence, **16**:400,n1
*Our Country's Flowers and How to Know Them* (Gordon), **14**:521,n1
*Outlook* (New York), **17**:306,n1, 456,n2; **18**:446-48; **20**:208,n1, 350,n1; **21**:243,-n2, 244n2, 620n1; **22**:172n1; **23**:300n, 514,n7, 548; **24**:274n2; **25**:125,n4
Overman, Lee Slater, **24**:273,n1
Owen, Edward, **15**:546
Owen, Elizabeth Sheldon (Mrs. Henry James), **15**:351
Owen, Isabella Sheldon, *see* Osgood, Isabella Sheldon Owen
Owen, Robert Latham, **18**:269; **22**:208,n1, 247, 248, 524,n2, 526; **23**:177,n3
Owen, Thomas McAdory, **15**:213,n4
Oxford, England, Church of St. Mary the Virgin, **14**:532, 553; Mitre Hotel, **14**:531, 532; Wilsons at, **14**:531-33, 556
Oxford, N. J., WW campaign speech, **21**:384
Oxford, University of, **14**:139-40, 511; **15**:324, 378, 396, 410, 421, 441, 445; **16**:4, 19, 37, 46, 58, 148, 254, 384, 413, 511; **17**:87, 166, 274, 276, 277, 286, 304, 348,n1, 359, 365, 463, 464, 535, 557, 558, 591; **18**:254, 304, 314, 579; **19**:128, 151, 152, 678; **20**:89, 434, 475; **22**:606; All Souls College, **17**:464; Balliol College, **15**:96-97, 396, 441; **17**:277, 332, 557; Bodleian Library, **14**:532; Christ Church, **17**:119, 277; Corpus Christi College, **17**:13,n1,2, 127, 461, 463, 465, 472, 558; Turnbull Sun Dial, 87-88, 127, 358, 359-60, 447n1, 461, 462, 463, 465, 509-10,n2, 558; Divinity School, **14**:532; Exeter College, **14**:532; Magdalen College, **17**:277, 557; Magdalen Tower, **15**:445; **19**:538; Merton College, **18**:388,n2; Oriel College, **17**:127, 463; Sheldonian Theatre, **14**:532; University College, **14**:531; Wadham College, **17**:557
*Oxford Book of English Verse 1215-1900* (ed. Quiller-Couch), **18**:357; **19**:350,n3
Oxford Movement 1833-1841, **16**:281
*Oxford Treasury of English Literature* (Hadow and Hadow), **18**:395,n3
*Ozark Folksongs* (ed. Randolph), **24**:252n1

P. P. Caproni and Brother, Boston art dealers, **14**:10,n4,71,79,97
Pach Brothers (photographers), **14**:40, 87
Pacific Navigation Co., **23**:41n6
Packard, William Alfred, **16**:199, 205, 245, 419, 429, 518; **17**:117; **18**:258; **19**:675; **20**:485n1, 489
Packard motor cars, **23**:557
Padua, **15**:357
Paestum, EAW at, **15**:235

Paganini, Niccolò, **19**:318-19n1
Page, Arthur Wilson, **21**:6n2; **25**:62,n2
Page, Frank, **23**:596,n2
Page, George True, **24**:291,n2
Page, Robert Newton, **23**:596,n2
Page, Thomas Nelson, **15**:393; **19**:556; **21**:602; **22**:30, 140, 377, 396n1
Page, Walter Hines, **14**:65; **15**:403; **16**:12-13, 324; **17**:449; **18**:259, 469, 590,n2; **20**:121, 257; **21**:5-6, 576, 579; **22**:413-14, 433-34, 439, 515, 518n3, 519n4, 520; **23**:135, 214-15, 285-86, 437, 596, 604; **24**:530-31, 543, 557; **25**:62, 515-17, 526, 618
Paget, Bermuda, **17**:8, 50,n1
Paget West, Bermuda, **25**:220n1, 552n1
Pahlow, Edwin William, **17**:164, 208, 213, 214, 219, 286, 557; **18**:271, 577-78; **19**:333-34, 351, 613
Pahlow, Gertrude Curtis Brown (Mrs. Edwin William), **17**:208,n1, 213; **19**:35,n1
Paine, Albert Bigelow, **25**:423n1
Paine, Thomas, **14**:281
Palisade Commission, **24**:266,n2
Palm Beach, Bermuda, **20**:133
Palm Beach, Fla., **16**:3, 29; **17**:5; The Breakers, **15**:580; WW at, **15**:579-80
Palma Vecchio (Jacopo Palma), **15**:359
Palmer, Alexander Mitchell, **21**:604,n1; **22**:26, 441n3; **23**:154, 156, 220, 221, 229, 230; **24**:7n1, 27, 29, 320-21, 392-94,n3, 396-97, 444, 453-54, 461, 467, 531, 537, 570; **25**:225
Palmer, Benjamin Morgan, **14**:332; **25**:457
Palmer, Edgar, **16**:398; **17**:346,n1; **19**:658
Palmer, George Herbert, **17**:128,n5; **20**:276,n1
Palmer, George M., **25**:143n2
Palmer, John McAuley, **23**:466, 470, 653
Palmer, Stephen Squires, **15**:28,n2, 123, 351, 526; **16**:398n1, 544; **17**:16, 39n1, 174, 175n2, 237-38, 272, 293, 340, 346, 349, 349-50, 351, 362, 368, 387, 393, 411; **18**:274-75, 277-78, 301, 336, 418, 451, 473, 475, 476, 514, 572, 615, 617; **19**:257, 277, 439, 450, 451, 458-59, 487, 626, 631, 632, 633, 634, 658, 662, 711, 733; **20**:183, 245, 321, 325, 353, 354, 357, 360, 361, 395, 403, 425, 427, 428, 431, 432, 433, 454, 470, 472, 476, 481, 483, 484, 485, 486, 489, 491, 494, 502; **21**:362n1, 385
Palmerston, Henry John Temple, 3rd Viscount, **22**:360, 403
Paltsits, Victor Hugo, **14**:352
Panama, Republic of, recognition of, **15**:60n1, 143
Panama Canal, **23**:419; **24**:33, 70, 107, 127, 184, 194, 195; **25**:16-17, 34-35,n2, 370-71, 574,n2, 587n3, 606,n1 ∆ J. D. Phelan, **24**:352; J. Smith, Jr., **22**:205n2
Panama-Pacific-Exposition, **24**:352

Pancoast, Charles, **23**:394
panic, **25**:343, 601-602
Panic of 1857, **17**:316-17
Panic of 1893, **25**:471-72, 514
Panic of 1907, **17**:96n1, 472-73, 490, 513, 519-20; **18**:315,n1, 317; **24**:533-34; **25**:384n7
*Papers of Thomas Jefferson* (ed. Boyd), **14**:360n1
*Paradise Lost* (Milton), **16**:103,n1
parcels post, **25**:15, 35-36, 308
Pardee, Ario, **19**:165
Paris, **14**:246; **15**:440, 441, 444; American Church, **14**:537; Chatham Hotel, **14**:552, 555; Collège de France, **19**:739; Crédit Lyonnais, **14**:548, 549; Eglise St.-Etienne-du-Mont, **14**:537; Foundation Thiers, **19**:739; Gare de l'Est, **14**:538; Gare de Lyon, **14**:541; Gare St.-Lazare, **14**:542; Hôtel de Cluny, **14**:555; Louvre, **14**:536; Notre-Dame, **14**:536; Palais du Luxembourg, **14**:536; Pantheon, **14**:537; Sainte-Chapelle, **14**:536; Université, **17**:556; **19**:739; Wilsons in, **14**:535-38, 541, 542, 555, 556
*Paris* (Baedeker), **14**:529
Paris, Texas, **23**:269, 286
Paris, William Francklyn, **16**:334,n1, 339, 340, 342
Paris *Herald*, **14**:539
Parish, Wainwright, **16**:535,n4
Parish & Schroeder, architects, **16**:535,n4, 536; **17**:147, 150-51, 153, 156-57, 158, 387, 564
Parker, Alfred L., **21**:24,n1
Parker, Alton Brooks, **17**:30,n2, 90, 92n2, 215; **19**:492; **20**:21, 22, 534,n2; **21**:5,n2, 322,n1; **22**:285; **23**:458, 463, 470; **24**:497n2, 500, 502, 531, 565, 571; Champ Clark, **24**:510; temporary chairmanship fight at Baltimore convention, **24**:491, 492,n2, 529-30, 547
Parker, George Frederick, **20**:534,n1
Parker, Sir (Horatio) Gilbert (George), **19**:191,n4
Parker, Theodore, **21**:519, 543
Parkhurst, Charles Henry, **21**:621,n1
Parkin, George Robert, **14**:336-37,n1, 398; **15**:180, 378
Parkman, Frances Parker (Mrs. Henry), **14**:90
Parkman, Francis, **14**:353, 518
Parkman, Henry, **14**:90
Parma, **15**:275
Parrish, Mr. (of Hamilton, Bermuda), **20**:140, 176; Mrs., **20**:140, 150, 176; **25**:556
Parrott, Thomas Marc, **14**:326; **15**:293; **16**:38, 421; **17**:164, 408; **20**:451
Parsifal (Wagner), **20**:173
Parsons, Herbert, **19**:756,n3; **23**:584
Parsons' Theatre (Hartford, Conn.), **25**:234n1

Parties and the Supreme Issue (Clark), 25:420n4
party government, 21:523
party organization, 24:232; 24:480
party politics, 25:79, 82, 93, 119-20, 131, 145, 155, 267, 334, 340-41, 347, 351, 437, 446, 480; bosses, 25:175-76, 187-88; *see also* under individual political parties, such as Democratic party
Pasadena, Cal., Annandale Country Club, 23:45; Auditorium, 23:51; Board of Trade, 23:51; California Club, 23:51; Hotel Maryland, 23:45, 51; Princeton alumni, 19:146; WW in, 23:45-48
*Pasadena Star*, 23:48n
Passaic, N. J., 23:233; 25:513,n1, 514n2; Acquackanonk Club, 15:61; Board of Trade, 15:61; charter, 19:729; High School, 21:493, 507; 23:222; Kenilworth Club, 14:328; WW addresses, 15:61-64; 21:493-502; 23:222
Passaic County, N. J., 21:7, 264, 380, 412, 584n1; 23:333, 334, 338, 349, 446, 461-63; 25:147n3, 513n1, 514n2, 582
*Passaic (N. J.) Daily Herald*, 20:558,n2, 570; 25:511n1
*Passaic (N. J.) Daily News*, 21:541
Passaic River, 21:497-98, 567
Patagonia, Princeton expeditions to, 16:507,n1, 550
patent monopoly, L. D. Brandeis on, 25:304
Paterson, N. J., 21:153, 158; 23:634n1; 24:358-60; High School, 18:563-64, 590-91, 612; 25:513,n1, 514n2; National Banks, 21:43; Opera House, 21:301; WW addresses, 19:171; 21:301-306; 23:461-63
Paterson Board of Trade, 24:324,n1
*Paterson Guardian*, 21:158, 158n1, 281n, 541; 22:77n1
*Paterson News*, 21:541
Patmos, 20:359
Patrick, Albert T., 16:557
patriotism, 14:365f, 403-404, 419f, 491f, 454; 22:493; 25:128, 131, 164, 171, 181
patronage, 24:412; 25:122, 444; civil service, 24:168, 173; Maine, 25:618; Negroes, 25:53, 65; Texas, 25:605, 624, 625-26
Pattee, Fred Lewis, 16:478,n1
Patten, Simon Nelson, 15:407
Patten, Thomas Gedney, 22:39,n13
Patterson, Archibald Williams, 23:653,-n3; 24:71,n6, 97
Patterson, George William, 15:5-6; Mrs., 15:6
Patterson, James A., 15:546
Patterson, Malcolm Rice, 18:7n1, 485n2; 23:289n2
Patterson, Robert Wilson, 16:377
Patterson, Samuel Alexander, 21:328,-n2; 16:487n1
Patterson, Thomas MacDonald, 22:584, 599; 23:21, 478

Patterson, William, 14:114; 15:519,n1
Patterson, Wylie Thomas, 19:19,n2
Patterson School, Legerwood, N. C., 16:487n1
Patton, Francis Landey, 14:22n2, 32, 45, 46, 47, 48, 50, 51, 69, 72, 77, 82, 115, 132, 144, 192, 192n2, 194, 253, 255-58,n2, 266, 289, 290, 291n5, 396n2,3, 438, 460, 550, 560; 15:14, 16, 26n2, 65, 94, 152, 205, 284n, 286n, 288n, 312, 410, 410n5, 412, 441; 16:102, 322, 329; 17:4n8, 26, 28n1, 99n2, 125; 18:286, 301; 19:621, 670, 671; 20:187n4, 266n4, 278; 21:26,n1; 22:397,n2, 404, 425-26; retirement fund, 14:47-48
Patton, Francis Landey, Jr., 14:438,n2
Patton, George Smith, Jr. (later General Patton), 23:32,n2, 45
Patton, George Smith II, 23:32,n2, 45
Patton, George Stevenson, 14:396n2,3; 15:155, 312, 410,n5, 441; 17:14,n1, 26, 408; 19:670, 671
Patton, James W., 24:293,n1
Patton, Jessie Campbell McIntyre (Mrs. Francis Landey, Jr.), 14:438n2
Patton, John Linn, 14:500
Patton, John MacMillan Stevenson, 17:4,n8, 14; 20:187,n4
Patton, Paul Richard, 14:55,n1
Patton, Rosa Antoinette Stevenson (Mrs. Francis Landey), 14:49-50, 77; 16:318, 322; 17:26
Patton, William D., 14:500,n3; Mrs., 14:500n3
Patton, Winifred Outerbridge (Mrs. George Stevenson), 15:155
Paul, John H., 23:536n1
Paul, Saint, 20:524-25, 526
Paulsen, Friedrich, 19:666,n2
Paxon, Frederic John, 14:20,n1; 15:216,n2
Paxton, William McGregor, 20:378n1
Paxton, Caroline Sophia Denny (Mrs. William Miller), 14:440,n2
Paxton Hotel (Omaha), 25:339n1
Payne, George W., 22:531,n3
Payne, Sereno Elisha, 19:191n1; 21:175
Payne, W. C., 21:616,n1
Payne, William Arthur, 16:177,n2
Payne-Aldrich Tariff of 1909, 19:191n1,2, 331,n2, 359f, 461, 462-63, 467-69; 20:38n5; 21:126, 175, 194, 219, 252, 255, 275, 327n1, 369n3, 456, 521, 565, 608n2; 22:478n3, 811n2, 567; 23:30, 130n1; 24:13, 18, 296,n2, 420, 478; 25:vii, 8, 242-43, 380,n4, 397, 407, 503; Schedule K, 25:243,n7, 409; W. H. Taft, 25:409; *see also* tariff
Peabody, Charles Augustus, 19:397,n5
Peabody, Charles Samuel, 25:609,n2
Peabody, Endicott, 16:192,n1; 17:125; 18:546,n2
Peabody, George (1795-1869), 24:213-14
Peabody, George Foster, 15:550-51,-n1,3,5; 17:95; 18:590,n2; 24:265, 401,

Peabody, George Foster, (*cont.*)
   472, 474, 491, 497; **25:**422, 608-609
peace, **23:**305-308; **24:**181-83
Peacock, Alexander Rolland, **16:**336,n13, 338
Peacock, Clarence Neilson, **16:**338,n1
Pearson, Edward Clarence, **22:**137,n3
Pearson, Karl, **19:**666,n2
Pease, Lewis Frederic, **14:**470,n1, 473
Peck, Harriet Roberts, **17:**607,n3, 612; **18:**450,n4, 481,n2
Peck, Mary Allen Hulbert (Mrs. Thomas Harbach Hulbert; Mrs. Thomas Dowse Peck; Mary Allen Hulbert after divorce July 9, 1912), **17:**29,n1, 48, 50, 93-94, 606, 607, 611, 612; **18:**372n8, 423-24, 436, 448-50, 466-68, 470-72, 478-81, 517; **19:**160-62, 174-75, 191-93, 214-15, 224-25, 229-30, 258, 261-62, 270-72, 289-92, 304-305, 307-10, 311-14, 317-19, 321-24, 324n2, 330-33, 349-51, 354-59, 382-86, 392-95, 442-44, 704; **20:**87, 118, 122, 126, 127, 138-41, 141-42, 148-51, 155-56, 172, 176, 177, 178-80, 180-81, 184, 185-88, 210-11, 248, 370-71, 408, 429, 473, 491-93, 500-501, 535-36, 575; **21:**26, 38-39, 48, 50-51, 64, 163-64; **22:**100, 139, 141-42, 204-205, 209-11, 292-93, 294-95, 323-25, 329-30, 331-32, 333-35, 362-64, 382, 391-93, 396, 407-408, 424-27, 438-40, 453-54, 477-80, 500-501, 509-11, 517-20, 531-34, 543-47, 548, 570-72, 581-83, 583n1, 597-98; **23:**11-12, 49-50, 80-81, 174, 184-85, 189-90, 193-94, 213-14, 220-21, 222-24, 225, 239-41, 256-57, 264-65, 267, 283, 329-30, 424-25, 559, 560, 590, 596-97, 606-607, 633-34, 654-55; **24:**5-6, 27, 43-44,n1, 58-59, 65-66, 98-99, 132-33, 150-51, 177-78, 218-19, 239-40, 249-50, 271-72, 305-306, 329, 385, 391-92, 409-10, 444-45, 451-52, 466-67, 481-82, 495-96, 541-42; *see also* Mary Allen Hulbert
Peck, Thomas Dowse, **17:**29n1; **18:**436, 481; **19:**160,n1, 192, 324n2, 382n2; **20:**181,n2; **22:**500,n1,4; **23:**241, 606n2; **24:**43n1
Peck, Tracy, **17:**114,n4, 588,n5
Peddie, Thomas Baldwin, **14:**356
Peddie Institute, Hightstown, N. J., **14:**356-57,n1
Pedricktown, N. J., **23:**394
Peel, Sir Robert, **22:**194n4; **23:**282,n4
Peirce, Charles Sanders, **14:**547,n3
Peirce, Mary Bisbing, **22:**285,n4
Peirce, Thomas May, **22:**285n3,4
Pekin, Ill., **24:**291
Pelter Bridge, Rydal, Westmorland, **16:**437n1, 450, 480; **18:**371, 376, 379
Pence, Thomas Jones, **24:**49n1, 65n1, 467-69, 475, 553
Peniston, Clarence, **17:**610n2

Penn, William, **14:**311
Penn Charter School, **15:**233
Penniman, Josiah Harmar, **14:**337n2
Pennington, Arthur Reginald, **18:**378,-n4, 383, 388
Penns Neck, N. J., Princeton Baptist Church, **20:**224,n1
Pennsgrove, N. J., **23:**392, 394
Pennsville, N. J., **23:**394
Pennsylvania, **23:**170, 229, 296, 426; **25:**419; Capitol building scandals, **23:**75,n1, 209; Democratic party and Democrats, **20:**307-308, 315-17, 352,-n1; **23:**220, 229-30,n1,2,3,5,6, 249n2, 262; **24:**27, 392-94, 397, 453-54, 461, 515, 538; Bryan Democratic League, **22:**522; primary results, **24:**330n3; State Committee, **23:**154,n3, 220, 220n,1, 221, 257-58; State Federation of Democratic Clubs, **23:**154-55, 156; electoral vote, **25:**527n1; free trade, **25:**242; Negroes, **25:**607; politics, **21:**446, 545; **23:**473; popular vote, **25:**527n1; railroad legislation, **24:**24; representative government, **24:**318, 319; Republicans, **23:**229; Supreme Court, **21:**342n7; WW addresses, **24:**138-40, 314-20; **25:**221-31, 462-66; western Pennsylvania, Princeton alumni, **14:**383, 446; **16:**32, 70,n2, 559; **18:**51
Pennsylvania, University of, **14:**337; **15:**100n3, 234n, 273, 407; **16:**250, 256, 272n1, 510; **17:**438, 445, 448, 555, 561, 619; **18:**67, 288, 575, 576; **19:**427, 677; **20:**108, 358n1, 539; baseball game with Princeton, May 21, 1904, **15:**345; Chapel, **16:**327; confers LL.D. on WW, **14:**381; faculty compared with Princeton's, **14:**121, 154; fraternities, **14:**480; Law School, **17:**223, 224n1; Settlement, **23:**128; students, **21:**421
Pennsylvania Academy of Fine Arts, **22:**329
Pennsylvania Bar Association, **23:**133
Pennsylvania College (now Gettysburg College), **16:**258
*Pennsylvania Magazine of History and Biography*, **21:**342n6
Pennsylvania Railroad, **15:**572,n1, 575, 576, 578; **17:**126; **18:**40-41, 247, 602; **19:**192; **20:**14,n2, 29, 310,n1, 353, 360, 403, 471; **21:**290, 312, 403,n3; **22:**114, 154, 370, 377, 522, 523; **23:**450n1; **25:**358, 431,n6; Kingston Branch, **15:**579; Princeton Branch, **15:**573n1, 576, 578, 579; Princeton University trustee committee to confer with officers, **15:**572,n1, 575, 576; Station (New York City), **24:**586
Pennsylvania Society of Sons of the Revolution, **16:**143
Pennsylvania State Bankers Association, **23:**133, 134

Pennsylvania State Sabbath School Association, **15:**126, 500-501, 520n3, 521, 522

*Pennsylvania: The Heritage of a Commonwealth* (Stevens), **23:**75n1

Penrith, Cumberland, **18:**364

Penrose, Boies, **17:**617; **22:**409n2; **24:**571

*Pensacola* (Fla.) *Journal*, **24:**257n

*People Awakened: The Story of Woodrow Wilson's First Campaign* (Bacon), **21:**220n1; **22:**50n2

*People's Law* (Lobingier), **22:**279,n4

People's Power League, **22:**255n5

Peoria, Ill., **23:**361n2; **24:**290, 291, 292, 308n1

Pepper, George Wharton, **19:**109

Pepys, Samuel, **18:**471

Perdue, William Lewis, **18:**579

Pericles, **15:**475

Periodical Publishers' Association of America, **21:**620-21; **22:**51; **24:**122-31

Perkins, Evelyn Ball (Mrs. George Walbridge), **19:**482

Perkins, George Walbridge, **15:**65n2; **18:**494,n3, 513; **19:**263-64, 479-80, 482; **20:**379-80; **22:**19, 72, 202; **23:**160n2, 408,n1, 409; **24:**346,n2, 400, 412n3; **25:**57,n1, 110, 160,n1, 381n6, 382-83

Perkins, Thomas Jefferson, **23:**82,n13

Pernice, Nicola, **24:**405, 406

Perrine, Emma Harmon Folsom, **16:**197,n3, 208

Perrine, Frederick Auten Combs, **15:**343n1

Perry, Annie Louise Bliss (Mrs. Bliss), **14:**44, 83-84, 88, 547, 551, 552; **16:**175, 180; **17:**123,n6, 333

Perry, Arthur Bliss, **17:**123,n6

Perry, Belmont, **23:**46,n3

Perry, Bliss, **14:**34-35, 44, 80, 83, 86, 88, 93, 101, 254, 309, 547, 551, 552; **15:**529,n1,2,3; **16:**170-71, 172, 174-75, 176, 180; **17:**92n2, 122-23, 333-34; **18:**525, 544; **21:**406

Perry, Claud W., **24:**146

Perry, Constance Goodnough (Mrs. Thomas M. Woodward), **17:**123,n6

Perry, Lawrence, **23:**30,n3

Perry, Lewis, **14:**55,n3

Perry, Margaret Smedley, **17:**123,n6

Perry, Ralph Barton, **16:**19-20,n1, 21-22

Persons, Charles Edward, **19:**615,n1, 677

Perth, Scotland, **18:**400

Perth Amboy, N. J., **21:**544f; **22:**294; Donahoe Auditorium, **21:**543n1, 560; strike, **24:**475-76,n1; WW addresses, **21:**543-55; **23:**437-42; Woodrow Wilson League, **23:**438

*Perth Amboy News*, **21:**541

Peru, Ind., WW in, **25:**332

*Peru*, Ind. *Evening Journal*, **25:**338n

Perugia, **15:**240, 303, 311, 323, 337, 338; Cambio, **15:**322; Oratoria di San Bernadino, **15:**323; EAW in, **15:**275, 322, 346

Perugino, Il (Pietro Vannucci), **15:**276, 322, 353

*Personal Memoirs of U. S. Grant*, **16:**119, 221

*Peter Ibbetson* (du Maurier), **18:**413

Peters, Andrew James, **24:**287,n1

Peters, Edith, **15:**267,n1

Peters, Ethel, **15:**267,n1

Peters, Harriet Felton (Mrs. Richard), **15:**268n1

Peters, Richard, **15:**268n1

Peters, William Elisha, **15:**393,n2

Petersburg, Ill., **24:**292

Petersburg (Va.) *Index Appeal*, **24:**465

Peterson, Emily O'Hanlon, **25:**572n2

Peterson, Geofrey Fraser, **25:**572n3

Peterson, John Magnus, **25:**572n3

Peterson, Magnus Fraser, **16:**440,n1, 481; **18:**366,n8, 402, 404-405, 417; **21:**619-20,n1; **25:**572; Mrs., **16:**440, 481; **18:**402, 404

Peterson, Merrill Daniel, **14:**360n1

Peterson, William, **14:**381

Petigru, James Louis, **19:**96; **21:**424,n4; **24:**203-204

Petition of Rights (English), **25:**237

Petrie, George, **15:**3,n1, 182-83,n1, 226, 237

Petroné, Antonio, **25:**59,n1

Pettigrew, Richard Franklin, **24:**269n1

Pettit, David, **15:**525

Pfeiffer, Timothy Newell, **19:**71,n3, 522n

*Phantom Ship, or the Quad System. Some Discussion of its Merits; Also of the Effect of its Continual Agitation upon Princeton University* (Annin), **20:**211,n1

Phelan, James (of Detroit), **25:**186n2

Phelan, James Duval, **24:**351-53,n1, 382-84,n1; **25:**558, 623

Phelps, Charles Edward, **16:**342,n2, 343

Phelps, William Lyon, **18:**53,n1

Phi Beta Kappa, **17:**104,n1, 274,n1, 410, 488n2; Maryland Alpha, **20:**402,n1; Massachusetts Alpha, **19:**11,n2, 270; Rhode Island Alpha, **14:**491; WW Yale address, **18:**68

Phi Kappa Psi fraternity, **14:**91,n2; **20:**244, 253, 256; **21:**105; at University of Chicago, **14:**225

Philadelphia, **18:**422, 467, 630n2; **21:**567; **22:**215, 216; **23:**227, 229, 230, 245, 314, 408, 605; **24:**262; Academy of Music, **19:**69; Academy of Natural Sciences, **18:**576; apartment house fire, **23:**590; Association Hall, **14:**415; Baptist Temple, **22:**486; Bellevue Hotel, **14:**380; Bellevue-Stratford Hotel, **16:**56; **18:**550, 564; **19:**112; **20:**242; **21:**558; **22:**148, 441,n1, 487n2; **23:**184; Broad Street Station, **23:**272, 275; Carpenter's Hall, **14:**352; Central

Philadelphia, (*cont.*)
    High School, **16:**71n1, 132, 256; Central Y.M.C.A., **15:**99; Chestnut Street wharf, **23:**273; City Club, **19:**500, 509; **20:**534; Contemporary Club, **19:**529, 531, 605, 606; **20:**223,n1, 242-43; DeLancey School, **20:**212, 221; Democratic City Committee, **23:**229n1; Democratic Club, **21:**584, 604; **22:**215,n2, 246-47, 435n1, 441, 450n, 451,n1; **24:**6; Durham ring, **21:**172,n2, 342,n6; Free Library, **16:**256; gang methods, **21:**551; Garrick Theatre, **15:**99; **20:**153n9; gas scandal, **21:**342,n6; Girard College, **15:**379; Grace Baptist Temple, **15:**179; Horticultural Hall, **14:**408; **15:**102; **17:**38, 39; Independence Hall, **14:**410; Northeast Manual Training School, **16:**225-26; Peirce School, **22:**285,n3,4; Pennsylvania Academy of the Fine Arts, **20:**189; Poor Richard Club, **23:**274; Princeton alumni, **14:**408, 415; **15:**79, 101-103; **17:**36, 38-40, 302, 303, 383, 383-84, 399,n1, 407-408; **18:**550; **19:**112-13, 146, 158, 159; **20:**247, 269, 310; **22:**487,n2; *see also* Princeton Club of Philadelphia; Reading ferry, **23:**273; Scotch-Irish Society, **16:**565,n1; Second Presbyterian Church, **15:**78, 98, 99; street-car riots (1910), **20:**153,n20, 188; Teachers' Association, **19:**554; Union League Club, **23:**500-501,n5; United Gas Improvement Co., **21:**342n6; University Club, **16:**38; Walton Hotel, **19:**509n1; water, **15:**148; William Penn High School, **19:**554; Wistar Institute of Anatomy, **18:**576; Witherspoon Hall, **19:**98; WW addresses, **14:**408-10, 415-17; **15:**79, 101-103, 177-78, 179, 494; **16:**38-39, 53, 56-67, 225-26, 327-28; **17:**38-40; **19:**49, 69, 98-100, 108-109, 112-13, 509-22, 554-56; **20:**223, 242-43; **24:**122-31; WW in, **19:**311; **21:**421; **23:**189, 273, 275
Philadelphia, S.S., **16:**179
Philadelphia and Reading Coal and Iron Co., **22:**215n1; **21:**343n9; **22:**215n1
Philadelphia County Sabbath School Association, **15:**177, 179
Philadelphia *Evening Bulletin*, **24:**165n1
*Philadelphia Inquirer*, **15:**99n, 179n; **24:**131n
*Philadelphia Negro* (DuBois), **21:**275n3
Philadelphia *North American*, **14:**11n2, 417n; **16:**39n, 143n, 302, 302n1, 303; **17:**39n; **19:**69n1, 113n, 556n; **21:**9,-n1,2, 158, 164, 165, 198-99, 243, 267,-n1,4; **22:**43,n3, 149n, 231,n4; **23:**157n, 215, 216,n2, 246,n1, 251, 314n1, 322n; **24:**6n, 131n, 183n, 288n, 408n; **25:**470n5
*Philadelphia Press*, **14:**11, 410n;

**15:**143n, 272, 401n; **18:**466n, 466, 467; **20:**385-87,n1,2, 397-98,n1; **23:**633n1
Philadelphia *Public Ledger*, **15:**100n, 103n; **16:**57n, 226n, 282n, 328; **17:**40n; **19:**100n; **20:**243n, 352n1; **22:**285n2; **24:**131n
Philadelphia Rapid Transit Co., **20:**153n10
*Philadelphia Record*, **20:**265n2; **21:**191n, 218n, 220n1, 221, 225, 243, 267n4, 287n, 320n, 385n1, 421n, 441, 449n, 476n, 502n, 518, 541, 555n, 564n, 576n; **22:**50n2, 367n; **23:**31n2, 215, 230, 346; **24:**131n; **25:**44n, 467n, 485n, 492n
*Philadelphia Times*, **25:**147
Philanthropy, **25:**81
Philbrook, Charles M., **14:**34, 51
*Philip Dru: Administrator, A Story of Tomorrow, 1920-1935* (House), **25:**550,n2
Philippine Islands and Filipinos, **14:**324, 433, 464; **15:**41, 143, 175; **16:**297, 317, 341, 367; **17:**544,n1; **18:**104, 477; **20:**309, 309n2, 312; **22:**14; **23:**267; **24:**105, 224,n1,3, 494, 560,n1,2,3,4, 566; **25:**14-15, 63, 316, 635, 649-50; Civil Government Act of 1902, **20:**309n2, 312n2; independence, **23:**235n3; Tariff bill, **16:**367n2
*Philippines and the United States* (Grunder and Livezay), **20:**309n2, 312n2
Phillips, Alexander Hamilton, **14:**218,-n7, 219, 220, 221, 227, 326, 426,n1, 432,n3, 434, 473; **17:**387, 408
Phillips, David Graham, **16:**375n1; **20:**372,n1
Phillips, John Herbert, **15:**226,n1
Phillips, John Sanburn, **19:**163,n1; **23:**136,n1
Phillips, Mabel Harriett Knight (Mrs. Alexander Hamilton), **14:**426,n2
Phillips, Mark F., **22:**253,n4, 367,n1
Phillips, William Wirt, **17:**221-22, 595; **18:**229; **19:**170-71; **20:**466,n3
Phillips Academy, Andover, **14:**25,n2, 165, 278; **15:**141n1; **16:**486-87; **17:**566; **18:**565-66,n1; **19:**498-99
Phillips Exeter Academy Christian Fraternity, **19:**498; *Exonian*, **15:**175n; **19:**499n; WW addresses, **15:**141, 175; **19:**498-99
Phillipsburg, N. J., **21:**383; Board of Trade, **22:**590; Lee House, **21:**385; Ortygian Hall, **21:**382, 390; WW campaign speeches, **21:**390-96; **23:**466-68
*Philosophia Ultima, or, Science of the Sciences* (Shields), **15:**544,n3
*Philosophy of Kant as Contained in Extracts from His Own Writings* (tr. Watson), **19:**666,n4
*Philosophy of the Enlightenment* (Hibben), **15:**301n4; **20:**208, 223

Phinizy, Bowdre, **22**:573,n1; **23**:552-53,n1, 554
phlebitis, **15**:571n1, 574, 580
Phoenix *Arizona Republican*, **25**:272n3
*Physics and Politics* (Bagehot), **18**:88
picture galleries, **23**:210
Piedmont Hotel, Atlanta, **22**:489
Pierce, Carlton Brownell, **23**:476-78; **24**:246
Pierce, Franklin, **17**:310; **18**:448n1
Pierce, Palmer Eddy, **16**:369-71,n1
Pierson, George Wilson, **15**:292n29; **19**:728n1
Pierson, John D., **23**:536n1
Pierson, Lewis Eugene, **18**:3
Pike County, Pa., **22**:144
Pilatus, Mt., Switzerland, Wilsons at, **14**:538
Pilgrim Fathers, **14**:209, 210
Pilgrims, The (of England), **15**:146,n5, 147
Pilgrims, The (of the United States), **15**:146-50
Pinchot, Amos Richards Eno, **22**:383n, 412n2
Pinchot, Gifford, **21**:546n3; **22**:32,n3, 144, 412n2; **25**:274
Pinchot, James Wallace, **22**:144,n3
Pingry School, Elizabeth, N. J., **16**:256; **19**:508
Pinturicchio (Bernardino di Betto), **15**:335
Piotrowski, Nicholas L., **24**:241-42,n1, 242-43; **24**:552; **25**:586
Pisano, Giovanni, **15**:322
Pisano, Niccolò, **15**:322
Pitass, J., **25**:28
Pitcairn, Robert (1836-1909), **15**:126,n1
Pitcairn, Robert, Jr., **15**:126,n1
Pitney, Henry Cooper, Jr., **14**:131,n1, 142, 144, 222, 247, 348, 349, 353-54, 355-56, 394, 495, 496, 497, 501; **15**:32-33, 48, 49, 51; **20**:31,n1
Pitney, John Oliver Halsted, **18**:559,n1; **19**:119, 120, 123
Pitney, Mahlon, **14**:290; **18**:229; **20**:511n4; **21**:16, 20, 27, 434,n1; **22**:28,n1
Pitt, William (the elder, 1707-1778), 1st Earl of Chatham, **14**:281
Pittman, Key, **25**:360,n2
*Pittsburg Dispatch*, **15**:47n; **16**:35n; **17**:101n; **18**:522n; **20**:368n; **24**:320n
*Pittsburg Post*, **18**:521n; **19**:230; **24**:310n, 316n
*Pittsburg Press*, **14**:386n
Pittsburgh, Pa., **16**:33; **18**:382, 385; **23**:229, 249n2, 426; Carnegie Music Hall, **15**:46; city councils, **21**:342n7; Duquesne Club, **15**:128,n2; East Liberty Y.M.C.A., **18**:507,n3,4,5, 520, 521; Emory Methodist Protestant Church, **15**:519; graft and bribery, **21**:342n7; Nixon Theatre, **21**:100,n1; Princeton alumni, **16**:377; **17**:378, 383,

384-85; **18**:218n1, 280-85; **19**:117, 118, 119, 124, 146, 155, 396, 401; **20**:53, 81, 85, 363-68, 370-72, 373-76, 377, 378-79,n1,2, 379-80, 380, 381, 386-87,n2, 387, 389, 390, 397-98, 398-99, 424,n1, 444, 453, 458; Schenley Hotel, **16**:32; **17**:64, 100; **20**:363, 366; Schenley Park, **15**:47n; Sixth United Presbyterian Church, **15**:519; Southern Society, **17**:617; Traffic Club, **18**:6,n1, 221-25; Tree of Life Synagogue, **23**:249n1; Union Club, **14**:383; University Club, **17**:384, 385; **20**:366; Voters' League, **21**:342n7; WW addresses, **14**:383, 385-86; **15**:126, 461, 510-20, 521; **16**:31-35, 559; **17**:64,n1, 100-101; **18**:221-25, 280-85; **20**:53, 81, 363-68, 368-69, 370, 372, 373-76, 377, 378-79,n1,2, 379-80, 380, 381, 386-87, 387, 389, 390, 397-98, 398-99, 424,n1, 444, 453, 458
Pittsburgh, University of, **16**:489,n4
Pittsburgh Academy, **16**:489n4
Pittsburgh *Chronicle-Telegraph*, **18**:576
*Pittsburgh Gazette*, **18**:576
Pittsburgh *Gazette Times*, **15**:520n; **17**:616; **20**:365n
Pittsfield, Mass., **18**:424n1, 441, 448, 449, 471, 472; **19**:229, 291, 312, 322, 324n2, 332, 382n2, 383, 385, 394; **20**:493; **23**:174, 184, 190, 220, 222, 224, 225, 256, 264, 606n2; Berkshire Athenaeum, **18**:436; Elmwood Court, **21**:48n1; **23**:189; First Congregational Church, **18**:424n2, 436; Wednesday Morning Club, **18**:436, 440, 449; **19**:309,n2; **21**:48,n5; WW addresses, **18**:436, 440-44; Wilsons visit, **19**:384,n7
Pius X, Pope, **18**:241, 250,n1, 267; **17**:32
Plainfield, N. J., **19**:464; **21**:173; **22**:22, 198-99, 238; **23**:468; **24**:272; Democratic Club, **19**:384,n8, 461, 464, 491-93; **22**:117, 244n1; Plainfield Theatre, **19**:461, 493; Princeton Alumni, **16**:418; **19**:155n1; Queen City Hotel, **23**:475; Reform Club Hotel, **21**:193,n1; WW address, **19**:461-64; **21**:193-98; WW in, **23**:475, 476
Plainfield, N. J., *Courier-News*, **24**:272n
Plains of Abraham, **14**:352
Plant, Thomas G., **25**:200,n3, 207
Plato, **14**:208; **18**:582; **19**:232, 597, 666
Platonists, **21**:618
Platt, Chester Charles, **25**:112
Platt, Dan Fellows, **17**:23-25,n1; **21**:11-12,n1, 22, 36, 41, 52, 56-57, 58, 140-42, 149, 172-73, 436; **22**:86-87; **24**:454
Plattdeutsch Volksfest Verein, **25**:48
Platzek, Marx Warley, **16**:322,n1
Plautus, Titus Maccius, **19**:597
Plaza Hotel, New York City, **18**:509; **22**:421, 425
Pleasantville, N. J., Wesley Methodist

Pleasantville, N. J., (cont.)
  Church, **23**:532; WW campaign speeches, **21**:325; **23**:531, 532
pleasure, WW on, **23**:306
Plimpton, George Arthur, **22**:209,n1
Pliny the Younger (Gaius Plinius Caecilius Secundus), **19**:597
Plunkitt, George Washington, **21**:303,n2
*Plunkitt of Tammany Hall* . . . (Riordan), **21**:303n2
Plymouth Harbor, **23**:642
Poe, Clarence (Hamilton), **17**:138-39,n1; **22**:437,n1, 499, 503,n, 509,n
Poe, Edgar Allan (1809-1849), **19**:34, 35, 606,n2
Poe, Edgar Allan (1871-1961), **20**:264,n1; **21**:600,n1; **23**:568
Poe, John Prentiss, **18**:278,n1
*Poems of Philip Freneau* (ed. Pattee), **16**:479n1
*Poems of Wordsworth* (ed. Arnold), **14**:521,n2
Poland, **25**:256
Polish-Americans, **24**:131-32, 134-35, 219, 226, 241-42, 243, 260, 269,n1, 270, 302; **25**:28, 400, 586
political bosses, **18**:210-11; **19**:88-89, 93, 98, 194, 509; **22**:448, 586, 593, 594, 602; **23**:276, 279, 296, 427, 567, 577-78, 613-14, 616, 627, 628, 629; **25**:175, 187-88, 189, 244, 267, 406, 432, 433, 437, 446 Δ R. Davis, **22**:26; G. S. Silzer, **22**:311-12; C. W. Kent, **22**:326
political contributions *see* campaign contributions
*Political Education of Woodrow Wilson* (Kerney), **20**:565,n1; **21**:583n2; **22**:86-n1, 113n2, 142n1, 357n2,4, 383n3, 503n2, 546n5; **23**:192n3
Political Evolution of a College President (Griffin), **23**:248,n1
*Political History of Europe Since 1814* (Seignobos), **14**:338 political machines *see* machine politics
political organizations *see* party organization
political parties, **21**:372f, 501-502, 530-33, 534; *see also* party politics and under the names of individual parties such as Democratic party
Political Predestination of Woodrow Wilson (Harvey), **22**:467,n1, 479
*Political Science Quarterly*, **16**:43n2; **18**:576; **20**:35n3
Political Transformation of Woodrow Wilson (*Current Literature*), **24**:140n1
politics, **22**:264f, 398; **23**:194-99, 277; **25**:31, 81, 91, 104, 144
politics and business, **23**:121-22
*Politics & Progress: The Rise of Urban Progressivism in Baltimore 1895-1911* (Crooks), **23**:573n1
*Politics of Prejudice: The Anti-Japanese Movement in California and the*

*Struggle for Japanese Exclusion* (Daniels), **24**:383n1
Polk, James Knox, **17**:310, 319
Pollard, Alonzo Wilder, **14**:52,n1, 57, 77
Pollard, Elise Welch (Mrs. Alonzo Wilder), **14**:52,n1, 77
Pollard, John Garland, **23**:138,n1, 152-53, 290-91, 313, 601-602, 605; **24**:51, 81
Pollock, Sir Frederick, **15**:162
Pollock, Walter, **15**:162
Pollock *v.* Farmers' Loan & Trust Co., **22**:535,n2
Pomerene, Atlee, **22**:161n1; **23**:135n2
Pompeii, EAW at, **15**:235
Ponce, S.S., **17**:12
Pontiac, Ill., **24**:292
Pontoosac Lake, Pittsfield, Mass., **19**:332
Poole, Monroe Van Brackle, **21**:324
Poole, Reginald Lane, **14**:140
*Poole's Index of Periodical Literature*, **22**:480
Pope, Alexander, **14**:503
*Popular Government* (Maine), **18**:103n3
*Popular Science Monthly*, **14**:21,n1,2, 22
Populist Party and Populists, **22**:220; **25**:82
Port Reading, N. J., **21**:560
Port Reading Railroad Co., **21**:343n9
Porter, Alice, Mrs., **20**:426
Porter, Burney, **23**:81,n1
Porter, Charles Darwin, **17**:407,n6
Porter, Gene Stratton, **17**:407n6
Porter, Horace, **16**:344,n1
Porter, James Jackson, **21**:16,n2
Porter, William, **25**:481,n9, 482, 484
Portland, Oregon, **22**:519n4, 533; **23**:41, 60; Armory, **23**:69, 76; Business Men's Club, **23**:70n2; Commercial Club, **23**:65, 68, 70n2; Committee of 100, **23**:70n2; Portland Hotel, **23**:64; Press Club, **23**:68; University Club, **23**:64, 70n2, 76; WW address, **23**:65-76; WW in, **23**:60, 63-76, 81, 147; YMCA, **23**:73
Portland Hotel, London, **14**:550
Portland *Morning Oregonian*, **23**:61, 63n, 63,n1, 65n, 66,n4, 68n, 69n, 72n, 76; **24**:175
Portland Oregon Daily Journal, **23**:68n2, 69n1, 72n
Portugal, politics, **21**:439,n1
Posada, Adolfo González, **14**:356,n1
Posillipo, EAW at, **15**:229, 230
Post, George Adams, **22**:484,n3, 485, 499
Post, Louis Freeland, **22**:278n2; **25**:608
postal rates, **22**:427
*Postscript* (Stuart), **18**:357,n2
Potter, Henry Codman, **14**:136,n1; **15**:146,n6, 147, 150; **16**:229n1
Potter, Rockwell Harmon, **17**:128,n7
Potter, Thomas, Jr., **16**:336
Potts, Franklin M., **16**:336,n8
Pottstown, Pa., WW address, **17**:49, 50
Pounds, Jessie Brown, **23**:379,n2

*Power and Responsibility: The Life and Times of Theodore Roosevelt* (Harbaugh), **21**:148n1

Poyntz, H. S., **20**:177,n3, 179; Mrs., 179, 179-80

Pratt, Joseph Hyde, **16**:527,n1; **22**:517,n3, 520

Pratt, Julius William, **17**:545n4

Pratt, Mary Dicus Bayley (Mrs. Joseph Hyde), **22**:517,n3, 520

Pratt, W. F., **16**:113

Pratt Institute, **16**:258

Praxiteles, **14**:71

Preceptor Idea at Princeton (editorial), **17**:456,n2

Preferential primary system *see* primary system and reform

prejudice, **24**:122 △ W. M. Trotter, **24**:558

Preliminary Report of the Princeton University Expedition to Syria (Butler and Littmann), **16**:186,n1

Prentice, William Kelly, **14**:245, 296, 297, 326, 327; **15**:251, 375, 376n1, 421, 435; **16**:130, 186, 492, 554; **17**:46,n1, 408, 415-16; **18**:579, 582

Presbyterian Board of Publication, **19**:395

Presbyterian Church, origins, **25**:453

Presbyterian Church in the United States (southern), **14**:330, 332; **22**:577n4

Presbyterian Church in the United States of America (northern), **14**:332; Board of Foreign Missions, **14**:196n1; **19**:109n1,3; **25**:390n1; General Assembly, **18**:339; *Minutes of the General Assembly*, **20**:84n2; New Brunswick Presbytery, **16**:105n2; **19**:208; Synod of New York, **17**:28-29; theological orthodoxy, **15**:169n2

Presbyterian College of South Carolina, **25**:549n1

Presbyterian Theological Seminary of Kentucky, **22**:21, 21n1

Presbyterian Union (Albany), **15**:168,n1

Prescott, William Hickling, **14**:134-35

Present Crisis (Lowell), **22**:335

presidency, E. M. House on length of term, **25**:565

President Woodrow Wilson and College Earnestness (Bridges), **17**:450n1

presidential campaign of 1896, WW on, **17**:77

presidential primaries, **25**:6, 15

*Presidential Problem* (Cleveland), **15**:306n4

Presidential Timber (editorial), **17**:121,-n2

*Presidents I've Known and Two Near Presidents* (Thompson), **25**:360n1

*Present College Questions: Six Papers Read before the National Educational Association, at the Sessions Held in Boston, July 6 and 7, 1903*, **14**:546n2

Present Peril to Liberal Education (West), **14**:546n2

Presidential Range, White Mountains, **14**:111

press *see* newspapers

Preston, Howard Willis, **14**:353,n4, 518

Preston, John Fairman, **19**:66,n2

Preston, Wilbur Fisk, **15**:22,n5

*Pretenders* (Triangle show, 1905), **16**:24,n2, 32

Price, Benjamin Marsden, **15**:378,n2, 391-92; **17**:364, 557; **18**:271

Price, Jacob Cole, M.D., **22**:325-26,n1, 378

Price, Jesse Dashiell, **24**:227,n2

Price, Luther Edmunds, **16**:460

Price, Robert, **17**:153,n1, 154

price-fixing, **25**:10

prices, **25**:10, 139, 201, 342

*Pride and Prejudice* (Austen), **15**:118

Priest, George Madison, **14**:45-46,n1, 277, 326, 327; **15**:14, 137; **16**:132, 257; **17**:408; **19**:211, 570, 571-72, 576; **20**:214

primary reform *see* New Jersey, primary elections and reform

primary system and reform, **24**:170-71, 232, 290-91, 297, 398, 442; **25**:236-37; importance of voting, **24**:433, 441-42; preferential, **24**:290-91, 320; *see also* New Jersey, primary elections and reform

Prime, William Cowper, **16**:18,n2, 246

*Primer of the Peace Movement* (Mead), **17**:92,n4

Primos, Pa., **20**:188,n3, 358

Prince, George, **23**:245,n1

Prince, John Dyneley, **22**:476,n2; **23**:401,n5, 446; **24**:529; **25**:523

Prince of Wales (afterward Edward VII), **15**:441

Prince William's Sound, Alaska, **19**:479

*Princess* (Tennyson), **14**:369,n2; **15**:171,n3; **16**:296-97n4, 529,n2; **22**:71,n5; **23**:19,n3

Princess Hotel, Bermuda, **17**:6, 8, 608,n9,12, 610n2, 616

Princeton, N. J., **21**:13, 323; **23**:10, 30, 174, 424, 540, 541, 590, 596, 606, 614, 633; Anderson's Saloon, **15**:215n4; Aqueduct, **14**:107; August weather, climate, **15**:245; **19**:115; ballots, **19**:510; Battlefield, **16**:143; Battle Monument, **19**:127,n1; Battle of Princeton, **20**:74, 466; beauty and charm, **14**:269; **19**:192; borough elections, **19**:91; Brackett property, **19**:398,n2; branch railroad line to Princeton Junction, **15**:573n1, 576, 578, 579; Broadmead, **18**:247n1; Canal Street property, **19**:238,n3; Dodge Lodge, **18**:546,n1; **20**:362,n2; **21**:385,-n2, 591; election night (1912), **25**:518-20; evangelists in, **18**:54-55, 504; First

Princeton, N. J., (cont.)
Presbyterian Church, **14**:140, 490,n1; **15**:16, 140, 306; **16**:92,n1,2, 207,n2, 219n2, 234, 235n1, 301,n1,2; **17**:98-99,n1,2, 259,n1, 567; **19**:149; **20**:312; **21**:597n1; **22**:234n1; Greenholm, **17**:569; G. Cleveland funeral, **18**:355; John Miller House, **16**:197,n1, 208; John St. degraded poor, **15**:154; Mac-Donald property, **19**:238,n4; Miss Fine's School, **14**:17,n1; Morven, **15**:544n1; **21**:606n1; Mrs. Wright's boarding house, **21**:132,n1; Nassau Apartment Building, **18**:243; Nassau Club, **15**:141-42,n2; **17**:381, 383; **18**:303; Nassau Inn, **18**:244; **19**:610, 611; Olden Tract, **17**:145-46, 166,n4; **19**:398,n2; Peacock Inn, **23**:10; Pennsylvania Railroad Station, **20**:471; Postal Telegraph office, **18**:244; Present Day Club, **20**:136n2,3, 148n, 412, 414,n1; **23**:52,n1; Princeton Bank, **17**:351n2; Princeton Cemetery, **19**:347n1; Princeton Inn, **14**:143, 146, 195, 387, 428; **15**:22, 57, 151, 161; **16**:36, 61, 102, 345, 374, 552; **17**:57, 58, 97, 115; **18**:260, 271, 300, 301; **19**:178, 226; **20**:326, 356, 383-84, 404, 536; **22**:149, 329, 334, 358, 407, 501, 544, 600n1; **23**:10, 52n1; **24**:461; St. Paul's Church (R.C.), **15**:117; Second Presbyterian Church, **14**:140; **15**:232; **16**:104-105, 206-207,n1,2, 218-19,n1,2,3, 234-35; Stanworth, **17**:142; Stony Brook, **14**:107; Trinity Church, **14**:452n1,3; **17**:68; **19**:8; **21**:117n1; Village Improvement Society, **15**:175n1, 316, 330-32; Witherspoon St. Presbyterian Church, **15**:148-49; Women's Employment Society, **15**:154; WW addresses, **19**:148-49; **23**:447-49; **24**:448-49; WW and Pennsylvania delegation, **24**:454; WW returns to quiet and freedom of, **25**:416; WW votes in primary, **25**:273; WW walks about, after election, **25**:523-25
Princeton Alumni Association of Cincinnati, **14**:448-49, 450
Princeton Alumni Association of the District of Columbia and the Southern States, **14**:447
Princeton Alumni Association of the New Northwest, **14**:426,n1, 445, 447
Princeton Alumni Association of Northern Ohio, **14**:447
Princeton Alumni Association of Omaha, **14**:447
Princeton Alumni Association of the Oranges, **15**:503,n1,2
Princeton Alumni Association of Western New York, **22**:14
Princeton Alumni Federation of New Jersey, **19**:155,n1
Princeton Alumni Weekly, **14**:147n, 170n1, 195n, 196n, 203, 203n, 330,

337n, 359n, 381n, 383n, 400n, 446n, 459n, 490,n2, 496; **15**:13n, 28n, 58n1, 79n, 112n, 161n, 182n, 200n, 227n, 252n, 272n, 273n, 313n, 376n1, 383n, 390n, 391n, 411n, 501n, 531,n2, 533n, 536n, 544n, 545n1, 577n, 580n; **16**:3n, 3n1, 7n6, 20-21n, 29n, 104n, 194, 212n, 213n, 292n, 308n1, 313n, 329n, 356n, 383n, 389n, 411n, 418, 419n, 420n, 459, 464n, 485n; **17**:7n16, 48n1,2, 71n2, 171, 198, 206n, 209n, 214, 215, 217,n1, 234, 238, 244, 247n2, 265, 266, 273, 274, 276, 279n, 280, 283, 284n2, 289, 291, 295n1, 300, 300n1, 351,n1,2, 353, 356, 378, 393, 395, 399,n1, 400n, 407, 410, 413-14, 415, 418, 426, 428-31, 433, 456n1, 487n, 550n3, 587n, 603; **18**:10, 13n, 34n, 219,n3, 228, 237, 247n1, 293,n1, 300n, 308, 308n1, 316, 333, 404, 482n2, 520, 556n1, 609n1; **19**:3n1, 102n, 145, 155, 177n, 196n1, 226n, 238, 238n, 255n, 276, 390n1, 398n1, 451n, 625,n1; **20**:57, 63, 66,n1, 67, 69, 83n, 84n2,4, 85, 101, 104,n2, 117,n2, 120, 121,n1, 135, 153n1,2, 215, 217,n1, 235n, 265,n2,3, 276n, 296n, 304,n2,3, 336, 348n, 357, 376n, 380, 466, 468, 511n4, 512n1, 519n1; **22**:79, 430n1, 487n3; **23**:599; **25**:521n
Princeton Architecture (Cram), **19**:303,-n1
Princeton Astronomical Expedition to South Africa, **16**:488
Princeton Club of Chicago, **14**:211, 223, 225, 226-27, 447; **16**:405; **18**:16, 17, 18,n2, 23, 645-46; **19**:33-46, 47, 117, 118, 124, 131, 146, 155, 479; **20**:262, 351,n1,3, 433-43
Princeton Club of Louisville, **14**:447
Princeton Club of Los Angeles, **23**:41,n4, 44, 60
Princeton Club of New York, **14**:46-47,n1,2, 268, 287-91, 294; **15**:251, 573; **17**:454; **18**:228,n1, 315; **20**:64,n2, 263,n1, 337-48, 466; **22**:287,n1; **23**:600; **25**:519
Princeton Club of Philadelphia, **14**:408, 415; **15**:79, 101-103, 272; **17**:36, 38-40, 302, 303, 383-84, 399,n1, 407-408
Princeton Club of St. Louis, **14**:447
Princeton Club of Western Pennsylvania, **14**:383, 446; **16**:32, 70,n2, 559
Princeton Entrance Requirements as Compared with Those of Harvard and Yale (Hoskins), **19**:625,n1
Princeton Expedition to Patagonia, **16**:550
Princeton Expedition to Syria (Butler), **15**:376n1; **19**:267
Princeton Glacier, Alaska, **19**:480, 482
Princeton Golf Club, **16**:139
Princeton Historical Association, **16**:479n1
*Princeton History*, **19**:755n2

*Princeton Ideal. A Permanent Plan to Se-
cure Social and Intellectual Coordination* (Brown), **20:**123,n2, 211-12
Princeton Lake *see* Princeton University, Carnegie Lake
*Princeton: Past and Present* (Collins),
**14:**439,n1
Princeton Preceptorial System (Wilson),
**17:**456,n1
Princeton Preparatory School, **16:**510,
511
*Princeton Press,* **14:**103n, 330n; **15:**67n,
175n1, 215n2, 333n, 385, 388n, 396;
**16:**105n2, 197n, 208n, 219n, 427n,
464n; **17:**17,n6, 99n, 351n2, 353;
**19:**149n, 263,n2; **20:**84n2, 148n, 312n,
512n1, 519n1, 538n; **21:**84n, 541;
**25:**273n

Princeton Press (C. S. Robinson & Co.),
**17:**351n2
Princeton Publishing Company, **17:**352-
n2
*Princeton, 1746-1896* (Wertenbaker),
**15:**284n6
*Princeton Theological Review,* **16:**425-
26n2; **17:**353
Princeton       Theological       Seminary,
**14:**257,n2, 290,n4; **15:**16, 184, 379,
462n2, 556; **16:**263, 516; **17:**559; **19:**65,
660, 686; **20:**233; **22:**501, 544; Library,
**16:**255;   Miller   Chapel,   **15:**16,n1;
Stuart Hall, **15:**16; Y.M.C.A., **16:**232
*Princeton Theological Seminary Bulle-
tin,* **17:**353

## PRINCETON UNIVERSITY

A.M., three-year, to be discontinued,
**19:**688
academic costume, **14:**122, 125
Academy Lot, **16:**21, 104, 329
administrative reorganization discussed,
**17:**552-53,n1
admissions compared, 1904-1905, **16:**
263-64; 1905-1906, **16:**516-17; 1906-
1907, **17:**559
Albany alumni, **14:**400; **15:**169; **16:**418
Alexander Hall, **14:**6, 187, 193, 195, 256,
259, 321, 490n1; **15:**179, 239n1, 296,
306, 313, 390, 464, 529n3; **16:**92, 137,
138, 498, 503; **17:**119, 120, 550, 564n1;
**18:**523; **19:**253; **20:**532; **22:**159, 501,
502, 528n1; **23:**447, 448
Alligators (eating club), **22:**28,n2
alumni, mentioned, **20:**18, 65, 72, 81, 85,
88, 90, 131, 157, 189, 208, 211n1, 254,
295, 311, 312, 320, 324, 376, 385, 401,
413, 427, 434, 460, 481, 514, 518, 519n,
529-30, 532, 535, 567; **21:**81-82, 149;
**22:**17, 18n2; **23:**252n1, 460, 465, 507,
548, 553, 558, 567, 594, 598, 600, 650
Alumni Commission, **18:**542; *see also*
Graduate Council
Alumni Council, **18:**554; **19:**80-81; *see
also* Graduate Council
*Alumni Directory,* **16:**418,n1; **18:**316;
**19:**412
alumni dormitory, proposed, **16:**308n1,
383, 389, 403, 417, 459, 463; **17:**32,n2,
37, 171, 550,n2,3, 560-61, 562; **18:**316;
**19:**145; *see also* Patton Hall
alumni dormitory committee (of the
classes of 1892-1901), **15:**249, 251-52,
414-16, 418-19, 432, 433, 435, 436,
440, 448, 461-62, 573, 577; *see also*
Patton Hall
Alumni Fund, **15:**422,n2, 425, 426, 435,
439, 526; **16:**134, 459, 460-61; **17:**171;
**18:**452; **19:**145,n2, 611, 683
alumni luncheons,   June   9,   1903,
**14:**485n1, 489; June 13, 1905, **16:**141;

June 12, 1906, **16:**424; June 11, 1907,
**17:**209; June 15, 1909, **19:**253-55, 274;
June 14, 1910, **20:**528-30, 532
*Alumni Princetonian, see Princeton
Alumni Weekly*
Alumni Review, *see Princeton Alumni
Weekly*
alumni smoker (classes of '78-'82), Hotel
Astor, New York City, Nov. 3, 1904,
**15:**528,n1
alumni trustees, **15:**167-68, 405, 406;
**17:**381; **18:**555, 618; **19:**117-18,n1, 119,
120, 123-24, 131, 155, 158, 159, 195-
96,n1; **20:**248, 264, 303, 320, 531-32;
**21:**39,n1
American    Philosophical    Association
meeting, Dec. 1903, **15:**111-12
American Whig Society, **14:**138-39, 256;
**15:**15-16; **16:**203, 204n1, 204, 205,n1,
266, 322, 325; **17:**120, 566,n2; **18:**583;
**19:**452, 749n1; **20:**315; **21:**170
Amherst (Mass.) alumni, **20:**320
Annual Reports of the President, Dec.
10, 1903, **15:**69-75; Dec. 8, 1904,
**15:**554-69; Dec. 14, 1905, **16:**245-65;
Dec. 13, 1906, **16:**506-19; Dec. 13,
1907, **17:**555-59; Jan. 1, 1909, **18:**569-
87; Jan. 1, 1910, **19:**674-95
anti-Semitism, **17:**222-24
architect,   consulting   (supervising),
**17:**71-72, 96-97, 108, 140, 170, 220-21;
*see also* Cram, Ralph Adams
architecture, campus, **17:**20-21, 35-37,
71-72; **22:**375
Art Museum, **15:**173,n1; **17:**119, 433-34;
**18:**12; William Horace Morse Collection, **15:**181,n2, 212
athletics: athletic grounds, **14:**6; baseball, **18:**321; team, **15:**22; Penn game,
May 21, 1904, **15:**345; Yale games,
June 6, 1903, **14:**488,n1; June 13,
1903, **15:**22,n4; Oct. 7, 1903, **15:**22;
June 9, 1906, **16:**419; June 8, 1907,
**17:**216,n1; June 6, 1908, **18:**310,n2;

*Princeton University, cont.*
June 12, 1909, **19**:195; June 11, 1910, **20**:519n1; basketball, **18**:321; football, **18**:321; **19**:556, 597, 672, 699, 700; Amherst game, Nov. 9, 1907, **17**:473,n4; Columbia game, Oct. 25, 1902, **14**:187,n1, 194; Yale games, Nov. 12, 1904, **15**:508,n3; Nov. 12, 1910, **22**:3-4,n1; Nov. 18, 1911, **23**:554,n7; WW talks to team, **22**:4-5; gymnastics, **18**:321; hockey, **18**:321; swimming, **18**:321; track, **18**:321; wrestling, **18**:321; University Athletic Association, Graduate Advisory Committee, **19**:704,n1

attendance, **15**:22-23, 75-76

Augustan age predicted by H. F. Osborn, **14**:54

B.S. and Litt.B. students, **19**:198

Baccalaureate sermons, Henry van Dyke, June 7, 1903, **14**:484; WW, June 12, 1904, **15**:364-74; June 11, 1905, **16**:119-28; June 9, 1907, **17**:187-96; June 7, 1908, **18**:323-33; June 13, 1909, **19**:242-51; June 12, 1910, **20**:520-28

Bachelors Club, **17**:167,n5; **19**:238,n2; **20**:105,n3

Baltimore alumni, **17**:43; **19**:146; **20**:27-28, 50,n1, 229-35, 247, 254, 265, 268, 269, 285, 311

Banjo Club, **14**:388

Bayles Farm, **15**:184,n3, 438; **16**:414n2

Bennett (Philo Sherman) Prize in Political Science, **16**:50-51,n1, 69, 199

bequest erroneously announced in Philadelphia newspapers, **17**:38-40, denied, 43-45, 48

biblical literature courses, **14**:293n2, 334, 396, 396n3; **16**:398-403

bicker, **19**:530,n2

Biological Laboratory, **16**:155

Biological Museum, **19**:680

Blair Arch, **14**:50n3, 486n1; **18**:302n1; **20**:15n2

Blair Hall, **14**:6, 21, 24, 36, 50n3, 256, 486n1; **15**:271, 577; **16**:308n1, 312, 312n1, 356, 498, 517, 518; **17**:119, 151, 386, 412; **18**:286, 302, 302n1, 523; **20**:130n1

Blair (John Insley) Professorship of Geology, **15**:438

Blair Tower, **20**:130n2

Bonner-Marquand Gymnasium, removal, **17**:386

Book Store, **16**:556n1

Boston alumni, **20**:252, 410, 413, 466, 469

*Bric-a-Brac*, **17**:42

Brokaw Field, **15**:398,n1,3, 436, 445, 577; **16**:308n1, 329, 403, 417, 459; **17**:32,n2, 37, 171, 550, 560, 561, 562, 566, 568, 585; **20**:124n2

Brokaw (Frederick) Memorial, **14**:256, 270

*Princeton University, cont.*
Brokaw tennis courts, **15**:577

Brooklyn alumni, **20**:247, 272-76

Brown (David) Hall, **14**:256; **15**:271; **17**:119; **18**:253

Brown (Susan Dod) bequest, **14**:396n2; **16**:134,n4, 135, 323,n1

Caledonian Club, **17**:390

calendar, **15**:183

Camden (N. J.) alumni, **19**:146

Campbell (John Alexander) Hall, **17**:388,n3, 550,n4, 561, 562, 567; **18**:242,n1, 302, 309n, 523, 580; **19**:241-42, 256, 402, 620

Campus Club, **14**:480n1, 482; **17**:42; **19**:398,n4

*Campus Songs 1903*, **14**:441n5

Cane Spree, **14**:279

Cannon Club, **14**:480n1, 482; **17**:42

Cap and Gown Club, **14**:480n1, 482; **17**:42, 221, 404; **18**:631

Carnegie Lake, **15**:57-58, 66-67, 549-50,n1,2, 575-76, 578-79; **16**:139; **17**:211; **18**:247n1, 248; **19**:320; formal opening, Dec. 5, 1906, **16**:497-503

*Catalogue*, **15**:443,n1; **17**:28-29,n3; **22**:358

Chancellor Green Library, **14**:125; **15**:545; **16**:27, 132, 204, 265, 391, 422, 468, 526; **17**:71, 198, 441, 594; **18**:255, 333, 458, 623; **19**:153, 435; **20**:4, 356, 485n1, 509; **21**:364

Chapel, attendance, **14**:279; **15**:23, 75-76; **16**:201-202, 223, 265; **17**:68; **20**:355, 356; choir, **14**:146; hymn books, **19**:386-87, 391, 395, 448, 453, 455; preachers, **14**:463, 550; **15**:425, 438, 442; **16**:552, 553; **17**:122, 125,n1,2,3,4, 127, 136, 137, 197-98, 233, 297, 334; **18**:286-87, 290; **19**:736; pulpit Bible, **19**:390, 456; services, **14**:131; **18**:448; chapel stage orations, **15**:68

Charter, Royal, **17**:359

Charter Club, **14**:480n1, 482; **17**:42

Chemical and Civil Engineering Laboratories, **17**:120

Chemical Building, **14**:211

chemical laboratory (proposed), **17**:120

Chicago alumni, **14**:211, 223, 225, 226-27, 447; **16**:405; **18**:16, 17, 18,n2, 23, 645-46; **19**:47-48, 117, 118, 124, 131, 146, 155, 479; **20**:262, 351,n1,3, 433-43

Chinese students on Boxer Indemnity, **18**:625,n1; **19**:120-21,n2

The Christian Student (statue), **19**:151,n1

Cincinnati alumni, **14**:448-49, 450; **19**:146; **20**:252,n2

Class of 1841, **16**:411

Class of 1860 Fellowship made University Fellowship, **15**:184

Class of 1873, **16**:38n2, 417; **18**:316; **19**:145

Class of 1876, **16**:459

Class of 1877, **16**:459; **17**:388,n3, 550,n4,

Princeton University, cont.
561; 18:242,n1, 273-74, 286, 316, 580;
19:145, 241-42, 402, 403; Professorship, 19:402,n2, 403
Class of 1878, 15:535
Class of 1879, 14:63; 15:70, 174, 185,
203, 535, 536; 16:275n1, 464, 488;
18:445-46, 549n1; 19:77n3, 123, 155,
190, 195, 252, 258, 260, 261, 424;
20:218, 247, 483; 22:28, 332n1, 519;
class dinner, Oct. 25,1902, 14:186-87,
195; Dormitory see Seventy-Nine Hall;
Class ode, The Pledge of Seventy-Nine
(Bridges), 15:388,n1, 389; Fifty Years
of the Class of 'Seventy-Nine Princeton, 15:388n1; gifts to Princeton,
15:390; Isham dinners, 14:330,n1;
15:131,n2; 17:31,n2; lions on Nassau
Hall (1889), 14:397,n1; Quindecennial
Record (1894), 15:27; Quindecennial
Reunion 1904, 15:203, 341, 360, 386,
387-90; Sexennial Record, 15:27;
Smith Farm, 15:528,n7; tigers on Nas-
sau Hall (1911), 14:397,n1; 18:549,
624; 19:63-64, 66-68; Witherspoon
Gang, 15:360,n1; see also Seventy-
Nine Hall
Class of 1880, 15:440, 535; 16:459
Class of 1881, 15:535; 16:417, 459;
18:316; 19:123, 145, 683
Class of 1882, 15:535; 18:543
Class of 1883, 19:231
Class of 1884, 16:459; 17:550,n3, 561,
566, 567, 568, 585; 18:316; 19:145, 253,
533n2, 537
Class of 1885, 19:683
Class of 1886, 15:52n1, 464, 465
Class of 1887, 16:459; 18:316
Class of 1888, 18:316; 19:145
Class of 1890, 18:316; 19:145
Class of 1892, 18:316; see also Princeton
University, Patton Hall
Class of 1893, 15:423; see also Princeton
University, Patton Hall
Class of 1894, 18:316; 19:145; 20:66,
67-68; see also Princeton University,
Patton Hall
Class of 1894 and Monday Night Club,
16:222,n2
Class of 1895, see Princeton University,
Patton Hall
Class of 1896, 18:316; 19:145; see also
Princeton University, Patton Hall
Class of 1897, 17:137; Fiftieth Anniver-
sary Book, 16:86n1; see also Princeton
University, Patton Hall
Class of 1898, 18:316; 19:145; see also
Princeton University, Patton Hall
Class of 1899, 18:316; 19:145; see also
Princeton University, Patton Hall
Class of 1900, 18:316; 19:145; see also
Princeton University, Patton Hall
Class of 1901, 18:316; 19:145; see also
Princeton University, Patton Hall
Class of 1902, 15:390; 16:459; 18:316;
19:145

Princeton University, cont.
Class of 1903, 16:459; 18:316; 19:145;
Decennial Record, 16:487,n1
Class of 1904, 15:67, 390; 16:459; 18:316;
19:145; 1904 Campus Songs, 15:323n
Class of 1905, 16:137f, 417, 459; 18:316;
19:145
Class of 1906, 16:261n2, 420, 459;
18:316; 19:145
Class of 1907, 18:316; 19:145; denomina-
tional affiliations, 15:24; horse p-rade,
15:507; reception at Prospect, 15:51
Class of 1908, 19:145; denominational
affiliations, 15:524; freshman recep-
tion, 15:492-93
Class of 1909, 16:188, 357; 19:226, 276
Class of 1910, 20:153n1, 314, 421, 511-
12; 21:98; 1910 Locomotive, 21:98n,
102n
Class of 1911, 17:396-97; 22:149-52, 323,
430
Class of 1912, 22:323
Class of 1913, 19:501,n3, 507, 523, 534;
22:323
Class of 1914, 21:169; 22:323
Class Officers Association, 16:462
class secretaries, 16:461-62
Class Secretaries Association, 15:151,
161
Cleveland alumni, 16:405-406
Cleveland Memorial Tower, 20:532, 533,
533n2; 21:434; 22:416
Cleveland-Wilson affair, 24:61; 25:232
Cliosophic Society, 14:138-39, 256;
15:15-16; 16:203, 204,n1, 205,n1, 266,
322, 325; 17:120, 566,n2; 18:583; 19:
749n1; 21:170
club problem, see Princeton University,
Quadrangle Plan and the upperclass
clubs
Coat of Arms, 15:468,n3
College Place, 20:485n1
Colonial Club, 14:480n1, 482; 17:42
Commemoration Day omitted 1904,
15:243n1, 504
commencement changes, 18:555,n3
Commencement, 1904, 15:307, 317, 320,
325, 341, 361, 362, 378, 379, 384, 385,
421, 528; 1905, 16:137; 1909, 18:559-
60; 19:190, 223, 225, 253, 258, 261;
1910, 20:209, 430, 457, 459, 483, 492,
496, 497, 498,n1, 501, 530, 531, 535,
536, 540; 1911, 22:430,n1; WW addresses, 1904, 15:379-83; 1905, 16:
137-41; 1909, 19:253-55; 1910, 20:
528-30
Committee of Fifty (originally Committee of Twenty), 15:528, 569-70; 16:3-5,
21, 69, 133-36, 137, 139, 204, 265,
282,n1, 291-92, 376, 382, 389, 415-18,
458-63, 518; 17:41, 170-72, 382, 383,
389-90, 435-36, 470; 18:315-17, 452-
56, 541, 542, 543, 568; 19:15n3, 17,
80-81, 128, 130, 131, 144-47, 166, 673;
report of sub-committee on plan and
scope, 18:452-56; report of committee

*Princeton University, cont.*

of trustees to consider report of Committee of Fifty, **18:**617-22

Committee on the Presidency, **22:**436

Commons, **14:**483; food served, **18:**608

congratulatory messages to WW on election to U. S. presidency, from J. G. Hibben, **25:**522; from faculty, 575-76

Connecticut Valley alumni, **20:**320-21,n1, 336

Converse (John Heman and John Williams) Scholarships, **15:**144, 155

Cottage Club, *see* University Cottage Club

Council Chamber, *see* Faculty Room

as a country club, **20:**131, 310, 369

Curator of Grounds and Buildings, **18:**613-14, 616

curriculum, **15:**17-19, 29-32, 55-56, 65,n1, 71-73, 117, 120, 121, 122, 135, 140, 154, 157-58, 164, 178, 264, 270, 277-95, 312, 323, 324, 326, 330, 343,n1,2, 344,n3, 375-76, 379-83, 403n2,4, 404, 443, 450-61, 493, 501,n2, 531, 536, 543, 554, 555, 558-66; **18:**18,n3, 58; **20:**230-31, 273f, 290-91, 292f, 339, 387; editorial note, The New Princeton Course of Study, **15:**277-92; elective courses, **19:**663, 710; Princeton's new Plan of Study (WW), **15:**450-60; reform, H. F. Osborn on, **14:**54; Dean West on, **22:**487n3; report of committee on revision of course of study, **15:**252-63

Cuyler (Theodore) Graduate Scholarship, **19:**153

*Daily Princetonian*, **14:**23n1, 132n, 134n, 139n, 163n2, 170n, 202n, 203n, 260n, 267n, 360n, 379, 387-88n, 399n, 458n, 463n, 486n; **15:**5n, 7n, 10n, 16n, 27, 47n, 51n, 52n1, 57n, 67n, 146n1, 162n1, 164,n1, 179n, 198n, 199, 199-200, 205n, 206n, 209n2, 297n2, 411n3, 491n, 493n, 494n, 495n, 503n, 503,n2, 506n2, 509n2, 509-10, 510n, 529n3, 545n, 576n, 577n, 579n; **16:**7n, 36-37, 37n, 62n, 84, 85n, 91n, 103n, 141n, 188n, 191n, 204n1, 206n, 224n, 232n, 243n, 261n2, 345, 346n, 357n, 375n, 379n, 491n, 559n; **17:**46n, 59n, 60n1,3,5, 85n2, 88n, 115n, 140n, 247n1, 351n2, 353, 395n, 397n, 404n, 411-13, 413n, 456n, 465n, 619n; **18:**26, 216n, 240, 260,n, 301n, 310n1, 323n, 335n, 422n, 466,n, 482n2, 519n, 520n4, 523n, 532n, 607; **19:**6,n6, 64n, 72n4, 115n1, 140n2, 148n, 178-79n, 181n1, 390n, 406n, 491n, 507n, 540n2, 551n, 581n; **20:**84n2, 153n1,2, 184, 229n, 256n, 327n, 401n, 404-407, 407n, 512n1; **21:**169, 171n, 178n, 471n; **22:**5n, 152n, 160n, 323n, 332n1, 600-601, 601n

Dean of Discipline proposed, **18:**587; *see also* Dean of the College

*Princeton University, cont.*

Dean of the College, **18:**612,n1, 613, 614, 616, 617; **20:**485n1; *see also* Elliott, Edward Graham

Dean of the Departments of Science, **18:**474n1, 481,n1, 513, 515, 586-87, 589, 591, 607, 614, 615, 616-17, 624; *see also* Fine, Henry Burchard

Dean of the Faculty, **18:**587, 613, 614, 615-16, 617; *see also* Fine, Henry Burchard

Dean of the Graduate School, **18:**513; *see also* West, Andrew Fleming

deanships, **19:**626

debating, **19:**140n1, 541; debates with Yale, March 25, 1904, **15:**164,n1, 207, 215; Dec. 6, 1907, **17:**564,n1

declared a non-sectarian university, **16:**468-69

degrees: A.B. degree recognized for admission to Netherlands Universities, **15:**194; B.S. degree, **15:**277n, 278n, 279n, 280n, 281n, 282n, 380, 381, 559n, 564-65; Litt.B. degree, **15:**252, 278n, 279n, 280n, 284n, 380-81, 458, 559n, 565; graduation thesis requirement for B.S. abolished, **15:**184

Delaware alumni, **17:**110; **19:**152,n1; **20:**336,n1

denominational affiliation of students, 1902, **14:**166; 1905-1906, **16:**201; 1906-1907, **16:**467; 1907, **17:**439; 1908-1909, **18:**586; 1909-1910, **19:**685

Denver alumni, **15:**552, 553; **19:**146; **20:**84,n4, 85

*Departments and subjects of instruction*: art and archaeology, **15:**56n1, 56, 73, 164, 255, 256, 259, 560; **17:**436; **19:**329; **20:**318-19, 369-70, 448-50; architecture, **20:**449; astronomy, **15:**56, 73,n3, 74, 560; **16:**80-83; **18:**587; **19:**139, 328-29; Biblical instruction, **19:**24-25; biology, **14:**119, 126-29, 155, 156; **15:**73n3, 164, 178, 256, 257, 262, 560; **16:**421, 550; **17:**39n1, 106, 110, 221, 271, 272, 387,n2, 409, 416, 561, 564; **18:**445, 587; **19:**16, 17, 69-70, 142, 328, 612-13, 680, 681, 686; **20:**232; chemistry, **14:**211-22; **15:**56, 73, 74, 184, 256, 257, 262, 324, 326, 560; **16:**10-11; **18:**587; **19:**328; **20:**409, 422, 426; civil engineering, **14:**166,n6, 212,n2, 465-67; **15:**55n1; **16:**64-67,n1, 262; **17:**439; **18:**586, 587; entrance requirements for the C.E. course, **18:**591,n1, 609-10; **19:**6, 8, 663, 710; classics, **15:**56, 73, 117, 255, 256, 259, 560; **17:**112-14, 117, 596; **18:**12, 20, 225, 355, 581, 582, 583; **19:**141, 591-97, 737-38; **20:**232, 450-51; **21:**30; constitutional law, **19:**589; departmental distribution of teaching force, **19:**242; duties of heads, **15:**74; reorganization, **15:**55-56, 73-74, 281n, 381,n2; **16:**421; economics, **14:**119, 155, 156; **15:**65; **19:**584, 586,

*Princeton University, cont.*
590, 591, 693; electrical engineering, **15**:55n1; **18**:337, 341, 355, 490,n3, 492-93, 517-18,n1, 518, 572, 573, 577, 587, 623n1; **19**:685; engineering, **16**:64-67,n1; English, **14**:85, 224, 329; **15**:56, 73, 110, 111,n2, 154, 255, 257, 260, 298-99, 302, 493, 560; **16**:38, 421, 570; **17**:59,n3, 70, 355; **18**:583; **19**:423, 748-52; **20**:451; experimental psychology, **20**:446-47; geodesy, **19**:139; geology, **15**:73n3, 164, 256, 257, 262, 560; geology and paleontology, **16**:550-51; **17**:39n1, 387,n2, 409, 564; **18**:587; **19**:16, 329, 680, 681, 682, 686; **20**:232; Greek, **15**:277nf; **19**:594-95; history, politics and economics, **14**:119, 155, 156; **15**:55n1, 56, 73, 120, 121, 122, 135, 233-34, 255, 256, 259, 330n3, 560, 561; **16**:7-8,n3, 8-9, 314, 379; **17**:286, 369; **18**:582; **19**:76-77, 183, 329, 409, 488-89, 557, 560, 581-91, 614, 616-19; **20**:371, 447-48; hygiene and physical education, **19**:3,n1, 4; **20**:361,n1, 569,-n1; jurisprudence and politics, **15**:55n1; **19**:584, 587, 589, 590, 591; Latin, **19**:593-94, 737; mathematics, **15**:55n1, 56, 73, 255, 257, 261, 560; **18**:20, 587; **19**:138, 142, 329, 693, 737; **20**:232; mental and moral philosophy, **15**:55n1; modern languages, **15**:55n1, 56, 73, 74, 154, 465, 560; **19**:562-76; **20**:451; Germanic section, **14**:145,n5; **15**:255, 257, 260; **19**:569-72, 575; Romanic section, **15**:255, 257, 261; French, **19**:572-74, 575; Italian, **19**:574; Spanish, **19**:574-75; natural sciences, **15**:55n1, 56, 73,n3, 74; philosophy, **15**:55n1, 56,n1, 73, 255, 256, 258, 560; **18**:582; **19**:329, 664-72, 688; **20**:446-47; physics, **15**:56, 73, 74, 140, 154, 184, 255, 257, 261, 560; **17**:39n1, 272, 369; **18**:322, 340-42, 354-55, 474, 489, 491-92, 572, 587, 623n1; **19**:16, 137, 142, 328, 450-51, 686; **20**:422; physiology, **20**:191-92; political economy, **15**:55n1, 504; psychology, **14**:145, 553; **15**:13-14, 55n1; science, **15**:55n1, 255, 257, 261; **18**:474; **20**:232-33; sociology, **15**:55n1
Dial Lodge, **19**:177n2
Dickinson Hall, **15**:293; **16**:133,n1; **17**:120; **20**:485n1
Dining Halls Committee, **18**:584
District of Columbia alumni, **14**:303n1, 337, 400, 447
Dod (Albert Baldwin) Hall, **14**:256; **15**:271, 445; **17**:119; **21**:169
Dodge Hall, **20**:228, *see also* Murray-Dodge Hall
dormitories, **15**:567; **19**:146
drinking at class reunions, **15**:151, 161,n1
East Orange (N. J.) alumni, **15**:503, 542
eating-club situation, M. T. Pyne report

*Princeton University, cont.*
on, **14**:479-84; *see also* Princeton University, Quadrangle Plan and the upperclass clubs
Edwards (George Kerr) Professorship of American History, **15**:438
Edwards Hall, **15**:271
Electrical Engineering School (proposed), **14**:159, 160, 223, 227, 271, 413
E[lizabeth] M[arsh] Museum of Geology and Archaeology, **15**:437; **16**:152,n2, 212; **17**:387, 409; **19**:680
Elliott's Ethics, or the Tragedy of Forty-Seven, **19**:502n3
Elm Club, **14**:480n1, 482; **17**:42, 362-63, 368, 371-72, 373
Elm Drive, **17**:120, 550
Endowment Fund, **18**:285; **20**:325
Englewood (N. J.) alumni, **19**:608
English, H. van Dyke memo on sophomore, **14**:329
enrollment: 1904-1905, **15**:556; decline of, **15**:531; limitation discussed by WW, **15**:552; 1905-1906, **16**:264; 1906-1907, **16**:517
entrance requirements and examinations, **15**:70, 145-46,n1, 160-61, 164, 183, 186-87, 233, 252, 253, 377, 555-56, 564; **18**:591,n1, 609-10; **19**:6, 8, 663, 710; dishonesty in examinations, **14**:25,n2, 165, 278; **15**:21, 186-87; papers stolen from printers and sold to students, **14**:154, 155, 156,n2, 156, 200,n1
exclusion of black students, **21**:171-72
*Faculty*: University faculty, **15**:155, 157-58, 183, 187-88, 247, 252, 264, 270, 271, 293-95, 296, 377, 396, 465, 491, 552, 570; **16**:102, 131, 201-202, 245f, 273, 280; **17**:46-47, 59, 62, 65, 68, 70, 84, 147, 161-63, 224, 265, 268, 270, 271, 274, 276, 280, 306, 308, 339, 343, 347-48, 358, 359, 367, 368, 380, 390, 391, 394, 402-403, 407-408, 409, 411, 418, 419, 420-22, 422-24, 425, 426, 432, 440, 448, 462, 466, 467-68, 470, 491, 496, 509, 552-53, 582, 586; **18**:421, 457, 504, 507, 591, 607, 609, 613, 615; **19**:8, 49, 74, 116, 442, 443, 446, 450, 453, 458, 534, 539, 553,n1, 576, 604, 605n2, 621,n1, 629, 630, 631, 632, 633, 654, 657, 660, 663, 673, 682, 686, 687, 695, 696, 702, 710, 734, 736, 753; **20**:18, 46, 51, 58, 65, 70, 71, 72, 73-74, 75, 76, 77, 79, 80, 82, 87, 93, 94, 108, 119, 124, 128, 130, 208, 213, 217, 228, 230-32, 233, 234, 237, 253, 263, 266n4, 270, 271, 272, 273, 275, 282, 283, 290, 291, 293, 294, 295, 296, 305, 317, 321-22, 323, 325, 339, 340, 341, 343, 347, 353, 355, 356, 357, 360, 361, 373, 387, 389, 396, 454, 456, 474, 478, 480, 482, 484, 500, 502, 507, 522, 530, 535, 537; **21**:434, 537; academic faculty, **14**:137,n1, **15**:23, 136, 165; com-

*Princeton University, cont.*

mittees dissolved, **14:**199, rules of order, **14:**137, 258-59; minutes of academic faculty quoted, **14:**137, 199, 207, 258-59, 296-97, 405; academic and science faculties established as subdivisions, **14:**137n1; academic and science faculties combined, **17:**552,n1; Clerk of the Faculty, **14:**144; committees reorganized, **14:**246; compared with Harvard, Yale, Columbia and Univ. of Pennsylvania, **14:**121, 154; graduate studies faculty proposed, **17:**553; meeting dates altered, **14:**207; H. F. Osborn remarks on, **14:**54; reorganization of 1903, **14:**474; resolution on WW resignation, **22:**79-81; science faculty minutes quoted, **14:**137n1, 277; *Faculty Songs, 1903,* **14:**441,n5; standing committees discharged, **14:**205; tribute to F. L. Patton, **14:**255-57; tribute to Wilson, **14:**257-58; University faculty minutes quoted, **14:**205, 255-58, 259n1, 326-27, 349, 470-71; **15:**14-15, 157-58, 293-95; **16:**64-65, 271; **17:**402-403, 407-408, 421-22, 432, 448, 467-68; **18:**285, 320-21; **19:**502n3, 547,n1

*Faculty committees and reports:* on absences, **15:**22-23; on attendance, **14:**326; **15:**14, 76; **16:**201-202; on catalogue, **14:**326; **15:**158, 340; on course of study; **14:**326, 349; **15:**65,n1, 71, 117, 120, 135, 140, 154, 157, 164, 183-84, 247, 258, 264, 270, 277n, 282n, 284n, 289n, 291n, 293-95, 296, 340; **16:**129; **17:**138, 155; **19:**454; report of committee on revision of course of study, mentioned, **15:**247, 293-95, 296; text, **15:**252-63; on discipline, **14:**326; **15:**75; **18:**243, 500, 608n1, 613, 616, 626n1; **19:**222, 502n3, 503, 527, 528, 534, 535, 539, 540n2, 577; on entrance, **14:**326; **15:**233; **16:**382; on examinations and standing, **14:**164, 296, 326; **15:**14, 23, 554; **18:**285,n1, 320, 585, 587, 613, 615, 626,n1; **19:**138, 454, 590, 676-77; on Graduate School, **14:**246, 326; **17:**156; **18:**626n1; **19:**77, 116, 117, 121, 122, 124, 134n1, 154, 172-73, 421, 426, 433, 436-37, 438, 454, 457, 458, 482, 549, 605n2, 621,n1, 622, 687-88, 696, 702, 705, 706, 712, 754; **20:**4, 6n, 7n, 8n, 91, 92, 93, 94, 96, 98, 116, 118, 119, 129, 130, 138, 143, 174, 175, 182, 266n3, 267, 270, 283, 284, 323, 394, 422, 427, 428, 431, 432, 433; report on site of Graduate College, **19:**426-33, 436; **20:**107-109; minority report, **20:**110-13, 286,n1; statement of Prof. H. C. Butler, **20:**113-14; memorial of Dean Fine and Profs. Capps, Conklin, Daniels to President, **20:**114-15; majority report on Graduate School, Oct. 19, 1909, **19:**754,n1; supplementary memorandum on the Graduate

*Princeton University, cont.*

School, **19:**753-55; on Library, **14:**326; **16:**142; on music, **14:**326; on nonathletic organizations, **14:**326; **18:**321; **19:**454; on outdoor sports, **14:**326; **16:**271-72, 371n5; **18:**321; on sanitation, **14:**326; **19:**454; on schedules, **14:**326; on scholarship, **14:**82,n3; **15:**287n, 288n; on special students, **14:**297, 327; on teachers and schools, **14:**326; on Trask lectures, **14:**326; on upperclass clubs, **19:**171; special committee to confer with trustees' committee on curriculum, **14:**254,n1

Faculty Room (Council Chamber, Senate Chamber, Fitz Randolph Hall), **16:** 145,n1, 152-53,n1, 176, 181-83, 185, 190-91, 212-13, 324, 387, 479, 485, 498; **17:**462, 466; **19:**506; **20:**7n, 354; **22:**425

*fund raising,* **15:**28,n1,3, 122-24, 124-26, 127, 128-29, 129-30, 135, 144, 158-59, 192, 219-20, 220-21, 223-24, 225-26, 246, 247-48, 249, 251-52, 271-72, 300, 341-43, 356-57, 394, 397, 399, 400, 402, 403, 404, 405-406, 407, 408-409, 417, 421, 422-23, 425, 426, 433, 435, 501, 525-27, 528, 569-70, 572-73, 577; **16:**3-5,n4, 75,n1, 133-36, 204-205, 302-303, 376-77, 379, 415-18, 458-63; **17:**16, 95-96, 99-100, 102-103, 170-72; **19:**144-47; appeal to General Education Board, **17:**60-62; Emergency Fund (Guarantee Fund, Special Fund), **15:**122-24, 124-26, 127, 128-29, 129-30, 144, 158, 192, 193, 219-20, 220-21, 224, 225, 246, 300, 342, 356-57, 397, 400, 402, 403, 404, 405, 407, 408-409, 417, 421, 422, 425, 426, 435, 439, 441, 446, 526-27; **16:**134, 204

Field Club, **22:**4

finances, **19:**320, 407-409, 434, 626

financial deficits, **15:**123, 124, 127, 128, 129, 158, 220, 224, 342, 422, 425, 435, 439, 525-26, 568; **19:**269n1

Financial Statement 1903-1904, **15:**437-39

Fitz Randolph Gateway and Fence, **15:**410,n4, 421-22, 435, 450n1, 467-68,n1,2,3, 264, 469-70; **16:**212, 329, 485

Fitz Randolph Hall *see* Faculty Room

floaters, **19:**568, 584, 665, 669, 670, 671, 672, 750

food and boarding-houses, H. F. Osborn on, **14:**54

Fortnightly Club, **15:**206,n1

founding, **17:**28-29

fraternities, **17:**278, 364, 429

Freshman Commons, **15:**199; **18:**584, 589; **19:**125

Freshman Debating Union, **16:**203,n1

Freshman Dormitory, *see* Holder Hall

Freshman Parade, **18:**457

freshman rules, **18:**608-609n1

freshmen and dormitories, **19:**672

general sanitation course, **14:**99,n1

*Princeton University, cont.*
Glee Club, **14:**134; **16:**289; **18:**231, 240
Globe-Wernicke building, *see* Patton Hall
Graduate Advisory Committee of University Athletic Association, **14:**297,-n1; **18:**456
Graduate Annex, **19:**431, 686; **20:**112
Graduate Club, **14:**202, 203; **15:**131
Graduate Club Committee, **18:**507

GRADUATE COLLEGE AND THE
CONTROVERSY OVER ITS LOCATION

**14:**157-58, 160, 182-83, 246, 361n1; **16:**31, 32-33, 34-35, 42, 140, 140n3, 263 413-14,n1,2,3,4, 458n1, 458, 468, 478, 480-81n1, 484, 490, 515, 516; **17:**20, 138,n1, 142-46, 164-68, 197; **18:**286, 291-93, 312, 314, 476; **19:**48-49, 52, 76-77, 114-15, 141-43, 189-90, 200, 201, 267-68, 293, 401, 404, 426-33, 435-39, 449-50, 456-57, 458-59, 481-82, 488, 540-41, 578, 608-609, 611-12, 621-22, 625-26, 628-30, 631-32, 633-34, 648, 649, 650, 650-51, 653-55, 655-56, 657-58, 659-60, 661, 662, 663-64, 673, 688-90, 695-97, 698-99, 701-702, 705-706, 709-10, 712-13, 727-28, 728, 729, 730-31, 731-33, 733-34, 735-36, 736, 739, 747, 747-48, 752-53, 753-55,n2; **20:**3-11, 12-13, 14-15, 16-20, 20-21, 23, 28-30, 31-32n1, 45-46, 47-48, 51-52, 56-58, 60, 61-64, 65, 67-71, 72-73, 73-78, 79-80, 81, 82, 83, 84-86, 87-88, 89-90, 90-91, 91-115, 116-17, 118-20, 120-23, 125, 127, 128-32, 137-38, 141, 142-44, 151, 152,n1,2, 156-57, 173-75, 182, 183, 190-92, 208-10, 211-14, 214-15, 216-22, 223, 224-25, 226, 227-28, 233-39, 241, 243-44, 245, 246-48, 249-54, 262-63, 264-72, 276, 277-82, 283-87, 289, 295-96, 303-305, 306-307, 310-11, 311-12, 314, 317-26, 327-28, 343-44, 353-55, 357, 359-63, 373, 377, 382, 387-89, 392-97, 403, 404, 407, 410-11, 413, 422-24, 424, 425, 427-28, 428, 431-33, 445, 454-57, 458, 459-61, 465-66, 469-73, 474, 476-83, 483-86, 488-91, 492, 493-95, 501-502, 506, 507-11, 512-13, 514, 528-32, 534, 535-36; **21:**3, 25; **22:**80, 487, 487n3; **23:**594; **24:**3-4, 28n2, 559,n1, 585n1
*Josephine Ward Thomson Swann Bequest,* **19:**143, 200, 398, 437, 438-39, 449, 456,n2, 488, 544, 559, 609, 610, 611, 621, 626, 629, 630, 631, 653, 654, 656, 659, 689, 690, 695, 708, 710, 728, 731, 733; **20:**4, 5, 19n2, 29, 31-32n1, 45, 47, 51-52,n1, 61-62, 66n2, 68, 96, 99, 101, 103, 117, 130, 131, 234, 281, 282, 286, 317-18, 319, 323, 394, 395, 403, 472, 480, 482, 506, 510-11
*William Cooper Procter offer,* **19:**125n1, 189-90, 194-95,n1, 196-97, 198-99, 199, 201, 237-38, 267-68, 293, 306, 354, 387, 388, 397,n1, 401n1, 403, 403-404, 404,

*Princeton University,*
*Graduate College, cont.*
406, 408, 409-10, 410n1, 411, 412-13, 413, 418, 420-21, 422, 423-25,n1,2, 426, 427, 433, 434, 435-39, 443, 445, 447-48, 449-50, 459, 481, 538, 609, 610, 611, 612, 620, 621, 626, 629-30, 631, 650, 652-55, 656, 659, 660, 662, 688-90, 695, 698, 701, 708, 710, 711, 712, 731, 733, 735, 736, 747, 748, 752; **20:**3, 4-5, 6n-9n, 10-11, 14, 15, 17-19, 20,·29, 30, 45, 46, 47-48, 51, 56-57, 60, 62, 64, 65, 66n2, 67, 69, 70, 75, 76n1, 80, 81n1; Procter offer withdrawn, 82,n1, 87,n1, 90, 100-101; report of Special Committee of Five on Procter offer, 92-115, 116, 117, 131, 156-57, 182, 209n1, 210, 211n1, 219, 221, 234, 235, 241, 252, 253, 256, 262, 265, 265n2,3,4, 268, 281, 282, 286, 295, 303-305,n4, 307, 307n1, 312, 317-18, 319-20, 322, 323, 324, 325, 343, 353, 354, 357, 361, 362, 363, 367, 373, 377, 381, 382, 382n5, 393-94, 395, 396-97, 403, 411, 423, 427, 428, 431-32, 454, 455, 470-71, 472, 474, 476, 480, 482, 484, 485, 486, 491, 492, 493, 500, 501; Procter offer renewed, 506, 507, 509,n2, 512, 513, 532; **21:**12
*Isaac Chauncey Wyman bequest,* **20:**452n3, 464,n2,3, 464-65, 467, 467-68, 469, 470, 471, 472, 474, 476, 477, 480, 482, 484, 491, 494, 502, 507, 510, 512-13, 530, 532, 542, 561, 573; **21:**12, 36
*Graduate College site discussion,* **17:**594; WW report, 590-94; **18:**8-9,n2, 13-14, 64-67, 308-309,n1; **19:**125n1, 198-99, 267, 304, 320, 397-98,n1,2,3,4, 403, 404, 406, 421, 434, 435-37; faculty committee reports, 426-33; trustee action, 435-39; 445, 447, 449, 456, 480; opinion of Mrs. Swann's executors, 488, 490, 538, 544, 620, 626, 628-30, 659-60, 689-90, 706, 709-10, 728, 731, 732, 735, 739, 753-54
Proposed Sites: Bayles Farm, **15:**184,n3; **16:**414n2; **20:**393, 396; Brackett-Young Observatory property (northeast corner of Prospect Avenue and Washington Road), **19:**398,n2, 732; **20:**128, 138, 210, 212; campus (central), **18:**225-26, 227, 248, 252-54, 261, 262, 295, 296-97; **19:**122,n1, 189, 198, 199, 304, 398, 401n1, 434, 437, 439, 628-30, 654, 689, 739; **20:**108, 112, 138, 212, 219, 394; Golf Links, **19:**238,n1, 304, 398, 403, 424, 432, 433, 436, 437, 439, 445, 447, 449, 456, 457, 480, 488, 538, 559, 609, 610, 612, 626, 628, 629, 650, 654, 655-56, 659, 660, 690, 695, 701, 702, 705, 731, 735, 736; **20:**3, 4-5, 29, 31-32, 46, 47, 52n1, 62, 74, 90, 93, 99, 103, 105, 106, 113, 217, 317, 324, 393, 394, 395, 396, 397, 427, 428, 432, 472, 474, 484; **21:**434; Merwick, **18:**247, 250, 251; **19:**200, 237, 398, 403, 428, 429-33, 436, 437; **20:**4, 93, 99, 105; Olden property (east side of Washington Road from Prospect Avenue to William Street), **19:**398,n2, 429, 732; **20:**103, 110,

*Princeton University,*
  *Graduate College, cont.*
212, 283, 322-23; Washington Road (both
sides, wooded knoll), **18:**66,n2, 247-
48,n1, 251-52; University Place and
Nassau Street, **19:**609,n1, 611, 674, 732;
two graduate colleges (University Hall
site and Golf Links), **19:**609, 610, 611-12;
**20:**7n, 9n, 10, 18, 19, 62, 394, 395, 427,
428; "anywhere in Mercer County,"
**20:**8n, 9n, 10, 19, 395
*Literature of the Controversy: Proposed
Graduate College of Princeton University*
(1903, West), **20:**4,n3, 8n-9n, 17-18, 20,
28, 30, 76n1, 92, 93, 95, 97, 101, 102, 103,
104-105, 117, 277, 278, 280, 322, 393,
394; *Narrative of the Graduate College
of Princeton University from its Proposal in 1896 until its Dedication in 1913*
(West), **20:**6,n3, 7n, 8n; *Residuary
Clause of the Will of Mrs. Josephine A.
Thomson Swann*, **20:**31,n1; *Legal Opin-
ions on Swann Bequest*, **20:**47; *Proposed
Graduate College. Record of the Project
from 1896 to 1910* (West), **20:**56,n1, 62;
*Phantom Ship, or The Quad System.
Some Discussion of its Merits: Also of the
Effect of its Continual Agitation upon
Princeton University* (Annin), **20:**211,n1;
R. F. McMahon letter to N. Y. *Sun*,
March 22, 1910, **20:**278-82, 311, 314,
320, 382,n3, 383,n6, 424; *The Gift*,
**20:**382n5; *The Graduate College and the
Quads* (McMahon), **20:**382,n6; *That
Pittsburgh Speech and Some Comment*,
**20:**424,n1, 444
Plans for Buildings, **19:**48, 52, 74-75,
76-77, 116-17, 121-22, 132-34, 134-35,
135-36, 141-43, 143-44, 304, 387, 388,
447, 450, 488, 540-41, 544, 549, 559-60,
621, 705-706; Cleveland Memorial
Tower, 533,n1, 537-38, 558-59, 609, 610,
612, 653
Graduate Council, **18:**454-56, 542, 620-
21; **19:**15,n3, 80-81; **20:**69n2, 543,n1,3,
573; plan for organization, **19:**128-31
Graduate House, *see* Merwick
*Graduate School* (*Graduate Department*),
**14:**23,n1, 81,n1, 82, 223, 256, 270, 361,
412; **15:**566; **16:**136, 140,n3, 171, 214,
262-63, 303, 460, 480,n1, 535; **17:**20,
138,n1, 165, 278, 356, 382, 424, 553n1,
582, 591, 592; **18:**20, 226, 335, 476,
494, 570; **19:**31, 52, 74-75, 79,n2, 114-
15, 121-22, 124,n1, 142, 424, 425, 435,
454, 457, 458, 593, 605n2, 626, 660,
673, 686-90, 696, 701, 702, 710, 712,
736, 753-55; **20:**4, 6n, 8n, 16, 46, 51,
57, 57-58, 61, 62, 74, 79, 81, 90-91, 98,
99, 100, 102, 115, 117, 119, 174, 191,
233, 234, 235, 243, 249, 279-80, 293-
96, 340-46, 355, 364, 395, 427, 428,
431, 478, 485, 502, 507-509, 513, 529,
532; **21:**538; **22:**80, 487n3; new by-
laws of trustees proposed, **19:**27-29,

*Princeton University, cont.*
31,n2; adopted, **19:**153-54; *see also*
Trustees, Committee on Graduate
School
Graduate School Dean, definition of posi-
tion, **19:**154; *see also* Andrew Fleming
West
Graduate Students' Association, **19:**491
Greek, Study of, **18:**245-46
Green (Andrew White) Scholarship,
**16:**223,n3, 225
Green (John Cleve) Engineering Building, **16:**66n1
Green Hall, **16:**66n1
Greensburg (Pa.) alumni, **19:**146
Grounds and Buildings Department,
**14:**45,n1; **17:**388; **19:**198
Gun Club, **18:**321
Guyot Hall (Natural History building,
geological and biological building),
named Arnold Guyot Hall, **18:**458;
**16:**490n1, 491, 535; **17:**39n1, 60,
141,n1, 142, 142n1, 147, 150-51, 156-
58, 168, 219, 220, 265, 271-72, 301,
387, 389, 437, 507, 564, 604, 605;
**18:**285; **19:**12, 14, 15-16, 21, 506, 612,
679-82, 682-83, 686; **20:**128, 138, 232,
345
Gymnasium (1903-1944), **14:**256, 485,-
n1, 486, 544; **15:**70, 192, 220, 225, 379,
418, 425, 436, 437, 444, 446, 577;
**16:**141; **17:**564, 567; **18:**334; **19:**254;
**20:**124n2; Guarantee Fund, **15:**192;
Ladies' rooms, **15:**140n1; Trophy room,
**15:**153n2
Halls, *see* American Whig Society,
Cliosophic Society
Hall Courses, **19:**749,n1, 750
Halsted Observatory, **16:**356
handbook needed, **14:**490,n4
Harrisburg alumni, **14:**362-64
Hartford alumni, **20:**284, 320-21,n1, 327,
335-36, 410
Harvard Fellowship, **19:**619
Harvard Fellowship in Chemistry,
**16:**192,n1
hatbands (hat-lines), **16:**521; **17:**183,
302,n1, 423, 439; **18:**304-305, 305;
**20:**537,n4
hazing and horsing, **14:**163-64,n1,2, 279;
**15:**22, 511, 523; **18:**608,n1, 611;
**19:**501,n4; *see also* Princeton University, student misbehavior
Hibben inauguration, **24:**43, 274-75,
284,n1, 391-92
Higginson (Henry Lee) gift, **16:**135,n7,
136
Hill School Club, **15:**57
history, **15:**532, 532n, 544-45
Holder Hall, **17:**241n1; **18:**256-57, 293,
301, 304, 309n, 317, 334, 481,n1, 508,
511-12, 554-55, 558, 565, 569, 589,
592; **19:**5, 5n1, 14n1, 68, 304, 533n2,
683; **20:**128n1, 137, 191, 495, 496, 498,
499, 507, 510

*Princeton University, cont.*

Holder Tower, **17:**241n1; **19:**533n2, 538, 559; **20:**495, 498, 499, 507, 510

Honor System, **14:**390; **15:**145-46,n1, 154, 155, 160-61, 164, 187, 200; **16:**284, 460; **17:**304, 440; **19:**524-25,n2

honorary degrees, **20:**411-12,n2

Honors: general and special, **15:**257-58, 282n-284n, 287n, 382-83

Honors Course in the Classical Humanities, **18:**581-83

Honors Course in Mathematics and Physics, **18:**581

horsing, *see* hazing

Hudson County (N. J.) alumni, **19:**155n1, 598, 599; **20:**290

Indiana alumni, **14:**447

Isabella McCosh Infirmary, **14:**270, 440; **15:**151, 161, 162, 215n4, 321, 437; Annex, **15:**422, 439; Ladies Auxiliary, **15:**140n1, 321,n1; **17:**141, 156, 157; **18:**322, 469,n1, 475; **21:**587n1

insurance premiums, **15:**422, 425

Inter-Club Treaty, **17:**83-85,n2, 108, 110-11, 182-84; **18:**232-33, 239; **19:**113-14,n1, 530

Ivy Club, **14:**325, 480n1; **16:**173; **17:**42, 184,n2, 209, 212, 294, 298, 372, 391, 404; **18:**630; **20:**152

Jacobus (Porter Ogden) Fellowship, **16:**214-15

Jefferson Medical College affiliation proposed, **19:**50,n2, 74,n1, 75-76,n2

Jersey City alumni, **20:**247, 256, 284, 290

Jesup (Morris Ketchum) Fund, **15:**422,n1, 425, 426, 439; **16:**134,n6, 135, 376, 416

John C. Green School of Science, *see* School of Science

John R[enshaw] Thomson Graduate College, *see* Graduate College

Joline letter, **24:**8

Joseph Henry House, **20:**485,n1, 489-90

Jurisprudence, School of (proposed), **14:**121, 159, 160, 223, 270, 412, 414, 447

Key & Seal Club, **17:**42; **18:**230n2

laboratory courses and facilities, **16:**139-40

Ladies' Auxiliary and subcommittee on the Infirmary, **15:**140n1

Law Club, **18:**216,n1; **20:**228-29

Lenox (James) Fund, **15:**438

Library, **14:**151, 155, 156; **15:**425, 437, 438, 491; **16:**255, 379-80, 390-95, 462, 472-74,n1, 483, 513; **17:**143; **18:**254, 609; **19:**6, 7, 451, 607, 676; **20:**269

Litt.B. Candidates in Scientific, then Academic Department, **18:**591,n2, 606-607, 615, 617n1

Little Hall, *see* Stafford Little Hall

Long Island alumni, **20:**272-76

Long (Mahlon) Scholarship, **14:**476,n2

Loomis (Anne M.) Recitals, **15:**492n3

*Princeton University, cont.*

Los Angeles alumni, **19:**146

Louisville alumni, **14:**447; **19:**155, 196, 212-14

Lower Pyne Hall, **14:**463

Lyme (Conn.) alumni, **20:**320

McCormick Hall, **16:**18n4

McCormick (Cyrus Hall Sr.) Professorship of Jurisprudence, **15:**438; **21:**471, 492, 493, 538-39, 577; **22:**44,n1,2

McCosh Hall (New Lecture Hall, 1907), **15:**528, 570; **16:**20-21, 104, 141, 145, 150-51, 153, 161-62, 176, 182, 211-12, 264, 292, 329, 518, 535; **17:**20, 120, 141n2, 157, 207, 281, 301, 345, 386, 388, 394, 466, 472, 510, 558; **18:** 253, 254; name rejected by Class of 1879 for its dormitory, **15:**374

McCosh Prize, **15:**412

McCosh (James) Professorship of Philosophy, **15:**438

McCosh Quadrangle, **17:**301, 462

McCosh Walk, **15:**493, 503n2, 509n2; **16:**151, 154, 211-12; **17:**120, 166, 340, 345, 349; **18:**252, 253, 296

Macdonald (Gordon) Fellowship, **18:** 490,n5, 623

MacDonald Property, **20:**105,n3

Magdalen tower proposed, **17:**566-68

Magnetic Laboratory, **17:**345

Marquand Chapel, **14:**6,n3, 131n1, 132, 133, 265, 429n1, 453; **15:**47, 140, 201, 306, 438, 491; **16:**21, 104, 153, 187, 329, 378n1; **17:**119, 394, 558; **18:**254, 421; **19:**389, 551; **20:**485n1; **21:**151

Marquand Library, **16:**18,n4

Marquand Professorship of Art and Archaeology, **20:**318, 369, 449-50

Marquand Transept of University Chapel (1928), **14:**7n3

Maryland alumni, **17:**43; **18:**10; **20:**27-28, 229-35, 268, 269

Maryland Alumni Association, **22:**158

Massachusetts alumni, **20:**262

Mather (Sir William) Sundial, **16:**472-n1,2,3, 487, 494, 536-37; **17:**13,n1, 87-88, 90-91, 105, 108-109, 126-27, 140,n1, 239, 281, 282, 301, 307, 338, 347, 358, 359-60, 387, 389, 391-92, 414, 442, 447n1, 460, 462-65, 466, 471-72, 509-10n2, 558

matriculation: 1902, 1903, **15:**24, fees, 183

Mechanical Engineering Building and School (proposed), **17:**157-58; **18:**587

Medical department suggested, **17:**40

Memphis alumni, **17:**48

*Merwick (Graduate House)*, **16:**140,n3, 262-63, 414n2, 515, 516; **17:**142-45, 165, 167, 559, 590,n1; **18:**64, 66,n1, 247, 250, 251, 291; **19:**194, 200, 237, 398, 403, 428, 430,n1,2, 431, 432, 433, 436, 437, 686, 755n2; **20:**4, 30, 58, 93, 99, 105, 108, 110, 111, 112, 113, 114, 280, 319

*Princeton University, cont.*
Mineralogical Museum, **19:**680
Ministerial Club, **19:**173,n1
Minneapolis alumni, **19:**146
Monday Night Club, **14:**463,n1; **16:** 222,n2; **19:**9,n1
Montclair (N. J.) alumni, **19:**155n1; **20:**76n1, 266,n3
Morphological Museum, **19:**680
Municipal Club, **16:**206; **17:**403-404; **18:**468,n2, 493, 530; **19:**157,n4
Munn (Orson Desaix) Fellowship in Electrical Engineering, **18:**490,n3, 492-93, 623
Murray-Dodge Hall, **14:**134, 201, 203, 256, 266, 399; **15:**7, 10, 15, 47, 131, 164, 197, 296, 492, 495, 506n2, 540n1; **16:**7, 91, 188, 189, 205, 280, 357, 378; **17:**140, 396, 404, 455; **18:**310; **19:**152n1, 173; **20:**228; **21:**169, 176
Murray (James Ormsbee) Professorship of English Literature, **15:**438
Museum of Geology and Archaeology, *see* Elizabeth Marsh Museum
Museum of Historic Art, **16:**17-18,n2,3,4
Museum of Mineralogy and Botany, *see* Elizabeth Marsh Museum of Geology and Archaeology
Museum of Natural History (proposed), **14:**127, 160, 223, 227, 271, 413, 414
Musgrave (George Washington) Professorship of Sociology, **15:**438
music instruction, **14:**470, 471n2, 473
Musical Clubs, **18:**321n1; **21:**170
name, change from College to University, **17:**511, 527, 545,n1
Nassau Hall, **14:**94,n2, 193, 290, 383; **16:**138, 144-45,n1, 153,n1,2, 154, 161, 181-83, 185, 190-91, 212-13, 318, 479, 485, 498, 501, 502; **17:**143, 359, 462; **18:**421, 549; **19:**506; **20:**465, 519n1; **22:**425,n1; museum in, **14:**127, 271; '79 lions (1889), **14:**397,n1; '79 tigers (1911), **14:**397,n1; **18:**549, 624; **19:**63-64, 66-68; **22:**332n1, 361
*Nassau Herald* (1879), **15:**27; (1906), 215n2
*Nassau Literary Magazine*, **18:**240; **19:**742-43,n1; **21:**16, 16,n4, 33n
Natural Science Museum, **19:**680
Negroes at, **15:**462,n2; **24:**558n2; **25:**60; reference in novel (*Hope Loring*) to charter preventing Negroes from graduating, **14:**380
New England alumni, **14:**360n1; **16:**357, 384-85; **18:**295,n1, 297-300,n1, 411; **19:**483, 497; **20:**262,n1
New Jersey Alumni Federation, **19:** 155,n1
New Lecture Hall, *see* McCosh Hall
New York alumni, **17:**381; **19:**131, 146, 158, 159; **20:**84, 85, 209, 247, 269, 310, 324, 382n4,5
Newark alumni, **14:**459; **19:**155n1, 171, 186-88, 652

*Princeton University, cont.*
newspaper publicity, **14:**490 nonsectarian institution, resolution on, **16:**468-69
North College, *see* Nassau Hall
Northern New Jersey alumni, **19:**608
Observatory of Instruction, **19:**139, 732
Old North, *see* Nassau Hall
Olden Farm, **16:**138-39
Omaha alumni, **14:**447, **19:**146
opening exercises, 1902, **14:**122, 125, 132; 1903, **15:**4-5; 1904, **15:**491; 1905, **16:**187-88; 1907, **17:**394; 1908, **18:** 421-22; 1909, **19:**389-90; 1910, **21:** 151-52
Orange (N. J.) alumni, **15:**503,n1,2; **16:**214, 215-18; **17:**273,n2, 383; **19:** 155n1, 316, 651,n1; **20:**76n1
Page (John Harding) Classical Fellowship, **15:**361
painting, vandalism, **14:**389, 390
Palmer Physical Laboratory, **16:**398,n2, 504, 544, 553; **17:**39n1, 60, 120, 141,n1,2, 142, 142n1, 150-51, 152, 156-58, 168, 172-73, 173-74, 237-38, 271-72, 293, 301, 340, 341, 344-45, 346, 349, 362, 369, 411, 558; **18:**241, 252, 253, 292, 322, 334, 336, 451, 475, 476, 572-74, 623; **19:**15, 16, 450-51, 506, 686; **20:**232, 345
Pasadena alumni, **19:**146
Patton Hall (gift of classes '92-'01, originally called Alumni Dormitory, also called Globe-Wernicke building and Decennial Dormitory), **15:**249, 251-52,n1, 398,n1, 423-24, 432, 435-36, 440, 444-46,n2, 461-62, 531, 533-34, 573, 574, 577; **16:**134,n5, 135, 173,n1, 177, 264, 291, 308,n1, 329, 356, 383,n2, 403, 417, 459, 517; **17:**20, 157, 171, 207, 436, 550n2,3, 560, 585; **19:**320; **20:**138, 212; *see also* Alumni Dormitory, proposed
Patton (John Linn) Scholarship, **14:**500,n3
pecuniary interests, effect of student disciplinary action on, **19:**539, 549
Pennsylvania, western, alumni, **14:**383, 446; **16:**32, 70,n2, 559
pensums, **14:**279,n1, 477; **15:**22-23, 76; **20:**355-56
personal hygiene course, **14:**99,n1
petition from the College of New Jersey to George III, June 25, 1766, **15:**532, 532n
Ph.D. degree, **19:**686-88
Philadelphia alumni, **14:**408, 415; **15:**79, 101-103; **17:**36, 38-40, 302, 303, 383-84, 399,n1; **18:**550; **19:**112-13, 131, 146, 158, 159; **20:**247, 269, 310; *see also* Princeton Club of Philadelphia
Philadelphian Society, **14:**133-34, 201, 265, 399, 457; **15:**7, 8,n1, 10, 162, 197, 492, 495; **16:**91, 188, 189, 248, 280, 377-79n1, 490; **17:**139-40, 296, 334, 454-56,n1; **18:**10, 310, 518; **19:**71, 495,

*Princeton University, cont.*
501; **20:**255-56; **21:**169, 170, 176;
**22:**159-60
Physical Society, **19:**443-44
physical training, **19:**3,n1
Pittsburgh alumni, **16:**336, 377; **17:**378,
383, 384-85; **18:**218n1, 280-85; **19:**117,
118, 119, 124, 146, 155, 396, 401;
**20:**53, 81, 85, 363-68, 368-69, 370, 372,
373-76, 376, 377, 378-79,n1,2, 379-80,
380, 381, 386-87,n2, 387, 389, 390,
397-98, 398-99, 424,n1, 444, 453, 458
Plainfield (N. J.) alumni, **16:**418; **19:**
155n1
Politics Club, **18:**293
*preceptorial system (tutorial system) and
preceptors*, **14:**153-54, 223, 226-27,
273-75, 414; **16:**4,n2, 6-7, 7-8,n1,2,3,
8-9, 19-20, 21, 21-22, 30, 31, 34, 37,
45-47, 51-53, 54, 55, 56, 58-61, 61-62,
67, 68, 68-69, 70-71, 79-80, 84-85,
87-88, 89, 90, 91-92, 92, 94, 95, 101-
102, 104, 106, 107-109, 110-11, 112-13,
128-32, 133, 136-37, 139-40, 141, 142-
43, 146-49, 152, 159-60, 185-86, 198,
200, 204, 214, 238, 244, 248f, 266, 274,
303, 306, 307, 308-309, 313, 314, 326-
27, 372, 380, 384, 385, 407, 417, 421,
426, 460, 464, 486, 509-11, 512-13,
519, 528; **17:**35, 58, 64, 70, 104,n2,
176-77, 180-81, 231, 235, 279, 292,
295, 333, 382, 386, 396, 411, 412, 450,
456,n1,2,3, 557-58, 589, 614-15;
**18:**18,n3, 19, 30-31, 58, 302-303, 439,
546, 593, 607, 610; **19:**6, 12n1, 70n1,
122, 160,n1, 167, 168-69, 256-57, 273-
74, 276n1, 311, 329, 330, 408, 409, 411,
451, 488-89, 495-96, 536, 569-75, 581,
583-84, 585, 586, 587, 588, 589, 593-
95, 613-14, 615, 616-19, 664-71, 690-
95, 701, 702, 734, 737-38, 748-51;
**20:**214, 230-32, 273f, 279, 293, 339,
340, 445, 448, 450, 451, 452, 506, 532;
**21:**537; **22:**79-80, 150, 487n3, 606
presidency, WW on, **22:**438
President: authorized to reorganize
teaching force, **14:**162, 168; birth-
places of Princeton presidents, **14:**
300,n2; control of the Graduate School,
**17:**144; relieved of responsibility for
Sunday Chapel services, **17:**197; salary and expense account set, **14:**144,
167-68; secretary authorized,
**14:**145,n4, 168; *see also* Princeton
University, Woodrow Wilson
President's Annual Reports, Dec. 10,
1903, **15:**69-75; Dec. 8, 1904, **15:**554-
69, mentioned, 580,n1; Dec. 14, 1905,
**16:**245-65; Dec. 13, 1906, **16:**506-19;
Dec. 13, 1907, **17:**555-59; Jan. 1, 1909,
**18:**569-87; Jan.1, 1910, **19:**674-95
President's House, *see* Princeton University, Prospect
Press Bureau, **14:**490n3; **16:**383, 389,
418, 459-60, 553n1; **17:**171-72; **18:**316,
455; **19:**145

*Princeton University, cont.*
Press Club, **16:**61-62, 374-75; **17:**115;
**20:**326; **21:**16; **23:**630
Princeton a College or University? H. S.
Pritchett on, **17:**511, 545,n1; WW re-
ply, **17:**527
Princeton Alumni Association of the
District of Columbia and the Southern
States, **14:**447
Princeton Alumni Association of Cin-
cinnati, **14:**448-49, 450
Princeton Alumni Association of the
New Northwest, **14:**426,n1, 445, 447
Princeton Alumni Association of North-
ern Ohio, **14:**447
Princeton Alumni Association of
Omaha, **14:**447
Princeton Alumni Association of the
Oranges, **15:**503,n1,2
Princeton Alumni Association of West-
ern New York, **22:**14
Princeton Alumni Federation of New
Jersey, **19:**155,n1
Princeton Alumni Wilson League, **21:**
82n1
Princeton Charter Club, **19:**72, 72n1,
529-30, 625
Princeton Club of Chicago, **14:**211, 223,
225, 226-27, 447; **16:**405; **18:**16, 17,
18,n2, 23, 645-46; **19:**33-46, 47, 117,
118, 124, 131, 146, 155, 479; **20:**262,
351,n1,3, 433-43
Princeton Club of Louisville, **14:**447
Princeton Club of Philadelphia, **14:**408,
415; **15:**79, 101-103, 272; **17:**36, 38-40,
302, 303, 383-84, 399,n1, 407-408
Princeton Club of St. Louis, **14:**447
Princeton Club of Western Pennsylvania, **14:**383, 446; **16:**32, 70,n2, 559
Princeton Expedition to Syria (1904-
1905), **15:**375,n1; **16:**17,n1, 186-87,n1
Princeton Lake, *see* Carnegie Lake
*Princeton Tiger*, **14:**383,n1; **18:**240,
520,n1,2; **19:**502n3
Princeton University Store, **16:**556,n1
Procter Fellowships, **20:**106, 107, 506
Procter Hall, **20:**106, 378n1, 480, 506,
533n2
Procter Towers, **19:**424
proctors, **14:**163, 164
pro-seminars, **15:**258, 330, 330n3, 566
Prospect, **14:**144n1, 194, 270, 439n1;
**15:**51, 52n1, 112, 360, 573n1; **16:**173,
185, 308n1, 314, 318, 322, 438, 493,
503, 535n1, 552; **17:**157, 466, 585;
**18:**218n1, 225-26, 226, 227, 248, 249,
250, 252, 254, 261, 262, 296, 322, 379;
**19:**189, 215, 223, 256, 260, 304, 310,
435, 437, 439, 444, 624, 689; **20:**30,
66n2, 105, 138, 212, 480; **21:**125, 167,
225, 289, 362n1, 385, 385n1, 412, 435,
539; **22:**4, 6, 9, 44, 86n1, 136n1, 141,
216, 329, 334; iron fence, **15:**493-94,
503,n2, 507, 508-509,n2, 509, 525; *see
also* Wilson, Woodrow, *Family Life
and Domestic Affairs*

*Princeton University, cont.*
Prospect Company, **18**:247n1
Prospect Drive, **15**:398
Prospect Garden, **17**:147, 345; **20**:501
Prospect Houses, **18**:247n1
Pyne Library (now East Pyne Building),
　**14**:6, 256; **16**:153n2; **19**:152n1
Pyne (Robert Stockton) University
　Fund, **16**:282,n1, 304
Quadrangle Club, **14**:480n1, 482; **17**:42,
　344n1; **20**:55,n1

QUADRANGLE PLAN AND THE
UPPERCLASS CLUBS

early intimations by WW of quadrangle
plan, **16**:214,n3, 218, 314-15,n1, 453,n2;
WW Supplementary Report to Trustees,
Dec. 13, 1906, **16**:519-25; M. W. Jacobus
comment on Supplementary Report,
**16**:528; G. Cleveland apprehensions,
**16**:535; WW on no antagonism between
graduate school plans and quad plan; to
see G. Cleveland about plan, **16**:536;
Trustees Committee appointed to consider Supplementary Report, also called
Committee on Social Coordination,
Committee on Social Conditions, and
Committee on Social Reorganization,
**16**:526; members, **17**:18-19; meetings,
March 9, 1907, **17**:51; Oct. 4, 1907,
**17**:400, 401, 404, 406, 410, 418,n1, 425-
27,n1; H. B. Thompson on club problem,
**17**:41-43; WW comment on H. B.
Thompson's analysis, **17**:47; undemocratic nature of clubs emphasized in
Supplementary Report, **17**:47,n2; WW on
plan as essential to academic and intellectual life of university, **17**:47,n4, 286-
87; C. H. Dodge on plan, **17**:49, 341,
405-406; M. W. Jacobus on Supplementary Report, **17**:57; C. F. Adams on plan,
**17**:105n2, 409-10, 417
WW on meeting with undergraduates
about inadequacy of interclub treaty in
light of radical reforms needed, **17**:110-
11; R. A. Cram on plan, **17**:118-19, 185-
86; D. B. Jones on club problem and quad
plan, **17**:147-48, 210-11, 273-75, 374-75,
392-93, 397-98, 404-405, 419; **18**:311-12,
336; **19**:79,n3; C. P. Brown on remedy for
club problems, **17**:169; report of Committee on Social Coordination, June 6, 1907,
**17**:176-86; WW on clubs as divisive ele-
ment in university life, **17**:180-86; F.
Murphy, Jr. on exaggerated influence of
clubs, **17**:187; Trustees adopt recommendations of Committee on Social
Coordination, and request WW
explanatory remarks be published,
**17**:198; WW explanatory remarks
printed in *Alumni Weekly*, **17**:199-203;
WW memorandum to club presidents
and reaction, **17**:204-206, 206-207, 216,
240-41, 246, 260-61,n1, 263, 264-65,
266-67, 273; WW announces at Alumni

*Princeton University, Quadrangle Plan,
cont.*
luncheon that Trustees sanction plan,
**17**:209; J. M. Rhodes, Jr. on need for
more democratic spirit among young,
**17**:209-10; L. C. Woods on serious nature
of club problem, **17**:211-12; F. Murphy,
Jr. on quad plan's possible effect on class
spirit, **17**:216-17; Tiger Inn opposed to
quad plan, **17**:216
WW on growth of clique feeling and im-
pulses of social ambition among undergraduates, **17**:217; Cap and Gown club
reaction to plan, **17**:221; L. M. Levy on
effects of club system on Jewish students, **17**:222-24; D. A. Story praises
plan and notes selfish spirit among undergraduates, **17**:224-25; R. S. Walker on
serious evils of club life, **17**:225; N. B.
Gaskill on evils of club system, **17**:230;
T. W. Hunt praises plan, **17**:231; W. B.
Scott on imperative need of social reorganization, **17**:231-32; J. C. Ten Eyck
supports proposed plan, **17**:232; H. Zeiss
on clubs as acme of snobbishness and
creative of undemocratic atmosphere,
**17**:234; L. R. Williams on plan as necessary to welfare of university, **17**:234-36;
J. H. Robinson believes new plan
greatest advance in Princeton life,
**17**:241-42; M. W. Jacobus on opposition
to plan in Hartford newspapers, **17**:244-
45; WW uneasy only about financial side
of quad scheme, **17**:245; G. S. Johns on
need for social coordination and maintaining equality in university life,
**17**:246-47; WW on clubs standing in way
of intellectual realization of university
life, **17**:261-62,n1; WW on Trustees'
adoption of central idea or principle of
plan, **17**:263, 282, 283, 292
WW on differences with Hibben, **17**:
263-64, 268-69; C. T. Grant on plan,
**17**:265-66; A. H. Osborn on plan,
**17**:266-67; A. F. West opposes plan,
**17**:270-71; H. van Dyke article in the
*Alumni Weekly* opposing plan, **17**:276-
79; WW replies to West, **17**:280; J. M.
Bennett, Jr. on plan, **17**:280; A. C. Imbrie on plan, **17**:281, 285, 293-95, 308;
WW replies to Imbrie, **17**:282-83, 297-
301; W. A. Wyckoff on plan, **17**:284,n2,
291; WW has had no flood of commenda-
tory letters but hopes for turn in tide
**17**:287; L. I. Reichner on reforming club
system, **17**:288-89; G. M. Harper on plan,
**17**:289-90; WW on clubs being secondary
to university's need for social organization most suited to intellectual training,
**17**:292; B. Henry on need for radical
changes in club life but doubts plan is
answer, **17**:301-306, 347-48; M. T. Pyne
on remedial effects on clubs of agitation
over quad plan, **17**:306-307; H. B.
Thompson on West's opposition to WW,
**17**:308-309; H. Holt on plan, **17**:333; WW

*Princeton University, Quadrangle Plan,*
*cont.*
on plan as most critical work of his administration, **17**:335; WW on alumni and
faculty support, **17**:338-39; W. M.
Daniels on WW's attitude, **17**:342-43;
L. C. Woods on plan, **17**:361, 378-79; Elm
club questionnaire on plan, **17**:362-64,
371-72; H. H. Armstrong on need for
more time among alumni to discuss plan,
**17**:364-65; WW replies to Elm club questionnaire, **17**:366-68, 373-74
WW on quad plan as essential to true
university spirit, **17**:370-71; WW on new
social organizations under plan, **17**:
373-74; H. B. Thompson on effect of quad
discussion on WW, **17**:379; on WW's interpretation of Trustees' action of June
10, 1907, **17**:380; on Trustee opposition,
**17**:380-81; H. G. Murray on alumni opposition to plan, **17**:381-83; Princeton
Club of Philadelphia to confer on plan,
**17**:383-84; faculty rejects club's request
to withhold action on plan, **17**:407-408;
Princeton Club of Pittsburgh seeks
meeting on plan, **17**:384-85; H. F. Osborn opposed to plan, **17**:389-91; W. R.
Wilder on starting quads on small basis,
**17**:393-94; F. Speir, Jr. opposes plan,
**17**:395-96; WW on misconceptions about
proposed quads, **17**:399; WW reference to
discussion with G. Cleveland, **17**:400;
WW on scholarship of clubmen, **17**:401-
402; faculty response to plan, **17**:402-
403, 407-409, 448; W. S. Myers on faculty meeting about plan, **17**:403; D. L.
Chambers on plan, **17**:407; W. S. Myers
on WW speech in faculty meeting,
**17**:408-409; C. F. Adams praises WW
initiative, **17**:409-10; *Daily Princetonian*
editorial on plan, **17**:411-13
P. van Dyke letter to *Alumni Weekly*
about plan, **17**:413-14; W. K. Prentice on
position of faculty, **17**:415-16; WW proposed statement to Trustees from Committee on Social Coordination, first
draft, **17**:418-19,n1; revised draft, **17**:
426-27,n1; WW address to faculty, Oct.
7, 1907, notes, **17**:420-21; faculty minutes, **17**:421-22; A. F. West abstract of
WW address, **17**:422-24; T. W. Hunt on
WW address to faculty, **17**:424-25; W. S.
Myers on WW address and scholarship of
clubmen, **17**:424; A. H. Joline letter in
*Alumni Weekly* opposing plan, **17**:428-
31; C.A.D. Burk commends plan,
**17**:431-32; M. W. Jacobus on proposed
report by Committee on Social Coordination to Trustees, **17**:432-33; G. B.
Stewart supports plan, **17**:433;
C. Wood proposes delay in plan, **17**:434;
H. B. Thompson on WW's inflexibility,
**17**:435; WW states Committee on Social
Coordination has no report for Trustees,
Oct. 17, 1907, **17**:441; Trustees recon-
sider action of June 10, 1907, withdraw

*Princeton University, Quadrangle Plan,*
*cont.*
adoption of committee recommendation,
discharge committee, Oct. 17, 1907, **17**:
441-42; WW reaction to Trustees' withdrawal of adoption, **17**:443-44, 450-54,
456-57, 458-59,n1, 468-69,n2, 470-71,
491, 599; WW on his complete defeat and
mortification, **17**:450-51
M. T. Pyne on definitely disposing of
quad plan, **17**:453-54; M. W. Jacobus on
Wilson's position after Trustees' rejection of plan, **17**:458-59, 468-69; R. Garrett
believes WW now free to discuss plan
before alumni and approach Trustees
again when time more ripe, **17**:459;
Trustees' news release on withdrawal of
adoption, **17**:459n1; W. M. Daniels' resolution in faculty meeting, **17**:467-68;
J. J. Forstall regrets giving up of quad
plan, **17**:512; WW notes for remarks to
Trustees about discussion of plan going
underground, **17**:589-90; WW appeal to
Carnegie for funds for plan, **17**:599,n1;
**18**:61-62, 61n3, 513,n1; **19**:18, 100-101;
WW thinks widespread excitement following the quad proposal has now sub-
sided, **18**:12,n4; WW knew from storm of
excitement following quad proposal he
had touched the vital matter, **18**:18,
18n4; WW states club system aborts intellectual life by forcing conformity,
**18**:26-32; WW on alumni being aroused
only when social life touched, **18**:58-59;
WW will not push plan for time being,
March 21, 1908, **21**:623; report on club
reforms by Trustees' Committee on Conference with Alumni, April 8, 1908,
**18**:229-41; reaction by pro and anti-quad
Trustees, **18**:444-45; Trustees take action on recommendations, Oct. 15, 1908,
**18**:458; J. M. Bowyer on club reforms,
**18**:304-305
WW on need to direct attention of students from social life to serious goals of
university, **18**:305-306; H. G. Murray
thinks agitation over quad plan reduced
alumni fund pledges, **18**:315; WW in
England, rested and content, barring
quad complications and consequences,
**18**:345; WW notes discussion in London
*Times* about his arrested plans, **18**:410;
WW says report of abolition of clubs
premature, **18**:465-66; appointment of
graduate committee to represent clubs,
**18**:489, 507, 510-11, 592, 630-31; **19**:
3,n3, 13,n2; WW opposed, **18**:444-45;
WW states opposition to quad plan by
candidate for alumni trustee no impedi-
ment to election, **18**:559; WW suggests
new commons rooms be of size suitable
for future use in quad plan, **18**:589;
M. W. Jacobus notes slow movement toward some scheme of residential quad,
**19**:6; J. S. Morgan's resignation and opposition to quad plan not related, **19**:6, 8;

*Princeton University, Quadrangle Plan,*
*cont.*

C. H. Dodge believes M. T. Pyne still worried about agitation over quad plan, **19:**15,n2; WW says must have money to effect quad plan or must turn from college administration, **19:**18-19

Effects of near abandonment of inter-club treaty proves wisdom of quad plans, **19:**113-15,n1, 116; J. B. Shea opposed to W. Farrand as alumni trustee because of his anti-quad, anti-administration reputation, **19:**118,n3; inter-club conference on reform, **19:**170-71; WW talk to seniors on University life and organization, **19:**241; enthusiastic reception, **19:**261-62; E. D. Duffield has more favorable view of quad proposal after WW address, **19:**265-66, 316-17; WW notes favorable outside comment about quad plans and hopes Princeton men will soon permit him to make clear exposition of plans, **19:**391; C. H. Dodge on effects on certain trustees if large sums available for quad plan, **19:**453; J. R. Mott offers to approach Rockefeller for money to support WW's plans, **19:**453, 456,n1; **20:**141,n1, 209,n7; WW feels tide is turning in his favor, **19:**459,n1; WW thinks time right for constructive article on quads in *Scribner's Magazine*, **19:**504; WW outlines article, **19:**536-37; The Country and the Colleges (unpublished), **20:**157-72,n2; J. N. Sayre understands quad idea after WW talk to Charter Club, **19:**529-30; R. S. Walker hopes WW will continue efforts to reform upperclass clubs and football, **19:**597-98

Princeton Alumni of Oranges appoint E. D. Duffield to confer with WW on quad plan, **19:**651-52, 708,n1; articles in New York *Herald* connect graduate school and quadrangle plan controversies, **20:**69n1,2; alumni statement in *New York Times*, Feb. 3, 1910, claims quad faction opposes Procter's gift on politics not on merits, **20:**76n1; C. P. Brown pamphlet on social and intellectual coordination at Princeton, **20:**123-24,n2, 211-12; M. T. Pyne supports WW administration except on quad plan and rejection of Procter gift, **20:**131; H. B. Fine recommends WW stop talking about undergraduate social reforms, **20:**191; quad question injected into graduate school discussion by R. E. Annin pamphlet, The Phantom Ship, **20:**211-12,n1; C. H. McCormick suggests special committee as consulting group for WW, **20:**213, 219, 220; C. H. McCormick criticizes timing of C. P. Brown pamphlet on quad system, **20:**213, 221; WW alleged to be letting club problem drift to increase need for quad plan, **20:**213-14; J. David Davis suggests WW emphatically state quad

*Princeton University, Quadrangle Plan,*
*cont.*

system not part of graduate school controversy, **20:**217; T. D. Jones thinks WW should not promise to abandon quad plan, **20:**219; H. van Dyke article claiming quad plan behind agitation over Graduate College, **20:**265n2; D. B. Jones describes opposing factions on Board of Trustees, **20:**266n4; J. DeWitt on WW's disastrous mistake in administration on Jan. 13, 1910, **20:**266n4, 268

WW claims quad proposal has never been revived since Trustees' rejection, **20:**274; R. F. McMahon on misconceptions of relation between graduate school and quad proposals, **20:**278-82; WW on shifting of graduate school discussion back to quad system, **20:**310; L. C. Woods still not ready to endorse quad scheme in all its details, **20:**387; WW declines request to write about college fraternities and aristocracy, **20:**399; A. C. Smith, Jr. opposed quad system but now believes WW acting solely from regard for Princeton, **20:**402; M. W. Jacobus reminds WW that A. D. Russell offered WW free hand in Graduate School plans for dropping quad system, **20:**410-11; WW has not given up conviction of need for social reorganization of university life, **20:**481

qualifying students (special students), **19:**685

rank of adjunct professor, **20:**452

Reading (Pa.) alumni, **19:**146

Registrar, **18:**614, 617; **19:**582, 583, 590

Registration 1908-1909, **18:**584-86; 1909-1910, **19:**684-85

report on social coordination of the university, text, **17:**176-86; *see also Princeton University, Quadrangle Plan and the Upperclass Clubs*

Residential College, *see* Graduate College

Reunion Hall, **20:**485n1

Rocky Mountain Club of Princeton alumni, **14:**447; **20:**84,n4; **22:**375

Russell Sage Freshman Dormitory, *see* Holder Hall

Sage Dormitory buildings, *see* Holder Hall

Sage Tower *see* Holder Tower

St. Louis alumni, **14:**436, 439,n1, 447; **18:**568; **19:**146, 505-506; **20:**253n1; **22:**262, 283

St. Paul (Minn.) alumni, **14:**424, 426, 445, 447; **19:**146

St. Paul's Society, **15:**9-10, 11

Salt Lake City alumni, **19:**146

Saybrook (Conn.) alumni, **20:**320

scholarship, scholarship deficiency, **15:**23, 70, 76-77, 187-88, 523-24; **16:**24-26, 325, 466; **17:**68-70, 438; **18:**244-45

*Princeton University, cont.*
scholarship funds, **19:**240
scholarships, **16:**169, 171
scholarships and tuition remission privileges extended, **18:**246,n4
School of Jurisprudence, proposed, **20:** 464, 467
School of Philosophy Fund, **14:**145
School of Science (John Cleve Green), **14:**45, 121, 127, 137n1, 145, 155-56, 165-66, 212,n1, 413, 500; **15:**14,n1, 23, 56n1, 70, 73, 74, 75, 126, 278n, 281n, 284n, 287n, 378, 381, 405, 452, 523, 524, 555, 565; **16:**21, 250, 257; **17:**20, 562; **18:**474; scholarship in, **15:**23, 187-88
Science Hall (now Green Annex), **17:**120
scientific study, J. M. Cattell on, **14:**22n
Scotch and Scotch-Irish church origins, **14:**261
Scranton (Pa.) alumni, **19:**146
Secretary of the University, **18:**543, 627; **19:**80; *see also* McAlpin, Charles Williston
Senior Council, **18:**230, 611; **19:**525,n4, 539,n2, 560-61, 579-81
Senior dinner to Wilson, 1909, **19:**226,276
Senior Parade, Oct. 13, 1906, **16:**466; **18:**457
Senior Society, **16:**261-62,n2
Sesquicentennial Celebration, Oct. 20-22, 1896, mentioned, **14:**193, 256, 295, 381, 387,n2, 435
Seventy-Nine Hall, Class gift as twenty-fifth memorial, **14:**149-50, 169; sod ceremony, **14:**194; death of architect W. Cope, **14:**198-99,n1, 199-200; B. W. Morris III chosen new architect, **14:**267,n2, 293, 335; cornerstone laying, Oct. 16, 1903, **15:**27; naming of, **15:**185,n1, 271, 374-75, 505,n1, 525, 528,n4,5,6, 530; dedication, **15:**387-88; Tower Room, to be office of president, **15:**388, 390; furnishing of, **15:**528; building vandalized, **15:**507,n2, 508, 509; mentioned, **14:**360; **15:**27-28, 64,n3, 70, 174, 203, 223,n3,4, 374-75, 400, 405, 425-26, 438, 445, 493-94, 508, 509n2, 534; **16:**174, 177, 178, 275,n1, 327, 333-34, 335-36, 339-40, 342, 357, 369, 405, 419, 463-64, 493; **17:**20, 32, 120, 142, 143, 157, 158, 159, 340, 345, 349, 387, 400, 401, 600; **18:**218n1, 226, 227, 243, 248n6, 249, 252, 253, 292, 295, 296, 297, 322, 591, 615; **19:**74, 76,n3,4, 143, 148, 199, 215; **20:**212, 314
Seventy-Seven Dormitory, Hall, *see* Campbell Hall
Smith Farm, near Monterey, Mass., **15:**528,n7
Social Hall, *see* University Club
sophomore clubs, **15:**199-200
Sophomore Commons, **18:**234-35, 236, 255, 285, 444-45, 584, 589

*Princeton University, cont.*
South-East Club, **17:**390
Special Fellowship in English, **16:**37-38,n2
special honors course in mathematics and physics, **16:**513-15
special students category eliminated, **19:**685
Special Trustee Committee on the Affairs of the University (1896-97) mentioned, **15:**285n, 288n
Spencer Trask Lectures, **14:**206,n1, 326; **15:**179, 296,n2, 529n3; **20:**84n2
Speyer (James) gift, **18:**516
Springdale Golf Club House, **19:**437; **20:**4
Springdale property, **16:**139
Stafford Little Hall, **14:**24, 50,n3, 256, 486n1; **15:**271, 418, 436, 577; **16:** 308n1; **17:**119, 151, 412; **18:**302n1, 523; **19:**136
Stafford Little Lectures, **14:**236n5; **15:** 306, 313; **18:**574; **19:**663; **22:**11-12,n3
Stanhope Hall, **16:**190-91; **20:**485n1
Stuart Professorships, **15:**13-14, 115n1, 438
student loans, **15:**101
student misbehavior: absences from class, unexcused, **20:**355-56; altercation with townies, two students shot, **15:**215,n2; chapel absences, **15:**75-76; **16:**201-202, 265; **17:**68; **20:**355, 356; chapel registration, false, **18:**243; dismissed or dropped students, **14:**164-65, 383, 390; disorderly conduct, **16:**24, 325; drinking, intoxication, **14:**162-63, 168, 278, 455-56, 477, 478,n1; **15:**21-22, 75, 186, 376-77; **16:**24, 325, 466; **17:**259, 439-40; **18:**243, 457; **19:**502n3, 508, 523, 534, 535, 538, 539, 543, 546, 547-49, 577; drunk brought to WW class, **15:**272-73; entrance examinations, dishonesty in, **15:**21; examination papers stolen from printer and sold to students, **15:**154, 155, 156,n2, 156, 200,n1; forgery, **14:**390; gambling, **19:**508; hazing, horsing, guying, **14:**163-64,n1,2, 279, 357; **15:**22, 511, 523; **18:**608n1, 611; **19:**501,n4; honor system violations, **14:**390; **17:**440; **18:**243; plagiarism on examination papers for McCosh prize, **15:**412; property daubed with paint, **15:**186; rough-housing, University Place fracas, **19:**501-502,n2,3, 503, 504-505, 507, 508, 525-29, 531, 534-36, 538-39, 539-40, 543, 545-49, 576-77; **20:**355; sexual immorality, **18:**243-44, 457; **19:**546, 547; thefts, **14:**278-79, 477
student parade following WW election, **22:**3
Swann (Josephine Ward Thomson) Bequest, **16:**414n4; **17:**590; *see also* Princeton University, Graduate College and the controversy over its location

*Princeton University, cont.*

Syracuse (N. Y.) alumni, **15**:169; **24**:307, 308

teaching fellows, **19**:605, 605,n2

Tennessee alumni, **16**:474-77; **17**:473, 474, 480, 488; **18**:342-43, 398-99, 420-21, 465, 467, 472, 473, 484

Terrace Club, **17**:42; **18**:230n2

Thomson (John Renshaw) College, **17**:143, 146; *see also* Graduate College and the controversy over its location

Thomson (John Renshaw) Fellowship, **16**:515-16; **19**:612

Tiger Inn, **17**:42, 187, 187n1, 216, 217, 404; **19**:13, 13n1, 32, 177n2

Tiger Inn Club, **14**:297, 480n1, 489

Tower Club, **14**:480n1, 482; **17**:42; **20**:537

track games, **18**:406

Treasurer (H. G. Duffield), **15**:101, 106, 132, 177, 180, 321, 400, 402, 403, 404, 424, 425, 535, 568; **16**:3, 162, 264, 291, 518; **18**:287; **19**:17, 125, 412, 622; **20**:54, 192, 378; **22**:165

trees, preserving the most beautiful on campus, **17**:207-208, 386; **18**:226

Triangle Club, **16**:24, 32; **18**:231, 240, 321n1; **19**:396, 505-506; 1907 show, The Mummy Monarch, **17**:64n1, 100,n1

trips of athletic and non-athletic organizations away from Princeton, **18**:231, 235-36, 255, 285, 320-21

#### TRUSTEES

**14**:119-21, 122, 125, 143, 149-50, 150, 162, 167-68, 169, 387, 408, 412, 414, 457, 469, 470, 476, 479, 553, 557; **15**:5, 13-14, 25, 52n1, 69, 75, 77-78, 103, 110, 112, 113-14, 115, 123, 127, 128, 130, 132, 133-34, 136, 163, 167, 174, 183, 189, 191-93, 194, 203, 270-71, 325, 326, 341, 342, 345, 361, 362, 374, 375, 376, 385, 399n1, 406, 414, 418, 434n3, 443, 444n2, 466,n1, 491, 504, 505, 509,n2, 525, 528, 530, 553, 569-70, 571, 572, 576, 577, 580n1; **16**:3, 4, 17, 22-23, 27, 29, 47, 51, 51n1, 52, 54, 55, 56, 58, 60, 61, 67, 79, 93-94, 94, 101, 112, 128-32, 132-36, 137, 139, 152, 198-99, 200-203, 204, 205, 245-65, 261n2, 265-66, 276, 303, 304, 312, 318, 321, 325, 371, 374, 386, 414n1,2,4, 416, 423, 424, 424n1, 425, 426, 435, 435,n2, 458, 462, 464, 466, 467-69, 478, 480, 481, 492-93, 493, 497, 506-26, 528, 536; **17**:18-19, 21, 36, 42, 49, 60, 61, 66, 67, 68, 70-72, 87, 91, 102, 103, 107-108, 111, 137, 139, 141, 144, 152, 158, 161, 165, 168, 173, 174-75, 176-86, 197, 198, 199-206, 206, 209, 210, 213, 214, 215, 217, 221, 232, 239, 244, 246, 260, 263, 264, 268, 270, 271, 273, 274, 275, 276, 280, 282, 283, 286, 291, 292, 295, 297, 299, 300, 301, 303, 304, 306, 308, 309, 335, 344, 348, 358, 359, 365,

*Princeton University, Trustees, cont.*

366, 375, 379, 380-81, 383, 388, 391, 392, 395, 396, 400, 402, 403, 405, 406, 417, 418-19, 422, 426-27, 429, 432,n1, 433, 433-34, 434, 436, 438, 441-44, 445, 446, 448, 449, 450, 452, 453, 454, 458, 459n1, 462, 466, 468, 470, 471, 496, 552-53,n1, 555-59, 566, 585, 586, 589-96, 596, 597, 598, 600, 602, 614, 615; **18**:8-9, 63, 64, 225, 226, 227, 228-29, 229-31, 233, 241, 242, 246n4, 247, 250, 252, 255-57, 257, 260, 261, 274,n1, 277, 287, 294, 295, 300, 308, 310, 312, 313, 317, 320, 333, 336, 337, 341, 355, 357, 359-60, 397, 418, 421, 423, 434, 444-45, 449, 451, 452, 453, 454, 455, 458, 466n1, 470, 472, 475, 476, 476n1, 480, 481n1,2, 481-82, 489, 493-94, 494n2, 507, 512-13, 514-15, 542, 544, 555, 559-60, 568, 591, 592, 607, 608, 609, 613-17, 618, 619, 621, 624-25, 630; **19**:3n1,3, 5, 6, 13, 16, 21, 27-29, 48, 51, 52, 64, 74, 77, 80, 100, 116-17, 122, 145, 150, 153, 153-54, 162, 183, 194, 195, 197, 200, 223, 228, 229, 238, 256, 257, 263, 264, 273, 275, 276, 311, 320, 323, 350, 388, 392, 401n1, 402, 403-404, 407, 410, 413, 418, 421, 423, 430, 435-39, 440, 442-43, 446, 447, 448, 449, 450, 453, 456, 459, 487, 488, 490, 495, 501, 539, 540, 544, 551, 609, 622, 625, 626, 629, 630, 648, 649, 650, 653, 654, 655, 656, 657, 659, 660, 661, 662, 663, 664, 674-95, 696, 698, 699, 701, 702, 703, 704, 706, 707, 709, 710, 711-12, 727, 728, 729, 731, 733, 734, 735, 736, 747, 748, 753; **20**:3, 4-5, 10, 12, 13, 17, 28, 29, 30, 45, 46, 48, 51, 52,n1, 56-57, 58, 60, 62, 63, 64, 65, 66n2, 67, 68, 69n2, 70, 71, 72, 73, 76, 76n1, 79, 80, 82, 83, 84n4, 87, 92-115, 116, 119, 121, 122, 124, 128, 131, 132, 133, 137, 143, 153n2, 157, 174, 182, 189, 208, 209n1,4, 210, 211n1, 213, 217, 221, 222, 225, 227-28, 228, 233, 234, 237, 238, 239, 243, 244-45, 246, 248, 253, 254, 262, 265-66n2,3,4, 268, 269, 270, 271, 274, 277-78, 280, 282, 283, 285, 287, 288, 296, 304, 305, 310, 311, 314, 317, 319n2, 319-20, 321, 323, 324, 325, 341, 343, 347, 354-55, 355-56, 356-57, 359, 361, 362, 370, 373, 387, 388, 392, 393, 394, 395, 396, 397, 399, 401, 410, 411, 412, 413, 422, 423, 427, 432, 445, 450, 452n3, 455, 470-71, 472, 474, 476, 477, 478, 479, 480, 481, 482, 485,n1, 486, 489, 491, 492, 493, 499n1, 501-502, 506, 507-11, 514, 519n1, 522, 530, 545, 573; **21**:39, 100, 136, 143, 146, 149, 166, 353, 362, 362n1, 377-78, 385n1, 434, 492, 577, 605, 623

*alumni trustees*, **14**:256,n1; **15**:167-68, 405, 406; **17**:381; **18**:555, 618; **19**:117-18,n1, 119, 120, 123-24, 131, 155, 158, 159, 195-96,n1; **20**:248, 264, 303, 320, 531-32; **21**:39,n1; *By-Laws* adopted Jan. 14, 1909, **18**:615-17; By-Laws on Graduate School changed April 8, 1909, **19**:153-54; By-Laws proposed, **18**:613-14;

*Princeton University, Trustees, cont.*
*Editorial Note* on meeting of Jan. 13, 1910, **20**:6-9; *Financial Secretary,* **19**:153; *Minutes* quoted, **14**:161-62, 169; **15**:25, 55, 77-78, 185, 528, 569-70, 572; **16**:27, 132-36, 204, 265-66, 422, 467-69, 526; **17**:70-72, 198, 441-43, 594-96; **18**:255-57, 333, 458, 623-24; **19**:435-39; **20**:4-5, 356-57, 509-11; **21**:364-66; **22**:17, 18n2, 44, 186, 358; **23**:479,n1, 543, 544, 594, 595, 598, 599; *Resolution* declaring university non-sectarian, **16**:468-69; Resolution on death of Grover Cleveland, **18**:451; Resolution of thanks to S. S. Palmer for Palmer Physics Laboratory, **18**:451; Resolution on WW resignation, **21**:536-39, 556,n1; *see also* Princeton University: trustee committees; Quadrangle Plan and the Upperclass Clubs; and Graduate College and the controversy over its location
*trustee committees: On the Catalogue,* **17**:232, 244; *On the Curriculum,* **14**:254, 464, 473-74; **15**:26,n2, 55, 115,n2, 343,n1,3, 345, 375-76, 531; **16**:15-16, 128-32, 198-99, 421, 464-65; **17**:57, 232, 425, 582,n1; **18**:337, 423, 424, 473-74,n1, 476, 555-56, 560, 585, 588-89, 591,n1,2, 593, 607, 609, 613, 614, 615-17, 617n1, 624; **19**:6, 8, 21, 22-23, 51, 70n1, 117, 152, 159, 167, 168, 197-98, 199, 228,n1, 242, 256-57, 273, 275, 276, 311, 320, 321, 407, 408, 409, 411, 422, 425, 489n1, 591, 625, 663, 664, 697, 710, 734; **20**:314, 321, 409, 410, 452n3, 499n1; report, **20**:445-52; **21**:539; **22**:44,n2; *On Faculty Minutes,* **16**:145, 146; *On Finance,* **14**:144-46, 167, 500; **15**:107,n1, 112, 113-14, 123, 128, 130, 131, 132, 183, 220, 224, 246, 361, 400, 402, 408, 525-27, 535, 569; **16**:136, 174, 435, 464; **17**:116, 117, 123, 130, 197, 417, 596, 597; **18**:246n4, 290, 337, 449, 593, 607; **19**:12, 14, 15, 16, 17, 21, 22, 31, 153, 167, 169, 242, 268, 269, 320, 321, 408, 426, 433, 434, 441, 452, 455, 481, 612, 674, 734; **20**:76, 128, 426, 510, 542-43, 561, 573; *On the Graduate School,* **15**:184,n2; **16**:414n2,4, 480, 484; **17**:138n1, 142-46, 164-68, 174,n1, 197, 590n1, 594; **18**:8,n2, 67n2, 226-27, 227, 229, 242, 247-50, 250-54, 262, 355; **19**:27, 31,n1, 48-49, 52, 74-75, 76-77, 115, 116-17, 121, 125n1, 143, 153, 154, 194,n1, 196, 198, 229,n1, 267, 268, 293, 306, 388, 397, 398, 401, 403, 404, 410, 410,n1, 412-13, 421, 422, 425, 426, 433, 435-37, 449, 456, 540-41, 558-59, 609, 622, 629, 634, 655, 686, 696, 698, 702, 709-10, 711, 712, 727, 731, 732, 733, 735, 748, 752, 753; **20**:4, 13, 14, 46, 56, 57, 62, 81, 93, 98, 119, 128, 129, 130, 137, 143, 190, 210, 211, 212, 215, 216, 219, 220, 221, 224-25, 225, 226, 227, 228, 236, 237-38, 239, 241, 245, 246, 254, 262,n2, 270, 271, 278, 323, 354-55, 357, 361, 394, 410, 461, 476, 491; *On Graduate College Site,* **18**:8, 52, 63,

*Princeton University, Trustees, cont.*
218, 242, 248, 249,n7, 250, 314; **19**:435-36; *On Grounds and Buildings,* **14**:149, 198; **15**:174, 415, 418, 432, 435, 436, 505n1, 507, 508, 509n2, 525, 528, 530; **16**:318, 321; **17**:19-21, 36-37, 48, 71-72, 153, 158, 160, 168, 169, 220, 281, 282, 339, 340, 344, 345, 349, 388, 391, 564; **18**:14, 52, 218, 236, 249, 255, 285-86, 290, 292, 293, 301, 302, 308, 314, 458, 580, 584, 589, 614, 616; **19**:52,n1, 68, 77, 115, 117, 132, 153, 320, 321, 621,n1, 634, 682, 683, 706; **20**:137, 480, 484, 489, 494, 498; *On Honorary Degrees,* **14**:388; **16**:22-23, 27, 274,n2, 492-93, 495; **17**:57; **18**:228-29, 624-25; **19**:697; **20**:411-12,n2, 413; *On the Library,* **16**:394-95, 483; **19**:153; *On Morals and Discipline,* **14**:162-66, 168, 255, 278-79, 389, 477-79; **15**:20, 75, 186-88, 376-78, 523; **16**:24-26, 145, 146, 167, 200-203, 265, 325, 466-67; **17**:68-70, 438; **18**:243-47, 457, 613, 614, 616; **20**:355-56; *On Nomination of Standing Committees,* **14**:465; **20**:476n2; *On Plan and Scope,* **18**:472; *On Procuring Funds for the University,* **15**:572-73; **16**:133-36
*Ad hoc committees: to confer with committee of alumni* (Thompson Committee), **17**:229-41, 595,n3; **18**:255, 313, 333,n1, 444-45, 458, 470, 489; **19**:3,n3; *Special Committee on the Curriculum,* **14**:254-55,n1,2; *Special Committee on the Halls,* **16**:204, 325; *to choose site for McCosh Hall,* **15**:572; *to approach N. J. Legislature for annual grant for scholarships,* **17**:594,n2, 600, 602; **18**:255-56; *to consult with officers of the Pennsylvania Railroad,* **15**:572,n1, 575, 576; *on physical training,* **19**:3,n1, 4, 5; *Special Committee of Five on Procter offer,* **20**:5, 9-10, 12-13, 17, 18, 20, 29, 46, 48, 57, 60, 62, 64, 65, 66n2, 67, 68, 87,n1, 122, 128, 130, 220, 283, 286; report, 92-115, 266n3

Trustees Room, **20**:356
tuition remission, **15**:14-15
tutorial system, *see* preceptorial system
undergraduate instruction, **19**:328-30, 330
university as academic and artistic background for club life, **17**:147-48
University Athletic Association, **16**:371n5
*University Catalogue,* **19**:330, 412
University Chapel (1928), **14**:7n3
university character, **20**:279
University Club proposed, **18**:233-34, 235, 239-40, 311-12, 458
University Cottage Club, **14**:333n1, 480n1; **15**:450; **16**:182, 329; **17**:42, 83-85, 110, 184,n2, 294, 298, 372, 404; **18**:631
University Dining Halls, **19**:610
University Field, **16**:242

*Princeton University, cont.*
University Hall, **14**:483; **16**:522n2; **17**: 143, 294, 297, 567, 585; **18**:234, 236, 255, 584, 589; **19**:609,n1, 610, 611, 612, 674
University Offices, *see* Stanhope Hall
University Power Company and power plant, **15**:70, 117, 425
University Pulpit, *see* Chapel Preachers
upperclass clubs, M. T. Pyne report on, June 8, 1903, **14**:479-84; social aims or university aims, **16**:314-15,n1; WW on club problem, **16**:519-26; servants in, **17**:143-44; Trustees' committee report on reform of club system, **18**:229-41; report of abolition premature, **18**: 465-66; **19**:320, 530,n2, 597; **20**:124n2, 279, 310-11, 399, 536-38; *see also Princeton University: Quadrangle plan and the upperclass clubs*
Upper Pyne Building, **16**:282n1
Varsity P, **15**:284n, 382
Vivarium, **17**:564; **19**:682
Wallace (William Clay) Scholarships, **15**:438
Washington (D. C.) alumni, **14**:303n1, 337, 400, 447; **19**:146; **20**:247
Washington's Birthday horsing, **18**: 608n1, 611
West College (West Hall), **16**:556n1; **17**:567, 568; **20**:485n1
Western Association of Princeton Clubs, **14**:440n1, 445, 446-47, 448-49, 450; **15**:128; **16**:47,n1, 48n2, 95,100,383,n4, 386, 389, 396, 405; **18**:51-52, 218n1, 280-85; **19**:211, 212, 505-506; **20**:209, 211, 212, 217, 220, 237, 238, 243-44, 252,n1, 252-53, 254, 256, 257, 262, 271, 284, 291-96, 303, 304,n2, 306-307n1, 311, 312, 320, 321, 322, 387, 410; **21**:623n2
Western Pennsylvania alumni, **14**:383, 446; **16**:32, 70,n2, 559; **18**:51
Wilkes-Barre alumni, **19**:146
Williamsport (Pa.) alumni, **19**:146
Wilmington (Del.) alumni, **19**:152,n1
Wilson, Ellen Axson, congratulations to John G. Hibben upon his election as president, **24**:149-50
WW election, reaction to, **25**:520n1
WW's remarks to students upon his election, **25**:520-21
Wilson's resignation, *see* Wilson, Woodrow, *Princeton University*
Wilson Hall suggested as name for Seventy-Nine Hall, **15**:271
Witherspoon Gang, **15**:360,n1; **19**:190,n1
Witherspoon Hall, **14**:192; **15**:271, 360,n1, 361; **17**:119; **19**:190n1
Witherspoon Prize proposed, **19**:239
Witherspoon (John) Scholarship, **19**:620, 622
Witherspoon's presidency, **19**:203, 204, 208, 210
Wood (Wistar Morris and Charles Morris) Scholarship, **15**:438

*Princeton University, cont.*
Woodhull Lecture Fund, **14**:99-100
Working Observatory (Observatory of Instruction), **17**:146
Wyman House, **20**:464,n3
Yale football game, Oct. 12, 1910, **21**:556,n4
Y.M.C.A., **19**:495

PRINCETON UNIVERSITY

*mentioned*, **14**:15, 20, 30, 44, 45, 62, 79, 83, 87, 102, 112, 115, 134, 139, 185, 223, 226, 246, 268, 269, 271, 295, 303, 337, 347, 385, 386, 402, 410, 411, 412, 415, 449, 459, 460, 461, 462, 480, 481; **16**:3, 17, 28, 32-35, 36-37, 45, 47, 59, 62, 68, 78, 96, 97, 131, 132, 143, 240, 272n1, 280, 281, 285, 299, 300, 305, 307, 321, 335, 337, 386, 406, 411, 417, 419, 426, 428, 429, 433, 437n1, 448, 453, 454, 472n2, 478, 479, 485, 486, 487, 499, 506; **17**:67, 68, 87, 88, 91, 94, 101, 102, 105, 106, 108, 110, 112-14, 122, 127, 130, 137, 144, 155, 173, 174-75, 184, 194, 227, 229, 238-39, 243, 264, 330-31, 334, 352n2, 491, 557, 566, 582n3, 586, 587, 588, 601; **18**:11, 16-34, 35, 52, 53, 54, 298, 335-36, 337, 339, 380, 382, 385, 391, 396n4, 399, 404, 406, 418, 421, 434n2, 435, 436, 437, 439, 450-51, 461, 472, 473, 474, 476, 480, 482, 488, 490, 491, 492, 505, 511, 512-13, 514-15, 534, 545, 546, 554, 561, 562, 564, 565, 567, 568, 569, 577, 578, 579, 580, 607, 633; **19**:20, 22, 51, 52, 64, 65, 79, 100, 102, 115-16, 124, 127, 128, 132, 142, 203, 204, 208, 210, 228, 231, 235, 238, 242, 243, 244, 253, 254, 255, 260, 263, 264n1, 265, 267, 274, 294, 315n1, 316-17, 323, 327, 328, 333-34, 350, 351, 353, 354, 358, 392, 407, 524, 535, 539, 541, 543, 556, 603, 606, 677, 678, 679, 713, 739; **20**:8, 29, 53, 54, 55, 56, 63, 66, 72, 74-76, 84, 85, 86, 88, 89-90, 116-17, 120, 123, 123,n2, 127, 131-32, 144, 156, 157, 187n1, 290, 313, 336, 337-48, 369, 374-76, 380-81, 383-84, 388, 393, 399, 402, 404, 406, 407, 408, 427, 431, 434-43, 459, 464, 465, 487, 513, 514, 521f, 528f, 538, 539, 540, 541, 546, 551, 555, 556, 557, 569, 570, 571, 573, 576, 577, 578; **21**:3, 6, 10, 11, 12, 14, 16, 21, 22, 24, 25, 27,n2, 30, 31n1, 36, 39, 49, 53, 55, 55n2, 81, 82, 86-88, 89, 90, 100, 104, 108, 109, 111, 112, 116, 121, 122, 129, 130, 132, 134, 136, 137n1, 141, 146, 147, 149, 151, 153, 154-55, 160, 166-67, 169, 169-71, 171, 174, 178, 193, 201, 238, 289-90, 301, 334, 336, 362, 362n1, 367, 369, 377-78, 406, 412, 434, 452, 478, 480, 483, 492, 520, 522, 555, 587, 588, 592, 595, 602, 603, 605, 614, 617, 623; **22**:28, 29, 33, 36, 47, 52, 58, 118, 131, 151, 160, 165-66, 177, 209, 217, 375, 410, 436, 450, 525, 556, 557, 600-601, 606; **23**:21, 27, 31, 40, 44, 46, 51, 65, 66, 82, 86, 87, 88, 93, 98, 110,

*Princeton University, cont.*
112, 137, 139, 140, 212, 227, 249n1, 301,
302, 366, 380, 396, 402, 425, 426, 427,
456, 485, 496, 497, 507, 543-44, 555, 564,
565, 567, 568, 573, 591n2, 595, 598, 599,

*Princeton University, cont.*
600, 607, 614, 628, 632, 657; **24:**148, 336,
448, 507, 512, 535; **25:**56, 181, 272, 273,
275, 459, 525, 534, 547, 553n1, 560, 561,
586

*End of Princeton University entry; see also*
WILSON, WOODROW, PRINCETON UNIVERSITY

Princeton University (Slosson), **19:**7n4,
122,n2
Princeton University and Her New Phi
Psi President (Helm), **14:**91n2
*Princeton University Bulletin*, **14:**170n1,
191n1, 258n3, 365,n1,2, 382n
*Princeton University Expedition to Abys-
sinia, 1905-1906* (Littmann), **16:**234,-
n1
*Princeton University Press*, **17:**351,n1,2,
352-57; style-book, 355-56, 357
*Princeton University Press: An Informal
Account* (Darrow), **17:**352n2
*Princeton University: Some Characteris-
tic Features* (1906), **16:**460,n2; **17:**172
*Princeton's New Curriculum* (Daniels),
**15:**403,n4, 501,n2
*Princeton's Quad System* (*Hartford
Times*), **17:**458,n2,3
*Princetonia* (asteroid), **18:**578
*Principles and Methods of University Re-
form* (Curzon), **17:**348n1
Pringle, Henry Fowles, **24:**412n3
Pringle Pattison, Andrew Seth, **15:**
410,n8
printing, spread of, **20:**400
*Prinzessin Irene*, S.S., **15:**307, 318, 339
prison labor, **24:**136, 277-78, 326 Δ E. C.
Davison, 100-101
prison reform, **24:**281,n1, 327,n10
Pritchett, Henry Smith, **14:**186,n1;
**16:**55n3, 78, 224, 304-305, 306, 419,
464, 546-47; **17:**103-104, 115, 122,n2,
149, 150, 154, 510-12, 527, 545-46,
549, 554; **18:**15, 52-53, 61-62, 220-21,
257-58, 260-61, 272, 289, 590,n2;
**19:**18, 51-52, 76, 101, 150, 162, 180-81,
182, 185, 188-89, 439, 441-42, 459-
60,n1, 480, 658; **20:**31, 464-65, 584;
**21:**20, 39-40, 160, 492-93, 540, 596-97;
**22:**23-24, 130-31,n4, 148, 283, 365-66,
548, 569-70, 572; **23:**83-84, 102-104,
226-27; **24:**503-504,n2
Private Secondary School Association,
**16:**327
*Proceedings of the National Conference of
Charities and Correction*, **24:**567n1
Procter, Charlotte Elizabeth Jackson
(Mrs. William Alexander), **20:**506
Procter, Jane Eliza Johnson (Mrs. William Cooper), **19:**320,n1, 404, 413, 450;
**20:**19,n4, 156, 432, 471, 500; **21:**434,
435
Procter, William Alexander, **20:**393, 486,
506
Procter, William Cooper, **15:**343n1;
**18:**397,n2,3; **19:**125n1, 189-90, 194-

95,n1, 196-97, 198, 199, 201, 237-38,
267-68, 293, 306, 354, 387, 388, 397-
98,n1, 401n1, 403, 403-404, 406, 408,
409-10, 410n1, 411, 412, 413, 418,
420-21, 422, 423-25,n1,3, 426, 427,
433, 434, 435-39, 443, 445, 447-48,
449-50, 459, 481, 538, 609, 610, 611,
612, 620, 621, 626, 629-30, 631, 650,
652-55, 656, 659, 660, 662, 688-90,
695, 696, 698, 701, 708, 710, 711, 712,
731, 733, 735, 736, 747, 748, 752; **20:**3,
4-5, 6n-9n, 10-11, 14, 15, 17-19, 20, 29,
30, 45, 46, 47-48, 51, 56-57, 60, 62, 64,
65, 66n2, 67, 69, 70, 75, 76n1, 80,
81n1, 82,n1, 87,n1, 90, 92-115, 116,
117, 131, 156-57, 182, 209n1, 210,
211n1, 219, 221, 234, 235, 241, 252,
253, 256, 262, 265, 265n2,3,4, 268,
281, 282, 286, 295, 303-305,n4, 307,
307n1, 312, 317-18, 319-20, 322, 323,
324, 325, 343, 353, 354, 357, 361, 362,
363, 367, 373, 377, 381, 382, 382n5,
393-94, 395, 396-97, 403, 411, 423,
427, 428, 431-32, 454, 455, 470-71,
472, 474, 476, 480, 482, 484, 485, 486,
491, 492, 493, 500, 501, 506, 507,
509n2, 512, 513, 532; **21:**362n1, 385,
434-35; **24:**4; portrait, **20**
Procter and Gamble Co., **19:**125n1,
425n2
Proctor, Alexander Phimister, **19:**63,
67-68
progress, **21:**510-11; **22:**91-92
*Progressive Democracy* (Croly), **20:**350,n2
Progressive Democrats of New York,
**22:**570, 570,n1
*Progressive Farmer* (Raleigh, N. C.),
**22:**437, 437n1
*Progressive Movement* (DeWitt), **17:**571
progressive movement and progressives,
**21:**344,n12, 447-48, 449, 547; **22:**387,
389, 390, 391; **23:**54, 131-32, 300, 394,
416, 421-22, 453, 464, 488n1, 493, 499,
500, 509, 515, 521, 538, 617; **24:**56,
127, 186, 203, 314, 346, 501-502, 505,
526; **25:**235-36, 378-80, 385 Δ H. E.
Alexander, **23:**262; A. L. Crothers,
**23:**266n2; S. Brooks, **23:**287n2; T. P.
Gore, **24:**65n1; L. Lea, **24:**546, 547, 548
Progressive Party (Bull Moose Party),
**25:**27n3, 47, 57-58, 85-86, 121-22, 149,
152, 153, 178, 181, 185, 192, 204, 208,
225, 245, 251, 261, 265, 266-67, 322,
323, 326, 378-80, 386-87, 388, 407,
408, 434-35, 469, 494-95, 499, 512,
543; and Democratic party, **25:**43-44,
289-94; and conservation, **25:**274; fol-

Progressive Party (*cont.*)
lowers, **25**:412-13; and monopoly, **25**:324, 371-72, 373-74, 380-82, 398; in New York, **25**:284, 378n2; and organized labor, **25**:264; platform, **25**:36,n3, 57n1, 71, 77; and Republicans, **25**:352, and social reform, **25**:311; and tariff, **25**:397-98; and trusts, **25**:289-94, 364-65, 380-82, 496; and woman suffrage, **25**:29n2

Progressive Republican League of New Jersey, **22**:366,n2

Progressive Voters of Labor, **21**:335n2, 463

*Progressives and Prohibitionists: Texas Democrats in the Wilson Era* (Gould), **22**:123n3; **24**:225n1; **25**:604n1

*Progressivism in Ohio, 1897-1917* (Warner), **22**:161n1

prohibition, **23**:231, 289n2; **25**:21n1, 625; statewide, **23**:175-76, 191, 231, 268, 601n1

*Prohibition and Politics: Turbulent Decades in Tennessee, 1895-1920* (Isaac), **18**:485n2; **23**:289n2

Prohibition Party, **25**:390n2

*Promise of American Life* (Croly), **20**:350,n1,2; **21**:322

property rights, **25**:176-77

*Prophets of Israel* (Cornill), **16**:400,n4

*Proposed Graduate College of Princeton University (1903)* [West], **14**:361, 412,n3; **16**:413-14,n3,4; **19**:189,n1, 689; **20**:4,n3, 8n-9n, 17-18, 20, 28, 30, 76n1, 92, 93, 95, 97, 98, 101, 102, 103, 104-105, 117, 277, 278, 280, 322, 393, 394; **23**:595n2, 599; **24**:559n1

*Proposed Graduate College, Record of the Project from 1896 to 1910* (West), **20**:56,n1

prosperity, **25**:99, 100, 101-102, 343, 598

protection *see* tariff

protective tariff *see* tariff

Protestant clergy, **23**:584

Protestant Episcopal Church, **18**:389

Providence, R. I., **16**:305, 310; **22**:390; Barnard Club, **16**:219,n1; Central Congregational Church, **21**:4n1; Commercial Club, **16**:309; First Baptist Church, **14**:494, 495; Narragansett Hotel, **16**:309; Trocadero, **16**:219,n1; University Club, **16**:222; WW address, **16**:219-22, 309-12

Providence *Evening Bulletin*, **14**:494n, 495n

*Providence Journal*, **16**:222n, 312n

provincialism, danger of, in U. S., **14**:264

Prudential Insurance Co. of America, **16**:455, 455n3; **18**:513n2; **22**:144

Prussia, government, **18**:90-92; Ministry of Education, **21**:48n4

*Psychological Review*, **14**:145

psychology, **18**:601

*Psychology* (James), **19**:666,n2

*Public* (Chicago periodical), **22**:278,n2; **25**:608

public domain, **21**:242

public opinion, **23**:87-88, 91; **24**:113, 114, 228, 229, 230, 236, 441; **25**:77, 79, 91, 95, 137, 173-74, 230, 268, 277, 347, 358-59

*Public Papers of Charles E. Hughes*, **19**:756,n1

*Public Papers of Woodrow Wilson: College and State* (Baker and Dodd), **24**:205n

public schools, **23**:363; **25**:183

public service commissions, **19**:461, 463-64, 469-70

public service corporations, **20**:316; **22**:110, 348-49, 448, 461, 469; **23**:297, 402, 434; **24**:427, 431

public utilities, **22**:310, 357n4, 455, 460f; *see also* New Jersey, Public Utilities bill and act

Public Utilities Commission (N. J.), **24**:25, 321-23, 324n1, 326n6, 431; **25**:308, 309, 431

publicity, **23**:614

Publishers Press, **19**:522

publishing, **24**:122-31

*Puck*, **25**:360n3

Puerto Rico, **14**:433; **16**:317; **17**:544,n1

Pujo, Arsène Paulin, **24**:577n1

Pulaski, Casmir, **24**:260

Pulitzer, Joseph, **21**:595

Pulitzer, Ralph, **24**:501, 556-57; **25**:118n3, 286, 534

Pullman, Raymond W., **25**:274,n3

Pullman strike of 1894, **15**:306, 313

Pulsifer, Frederick K., **22**:117,n1

Pulsifer, William Edmond, **14**:379-80,n1

Purcell, William Edward, **22**:226,n2

Purcell's restaurant, Manhattan, **15**:201

Purdy, Edward Amos, **24**:487,n1

Purdy, James E. (Boston photographer), **14**:64n1, 76, 93, 97, 99, 101

Pure Food and Drug Act (1906), **25**:150n4

*Pure-Food Issue: A Republican Dilemma, 1906-1912* (Anderson), **25**:150n4

Pure food laws, **25**:149-52, 153, 282

pure science vs. professional training, **15**:562-63

Puritans, New England, **17**:52, 53, 56

Purves, George Tybout, **14**:428

Purves, Rebekah Bird Sellers (Mrs. George Tybout), **14**:428

Putnam, George Haven, **18**:647,n1

Putnam, Herbert, **18**:525,n3, 544

Pyle, Adelaide McAlpin (Mrs. James Tolman), **16**:448,n2

Pyle, David Hunter McAlpin, **25**:560-61,n1

Pym, John, **19**:207

Pyne, Margaretta Stockton (Mrs. Moses Taylor), **14**:382, 440; **15**:232, 426, 432;

**16:**438n1; **17:**309; **19:**406, 413, 450, 622; **20:**47, 48, 397, 432; **21:**435
Pyne, Moses Taylor, **14:**43,n1, 47, 67, 90, 92, 94, 111, 112, 144, 168n1, 198, 335, 382, 440, 479-84, 484, 490, 500; **15:**60, 103, 104, 106, 107-108, 108, 109, 110, 112-13, 121, 123, 128, 130, 184, 232, 301n2, 399, 409, 413, 414, 422-23, 423-24, 424-26, 432, 433, 434-35, 436-39, 439, 440, 508, 527, 534, 569, 570, 572, 573n1, 573, 575; **16:**21n1, 69, 102, 140n3, 144-45, 152, 153, 161, 162, 172, 175, 175-76, 176, 177, 181, 184, 204, 225, 262,n4, 277-78, 278-79, 282, 289, 304, 308, 323-24, 382, 389, 422, 427, 428, 431,n2, 434, 437n1, 442, 448, 453,n1, 454, 472, 473, 482-83, 497, 500, 503, 506n1, 526, 541-42, 547, 552, 553-54; **17:**16,n3, 19, 48, 51, 62, 63, 110, 116-17, 152, 155, 174, 207, 210, 220, 221, 274, 300, 301, 306-307, 308-309, 339, 351n2, 382,n1, 392, 393, 395, 400, 401, 411,n2, 419, 427, 427n1, 435, 441, 442, 453-54, 468,n2, 496, 549-50, 552, 560-61, 562, 566, 568-69, 590n1, 595, 600, 602, 604-605; **18:**229, 246n4, 255-56, 261, 273, 285, 286-87, 290, 292, 293, 301, 304, 308, 314, 472-73, 490-91, 514, 591, 593, 606-607, 610, 615; **19:**10, 11n2, 12, 15,n1, 16, 17, 21, 27-28, 29, 48-49, 52, 68, 74, 76, 78, 115, 121, 122, 126, 131-32, 153-54, 194-95, 200, 201, 237, 241, 267, 268, 269n1, 293, 303, 306, 320, 397, 398, 403, 404, 406, 409, 410-11, 413, 418-19, 421, 422, 425, 426, 434, 435, 436, 437, 439, 447-48, 449-50, 453, 456, 480, 481-82, 488, 533, 537, 538, 540-41, 544, 549, 558, 559, 559-60, 578, 608-609, 610, 611-12, 620, 621-22, 625, 626, 627, 628-31, 631, 633, 634, 649, 650, 655, 656, 657, 658, 659, 660, 661-62, 672-73, 695, 696, 698, 701, 703, 706, 707, 709, 710, 711, 712, 727, 728, 729, 730, 731, 732, 733, 734, 736, 739, 747-48, 748, 752-53; **20:**3, 6n-9n, 12, 13, 14,n1, 17-19, 19-20, 23, 28-29, 29-30, 31-32, 45, 46, 47-48, 52, 56-57, 62, 63-64, 65, 68, 76n1, 80,n1,2, 81,n1, 90, 96, 97, 99, 105, 105-107, 124, 131-32, 152, 156, 174, 182, 190, 209n4, 210, 220, 224-25, 225, 226, 227, 228, 236-37, 237, 239, 241, 245, 254, 262, 264, 266n4, 269-70, 271, 278, 284, 322, 323, 324, 324-26, 353, 354, 355, 357, 359, 361, 362, 377-78, 393, 395, 396-97, 422-24, 425, 427, 428, 431-32, 433, 435, 445, 454, 456, 458, 460, 461, 465-66, 470-71, 474, 476, 480, 484, 485, 486, 489, 491, 492, 494, 495, 500, 506, 509, 518-19,n1, 533; **21:**152, 353, 362n1, 366, 385, 385n1, 434-35, 435,n1,2, 444; **22:**17 436,n2; **23:**139; portrait, **20:**illustration section

Pyne, Percy Rivington, **15:**248, 526; **16:**5, 21n1; **20:**254,n1
Pyne, Robert Stockton, **14:**382,n1; **16:**282n1

Quay, Matthew Stanley, **19:**711,n1
Queen City Hotel, Plainfield, N. J., **23:**475
Queen Margaret College, Glasgow, **16:**507
Queens University, Kingston, Ontario, **18:**578
Quezon, Manuel Luis, **24:**224,n1,3, 560n1
Quiller-Couch, Sir Arthur Thomas, **14:**526,n5; **19:**351n3
Quinn, Arthur Hobson, **16:**495, 504-505

Rachmaninoff, Sergei Wassilievitch, **20:**181
Radcliffe College, **18:**577
radicals and radicalism, **22:**449; **23:**93, 185, 209-10, 371-72, 399, 460, 504, 505, 547, 601n1, 616, 626; **24:**14-15, 69, 118, 181, 204-205, 350, 414; **25:**234, 241
Ragan, Adolphus, **19:**272,n1, 292; **21:**14,n1
Rahway, N.J., **23:**290, 468; Reformatory, 305
railroad bribery, **23:**122
railroad employees, **23:**467,n2
Railroad Employees and Investors Association, **23:**357,n2
railroads, **17:**124,n1; **21:**42-43, 63, 126, 134, 242, 311-12, 340n2, 402-403, 449,n1, 453, 571; **24:**24, 106-107, 194, 321-23,n1, 324-25, 326,n6; **25:**156-57, 195, 208-209, 227, 262-63, 297, 344, 371; grade crossings, **24:**321-23,n1, 324-25, 326,n6; **25:**309; management of, **17:**502; monopoly hearings, **25:**274,n2; platform plank, **24:**480; regulation of, **23:**235n3
*Railway Age*, **18:**262
Rainey, Henry Thomas, **24:**67
Rainsford, William Stephen, **14:**115
Raleigh, N. C., **22:**406; **23:**139; **24:**389, 461n2, 464n1; Capital Club, **23:**111n1; WW address, **23:**110,n1; WW in, **23:**139, 140
Raleigh, Sir Walter, **14:**552
Raleigh Hotel, Washington, D. C., **23:**566; **24:**9n1
Raleigh (N. C.) *News and Observer*, **22:**121,n1, 407,n2, 435, 499,n1, 509; **23:**111n, 139, 140; **24:**49n1, 59n1, 60n1, 64n1, 65n1, 380, 399,n1, 471,n2; **25:**585n1
Ralph, Henry William, **19:**139,n4
Ralston, Samuel Moffett, **25:**327-28,n5
Ramsay, Darley Hiden, **23:**550,n1

Ramsay, William Ernest, M.D., **22:** 328,n2, 481,n3
Ramsdell, Fred Winthrop, **23:**82,n9
Randall, John Herman, **19:**314,n5
Randolph, Charles Brewster, **16:**61
Randolph, Corliss F., **16:**381
Randolph, Harrison, **14:**5,n1, 56n2, 86
Randolph, Vance, **24:**252n1
Randolph-Macon College, **20:**408,n3
Rankin, Edwin Moore, **14:**474; **15:**375; **16:**67, 131, 254, 528; **17:**161,n1, 162,n8, 408
Rankin, Walter Mead, **14:**126,n1, 128, 277, 326, 327; **15:**375; **17:**408, 561; **19:**70, 100,n1
Rankin, William, **19:**100,n2
Ransom, Edward A., Jr., **23:**536n1
Raper, Charles Lee, **18:**311,n2, 311
Raphael (Raffaello Sanzio), **15:**250, 251, 276, 322, 358; **22:**218
Raphael, Emanuel, **16:**556-57,n1; **17:**88, 394n5
Raritan, N. J., **23:**475
Raritan River, **15:**579
rate-making, **22:**84
Raven Crag, Westmorland, **18:**395
Ravenna, Italy, **14:**246
Rawnsley, Hardwicke Drummond, **16:** 451,n1; **18:**369n3, 378,n7, 395; **24:**540-41
Rawnsley, Willingham Franklin, **18:** 369,n3, 370, 378
Ray, George W., **23:**511
Raycroft, Joseph Edward, **19:**3,n1
Raymond, Andrew Van Vranken, **15:**496,n2, 500; **16:**292n1
Raymond, Bradford Paul, **14:**515; **16:**68,n2, 80, 243
Raymond, George Lansing, **14:**559,n1; **16:**140n3, 263; **17:**565-66
Raymond, Jennie Abbott Ward (Mrs. John Marshall), **19:**225,n2
Raymond, John Marshall, **19:**225,n2; **20:**464,n1, 466, 467, 482, 542, 561, 573
Rea, James Childs, **23:**128n1
Rea, Julia Dodge (Mrs. James Childs), **23:**128,n1
Rea, Samuel, **16:**336,n3
Read, Conyers, **19:**190,n2, 678
Read, William T., **23:**365n2
Read House, Chattanooga, **16:**476
Reading, Pa., **24:**138; Princeton alumni, **19:**146
Reading Railroad, **21:**560; **23:**450n1
Reagan, John Henninger, **23:**499,n3
Real Estate Exchange of Boston, **24:**126
Ream, Edward King, **15:**272n1; **19:**165
Ream, Norman Bruce, **15:**271-72,n1, 527; **16:**303, 336, 376-77, 389, 547, 552, 552n2, 553
Reazor, Frank Burrows, **17:**4,n7
Reber, Louis E., **23:**480n1
recall, *see* initiative, referendum and recall

*Recht des Modernen Staates* (Jellinek), **14:**322
reciprocity, **23:**622
Reciprocity (Shipp), **23:**655n1
reciprocity with Canada, **22:**478n3, 486, 592, 601; **23:**41, 90-91, 131-32,n1, 132n1, 369, 422, 442-43, 622
*Reciprocity, 1911: A Study in Canadian-American Relations* (Ellis), **22:**478n3
*Recollections of a Long Life: An Autobiography* (Cuyler), **14:**347,n1
*Recollections of Fifty Years of West Virginia* (MacCorkle), **16:**565n
Reconstruction era, **14:**33, 312, 344; **17:**321
Record, George Lawrence, **21:**244n2, 249,n3, 258n10, 259, 274, 275, 290, 290n1, 291, 293, 296, 297, 338-47, 348, 379n1, 380, 406-11, 412, 415-16, 433n1, 435, 436, 442, 443, 449, 450, 451, 453, 457, 464, 503, 580, 596; **22:**13, 77n1, 231,n3, 357n4, 357-58, 382-83n3, 546n5; **24:**546
*Records of the Federal Convention of 1787* (ed. Farrand), **21:**309n2
*Records of the Presbyterian Church, U.S.A.* (ed. Roberts), **17:**28,n2
*Rectorial Address Delivered to the Students in the University of St. Andrews, 22nd October, 1902* (Carnegie), **14:**306,n1
Red Bank, Cumberland, England, **18:** 413
Red Bank, N. J., **20:**541n1; **23:**447; **25:**511; Frick Lyceum, **21:**213,n1; WW campaign speeches, **21:**213-18; **23:** 442-47
Red Cross, **22:**416
Red Star Line, **19:**306
Redfield, William Cox, **23:**560-61,n1,2, 589, 638n2, 641, 644, 647; **24:**238n3, 579-80
Reed, Adèle Wilcox (Mrs. David Aiken), **17:**4,n5, 14, 18
Reed, David Aiken, **14:**100; **17:**4,n4, 10, 14, 18
Reed, Edward Bliss, **24:**166n2
Reed, Eugene Elliott, **24:**272,n2, 286
Reed, Horace Garner, **19:**544,n3
Reed, James Alexander, **23:**291,n2
Reed, James Hay, **14:**99-100; **15:**124-26, 129n2, 356-57, 527; **17:**4,n6, 14, 18; **18:**6, 217-18
Reed, James Hay, Jr., **14:**100; **15:**126
Reed, Kate J. Aiken (Mrs. James Hay), **15:**126; **18:**6
Reed, Katherine, **15:**126; **17:**4,n5, 11, 14, 18
Reed, Richard Clark, **14:**331
Reed, Thomas Baird, **16:**375
Reed, Thomas Brackett, **14:**192, 194, 258; **18:**127; **20:**415,n3

Reed, William Belden, Jr., **14**:465-67; **17**:362-64,n1, 366-68, 371-72, 373-74
Reed, William Maxwell, **16**:81,n1
*Reed's Rules. A Manual of General Parliamentary Law . . .* (Reed), **14**:258
Reelfoot Lake, Tennessee, **18**:485n1
Rees, Bird Le Grand, **16**:375
Reese, James Mitchell, M.D., **22**:590
referendum, *see* initiative, referendum and recall
*Referendum in America* (Oberholtzer), **17**:262,n2
Reform Club of New York, **24**:284n1, 391,n1, 394
*Reform of Legal Procedure* (Storey), **21**:386n2
Reformation, **18**:93, 330
reformers, **21**:360
registration, *see* voter registration
Reichmann, Alexander Frederick, **24**:151n2
Reichner, Louis Irving, **15**:103; **17**:288-89,n1, 292; **22**:450-51
Reid, Edith Gittings (Mrs. Harry Fielding), **14**:3, 146, 167, 196, 277, 347-48; **15**:8,n4; **16**:308-309; **17**:59, 72; **20**:402, 407; **24**:445-46; **25**:422-23, 551-52
Reid, Harry Fielding, **14**:3, 146, 167, 196, 347; **25**:552n2
Reid, John, **16**:344
Reid, Legh Wilber, **15**:351,n4; **18**:416n1, 466,n1
Reid, Mrs. Legh Wilber, **15**:351,n4; **18**:416,n1, 466,n1
Reid, Elizabeth Mills (Mrs. Whitelaw), **18**:398,n1, 399-400
Reid, Ogden Mills, **18**:400,n9
Reid, Whitelaw, **18**:398, 399-400; **21**:592,n2, 615
Reilly, Peter E., **21**:487
Reilly, Thomas Lawrence, **24**:287,n1
Reinhart, J. Albert, **18**:563, 612; **19**:171,n1
religious education, **23**:373
*Religious Perspectives in American Culture* (ed., Smith and Jameson), **19**:253n1
*Reminiscences* (Carlyle; ed. Froude), **18**:362n2
Remsen, Elizabeth Mallory, **24**:65,n1
Remsen, Ira, **14**:337, 515; **24**:65, 82-83; **25**:150,n5, 151n6, 282,n1, 547, 578
Renaissance, **23**:363
*Renascence Portraits* (van Dyke), **14**:82,n4
Rendall, F. H., **17**:613,n3
Rennert Hotel, Baltimore, **24**:489
Reno, Nev., **24**:404
Reno *Nevada State Journal*, **25**:359n1
Rensselaer Polytechnic Institute, **16**:239
Rentschler, Gordon Sohn, **22**:214
*Répertoire encyclopédique du droit français* (Labori and Schaffhauser), **15**:434n2

Repetto, Louis A., **23**:523
*Report on the Miners' Strike in Bituminous Coal Field in Westmoreland County, Pa.*, **23**:249n2
*Report of the Secretary of the Treasury on the Subject of Manufactures* (Hamilton), **18**:538
*Reports of the Princeton University Expeditions to Patagonia, 1896-1899* (ed. Scott), **16**:507,n1
Repp, Charles A., **21**:584n1
representative government, **22**:464, 595; **23**:619-20; **24**:10, 94, 112, 128, 200, 229, 230, 234, 235, 318; **25**:7, 124, 239
*Representative Government. Circular of the "Direct Legislation League". . .* **22**:247,n1
Republican National Committee, **18**:640; **24**:494; **25**:396n3
Republican party and Republicans, **15**:547, 550, 551n4; **16**:533, 533n1; **17**:77, 320, 321, 584,n1; **18**:215, 269, 479, 479n1; **19**:362, 365-66, 367; **20**:297, 298, 299, 425, 442, 503, 504, 505; **21**:9, 21, 21n1, 46, 88n3, 96, 124, 125, 126, 129, 141, 145, 174, 183, 185, 194, 197, 211, 212, 214, 215, 218, 219, 223, 227, 248-49, 253, 256, 272, 276n2, 284, 292, 300, 329, 330, 339, 342n6, 343n11, 344n12, 357, 367, 427, 431n6, 432, 448, 454, 474, 501, 535, 565, 591, 598, 603, 608n2, 621; **22**:7, 34, 61, 85, 164, 181, 207, 212, 214, 216, 217, 218, 219, 220, 221, 222, 225, 226, 274-75, 291n2, 334, 335, 372, 376, 378, 405, 423, 429, 442, 444, 445, 446, 465, 474, 475, 476, 478n3, 488, 491, 534, 536, 543, 556, 559, 565, 568, 573, 584n2, 587, 594, 595; **23**:7, 45, 62, 89, 90, 102, 105, 107-108, 123, 130n1, 131, 132, 156, 165, 234n5, 247, 276, 287n2, 294, 310n3, 413, 414-17, 441, 466, 489, 503, 509, 515, 521, 578, 597, 607, 623, 624, 638-39, 642-43, 645, 647, 648; **24**:11, 109-10, 116, 141-42, 155, 156, 195, 202-203, 294, 317-18, 340, 362-63, 365, 367, 373, 374, 407, 411, 420, 485, 494, 498; **25**:17, 44, 69, 71, 81, 82-85, 89, 93, 120-21, 125, 127, 141, 148, 174, 185, 204, 230, 242, 243, 246-47, 261, 322-23, 326, 334-35, 349, 351-52, 355, 364, 371, 375-76, 378-80, 388, 404, 427-28, 433, 434-36, 439-40, 444-45, 462, 466, 469, 470, 485, 489-90, 494, 499, 503, 506-507, 511-12, 605; campaign of 1908, **18**:639-40; in Congress, **25**:260-61; Convention of 1860, **18**:110; corporate campaign contributions, **25**:396,n3; division in, **25**:472, 475-76, 489; expenditures in 1904, **25**:396n3; insurgents, **21**:447; monopoly, **25**:324-25, 398; negroes, **25**:607; number in House of Representatives, **25**:503; panic of 1893, **25**:471; presidential

Republican party and Republicans, (cont.)
term, **25**:565; and Progressive Party,
**25**:181; progressives in, **25**:46, 379-80;
tariff, **25**:7-8, 209, 261, 324-25, 366-67,
397-98; Wall Street, **25**:411
in California, **21**:447; **22**:31-32, 32n;
**23**:251, 473; in Delaware, **23**:436,n2;
in Illinois, **23**:311; **25**:392; in Iowa,
**24**:220-21; **25**:439; in Kansas, **21**:248,
447; **23**:291; **25**:378-80, 621n2; in
Maine, **21**:447; **25**:619n1; in Maryland,
**23**:264n1, 573,n2; **24**:448; in Michigan,
**23**:263; in Nebraska, **25**:340-41; in
New Hampshire, **21**:447; **23**:473, 474
in New Jersey, **16**:455; **21**:7, 7,n4, 9,
11, 16, 18, 19, 20, 23, 27, 37, 50, 57,
107, 114, 161, 168, 214, 217, 219n1,
226, 231, 232, 235, 236, 240, 241, 244,
244n2, 247-50, 251, 252, 255, 258, 259,
260-61, 272, 273, 275, 278-79, 283,
284-87, 290n1, 293, 303, 311, 312-13,
314, 315, 324, 326, 327, 329, 331,
343n9, 345-48, 351, 352, 354, 357-59,
369-70, 369n3, 380, 388, 389, 390, 392,
393, 394, 395, 396, 398, 404, 409, 411,
413, 416, 418, 419, 420, 424, 426, 427,
429, 430, 431, 438, 441, 446, 447, 448,
449, 457, 458, 461, 491, 495, 503-505,
510, 511, 520, 521, 529, 530, 545, 547-
49, 552-53, 561, 566, 568-69, 572,
584n1; **22**:22, 27, 47, 77n1, 125, 155-
56, 164, 173, 204, 212, 216, 217, 219,
249, 250, 284, 294, 297, 298, 301, 308,
357-58, 366, 412,n2, 454, 455, 458,
460, 476, 513, 513n2, 517, 518, 531,
535, 537n4, 561, 569, 571, 582, 588,
589, 602; **23**:68, 203n4, 262, 333, 334,
338, 346, 347, 364, 365, 381, 384, 393,
394-95, 398, 400, 401, 404-406, 409,
411, 419, 429, 431, 432n9, 439, 445,
446, 453, 455, 456, 461, 462, 464, 465,
468, 469, 472, 475, 522n1, 524, 529n3,
530, 532-33, 535, 536, 536n1, 538, 540,
544, 544n1, 546, 627, 628, 629; **24**:180,
324-28, 434-35, 444; **25**:86, 121, 246,
322, 336, 351, 379, 428-29, 474-75,
479, 513, 523; Board of Guardians,
**21**:219,n2, 226, 230-31, 266, 272, 301,
303, 303-304, 315, 346-47, 347, 359,
378-79, 380, 408-409, 429, 443, 503;
**22**:249, 300; **23**:391-92, 449-50, 467,
471; Cape May Co., **25**:480; card index
of expected campaign contributors,
**21**:226, 232; Fitzherbert scandal,
**24**:244n1, 246; Geran Act, **24**:431-34;
grade crossings, **23**:476-78; **25**:309;
New Idea progressives, **21**:7,n7, 19,
172, 214,n3, 219n1, 256n9, 275, 297,
301, 346, 347, 380, 409, 510; **22**:225n3,
297; and WW vetoes, **25**:309
in New York, **21**:252n6, 598; **25**:284,
380,n3; Old Guard, **21**:252n6, 598; in
Ohio, **21**:248, 379; in Oregon, **23**:350;
**25**:492; in Pennsylvania, **21**:608n2;
**22**:409n1,2; **23**:229; in Tennessee,
**23**:288, 289n2; in Wisconsin, **23**:253,
540; **25**:379
Reserve Association of America, **23**:
293n3
"Residential Quad" idea at Princeton
(van Dyke), **17**:276-79
*Residuary Clause of the Will of Mrs.
Josephine A. Thomson Swann*, **20**:
31,n1
retirement and pensions of college pro-
fessors, **19**:460,n1, 480
Rettger, Ernest William, **14**:145,n6
Reuter's news agency, **17**:92, 472
*Review of Reviews* (New York), **14**:40,n4;
**17**:333,n1; **19**:597,n2; **21**:175, 300,n1,-
2,3; **22**:139,n2; **23**:10,n4
Revolution, *see* American; French
revolution predicted by WW, **20**:363,
366, 368
Revolution Impending (Chamberlain),
**14**:443,n3
Reynolds, James Burton, **16**:442-43
Reynolds, Joseph S., **23**:555,n8
Rhee, Syngman, **20**:556,n1
Rhees (Benjamin), Rush, **17**:128,n2
Rhode Island, **22**:390; **25**:33
Rhodes, Ann Card (Mrs. James Ford),
**20**:475,n2, 496
Rhodes, Cecil John, **14**:337, 462;
**15**:204-205, 273; **20**:475
Rhodes, James Ford, **14**:282; **20**:430, 457,
475, 483, 496,n1, 499; **22**:27, 49
Rhodes, James Mauran, Jr., **17**:209-10
Rhodes Scholarships, **14**:336, 398, 416;
**15**:180, 204-205, 273, 324, 378, 391,
391-92; **16**:538-39; **17**:557; **19**:159;
Rhodes Scholarship Trust, **14**:337n1;
**15**:180; **16**:538-39
Rice, Melvin A., **23**:183; **24**:507,n2, 551,
561
Rice, Richard Henry, **22**:411,n1
Rice, William Marsh (1816-1900), **16**:
556n2; **17**:394n3; **18**:570,n1
Rice, William Marsh (Princeton '79),
**17**:394,n3, 448, 449
Rice Institute (now Rice University),
**16**:556-57,n1,2,3; **17**:66n1, 88, 394,
394n3,5, 448-49, 586,n1; **18**:570-71,n1;
**19**:558; **20**:580
Rich, Samuel Joseph, **23**:64,n7
Richards, Alfred Ernest, **16**:198; **19**:
569-70, 570-71, 576
Richards, Emerson, **23**:522n1, 529n3
Richards, William Rogers, **14**:550,n3;
**17**:125,n1
Richardson (at Bermuda), **20**:177, 179
Richardson, Charles Patton, **15**:343n1
Richardson, David Crockett, **24**:101n2,3,
119
Richardson, Donald William, **15**:375
Richardson, Ernest Cushing, **14**:326;
**15**:207,n4; **16**:379-80, 390-95, 472-74;
**20**:217,n1, 269-70

Richardson, Evans Tulane, 25:271-72,n1
Richardson, Grace Ely (Mrs. Ernest Cushing), 15:207,n4
Richardson, Hugh, 22:488,n1
Richardson, Katherine Augusta Mayo (Mrs. Evans Tulane), 25:272,n5
Richardson, Katherine Beecher, 25:272,n5
Richardson, Lilian Maud Wilson (Mrs. Owen Willans), 16:433,n2, 442; 18:355
Richardson, Sir Owen Willans, 16:428,n2,3, 433, 434, 434-35, 442, 454, 465, 507; 17:152, 155, 240, 241, 408; 18:340-42, 354
Richardson, Rufus Byam, 15:141,n3
Richardson, Rupert N., 25:550n2
Richardson, Samuel, 14:503
Richelieu, Duc de (Armond Jean du Plessis) (Cardinal Richelieu), 24:488
Richmond, Archibald Murray, 21:146,n1
Richmond, Charles Alexander, 15:169,n3; 19:19-20,n1,2, 223, 229, 231-37; 21:146
Richmond, Mass., 23:220
Richmond, Va., 14:238; 18:601; 23:133, 138, 290, 327, 359, 390, 601, 653; 24:71, 79, 97, 117-22; WW address to City Council, 24:101-17, 339; Woodrow Wilson Club, 23:563n2; 24:79
Richmond Academy, 24:117
Richmond College, 24:117-19
Richmond, Va., News Leader, 23:563n2; 24:101n, 136n
Richmond, Va., Times-Dispatch, 21:539,n2; 23:328n2, 563n2, 591n2, 601, 601n1, 604; 24:97n2, 122n, 486; 25:632n1, 640n, 647,n1
Richmond, University of, 23:133n1
Ricketts, Eliza Getty (Mrs. Palmer Chamberlaine, Sr.), 14:8, 428; 16:544,n4; 17:410-11,n1
Ricketts, Henrietta, 14:8, 425, 428, 429; 15:120, 134, 140, 152, 162, 277, 312; 16:544,n4
Ricketts, Louis Davidson, 15:152,n1
Ricketts, Palmer Chamberlaine, Jr., 15:312,n3; 16:102
Ridder, Herman, 25:441,n1
Riddle, William, 25:129,n1
Rideing, William Henry, 16:496-97,n1, 534, 538; 22:406
Rider, Frederic, 22:357,n3
Ridgely, William Barret, 14:298
Ridgewood, N. J., Methodist Church, 20:385; WW addresses, 20:385; 23:449-51
Riegelman, Henry, 24:221,n1
Riggs, Clinton Levering, 23:568,n3
Riggs, Grace Cutting (Mrs. Herman Clarence), 15:166,n5
Riggs, Herman Clarence, 15:166,n5
Riggs, Lawrason, 16:5, 167,n1; 20:264,n1; 24:82,n1

Right-Hand Man: The Life of George W. Perkins (Garraty), 15:65n2; 24:346n2
Right of Sanctuary in England: A Study in Institutional History (Trenholme), 16:41,n4
Riis, Jacob August, 16:227n2
Riker, Adrian, 14:195; 15:388; 16:5; 19:171,n1
Riker, Thad Weed, 14:474
Rimini, Italy, 14:246
Rinaldi, E. A., Madam, 15:228, 230, 241, 265, 267, 300
Rinaldi, Ninni, 15:267, 275-76, 300
Rio Grande, N. J., 23:274
Riordan, William L., 21:303n2
Rise and Growth of American Politics: A Sketch of Constitutional Development (Ford), 14:14; 17:619; 18:208n5, 576; 20:35n3, 198; 22:399,n1
Rise of the Greek Epic: Being a Course of Lectures Delivered at Harvard University (Murray), 17:106n2
Ritchie, Richmond Thackeray, 15:97,n4
Ritter, Frederick W., 14:475
Ritz-Carlton Hotel, New York City, 22:474, 477
River Duddon (Wordsworth), 18:371n6
Riverdale, New York, 23:193, 214, 479
Rivers, William James, 14:342,n5
Rivers family of Charleston, S. C., 19:229,n3
Rives, George Lockhart, 14:289-90; 25:587,n1
Road to the White House (Link), see Wilson: The Road to the White House
Roanoke Camp of Confederate Veterans, 22:604n2
Roanoke College, 22:604,n1,2
Roanoke Times, 22:604n2
Robb, James Hampden, 22:40,n29
Robbia, Luca della, 15:353
Robbins, Adam O., 23:411,n2
Robbins, Edmund Yard, 14:5,n3, 137,n3, 144, 297, 326, 327, 394; 15:136, 301; 17:408
Robbins, Emeline Place Hayward (Mrs. Edmund Yard), 15:136, 301, 321
Robbins, Wilford Lash, 17:125,n2; 18:229
Roberdeau, Roger Courtland, 23:268,n4
Robert M. LaFollette (LaFollette and LaFollette), 22:412n2
Roberts, Algernon Brooke, 16:5
Roberts, Frank Calvin, 16:5
Roberts, Guy Hall, 16:388,n2
Roberts, Henry Chalmers, 25:448,n1
Roberts, Jonathan William, 15:51,n1, 52
Roberts, William Henry, 14:253; 16:228,n2; 17:28-29,n1,2,3; 18:339,n1; 19:51,n1
Robertson, Daniel Leslie, 16:243
Robertson, James William, 18:590,n2
Robertson, John Charles, 23:507,n4
Robinson, Belle R., 14:406n3

Robinson, Charles Alexander, **14**:471,n4; **15**:14

Robinson, Charles S., **15**:154,n1, 187, 385; **17**:351n2, 352

Robinson, Corinne, **16**:243

Robinson, Corinne Roosevelt (Mrs. Douglas), **16**:243

Robinson, Douglas, **16**:243

Robinson, Frederic H., **16**:313,n2

Robinson, Harvey L., **15**:22,n2, 154,n1

Robinson, Joseph Haswell, **17**:241-42,n1

Robinson, Lois Ball (Mrs. William S.), **18**:390,n6; **19**:313,n3; **23**:81,n2

Robinson, Lydia S. M., **20**:149,n2

Robinson, Lydia Biddle (Mrs. Moncure), **20**:133,n8, 139, 149, 179, 181,n4; **22**:324,n2

Robinson, Morgan Poitiaux, **15**:32,n1

Robinson, Philip Ely, **16**:465, 508; **17**:408

Robinson, Stewart MacMaster, **20**:380,- n2, 381

Robinson, William Courtland, **20**:380- 81,n1

Robinson, William S., **18**:390n6; **19**: 313,n1; **23**:81,n2

Roby, Henry John, **18**:368,n7, 383, 388, 396, 413

Rochambeau, Jean Baptiste Donatien de Vimeur, comte de, **14**:352

Rochelle, Ill., **24**:301

Rochester, N. Y., **19**:707; **23**:481,n2

Rochester, University of, **16**:240

Rochester Movement (Ward), **23**:481n1

Rockefeller, John Davison I, **14**:454n1; **15**:129n1; **16**:303; **17**:51n1, 63n2, 102; **19**:65, 65n3, 424, 453, 544,n3; **20**:141n1, 209,n7; **23**:118n4, 583

Rockefeller, John Davison, Jr., **19**:65,n2, 453

Rockefeller Foundation, **19**:544n3

Rockwell, William Locke, **25**:467,n3

Rockwood, Charles Greene, Jr., **14**: 277, 326, 327; **15**:14; **16**:17, 27, 130, 245, 246

Rockwood, Hettie H. Smith (Mrs. Charles Greene, Jr.), **16**:17

Rocky Mountain Club of Princeton alumni, **14**:447; **20**:84,n4; **22**:375

*Rocky Mountain News, see* Denver *Rocky Mountain News*

Rodin, Auguste, **19**:36

Roe, Gilbert E., **22**:412n2

Roebling, Cornelia Witsell Farrow (Mrs. Washington Augustus, II), **19**:229,n1, 230n4, 312; **20**:127,n1; **22**:583n1; **23**:50n4, 80, 174, 184, 220, 241, 257

Roebling, Ferdinand William, Sr., **23**: 223,n4

Roebling, John Augustus, II, **18**:472n1; **21**:450,n1; **23**:109n4

Roebling, Siegfried, **18**:472,n1

Roebling, Washington Augustus, **21**: 450n1; **22**:583,n1; **23**:50n4, 174

Rogers (nurse), **23**:83,n16

Rogers, Armoth D., **23**:268,n8

Rogers, Arthur Kenyon, **14**:547n2

Rogers, G. Tracy, **21**:343n10

Rogers, Guy Wright, **16**:243

Rogers, Henry Wade, **24**:381,n3

Rogers, Howard Jason, **14**:395n1; **15**: 60,n2, 491n

Rogers, James Edwin Thorold, **14**:558,n1

Rogers, James Slocum, **21**:153,n1

Rogers, Robert William, **19**:381n4

Rogue River University Club, **23**:63

Rogue River Valley, **23**:62-63

Rohlfs, Mrs. Charles, *see* Green, Anna Katherine

Rollins, Philip Ashton, **20**:64,n1, 263

Romagna, Jack, **25**:xii, xiii

Roman Catholic Church, **18**:638; **19**:60, 264,n1, 266, 743; **20**:329; **21**:180, 319; **22**:277, 305, 491; **23**:94; **24**:294; **25**:63,n3, 452; clergy, **23**:584

Roman Catholic voters, **21**:541-42

Roman fever, **15**:323

Rome, **14**:246; **15**:302, 303, 306n3,4, 308, 310, 338, 339, 354, 358; **20**:400; **21**:428; Appian Way, **15**:251; Barbarini Palace, **15**:241; Catacomb of St. Calixtus, **15**:251; Corsini Gallery, **15**:250; Forum, **15**:268, 269, 306; Fountain of Trevi, **15**:297; Museo e galleria Borghese, **15**:251; Palatine Hill, **15**:274, 298; Pincian Hill, **15**:251; Pensione Rinaldi, **15**:339; Presbyterian Church, **15**:241; Protestant Cemetery, **15**:250; St. Peter's basilica, **15**:241, 338; Sta. Maria Maggiore, **15**:276; Sistine Chapel, **15**:250, 251, 266, 274, 298; United Free Church of Scotland, **15**:273-74n3; Vatican Musuem, **15**: 266, 268, 274, 298, 322; EAW at, **15**:228, 240, 241, 244, 246, 250-51, 264, 265-67, 270, 273, 274, 275, 297, 298, 300, 303, 306, 334, 338

Rome, Ga., **23**:655; **25**:569

*Romeo and Juliet* (Shakespeare), **21**: 335n2

Rood, Henry Edward, **16**:470,n1

Roosevelt, Edith Kermit Carow (Mrs. Theodore), **15**:142; **16**:213, 243

Roosevelt, Franklin Delano, **22**:161n1

Roosevelt, Kermit, **18**:546,n3

Roosevelt, Theodore, **14**:8, 147-48,n1, 148, 193, 265, 303, 337-38, 348, 358,n1, 374, 387, 419, 420, 437, 454, 492; **15**:60n1, 61,n1, 127, 142, 147, 172, 471, 539,n3; **16**:15n1, 50n3, 172- 73, 175, 206, 213, 233, 235, 242-43, 319, 531n3, 559n3, 569; **17**:92n2, 96n1, 175, 247, 459, 490, 513, 518-19, 521, 584n1; **18**:119, 186n4, 265n1, 269, 293, 299, 352, 384, 386,n1,2, 546; **19**:82, 479, 518,n5, 746,n2; **20**:202; **21**:47n1, 124, 129, 132, 136, 147,n1, 154, 160, 176, 252n6, 275n2, 284,n3, 294, 322, 322n1, 475, 563, 584n1, 591, 598, 599,

609n1, 621; **22:**44n3, 47, 48, 52, 59,n3, 140, 164, 207n4, 209, 285, 375, 427n1, 429, 500, 536,n3, 562; **23:**21, 23,n1, 40,n1, 42, 53, 64, 69, 105, 106, 186, 223, 234n5, 238, 243n3, 287n2, 311n4, 500-501,n5, 516, 573, 593, 597, 610, 615, 616, 655; **24:**8, 9, 61, 67, 114, 165, 185, 187, 220, 221, 316-17, 362, 368, 373, 391, 407, 412,n3, 435, 444, 446, 447, 448,n1, 450n1, 494, 495, 497, 499, 502, 518, 531, 535, 537, 546, 550, 553, 560, 566-67,n2, 571; **25:**20, 22, 24, 51-52, 55-56, 57n1, 62, 71-72, 111,n2, 113, 124-25, 141, 149, 150, 192, 204, 214, 215, 225, 233, 248, 260, 271, 277, 286n1, 287, 323-24, 325, 352, 361, 366, 372, 374, 382, 386, 388-89, 391, 394, 407, 411, 453, 526, 581; Arizona, **25:**271-72,n3; assassination attempt, **25:**418,n1, 421, 423, 424-25; campaign contributions (1904), **25:**396n3; campaign contributions (1912), **24:**254; candidacy, **24:**137,n3; *Collier's* support of, **25:**449n1; congratulatory message to WW, **25:**521; electoral vote, **25:**518n1; and W. J. McDonald, **25:**423,n1; and J. C. McReynolds, **25:**557; monopoly, **25:**353, 380-81; Panic of 1907, **25:**384n7; Pennsylvania vote, **25:**527n1; platform, **24:**554; popular vote, **25:**518n1; resumes campaigning, **25:**461; speech preparation, **25:**361; social workers, **25:**312; straw vote of American missionaries in Japan, **25:**390; tariff, **25:**334, 380, 410; trusts, **25:**261-62, 381,n6, 384,n7; woman suffrage, **25:**26, 29; portrait, **25:**illustration section
Roosevelt Borough, N. J., **21:**560
*Roosevelt Policy* (T. Roosevelt), **23:**501n5
Root, Elihu, **15:**145,n2, 237, 408; **16:**47n1, 243, 533, 569,n1, 571; **17:**92n2, 226n1, 227; **18:**546, 626n1; **21:**166, 615, 615n2; **22:**184, 514n1; **25:**285,n1, 461, 587n3
Root, Oren (Hamilton College, 1833), **16:**47n1
Root, Oren (Hamilton College, 1856), **16:**45-47,n1
Root, Robert Kilburn, **16:**37, 70-71,n1, 132, 256; **17:**408
Roper, William Winston, **20:**487n1, 547-48,n1, 560; **23:**448, 449
Rosalsky, Otto A., **22:**183,n3
Rosebery, Archibald Philip Primrose, 5th Earl of, **23:**292,n1
Roselle, N. J., **23:**468
Rosemary Hall, Greenwich, Conn., **17:**556
Rosenkrans, Martin, **23:**465,n1
Rosewater, Victor, **15:**182,n1; **18:**639-40; **23:**99,n1
Ross, Millard Fillmore, **20:**563,n2, 565n; **22:**101,n3, 145, 328; **23:**265

Ross, William Borland, **23:**535
*Roster of the Round Table Club, New York,* **14:**306n3
Rothay Bridge, Westmorland, **18:**379
Rothay Holme, Westmorland, **18:**369
Rothay Hotel, Grasmere, Westmorland, **14:**523; **18:**364n1, 370, 373, 375, 394, 396, 402, 413
Rothay River, Westmorland, **16:**437n, 480, 493; **18:**371
Rothwell, Laura P., Mrs., **21:**115
Rotterdam, **15:**441
Round Table Club, New York City, **14:**306,n3, 381n1, 397; **17:**417n1; **19:**23,n4, 33, 500n2, 552, 658; **25:**587
Roundtree, Irwin William Langston, **15:**462n2
Rouse, Ruth, **22:**385n2
Rousseau, Jean-Jacques, **19:**315n2
Rowe, Leo Stanton, **17:**555,n1, 619; **18:**259,n1; **21:**614,n1
Rowland, Reginald, **22:**480,n1
Roxbury, N. J., **21:**385
Royal County Hotel, Durham, England, **14:**525,n4
Royal Hotel, Edinburgh, **16:**444, 452
Royal Military College of Canada, **16:**159
Royce, Josiah, **15:**116, **18:**378
Rozell, William, **24:**543
Rudd, Edward Huntting, **15:**248n1; **16:**384
Rudolph, Frederick, **15:**291n26
Rue, John Davison, Jr., **16:**465, 512
Ruef, Abraham, **21:**342,n5
Ruffin, Edmund, **17:**620,n1
Rugby, Warwickshire, Wilsons in, **14:**530
Rugby School, **17:**327
rule of reason, **23:**235n3, 284, 361n3
Rulon-Miller, John, **16:**336,n5
Rulon-Miller, John, Jr., **16:**336n5
Rulon-Miller, Sumner, **16:**336n5
Runnymede, Surrey, **18:**70, 73, 104, 174; **23:**15
Rupp, Laurence Henry, **24:**138,n1
Rush, Benjamin, M.D., **17:**249
rushbearing (English ceremony), **18:**378,n6, 383, 391, 407
Rushforth, Gordon McNeil, **14:**246,n5
Ruskin, John, **15:**223n2, 358, 359,n4, 365,n1, 476, 479, 499
Ruspoli, Emanuele, Principe di Poggio Suasa, **15:**274n4
Russell, Albertina Pyne (Mrs. Archibald Douglas), **15:**425,n3, 426, 527; **16:**21n1, 323,n2; **19:**166-67
Russell, Archibald Douglas, **15:**301n4, 379n1, 426; **16:**5, 21n1, 175, 312,n2, 500; **17:**20-21, 36-37, 71-72, 169, 172, 219, 352n2, 411,n2, 564, 595, 600; **18:**286, 301, 458, 515; **19:**132, 439, 711, 712; **20:**254,n1, 362,n3, 410, 413, 484, 489, 490

Russell, Charles Edward, **21**:342n7
Russell, Daniel, Jr., **14**:253
Russell, Henry Norris, **14**:112; **16**:80,n1, 81-83,n2; **18**:578-79; **19**:139
Russell, Isaac K., **25**:107, 114, 360n2
Russell, Joseph Ballister, **20**:145,n2, 177, 180
Russell, Lucius Thompson, **20**:288,n1; **22**:137
Russell, May Pomeroy (Mrs. Frank), **22**:100,n1
Russell, William Eustis, **20**:145,n2
Russell Sage Foundation, **22**:177; **25**:310,n1, 311,n5
Russia, **23**:583-87; **25**:54, 576-77, 610; government, **18**:87; Jewish-Americans in, **23**:191,n2, 329
Russia, Tsar of, **15**:471
Russian-American Commercial treaty of 1832, **23**:192n2, 585-86
Russo-Japanese War, **15**:149-50,n1,3; **16**:29, 50n3
Rutgers College, **14**:167,n2; **15**:273; **16**:239, 335n3, 427; **20**:446; **21**:438; **23**:440; Alumni Association, **17**:31,n1; **21**:620
Rutherford, N. J., **21**:141, 608; Town Hall, **21**:446; WW campaign speech, **21**:412, 446-49
Rutledge, Edward, **17**:249
Ryan, Thomas Fortune, **16**:276n1, 533,-n8, 534; **17**:65, 66, 93,n1; **22**:39,n22, 160,n2, 184, 274, 282n1, 393, 429; **23**:603n1; **24**:60,n1, 78, 80, 81,n1, 486, 529, 531
Ryan, Thomas J., **23**:229,n2; **24**:393
Rydal, Ambleside, Westmorland, **16**:430, 431, 432, 433, 434, 435n1, 435, 436, 437, 438, 439, 440, 441, 442, 443, 444, 445, 447, 448, 449, 450, 451, 453, 454, 463, 469, 470, 479, 480, 485, 493; **17**:366; **18**:313, 356, 364, 368, 379n8, 389, 416, 417
Rydal Mount, Westmorland, **18**:368, 369, 376; Wilsons at, **14**:521
Ryder, Arthur William, **14**:25n2

Sachs, Julius, **14**:267-68
Sachs, Samuel, **22**:39,n20
Sackett, Clarence, **21**:502n, 518n, 536n; **22**:50, 171, 200, 215
Sackett, William E., **20**:566n5; **21**:343n9; **23**:295n5
Sadler, Wilbur Fisk, Jr., **22**:54, 482-83,n1, 532; **23**:190,n1, 194, 223,n3, 241; **24**:475-76
safe and sane, words much abused by standpatters, **22**:594
Sag Harbor, L. I., Pierson High School, **18**:309,n1
Sagaponack, L. I., **14**:7,n1, 95
Sage, Margaret Olivia Slocum (Mrs. Russell), **17**:240,n1; **18**:34,n1, 35, 217,

256-57, 286, 290, 302, 302-303, 304, 309, 317, 334, 380, 481,n1, 483, 491, 508, 511, 514, 515, 554-55, 557, 558, 565, 569, 580-81; **19**:80, 533n2, 683, 728n1; **20**:191, 495, 496, 497, 498, 498-99, 507, 510
Sage, Russell, **17**:241n1, 243, 245, 265
St. Andrews, University of, **15**:421; **16**:507
Saint Andrew's Golf Club, Chauncey, Westchester County, N. Y., **19**:480,n1
St. Andrew's Society of the State of New York, **15**:50, 58, 67
St. Augustine, Fla., **17**:8; **23**:550, 553, 554, 555, 556, 563
St. Denis Hotel, New York, **15**:79n1, 328, 500, 505
St. Enoch Hotel, Glasgow, **16**:494
Saint-Gaudens, Augustus, **14**:306n3
St. Hubert's, Essex Co., N. Y., **17**:220n1, 246, 261, 268, 270, 280, 282, 283, 284, 286, 287, 292, 295, 297, 309, 334, 338, 339, 341, 342, 343, 344, 349, 365, 366, 368, 369, 370, 373, 375; **18**:352n3; **19**:321; **21**:13,n4, 49-50
St. John, William W., **21**:581-83,n1; **22**:73,n3, 76-77, 81, 86n1, 137,n2, 155, 200
St. John-Stevas, Norman, **22**:194n4
St. John's College, Cambridge, **14**:530; **15**:410,n3, 421; **19**:739
St. Louis, Mo., **20**:43; **23**:360, 459, 517, 549; City Club, **22**:276; Civic League, **18**:516-17, 532-33, 567; **19**:81-97; International Congress of Arts and Sciences, 1904, **14**:394,n1; **15**:105-106, 116, 157, 433-34,n2,3, 468n3, 469, 472n1, 478, 491n; Jefferson Hotel, **19**:101; Louisiana Purchase (or Universal) Exposition, 1904, **14**:395n1, 434,n1, 437, 439; **15**:60,n1, 105-106, 318, 443, 463, 472n1; Normal High School, **16**:258; Princeton alumni, **14**:436, 439,n1, 447; **18**:568; **19**:146, 505-506; **22**:262, 283; Southern Hotel, **22**:262; University Club, **14**:431, 433, 434, 436; **19**:97; Virginia Society, **18**:567, 568, 593; **19**:97; WW address, **15**:472-91; **19**:81-97, 101, 101-102; **20**:211, 212, 220, 237, 238, 243-44, 252, 252-53, 254, 256, 262, 271, 284, 291-96, 303, 304,n2, 306-307n1, 311, 312, 320, 321, 322, 387, 410; **25**:395-99; WW in, **14**:431, 434, 436, 437, 439, 440, 448; **15**:433, 468n3, 469; **22**:210,n4, 211, 260, 262-63, 263-72, 272, 276-77, 283, 292
*St. Louis Globe-Democrat*, **14**:434n, 436n
St. Louis, Iron Mountain & Southern Railroad, **14**:145-46
*St. Louis Post-Dispatch*, **15**:20n1; **17**:247n1,3; **19**:97n; **20**:306,n1; **22**:262, 263n; **24**:573n,n1; **25**:124
St. Louis *Republic*, **15**:318
St. Louis *Star*, **15**:318

*St. Mark's Rest: The History of Venice...* (Ruskin), **15**:359n4, 476-77

St. Mary's Hall (Hoboken, N. J.), **25**:213n1

St. Mary's School, Raleigh, N. C., **16**:470, 481-82, 526; **17**:33, 344n1

St. Paul, Minn., **22**:519n4; **23**:88; Association of Commerce, **23**:84; Minnesota Club, **14**:424, 426, 445; Princeton alumni, **14**:424, 426, 445, 447; **19**:146; St. Paul Hotel, **23**:86, 87; WW in, **14**:421, 423, 424, 426, 445; *see also* Minneapolis

*St. Paul Dispatch*, **23**:95n

St. Paul Hotel, St. Paul, Minn., **23**:86, 87

*St. Paul Pioneer-Press*, **23**:86n, 92n; **25**:184n

St. Paul's School, Concord, N. H., **16**:252; **17**:128; **18**:436-37,n1, 450, 450-51; **19**:201, 222, 226-28, 229, 238, 239, 390; WW address, **19**:226-28

St. Peter's College, Jersey City, **22**:400n1

Salem, Mass., **14**:4; **19**:225, 225n1,2; **20**:464, 465, 470, 561; WW in, **14**:57, 65

Salem, N. J., **21**:463; **23**:391; Grand Opera House, **21**:423,n1, 463; **23**:393; WW campaign speech, **21**:412, 423-33, 463

Salem, Oregon, **23**:66, 67

Salem County, N. J., **21**:584n1, **23**:391, 393, 395; **25**:582

*Salem* (N. J.) *Sunbeam*, **21**:463

Salerno: Maiori, Minora, EAW at, **15**:236

Salisbury, N. H., **18**:632-33

Salisbury, Robert Arthur Talbot Gascoyne-Cecil, 3rd Marquis of, **14**:233-34; **15**:238

Salisbury, Wilts, **15**:396; cathedral, **14**:534; Wilsons in, **14**:533-34

Sallust (Gaius Sallustius Crispus), **19**:597

Salmon, Edward Seiler, **21**:105-106,n1

Salmon, J. R., **22**:173n1

Salomé (Strauss), **20**:173

Salt Lake City, Princeton alumni, **19**:146

Salter, Harry Broughton, **21**:226,n1

Salvation Army, **22**:386

Sampey, John Richard, **16**:332,n1

San Antonio, Texas, **16**:252

San Antonio *Express*, **23**:231n1

San Bernardino, Cal., **23**:44

San Damiano, EAW in, **15**:338

San Francisco, **22**:519n4, 533; **23**:41, 41n6, 42; Argonaut Hotel, **23**:53; Fairmont Hotel, **23**:53, 54, 55; Harvard Club, **23**:54, 55; Princeton Club, **23**:54, 55, 60; school segregation, **16**:558,n3,4; traction graft, **21**:341-42,n5; University Club, **23**:53; WW in, **23**:49, 50-58; Yale Club, **23**:54, 55

*San Francisco Chronicle*, **23**:55n, 60n

*San Francisco Examiner*, **23**:57n5, 58n; **24**:383n1, 391, 520-21

San Jose, Ill., **24**:292

Sandanwede, **24**:452, 466, 552; **25**:21, 461

Sanders Theatre (Cambridge, Mass.), **24**:93

Sanderson, Edward Frederick, **17**:128,n8

Sands, James Hoban, **16**:243

Sandys, Sir Edwin, **14**:352

Sanford, Henry Gansevoort, **19**:156

Sangamon County Courthouse, Springfield, Ill., **25**:390n1, 391

Santa Cruz, Cal., *Surf*, **14**:16,n3

Santiago Bay, Battle of, **22**:371,n5

Saratoga, Battle of, **14**:281

Sardis, excavation of, **17**:102, 108, 111-12,n1

Sargent, John Singer, **14**:381; **15**:238,n2

*Satires* (Horace), **19**:594, 597

Sato, Shosuke, **22**:139,n1

Satterlee, Henry Yates, **14**:191, 192

Satterthwaite, Pennington, **15**:414-15, 418

Satterwhite, Benjamin Offutt, **15**:7

*Saturday Evening Post*, **17**:240,n2

*Saturday Review* (London), **15**:148, 162,n1

Saulsbury, Annie Melby Ponder, **25**:52n1

Saulsbury, Willard, **23**:436,n1, 285, 329-30, 353-54, 356, 379-80, 382, 447, 450, 469, 471; **25**:52, 425,n2; portrait, illustration section, Vol. 24

Saunders, Mrs. (Mother of Nancy Saunders Toy), **14**:406,n3

Saussy, Frederick Tupper, **23**:558,n11

Savage, Charles Winfred, **20**:539

Savage, Minot Judson, **16**:230-31, 232-33

Savannah, Ga., **22**:543, 576; **23**:239, 553, 554, 556, 557; **24**:268, 349-51, 387; Ardsley Park, **23**:557; Bonaventure Cemetery, **23**:557,n5; Chatham County Court House, **23**:557, 558; Chatham Crescent, **23**:557; Citizens & Southern Bank, **23**:557; Cotton Exchange, **23**:557; Hibernian Society, **22**:466,n4, 532n6, 543,n2; Independent Presbyterian Church and Manse, **23**:557; Ocean Steamship Terminal, **23**:557; WW in, **23**:557-58

*Savannah Morning News*, **23**:557, 557,-n6

*Savannah Press*, **22**:466n4, 491n6, 516-n1, 543,n1; **23**:557, 558n; **24**:306,n2, 351n

Savanorola, Girolamo, **15**:347

Savoy Hotel, New York City, **14**:253; **16**:243

Sawyer (of Savannah), **23**:557

Sawyer, Walter Hulme, **19**:181-82n1, 184, 185n1

Saybrook, Conn., Princeton alumni, **20**:320

Saybrook Junction, Conn., **19**:307-308

Sayce, Archibald Henry, **16**:93,n2
Sayers, Joseph Draper, **23**:458n1
Sayles, John, **23**:559,n1
Sayre, John Nevin, **19**:529-30,n1
Says Bosses Named Wilson (N. Y. *Evening Post*), **25**:111,n2
Sca Fell, Cumberland, **18**:374
Scale How (Miss Mason's School) Ambleside, **18**:415
Scarborough, John, **14**:192
Scarborough-on-Hudson, N. Y., **21**:38; **22**:187n2
scarlatina, **14**:196
Schaeffer, John Nevin, **19**:678
Schaffhauser, Émile, **15**:434n2
Scharnagle, Barbara, **22**:356,n3
Schauffler, Adolphus Frederick, **14**:114; **19**:543,n1, 547-48
Schauffler, William Gray, M.D., **22**:550n2; **23**:183,n1, 216
Schedule K, *see under* Tariff
Schellinger, Ralph, **23**:273,n5
Schenectady, N. Y., **19**:229; First Presbyterian Church, **15**:496,n1; WW address, **19**:231-37
Schenley, Mary E. Carson (Mrs. Edward W. H.), **15**:46,n1
Schenley Hotel, Pittsburgh, **16**:32; **17**:64; **20**:363, 366
Schiff, Jacob Henry, **14**:298,n1
Schirmer, Rudolph Edward, **14**:26-27,n1; **16**:210n1; **18**:355,n2; **21**:617
Schlesinger, Arthur M., Jr., **25**:57n1
Schlesinger, Louis, **22**:39,n15
Schmedeman, Albert George, **23**:254,n4
Schmitz, Adolph John, **22**:57
Schmitz, Eugene E., **21**:342n5
Schomburgk (Sir Robert) Line, **22**:11
School of Fine Arts (Paris) *see* École des Beaux Arts
Schools—The Main Spring of Democracy (White), **19**:163,n2
Schroeder, Alwin, **15**:153n2
Schroeder, James Langdon, **16**:535,n4; **17**:219, 220, 221, 271, 272, 387, 409; **18**:285
Schroeder, Nathan Southwick, **15**:252
Schuetzen Park (N. J.), **25**:47, 48
Schulz, Carl Gustav, **19**:542-43,n1
Schumaker, Isaac Ripple, **17**:557
Schurman, Jacob Gould, **19**:416,n3; **21**:611,n1; **22**:30, 130, 359, 399-400; **23**:584; **24**:503, 504
Schuyler, Philip, **16**:495,n1
Schwab, Charles Michael, **14**:450
Schwab, John Christopher, **14**:344,n8
Schwartz, Anna J., **15**:29n1
*Science* (New York), **14**:22
*Scientific American*, **16**:173n1
Scotch-Irish, **22**:418
Scotland, **18**:393; city government, **23**: 149, 166, 579; self-government, **21**:439
Scott, Austin, **14**:398n2; **15**:180, 204, 273, 324, 378, 391, 392; **16**:538; **23**:440

Scott, Charles Ernest, **19**:65-66,n1, 177-78
Scott, Dred, **17**:316
Scott, Francis, **15**:61; **19**:171,n2
Scott, Sir Giles Gilbert, **18**:352-53
Scott, Hugh Lenox, **20**:391,n1, 429
Scott, Mary Blanchard, **15**:323,n4
Scott, Mary Merrill (Mrs. Hugh Lenox), **20**:391, 429
Scott (of Nashville), **23**:288,n1
Scott, Richard Carter, **22**:383,n4
Scott, T. Fraser, **16**:88,n1
Scott, Thomas McGee, **23**:269,n9
Scott, William, **16**:5
Scott, William Berryman (Wick), **14**: 126,n1, 127, 128, 326, 395; **15**:56, 73n3, 74, 264,n2, 323n4, 425,n2; **16**:92, 97n2, 157,n6,7, 507n1, 536; **17**:231-32, 301; **19**:69, 70; **20**:391n1
Scott, William Earl Dodge, **15**:411,n2,3
Scott, William H., **21**:21n1
Scottish-Americans, **25**:97
Scranton, Pa., **23**:356; First Presbyterian Church, **16**:537,n1; Princeton alumni, **19**:146; WW campaign speech, **25**:221-31
*Scranton Times*, **25**:221n2, 231n
Scribner, Arthur Hawley, **15**:184; **16**: 379-80,n1
Scribner, Charles (Princeton 1875), **14**:79, 85, 303-304; **15**:184, 421, 569; **16**:5, 37-38,n2; **17**:351, 351n2; **18**:420; **19**:390, 391, 455-56, 504,n2; **20**:543, 573; **21**:104, 144; **22**:51-52
Scribner, Charles (Princeton 1913), **19**: 390,n3, 391
*Scribner's Magazine*, **19**:347n, 348, 390, 391, 503,n1, 504, 530, 536; **20**:133, 148n, 161n, 172,n2, 177, 180, 378n1
Scribner's Sons, Charles, **14**:104,n1, 136; **15**:223n1, 238, 300; **17**:352n2; **18**:517
Scudder, Edward Wallace, **21**:175-76,n1, 388-89, 449,n1, 450; **22**:233-34
Scudder, Wallace McIlvaine, **22**:225-26, 245, 357
Scully, Michael Welsh, **21**:131,n1
Scully, Thomas Joseph, **21**:213,n2; **24**:287,n1, 481; **25**:511
Sea Girt, N. J., **23**:10,n2, 30, 194, 213, 214, 215, 217, 218, 220, 221, 224, 225, 226, 232, 234n1, 239, 241, 242, 244, 250, 254, 257, 258, 266, 267, 283, 284, 285, 286, 290, 302, 305, 312, 313, 316, 327, 329, 330, 339, 340, 341n1, 357, 361, 367, 424; **24**:466, 474, 481-82, 488, 491, 501, 505, 522, 545, 586; **25**:27,n1, 43, 66; Camp Wilson, New Jersey National Guard, **23**:225, 256; celebration, **24**:527; Charles McCarthy, **24**:554n1; Governor's Day at Sea Girt, **23**:250,n2, 367, 628; photographs of WW in, Vol. 24, Vol. 25; WW remarks to Democratic women, **25**:44-45; WW remarks to Italian Americans, **25**:107-109

Seal Harbor, Maine, **16**:446, 448; **20**:475
Seaman, Marjorie Luce (Mrs. William I.), **19**:425n1
Seaman, William I., **19**:425,n1
Searle, John Preston, **16**:335,n1
Seattle, **22**:519n4, 533; **23**:41, 60, 245,n2, 597; Commercial Club, **22**:416; Dreamland Pavilion, **23**:79; Press Club, **23**:79-80; Washington Hotel, **23**:78, 80; Wilson Club, **23**:598; WW in, **23**:76-81
*Seattle Daily Times*, **23**:78n, 80n
*Seattle Post-Intelligencer*, **23**:79n
Seaview, Wash., **21**:12
Secor Hotel, Toledo, Ohio, **18**:524
Secret Service, **25**:532
Seely, Fred Loring, **23**:328-29,n1
Seibold, Louis, **24**:512n1
Seignobos, Charles, **14**:338,n2
Seitz, Don Carlos, **22**:455
Selden, Charles Albert, **22**:101,n1, 127, 135, 287, 288, 307
Select Classical School (Augusta, Ga.), **25**:542n2
*Selected Letters of Cicero* (ed. Abbott), **18**:575
Seligman, Edwin Robert Anderson, **23**:516,n9
Selkirk, Scotland, **15**:410
Selleck, William Alson, **23**:96,n1
Selling, Benjamin, **23**:64,n9, 70
Sells, Cato, **23**:268, 509; **24**:254
Selma, Ala., WW address, **16**:72-73
Semple, James Lithgow, **14**:206,n1
Senate (N. J.), *see* New Jersey, Legislature
Senate (U. S.), *see* United States Congress, Senate
Senators, direct election of, **23**:235n3, 350, 369; **25**:6, 15, 237-39, 306
Sensenbrenner, Frank Jacob, **19**:494,n2
Sensenbrenner, John Stephen, **19**:495n2
Seth, James, **14**:26
Seth Pringle Pattison, Andrew, **15**:410,n8
*Seven Lamps of Architecture* (Ruskin), **15**:499,n4
Seventeen Hundred Rural Vote-Sellers (Blair), **23**:75n2
*Seventy Years of the Red-Fire Wagon from Tilden to Truman Through New Freedom and New Deal* (Guffey), **21**:623n
Sevier, Edith Rogers Love (Mrs. Joseph Ramsey), **23**:553,n3, 556
Sevier, Joseph Ramsey, **23**:553,n3, 556
Sewanee *see* University of the South
*Sewanee Review*, **18**:575
Sewald, William Henry, **17**:314, 320; **18**:110, 602
Sewickley, Pa., Edgeworth Club, **17**:617
Sexton *v.* the Newark District Telegraph Co., **23**:324n2
Seymour, Arthur B., **21**:520
Seymour, Edmund Bayly, Jr., **17**:383-84, 399

Seymour, Horatio, **21**:335
Seymour, Thomas Day, **17**:587,n1, 588
Seymour, Warren Ilsley, **20**:363,n1, 367, 373, 398
Shaeffer, Charles G., **16**:381
Shafer, Robert, **21**:16,n5
Shafroth, John Franklin, **22**:388n1, 584; **23**:21, 478; **25**:545,n1
Shakespeare, Anne Hathaway (Mrs. William), **14**:531
Shakespeare, William, **14**:259, 531; **15**:238,n1, 340, 397n4, 488; **16**:316, 445n3; **19**:35, 750, 751; **20**:161, 185, 555, 559,n3; **21**:335n2; **22**:270; **23**:16, 375
Shaler, Nathaniel Southgate, **17**:547n6
Shaler, Sophia Penn Page (Mrs. Nathaniel Southgate), **17**:547,n6
*Shall We Work or Be Worked? Being an Appeal to the Colored Republican Voters of Essex County . . .*, **21**:161n2
Shallcross, Thomas, **16**:225,n4
Shallenberger, Ashton Cokayne, **21**:622,n1
Shalvoy, Frank P., **22**:253,n4, 367,n1; **23**:333, 336, 337, 385, 388, 390
*Shame of the Cities* (Steffens), **16**:43n2
Shannon, Joseph Bernard, **24**:186,n4
Shannon, Thomas Berry, **22**:598-99,n1; **25**:21,n2
Sharpe, John C., **21**:476,n2
Sharpless, Isaac, **18**:67,n1, 459
Shaw, Albert, **16**:415,n1, 495-96; **18**:590,n2; **19**:155, 156, 597,n2, 606; **21**:300; **25**:581, 617
Shaw, Elsie Forrest (Mrs. Thomas), **18**:400,n7, 402
Shaw, James Prestley, M.D., **16**:33,n2
Shaw, John Irwin, **16**:5
Shaw, Leslie Mortier, **14**:515; **15**:29n1; **16**:433, 434; **17**:78n1
Shaw, Thomas, **18**:400,n6, 401, 401-402
Shaw, William B., **21**:300
Shaw, William Hudson, **18**:525,n4, 544
*She Stoops to Conquer* (Goldsmith), **14**:503; **20**:172
Shea, Joseph Bernard, **15**:570, 573; **16**:5, 32,n1, 33, 424n1; **17**:199n3, 206, 212, 382, 385; **18**:51-52; **19**:117-18, 119, 131, 158, 211, 268, 418, 437, 439, 544, 608-609, 698, 703, 707, 711, 735; **20**:6n, 19-20, 23, 63, 224, 225, 245, 247, 262, 321, 354, 361, 387, 388, 392, 404, 458, 460, 476, 491; **21**:81-82
Sheehan, William Francis, **22**:161n1, 359,n3, 361, 429, 429n1, 430n1
Sheldon, Charles Monroe, **19**:252,n1
Sheldon, Edward Wright, **14**:206; **15**:219-20, 351n3, 388, 569, 573; **16**:5; **17**:89-90, 94, 595; **18**:9n2, 64, 218, 225, 227, 236, 247-50, 248,n2, 250-54, 261-62, 285, 458, 592, 625; **19**:27-28, 122, 238, 266-68, 268-69, 293, 305, 306, 320-21, 354, 397, 407-10, 412-13, 418, 426, 433-34, 436, 437-38, 439, 440,

Sheldon, Edward Wright, (*cont.*)
444-45, 452, 455, 456, 482, 501, 609, 631, 632, 633-34, 649, 655-56, 657, 658, 672, 698, 699, 707, 709, 711, 730-31, 732, 733, 735, 752, 753; **20:**7n, 14, 16-17, 51-52, 61-63, 63, 68-69, 76, 105, 118-19, 128, 130, 137-38, 144, 174, 182, 183, 190-91, 191, 208, 209, 211-14, 219, 220, 221-22, 223, 224-25, 225, 226, 227-28, 228, 236-37, 237-38, 238-39, 241, 245, 246, 252, 254, 270-71, 283, 284, 321-24, 354, 354n1, 355, 361, 362, 393, 403, 425, 426, 427-28, 428, 431, 432, 433, 445, 454-55, 455,n1,2, 456-57, 458, 460-61, 474, 476-77, 479-81, 481, 483, 485n1, 486, 488-90, 491, 493, 510, 542-43, 544, 551, 551-52, 552, 554, 561, 572-73, 576, 579; **21:**143, 298, 353, 362n1, 385n1, 594; **22:**13, 165, 177, 186-87; **23:**594; **25:**109n2, 110n5

Sheldon, Merriam Ward, **19:**252,n2,3
Sheldon, Wilmon Henry, **16:**131, 249; **17:**408; **19:**676
Shelley, Percy Bysshe, **14:**503, 531
Shepard, Edward Morse, **15:**207,n5; **22:**125,n2, 161n1, 287, 289, 361; **24:**472,-n2
Shepard, James Edward, **19:**399-400,n1; **22:**98-99,n1
Shepardson, Francis Wayland, **14:**248-52
Shepherd, Henry Elliot, **19:**150,n1; **20:**31,n2, 584
Shepherd, William Robert, **22:**469n3
Shepperd, Gwynn T., **16:**290, 543-44
Sherer, William, **14:**298,n1
Sherley, Joseph Swagar, **24:**80,n2
Sherman, James Schoolcraft, **19:**65n4, 363n1; **21:**252n6; **23:**521
Sherman, John, **24:**394, 449
Sherman, William Tecumseh, **19:**34
Sherman Antitrust Act of 1890, **18:**48, 50, 265; **21:**505; **23:**55n3, 118, 118n5, 120, 157n1, 361n2,3, 370, 408, 447, 504n6, 593; **24:**89n3, 196, 394, 395, 449, 549; **25:**10, 58; Benjamin M. Anderson, Jr., on, **25:**420; Louis D. Brandeis on, **25:**290, 292, 293, 294, 295, 299, 300, 301, 302; John Bates Clark on, **25:**420
Sherman Hotel (Chicago), **24:**303, 304-n1, 307
*Shield of Phi Kappa Psi*, **14:**91,n1,5
Shields, Charles Woodruff, **14:**258; **15:**491,n2, 544,n1,3, 556-57; **22:**425,n2
Shields, Edmund Claude, **24:**484,n3
Ship that Found Herself (Kipling), **15:**537; **20:**135,n4
Shipley, Arthur Everett, **15:**409-10,n1; **16:**23,n8, 428,n1
Shipman, Henry Robinson, **16:**84, 88, 92, 104, 131, 251, 306; **17:**408; **18:**271, 294; **19:**613, 619; **20:**153,n8, 173

Shipp, Margaret Busbee, **23:**655n1
Shively, Benjamin Franklin, **25:**327,n4
shoe manufacture, **25:**200,n3,4, 207-208; Louis D. Brandeis, **25:**296-97, 303
Shoemaker, Lynden Brown, **16:**465
Shoemaker, Samuel Moor, **15:**343n1
Shope, Bella Wilson (Mrs. William Krebs), first cousin of WW, **15:**166,n3
Shoreby (Bermuda), **25:**556,n1
Shoreham Hotel, Washington, D. C., **20:**211, 225; **22:**20; **23:**566; **24:**17
Shorey, Paul, **14:**429,n3; **17:**173,n1
short ballot, **19:**510f, 756, 756n1; **20:**32f, 205f; **23:**25, 71-72, 169, 371, 456, 457
Short Ballot League, **22:**258
Short Ballot Organization, **19:**307, 311, 419-20,n5, 446-47, 510, 553, 579, 661, 756; **20:**32-43; **22:**59, 197n2
*Short History of British Colonial Policy* (Egerton), **14:**443,n3
*Short History of Rome* (Abbot), **18:**575
*Short History of the American People* (Turpin), **19:**273n1
*Short History of the English People* (Green), **14:**310, 340, 350, 516
*Short History of the Hebrews to the Roman Period* (Ottley), **16:**400,n1
*Shorter Catechism* (Westminster Assembly of Divines), **17:**347n1; **23:**379-80
Shoulthwaite Fell and Rock, Westmorland, **18:**395
Showerman, Grant, **15:**375,n2, 558; **16:**130
Shreveport Rate Cases, **22:**122n2
Shrewsbury, Charles Henry John, 20th Earl of, **15:**448
Shultice, Robert W., **22:**99,n1
Shurts, George, **24:**139
Siam, Crown Prince of, **14:**195,n1
*Sic et Non* (Abelard), **20:**64
Sidgwick, Henry, **15:**410,n2; **19:**666
Siegrist, Jacob J., **24:**311,n2
Siena, **15:**275, 311, 314
sight-seeing railroad engine, **23:**273
Sigrid (servant), **20:**153,n7, 190
Sihler, Ernest Gottlieb, **17:**543,n3
Sill, Edward Rowland, **18:**411
Sill, Herbert Fowler, **14:**217,n6, 218, 221
silver, free coinage of, **17:**77; **23:**653
*Silver Butterfly* (Woodrow), **18:**520,-n1,2,3
Silver How cottage, **18:**370
Silvester, Charles Frederick, **14:**126,n1; **19:**70
Silvester, George Winfred Putman, **14:**145
Silzer, George Sebastian, **21:**7,n2, 35n1, 37n1, 97, 436, 585n1; **22:**243, 311-12, 328, 357, 550n2; **24:**246, 247
Sime, James, **19:**571
Simmons, Furnifold McLendel, **18:**269
Simmons, Harry J., **24:**186,n4
Simmons, Maurice, **25:**129n1

Simmons College, **18**:578
Simon de Montfort, Earl of Leicester, **18**:73
Simons, Edwin Sidney, **15**:248n1, 528,-n2; **19**:501-502,n1, 507, 576
Simons, John Farr, **19**:501,n2,3, 507, 508
Simpson, Catherine, **18**:368,n6, 370
Simpson, Charles E. S., **22**:481; **23**:343, 401,n6, 536n1
Simpson, Eleanor, **18**:368,n6, 370
Simpson, Gertrude, **18**:368,n6, 370
Simpson, Harriette Abby (Mrs. William Frederick), **18**:368n6, 370, 378, 381, 383, 388, 389, 392, 394, 395, 406, 407, 412, 415
Simpson, Mrs., **14**:10
Sinclair, William John, **16**:199; **17**:231,-n2
single tax, **14**:200; **22**:2, 278n1
Sioux City, Iowa, **25**:148-56, 162-64, 282
*Sioux City* (Iowa) *Journal*, **25**:156n, 164n
Sioux City Stock Yards Co., **25**:148n2
Sioux Falls, S. D., **25**:158-61, 162
Sioux Indians, **25**:162-63, 169
Sins of the Father (Dixon), **22**:96,n3
Sire de Malétroits' Door (Stevenson), **15**:397,n7
Sismondi, Jean Charles Leonard Simonde de, **14**:344
Sister A (Sister Annie), *see* Howe, Annie Wilson
Sitting Bull, **14**:250, 445
Skelwith Bridge, near Grasmere, Cumberland, **18**:412
Skibo Castle, Sutherlandshire, **18**:344, 349, 391, 392, 398, 399, 401, 405, 406; WW at, **18**:399-402
Skillman, N. J., **23**:290
Slattery, Daniel G., **22**:283,n1
Slaughter, Coleman C., **17**:492,n1
Slaughter, Evans Griffiths, **22**:203,n1; **23**:272,n2, 274, 275
slave women, **22**:604n2
slavery, **14**:313, 380, 519; **17**:53; **18**:184-85, 213; **25**:596; extension of, **17**:311
Sleeper, Charles F., **22**:164-65,n1
Sloane, James Renwick, **14**:78,n5, 97
Sloane, W. & J., **14**:43,n2
Sloane, William Milligan, **14**:78n5, 290, 325, 388; **15**:544,n3; **16**:30, 140n3, 457, 458; **17**:142, 145, 146; **18**:227, 261; **19**:488; **20**:31,n2, 117, 506
Slocum, John Wesley, **24**:246, 247
Slocum, William Frederick, **23**:21,n5
Slosson, Edwin Emery, **19**:7n2,3, 122n2; **20**:468,n1,2
Small, Albion Woodbury, **14**:395
Small, John Humphrey, **24**:287,n1
Small and Select Democracy (N. Y. *World*), **15**:550,n4
small business, **25**:191-92, 200, 207, 245, 255, 265, 372, 427, 445
Smalley, William W., **23**:476, 541,n1
Smathers, Frank, **22**:310n5, 413,n1

Smick, Isaac S., **23**:394
Smietanka, Julius F., **24**:302,n2
Smith, Adam, **14**:339, 343, 505
Smith (of Men's Association of Brick Church, New York), **14**:267
Smith, Albridge Clinton, **17**:273n1
Smith, Albridge Clinton, Jr., **17**:273,n1, 283; **20**:402,n1
Smith, Arthur Lionel, **14**:407,n4
Smith, Caroline W. Guppy (Mrs. Charles R.), **19**:503,n1
Smith, Charles R., **19**:503n1
Smith, Charles Robinson, **15**:405,n2
Smith, Charles Sprague, **16**:332n1
Smith, Charles Stephenson, **23**:288,n1
Smith, Chatford, **21**:421
Smith, Clement Lawrence, **17**:588,n3
Smith, Courtland Ninde, **16**:375
Smith, Donald Pritchard, **18**:579
Smith, Edgar Fahs, **15**:539,n1; **16**:57,n1; **20**:357,n2
Smith, Ellison DuRant, **24**:273,n1, 287,-n1, 467
Smith, Ford Cushing, **14**:500; **15**:375
Smith, Francis Henry, **17**:86,n2
Smith, Francis Hopkinson, **15**:546; **20**:25,n1, 26
Smith, George Adam, **19**:22,n2,3
Smith, George Doane, **22**:142n1, 392,n2
Smith, George N., **23**:272,n3
Smith, Goldwin, **14**:249, 387,n1, 391; **15**:500,n1
Smith, Harold Cornelius, **14**:440; mother, 440
Smith, Henry L., **15**:50
Smith, Henry Marston, Jr., **24**:71,n1, 489
Smith, Herbert Boughton, **15**:528,n7
Smith, Herbert Knox, **24**:412n3
Smith, Herbert Stearns Squier, **14**:277, 326, 327; **15**:246, 248; **17**:408
Smith, Hoke, **17**:484,n3; **22**:480,n1, 488, 489, 491n1; **23**:236n3; **24**:273, 287,n1, 288, 335, 336, 337; **25**:563, 622, 646
Smith, Helen Dominick (Mrs. Howard Alexander), **16**:89
Smith, Howard Alexander, **16**:19,n1, 89
Smith, James (c. 1719-1806), **17**:249
Smith, James, Jr. (1851-1926), **16**:455n1, 541n1, 561n2; **17**:23-24,n2; **19**:328,n2; **20**:147, 215n1, 352n1, 519-20,n2, 540, 541, 541n1, 544, 548, 556, 557, 561, 562, 563,n1, 564, 565n, 568; **21**:7, 23, 27, 34, 35, 40n1, 52, 57, 62, 88,n4, 90, 99, 141, 142, 200,n1, 261, 345, 345n13, 347, 348, 349, 367, 378, 388, 389, 409, 503, 590; **22**:15, 41-42,n2, 43,n2, 46, 47, 72,n3, 77n1, 81n1, 82, 83, 84, 86, 86n1, 94, 97, 98n1, 100, 101, 113,n1,2, 114-16, 117, 119, 120, 121, 126, 127, 128, 129, 132-33, 133-34, 134-35, 135-36,n1, 136, 137, 137n1,3, 141,n1, 143, 145, 146, 153, 154, 155-56, 160, 160n1, 162, 163-64, 166-67, 169-70, 170n1,

Smith, James, Jr., (cont.)
173-74n1, 175, 181, 181n1, 185, 197, 198, 199, 201, 204,n2, 206, 210, 212, 214, 217, 224, 225, 225n1, 226, 229-30,n1, 231, 231n3,4, 232-33, 235-36,n2, 237, 238, 239, 240, 241, 242n2, 245, 245n2, 247, 248-52,n2, 253, 257, 258, 259, 260, 262, 272-74, 278, 280, 281, 283, 286n2, 287, 288, 289, 292, 295-307, 309, 312n1, 321, 325, 328, 331n1, 334, 336, 337, 339, 340, 357, 361, 363, 367, 376, 377, 382, 384, 392, 393, 453n1, 513, 518, 582, 583; **23**:109, 220, 255, 311, 332n2, 361, 361n, 365, 447, 449n3, 531,n1, 544n1, 546, 627-28; **24**:98,n2, 295, 361, 411,n2, 429, 430-31, 432, 436n5, 440,n8, 449n1; **25**:63-64, 93, 116-18, 129, 214, 215, 217, 271, 272, 345-46, 566n1, 582; primary vote, Sept. 24, 1912, **25**:236n3
Smith, James III, **22**:392,n2
Smith, James R., **24**:335,n1
Smith, James Ward, **19**:253n1
Smith, John Alexander, **15**:441,n2
Smith, John Blair, **15**:496n3
Smith, John Henry, **22**:392,n2
Smith, John Walter, **22**:15-16,n1
Smith, Joseph Lyndon, **22**:392,n2
Smith, Katharine R. Nugent (Mrs. James, Jr.), **20**:215n1
Smith, Leon Rutherford, **24**:482-83,n1,2
Smith, Lucy Marshall, **15**:202, 202n1, 208, 209, 211, 228, 230, 233, 240, 265, 297, 301n5, 304, 306,n1, 308, 310, 333, 334, 336, 339, 346, 347, 355, 356, 357, 358; **23**:112,n1, 597,n2
Smith, Marie, **22**:50n3
Smith, Mary Randolph, **15**:202, 202n1, 208, 209, 211, 228, 230, 233, 240, 265, 267, 297, 301n5, 304, 306,n1, 308, 309, 310, 333, 334, 336, 339, 346, 347, 355, 356, 357, 358; **23**:112,n1, 597,n2
Smith, Mortimer, **20**:402n1
Smith, Norman Kemp, **16**:398,n1, 451,-n2, 454, 465, 507; **17**:290; **18**:582; **19**:670
Smith, Samuel, **16**:197
Smith, Samuel Archibald, **19**:508,n1, 527-28
Smith, Samuel Macon, **14**:331
Smith, Samuel Stanhope, **16**:191n1
Smith, Schuyler, **16**:19,n1
Smith, Thomas, **15**:494,n3
Smith, Walter, **15**:441,n3
Smith, Warren Ridgeway, **19**:502n3, 503,n2
Smith, William Robert, **24**:287,n1
Smith, William Roy, **16**:41,n1,2
Smith, Wilson Schuyler, **17**:221,n2
Smith, Wilton Merle, **14**:114; **16**:29
Smith College, **17**:547; **20**:583
Smith of New Jersey: A Biography of H. Alexander Smith, United States Senator from New Jersey, 1944-1959 (dissertation, Leary), **16**:89n1

Smither, Harriett, **17**:50n1
Smollett, Tobias George, **14**:503
Smyth, Charles Henry, Jr., **16**:112, 130, 247; **17**:408
Smythe, Augustine Thomas, **22**:34
Snedden, David, **23**:103
Snell, Frances, **14**:16,n2, 31, 52, 70, 96
Snitcher, Harriet Peck, **21**:48,n6, 50; **23**:224n8
Snow, Thomas L., **15**:467, 470, 520-21, 523; **17**:334
Snow, Mrs. Thomas L., **15**:520, 521, 523
Snowden, Robert Brinkley, **17**:473,n2, 474
Snowden, Sarah Day (Mrs. Robert Brinkley), **17**:473n2
Snyder, J. M., **23**:383
Sobel, Herman, **22**:100,n2
Social Center Association of America, **23**:480n1
Social Center Development (Rochester, N. Y.), **25**:546,n1
social classes, **25**:369
*Social England: A Record of the Progress of the People* (ed. Traill), **14**:339,n3; **15**:482, 483, 484, 485
*Social Evolution* (Kidd), **18**:443,n1
social reform, **25**:71, 77, 125, 412-13, 434, 469, 472, 497; and Progressive party, **25**:365 Δ A. J. McKelway, **24**:566-67; **25**:310-12, 543
Socialist Party, **25**:82
socialists and socialism, **16**:320, 341, 361, 365, 477; **17**:101; **18**:11, 426-27; **19**:194, 509; **21**:63, 268, 352-53, 386-87, 440, 584n1; **22**:222, 280, 354-55, 452,n2; **23**:42, 54, 105, 107, 116, 609; **24**:313, 345-46, 351, 365-66, 376-77, 427-28; **25**:333
socialism, Christian, **14**:555
*Socialism and the Child Labor Problem* (Spargo), **22**:452n2
*Society and Politics in Ancient Rome: Essays and Sketches* (Abbott), **19**:393
Society for the Prevention of Cruelty to Animals, **17**:580
Society for the Promotion of Engineering Education, **14**:171,n2
sociology and sociologists, WW on, **14**:240-41
Socrates, **23**:498
Solari, Luigi, **25**:28
Solingen, Prussia, **19**:363
Solon, **14**:375
Soltan-Symons, L. C., **17**:14,n2
*Some Memories of a Palaeontologist* (Scott), **16**:157n7
*Some Modern College Tendencies* (Adams), **17**:105,n2, 410, 417; **20**:265n2
*Some Southern Questions* (MacCorkle), **16**:565,n3
Some Talks with Mr. Roosevelt (Brooks), **23**:287n2
Somers, Sir George, **20**:224

Somerset, Bermuda, **20**:139
Somerset County, N. J., **22**:532; **23**:540; **25**:582; Democratic Committee, **21**: 131, 354, 610; schools, **23**:475; WW campaign speeches, **23**:470-76
Somerville, N. J., **21**:361, 380; **23**:471; Armory, **21**:354; WW campaign speech, **21**:354-61
Sommer, Frank Henry, **22**:225,n3, 310
Sons of the Revolution, **21**:482; in New York, **15**:151, 153,n1; **16**:11-12; in Pennsylvania, **16**:143
Sophocles (Greek portrait statue in Lateran Museum, Rome), **15**:276
Sorbonne, **15**:444n2
Sorley, William Ritchie, **15**:410,n2
Sorrento, EAW at, **15**:240, 270
Souffer, B. O., **23**:64,n9
*Souls of Black Folk* (DuBois), **21**:275n3
*Source of His "Wisdom,"* **21**:335n2
South, the, **18**:640-41; **21**:335n2; **22**:189f, 419-20, 478, 490, 492f, 532n6, 598, 604n2; **23**:105, 568, 569f; representative government, **23**:550
South and the Democratic Campaign of 1910-1912 (dissertation, Link), **22**:282n1; **24**:332n2, 398n1
*South and the National Government* (Taft), **19**:10n2
South Africa: British Association meeting at, **16**:157,n7, 164
South and the Democratic party, **15**:547-48, 551
South Carolina, **22**:68; **23**:124, 125, 173; **25**:129; delegation to National Convention, **24**:486; primary results, **24**:387,n1; purchase of WW boyhood home in Columbia, **25**:539-40; state convention, **24**:400,n4
South Carolina, University of, **16**:87,n2; **22**:140
South Carolina College for Women, **16**:87n3
South Carolina Presbyterian Institution for Young Ladies, **22**:577n4
South Carolina Press Association, **22**:499,n2, 507; **23**:114
South Carolina Society of New York City, **17**:78n1
South Dakota, **25**:156-61; delegation to Democratic National Convention, **24**:502, 507,n1
South Dakota, Bishop of, **18**:388,n4
South Jersey political situation, **23**:537
Southampton, Hants, **18**:346
Southern Amusement Co., **22**:96n1
Southern Commercial Congress, **22**:478, 480; *Proceedings . . . ,* **22**:498n
Southern conservatism, **16**:286-88
Southern Educational Association, **18**:589-90
Southern Educational Council, **15**:227
Southern Hotel, St. Louis, **22**:262
Southern Methodist University, **23**:511
Southern Pacific Railroad, **22**: 32n2; **23**:41n6, 101, 296; **25**:240-41
Southern Railway, **16**:495; **22**:140; **23**:552
Southern Society, of New York, **25**:589, 593-603
*Southerner: A Romance of the Real Lincoln* (Dixon), **25**:578n2
*Southwestern Historical Quarterly,* **22**:123n3; **23**:267n1; **24**:225n1
Southwestern Life Insurance Co., **22**:123, 422
Southwestern Presbyterian University, **17**:153n1, 154
Southwestern Railroad Co., of Georgia, **14**:499
Spaeth, John Duncan, **16**:71, 132, 256; **17**:408
Spaeth, Sigmund Gottfried, **16**:465, 511
Spain, EAW in, **15**:211
Spanish-American War, **14**:344, 352, 442; **15**:41; **18**:108, 121; **20**:293; **22**:371; **23**:641; **25**:129, 129-34
Spargo, John, **22**:452,n2
Sparta, N. J., **21**:413
Spaulding, Edward Gleason, **16**:131, 249; **17**:408
Spearing, James Zacharie, **24**:274,n2, 286
special interests, **24**:13-14, 158, 176, 228, 230, 301, 337-38, 365, 433; **25**:33, 71, 85, 122, 157, 175, 178, 185, 187, 189, 196, 252, 280, 346, 359, 380, 397, 433, 439, 472, 476, 501; New Jersey, **25**:483
special privilege, **23**:185; **25**:8, 122, 214, 245, 250, 254, 324, 330, 370, 371, 379, 388, 391, 398, 402, 403, 413, 470-71, 485, 495
Speck von Sternburg, Hermann, **16**:233-n4
Speck von Sternburg, Lillian Lanham (Mrs. Hermann), **16**:233n4
*Spectator* (London), **14**:535
*Speeches at the Lotos Club* (ed. Elderkin et al.), **16**:299n, 301n
*Speeches of William Jennings Bryan,* **23**:237,n1, 284n1
Speer, Robert Elliott, **14**:114; **16**:228; **17**:128, 296,n2; **19**:109,n3; **21**:334,n1
Speer, Robert Walter, **22**:338n1, 584
Speer, William Henry, **22**:469,n3
Speir, Francis, Jr., **17**:382, 383, 395-96,n1; **20**:31,n1, 76,n1; **22**:72,n1, 94
Spello, EAW at, **15**:335, 349
Spence, Bartholomew John, **19**:137, 139, 679
Spence, C. L., **16**:234
Spence, Marion, **16**:234
Spence, William Hamilton, **16**:552,n1, 553
Spencer, B. W., **15**:61
Spencer, Charles Worthen, **16**:84, 88, 92, 101-102, 131, 251, 376,n3, 380; **17**:408; **18**:271, 294; **19**:613-16, 615, 615-19
Spencer, Henry Russell, **16**:376,n4, 380, 509; **17**:87, 286, 557

Spencer, Hubert, 15:98
Spencer, Samuel, 16:495,n1
Spencer, Selden Palmer, 20:21,n5
Spenser, Emma C., 14:328,n1
Speyer, James Jospeh, 18:490,n4,5,6, 491, 516, 623; 21:48n4
*Spirit of the Laws* (Montesquieu), 14:13
Spohn, George Samuel, 19:576
Spokane, Wash., preferential ballots, 23:456
Spoleto, EAW at, 15:335, 349
Spooner bill of 1901, 20:309n2
Spraggins Traverse Alexander, 23:232,n1
Sprigg, James Cresap, 21:62-63, 309, 310; 22:245, 413, 433
Spring Lake, N. J., 23:316, 440; 24:514; Governors' Conference, Sept. 12-16, 1911, 23:317-24
Springfield, Ill., 24:290, 292, 292-98; WW speeches, 25:390-95
Springfield, Mass., 23:248, 367, 413n3, 414, 435; 25:230
Springfield *Illinois State Register*, 24:298n; 25:395n
Springfield (Mass.) *Republican*, 19:293-94,n1, 332; 21:35; 23:243n3, 248; 25:282, 531n1, 554
*Springfield Weekly Republican*, 22:604
Sprunt, James, 15:154n1, 178, 218, 227; 20:31,n1, 584; 24:464, 478-79
Sprunt, Mrs. James, 15:218
Sprunt, James Laurence, 15:178
Squier, A. C., 14:331
Stadler, Adolf, 19:327,n1
Stagg, Amos Alonzo, 20:539
Stahlman, Edward Bushrod, 22:376,n1
Stamp Act, 15:148
Standard News Association of New York, 23:215
Standard Oil Company, 17:503n3, 518-n2, 583; 20:558n2; 24:373, 374, 394n1; 25:206; L. D. Brandeis on trusts, 25:291, 292, 297, 300, 301, 302; 1904 Republican campaign contribution, 25:396n3; Supreme Court decision, 23:5n1, 54,n3, 59, 62, 76, 78, 118,n4, 238, 361n2
Standard Oil Company of Indiana, 17:503n3; *see also* Standard Oil Company
Standard Oil Company of New Jersey, 17:503n3; 23:54,n3; *see also* Standard Oil Company
Standard Underground Cable Company, 24:475n1
standpatters, 22:593, 594; 24:155, 186, 221, 261; 25:170, 182
Stanford Academy, Kentucky, 16:254
Stanford (Leland, Jr.) University, 15:100n3, 291n; 16:33; 22:130
*Stanford University: The First Twenty-five Years* (Elliott), 22:131n3
Stanlaws, Penrhyn (Penrhyn Stanley Adamson), 14:59-60,n1

Stanley, Augustus Owsley, 23:157n1; 25:287
Stanley, Peter William, 24:224n3, 560-n1,4
Stanley bill, 25:287, 288; *see also* La Follette-Stanley antitrust bills
Stanley Committee, 24:15, 89,n3, 143, 159, 196, 346n2, 358n1, 567n2; 25:612n2
Stanwix, near Carlisle, Cumberland, 18:402; St. Michael's Church, 18:402
Stark, George Shippen, 15:462n2; 19:149
Starr, Moses Allen, 15:192,n3
state, 19:636f; definition, nature and powers of, 22:104f; 23:500f
*State of Alaska* (Gruening), 23:175n2
state constitutions, 22:255n2
state government administration, 20:317
state insurance, 22:143-44
state rights, 14:380, 518-19; 22:104; 23:100, 101, 235n3, 294, 618-19
state universities and Carnegie pensions, 17:149-50, 510-11, 527, 545; 18:15, 52-53, 61,n1, 220-21
state *vs.* federal control of corporations, 22:312f
Staten Island, 23:213, 295,n5,6
*Statendam*, T.S.S., 15:360, 384
statesman, definition of, 21:461-62
Statue of Liberty, 24:343-44, 379
Staunton, Va., 22:9, 118; 23:550, 551; 24:80, 101,n4, 133; 25:553,n1; First Presbyterian Church, 15:49,n1,2, 522; 22:118; WW addresses, 25:626-40; Woodrow Wilson Democratic Club, 22:96, 118
Staunton Military Academy, 25:632n1
Steadman, Charles, 14:490n1
Stearns, Alfred Ernest, 14:25n2; 16:486-87, 489; 17:566
Steck, David W., 21:17n; 22:199n
Stedman, Charles Manly, 24:287,n1
Stedman, Edmund Clarence, 14:40n1, 192, 194, 407
steel industry, 25:152, 153, 193, 249; pricing, 15:195; tariff, 25:244; trust, 23:157, 299; 25:160, 331, 381,n6
Steele, Robert V. P. (*pseud.* Lately Thomas), 19:500n3
Steen, John Ewing, 14:134, 265
Steffens, Lincoln, 16:43n2; 22:412n2
Stein, Alfred Anthony, 24:493,n1
Stein, Anthony H., 19:171
Steinson, Harry G., 23:594-95,n1, 598
Steinway & Sons and their pianos, 16:318, 482
Stele Inscription in the Roman Forum (Warren), 17:546,n3
Stelle, Frederick William, 19:73n3
Stengel, Alfred, M.D., 16:412n1, 430, 445,n2; 24:190,n2
Stephen, Sir James Fitzjames, 14:13
Stephens, Alexander Hamilton, 14:517

Stephens, Lawrence Vest, **22**:198,n2
Stephenson, Nathaniel Wright, **23**:293-n3
Sterling, Ill., **24**:299, 300
Sterling (of Lyme, Conn.), **21**:52n1; **23**:112,n4
Sterling Hotel, Trenton, **22**:583; **23**:136, 190,n2, 277,n1
Sterne, Laurence, **14**:503, 505
Stetson, Francis Lynde, **22**:39,n21, 121
Steuert, Frederick A., **14**:108, 110, 115, 122, 440,n1; **19**:603,n1; **21**:594
Steuerwald, Philip, **23**:536n1
Stevens, Clyde Garfield, **15**:22,n5
Stevens, Edwin Augustus (1795-1868), **16**:541n1
Stevens, Edwin Augustus (Princeton 1879), **16**:539-41,n1, 545, 547, 548-49, 549, 550, 555, 555n1, 561n1, 561-62, 563; **17**:10n2,3,4, 23, 25; **21**:150n1, 198, 601; **22**:113, 173-74, 415n1; **23**:290
Stevens, Martha Bayard Dod (Mrs. Edwin Augustus), **21**:150n1
Stevens, Mary Stuart Whitney (Mrs. Robert Livingston), **23**:634,n3
Stevens, Sylvester K., **23**:75n1
Stevens Institute of Technology, **16**:239, 540n1; **22**:39n24, 410-11
Stevenson, Adlai Ewing (1835-1914), **24**:291; **25**:623
Stevenson, Alexander Russell, **14**:435,n5
Stevenson, Joseph Ross, **14**:114, 428,n1
Stevenson, Robert Louis, **15**:397,n7; **23**:513
Stewardson, Emlyn Lamar, **15**:423,n1
Stewardson, John, **15**:423,n1
Stewart, George Black (Princeton 1876), **15**:16; **16**:27, 131, 145, 146, 199, 279; **17**:71, 423; **18**:9, 615, 617; **19**:438, 439, 449, 626, 649, 659, 662, 698, 703, 733, 736; **20**:245, 247, 314, 321; **21**:367,n2
Stewart, George Black, Jr. (Princeton 1906), **16**:203,n3
Stewart, John Aikman (1822-1926), **14**:144, 168, 169; **15**:77, 219, 220; **16**:277; **17**:198, 594; **18**:8-9, 333, 449,n1, 458, 494, 512, 624; **19**:79, 439, 631, 632, 633, 634, 650, 656, 657, 699, 711; **20**:4, 190, 222, 245, 278, 283, 362, 455, 476, 477, 493; **21**:362n1, 364, 366, 434, 435; **22**:436,n3
Stewart, John Aikman III (Princeton 1905), **19**:72,n2
Stewart, Roscoe Winfield, **24**:94,n1
Stewart, Sir Robert MacGregor, **17**:4,n10
Stewart, William Alexander Campbell, **18**:414n1
Stiger, Mrs. M. A., **19**:125
Stillman, James, **14**:298
Stimson, Frederic Jesup, **18**:446,n1
Stimson, Henry Lewis, **19**:364n2; **21**:252n6, 591,n1; **23**:62, 295n6
Stires, Ernest Milmore, **14**:210,n1

Stirling, England, **18**:356; WW at, **18**:349-51
stock watering, **21**:99
Stockbridge, Frank Parker, **21**:309n, 309n2, 320n, 334n, 443n, 462n, 502n, 536n, 555n, 576n; **22**:519, 519,n4, 533, 581; **23**:11, 27,n1, 30, 40n, 43, 60, 85, 93, 135, 135n3, 252, 286, 308, 315, 329, 424n, 591n1; **24**:ix
stockings, Scotch *vs.* American, **21**:216
stocks, **25**:207, 224
Stockton, Bayard (Princeton 1872), **15**:544,n1,3; **16**:197, 208, 457, 458; **18**:227, 261; **19**:488; **20**:31,n2, 506; **21**:131
Stockton, Bayard (Princeton 1906), **15**:544n1
Stockton, Charlotte Julia Shields (Mrs. Bayard I), **15**:544n1
Stockton, Helen Hamilton Shields (Mrs. Bayard II), **15**:544n1; **22**:425,n3
Stockton, Richard (Princeton 1748), **15**:544n1
Stockton, Richard (Princeton 1909), **15**:544,n1
Stockton, Samuel Witham, **15**:544n1
Stoddard, Harry Galpin, **22**:574,n4
Stoddard, Lothrop, **21**:342n8
*Stoic and Epicurean* (Hicks), **15**:301n4
Stoke-on-Trent, Staffordshire, **15**:448
Stokes, Anson Phelps, Jr., **15**:100,n7; **16**:189-90; **17**:122, 125, 127-28, 129-30, 136; **19**:728n1; **20**:52,n1
Stokes, Edward Casper, **21**:90,n3, 219n2, 263,n5, 277, 293, 346, 409, 503, 503-507, 584n1; **23**:392; **25**:474,n3
Stone, Claudius Ulysses, **24**:287,n1
Stone, Melville Elijah, **21**:243,n1, 245
Stone, William Joel, **24**:290, 292, 298, 507, 510
Stone Harbor, N. J., **23**:185
Stoneleigh Abbey, Warwickshire, **15**:446
Stony Brook (Princeton, N. J.), **15**:66, 576
Storer, George Butler, **18**:530,n1
Storey, Moorfield, **21**:386,n1,2; **25**:649-50
Stories of the Nations series, **18**:647
Storrs, Caryl B., **14**:428
Story, Daisy Allen (Mrs. William Cumming), **17**:224-25,n1
Story, Joseph, **14**:373
*Story of Bermuda* (Strode), **17**:50n1, 610n1
*Story of Mrs. Peck: An Autobiography of Mary Allen Hulbert*, **17**:30n1
*Story of the Rockefeller Foundation* (Fosdick), **19**:544n3
Stoughton, William, **22**:89,n2
Stovall, Pleasant Alexander, **22**:491,n6, 516, 532n6, 543; **23**:239, 557,n2; **24**:268, 306, 349, 387
Stowell, Mrs., **14**:92, 99, 113, 117
Stoy, Franklin Pierce, **21**:47,n2
Strachan-Davidson, James Leigh, **15**:96,n3

Stradivarius, Antonio, **25**:318
Straight, Willard, **20**:350n2
Strassburg, University of, **19**:267, 305, 327, 328
Stratford, Arthur Chazotte, **24**:68,n4
Stratford-on-Avon, Warwickshire, Anne Hathaway's House, **14**:531; Church of the Holy Trinity, **14**:531; Guild Hall, **14**:531; Shakespeare's house, **14**:531; Wilsons at, **14**:531
Stratton, George Malcolm, **15**:117,n3
Stratton, Morris Hancock, **21**:423,n2
Straus, Isidor, **21**:18n1, 613,n1
Straus, Nathan, **21**:18,n1, 613; **24**:95; **25**:378, 422, 649
Straus, Oscar Solomon, **21**:18n1; **25**:284, 378n2
Strauss, Johann, **25**:55n1
Strauss, Richard, **20**:173,n4
Street, Jacob Richard, **24**:307,n3
Street Railway Association of the State of New York, **21**:343n10
Streitwolf, August C., Jr., **22**:101,n2, 145, 233, 243-44, 308, 309, 328; **23**: 265-66
Stribling, Carrie, **16**:432,n2
Stribling, Robert M., **16**:433n2
Strode, Hudson, **17**:50n1, 610n1
Stromquist, Carl Ebin, **14**:474; **16**:160, 162, 165,n2; **18**:578; **19**:137, 138, 139, 676
Strong, Augustus Hopkins, **19**:381n4
Strong, Josiah, **19**:71, 72; **23**:480n1; **24**:498-500
Strong, Theodore, **21**:260,n2, 378
Strong, Thomas Nelson, **23**:70n2
Strong, William Lafayette, **19**:86n1
Strong & Cadwalader, **23**:238n3
Stryker, Samuel Stanhope, M.D., **17**: 384,n1
Stuart, Donald Clive, **16**:465, 511; **19**: 572, 576
Stuart, Duane Reed, **16**:51-52, 60, 87-88, 101, 132, 254, 528; **17**:46, 163,n9, 408, 557; **20**:450
Stuart, Duane Reed, Jr., **16**:52n
Stuart, Eleanor, *pseud.* of Eleanor Stuart Patterson (Mrs. Harris Robbins) Childs, **18**:358n2
Stuart, Ellen Douglas, **25**:633,n3
Stuart, Emilie Eugénie Meddaugh (Mrs. Duane Reed), **16**:87-88
Stuart, Zaidee Townsend, **15**:99
Stuart Hall School (Staunton, Va.), **25**:633n3
Stubbs, Walter Roscoe, **22**:180,n1; **24**: 187,n1; **25**:621n2
Studdiford, Samuel Miller, **16**:207,n4
student self-help, **15**:32
Student Volunteer Movement, **14**:266; Rochester convention, **19**:707,n1
*Students and the Present Missionary Crisis*, **19**:707n1
Students' Christian Movement, **14**:265-67

*Studio* (London), **18**:406n2
*Study in Boss Politics: William Lorimer of Chicago* (Tarr), **21**:343n11
*Study of American Colonial History* (Osgood), **14**:443,n2
Sturges, Frederick, Jr., **19**:165
Suez Canal, **25**:34
suffrage, **25**:61; *see also* woman suffrage
suffragette speaker in Grasmere, **18**: 410-11, 411
Sugar Trust, **19**:364,n2; **21**:206, 304,n3; **22**:113n2, 173, 177; **23**:531; L. D. Brandeis, **25**:297
*Suggested Plan for Monetary Legislation, Submitted to the National Monetary Commission by Hon. Nelson W. Aldrich* (two versions), **23**:293,n3
Sullivan, Catherine Driscoll (Mrs. Mark Anthony), **22**:401,n1
Sullivan, G. McArthur, **19**:529,n1, 550, 557-58
Sullivan, George Hammond, **21**:541,n1, 543
Sullivan, Jerry Bartholomew, **23**:247,n2, 310, 341,n1; **24**:221; **25**:555, 623
Sullivan, Mark Anthony, **21**:19,n5, 57, 346,n15, 433; **22**:22-23, 87n2, 119, 228, 229n1, 304, 357, 400, 404, 413,n1
Sullivan, Roger Charles, **20**:519n2, 562, 562n1, 564, 568; **21**:99, 584; **22**:74,n2; **24**:521,n4; **25**:111,n2, 135n1, 400n2
Sulzburger, Solomon, **25**:28
Sulzer, William, **16**:539; **20**:390,n2; **21**:616; **23**:584; **25**:112, 134, 284n4, 329, 361, 441, 492, 493n1, 587, 617n4
Sulzer bill, **25**:614
Summerill, Joseph J., **23**:395n1
Summerville, Ga., Tanglewood Hall, **23**:556
Summit, N. J., **23**:468, 634n1; Athenaeum Club, **19**:533-34,n3, 599; WW address, **19**:599-601
Sumner, Charles, **17**:314
Sumner, Charles A., **24**:186,n2
Sumner, William Graham, **14**:306n3; **19**:315n2
Sumter, S. C., **20**:453
Sun Yat-sen, **25**:576,n1
supply and demand, **25**:10, 139
*Suppression of the African Slave-Trade to the United States of America, 1638-1870* (DuBois), **21**:275n3
Supreme Court *see* United States Supreme Court
Susquehanna Institute, Towanda, Pa., **16**:255
Susquehanna Railroad, **23**:450n1
Surf City, N. J., **25**:584
Sussex, N. J., Boy Scouts, **23**:465; Hornbeck's Hall, **23**:465; WW campaign speech, **23**:465
Sussex Borough, N. J., WW campaign speech, **21**:413
Sussex County, N. J., **21**:396, 404, 413,

569; **22**:253, 370, 378; **24**:179-81, 582; Grangers, **23**:465-66,n2; WW campaign speeeches, **23**:464-66

Sussex Society, **24**:179-81

Suter, Herman Milton, **17**:492,n2

Sutherland, Evelyn Greenleaf, **14**:527n7

Sutherland, Florence, **16**:234

Sutherland, Margaret, **16**:234

Sutphen, William Gilbert van Tassel, **20**:127,n1

Sutro, F. C., **22**:173n1

Suttner, Arthur Gundaccar, Freiherr von, **18**:400n1

Suttner, Bertha Felicie Kinsky (Freifrau von), **18**:400,n1,2, 405

Sutton, Carr Kemper, **16**:154,n1

Sutton (construction superintendent), **15**:223,n4

Suzzallo, Henry, **23**:103

Swackhamer, Samuel S., **22**:173n1; **23**:476

Swain, George F., **25**:414

Swan, Carla Denison (Mrs. Henry), **23**:21,n12

Swan, Henry, **23**:21,n12

Swan Hotel, Wells, Somerset, **14**:533

Swann, Josephine Ward Thomson (Mrs. John Renshaw Thomson; Mrs. Edward Swann), **14**:117,n1; **16**:414n4, 457,n1, 458, 515, 516; **17**:197, 590; **18**:64, 65, 227, 228n1, 247, 249, 261, 262; **19**:143, 200, 398, 437, 438-39, 449, 456,n2, 488, 544, 559, 610, 611, 621, 626, 629, 630, 631, 653, 654, 656, 659, 689, 690, 695, 708, 710, 728, 731, 733; **20**:4, 5, 19n2, 29, 31-32n1, 45, 47, 51-52,n1, 61-62, 66n2, 68, 96, 99, 101, 103, 117, 130, 131, 234, 281, 282, 286, 317-18, 319, 323, 394, 395, 403, 472, 480, 482, 506, 510-11; *see also Princeton University, Graduate College and the controversy over its location*

Swann, Thomas, **14**:117n1

Swanson, Claude Augustus, **23**:311, 359,n2; **25**:642n3

Swarthmore College, **16**:240, 488; Parrish Hall, **16**:267; *Swarthmorean*, **16**:271n; WW address, **16**:267-71

Swarthmore College Peace Collection, **25**:20n4

Swearingen, John Eldred, **25**:539

Swedish Americans, **25**:108

Sweeney, Algernon Thomas, **23**:588,n4

Sweeney, Michael F., **15**:57

Sweet, Emma, **23**:21,n11

Sweetwater, Texas, **25**:528, 548

Sweny, William H., **21**:59

Swem, Charles Lee, **23**:211n; **24**:xi, xii-xiii; **25**:ix-xiii, 140n3, 452,n1, 518, 566

Swettenham, Sir Alexander, **17**:14-15,n3

Swift, Elijah, **17**:557; **19**:138, 139, 678

Swift, Jonathan, **14**:503; **15**:511; **17**:483; **19**:476; **21**:253, 317; **23**:640

Swift & Co., **16**:382, 382n1

Swinburne, Algernon Charles, **14**:101, 108

Switzerland, **23**:591, 601n1; Wilsons in, **14**:539, 540-41, 556

*Switzerland* (Baedeker), **14**:529

Sykes, [Benjamin William] McCready, **23**:65,n2

Syracuse, N. Y., Century Club, **15**:169; Chamber of Commerce, **24**:307; Democratic convention, **25**:283,n2, 284; Princeton alumni, **15**:169; **24**:307, 308; University Club, **15**:169; WW in, **24**:307-308; WW speeches, **24**:307; **25**:137-46

*Syracuse Herald*, **15**:173n

Syracuse *Post-Standard*, **24**:305, 308n; **25**:146n

Syracuse University, **16**:239

Syria, Princeton Expedition to, **15**:376n1

Syria: Publications of the Princeton University Archeological Expeditions to Syria in 1904-1905 and 1909, **15**:376n1

Syrian Protestant College, Beirut, **16**:248; **18**:578

*Tables of the Motion of the Moon* (Brown), **16**:489,n3

Tacitus, Cornelius, **18**:575; **19**:597

Taft, Helen Herron (Mrs. William Howard), **16**:233; **25**:565

Taft, Henry Waters, **19**:396,n3; **23**:238,n3

Taft, William Howard, **16**:213,n2, 233, 318; **17**:159; **18**:479n1; **19**:9,n2, 64, 363n1, 365, 561, 602; **20**:22, 38n5, 309, 309n2, 312, 312n2; **21**:21n1, 47n1, 115, 124,n3, 132, 175, 251, 252, 253, 275n2, 284n3, 454, 456, 468, 475, 546n3, 573, 608n2, 615, 615n2, 621; **22**:32n3, 38n3, 44n3, 85n3, 88, 140, 184, 220, 248, 291n2, 362, 427n1, 478, 478n3, 486, 488, 491, 500, 514,n1, 515, 573, 592n2; **23**:45, 62, 130n1, 173, 175n2, 192n2, 234n5, 238, 251, 284, 287n2, 303n1, 361,n2, 369, 395, 399n4, 415, 442, 443, 447, 505n7, 515, 516, 597, 605, 611, 612; **24**:75, 165, 220, 257,n2, 352, 362, 373, 392, 407, 412,n3, 435, 447, 448n1, 494, 510, 546, 553, 565, 566; **25**:29, 33, 46, 51-52, 56, 57, 181, 204, 214, 215, 233, 248, 260, 285n1, 323, 335, 352, 361, 382, 394, 397, 407, 408, 419, 426, 451, 466, 526, 564, 565-66, 574,n3; campaign funds, **24**:254; Catholic vote, **25**:63; congratulatory message, **25**:521; electoral vote, **25**:518n1; followers, **25**:413; R. M. LaFollette on, **25**:475; Edwin Doak Mead on, **25**:20; panic of 1893, **25**:471; Pennsylvania vote, **25**:527n1; popular vote, **25**:518n1; straw vote of American missionaries in Japan, **25**:390; tariff, **25**:249, 380, 409; trusts, **25**:381n6; and

Taft, William Howard, (*cont.*)
WW meet in Boston, **25**:269-71; portrait, **25**:illustration section
Taft Hotel (New Haven), **24**:166n1; **25**:271
Taggart, Thomas, **20**:562n1, 568; **25**: 111,n2, 135n1
Taine, Hippolyte Adolphe, **14**:345
Takahashi, Motokichi, **16**:557-58
Takahira, Kogoro, **18**:229; **19**:31,n3
Talbot, Ethelbert, **14**:114, 441,n3, 452,-n1,3; **17**:125, 127, 130,n1
Talbot, Howard, **14**:288n1
Talcott, Charles Andrew, **14**:195; **15**: 360n2, 361, 388; **19**:215, 252; **21**:298, 338, 578, 583, 590, 591; **22**:12, 456; **24**:287,n1
*Tale of Two Conventions, A* (Bryan), **25**:533n1
Tallman, Clay, **25**:360,n2
Talton, John L. F., **24**:484-85,n1
*Tammany* (song), **16**:318,n7
Tammany Hall, **14**:376; **16**:43, 218, 323n1; **18**:60n3; **19**:512; **20**:76n1, 402n1; **21**:303n2, 342n8, 344n12, 523; **22**:161n1, 602; **23**:259; **25**:24, 112n3, 134, 233, 284n3, 361, 649n6
Tammany Publishing Company, **16**:415
*Tammany Times*, **16**:415n1; **22**:229, 376n1
Tamworth, N. H., **18**:346,n7
Tang Shao Yi, **18**:560
Tarbell, Ida Minerva, **20**:135,n3
Tardy, William Thomas, **23**:519
tariff, **14**:232-33; **16**:367, 530; **18**:639, 644; **19**:193, 213, 258, 331, 358, 359-80, 461-63, 467-69; **20**:301-302, 315, 420, 504, 546; **21**:46, 88n3, 194, 196-97, 206, 214-16, 251, 253-56, 280, 338, 454, 456, 468, 474, 475, 521, 525, 530; **22**:7, 219, 220, 222, 223, 267, 301, 359, 556, 567, 592; **23**:4-5, 25, 90, 91, 123, 155, 286, 367-69, 399, 504, 531, 560, 561, 611f, 617, 621-22, 622-23, 637-50; **24**:13, 52, 84, 87, 111, 125, 126, 142, 156, 192, 196, 236n8, 238, 259, 291, 295-96, 302, 314, 330-32, 340, 391,n1, 394-95, 412, 417, 418-20, 580n1; **25**:5, 7, 16, 38-39, 100-101, 103-104, 117, 120, 122, 133, 137-43, 151, 166, 188-89, 194, 204, 205, 209, 225, 242-43, 248-50, 261, 268, 324, 331, 334, 335, 341-42, 354-55, 364, 366-67, 371, 380, 386-87, 394, 407, 412, 413, 428, 429, 430, 433, 439, 443-44, 470,n5, 471, 501-502, 567n3, 593n1; and farmers, **25**:32-34; platform plank, **24**:478-79; Progressive Party, **25**:495; Republican Party, **25**:490; Schedule K, **23**:130,n1, 131; **25**:140-41, 249, 430 Δ N. W. Aldrich, **25**:437; E. B. Andrews, **24**:540; G. Bradford, **22**:138; L. D. Brandeis, **24**:580; W. J. Bryan, **23**:235n3, 238; congress, **23**:130n1; M. P. Devlin,

**22**:128; Charles William Eliot, **25**:286n1; J. J. Fitzgerald, **21**:327,n1; G.B.M. Harvey, **19**:191; H. L. Higginson, **21**:612; T. D. Jones, **25**:115, 133; F. F. Kane, **24**:496; E. Kelly, **21**:175; W. Kent, **22**:32; J. A. O'Gorman, **22**:601; Walter Hines Page, **25**:516; G. L. Record, **21**:345; W. C. Redfield, **23**:560,n2; reform bill of 1894, **21**:344n13; Republican platform, **23**:399n4; T. Roosevelt, **25**:410; James Smith Jr., **22**:205n2; **25**:214, 345; W. H. Taft, **22**:478n3; **25**:249, 380, 409; S. Untermyer, **23**:605n1; H. Watterson, **23**:303n1; J. S. Williams, **21**:557; **22**:197
*Tariff Address by Governor Woodrow Wilson . . . January 3, 1912*, **23**:650n
Tariff and the Tariff Commission (Taussig), **23**:643n3
*Tariff History of the United States* (Taussig), **23**:611n2, 643n3
Tariff of abominations, 1828, **24**:419
Tariff of 1816, **14**:518
Tariff of 1824, **18**:184
Tariff of 1828, **18**:538
Tarkington, Booth, **14**:31n1, 527n7
Tarkington, Laura Louisa Fletcher (Mrs. Booth), **14**:31,n1
Tarr, Joel Arthur, **21**:343n11
Tarrant, Warren Downes, **22**:56,n1, 61,n2
Tarrytown, N. Y., **16**:154; **21**:38
Taussig, Frank William, **15**:65,n2; **16**: 372,n1; **23**:611n2, 643, 643n3; **24**:536-37
Tawney, James Albertus, **22**:207,n6
taxation, **19**:463, 468-69; **20**:317; **22**:349-50, 530-31; **23**:25; **24**:172, 216-17; **25**:409; New Jersey, **25**:307, 310
*Taxation in America* (Burke), **14**:14
Taylor, Charles E., **23**:517
Taylor, Edward Thomas, **24**:287n
Taylor, George, **17**:249
Taylor, Hillsman, **18**:485n1
Taylor, James Monroe, **19**:499-500,n1, 532-33
Taylor, Leon R., **24**:324,n2; **25**:566n1, 581, 583
Taylor, Malcolm Slicer, **16**:487,n1
Taylor, Robert Love, **23**:289n2, 291, 588
Taylor, Zachary, **17**:319
Taylors (of Westmorland), **16**:443, 444
Teal, Joseph Nathan, **25**:645,n5
Tchaikovsky, Pëtr Ilich, **15**:153n2
Teachers College, Columbia University, **16**:282; **18**:612
Teachers Insurance and Annuity Association of America, **16**:55n3; **17**:104n1
Teall, Edward Nelson, **16**:30
technical education, **16**:381, 384
*Technique of Shorthand Reporting* (Swem), **25**:xi
Tedcastle, Agnes Vaughn (Mrs. Arthur

W.), **14**:4, 5n1, 7, 9, 10, 12, 16, 17, 18, 23, 25, 28, 35, 39, 48, 50, 51, 53, 87, 96, 118, 254, 424; **16**:357; **19**:270n2, 290-91, 293

Tedcastle, Arthur W., **14**:4, 5n1, 7, 8, 9, 12, 16, 19, 31, 48, 49, 51, 52, 70, 72, 77, 95, 118, 254, 424, 438; **16**:357; **19**:270,n2, 290-91, 292-93

telephone, **20**:400

telegraph, **20**:400

*Tempest* (Shakespeare), **20**:224

Templecombe, Somerset, Wilsons at, **14**:534

Ten Eyck, John Conover, **16**:460, 461; **17**:232,n1

Ten Eyck Hotel, Albany, **15**:168

Tener, John Kinley, **22**:409n2; **23**:229,n4

Tennant, George Grant, **18**:487,n2

Tennent, Gilbert, **15**:66

Tennent, Hattie Taylor, **14**:406

Tennessee, **23**:634; **24**:78, 403,n1; **25**: 611-13, 621; Democrats, **23**:213n1,2,3, 218n2, 288-89,n2; night riders, **18**:6,n1, 483,n1; pre-convention trip, **24**:190-216; Princeton alumni, **16**:474-77; **17**:473, 474, 480, 488; **18**:342-43, 398-99, 420-21, 465, 467, 472, 473, 484; Prohibition, **23**:289n2; Republicans, **23**:288, 289n2; State Fair, **23**:244; state comptroller, **19**:515-16; Wilson movement, **23**:212,-n2

Tennessee, University of, **16**:512

Tennessee Coal & Iron Company, **25**: 384n7

*Tennessee Historical Quarterly*, **18**:485-n2; **23**:289n2

*Tennessee Teetotalism: Social Forces and the Politics of Progressivism* (Lacy), **18**:485n2; **23**:289n2

tennis, **20**:176

Tennyson, Alfred, 1st Baron Tennyson, **14**:104, 369,n2; **15**:171,n3, 276, 442; **16**:297n4, 529,n2; **18**:369n; **19**:34; **20**:264; **22**:71,n5; **23**:19,n3, 459,n1

Terence (Publius Terentius Afer), **17**: 546; **19**:593, 597

Terrell, Alexander Watkins, **23**:500,n4

Terry, David John, **19**:174

Terry, Ellen, **15**:391,n4; **16**:444,n3

Texarkana, Ark., WW in, **23**:519-20

Texas, **22**:122-23, 422-23, 466, 466,n3, 584; **23**:176, 191, 231, 233, 258, 259n1,2, 512; **24**:164, 225, 248, 254, 384,n2, 385, 386, 387, 489, 515; **25**: 532, 624; Democrats, **23**:231, 258,n1,2, 260-61, 267-69, 302, 458, 470, 540, 589; **25**:603-606; legislation regulating corporations, **17**:518,n2; legislature, **22**:422; **23**:260; political appointments, **25**:603-605; progressives, **23**:499; prohibition, **25**:625; State Fair, **22**:576, 584; **23**:231, 242, 255-56, 260, 261, 499,n1, 506, 508, 509, 510; State Fair:

Woodrow Wilson Day, **23**:506; State Press Association, **23**:268; Woodrow Wilson movement and Association, **23**:256, 507; Woodrow Wilson State Democratic League, **23**:260, 260n2, 261, 267-69, 286

Texas, University of, **16**:132, 252, 465, 511; **19**:677; **23**:268

*Texas Rangers: A Century of Frontier Defense* (Webb), **25**:423n1

textile workers, **25**:430

Thach, Charles Coleman, **15**:12,n2

Thacher, John Hamilton, **16**:47,n2, 95, 405

Thacher, John Seymour, M.D., **17**:236n1

Thackeray, Hotel, London, **16**:436,n2, 438, 444

Thanksgiving Day, **22**:87f

*That Pittsburgh Speech and Some Comment*, **20**:424,n1, 444

Thayer, Harvey Waterman, **16**:112-13, 132,257-58, 421;**17**:408; **19**:570,571,576

Thayer, William Roscoe, **19**:293

Theodore L. De Vinne and Co., New York City, **20**:277

*Theodore Roosevelt and Japan* (Esthus), **16**:559n3

*Theodore Roosevelt and the Art of Controversy* (Gatewood), **18**:387n1,2

*Theodore Roosevelt and the Bureau of Corporations* (Johnson), **16**:15n1

*Theodore Roosevelt and the Japanese-American Crises* (Bailey), **16**:559n3

*Theodore Roosevelt and the Progressive Movement* (Mowry), **19**:191n1; **21**:148-n1, 344n12

Theta Delta Chi fraternity, **22**:250n2

Thilly, Frank, **15**:114-15,n1, 115, 119, 134, 135, 136, 152, 152-53,n1, 156, 163, 183, 188-89, 197, 198, 202-203, 207,n3, 245, 439-40, 448, 535, 557; **16**:398n1, 428, 507; **18**:519, 528; **19**:666n2; **22**:35-36,n1

Thilly, Frank, Jr., **15**:448,n2

Thilly, Jessie Matthews (Mrs. Frank), **15**:135, 189, 245, 440, 448; **18**:519,n3, 528

*Third Degree* (Charles Klein), **20**:153,n9

Thirlmere, Westmorland, **16**:444; **18**: 374, 395

*Thirteen for Good Luck* (Jones), **19**: 502n3

Thomas, Augustus, **14**:329; **25**:493n1, 596,n2, 602

Thomas, Calvin, **19**:570

Thomas, Charles Spalding, **22**:376, 388-n1, 574, 584, 599; **23**:21, 478, 652-53; **25**:545-46,n1

Thomas, Claude M., **24**:146

Thomas, Daniel Lindsay, **15**:3n2

Thomas, Harvey, **22**:309-10,n1; **24**:253, 289,n1, 453

Thomas, Lately (*pseud*. of Robert V. P. Steele), **19**:500n3

Thomas, Martha Carey, **14**:6,n2, 319-20; **16**:58,n1, 79; **18**:395

Thomas, Norman [Mattoon], **16**:138,n2; **17**:223n3; **18**:335-36,n1

Thomas, Phillips, **16**:512

Thomas, Seymour, oil painting of WW, **25**:illustration section

Thomas à Kempis, **15**:110, 117, 119

*Thomas Carlyle* . . . (Froude), **18**:362n2

Thomas Cooke and Son, **14**:534,n13; 538, **15**:228, 229, 240, 275, 304, 315, 322

Thomas G. Plant Shoe Co., **25**:200,n3, 207

Thomas H. Prior and Sons Co, **16**:156n1, 172

Thomas Jefferson Memorial Association of the United States, **14**:131,n3, 360,n1

Thomas Y. Crowell and Co., **17**:457

Thomas G. Plant Shoe Co., **25**:200,n3, 207

Thompson, Alexander Marshall, **20**:85-86,n1, 131-32; **24**:535n1, 579

Thompson, Berenice Morrow, **25**:360-62

Thompson, Charles Willis, **20**:570,n1; **25**:360-62, 588

Thompson, Elinor, **20**:579

Thompson, Florence Jones (Mrs. James MacNaughton), **15**:432

Thompson, Henry Burling, **15**:509, 527; **16**:5, 274-75, 424,n1; **17**:41-43, 47,n1, 49, 110, 219, 220, 265, 271-72, 281-82, 285, 301, 302, 303, 308-309, 334, 339, 341, 346, 349, 351, 362, 369, 379-81, 383, 386-89, 391, 405, 409, 410-11, 434-35, 564, 595; **18**:14, 52, 229-36, 236, 285-86, 290, 301-302, 302-303, 304, 308, 313, 360, 380, 418, 423, 444-45, 458, 473-74, 475, 477, 489, 507, 510, 511, 512, 514, 515, 554, 584, 589, 592, 615, 622, 630-31; **19**:3,n1, 4, 5, 68, 80, 122, 152, 159, 168-69, 197-98, 228, 256-57, 273-76, 276-77, 320-21, 439, 612-13, 620-21, 624, 631, 632, 649, 657, 663, 664, 672-73, 697, 698, 705-706, 711, 712-13, 727, 730, 731-33; **20**:5, 6n, 8n, 12, 13, 14-15, 16-17, 45-46, 48, 60, 62, 87, 97, 128, 137, 183, 190, 209, 223, 226, 238-39, 241, 245, 246, 252, 254, 324-26, 359, 361-62, 413, 485n1, 488-90, 498, 509, 578-79; **21**:49, 104, 138, 299, 385n1, 435, 435n2, 593; **22**:436

Thompson, Henry Dallas, **14**:81, 296, 326, 394; **15**:164, 301, 330,n2, 340, 443; **16**:145, 152, 153, 159-60, 162, 162-63, 165, 176, 179, 448; **17**:408; **19**:328; **21**:606; **24**:274-75, 284

Thompson, James MacNaughton, **14**:45, 49,n2, 53, 55, 57, 60, 65, 66, 67, 71, 72, 77, 78, 83, 86, 99-100, 109, 326,n3, 490; **15**:321, 415, 416, 425,n1, 432, 436, 493

Thompson, John N., **15**:156,n2, 186-87,-n1

Thompson, Joseph, **23**:552n1, 529n3

Thompson, Julia Dickinson Watson (Mrs. Slason), **14**:454,n5

Thompson, Katherine, **20**:579,n1

Thompson, Mary, **20**:579,n1

Thompson, Mary Wilson (Mrs. Henry Burling), **21**:593,n1

Thompson, Miss (C. W. McAlpin's stenographer), **14**:498, 499

Thompson, Richard W., **14**:290, 291

Thompson, Robert Ellis, **16**:71,n1

Thompson, Samuel Huston, **20**:84,n3; **24**:534,n1, 579

Thompson, Samuel Huston, Jr., **20**:84,n1, 85; **21**:130, 149; **22**:375-76, 405, 521, 523, 527, 574, 577-78; **23**:23, 650; **24**:535n1, 579; **25**:550

Thompson, Slason, **14**:454,n5

Thompson, Suzanne Dawes, **21**:13,n2

Thompson, William Barlum, **25**:186n3

Thompson, William Henry, **23**:97,n3; **25**:347n2

Thompson, William Howard, **25**:621n2

Thompson, William Pitt, **23**:341,n3

Thompson & Summerfeldt, auditors, **17**:357

Thomson, John Renshaw, **14**:117n1; **16**:458n1; **19**:689

Thomson, Sir Joseph John, **16**:157,n3, 163, 164, 165

Thomson, Josephine Ward (Mrs. John Renshaw), **14**:117,n1

Thomson, Rose Elizabeth Paget (Lady Thomson), **16**:165

Thorne, Gabriel Wisner, **18**:551,n1

Thornton, William Mynn, **16**:281,n2, 284, 322

Thornwell, James Henley, **14**:332

Thorp, Willard, **19**:253n1, 754n2

Thorpe, James Francis, **21**:53n1

Thorstenberg, Herman Justus, **22**:604n2

*Three Centuries of Harvard* (Morison), **16**:520n1

Three Doctors Who Can Cure Football, **19**:556n1

*Three Phi Beta Kappa Addresses* (Adams), **17**:104,n1, 274,n1, 410

Throop Hotel (Topeka, Kansas), **24**:187

Thruston, Gates Phillips, Jr., **23**:288,n1

Thucydides, **14**:287

Thum, William, **23**:45,n1

Thunderbolt, near Augusta, Ga., **23**:557

Thwaites, Reuben Gold, **14**:430; **16**:144n3,4; **20**:582, 583n1

Thwing, Charles Franklin, **16**:91,n1; **22**:53; **23**:657

Tibbits (Thibits), Miss (of Lyme, Conn.), **16**:154,n1

Tiberius, **17**:483; **19**:43

Tice & Lynch, **15**:173

Tide-Water Bldg. Co., **15**:449

Tiffany, Louis Comfort, **14**:7n3

Tiffany & Company, **14**:145

Tiffany clock, **19**:405

Tiffany Studios, New York City, **15**:449

Tiger, Alaska Glacier, **19**:480, 482

tigers, **19**:65-68
Tiger's Tail, Alaska glacier, **19**:480, 482
Tilden, Samuel Jones, **17**:75; **19**:272; **23**:200n1, 243n3, 249n1, 303,n1; **24**:46, 59n1
Tildsley, John Lee, **18**:533-34,n1, 541
Tillman, Benjamin Ryan, **22**:28,n1; **23**:592n3; **24**:80,n1,2, 273, 400, 468, 485-86, 588n2
Tillyard, Alfred Isaac, **17**:348n1
Timlow, William Ferree, **18**:456
Tindall, George Brown, **19**:10n2
Tintoretto, Il (Jacopo Robusti), **15**:359
Tippin, H. H., **16**:113
Tippin, W. H., **16**:113
Tirrell, George L., **16**:329,n1, 330, 372
Titian (Tiziano Vecelli), **15**:229, 350n1, 354, 359, 477
Titsworth, Charles Grant, **16**:48,n2
Titus, Columbus A., **23**:52,n6
Titus, George E., M.D., **25**:509,n1
Titus, Nelson Woodhull, **14**:76,n2, 77, 117, 164,n3
Tivoli, Hadrian's Villa, EAW at, **15**:274
Tivoli, Italy, Wilsons at, **14**:540
Tivoli Hotel, Luzern, **14**:539,n10
*To Advance Knowledge: A Handbook on American University Press Publishing* (Hawes), **17**:352n2
*Tobacco Night Riders of Kentucky and Tennessee 1905-1909* (Nall), **18**:7n1, 485n1
tobacco trust, **18**:7n1; **23**:361n2; L. D. Brandeis, **25**:291, 292, 296-303; J. C. McReynolds, **25**:557-58
tobacco-chewing, **23**:87
Tobin, George Timothy, **15**:223,n2, 238; drawing of WW, illustration section Vol. 15
Tocqueville, Alexis Charles Henri Maurice Clérel de, **14**:14; **15**:62; **16**:269, 296, 530; **17**:506; **18**:86, 167, 443, 447; **19**:518; **20**:329, 367-68; **21**:512; **23**:127n10; **25**:427
Tod, Robert Elliott, **19**:539,n3,4
Todd, Ambrose Giddings, **15**:248n1
Todd, Frederick, **22**:121-22,n1, 185-86
Toledo, Ohio, **18**:528, 530; Chamber of Commerce, **18**:524, 526, 527, 530; Secor Hotel, **18**:524; Valentine Theater, **18**:524, 526, 530; WW address, **18**:524, 526-28
*Toledo Blade*, **18**:524n
*Toledo Manuscript of the Germania of Tacitus* (Abbott), **18**:575
*Toledo News-Bee*, **18**:528n
tolerance, **22**:91
Tolson, John, **16**:431n1
*Tom Brown's School Days* (Hughes), **17**:327
Tome Institute, Port Deposit, Md.,**19**:677
Tomkins, Floyd Williams, **14**:114; **15**:492,n3; **19**:394,n4
Tomlinson, Ben, **20**:430,n2
Tompkins, F. C., **16**:415

Tompkins, Walter Knapp, **14**:391-92
Toms River, N. J., **23**:380; WW campaign speech, **21**:325-26
Tonks, Oliver Samuel, **16**:106, 131, 252; **17**:408; **20**:318, 449
Topeka, Kans., **23**:292; **24**:187-88, 188-89; **25**:272n3, 378-85
Topeka *State Journal*, **24**:188n, 189n
Topley, John William, **15**:21,n1; **17**:440
Tories, **22**:594, 596
Toronto, **21**:341; WW at, **15**:448
Toronto, University of, **16**:88, 159, 258, 266; **20**:451n2; Press, **17**:352n2
Touraine Hotel, Boston, **20**:466,n4
Tower, William Hogarth, **20**:68,n1
town meeting government, **20**:194
*Town Topics, The Journal of Society* (New York), **19**:322,n2; **22**:324,n5
Towne, Charles Arnette, **25**:213,n3
Townend, Troutbeck, Westmorland, **16**:439n1
Townsend, Edward Davis, **19**:139n4, 679
Townsend, Edward Waterman, **21**:521,-n1; **23**:129; **25**:468,n4
Townsend, James J., **25**:400n2
Toy, Crawford Howell, **14**:406,n2; **20**:475n1
Toy, Nancy Saunders (Mrs. Crawford Howell), **14**:406,n2,3; **15**:121; **20**:475,-n1; **25**:232
trackless trolley bill, **24**:279, 326
Tractarian movement, **14**:555
trade, **24**:35, 36, 39, 106, 125, 185, 195; **25**:16, 100, 101, 104-105, 341-42, 343, 371; L. D. Brandeis, **25**:295-96; harbor development, **24**:183-84; Panama Canal, **24**:33-34, 195
trade unions, **19**:245, 255, 269-70, 309-10
Traill, Henry Duff, **14**:339,n3; **15**:482, 483, 484, 485
Trainer, William Booth, **19**:165
*Transcript*, **25**:xin1
*Translation of Giovanni Boccaccio's Life of Dante* (tr. Carpenter), **19**:703,n1
Travelers' Protective Association, **24**:261
Travell, Ira Winthrop, **14**:69, 262
*Traveller* (Goldsmith), **14**:435,n2
Travis, John Linn, **23**:68,n1
Traymore Hotel, Atlantic City, **23**:522
Treacy, John Joseph, **22**:163,n1, 304, 357; **23**:350
Treadway, Lyman Hambright, **17**:497-n1, 498, 507-508n1, 508, 509
*Treason of the Senate* (Phillips), **16**:375n1; **20**:372n1
*Treasures of a Hundred Cooks: A Collection of Distinctive Recipes for Lovers of Good Food* (Hulbert), **17**:30n1
*Treaties and Agreements with and concerning China, 1894-1919* (MacMurray), **15**:143n2
*Treatise on the System of Evidence in Trials at Common Law . . .*, **25**:611n1
Treaty of Paris (1783), **14**:341

Tree, Sir Herbert Beerbohm, 15:396,n4; 16:445n3
Treman, Charles Edward, 25:134,n3
Trench, Richard Chenevix, Archbishop of Dublin, 15:296
Trenholme, Norman Maclaren, 16:41,-n1,3,4
Trent affair, 14:250, 445
Trenton, N. J., 15:579; 19:349, 351; 21:25, 33, 167, 226, 228, 430; 22:379-82; 23:134, 135, 136, 140, 143, 148, 152, 153, 160, 164, 165, 166, 174, 182, 183, 184, 189, 191, 192, 193, 199, 200, 216, 217, 218, 220, 227, 231, 233, 246, 257, 262, 262n3, 267, 270, 271, 275, 329, 352, 366, 381, 398, 400, 409, 416, 424, 425, 426, 427, 428, 437, 440, 449, 463, 466, 478, 479, 480, 504, 518, 520, 539, 542, 546, 547, 559, 560, 563, 567, 584, 591, 592, 594, 603, 604, 605, 630, 631, 634n1, 636, 650, 651, 653; adopts commission government, 23:161,n1; Association Hall, 16:63; ballots, 19:510; Board of Trade, 22:483; Central Labor Union, 21:23n1; 22:259; Chamber of Commerce, 22:482, 575n1; 23:223,n5; City Commission League, 23:164; city government, 23:148, 150, 152; Common Council, 19:522,n2; Country Club, 22:532, 582; Democratic League, 21:24n1; Fifth Presbyterian Church, 22:259; First Methodist Episcopal Church, 22:385, 386; First Presbyterian Church, 16:105n2; 22:380, 452; Green properties, 21:606; Dr. John Hall, 25:457; Har Sinai Temple, 22:87,n1; Manhattan Hotel, 23:184; Masonic Temple, 21:351n1; 23:385, 428; New Jersey State Home for Girls, 25:536n1, 537; police force, 23:143-44; Public Library, 15:273; 16:538; Second Regiment Armory, 23:372,n1; State House, 23:277,n1; Sterling Hotel, 22:583; 23:136, 190,n2, 277,n1; Taylor Opera House, 21:91n1, 104, 229; 22:53, 504n1; 23:425n1; Trenton Fair, 21:217; WW addresses, 14:354-55; 16:63-64, 279-80; 21:229-38; 23:425-36; 24:389-90; 25:304-305, 453-57; Winkler's orchestra, 22:380; Y.M.C.A., 16:63; 22:379
Trenton Evening Times, 14:358n; 19:554n3; 20:566n8, 577n2; 21:23,-n1,4, 26,n2, 31, 52, 53, 54,n1, 55n2, 91n, 94n, 100n, 120, 125n, 142n1, 191n, 198n, 238n, 541, 582, 590n; 22:9, 73,n3, 77,n1, 99n, 129, 136n1, 142n1, 154n, 182, 216n3, 229n1, 252n, 382n, 416n, 455, 476n, 505n, 575n; 23:26n, 131n, 152n, 191n, 277n, 290n, 302, 409, 436n, 449n; 24:574n; 25:40n, 118n, 305n, 310n, 451n, 452n, 539n, 556n, 590n, 591n
Trenton Potteries Co., 22:379
Trenton State Gazette, 21:62

Trenton Sunday Advertiser, 21:34,n1
Trenton True American, Daily True American, Evening True American, 14:355n, 475n; 16:64, 280n, 338n; 19:522n1; 20:564,n2; 21:5, 9, 16n, 22, 23, 24n, 24, 26,n2, 28n3, 33-34, 37,n1, 40, 54, 58, 61n, 62n2, 94n, 96n, 120n, 152n, 181n, 259n, 290n, 327, 351n, 433n, 527n, 584n1; 22:73,n3, 81n1, 93n, 152n, 154n, 155, 238n1, 277n, 307n, 387n1, 399n, 427n, 453n, 474n, 484n3, 486n, 502, 503n, 504n1, 537n4, 546n5, 576n, 579n; 23:20n, 52,n4, 53n4, 152n, 160,n2, 177n1, 177n, 215, 262n3, 305n, 313n, 361n, 364n, 372n1, 380n, 432n9, 540n, 542n, 544n1, 656n; 24:100n2, 328n, 409n, 434n, 449n, 584n; 25:xi,n2, 60n, 110n3, 453n, 457n, 492n, 510n, 512n, 518n
Trevelyan, George Otto, 14:352
Triggs, Henry Inigo, 16:472,n1,2, 536; 17:359, 360
Trimingham, Elizabeth Fenton, 25:573-n3
Trimingham, Thomas Darrell, 25:573,n3
Trimingham Brothers, Ltd., 25:573n3
Trinity College (now Duke University), 16:255; 22:489,n4; 24:257n1,3
Trinity College, Cambridge, 16:246, 247, 507
Trinity College, Dublin, 14:295; 16:506
Trinity College, Hartford, Conn., 16:239, 353; 20:335, 336
Trippe, James McConky, 24:227,n1
trolleys, 21:226, 312, 341, 343n10
Trollope, Anthony, 14:13; 15:334
Trone, Royal Eugene, 16:199
Trossacks, Perthshire, Wilsons at, 14:523
Trotter, William Monroe, 21:21n1, 275,-n5; 22:50; 24:556, 558,n3
Troutbeck, Westmorland, 16:437, 438, 439; 18:381, 383, 409, 410; Mortal Man Inn, 18:381
Trowbridge, Augustus, 16:465, 508; 17:86, 86n2, 408; 18:354; 19:137, 139; 20:91; 21:13
Trowbridge, Cornelia Polhemus Robertson (Mrs. George Alfred), 20:91,n1
Trowbridge, John Townsend, 17:122,n1
True Americanism (Philadelphia North American), 23:216n2
Trueblood, Benjamin Franklin, 18:419-20,n1
Truesdale, Joseph Robinson, 14:388; 15:57; 18:456
Truesdale, William Haynes, 23:352, 356,n1
Trust Company of America (N.Y.C.), 24:533
trusts, 16:14-15, 475; 17:515, 517, 518; 19:324f, 463, 469; 20:300-301, 316, 504; 21:45, 60, 426; 22:312; 23:118, 121, 296, 612f, 621, 646; 24:14, 158, 340, 374, 395; 25:5, 8, 10, 11, 12, 32,

59-60, 88, 117, 142, 152-53, 154, 158, 175, 178-79, 192, 193, 194, 214, 261-62, 265, 266, 268, 269, 323, 324, 364-65, 367-68, 370, 371, 373, 374, 379-85, 394, 398, 412, 427, 430, 433, 434-35, 495, 496, 502, 503, 504-505 Δ B. M. Anderson, Jr., **25**:419-21; L. D. Brandeis, **25**:58, 288, 289-94, 295; W. J. Bryan, **24**:571; J. B. Clark, **25**:419-21; A. H. Gore, **19**:541, 557; C. E. Hughes, **17**:248; D. B. Jones, **24**:549-50; T. D. Jones, **25**:133; W. B. Killingbeck, **21**:268, 269; and organized labor, **25**:262-63; C. A. Lindbergh, **23**:605n1; C. S. Moore, **23**:593; platform plank, **24**:470, 477-78, 489; T. Roosevelt, **25**:261-62; shoe industry, **25**:207-208; W. H. Taft, **25**:381n6; *see also* monopoly and under the particular industry, such as, steel, tobacco

Trusts, the People and the Square Deal, (Roosevelt), **25**:125,n4

Trust the People (Richmond *Times-Despatch* editorial), **25**:647n1

truth, **23**:308

tuberculosis, N. J. laws, **25**:309

Tucker, Guy B., **23**:518

Tucker, Henry St. George, **16**:542-43,n1; **20**:21; **22**:282,n1, 287, **23**:559, 601; **24**:118, 465-66, 469, 489, 568-69; **25**:647

Tucker, John Randolph, **24**:568

Tucker, Luther Henry, **15**:169

Tucker, William Jewett, **19**:413,n1; **21**:31,n1

Tuckerman, Bayard, **14**:471,n3, 473

Tuckerton, N. J., **22**:375; WW campaign speech, **21**:326

Tudor architecture, **15**:445

Tulane University, **25**:557n1

Tumulty, Joseph Patrick, **21**:19,n6, 141, 346,n15, 433, 589; **22**:81n1, 87n2, 98n1, 118-20, 134, 136n1, 142n1, 145-46, 200, 228, 229n1, 233, 245, 288,n1, 295,n2, 304, 312, 328-29, 356, 357, 439, 451-52, 510, 582, 588; **23**:69,n2, 137, 245, 252, 260, 271; **24**:42, 453, 458, 509n1, 519,n3, 524n3; **25**:xii, 24, 27, 114, 282n2, 423, 514, 518, 519, 561, 566, 579-80, 581-84, 584, 589, 603, 610

Tumulty, Mary Byrne, **25**:514,n4, 561

Tumulty, Philip Anthony, **25**:514,n3, 561

Turgeon, Newton E., **24**:311,n2

Turkey, **25**:610

*Turmoil and Tradition: A Study of the Life and Times of Henry L. Stimson* (Morison), **19**:364n2; **21**:252n6

Turnbull, Charles, **16**:472n2; **17**:87, 558

Turnbull, Edwin Litchfield, **24**:473-74,-n1

Turner, Caroline Mae Sherwood (Mrs. Frederick Jackson), **14**:430; **16**:58

Turner, Frederick Jackson, **14**:430,

516-19; **16**:58; **17**:164, 208, 213, 214; **19**:405n2; **21**:602

Turner, Grace M., **15**:162,n2

Turner, Horatio Whitridge, **18**:468,n1, 493

Turner, Joseph Mallord William, **15**:359

Turpin, Edna Henry Lee, **19**:272-73,n1, 382

Tuscan art, EAW on, **15**:334, 335

Tuttle, Harry Warren, **16**:154

Tuttle, Joseph Parsons, **25**:234n2

Tuttle, William Edgar, Jr., **23**:129; **24**:287,n1

Tuttle, William T., **21**:383

Twain, Mark, **14**:192, 194; **15**:334; **17**:607-608, 610n2, 612; **20**:133,n3, 139, 188, 378n1

Tweed Ring, **19**:513-14; **20**:40, 331; **22**:59; **23**:574-75

Tweedy, Henry Hallam, **17**:128,n9

*Twelfth Night* (Shakespeare), **14**:259, 260; **15**:238,n1

*Twentieth Century Socialism . . .* (Kelly), **21**:174,n2, 175, 179

*Twenty-Seventh Annual Dinner of the New York Southern Society*, **25**:603n

Twichell, Joseph Hopkins, **18**:358,n3

Twin City Princeton Society, **23**:95

*Two Notable Articles About Woodrow Wilson*, **23**:629n2

Tyburski, S. J., **25**:28

Tyler, Charles W., **24**:400,n1,2

Tyler, John, **17**:319

Uhlig, Johannes Karl Robert, **16**:316

Ullswater, Cumberland, Westmorland, Wilsons at, **14**:521, 523; **18**:422

Ulpha Fell, Cumberland, **18**:371

*Ultime Lettere di Jacopo Ortis* (Foscolo), **19**:573

Umbrian Hills, **15**:314

Umbrian school of art, **15**:322, 349

Underhill, Anthony Lispenard, **16**:160, 162, 198

Underhill, Edward D. S., **23**:506

Underwood, Oscar Wilder, **22**:95,n1; **23**:130n1, 513n4, 553, 593, 601, 615; **24**:165,n2, 237,n2, 248, 268, 288, 306n2, 386, 388, 389, 396, 468, 472, 473, 494, 503, 510, 514, 525, 527,n8, 530, 531, 540, 542-43, 545, 560, 565-66, 567; **25**:493n1, 562, 566, 593,n1; campaign funds, **24**:254; Democratic National Convention balloting, **24**:507n1, 516n1; meeting with WW, **24**:555; primaries, in Florida, **24**:382n1; in Georgia, **24**:381n2, 522n1; in North Carolina, **24**:399n1, 464n1, 471n2; in Tennessee, **24**:78, 403n1; in Virginia, **24**:486; portrait, illustration section, Vol. 24

*Underwood Presidential Movement in 1912* (Link), **23**:513n4

unemployment insurance, **22**:144

Unger, Gladys, **25**:55n1
Union City, Ind., **25**:148
Union College, Schenectady, N. Y.,
 **15**:496,n1, 500; **16**:239; **17**:328, 329;
 **19**:19-20,n1, 223, 229, 231-37
*Union College Bulletin*, **19**:237n
Union County, N. J., **21**:83, 464; **22**:22,
 114, 137, 153, 243, 278, 309; **23**:546;
 **25**:582; WW campaign speeches,
 **23**:468-69
Union Hill, N. J., **25**:48
union labor, **19**:245, 255, 269-70, 309-10;
 **24**:258
Union Pacific Railroad, **14**:144; **25**:240
Union Theological Seminary, **16**:248,
 282, 448; **18**:336n1
*Union University Quarterly*, **15**:500n
unions *see* labor unions
unit rule, **24**:501, 502, 503; and platform
 plank, **24**:480; and Kansas delegation
 to the Baltimore Convention, **24**:248-
 n1; Louisiana delegation, **24**:483; Virginia delegation, **24**:469, 486
Unitarians, **16**:228,n3, 230-31
United Carmen's Association, **20**:153n10
United Daughters of the Confederacy,
 **22**:604n2; **25**:574n3
United Mine Workers of America,
 **14**:133n1; **23**:249n2; **25**:399,n1,2, 417
United Negro Democracy of New Jersey,
 **24**:574
United Polish Societies of South Brooklyn, **24**:131-32, 219, 223n1
United Press, **19**:522; **25**:451
United Railways of New Jersey, **18**:40
United Shoe Machinery Co., **25**:296-97,
 303, 414,n2
United Spanish War Veterans, **25**:129-
 34
United States and United States Government:
arbitration treaties, **23**:520, 592,n2; *Attorney General*, **23**:273; *cabinet*, **18**:111-
 13, 117, 118f; **23**:133; Children's Bureau,
 **22**:207,n4; Circuit Court for N. J.,
 **23**:504; Circuit Court for the Southern
 District of New York, **23**:118n5; *Department of Commerce and Labor*, **16**:15n1;
 **22**:207n4; **23**:612; Confederation, **21**:73;
 corrupt practices act, **21**:96; courts,
 **18**:162-82; customs service, **19**:364n2;
 *Department of State*, **19**:363, 363n1;
 **20**:38,n5; **21**:518; District Court, Southern district of New York, **19**:364n2;
 Bureau of Education, **22**:207; farmer's
 free list bill, **22**:592,n2; flag, **21**:120;
 foreign relations, **18**:120-21; Geological
 Survey, **18**:579; Industrial Commission
 Report, **21**:323; *Interior Department*,
 **23**:174,n1; *Interstate Commerce Commission*, **21**:496; **22**:96, 122n2; **23**:228n3,
 408n1; *Justice Department*, **23**:361n3,
 504n6; *Bureau of Labor*, **18**:186n4; Library of Congress, **22**:226; Military

Academy, **16**:172, 175, 235, 239, 243;
 **17**:121; **19**:213-14; **20**:391, 391n1, 439,
 539; National Monetary Commission,
 **19**:94n3; **20**:26,n1, 38,n4; **23**:293,n3, 625;
 Naval Academy, **16**:46, 173, 175, 235,
 243, 272n1; **19**:213-14; **20**:539; navigation laws, **23**:186; party government,
 **18**:199f; party system, **18**:109f; Philippine Commission, **14**:464; **20**:312n2; *Post
 Office Department*, **22**:427n1; *president*,
 **18**:104f, 153, 202; **19**:518-19; **20**:179;
 **21**:573; and state government, **18**:182-
 99; *Supreme Court*, **16**:298; **18**:48, 115,
 150, 168, 172, 174, 175, 178, 180, 187,
 198; **21**:69, 147-48,n1; **22**:313, 314,
 511,n2, 535,n2, 546n5; **23**:54,n3, 59, 62,
 76, 118, 118n4,5, 120, 206, 295n5, 361n2;
 **25**:300; Tariff Commission, **23**:611,n2,
 622-23, 645, 649; *Treasury Department*,
 **17**:108-109, 126; vice-president, **18**:111,
 156; *War Department*, **23**:295n6
*Congress*, **18**:115f, 190, 479n1; **19**:213;
 **21**:358, 454, 474, 505, 564, 573, 596;
 **22**:102, 104, 316; **23**:92, 128-30, 284, 543,
 612, 622, 638; **25**:87, 362-63, 516-17,
 564-65; courts, **18**:176; extraordinary
 session, **25**:567,n3, 588; tariff, **25**:10;
 *House of Representatives*, **18**:123f
 **21**:344n12, 345n13, 454, 456, 608n2;
 **23**:91, 130n1, 131, 132, 192n2, 249,n5,
 383, 504, 649; **25**:87, 160, 242, 247, 248,
 467, 468, 478, 499; committees, **18**:128-
 29; Committee on Insular Affairs,
 **20**:312n2; party make-up, **25**:260-61,
 503; Rules Committee, **20**:258n1;
 speaker, **18**:129f; Stanley Committee,
 **23**:157n1, 423; *United States Steel Corporation. Hearings before the Committee
 of Investigation of United States Steel
 Corporation*, **23**:157n1; Ways and Means
 Committee, **19**:361, 368; **23**:229, 368,
 369; **24**:419; **25**:9, 32, 72, 106, 189, 242,
 370, 438, 588
*Senate*, **16**:375,n1; **18**:140f; **21**:343,n11,
 345n13, 348, 349, 388, 407, 454, 456,
 475, 582, 608n2; **22**:514n4, 515; **23**:4, 8,
 91, 129, 131, 132n, 132n1, 234, 381,
 399n4, 643; **24**:417, 419, 473,n5; **25**:87,
 237-39, 242, 247, 467, 468, 477, 487, 489,
 499, 503, 524, 585,n1, 611-12; Samuel
 Chase Trial, **25**:600; Clapp Committee,
 **25**:109,n1; committees, **18**:157f; direct
 election of senators, **21**:31, 89n3, 96, 126,
 204, 263, 339, 348; **22**:205n2, 355, 371n4,
 578, 592, 601, 603; **23**:235n3, 350, 369;
 election of senators, **18**:151-54; Finance
 Committee, **19**:361, 363, 363n1, 368;
 **20**:38,n5; **21**:474; **23**:368; **24**:419, 577n1;
 **25**:9, 32, 72, 106, 189, 242, 370, 438, 563;
 Maine, **25**:618-19; money trust,
 **24**:577n1; Nevada elections, **25**:359-60;
 panic of 1893, **25**:47; party make-up,
 **25**:260-61; special interests, **25**:431;
 tariff, **25**:407, 437; presidential term of

office, **25**:564-65; presiding officer, **18**:156f
*Constitution*, **15**:537; **16**:310, 364, 501; **18**:74, 96f, 170f, 191, 195; **19**:371, 518-19, 601; **20**:37, 467; **21**:250, 505; **22**:10, 11, 12, 442, 511n1,2, 535n2, 546n5, 562, 595-96; **23**:94, 280; **24**:127, 193, 416, 417, 418; **25**:238, 480; and commercial interests, **14**:231-32, 315, 318; Convention of 1787, **18**:160, 191, 201, 644; **19**:208; **23**:127; Fourteenth Amendment, **19**:352; Sixteenth Amendment, **22**:511,n1,4, 534-35; **24**:216-17 Δ A. Ragan, **19**:272; C. W. Eliot, **25**:286n1
*United States, Annual Report, 1912* (J. Bryce), **24**:507n1
United States Bank, **15**:551
United States Indian Industrial School, Carlise, Pa., **21**:53,n1
United States Mortgage and Trust Co., **19**:308
*United States Reports*, **23**:118n5
United States Steel Corporation, **16**:55, 223; **22**:461; **23**:157n1, 228n3, 246n4, 299n8, 314n2, 504n6; **24**:143, 346,n2, 358,n1, 373, 395, 567,n2; **25**:153, 160, 161, 168, 193, 195, 206, 208, 214, 223, 225, 381,n6, 382, 384n7, 389, 612n2
United States Trust Co., **19**:308
United States *v.* American Tobacco Co., **23**:118n5
United States *v.* United States Steel Corporation *et al.*, **23**:504n6
United Trades and Labor Council of Buffalo, **25**:69n1,2, 92
Universal Exposition, *see* Louisiana Purchase Exposition, St. Louis, 1904
Universal Peace Society, **24**:183n1
Universal Peace Union, **24**:181-83
universities, **21**:305; urban vs. rural, **14**:283
University Club, New York, **16**:143, 301; **24**:586, 587
University Club of Brooklyn, **16**:289
University Club of Buffalo, **24**:309-10, 312
University Club of Detroit, **16**:43
University Club of New York, **25**:553n1
University Club of Philadelphia, **16**:38-39
University College, Oxford, **14**:531
University Extension Society, **19**:98-100, 108-109
University Military School, Mobile, Ala., **15**:325n1, 402-403
University of California Press, **17**:352n2
*University of Chicago Magazine*, **19**:544n3
University of Chicago Press, **17**:352n2, 356
*University of Missouri, A Centennial History* (Viles *et al.*), **15**:157n4
University of Pennsylvania Press, **17**:352n2

*University of South Carolina* (Hollis), **16**:87n2; **22**:577n4
University of the City of New York, *see* New York University
University of the South, Sewanee, Tenn., **16**:90
University of Toronto Press, **17**:352n2
*University of Wisconsin: A History* (Curti and Carstensen), **17**:241n3
*University Record* (of the University of North Carolina), **23**:110n
University School, Cleveland, **16**:510
Untermyer, Alvin, **24**:534,n1
Untermyer, Samuel, **23**:314, 314n1, 325, 340-41, 605,n1, 631; **24**:532, 577-78, 581; **25**:415, 528-29, 542
Upham, Samuel Foster, **14**:435,n4
Upshur, Agnes Maxwell Kearny (Mrs. John Henry), **20**:148,n1, 181
Upshur, John Henry, **20**:148,n1, 181
Upson, Irving Strong, **14**:167,n1
Urban, Wilbur Marshall, **20**:335-36,n1
U'Ren, William Simon, **19**:419,n2, 446; **22**:197,n1, 255n5; **23**:60, 66-67, 70n2, 73, 147, 282, 619; **24**:175-76
Ursinus College, **16**:131, 240, 251; **18**:577; **19**:677
*Utica Observer*, **23**:632
*Utilitarianism* (Mill), **19**:666
Uzzah, **17**:393,n1; **20**:218,n1

Vaca Valley, California, **24**:352
Vail, J. Howard, **23**:533n3
Van Anda, Carl Vattel, **23**:325,n3, 352; **25**:114
Van Arsdall, George B., **23**:21,n7
Van Benthuysen, Boyd, **15**:415
Van Berckel, Pieter Johan, **16**:502
Van Buren, Martin, **17**:319
Vance, Zebulon Baird, **21**:423
Vanderbilt, George Opdyke, **22**:415n2
Vanderbilt, Kermit, **15**:422n2
Vanderbilt Hotel, New York, **25**:415, 507
Vanderbilt University, **16**:247, 254, 564; **17**:457; **20**:539; **23**:103, 511n3
Vanderbilt University Law School, **23**:211
Vanderlip, Frank Arthur, **16**:78,n1, 224; **18**:219, 471, 494, 513, 529-30; **19**:18-19, 29-30, 101, 181, 259-60, 601-602, 604, 607, 609-10; **21**:38, 59; **22**:187,n2, 234; **23**:293n3
Vanderlip, Narcissa Cox (Mrs. Frank Arthur), **18**:471; **21**:38
Van Deventer, Harry Brown, **17**:163,-n11, 557
Van Doren, E. Gertrude (Mrs. John V.), **14**:71,n3
Van Doren, John V., **14**:71,n3
Van Doren, Peter Alfred Voorhees, **14**:195
Van Doren, William Voorhees, **16**:138
Vandruff, Samuel S., **23**:465

Van Duyn, John, **15:**170,n1
Van Dyck, Sir Anthony, **15:**229
Van Dyke, Ellen Reid (Mrs. Henry Jackson, Jr.), **14:**253; **15:**442,n2
Van Dyke, Henry [Jackson, Jr.], **14:**115, 191,n1, 192, 253, 265, 267, 325, 326, 329, 484, 550; **15:**4-5, 119, 134, 136, 296, 442, 491; **16:**38, 38n2, 102, 140n3, 412, 420n1, 448, 485; **17:**58-59, 59-60, 66, 67, 68, 70-71, 92n2, 125, 129, 143, 246, 260-61, 263, 273-75, 276-79, 297n1, 309, 343, 380, 402, 403, 408, 410n1, 428; **18:**579; **19:**551, 673, 739; **20:**254, 265,n2, 268, 362n4; **21:**16,n4,5; **23:**302n2; **24:**4n1
Van Dyke, Henry Nevius, **14:**326,n1, 497; **16:**104,n1, 105, 206, 207, 234, 235; **18:**554
Van Dyke, John Charles, **23:**183
Van Dyke, Katrina Trask, **15:**443
Van Dyke, Paul, **14:**82, 326, 453; **15:**120, 233, 234, 295; **17:**99n2, 108, 110, 125, 129, 197, 233, 263, 343, 408, 413-14; **18:**271, 293; **19:**586; **20:**152, 214-15, 223,n2, 235-36, 249-51, 254, 422-24
Van Dyke, Tertius, **17:**296,n1
Van Dyke, William Duncan, **15:**248
Van Hise, Alice Bushnell Ring (Mrs. Charles Richard), **19:**550,n3
Van Hise, Charles Richard, **14:**430; **15:**145,n1; **16:**539; **17:**240,n3, 551; **19:**550,n1; **23:**480n1; **24:**546,n1, 554
Van Hoesen, Henry Bartlett, **18:**355,n1; **19:**678
Van Hook, La Rue, **16:**101, 132, 254, 528; **17:**162,n9, 408; **20:**451
Van Ingen, Gilbert, **14:**474; **17:**272, 301, 387; **18:**579; **19:**679-82
Van Laer, Alexander Theobald, **23:** 10,n5, 128
Van Meter, John Blackford, **16:**544,n2
Van Nest, John Stout, **14:**215, 217, 218, 220, 221, 474; **16:**10-11
Van Noppen, Charles Leonard, **16:**187,-n2
Van Norden, Warner, **14:**253
Van Pelt, E. L., Mrs., **14:**538,n15, 542, 556
Van Rensselaer, Alexander, **14:**409; **15:** 122-24, 127, 409, 527; **16:**5, 277; **17:** 303,n1; **19:**165, 305, 712; **20:**6n, 15, 245, 247
Van Rensselaer, Sarah Drexel Fell (Mrs. Alexander), **15:**124
Van Reypen, William Knickerbocker, **15:**200
Van Slyke, George Martin, **25:**588,n2
Van Syckel, Bennet, **20:**31,n1; **21:**274,n1
Van Tyne, Claude Halstead, **14:**441-45; **16:**92,n1, 106, 111, 111-12
Vanuxem, Louis Clark, **15:**64,n4, 67
Van Valkenburg, Edwin Augustus, **21:**9,n1, 158, 164-65, 198-200, 241-42, 267; **22:**44n3, 231,n4

Van Valzah, William Ward, M.D., **14:** 424,n3
Van Vleet, Angus McKay, **17:**476n2
Van Vleet, Peter Percy, **17:**474,n1, 480n1
Van Wickle, Augustus Stout, **15:**468n1; **16:**212,n1, 485
Van Wickle, Marjorie, **16:**485
Van Wisselingh Gallery, London, **16:** 506, 506n2
Vardaman, James Kimble, **22:**28,n1; **24:**237,n2, 558n2
*Varieties of Religious Experience: A Study of Human Nature, Being the Gifford Lectures on Natural Religion Delivered at Endinburgh in 1901-1902* (James), **14:**295,n2
Vassar College, **19:**533,n1
Vauclain, Jacques Leonard, **16:**336n9
Vauclain, Samuel Matthews, **16:**336,n9
Vaughan, Clement Leslie, **17:**557
Veblen, Oswald, **16:**160, 162, 178-79, 198, 258; **17:**408
Venable, Helen Skipworth Wilmer (Mrs. Edward Carrington), **14:**102,n2
Venable, Edward Carrington, Jr., **14:** 102,n2
Venable, Francis Preston, **14:**204,n3,4, 467; **16:**435,n3; **18:**561,n2, 588, 634; **22:**20,n1, 517,n1, 520
Vendome Hotel, Boston, **18:**297n1; **20:** 466
Venezuelan boundary controversy, **14:** 282; **22:**11-12,n3
*Venezuelan Boundary Controversy* (Cleveland), **22:** 12n3
Venice, **15:**275, 314, 325; Accademia delle Belle Arti, **15:**359; Grand Canal, **15:**358; Lido, **15:**359; Palazzo Ducale, **15:**359; Piazza San Marco, **15:**359; Ponte dei Sospiri (Bridge of Sighs), **15:**359; San Giorgio degli Schiavoni, **15:**359; San Marco, **15:**359; EAW in, **15:**355-56, 358-59
Venus de Milo, **15:**298
Verdery, Annie Winter (Mrs. Eugene E.), **23:**556,n1
Verdery, Eugene E., **23:**556,n1
Verdery, Marion Jackson, **16:**529,n1; **18:**532,n2, 563; **22:**201-203,n1, 257, 552-53
Vermont, **23:**134; **24:**429; **25:**51, 52, 157,n1; Democratic party, **25:**126
Vermont, University of, **15:**379; **16:**249, 252, 255; **17:**556
Vernon, Ambrose White, **16:**189,n2, 190; **17:**125; **18:**10,n1; **25:**568
Verona, Italy, **14:**246
Versailles, **15:**441; Grand Trianon, **14:**536; Wilsons at, **14:**536, 555
Vessey, Robert Scadden, **20:**43n8
Vesuvius, Mount, **15:**235
Veysey, Laurence R., **15:**292n28

*Vicar of Wakefield* (Goldsmith), **14**:503; **20**:190n4

Vicario, John, **25**:28

Vick, Walker Whiting, **21**:115-16,n1, 608; **24**:461

Viles, Jonas, **15**:157n4; **16**:41,n7, 68-69, 88,n1

Villard, Fanny Garrison (Mrs. Henry), **17**:609n1

Villard, Henry, **17**:609n1

Villard, Oswald Garrison, **17**:609,n1; **20**:141; **21**:58-59, 618; **22**:26, 83, 101-102, 127, 135-36, 287, 288-89, 307, 308, 454-55; **23**:560-61, 589, 632, 633; **24**:59, 63, 72-74; **25**:24-26, 26-27, 29, 41, 52-53, 60-61

Vincent, George Edgar, **23**:82,n15, 83, 86-87, 87, 93, 112; **25**:169,n1

Vincent, John Martin, **19**:405n2

Vineland, N. J., **23**:290, 300; Mystic Chain Hall, **23**:532; Soldiers' Home, **23**:532-33,n2; WW campaign speech, **23**:531, 532-33

Vinogradoff, Paul Gavrilovitch, **17**:226-n1

Virgil (Publius Vergilius Maro), **15**:118, 229; **16**:90

Virginia, **16**:299, 300; **17**:51-56; **22**:282, 287, 604n2; **23**:241, 313, 591n2; **24**:96, 237, 469, 489, 514, 536, 543, 568-69, 578; **25**:129, 530, 647,n1,2; Anti-Saloon League, **23**:328n2; Bill of Rights, **23**:648; Constitution, **18**:71, 637; Democratic National Convention (1912), **24**:463, 522; **25**:638; first ballot votes, **24**:471,n1; forty-third ballot vote, **24**:521n5; Democrats, *see* Democratic party and Democrats in Virginia; Harvey-Watterson affair, **24**:71; history, **25**:596, 631-32, 634, 640; legislature, **23**:631; liquor interests, **23**:327; Thomas S. Martin, **24**:72n9; politics, **23**:559; representative government, **23**:550; state convention, **24**:398n1; unit rule, **24**:469, 486; WW addresses, **25**:626-40; **24**:101-17, 117-22

*Virginia*, S.S., **22**:597

Virginia, University of, **14**:32, 188, 189,-n2, 203-204n2,4; **15**:60, 79-80, 100,n4, 213, 393-95,n3, 507-508,n1,2,3, 574; **16**:35-36,n1, 193-94, 195-97, 256, 284, 509; **17**:557; **18**:31, 567; **19**:109; **20**:256, 371n2, 539; **21**:595, 597-98; **22**:118, 140, 383-84, 558, 559; **23**:549, 550; **24**:72n9, 121, 163, 474; **25**:553, 627; Cabell Hall, **23**:550; *College Topics*, **16**:197n; Fayerweather Gymnasium, **23**:549; Glee Club (Octette), **22**:383,n3, 384; Jefferson Literary Society, **15**:508,n3; **22**:383,n2; **23**:550; Lambeth Field, **23**:550; Madison Hall, **16**:161, 193-94, 195-97; Society of Alumni, **15**:16,n1; Washington Society, **15**:508,n3; WW address, **16**:195-97; Woodrow Wilson Club, **23**:550; Y.M.C.A., **22**:326,n1, 333

Virginia Bill of Rights, **24**:114-15, 130, 180, 235, 339; **25**:186, 248, 639

*Virginia: Bourbonism to Byrd* (Moger), **24**:398n1; **25**:632n1

Virginia Press Association, **23**:328,n2

Virginia Society of Colonial Dames, **14**:396

Virginia State Bar Association, **21**:117; **23**:139,n2

Vittorio Emanuele III, King of Italy, **15**:273n1, 297, 353

Vlasto, S. J., **25**:29

Vlissingen (Flushing), Holland, **15**:441

vocational education, **24**:223; **25**:36, 37-38

*Voce del Popolo* (Philadelphia), **24**:133n1

*Voice of Independence* (Washington, D. C.), **21**:616,n2

Voorhees, Daniel S., **24**:430,n1

Voorhees, Foster, **21**:277, 378

Voorhees, James Dayton, **16**:24n2

Voorhees, John Hunn, **16**:406, 411

Voorhis, Eleanor Glasgow, **16**:143,n1, 150

Voorhis, Julia Clark, **16**:144n1, 150

Votaw, Clyde Weber, **14**:198

voting registration, **25**:328, 338

voting, **25**:91, 127-28

Vreeland, Edward Butterfield, **24**:238,n1

Vreeland, Williamson Updike, **14**:137,-n3, 296, 326; **15**:29-32, 52n1, 56, 74, 183, 189, 205; **16**:27, 61, 68, 80, 154, 167; **17**:408; **19**:562-76; **21**:154-55

Vroom, Garret Dorset Wall, **22**:415n2

Waco (Texas) *Tribune*, **23**:268,n7

Wade, Benjamin Franklin, **17**:314

Wadham College, Oxford, **17**:557

Wadsworth, James Wolcott, Jr., **19**:756,n2; **20**:33,n2, 43n8

wages, **25**:268, 342

Wagner, Richard, **15**:212

Wagner, Jay J., **22**:291n2

Wainwright, Musson, **25**:551n1

Wake County, N. C., **24**:461

Walbridge, Marguerite, and mother, **15**:241,n2, 269, 276, 347, 356, 357

Wald, Lillian D., **22**:157n1, 297n14

Waldorf-Astoria Hotel, New York, **14**:288, 298; **15**:68, 545; **16**:320, 344, 362-n1, 369n, 529; **17**:65, 78n1; **18**:532; **19**:175, 601; **20**:23, 25, 66, 402n1, 556; **21**:265, 621; **22**:51, 274, 389, 392, 453n1; **25**:527n2, 589, 617n3,4

Waldron, John Milton, **21**:21n1, 275,-n1,3, 292, 387; **24**:556; **25**:52, 60, 65-66, 548, 620

Walker, Byron Edmund, **18**:430,n4

Walker, Edward Washburn, **17**:225,n2; **19**:597,n3

Walker, James Henry, 19:73n3
Walker, John Brisben, 15:450n1, 460-61, 462-63,n1
Walker, Robert Scott, 17:225,n1; 19: 597-98,n1
Walker, William David, 17:115,n2,3
Walker, Williston, 19:381n4
Wall, Albert Chandler, 16:215,n2
Wall, Joseph Frazier, 16:55n3, 305n4
Wall Street, the Interests, 20:562n1, 568, 570; 21:5, 29, 55n2, 98-99, 335n2, 554; 22:77n1, 199, 237, 261, 275, 292, 495; 23:246n1, 437n2, 632; 24:60, 164, 165, 254n1, 502; 25:330, 357, 411; anti Bryan men on, 24:400
Wallace, George Riddle, 15:103; 16:406
Wallace, Henry, 25:62,n1
Wallace, Hugh Campbell, 25:507,n2
Wallace, Sir Richard, 14:528n9
Wallace, William Hockaday, 24:186,n2
Wallace's Farmer, 25:62n1
Wallenstein, David, 24:461,n1
Waller, Elizabeth Wallace (Mrs. James Breckinridge), 14:453,n2
Waller, James Breckinridge, 14:195, 453,n2; 15:64,n4; 16:5
Waller, Lewis, 14:527n7
Walpole, Sir Robert, 14:502; 16:499
Walsh, Allan Bartholomew, 22:29,n1, 504n1, 546n5, 574n1,4; 23:109,n4; 25:345-46,n3
Walsh, Francis Patrick, 25:310,n3, 543
Walsh, Thomas F., 14:130,n2
Walsh Act for commission government N. J.), 24:431
Walters, Alexander, 21:21n1, 47n1, 275,n2,4; 25:448-49,n, 450, 571, 606-608
Walton Hotel, Philadelphia, 19:509n1
Walworth, Arthur, 20:582n, 583n
Walz, William L., 24:57
Wanamaker, John, 14:253; 15:160n3, 520,n3; 16:227n2, 336; 21:431n6, 601; 24:13n3
Wanamaker, [Lewis] Rodman, 16:302,-n2, 303, 336; 21:267,n4
Wanamaker, Mary Lowber Welsh (Mrs. Thomas Brown), 21:267,n3
Wanamaker, Thomas Brown, 15:141; 16:302,n1,3, 303, 307, 336; 21:267,n2,4
Wanamaker (John) Store, New York City, 14:61, 92, 111
Wansfell Pike, Westmorland, 16:437, 438, 443; 18:371
War of 1812, 14:344, 444
Warburg, Paul Moritz, 23:293n3
Ward, Edward Joshua, 23:255, 256, 258, 481n2; 25:546,n1
Ward, James, 15:506,n2
Ward, Jane Shaw, 23:21,n13
Ward, Mary Augusta Arnold (Mrs. Humphrey), 15:97,n5; 18:4,n2
Ward, William Hayes, 14:11,n3
Ware, Henry Burt, 21:463,n1

Ware, Daisy Davidson (Mrs. Leonard Everett), 15:265,n4, 384,n1
Warfield, Benjamin Breckinridge, 17:17,n8
Wahrheit, Die, 24:28,n3
Warner, E. Walpole, 14:114
Warner, Everett Longley, 23:81,n5
Warner, Hoyt Landon, 22:161n1
Warren, Catherine Carter Campbell (Mrs. Howard Crosby), 20:412, 414
Warren, Estelle Ward Carey (Mrs. Frederick Morris), 15:166
Warren, Francisca Machado (Mrs. Augustus Gibson Paine), 17:546,n5
Warren, Frederick Morris, 15:166-67
Warren, Henry White, 23:21, 21,n4
Warren, Herbert Cleveland, 18:522,n1
Warren, Howard Crosby, 14:553,n3; 15:135,n1, 136; 17:408; 20:412n1
Warren, Minton, 17:546n1,3, 548, 549, 565, 587, 588
Warren, Minton Machado, 17:547,n4
Warren, Salomé Machado (Mrs. Minton), 17:546-48,n1, 548-49, 554, 565
Warren County, N. J., 21:382-85; 22:370; 23:270-72; 25:582; Farmers' picnic, 23:270; WW campaign speech, 23:466-68
Warrenton, N. C., 19:324n2; 23:606n2
Warwick, Bermuda, Christ Church, 17:27-28,n1
Warwick, England, Wilsons in, 14:530, 531
Wasdale Hall, Cumberland, 18:374
Washington, Booker Taliaferro, 14:192, 15:502; 18:386,n1; 19:69n1; 21:21n1, 275n3,5
Washington, George, 14:311, 352, 365, 507; 15:44, 174, 213; 16:11-12, 53, 57, 206, 316-18, 359, 502; 17:49, 50, 74, 455, 462, 620n3; 18:6, 98, 112, 117, 119, 122, 179, 202, 635; 19:65-66, 203, 205, 272, 506; 21:138, 180, 184, 196, 309, 404,n4, 425, 480, 518, 598; 22:4, 229, 389; 23:23, 89, 127, 282, 292-93, 309, 367, 591n2, 648; 24:120; Farewell Address, 24:225; Houdon bust of, 14:71,n2
Washington, D. C., 23:234, 566, 592, 593; 24:287; 25:472, 543-44, 549-50; Church of the Covenant, 19:64n1; Democracy of the District of Columbia, 23:566; Jackson Day dinner, Jan. 1912, 23:602n1; 24:9; National Press Club, 22:377n1, 396, 404; Princeton alumni, 14:303n1, 337, 400, 447; 19:146; 20:247; Raleigh Hotel, 23:566; Shoreham Hotel, 20:211, 225; 22:20; 23:566; University Club, 16:315; 23: 292,n2; Willard Hotel, 14:400; 23:129, 131; WW addresses, 14:400-403; 16:315-18; 19:202-210; 24:9-16, 16-17; WW in, 19:578; 23:128-32
Washington, Mount, 14:111
Washington, N. J., 21:382-83; Baker's

Hotel, **21:**383; WW campaign speech, **21:**383; **23:**467
Washington and Jefferson College, **16:** 106-107, 130, 248
Washington and Lee University, **14:**87; **17:**556; **23:**327
Washington Association of New Jersey, Morristown, N. J., **14:**131,n1, 142, 144, 222, 247, 348, 349, 354, 356, 365, 378, 394, 495, 496, 497, 501; **15:**32-33, 48, 49, 51,n1,2, 52
*Washington Evening Star*, **16:**318n; **21:** 275n2; **22:**34,n3; **25:**544
*Washington Herald*, **21:**275n2, 387n1; **22:**160,n1; **25:**544
Washington Hotel, Seattle, **23:**78, 80
Washington Park, N. J., **25:**31
*Washington Post*, **14:**403n; **16:**302n; **21:** 275n2, 615n2; **22:**255n1, 399n; **25:**274n3, 544
Washington state, **22:**395, 519; **23:**323; **25:**397, 645; Democrats, **23:**598; preferential ballots, **23:**456; Wilson League, **23:**598
Washington University, St. Louis, **16:** 132, 254; **19:**101-102; **23:**560n1
Wast Water, Cumberland, **18:**371, 373-74, 379, 386
watered stock, **22:**69, 461; **25:**207
Waters, Henry Jackson, **25:**645,n8
Waters, W. T., Jr., **24:**333-35, 344-47
Waters-Pierce Oil Company, **25:**604n1
Watkins, Edmund, **18:**399,n1
Watkins, Idelette Christian Dial (Mrs. Edmund), **18:**399,n1
Watkins, Walter Hudson, **18:**342-43,n1, 398-99, 420-21, 465
Watson, Clarence Wayland, **23:**215,n1; **25:**23,n3
Watson, David Thompson, **24:**317n1
Watson, Gertrude, **21:**48,n1
Watson, John, **19:**666,n4
Watson, Thomas Edward, **25:**493,n1
Watters, Philip Sidney, **20:**405,n1
Watterson, Henry, **14:**17n3; **16:**532,n2, 534; **18:**271-72; **20:**541n1, 544, 556; **21:**433, 435; **22:**140, 143, 160, 181n1, 184-85, 212, 274, 286, 393-94, 435,n1; **23:**153-54, 182-83, 199, 221-22, 226, 303, 560n2, 603, 603n1; **24:**40-42,n1,2, 45-47, 48-50, 52, 59n1, 60,n1, 61-64, 68, 73, 76, 77-78, 80,n1,n2, 95, 97-98,n2, 332n2, 400, 529; *see also* Harvey-Watterson affair
Watterson, Rebecca Ewing (Mrs. Henry), **22:**274, 393, 394; **23:**154,n2, 183, 199, 221, 226, 303n2
Waycross, Ga., **24:**347
Wayland, Chandler Norton, **22:**331,n3
Wayland, Francis, **17:**328, 329
Wayland, Lucy Elton (Mrs. Chandler Norton), **22:**331,n4
Wayland, Mary Isabel Scovill (Mrs. John Elton), **24:**58,n1
Ways and Means Committee, *see* United

States Congress, House of Representatives
Wayt, Hampton H., **22:**9, 96
Wazeter, Leon F., **25:**28
wealth, **25:**98-99
*Wealth of Nations* (Smith), **14:**505
Weatherford College, Texas, **16:**254
Weaver, James Baird, **24:**221n3
Weaver, James Bellamy, Jr., **24:**221,n3
Weaver, Jonn, **16:**225,n1; **21:**342n6
Webb, Clement Charles Julian, **15:** 441,n1
Webb, John, **20:**136
Webb, Walter Prescott, **25:**423n1
Webb, William Robert, **16:**235,n3
Webb & Prall (New York Stockbrokers), **14:**499
Webb School, Bell Buckle, Tenn., **16:** 235,n3
Webster, Daniel, **14:**251, 282, 519; **15:**45; **16:**53; **17:**312, 319; **18:**101, 632-33, 637; **22:**218; **24:**417; **25:**633-34
Webster, James Edwin, **15:**361; **19:**252; **20:**50; **21:**555,n5; **23:**568,n11
Webster Hotel, New York City, **19:**229n3
Wedderburn, Joseph Henry Maclagan, **19:**138, 139, 678
Wedel, Karl, Graf von, **19:**327,n2
Weden, Nicholas P., **25:**582,n2, 583
Weehawken, N. J., **21:**43; Public School No. 3, **23:**537
*Weekly News* (Palmyra, N. J.), **22:**164n1
Weinstein, Edwin Alexander, M.D., **16:** 412n1
Welch, William Henry, M.D., **20:**31,n3, 368, 538; **21:**129-30; **22:**396n1
welfare, **24:**566
Welles, Caroline McMurty (Mrs. Henry Hunter), **18:**383n5, 389
Welles, Charlotte Rose, **18:**383n5
Welles, Harriet Woodrow (Mrs. Edward Freeman), **23:**12,n3, 28; **25:**627n2,3
Welles, Henry Hunter, Jr., **15:**471,n3; **18:**383,n5, 389
Welles, Henry Hunter III, **18:**383n5
Welles, Katherine Ryerson, **18:**383n5
Wellesley College, **19:**677
Wells, Carolyn, **25:**458,n1
Wells, Edward J. A., **23:**532
Wells, Somerset, Cathedral, **14:**533; Episcopal Palace garden, **14:**533; Swan Hotel, **14:**533; Wilsons at, **14:**532, 533
Wells, Rolla, **16:**5; **24:**587,n1; **25:**49
Wells, Thomas Bucklin, **16:**143,n2
Wells College, **16:**255
*Weltgeschichte* (ed. Helmolt), **14:**339,n3
Weltnar, Akos, **24:**548-49,n1
Wendell, Barrett, **16:**170; **19:**315n2, 349,n1; **20:**475,n3
Wendell, Edith Greenough (Mrs. Barrett), **19:**349,n2
Wendell, Evert Jansen, **15:**165,n1
Wertenbaker, Charles Christian, **20:** 371,n3

Wertenbaker, Thomas Jefferson, **15:** 284n6; **20:**371,n2, 430

Werts, George Theodore, **21:**258n10; 343n9; **22:**173,n3

Wescott, John Wesley, **21:**103,n1, 137, 152, 421, 604; **22:**42-43, 169-70, 206, 261-62, 289, 394, 413, 414-15, 451-52, 516, 520-21, 548-49; **23:**411, 424, 425, 518-19; **24:**179, 189-90, 449-50, 452, 462, 511n2, 512; **25:**146-47, 184,n1, 217, 218

Wesley, Charles, **14:**510

Wesley, John, **14:**421,n3, 502-15; **24:**381

Wesley, Samuel (1662-1735), **14:**506

Wesley, Susannah Annesley (Mrs. Samuel), **14:**506

Wesley College, University of Manitoba, **16:**159

Wesleyan Female College (Macon, Ga.), **24:**354-55,n2

Wesleyan University, **16:**68, 80, 239; **17:**557; **18:**62n2, 383,n3,4; **19:**475n3; New York alumni, **16:**243; Oregon alumni, **23:**66; *1703-1903, Wesley Bicentennial,* **14:**515n; Wesley Bicentennial Celebration, **14:**515

Wesser, Robert Frank, **19:**26n6

West, Andrew Fleming, **14:**23, 26, 36, 61, 81,n1, 87, 139-40, 157, 158, 245-47, 258,n3, 295, 326, 336, 361, 361n1, 394, 395n, 400, 411, 436, 448, 546,n2; **15:**15, 56, 60, 73, 96,n2, 117, 119, 135, 164, 184-85, 185n3, 258, 274n5, 340, 533, 533n1; **16:**32, 35, 60, 70, 87, 95, 101, 104, 140, 184, 205, 215, 386, 406, 414n2, 423, 435, 458, 464, 467, 468, 478, 480, 480n1, 515; **17:**46, 66, 138, 142-46, 154-55, 155-56, 160, 164, 165, 166, 270-71, 280, 309, 343, 382, 408, 422-24, 462, 553n1, 587, 590, 590n1, 591, 592, 594; **18:**67n2, 227, 242, 279, 292, 295, 296, 300n2, 301, 304, 314, 346, 355, 355-56, 373, 472,n2, 484, 490, 494, 626n1; **19:**8-9, 12, 48, 79,n2, 114, 116, 117, 124,n1, 172, 189-90,n1, 195, 237, 240, 398, 403-404, 413, 420-21, 421-22, 426, 433, 436, 437, 442-43, 456, 457, 458, 459, 482, 604-605,n2, 626, 628, 629, 631, 632, 650-51, 652-55, 659, 660, 662, 673, 688-89, 695, 696, 706, 710, 712, 735, 736; **20:**4,n2, 6n-9n, 10-11, 16, 17, 18, 28, 29-30, 30, 46, 47, 51, 56, 57, 57-58, 62, 63, 74, 76n1, 79, 81, 82, 84, 87, 92, 93, 95, 96, 97, 98, 99, 101-102, 104-105, 107, 115,n6, 116, 119, 121-22, 125, 128-29, 130, 138, 143, 144, 148n, 153n2, 156-57, 174, 175, 182, 183, 189, 208, 209n1, 210, 222, 225, 249, 267, 269, 270, 277-78, 280-81, 282, 303-305, 310, 319, 322, 323-24, 326, 354-55, 394, 395, 396, 410, 411, 422-24, 427, 428, 431, 432, 433, 454-55, 457, 461, 464, 465-66, 470, 471, 472, 474, 476, 479, 481, 482, 484, 485, 491, 494, 500, 502, 510, 536; **21:**13, 25, 36; **22:**436, 438, 487, 487n2,3; **23:**139, 302, 599, 600; **24:**3-4, 559n1; **25:**232; dilettante ideals, **19:**755n2

West, Clara Lindforth, **15:**274,n5

West, Nathaniel, **16:**435,n1; **20:**84,n2

West, Oswald, **21:**608n2; **23:**66,n3

West, Willis Mason, **23:**93,n1

West (U. S.), enslavement to East, **23:**106; political discontent in, **23:** 608-609

West Chester, Pa., **25:**462-66; State Normal School, **16:**282; WW address, **16:**282

West Hoboken, N. J., **23:**634n1; St. Michael's Hall, **21:**473; WW campaign speech, **21:**473

West Hotel, Minneapolis, **23:**86

West New York, N. J., **23:**634n1; St. Joseph's Hall, **21:**473; WW campaign speech, mentioned, **21:**473

West Point, *see* U. S. Military Academy

West Shore Railroad, **20:**391

*West Tennessee Historical Society Papers,* **18:**485n1

West Tennessee Land Company, **18:** 485n1

West Virginia, **25:**129, 419; delegation to Democratic National Convention, **24:**521n5

Westcott, Edith F. Sampson (Mrs. John Howell), **14:**50, 57, 86, 93, 95, 111, 118, 555; **16:**89,n1, 159,n1, 171, 180

Westcott, Edward Noyes, **14:**72n6; **22:** 331n5

Westcott, John Howell, **14:**50, 57, 86, 93, 95, 98, 111, 118, 296, 326, 327, 394, 411, 555; **15:**17-19, 291n, 304, 306-307; **16:**88-89, 97n2, 423, 528; **17:**46-47,n3, 112, 114, 139, 161-63, 218, 290, 333, 408, 587, 588, 601, 613-15; **18:**12,n5, 271, 582; **19:**737, 738

Westcott, Marian Bate (Mrs. John Howell II), **17:**613-14,n1; **18:**12,n5

Westcott, William Augustus, M.D., **22:** 261,n1

*Western Architect,* **24:**487n1

Western Association of Princeton Clubs, **14:**440n1, 445, 446-47, 448-49, 450; **15:**128; **16:**47,n1, 48n2, 95, 100, 383,-n4, 386, 389, 396, 405; **18:**51-52, 218n1, 280-85; **19:**211, 212, 505-506; **20:**209, 211, 212, 217, 220, 237, 238, 243-44, 252,n1, 252-53, 254, 256, 257, 262, 271, 284, 291-96, 303, 304,n2, 306-307n1, 311, 312, 320, 321, 322, 387, 410; **21:**623n2

Western Electric Company, Chicago, **16:**512

Western Pennsylvania alumni, **14:**383, 446; **16:**32, 70,n2, 559; **18:**51

Western Reserve University, **16:**91-92n1, 249; **19:**333,n1

Western Theological Seminary, Pittburgh, **16**:306,n7
Western University of Pennsylvan__ (now University of Pittsburgh), **16**:489,n4
Westervelt, Harry Clarkson, M.D., **18**:507-508
Westfield, N. J., **23**:468
Westinghouse, George, **22**:478,n2
Westinghouse Electric and Manufacturing Company, **18**:577
Westminster Assembly of Divines, **17**:347n1
Westminster College, Fulton, Mo., **19**:679
Westminster School, Simsbury, Conn., **16**:509
Westmoreland County, Pa., bituminous coal strike, **23**:249,n2,3,4,5
Westmorland, England, **24**:524
Westmorland Music Festival, **18**:378
*Westover Manuscripts* (ed. Ruffin), **17**:620,n1
Westport, Mo., Country Club, **16**:100
Wetmore, Edmund, **16**:11,n1
Weyl, Walter, **20**:350n2
Weyman, Stanley John, **15**:115,n1
Wharton, Joseph, **16**:336,n10
What Happened to the *World*? (Philadelphia *North American*), **23**:246n1
What's the Matter with Kansas? (White), **14**:239,n6, 369, 420, 492; **15**:171,n4; **25**:385,n8
What's the Matter with the Public Schools? (Dorr), **18**:62,n2, 68,n1
*What Woman is Here?* (Bakewell), **24**:316n3
Wheatley School (Kansas City, Mo.), **24**:484n1
Wheaton, Harry C., **25**:481,n8, 482,n10, 484
White, John Barber, **25**:62,n1
Wheeler, Arthur Ledlie, **18**:550,n1, 564
Wheeler, Benjamin Ide, **16**:112,n1; **22**:54; **23**:55,n4, 59
Wheeler, Joseph, **24**:122
Wheelock, Ralph W., **23**:85
Whelen, Charles Smith, **15**:161,n2, 162
Whelen, Mrs. Charles Smith, **15**:162
Whelen, Charles Smith, Jr., **15**:161n2, 162
When, in disgrace with Fortune and men's eyes (Shakespeare sonnet), **20**:185
When Earth's Last Picture is Painted (Kipling), **23**:398,n3
When Merwick was the University's "Graduate House" 1905-1913 (Thorp), **19**:755n2
Whig Party, **17**:319
Whipple, George, **18**:64n19, 248; Hazen & Whipple, Consulting Engineers, New York, **18**:64n1
whisky, **16**:456

Whistler, James Abbot McNeill, **18**:349
Whitacre, John Jefferson, **24**:467
White (a pro-Boer), **14**:325
White, Andrew Dickson, **15**:502; **17**:92n2; **23**:584
White, Charles A., **21**:343n11
White, Daniel S., **23**:522n1, 523, 529n3
White, David Irvine, **15**:226,n2
White, Edward Douglass, **23**:55n3; **25**:563, 565
White, Harry, **16**:406
White, Henry, **16**:570,n2; **19**:658,n1
White, Henry Alexander, **14**:331
White, Horace, **24**:153
White, Howell North, **15**:375
White, Israel Losey, **20**:512-13,n1, 530-31
White, John Albert, **15**:150n3
White, John Barber, **25**:312n2
White, John Josiah, **23**:316,n1
White, John Williams, **14**:382; **17**:588,n4
White, Mrs. (nurse for J. R. Wilson), **14**:197
White, Thomas Henry, M.D., **16**:33,n4
White, William Allen, **14**:239n6; **15**:171,n4; **17**:260n1; **19**:163,n2, 661; **20**:362n4, 566n; **25**:385n8
*White Chief: James Kemble Vardaman* (Holmes), **24**:237n2
White Hart (hotel), Lincoln, Lincs, **14**:526
White Mountain, **14**:73, 99; **23**:263; presidential range, **14**:111
Whitefield, George, **14**:507, 508, 510; **24**:211
Whitley, Joseph, **14**:28,n1, 43, 92
whitewashed men, **21**:480
Whitlock, Brand, **21**:607,n1; **22**:161n1
Whitmer, George R., **25**:163
Whitmore, Edith M., **24**:100,n1, 140
Whitney, George Washington Tapley, **17**:556; **20**:446
Whitridge, Frederick Wallingford, **20**:187,n2
Whitridge, Lucy Charlotte Arnold (Mrs. Frederick Wallingford), **20**:187,n2
Whittier, John Greenleaf, **14**:517
Whittlesey, Walter Lincoln, **16**:385,n1, 385, 465, 511; **17**:286; **19**:73,n1, 77, 615
Whitty, James Howard, **19**:606-607,n1,2
Why Did Governor Wilson Snub the Old Soldiers and Their Wives? (Camden, N. J. *Daily Courier*), **23**:533n2
Wickersham, George Woodward, **19**:552; **20**:312n2; **22**:600,n3; **23**:361,n3, 443; **25**:558,n5
Wickham, Julia P., **16**:534,n1, 536
Wiehle, Paul, **16**:177,n1, 185
Wiggins, Benjamin Lawton, **14**:139; **16**:90,n1
Wight, George, **23**:304,n1
Wightman, McQueen Salley, **14**:145n4, 422,n1; **15**:118,n1, 119, 120

Wigmore, John Henry, **25**:611,n1
Wikoff, James Holmes, M.D., **15**:222, 231, 311,n5
Wilbur, George Franklin Fort, M.D., **14**:63, 65
Wild, Georgio, M.D., **15**:302,n3, 303, 322
Wilde, Edward Seymour, **22**:41-42,n1
Wilder, William Royal, **14**:46, 47, 63, 195; **15**:151, 161, 270, 374-75, 528,n6, 528-29; **16**:419; **17**:393-94, 448; **19**:64, 424; **20**:22, 65-66, 67, 218; **21**:129, 150; **22**:358-59, 361
Wildwood, N. J., **23**:272, 364; **25**:474n1, 478n6; Five Mile Beach, **23**:275; Hippodrome, **21**:281n1, 283; Wildwood Manor, **23**:274, 275; WW speeches, **21**:281-87; **25**:479-85
*Wildwood (N. J.) Beach Weekly Journal*, **23**:275n
Wildwood Crest, N. J., **23**:274; borough council, **23**:274
Wiley, Harvey Washington, **25**:150,n4, 282,n1, 535
Wiley, Louis, **16**:231; **17**:565; **23**:287,n1, 325, 352, 355-56; **25**:107, 114, 115
Wilhelm II, Emperor of Germany, **15**:353; **21**:48
Wilhelmina, Queen of Holland, **15**:236,n1, 240, 353
Wilkes-Barre, Pa., **18**:383; **21**:211; Princeton alumni, **19**:146
*Wilkes-Barre News*, **17**:121,n1,2
Wilkins, John Franklin, **16**:5
Wilkins, Robert Crew, **19**:165
Wilkins, Walter Maurice, **20**:373,n2, 421,n1; **21**:98,n1, 102
Willard, Ralph Claude, **18**:579; **19**:73,n1, 77
Willard Hotel, Washington, **23**:129, 131
Willcox, Thomas H., **22**:596
Willey, Day Allen, **14**:11,n1
William III, Prince of Orange, **14**:504; **16**:501-502; **18**:119
*William Howard Taft: A Conservative's Conception of the Presidency* (Anderson), **22**:427n1
*William Jay Gaynor: Mayor of New York* (Smith), **20**:402n1
*William F. McCombs, the President Maker* (Lyons), **24**:509n1
*William Wordsworth: His Life, Works and Influence* (Harper), **15**:111n
Williams, Billy, **23**:85,n6
Williams, Carl Sheldon, M.D., **20**:539
Williams, Charles Richard, **17**:569,n2, 574; **22**:52,n1, 525,n1, 557,n3
Williams, George Fred, **23**:242,n2; **24**:269,n1, 270, 364, 391; **25**:578
Williams, George Goodwin, **19**:323,n3
Williams, George Weems, **20**:264,n1
Williams, Henry L., **20**:539
Williams, James Thomas, Jr., **20**:372,n1, 390
Williams, Jeannette Hunt (Mrs. George Goodwin), **19**:323,n3

Williams, Jesse Lynch, **14**:297, 417, 490; **20**:249; **23**:599
Williams, John, **15**:449, 450, 470; **23**:340, 340,n5
Williams, John Rogers, **14**:490n4, 499; **15**:431n, 434n1, 436, 443, 462, 575; **16**:170, 171, 431, 478,n1,3
Williams, John Sharp, **21**:557,n1; **22**:93-94, 197; **24**:273, 287,n1, 371, 372, 378, 411, 468, 470n1, 474, 489, 507n1, 531
Williams, Linsly Rudd, M.D., **17**:234-36,n1
Williams, Marnay, **25**:310,n2
Williams, Percy Herbert, M.D, **19**:165
Williams, Stevens Edwin, **24**:386,n1, 388, 390
Williams, Stevenson Archer, **14**:358
Williams, Talcott, **14**:388
Williams, Thomas, **22**:50,n3
Williams, Thomas T., **20**:402n1
Williams, Walter, **15**:156,n1; **16**:69,n1
Williams, William D., **23**:512,n3
Williams College, **15**:86, 234, 330n3; **16**:46, 132, 198, 248, 249, 253, 257; **17**:284, 307, 329, 392, 528, 556; **18**:271, 347-48, 369, 382-83, 437-39, 467, 570, 571, 578, 579; **19**:71, 679; **20**:318, 449; **21**:421, 558, 559n1; **23**:242,n1; *The Induction of Harry Augustus Garfield, LL.D. into the Office of President*, **18**:439n; WW speech to New York alumni, **19**:30-31; **22**:490,n5
Williamson, Edgar, **21**:55-56,n1, 59-61, 61n1, 83, 85, 89, 115, 180
Williamsport, Pa., Princeton alumni, **19**:146
Williamstown, Mass., **18**:382, 419, 423, 448, 467
Willis, Henry Parker, **25**:531,n1, 589, 608, 641n1, 643-44, 650
Willoughby, Westel Woodbury, **17**:555,-n1, 563; **19**:405n2; **20**:407,n1
Willoughby, William Franklin, **19**:405-n2
Wills Point, Texas, **23**:268,n6
*Wills Point* (Texas) *Chronicle*, **23**:268,n6
Willson, Augustus Everett, **18**:7n1; **22**:172, 214-15
Wilson, Frederick Newton, **14**:440,n1; **17**:259
Wilmington, Del., **24**:353; Princeton alumni, **19**:152,n1; WW addresses, **19**:152,n1; **25**:425-32
Wilmington, Del. *Every Evening*, **19**:152n1; **25**:432n
Wilmington, N. C., First Presbyterian Church, **15**:154,n2, 218; **21**:115
Wilmot, David, **17**:320
Wilson, Albert Harris, **14**:326,n2; **15**:14
Wilson, Alfred McCalmont, **23**:64,n3; **25**:541
Wilson, Alice (niece of WW), **15**:319,n2; **16**:537; **17**:376; **18**:484; **20**:45, 50, 239; **21**:115; **25**:613

Wilson, Arthur Jewell, Jr., **15:**462n2
Wilson, Edmund (Princeton 1885), **19:** 170,n3; **24:**321n1
Wilson, Edmund (Princeton 1916), **19:** 170n3
Wilson, Edmund Beecher, **14:**128,n3; **17:**106-107,n1, 110, 450
Wilson, Edwin Bird, **23:**227,n1; **25:**27, 42
Wilson, Edwin Clinton, **21:**162n1
Wilson, Edythe Pardee (Mrs. Alfred McCalmont), **23:**64,n4
Wilson, Eleanor Randolph (Nell, Nellie, Nen; *afterwards* Mrs. William Gibbs McAdoo), **14:**39, 42, 50n4, 53, 78, 97, 101, 468,n3, 498, 555; **15:**117, 201, 202, 210, 222, 230, 231, 232, 237, 238, 243, 247, 264, 265, 266, 268, 269-70, 276, 295, 296, 300, 312, 323, 325, 339, 340, 345, 351, 352, 353, 354, 360, 384, 397; **16:**432, 436n1, 441, 470,n5, 481, 493, 526-27, 544,n1, 546, 547,n1, 553, 563; **17:**9,n18, 11, 12, 26, 33, 34, 343-44,n1; **18:**368, 375, 377, 390, 391, 412, 416; **19:**192, 193, 260, 262, 270, 306, 307, 351,n4, 385; **20:**137, 153, 172, 181, 184, 187, 188, 358; **21:**225,n3; **22:**329, 501, 544; **23:**30, 112, 220, 590, 596, 634; **24:**27, 151, 218, 239-40,n2, 482, 523, 528; **25:**518, 556-57, 560; photograph, **25:**illustration section
Wilson, Elizabeth, **23:**64
Wilson, Elizabeth McCalmont (Mrs. Edwin Clinton), **21:**161

## ELLEN AXSON WILSON

**14:**3, 4-5, 6-7, 7-8, 9, 10, 11-12, 15-17, 17-19, 20-21, 22-23, 24-25, 26-29, 31, 33, 34, 35-37, 38-43, 44, 48-50, 51-54, 55-56, 56-57, 60-62, 64-65, 66-67, 67-69, 70-72, 73-74, 75-78, 79-81, 82, 83-84, 85-86, 87-88, 89-95, 96, 96-98, 99, 100-102, 103-106, 106-108, 108-10, 110-11, 112, 113, 116-19, 123, 137, 138, 140, 142, 143, 146, 167, 186, 188, 189, 195, 196, 197, 206, 247, 277, 293-94, 295, 328, 330, 346, 347, 348, 359, 364, 397, 407, 415, 418, 421-27, 428-33, 434-35, 437-40, 440-41, 447-48, 451-54, 498, 499, 500, 521, 524, 525, 527, 532, 541, 542, 543, 544, 545, 546, 548, 549, 550, 551, 552, 553, 555, 556, 557; **15:**7-9, 13, 52n1, 112n1, 117, 118, 119, 134, 136, 140, 142, 147, 152, 153, 155, 156n1, 156, 157, 162, 163, 165, 167, 191, 201-202, 207-12, 221-22, 227-33, 237-38, 240-42, 243-44, 245, 246-47, 250-51, 263-70, 273-77, 295-98, 299, 300-301, 302-12, 313-16, 317-18, 320-23, 324-26, 333-37, 337, 337-39, 340-41, 344-56, 357-60, 383, 384, 385, 387, 397, 398, 399, 410, 417, 426, 440, 448, 461, 467, 470, 521, 523, 529, 533, 575; **16:**13, 23, 28-29, 86, 88, 102, 131, 153,n1, 155, 158, 159, 168, 170, 171, 173, 175, 180, 181, 191, 192, 194, 213, 234, 235n4, 283, 338, 357, 423-24, 431, 436-42, 443-46, 448-49, 450-51, 452, 482, 493, 535, 544-45, 563; **17:**3-9, 10-12, 13, 14-16, 17, 25-27, 33-35, 73, 91, 95, 98, 109, 117, 127, 137-38, 141, 150, 159, 215, 218, 233, 238, 242, 263, 264, 265, 268, 290, 308, 334, 342, 362, 372-73, 377, 392, 431, 450, 451, 466, 467, 469, 471, 472, 524, 547, 549, 562, 563, 565, 566, 569, 598, 606-608, 611-13; **18:**4, 12, 63, 321, 322, 340, 343-47, 348-54, 356-58, 361-67, 368, 369-72, 373-76, 377-80, 381-84, 386, 387-90, 392, 393-96, 398, 399-403, 404, 405-16, 416-17, 419, 422, 424, 448, 449, 450, 466, 467, 471, 472, 481, 491, 519, 520,n1,3, 532, 545, 560, 568, 589, 610, 625; **19:**26, 48, 79, 100, 152, 177n2, 190, 192, 193, 195, 196, 260, 270, 292, 293, 307, 311, 313, 320, 323, 333, 351, 357, 358, 383, 384n2, 384, 385, 388, 394, 411, 485, 507, 529, 550, 553, 606, 622; **20:**22, 27, 59, 78, 125-26, 132-34, 134-37, 144-46, 147n, 148n, 152-53, 172-73, 175-77, 181, 183-85, 187, 188-90, 239, 240, 306, 358, 362, 391, 424, 475, 479, 532, 538, 569, 576, 579, 580; **21:**10, 13, 49, 84, 101, 107, 130, 146, 167, 225, 378, 385, 519, 588, 589n1, 592, 594, 595, 600, 602, 606, 609, 611; **22:**21, 33, 45, 95, 131, 143, 187, 211, 232, 234-35, 274, 287, 293, 329, 356, 394, 425, 501, 502, 502n2, 507, 517, 534, 544; **23:**10-11, 21, 22, 30-31, 31n1, 49, 51-52, 81-83, 111-13, 127-28, 153, 160, 172, 174, 213, 222, 224, 241, 250, 257, 265, 267, 283, 290, 300, 301, 342n5, 555, 557, 557n1,4, 559, 597, 655, 657; **24:**27, 43-44, 44, 65, 77, 79, 147-49, 149-50, 189-90, 244, 256, 275, 285, 355, 401, 446, 462, 502, 505, 507, 509n1, 511, 522, 523-24,n3, 536, 552, 572, 576; **25:**66, 221, 232, 359, 390, 416, 418, 422, 423, 448, 461, 513, 530, 533, 535, 540, 552, 556-57, 565, 573, 574, 579, 617,n3, 621, 624; describes WW, **24:**573,n1; drawing by F. Yates, **16:**482; election night, **25:**518; Georgia reception, **24:**333, 335; Harvey-Watterson affair, **24:**40-42,n1,3; at nunnery in Naples, **15:**222,n2, 228, 229, 230, 232, 240, 241; resemblance to Titian's Flora, **15:**354; photographs, **25:** illustration section

### HEALTH

cold, **15:**140, 142, 147; ill, **15:**155, 156; swellings in ears, **15:**159

*Ellen Axson Wilson, cont.*
OPINIONS

I didn't know [Henry Cabot Lodge] was so rich; he seems to be, like Roosevelt, one of fortune's all round favorites, 14:8; [At church convocation in St. Peter's, Rome] I had an opportunity to study his [Pope Pius X] face—a very beautiful & noble one. 15:251; [In Rome, 1904] This is certainly the woman's century! They have taken possession of the *earth*! Everywhere one goes there are at least nine women to one man—women travelling alone—women of *all* nationalities from Swedes & Russians down to the Indies—all, all equally emancipated! 15:275

READING

William Nathaniel Harben, *Abner Daniel*, 14:72,n5
Rudyard Kipling, The Ship that Found Herself, 20:135,n4
Algernon Charles Swinburne, 14:101

*End of Ellen Axson Wilson entry*

*Ellen Axson Wilson, cont.*
Edward Noyes Westcott, *David Harum*, 14:72,n6
Owen Wister, *Lin McLean*, 14:453,n3
Charles Dickens, 15:334
Oliver Goldsmith, The Deserted Village, 15:310n4
John Ruskin, *St. Mark's Rest: The History of Venice . . .*, 15:359n4
Alfred Tennyson, 1st Baron Tennyson, 15:276
Anthony Trollope, 15:334
Mark Twain, *Joan of Arc*, 15:334

TRAVEL

Summer vacation at Clifton, Mass., July, 1902, 14:4-5n1, 7-8, 11, 15-16, 18-19, 21, 25, 28, 31, 36, 41, 42-43
vacation trip to Britain and the continent with WW, July 10-Sept. 22, 1903, 14:521-43, 545, 546, 547, 548, 550, 551, 552, 553, 555, 556
European trip of 1904, March-June, 15:201-383 *passim*

Wilson, Ellen Dickson (Mrs. William Potter), 18:630,n2
Wilson, Eva C. Larkin (Mrs. Gamaliel B.), 20:49, 239,n2
Wilson, George (of New York), 15:150
Wilson, George (of Philadelphia), 17:377
Wilson, George C., 16:377
Wilson, George T., 15:60,n6
Wilson, Hugh Irvine, 18:630n2
Wilson, Ida Gordon (Mrs. John Adams), 17:64,n2
Wilson, Jackson Stitt, 23:42,n8, 60n1
Wilson, James (1742-1798), 17:249
Wilson, James (1787-1850), grandfather of WW, 21:223
Wilson, James, Secretary of Agriculture, 1901-13, 16:315,n2; 25:282
Wilson, Janet Woodrow (Mrs. Joseph Ruggles), 14:328, 417; 18:363, 631; 19:175; 21:225, 478; 25:539
Wilson, Jessie Woodrow, daughter of WW and EAW (*afterwards* Mrs. Francis Bowes Sayre), 14:17, 18, 19, 42, 50n4, 53, 69, 97, 196, 198, 199, 293, 438, 468,n3, 498, 555; 15:9, 118, 134, 202, 202n1, 208, 209, 211, 230, 231, 233, 236, 240, 244, 250, 251, 264, 265, 266, 269, 274, 276, 277, 298, 301, 302, 303, 304, 306, 308-309, 310, 311, 313, 314, 315, 316, 318, 320, 321, 323, 325, 326, 333, 334, 336, 338, 339, 340, 344, 345, 346, 348, 349, 351, 352, 353, 354, 355, 356, 357; 16:28,n2, 234, 423,n1, 436n1, 439, 441, 442, 444, 469, 470,n4, 481, 544, 546; 17:33, 34, 242, 269; 18:278, 319,n1, 321, 367-68, 375, 387, 391-92, 402, 408, 449-50, 468, 471, 472; 19:193, 260, 262, 270, 306, 307, 351,n4, 385; 20:16n3, 135, 137, 152, 153, 173; 22:329, 501, 544; 23:30, 112, 128, 220, 300, 301; 24:27, 74,n2, 334,n1, 523, 528; 25:423, 518, 556-57, 560; photograph, 25:illustration section
Wilson, Jessie Woodrow, niece of WW, 15:319n
Wilson, John, uncle of WW, 15:166,n2
Wilson, John Adams, first cousin of WW, 15:184,n3; 16:33n5; 17:64-65; 21:161-62; 23:64n3
Wilson, John Glover, 14:386,n1
Wilson, John Moulder, 14:192
Wilson, John P., 17:397,n1, 401, 402, 404-405; 24:549-50n1
Wilson, Joseph R., Jr., brother of WW, 14:68, 74, 405; 15:235n, 318-19; 16: 235, 481, 537-38; 17:376-77,n1, 488, 489; 18:467, 483-85,n1,2; 20:49-50, 239-40; 21:114-15; 22:95-96; 23:288-89, 634, 657; 24:78-79; 25:24, 118,n2, 568-69, 585-86, 611-12, 612-13, 617-18, 621
Wilson, Joseph Ruggles, father of WW, 14:5n1, 6, 7n4, 23, 24, 25, 27, 28, 31, 39, 42, 43, 49, 50, 56, 65, 66, 68, 69, 71, 74, 77, 86, 88, 90, 94, 95, 98, 99, 101, 102, 104, 105, 106, 108, 109, 113, 116, 117, 119, 197, 294, 303n1, 417; death of, 14:330,n1, 335, 335-36, 337, 346, 347-48, 348, 349, 359, 360n2, 378-79; funeral, and obituary tributes, 14: 330-33; estate of, 405-406, 436; mentioned, 15:6, 49, 79, 137, 218, 513, 581; 16:350, 430; 17:17, 153n1, 573, 575, 578,n5; 18:488, 631; 19:33, 103; 20:331; 21:223; 22:21,n3; 23:446, 553,

554, 555, 556; **24**:456, 578; **25**:405,
455,n4, 456, 539
Wilson, Kate Wilson (Mrs. Joseph R.,
Jr.), **14**:68, 74; **15**:235n, 319,n2; **16**:
235, 537; **17**:376, 377; **18**:484; **20**:49-
50, 239-40; **21**:115; **23**:289; **25**:613
Wilson, Kathleen Gordon, **17**:64,n2
Wilson, Lucius Edward, **24**:52,n1
Wilson, Margaret Woodrow, daughter of
WW and EAW, **14**:6, 15, 16, 17, 18,
23n1, 38, 38n2, 39, 50n4, 53, 294, 346,
468,n3, 498, 555; **15**:7-9, 117, 118, 210,
214-15, 222, 230, 231, 238, 243, 247,
264, 265, 266, 268, 270, 295, 296, 300,
304, 306, 308, 312, 323, 325, 337, 338,
339, 345, 351, 360; **16**:28,n2, 158, 234,
436,n2, 436, 438, 439, 440, 441, 442,
443, 444, 445, 446, 448-49, 470, 479,
482, 527; **17**:12, 34, 137, 607;

**18**:321,n2, 368, 382, 390, 402, 412;
**19**:192, 193, 260, 307, 320, 385,n1;
**20**:137, 153, 173, 176; **22**:329, 425, 454;
**23**:30, 83, 112; **24**:27, 44, 65, 218,
334,n1, 523, 528, 572; **25**:518, 560,
589; photograph, **25**:illustration section
Wilson, Norman Richard, **16**:159,n1,
160, 162
Wilson, Samuel Mackay, **24**:333,n3
Wilson, Thomas, **19**:493, 494, 605
Wilson, Wayne MacVeagh, **18**:630n2
Wilson, William Bauchop, **23**:155,n4,
249n5; **24**:287,n1; **25**:544, 615
Wilson, William Lawrence, **20**:351,n1,
353; **21**:20-21,n1; **22**:71,n1; **23**:218,n1,
315, 568
Wilson, William Lyne, **21**:345n13

# WOODROW WILSON

## I

APPEARANCE, 277
HEALTH, 278
HABITS AND CHARACTERISTICS, 278
OPINIONS AND COMMENTS, 278
FAMILY LIFE AND DOMESTIC AFFAIRS, 283
READING, 284
RELIGIOUS ACTIVITIES, 287
RECREATION, 288
TRAVEL, 288

## II

PROFESSIONAL ACTIVITIES, 288
PRESIDENT OF PRINCETON UNIVERSITY, 289
POLITICAL CAREER, 292
GOVERNOR OF NEW JERSEY, 295
POLITICAL, RELIGIOUS, AND
EDUCATIONAL ADDRESSES, 296
INTERVIEWS, 312
WRITINGS, 312
PORTRAITS AND PHOTOGRAPHS, 314

---

## I

### APPEARANCE

He is tall and lank, like Abraham Lincoln and Uncle Sam, with a touch of
the awkwardness that one associates
with the sons of New England, **14**:427
Dr. Wilson wore the conventional frock
coat, but he wore it with an air in
great contrast to the man of society,
**15**:46
Striking resemblance to George Ade,
**16**:115-16
This lantern jaw of mine, **17**:4
Printed likenesses fail to indicate the
lighting up of his face as he talks,
**17**:474
His face is generally in repose but is
lighted every now and then by a de-
lightful smile, **18**:4
Look of seasoned scholarliness about
him . . . long, lean face, **18**:17
I wish I had an eighteenth century costume to match my face, **20**:151
There is something in his makeup that

suggests the timber of which superior
men are made, **21**:124
The President of Princeton . . . is an old-
young man, **21**:134
He has what is sometimes called "a
strong face." The brow is both high
and broad, the eyes are deep set, the
nose long and the mouth quite straight
and not very large . . . , **21**:135
When you look at the face in profile it is
decidedly aquiline . . . The mouth is
large and full-lipped, but drawn into a
straight, firm line. When he smiles he
shows fine large teeth. The eyes are
blue-gray, clear and penetrating, un-
dimmed by the glasses, **21**:220
His cheek bones are high, like a Mult-
nomah Indian's, and he runs to chin
excessively, **21**:478
His eyes are gray, shrewd and calm.
Sometimes they twinkle, **21**:525
He has the head and visage of a
mediaeval scholar, **22**:217
A tall, spare man, one might almost call

*Woodrow Wilson, Appearance, cont.*
him lean. He has long limbs, a long neck, and a very long, narrow, big-boned face, with a high forehead and long, square jaw, **23:**610-11
The most prominent feature of his face is his jaw. It's of the steel variety, long and square, **24:**75
There is only one man whom I know that has as large ears, **24:**75
The tall spare figure, **25:**260
For beauty I am not a star . . . , **24:**371; **25:**174
Described by EAW, **24:**573
My personal beauty is not the kind to excite admiration, **25:**322
He may be all right, but he ain't good-looking, **25:**361

HEALTH

sore throat, **14:**400
congestion of throat, **15:**4, 7; cold, 9; grippe, neuralgia, 114, 115; distressing headache, 119; upset in bowels, 155; in house all day, 156; shaky, 159; hernia operation, Dec. 1904, 571n1, 574, 576, 577; phlebitis, 574, 580; rest, following operation, at Palm Beach, Fla., 579
recuperation from hernia operation and phlebitis at Palm Beach, **16:**3, 12-13, 28-29; stroke of May 28, 1906, blindness in left eye caused by disease of arteries, 412,n1, 413, 423, 424, 425, 426, 427, 428, 429, 429-30, 431, 432, 435, 439, 444, 445-46, 450, 457, 463; midwinter vacation in Bermuda (Jan. 12-Feb. 9, 1907), 535n3, 536, 541,n1, 554, 559
seasick, **17:**3; hernia operation and phlebitis (Dec. 1904), mentioned, 34, 611n1; stroke of May 28, 1906, mentioned, 34; H. B. Thompson comment on WW's physical and mental condition, 379; slight stroke (Nov. or Dec. 1907); numbness and pain, "neuritis," in right arm until autumn of 1908, 549,n1, 562, 563, 564, 568, 585, 587, 599, 603, 604; "perfectly well," 607; falls and twists left knee, 611n1
small stroke of 1896 mentioned, **18:** 345,n3: *correction:* note should read: Because he had suffered a small stroke in the spring of 1896, about which *see* WW to Harper and Brothers, May 27, 1896, **9:**507n2; pain in knee, 351, 381; phlebitis, 351; cold and "the blues," 467, 468, 471, 472, 475, 478; stiff thumb, 468; torture with dentist, 479
imperfect vision of left eye, partially blinded by stroke of 1906, **19:**193,n6, 318; dilapidated tooth replaced and sessions with dentists, 311-12, 318, 319

*Woodrow Wilson, Health, cont.*
deeply affected, "in my nerves," by the abuse which has recently been heaped on me, **20:**125; This rest [in Bermuda] has been splendid, invaluable, but its object has been attained: it has been enough to render me normal at home once more, 184; savage cold which has descended upon my throat, my most used member, 413; ugly throat of mine is giving me a great deal of trouble, 429
has stood the work of campaigning wonderfully well, **21:**412
bowel upset, **22:**544, 546; attack of acute indigestion at banquet, 590
broken thumb, **23:**93, 112; bilious attack, 329; thoroughly exhausted after day of campaign speeches, 443; sick headache, 560
phlebitis, **24:**75n4; sight poor in right eye, 75,n5; EAW's concern, 189-90; Dr. Stengel gives clean bill of health after exhaustive examination, 190; severe cold, sore throat, 370; laid up with a cold, 384; in bed with a cold, 385; in bed with desperate cold, 387; cold has almost disappeared, 392; sore throat, 398; in bed with cold on May 6, 1912, 401; sore throat, 403; teasing sick headache, 482
sick headache and indigestion, **25:**67; lost voice on tour, 416; head wound in auto mishap, 508-10, 523-24, 525; attack of indigestion, 561, 562-63; feeling fine on return from Bermuda, 589; in bed with severe cold, 641n1

HABITS AND CHARACTERISTICS

use of typewriter, **14:**60, 245, 336, 558, 559; **15:**420, 522; **25:**452
rides bicycle to lectures, **14:**147
reason he dropped "Thomas" from name, **14:**328
shorthand, **24:**529, 564; **25:**ix, 452
speechmaking: use of gestures, **16:**115-16; extemporaneous style, **24:**220; **25:**111,n1, 493,n1
baseball fan, **25:**390-91
indiscriminate reader of detective stories, **25:**458

OPINIONS AND COMMENTS

*(Some of which are paraphrased)*

The rewards of my [Princeton] presidency seem to be coming to me now (lest they should lack at the end?), **14:**20
Hereafter [July 1902] comes hard work, the deep waters of responsibility, for Princeton is to be handled at a crisis in her development, **14:**20

*Woodrow Wilson, Opinions and Comments, cont.*

Never before treated himself as a professional "educator," **14**:27

A certain Unitarian (or Universalist) parson judged imperfectly religious by systematic way he does *not* bring up his children, **14**:104

A University career is, in this country, becoming, not more, but less and less attractive to men of real capacity and strong ambition (1902), **14**:152

I don't know what sociology is; moreover I am convinced that there isn't a man living who does; whenever a man is studying anything queer he calls it sociology, **14**:240

The men who founded [Princeton] university were for the most part of the Scotch and Scotch-Irish Church, and the institution was started with a definite purpose, and there is no danger that we will depart from that purpose, **14**:261

I am more and more convinced that carnal man was never intended to sit down and read books, **14**:263

I have ceased to be an historian, and have become a man of business, **14**:267

By the very simple device of constructing our new buildings in the Tudor Gothic style . . . we have added a thousand years to the history of Princeton by merely putting those lines in our architecture which point every man's imagination to the historic tradition of learning in the English-speaking race, **14**:269

The university robbed by its urban location of the community atmosphere is a failure in the highest and best definition of the American university, **14**:283

It is not necessary for a man to be cultured, in order to be educated, **14**:316

In the classroom the man is on his guard against allowing anything to enter his mind, and it takes almost a surgical operation to get anything into some men, **14**:317-18

Tells E. G. Elliott that his mind is not philosophical, **14**:322

The flag of the United States stands for the biggest *kick* on record. It stands for deliberate non-conformity; it stands for the things which men who are resisting authority stand for, **14**:367

When I look at that flag, I sometimes think that its stripes are alternating stains of blood on old parchment. . . . In white stripes are written the immemorial principles of individual liberty, and the red stripes are streaks of blood which have sealed those principles, **14**:367; **24**:53, 103, 128; **25**:377

*Woodrow Wilson, Opinions and Comments, cont.*

There is nothing that gives a man more profound belief in Providence than the history of this country, **14**:371

The best college is the one where the faculties are generalized. The man who aspires to a restricted technical task, is not the man for a university, **14**:401

One of the greatest evils we have to deal with in this democratic country is similarity. . . . We must inaugurate a fight against this tendency to level men's views, **14**:402

Education, after all, is chiefly the interchange of ideas, and the best way to cultivate the mind is by subsequent discussion, **14**:402

His theory of writing history, **14**:444,n4

A nation which calls its chief executive "Teddy" is not in a way to take itself very seriously, **14**:492

I have the highest respect and admiration for the men who earn their own education by work outside, but I think it is every man's duty to choose the sort of work which will maintain his self-respect and social standing, **15**:32

The best [public] service has been rendered by men who have not made a living out of it, **15**:198

I have suffered so many unspeakable things from reporters myself, that I am not likely to take their word too seriously with regard to others, **15**:202

No majority ever rules anything. Majorities are manipulated. The concerting minority invariably determines what the majority shall do, **15**:329

Leaders in the world of finance manipulate the destinies of the Nation to-day [1904], **15**:329

The men who put themselves through the Greek [language] training put themselves through the training that produced the intellectual movements of the modern world, **15**:380, 457-58

Culture is a word that it is easy to drawl and make too mawkish distinctions about: but it represents a splendid thing, after all, which is too hard to find in America, **15**:421

Conservative, but not illiberal, Princeton has always stood for system as against miscellany in studies, **15**:459

While there is nothing in the law of [Princeton] University to prevent a negro's entering, the whole temper and tradition of the place are such that no negro has ever applied for admission and it seems extremely unlikely that the question will ever assume a practical form, **15**:462

*Woodrow Wilson, Opinions and Comments, cont.*

I do not believe in hazing, but I do believe that there are some things worse than hazing. And I have suffered worse things from my fellow-men since I got out of college than I suffered while I was in college, **15:511**

The process of culture, the process of civilization, and the processes that can be bought with wealth, are largely processes of exemption from the harder classes of the school of life, **15:512**

There are two beings who assess character instantly by looking into the eyes,—dogs and children, **15:516**

The Middle States have always seemed to me the most typically American part of the United States, **15:540**

The intimation . . . that the Grand Army of the Republic is at liberty to call their fellow-citizens to account for public utterances, *seems to me both offensive and ridiculous*, **16:35**

Salvation by character: I regard such an enterprise as one of despair. . . . I would not care to offer [my character] as a certificate of my salvation. If I started out to make character I would be a prig, **16:228**

The most conservative persons I ever met are college undergraduates. The radicals are the men past middle life. . . . These are the desperate radicals— the men who would clear the stage that they might begin anew. It is not the youngster of hope, but the man near the darkness of despair who is your man of destruction, **16:228-29; 20:242**

There is a mighty task before us. . . . It is to make the United States a mighty Christian nation, and to christianize the world, **16:228, 230**

The pushing things in this world are ideals, not ideas. One ideal is worth twenty ideas in propulsive force, **16:229**

Some men pad themselves about so well with doctrine that virtually they are in padded cells, **16:230**

Of all the menaces of to-day the worst is the reckless driving in automobiles [1906], **16:320**

Nothing could be further from my thoughts than the possibility or desirability of holding high political office [1906], **16:331**

The Roman Catholic priesthood, when its members have really remembered their consecration and lived true to it, have made a deeper impression upon the communities they lived in than the Protestant clergy, **16:347, 352**

I have had the unspeakable joy of having

*Woodrow Wilson, Opinions and Comments, cont.*

been born and bred in a minister's family, **16:350**

[Jefferson] never realized the practical difficulty of Democracy. The difficulty in believing in the people is that you know so many of them, **16:364**

We shall reject, as we would reject poison itself, the prescriptions of Socialism, **16:365**

I do not see how any man can fail to perceive that scholarship, that education, in a country like ours, is a branch of statesmanship, **16:408**

Many a man would be morally independent if he were in fact independent, but he is carrying the fortunes of others [the woman he loves, the children he loves], **16:409**

I do not deem myself a suitable person to be a presidential candidate on the ticket of a party so divided and so bewildered as the Democratic party is at present; still less do I deem myself a suitable person to be President [1907], **16:531-32**

I made an address last Sunday evening [at St. Andrew's Presbyterian Church in Bermuda]. It made me very unhappy, as a religious address always does, **17:25**

Your professional reformer is an unmitigated nuisance, **17:484**

Women do not really want the franchise and it would not be an unmixed blessing for the rest of the world if they had it, **18:3**

As a rule, women prefer goodness as a quality, to ability, and are apt to be not a little influenced by charm of manner, **18:4**

I went to the Galleries [in Glasgow] and saw, as well as the glass which covered it would allow, Whistler's wonderful Carlyle (how could that absurd Mephistopheles do such grave and masterly things?), **18:349**

Mrs. Yates, whose mind, for all her loveliness, has the quite hopeless New England limitations, **18:411**

Women, whether by nature or circumstances, draw their conclusions about public affairs from logical reason, whereas safe and wise conclusions in such affairs can be drawn only from *experience* such as women have not had and cannot have, **18:417**

If there is a place where we must adjourn our morals, that place should be in what we call the private life. It is better to be unfaithful to few people than to a considerable number, **18:442**

Men who are saints in private life may be poor leaders, **18:442**

I do not know of a single generalization

*Woodrow Wilson, Opinions and Comments, cont.*

that is true of a half dozen men, **18**:443

I have no ambition to be president of a country club, **18**:503-504

Burke [is] the only entirely wise writer upon public affairs in the English language, **18**:594

I do not believe in a democratic form of government because I think it the best form of government. It is the clumsiest form of government in the world [but] it is an incomparably resourceful arrangement, **18**:638

Every successful business man, while he may not be guilty of accepting money for anything, has already been bribed. Society as it stands has allowed him to have some of its prizes. Therefore, he stands bound to keep society as it stands, **19**:96

The lad who is to inherit money is foredoomed to obscurity, **19**:227

The sort of people I like least, the restless, rich, empty-headed people the very sight of whom makes me cynical, **19**:312

I have come to feel that the finest word in the language is loyalty and the finest guide in life is certainly courage, **19**:331

No one has ever dreamed of imparting learning to undergraduates. It cannot be done in four years. To become a man of learning is the enterprise of a lifetime, **19**:335

Work, well done, is the only thoroughly satisfactory thing in the world, and, if done with zest, is the only entirely wholesome thing, **19**:359

One of the saddest things that has ever happened to us is that we have studied pedagogical methods, **19**:418

The only responsibility to which human society has ever responded or ever will respond, is the responsibility of the individual, **19**:474

Every man has to live with himself privately—and it is a most uncomfortable life, **19**:474

Every turning point in the history of mankind has been pivoted upon the choice of an individual, **19**:474

I have often preached in my political utterances the doctrine of expediency, and I am an unabashed disciple of that doctrine, **19**:476

No man in public life irritates me and repels me more than Senator Aldrich of Rhode Island, except Mr. Joseph G. Cannon, **19**:604

People are divided into the exhaustible and the inexhaustible, **20**:149

I am a man's man, and exasperate even men by confident opinions of my own. I am, at any rate, now fully authenti-

*Woodrow Wilson, Opinions and Comments, cont.*

cated as a man by the number of enemies I have made, **20**:150

Every college man thinks of his college with his eye over his shoulder. The past is its domain in his thought. He dreads to see it changed. Those who are responsible for the administration of the colleges, on the other hand are only too keenly aware that they must in some degree ignore this sentiment. It is their duty to look forward, not backward, **20**:159

The duty of the young man is to make everybody reexamine his standards of right, **20**:242

Our political parties are falling apart, so that they do not know where they stand (1910), **20**:243

Men are not afraid of the penalties of the law; but men are afraid of the look in the accusing eyes of their friends and acquaintances. The most terrible punishments are spiritual punishments, **20**:332

The Protestant churches have dissociated themselves from the people. They serve the classes, not the masses, **20**:364

The state university is being lifted in popular esteem and the privately endowed institution is being lowered. The future is for the state university and not for the privately endowed one, **20**:364

If she loses her self possession America will stagger like France through fields of blood before she again finds peace and prosperity, **20**:366

Unfortunately, my mind is a one-track affair on which I can run only one through train at a time, **20**:378

I don't drink, but I am not a prohibitionist. I believe that the question is outside of politics, **20**:565n

His philosophy of education, **21**:32-33

I have always been the warm friend of organized labor, **21**:60-61

Publicity is one of the purifying elements of politics, **21**:232-33

I come of a Scotch-Irish stock that cannot help fighting to save its life. I always think I am right, and although I try to be courteous to the men I differ from, I am always sure they are wrong, **21**:250

Our universities are not intended to enjoy their own fraternity, but to make the torches which light men's paths through the world, **22**:160

I do not *want* to be President. There is too little play in it, too little time for one's friends, too much distasteful publicity and fuss and frills. I dote on going my own way (Jan. 1911), **22**:293

*Woodrow Wilson, Opinions and Comments, cont.*

The atmosphere of books is not the atmosphere of life; nations do not live in libraries, 23:442

University intended to make young people just as unlike their fathers as possible, 23:484; 25:172

[Dean West] wished his Graduate College, which was (in fact) only to be an elaborate hall of residence, to be surrounded by gardens,—set off at a distance from the rest of the University. . . . I, for one, could not support such a plan, 24:3

Dean West's influence on Cleveland as trustee of Princeton, 23:3-4

I believe in the judgment of the people because I feel safer in the great common judgment than I do in the specialized judgment, 24:53

Progressive Republicanism is but another way of spelling Democrat, 25:56

Drop the hyphens and call them all Americans, 24:57-58, 260

America has the most lively mind and the most conservative disposition in the world, 24:314; 25:176

Human freedom consists in perfect adjustment of human interests to one another, 24:112, 128

A President of the United States is not now tolerated if he follows, if he listens, to little groups of men. He is expected to hear the unspoken voice of a great mass of people, be their servant and their leader, 24:129

Heroism is not originated in doing popular things. Heroes have been bred out of those men who were willing to do what they thought was right before anybody agreed with them or thought it was right, 24:215

This has been a petty and barren legislature. It has done nothing worth mentioning except try to amend and mar the wonderful things we accomplished last year, 24:271

I am heartily in favor of legislation requiring publicity of contributions to presidential campaign funds, 24:305

Scores university men for their exclusiveness and advises them to get out and share life with the ordinary working man, 24:309-10

All my life I have been an insurgent against the class in which I was born, 24:310

Has not made his mind up on woman suffrage, 24:315, 355

The South has been touched by the stimulation, but she has not been touched by the corruption of the age in which we live, 24:341-43

*Woodrow Wilson, Opinions and Comments, cont.*

The lesson of history is that every set of institutions and every nation is renewed out of the mass of unknown men, 24:377

The whole question [of immigration] is one of assimilation of diverse races. We cannot make a homogeneous population out of people who do not blend with the caucasian race, 24:382-83, 405-407, 564

Explains why he avoids attending Hibben's inauguration as president of Princeton, 24:391-92

The whole problem of life, gentlemen, is to understand one another; the whole problem of politics is to get together, 24:415-17

Every voter in this commonwealth is a trustee for the general good, and if he does not vote he is recreant to his trust, 24:441-43

If I did not believe in Providence I would feel like a man going blindfolded through a haphazard world, 24:443

I believe that God planted in us visions of liberty . . . that we are chosen and prominently chosen to show the way to the nations of the world how they shall walk in the paths of liberty, 24:443

Campaigning brings distasteful personal notoriety, 24:482

Vast corporative confederacies . . . bound together by the fact that the ownership of their stock and the members of their boards of directors are controlled and determined by comparatively small and closely interrelated groups of persons, 25:12

The effect of personalities on a Presidential campaign is not only to inject bitterness but to obscure the issues, 25:18, 327, 451

Politics ought to be considered as a branch of the national business, 25:31

Public politicians are amateurs compared with college politicians, 25:68

All my interest is that you [editors of foreign language newspapers] shouldn't regard the language in which you print your periodicals as a foreign language when printed in America for the conveyance of American thinking, 25:97

Peace will supplant war when it becomes as distinguished, 25:130

A man borrows greatness, doesn't possess it, 25:131-32

Universities should provide a map of life, 25:171-72

I, for my part, do not consent to regard that light [of individual liberty, of untrammeled enterprise] as an *ignus fatuus* which we have been following

*Woodrow Wilson, Opinions and Comments, cont.*

as if we were pursuing a mirage. I believe that light to shine out of the heavens that God himself has created, **25**:196-97

I believe in human liberty as I believe in the wine of life, **25**:197

I must listen, if I be true to the pledges of leadership, to the voices out of every hamlet, out of every sort and condition of men, **25**:211

There are men connected with big business in this country who believe that business is the necessary providence to take care of. And we know it is that kind of providence which God in his wisdom will sooner or later crown with a destroying disapproval. For there is a God in the Heavens. There is Justice in the souls of men, **25**:219

America must be fertile, or she cannot be great, and if you confine the processes of your industry or the processes of your politics to these lines where there may be or has been monopoly, you impoverish the great country which we would enrich, **25**:229

Government *for* the people is sooner or later autocracy and tyranny, no matter whether it is benevolent or not, **25**:267

College men have not borne a very active relationship to public life in this country in the past, **25**:275

Academic point of view unserviceable when there is a failure to admit into reckoning the most practical circumstances of life, **25**:277-78

There is no group of men wise enough to dominate a great free nation. Because if they do dominate it, then it would be proof positive that it had ceased to be free, **25**:280

When they call me "kid" and "Woody," and all the rest of it, I know that I am all right, **25**:348

I believe that part of the sadness we now suffer from, because of that atrocious assault upon Mr. Roosevelt, is a feeling that there is anybody in the United States who would dare attempt to interrupt the orderly course of politics and public affairs of this country by the violence of his own hand, **25**:424

Always be afraid of the man who is indifferent to his own success and certain of the success of the thing that he represents. Stand out of his way, for he has behind him the hosts of the Almighty. . . . I think it is enough for the salvation of the world if any particular congregation produces one such man a generation. If it produces two, that is largess; if it produces three, that is the

*Woodrow Wilson, Opinions and Comments, cont.*

revolution of the community; if it produces four, the millenium is approaching. One is enough for a generation, because your generation cannot get away from that, **25**:456

This great middle class from which the energies of America have sprung is being crushed between the upper and the nether millstones, **25**:463-64, 472-73

The world is lifted by example. The world is purified by its saints. . . . It is purified by the rare instance, the conspicuous instance. Biography, so to say, contains the seed of all great improvements, **25**:538-39

[Bermuda] is an unreal country. It's a land of witchcraft, a fairy land, a land of make-believe, **25**:588

Prosperity does not exist for a nation unless it be pervasive. Prosperity is not a thing which can be consumed privately or by a small number of persons, and the amount of wealth in a nation is very much less important than the accessibility of wealth in a nation, **25**:598

When I take the oath of office I shall deem myself bound to transact the business of the nation, so far as it falls to the Executive, and I shall feel bound to cut out everything that does not touch that business, **25**:599

Are you giving anything to society when you want to take something out of society? Is the question to be put to them. A large part, too large a part, of the fortune making of recent decades has consisted in getting something for nothing, **25**:629-30

FAMILY LIFE AND DOMESTIC AFFAIRS

Library Place house: remodeling of chimneys, **14**:6,n5, 16, 21, 24, 25, 27-28, 35-36, 39, 40, 43, 71, 77, 83, 109; renting or sale of house discussed, **14**:16, 84-85, 93, 96; house sold to Robert Garrett and John Work Garrett, **14**:123, 147

Prospect, **14**:85, 85-86, 90-91, 92, 93, 94, 99, 100, 102, 106, 107-108; moves into, Oct. 1902, **14**:147; Pyne-Cuyler fund for furnishings, **14**:43n1, 110-12, 117; furnishing and remodeling, **14**:4,n5, 10, 12, 16, 17, 19, 20-21, 22-23, 25, 28, 39, 43, 49, 55-56, 57, 61, 65, 68, 71, 76, 78, 80-81, 83; the family at, **14**:167, 196, 198, 296, 320, 498; quarantined by illness of Jessie Wilson and Annie Howe with scarlatina, **14**:196, 293; JRW dies at, Jan. 21, 1903, **14**:330

Woodrow Wilson, Family Life and Domestic Affairs, cont.

WW executor of his father's estate, 14:405-406

Summer vacation at Judd Haven, Muskoka district, Ontario, July 1904, 15:411f; mentioned, 383,n4, 391; WW property at Lake Rosseau, Muskoka, Ontario, 467

Summer vacations at Lyme, Conn., 1905, 16:153,n1, 154,n1, 155 passim; 1909, 19:193, 262, 270; 1910, 20:501 passim; 21:4 passim; English lake holiday, June 30—Oct. 14, 1906, 16: 424, 427, 429-93 passim

Summer vacation at St. Hubert's, Essex Co., N. Y., 1907, 17:268-375 passim; mentioned, 17:220n1, 246, 261

Income supplemented by friends, 22:333

Moves to 25 Cleveland Lane, Princeton, 23:424-25; electric meter at 25 Cleveland Lane, 438

Carnegie retirement pension, 23:564-66,n1, 583,n1, 590, 592; 24:147-49

Home milieu, 24:74; "Tommy," 76; household—everyday, 77; Irish heritage, 251; marriage license, 349; days in Sea Girt, 505-507, 509-11, 516; umpires ballgame, 518; last day as candidate, 525; escape to Drynock Farms, 551; EAW description of WW, 573

Loss of privacy, 25:21, 55; votes in primary election, 273; rumors of implication in Hulbert-Peck divorce proceedings, 285; heritage, 400; Ohio heritage, 405; boyhood admiration for Jefferson, 413; Captain Bill McDonald as bodyguard, 423-24; election night reactions, 518-20; day after election, 523-24; boyhood home in Columbia, S. C., 539-40; vacation in Bermuda (Nov. 18—Dec. 16, 1912), 551-89; annoyed at photographers in Bermuda, 556; intention to remain N. J. resident, 591-92, 596-97; recalls visits to Staunton, Va., 627-28; presented with miniatures of parents, 633

READING

I am more and more convinced that carnal man was never intended to sit down and read books, 14:263

My days are full of business, my head goes round with the confused whirl of university politics, I read no books, no, nor anything else that might renew my mind or quicken my imagination, 19:261

I am . . . reduced to so maudlin a state by the winter's fatigue that I can read nothing but detective stories with zest and comprehension, 19:309

I haven't had time in the last eight

Woodrow Wilson, Reading, cont.

years, since I came here [to Prospect], to arrange my library. . . . I don't have time, either, to keep up with the present books, though I get some idea of the best of them from what my friends tell me, 21:136

The fact is that I am a somewhat indiscriminate reader of detective stories, 25:458

*Authors and works, read, cited, alluded to*

Frank Frost Abbott, Handbook for the Study of Roman History, 18:575; A History and Description of Roman Political Institutions, 18:575; A Short History of Rome, 18:575; (ed.) The Selected Letters of Cicero, 18:575; Society and Politics in Ancient Rome: Essays and Sketches, 19:393; The Toledo Manuscript of the Germania of Tacitus, 18:575

John Emerich Edward Dalberg Acton, 1st Baron Acton, ed., Cambridge Modern History, 15:482-84, 485

Charles Francis Adams (1835-1915), Some Modern College Tendencies, 17:105,n2, 410, 417; Three Phi Beta Kappa Addresses, 17:104,n1,2, 410, 417

Aristotle, 14:208

Matthew Arnold, The Future, 15:371n2

Karl Baedeker, London and Its Environs: Handbook for Travellers, 16:436; Paris, 14:529; Switzerland, 14:529

Walter Bagehot, 17:483; The English Constitution, 14:13; Physics and Politics, 18:88, 95

John Spencer Bassett, The Federalist System, 20:583

Augustine Birrell, 17:227

Giovanni Boccaccio, A Translation of Giovanni Boccaccio's Life of Dante (tr. Carpenter), 19:703,n1

David Josiah Brewer, American Citizenship, 14:136,n1

Robert Bridges, President Woodrow Wilson and College Earnestness, 17: 450n1

Robert Browning, 18:638; 19:723; Luria, a Tragedy, 18:328n1; 19:41,n2

Samuel Henry Butcher, Harvard Lectures on Greek Subjects, 16:28n1

James Bryce, Viscount Bryce, The American Commonwealth, 14:14

Edmund Burke, Conciliation with America, 14:14; Letter to the Sheriffs of Bristol, 14:14; Taxation in America, 14:14

Samuel Butler, Hudibras, 17:13

Julius Caesar, Commentaries on the Gallic War, 16:119, 221; 17:542

Thomas Carlyle, 17:481-82, 504; History

Woodrow Wilson, Reading, cont.
of the French Revolution, 18:83n2;
Love Letters of Thomas Carlyle and
Jane Welsh (ed. A. Carlyle), 18:362,n1;
New Letters of Thomas Carlyle (ed.
A. Carlyle), 18:362,n1; Reminiscences
(ed. Froude), 18:362,n2
Andrew Carnegie, Ezra Cornell . . . ,
17:124,n1; A Rectorial Address Deliv-
ered to the Students in the University of
St. Andrews, 22nd October, 1902,
14:306,n1
Benvenuto Cellini, Autobiography, 15:
477
Sir Mackenzie Dalzell Chalmers, Local
Government, 14:14
Mellen Chamberlain, The Revolution
Impending, 14:443,n3
The Chapel Hymnal, 19:395
Gilbert Keith Chesterton, 15:506,n3;
20:242; Orthodoxy, 19:521,n7, 714
Marcus Tullius Cicero, 14:208, 209
Grover Cleveland, The Independence of
the Executive, 14:236,n5
Price Collier, England and the English
from an American Point of View,
19:262,n3
John Corbin, Wisconsin: The Utilitarian
University, 17:240,n2
Carl Heinrich Cornill, The Prophets of
Israel, 16:400,n4
Samuel McChord Crothers, The Anglo-
American School of Polite Unlearning,
17:534-35,n1
Dante Alighieri, The Divine Comedy,
19:367,n5
Goldsworthy Lowes Dickinson, Letters
from A Chinese Official: Being an
Eastern View of Western Civilization,
16:121,n1
Sir Charles Dilke, Greater Britain, 14:14
Dr. Wilson's Plans at Princeton, Review
of Reviews, 17:333,n1
Marcus Dods, The Bible: Its Origin and
Nature, 16:400,n2
Rheta Childe Dorr, What's the Matter
with the Public Schools? 18:62,n2,
68,n1
George du Maurier, Peter Ibbetson, 18:
413
Hugh Edward Egerton, A Short History
of British Colonial Policy, 14:443,n3
Edward Eggleston, Beginners of a Na-
tion, 15:484
Henry William Elson, History of the
United States of America, 16:387,n1
The Federalist Papers, 14:13; 15:44
Guglielmo Ferrero, Characters and
Events of Roman History, from Caesar
to Nero, 19:262,n3
Henry Fielding, History of Tom Jones, a
Foundling, 14:503,
Henry Jones Ford, The Rise and Growth
of American Politics: A Sketch of Con-

Woodrow Wilson, Reading, cont.
stitutional Development, 14:14; 18:
208n5, 576; 20:35n3, 198
Benjamin Franklin, Autobiography, 15:
477
Edward Gibbon, The Decline and Fall of
the Roman Empire, 15:473
Oliver Goldsmith, She Stoops to Con-
quer, 14:503; The Traveller, 14:435,n2
William John Gordon, Our Country's
Flowers and How to Know Them,
14:521,n1
Kenneth Graham, The Golden Age,
15:510
Ulysses Simpson Grant, Personal
Memoirs of U. S. Grant, 16:119, 221
John Richard Green, 18:89; History of
the English People, 14:141; Short His-
tory of the English People, 14:310, 340,
350, 516
Alexander Hamilton, Report of the Secre-
tary of the Treasury on the Subject of
Manufactures, 18:538
James Hastings, ed., A Dictionary of the
Bible . . . , 16:400,n3
Nathan Wilbur Helm, Princeton Uni-
versity and Her New Phi Kappa Psi
President, 14:91,n2
Hans Ferdinand Helmolt, ed., Weltge-
schichte, 14:339,n3
John Grier Hibben, Hegel's Logic: An
Essay in Interpretation, 14:104,n1; The
Philosophy of the Enlightenment,
20:208,n1, 223
Oliver Wendell Holmes, The Autocrat of
the Breakfast Table, 16:226,n5; 17:
486,n4
Hamilton Holt, The Approaching Na-
tional Peace and Arbitration Confer-
ence, 17:92,n4
Homer, Iliad, 17:535
Thomas Hughes, Tom Brown's School
Days, 17:327,n1
Edward Ingle, New England and the
North in Early Southern Life,
14:89,n1
Georg Jellinek, Gesetz und Verordnung,
14:322, 324; Das Recht des Modernen
Staates, 14:322
George Sibley Johns, A College Democ-
racy (St. Louis Post-Dispatch),
17:247,n3
Juvenal (Decimus Junius Juvenalis),
14:209
Benjamin Kidd, Social Evolution, 18:
443,n1
Rudyard Kipling, The Ship that Found
Herself, 15:537; 23:104; When Earth's
Last Picture is Painted, 23:398,n3
George William Knox, Arthur Cushman
McGiffert and Francis Brown, The
Christian Point of View: Three Ad-
dresses, 16:400,n5
Ernest Lavisse, ed., Histoire de France

*Woodrow Wilson, Reading, cont.*
  *depuis les origines jusqu'à la Revolution*, **14**:339,n3
Richard Lovelace, To Lucasta: Going to the Wars, **23**:110,n6
Abbott Lawrence Lowell, *Essays on Government*, **14**:14; *Governments and Parties of Continental Europe*, **14**:14
Edward Verrall Lucas, *The Open Road. A Little Book for Wayfarers*, **18**:411,n3
Titus Lucretius Carus, **14**:208
Thomas Babington Macaulay, 1st Baron Macaulay, **15**:473
Sir Henry James Sumner Maine, *Popular Government*, **18**:103n3
Frederic William Maitland, *The Constitutional History of England*, **18**:356-57,n1
Lucas Malet, *The History of Sir Richard Calmady*, **14**:529,n12
Paul Mantoux, Anatole France on Childhood, **14**:440n2
Lucia Ames Mead, *A Primer of the Peace Movement*, **17**:92,n4
John Stuart Mill, **14**:242
Theodor Mommsen, *History of Rome*, **15**:485
Lucius Hopkins Miller, Modern Views of the Bible and of Religion, **18**:273,n2
Charles de Secondat, Baron de La Brède et de Montesquieu, *The Spirit of the Laws*, **14**:13
John Morley, Viscount Morley of Blackburn, *The Life of William Ewart Gladstone*, **15**:116,n1, 117, 119
Elisha Mulford, *The Nation*, **14**:14
Ethel Watts Mumford, Oliver B. Herford, and Addison Mizner, *The Entirely New Cynic's Calendar of Revised Wisdom 1905*, **18**:428n3; **19**:235,n2
Hugo Münsterberg, *Die Amerikaner* (transl., *The Americans*), **14**:76,n1
Ellis Paxson Oberholtzer, *The Referendum in America*, **17**:262,n2
Frederick Scott Oliver, *Alexander Hamilton: An Essay on American Union*, **20**:339-40,n1
Henry Fairfield Osborn, *The Medieval and the True Modern Spirit in Education*, **14**:54,n1, 61
Herbert Levi Osgood, The Study of American Colonial History, **14**:443,n2
Michael J. O'Toole, Presidential Timber (*Wilkes-Barre News*), **17**:121,n2
Robert Lawrence Ottley, *A Short History of the Hebrews to the Roman Period*, **16**:400,n1
Samuel Pepys, *The Diary of Samuel Pepys, M.A., F.R.S.*, **18**:471
Bliss Perry, *The Amateur Spirit*, **15**:529,n1,2
David Graham Phillips, The Treason of the Senate, **16**:375n1
Plato, **14**:208

*Woodrow Wilson, Reading, cont.*
Henry Codman Potter, *The Citizen in His Relation to the Industrial Situation*, **14**:136,n1
William Hickling Prescott, *The Works of William H. Prescott*, **14**:134, 135,n1
Howard Willis Preston, ed., *Documents Illustrative of American History*, **14**:353,n4, 518
Sir Arthur Quiller-Couch, ed., *The Oxford Book of English Verse 1215-1900*, **18**:357; *The Laird's Luck and Other Fireside Tales*, **14**:526,n5
Hardwicke Drummond Rawnsley, *Literary Associations of the English Lakes*, **16**:451,n1
Thomas Brackett Reed, *Reed's Rules. A Manual of General Parliamentary Law . . .*, **14**:258
William Henry Roberts, ed., *Records of the Presbyterian Church. U.S.A.*, **17**:28,n2
James Edwin Thorold Rogers, *A History of Agriculture and Prices in England from the Years after the Oxford Parliament*, **14**:558
Edmund Ruffin, ed., *The Westover Manuscripts*, **17**:620,n1
John Ruskin, **15**:479; *The Crown of Wild Olive*, **15**:365n1; *St. Mark's Rest: The History of Venice . . .*, **15**:476-77; *Seven Lamps of Architecture*, **15**:499,n4
William Berryman Scott, ed., *Reports of the Princeton University Expeditions to Patagonia, 1896-1899*, **16**:507,n1
William Shakespeare, **15**:488; *As You Like It*, **15**:340, 345; *Mid-Summer Night's Dream*, **15**:340; *Much Ado About Nothing*, **15**:340
Edward Rowland Sill, **18**:411,n4
Adam Smith, *The Wealth of Nations*, **14**:505
Lincoln Steffens, *The Shame of the Cities*, **16**:43n2
Sir James Fitzjames Stephen, *Liberty, Equality, Fraternity*, **14**:13
Laurence Sterne, *The Life and Opinions of Tristram Shandy*, **14**:503
Eleanor Stuart (pseud. of Eleanor Stuart Patterson, Mrs. Harris Robbins Childs), *The Postscript*, **18**:357-58,n2
Jonathan Swift, **15**:511; **17**:483
Alfred Tennyson, 1st Baron Tennyson, *The Princess*, **14**:369,n2; **15**:171,n3; **16**:296-97n4, 529,n2
Thomas à Kempis, *Imitation of Christ*, **15**:110
Reuben Gold Thwaites, *The Colonies*, **20**:582
Alexis Charles Henri Maurice Clérel de Tocqueville, **17**:506; *Democracy in America*, **14**:14; **20**:329; **23**:127n10
Henry Duff Traill, *Central Government*, **14**:14; (ed.) *Social England: A Record*

*Woodrow Wilson, Reading, cont.*
of the Progress of the People, **14:**339,n3;
**15:**482, 483, 484, 485
Norman Maclaren Trenholme, *The Right of Sanctuary in England: A Study in Institutional History,* **16:**41,n4
Anthony Trollope, *The Life of Cicero,* **14:**13
Mrs. Humphry Ward, *Lady Rose's Daughter,* **15:**97,n5
John Wesley, *Journal of the Rev. John Wesley,* **14:**421,n3, 512
Andrew Fleming West, *The Proposed Graduate College of Princeton University,* **14:**361; **16:**414,n3,4
Westminster Assembly of Divines, *Shorter Catechism,* **17:**347n1
Stanley John Weyman, *The Long Night,* **15:**115,n1
William Allen White, *What's the Matter with Kansas?* **15:**171,n4
Justin Winsor, ed., *Narrative and Critical History of America,* **14:**443n3; **15:**482
Mrs. Wilson Woodrow, *The Silver Butterfly,* **18:**520,n1,2,3
William Wordsworth, Lines Composed a Few Miles above Tintern Abbey, **16:**378,n2; **17:**192-93,n1; Michael. A Pastoral Poem, **18:**415,n4; *The Poems of Wordsworth* (ed. Arnold), **14:**521,n2; *The River Duddon,* **18:**371n6
Thomas H. Wynne, ed., *History of the Dividing Line, and Other Tracts,* **17:**620,n2

RELIGIOUS ACTIVITIES

Talk at vesper service, Marquand Chapel, Sept. 21, 1902; notes, **14:**133; God is Love, address to Trenton Y.M.C.A., Feb. 8, 1903; news report, **14:**354-55; The Laws of the Lord, address to Philadelphian Society, Murray Hall, March 26, 1903; news report, **14:**399; address to Philadelphian Society on Romans viii, Murray Hall, May 14, 1903; news report, **14:**457-58
Religious talk before St. Paul's Society, Sept. 30, 1903; announcement, **15:**9; notes, **15:**9-10, 11; talk before Philadelphian Society, Oct. 1, 1903, **15:**9,n1; news report, **15:**10; conducts service preparatory to communion service in Marquand Chapel, Dodge Hall, Nov. 7, 1903; mentioned, **15:**47; leads Class of 1904 prayer meeting, Dodge Hall, Dec. 6, 1903; notice, **15:**67; The Church and Society, address at the Second Presbyterian Church, Philadelphia, Dec. 13, 1903; news report, **15:**98-99; notes, **15:**78; The University and the Church, address to the Presbyterian Union of Albany, Ten Eyck Hotel, Feb. 15, 1904;

*Woodrow Wilson, Religious Activities, cont.*
news report, **15:**168-69; The Young People and the Church, address at Grace Baptist Temple, Philadelphia, Feb. 26, 1904; notes, **15:**177-78; news report, **15:**179; talks before Philadelphian Society, Murray Hall, March 17, 1904; news report, **15:**197-98; Sept. 28, 1904, news report, **15:**495; The Young People and the Church, address on Christian Education in Pittsburgh, Oct. 13, 1904, text, **15:**510-19; news report, **15:**519-20; mentioned, **15:**126,n2, 461, 492, 521-22
Address to conference of leaders of Christian work among students, Murray-Dodge Hall, Feb. 19, 1905, mentioned, **16:**7,n1; address to Philadelphian Society, Murray Hall, May 4, 1905; news report, **16:**91; tribute to Rev. Dr. J. H. de Vries, written as elder of the Second Presbyterian Church of Princeton, **16:**105; University spirit, address to the Philadelphian Society, Sept. 28, 1905; news report, **16:**189; efforts to unite two Presbyterian Churches of Princeton, Nov. 1905, **16:**219n2; address to prayer meeting of the Princeton Theological Seminary Y.M.C.A., Stuart Hall, Nov. 22, 1905; news report, **16:**232; resigns as elder and withdraws from Second Presbyterian Church of Princeton, Nov. 25, 1905; WW and EAW take letter of dismission and join First Church, Nov. 29, 1905, **16:**234-35,n1; Newness of Spirit, address to the Philadelphian Society, Murray Hall, Jan. 11, 1906; news report, **16:**280-81; proposed for elder of First Presbyterian Church, Feb. 3, 1906; declines, **16:**301,n2; The Minister and the Community, address at Hartford Theological Seminary, Mar. 30, 1906, **16:**346-52; addresses class of 1909 prayer meeting, Dodge Hall, April 7, 1906; notice, **16:**357; address to Philadelphian Society, Murray Hall, April 26, 1906; notes, **16:**377-78; news report, **16:**378-79; address to Philadelphian Society, Nov. 22, 1906; news report, **16:**490-91
Address at St. Andrew's Presbyterian Church, Hamilton, Bermuda, Jan. 27, 1907, **17:**22; notes, **17:**22-23; mentioned, **17:**25; sermon at Christ Church, Warwick, Bermuda, Feb. 3, 1907; notes, **17:**27-28
Address to the Presbyterian Union of Baltimore, Feb. 19, 1909; text, **19:**52-63; mentioned, **19:**48-49, 76,n5; address to Philadelphian Society at Murray Hall, April 1, 1909; news report, **19:**147-48; What Ought a Man to Do? address at the Witherspoon St. Presbyterian Church, March 31, 1909; news report, **19:**148-49; The Claims and Character of the Chris-

*Woodrow Wilson, Religious Activities, cont.*

tian Ministry, address to the Ministerial Club, April 26, 1909; news report, **19**:173-74; The Present Task of the Ministry, address at the 75th Anniversary of Hartford Theological Seminary, May 26, 1909; text, **19**:215-22; mentioned, **19**:214, 229,n2, 274, 310-11, 319, 441,n2, 473,n1, 487; statement about the Bible, **19**:406; The Ministry and the Individual, address at McCormick Theological Seminary, Chicago, Nov. 2, 1909; text, **19**:471-79; mentioned **19**:398-99, 481, 485, 486-87; address to the Christian Fraternity of Phillips Exeter Academy, Exeter, N. H., Nov. 11, 1909; news report, **19**:498-99; Religion and Citizenship, lecture at Harvard Church, Brookline, Mass., Nov. 12, 1909; notes, **19**:496; news report, **19**:497; mentioned, **19**:383,n6

Address to the Philadelphian Society, March 17, 1910; news report, **20**:255-56; lecture under the auspices of the Brotherhood of the First Presbyterian Church of Princeton, March 31, 1910; news notice, **20**:312; talk at Senior Prayer Meeting, April 3, 1910; notes, **20**:314; The Function of the Country Church, address at the dedication of the new meeting-house of the First Congregational Church, Old Lyme, Conn., July 1910; mentioned, **20**:538,n1; news report, **21**:4-5

The Bible and Progress, address in Denver Auditorium, May 7, 1911, **23**:12-20; address at the dedication of the Oheb Shalom Synagogue, Newark, Sept. 7, 1911, **23**:305-308; address before Sunday School rally in the Second Regiment Armory, Trenton, Oct. 1, 1911, **23**:372-80; Life and the Bible, address at the First Baptist Church, Dallas, Texas, Oct. 28, 1911, **23**:494-99; address in Nashville on behalf of the Y.M.C.A., Feb. 24, 1912, **24**:206-16; address on the two hundredth anniversary of the First Presbyterian Church of Trenton, **25**:453-57

RECREATION

Attends Keith's Theatre in Boston, **14**:70; attends *Monsieur Beaucaire* (Tarkington), Comedy Theatre, London, July 30, 1903, **14**:527; *The Admirable Crichton* (Barrie), Duke of York's Theatre, London, Aug. 3, 1903, **14**:528,n8; *The Bishop's Move* (Hobbes and Carson), Garrick Theatre, London, Aug. 5, 1903, **14**:529,n10; golf, **19**:318, 322, 323, 332, 351, 356; **20**:180, 568; **21**:51, 136; horseback riding, **21**:136; baseball fan, **25**:390-91; indis-

*Woodrow Wilson, Recreation, cont.*

criminate reader of detective stories, **25**:458

TRAVEL

Summer vacation at Clifton, Mass. in Aug. 1902, **14**:48-98; at Gorham, N. H., Aug. 19-31, 1902, **14**:93-121; Chicago visit, Nov. 1902, **14**:210-11, 223, 226-27, 228-45, 247-48; news item, **14**:225-26

Western trip of April-May, 1903, **14**:445, 459, 461; at Ann Arbor, **14**:418-21, 425; Chicago, **14**:421, 422, 424, 429, 431, 448, 451, 453-55; St. Paul, **14**:423, 424, 426-28, 445, 446; Madison, Wisc., **14**:430, 435; St. Louis, **14**:431, 433-35, 436-37, 439, 440, 445, 448; Cincinnati, **14**:439, 440, 446-47, 448-51

Vacation trip to Britain and the continent with EAW, July 10—Sept. 22, 1903, **14**:521-56; European trip of 1903, mentioned, **15**:13; southern trip, planned for April and May 1904, given up, **15**:272, 308, 420; summer vacation at Judd Haven, Muskoka, Ontario, July 7—Sept. 10, 1904, **15**:411-62; recuperation in Palm Beach, Florida, Jan. 21—Feb. 15, 1905, **15**:579; **16**:3, 29; English lake holiday, June 30—Oct. 14, 1906, **16**:424, 429, 429-93 *passim*

Vacation at Hamilton, Bermuda, Jan.—Feb. 9, 1907, **17**:3-29; summer vacation at St. Hubert's, N. Y., July 9—Sept. 10, 1907, **17**:268-375 *passim*; vacation at Hamilton, Bermuda, Jan. 20—Feb. 27, 1908, **17**:606-19; summer vacation in Scotland and England, June—Sept. 1908, **18**:343-419; summer vacation in Old Lyme, Conn., July 13—Sept. 18, 1909, **19**:304-84; vacation at Hamilton, Bermuda, Feb. 12—March 5, 1910, **20**:122-21; summer vacation in Old Lyme, Conn., 1910, **20**:501-81 *passim*; **21**:4-89 *passim*; 1911, **23**:139-74 *passim*; at Governor's summer residence, Sea Girt, N. J., July 16—Sept. 27, 1911, **23**:213-362 *passim*; June 16—Sept. 14, 1912, **24**:481-585; **25**:3-147 *passim*; at Paget West, Bermuda, Nov. 18—Dec. 16, 1912, **25**:551-89

# II

PROFESSIONAL ACTIVITIES

Declines R. W. Gilder's request to write a biography of Robert E. Lee, **14**:58

Declines invitation to deliver series of lectures at Yale on the Responsibilities of Citizenship, **14**:135-37, 138

*Woodrow Wilson, Professional Activities, cont.*

LL.D. conferred by Rutgers College, June 18, 1902, **14**:167

Elected to membership in the Round Table Club, New York City, Dec. 1902, **14**:305-306

LL.D. conferred by University of Pennsylvania, Feb. 21, 1903, **14**:381

LL.D. conferred by Brown University, June 17, 1903, **14**:494-95

President of the Nassau Club of Princeton, 1903-1904, **15**:141-42,n2

Member of the N. J. Committee of Selection for Rhodes Scholars, **15**:204

Classmate hopes to cast future vote for him as Democratic nominee for President, **15**:472

Delegate to Columbia University's 150th anniversary celebration, Oct. 31, 1904, **15**:533,n1

Elected a vice-president of the American Academy of Political and Social Science, **16**:313

Elected president of the Association of Colleges and Preparatory Schools of the Middle States and Maryland for 1906-1907, **16**:495

Member of the General Committee for the National Arbitration and Peace Congress, New York, April 1907, **17**:92n2

LL.D. conferred by Harvard University, June 26, 1907: citation by President Eliot, **17**:225-26n1; mentioned, **17**:219, 334

LL.D. conferred by Williams College, Oct. 7, 1908, **18**:347-48, 382-83; citation, **18**:439

Trustee of the Cleveland Monument Association, **18**:559,n2,3, 645; member of site and plans committee, **19**:78

Corresponding member of the Southern Educational Association, **18**:589-90

Member of the Committee of Christian Education in China, **19**:109,n4, 544

Elected trustee of the Mutual Life Insurance Co. of New York, **19**:396-97, 454-55

LL.D. conferred by Dartmouth College, Oct. 14, 1909, **19**:414,n2

President of the Short Ballot Organization, **19**:420,n5, 446

Approached on possibility of accepting the presidency of the University of Minnesota, **19**:457-58, 485-86, 493-95, 532, 542-43, 605

Invited to deliver Commencement Address at University of Michigan; declines, **20**:16

Invitation to presidency of University of Minnesota, mentioned, **20**:357,n3

LL.D. conferred by Princeton, Nov. 3, 1910, **21**:539

*Woodrow Wilson, Professional Activities, cont.*

Carnegie retirement pension, **21**:540,n2; **22**:130-32,n4, 148, 283,n2, 287n2

Elected vice president of the National Civil Service Reform League, **22**:256

PRESIDENT OF PRINCETON UNIVERSITY

To continue teaching following his assumption of presidency, courses noted, **14**:12,n2

Talk before freshmen at reception of Philadelphian Society, Sept. 20, 1902; notes, **14**:133; news report, **14**:133-34

Talk at Vesper Service, Marquand Chapel, Sept. 21, 1902, notes, **14**:133

Salary as president fixed at $8000 plus $2000 for entertainment and maintenance at Prospect, **14**:144

statement to trustees at the beginning of his administration, Oct. 21, 1902, memorandum, **14**:119-21; text, **14**:150-61

Inauguration as 13th president of Princeton University, Alexander Hall, Oct. 25, 1902, **14**:47, 60, 63, 64, 67, 75, 137, 139, 140, 142-43, 143, 147, 148, 149, 161, 169, 186, 187-88, 189, 197, 198, 199, 203, 280, 328, 330, 407; Inauguration Committee, **14**:67, 134; medal proposed, **14**:94,n1, 97; news report, **14**:191-95; oath, **14**:195

*Princeton for the Nation's Service*, inaugural address, Oct. 25, 1902, text, **14**:170-85; preparation of, **14**:8,n2, 12, 17, 21, 22, 24, 27, 38, 40, 42, 58,n1, 61, 147; mentioned, **14**:186, 187, 188, 190, 197, 397; **15**:27; **16**:414n3; quoted, **15**:289n-90n

Address to students and public on steps of Nassau Hall following his installation as president, Oct. 25, 1902; news report, **14**:193-94

Remarks at the ground-breaking ceremonies for '79 Hall, Oct. 25, 1902, mentioned, **14**:194

Speech at Class of 1879 dinner, Oct. 25, 1902, mentioned, **14**:186-87,n1, 195

Authorized to reorganize teaching force and create vacancies, **14**:162, 168

First appearance before constitutional government class after inauguration, **14**:203

Memorandum on Revision of Academic Course of Study, **14**:207-209,n1

Address of welcome at Whig-Clio mass meeting, Oct. 3, 1902, mentioned, **14**:138

*The True University Spirit*, address to Philadelphian Society, Nov. 6, 1902, news report, **14**:201-202

*The Objects of Graduate Study*, talk be-

*Woodrow Wilson, President of Princeton University, cont.*

fore Graduate Club, Nov. 7, 1902, notes, **14**:202; news report, **14**:203

Response to toast, Princeton University, at *Daily Princetonian* banquet, Princeton Inn, March 10, 1903, news report, **14**:388

Address to Philadelphian Society on The Laws of the Lord, March 26, 1903, news report, **14**:399

Address to the Philadelphian Society on Romans viii, May 14, 1903, news report, **14**:457-58

Sir Henry Maine, a Lawyer with a Style, address before the Monday Night Club in 9 Lower Pyne, May 25, 1903, news report, **14**:463; read to Graduate Club, Dodge Hall, Jan. 15, 1904, mentioned, **15**:131; text in vol. **10**, 443-61

Address to seniors at Baccalaureate Service, June 7, 1903, news report, **14**:484

Remarks at the alumni luncheon of 1903, Gymnasium, June 9, news report, **14**:485-86

Religious talk before St. Paul's Society, Sept. 30, 1903, announcement, **15**:9; notes, **15**:9-10, 11

Address to Philadelphian Society, Oct. 1, 1903, **15**:9,n1; news report, **15**:10

Remarks at mass-meeting of American Whig and Cliosophic Societies, Oct. 9, 1903, news report, **15**:15

Address on class sentiment delivered at the laying of the cornerstone of Seventy-Nine Hall, Oct. 16, 1903, mentioned, **15**:27

Conducts service preparatory to Communion service in Marquand Chapel, Dodge Hall, Nov. 7, 1903, **15**:47

Remarks at Hill School Club Dinner, Princeton Inn, Nov. 20, 1903, mentioned, **15**:57

Leads Class of 1904 prayer meeting, Dodge Hall, Dec. 6, 1903, notice, **15**:67

Annual Report to the Board of Trustees, Dec. 10, 1903, **15**:69-75

Address of Welcome to members of the American Philosophical Association in Princeton, Dec. 29, 1903, notes, **15**:111-12

College lectures: on contracts, mentioned, **15**:121,n1; on torts, mentioned, **15**:135

Religious talk before Philadelphian Society on Public Life, Murray Hall, March 17, 1904, news report, **15**:197-98

Response to toast "Princeton" at the annual dinner of the *Daily Princetonian*, March 16, 1904, mentioned, **15**:200

Leaders of Men, address to Fortnightly Club, Princeton, March 23, 1904, news report, **15**:206; text, vol. **6**, 646-71

*Woodrow Wilson, President of Princeton University, cont.*

Remarks at the dedication of Seventy-Nine Hall, June 11, 1904, news report, **15**:388; mentioned, **15**:389

Talk given at Class of 1879 dinner in Seventy-Nine Hall, June 11, 1904, mentioned, **15**:388

Baccalaureate Sermon, June 12, 1904, text, **15**:364-74; mentioned, **15**:182, 323, 345, 387

The Revision of the Courses of Study, address at the alumni luncheon, Gymnasium, June 14, 1904, text, **15**:379-83

Commencement address, 1904, Alexander Hall, June 15, 1904, news report, **15**:391

Powers and duties as President of Princeton, **15**:393-95

Princeton's New Plan of Study, unpublished article, Aug. 29, 1904, **15**:450-60

Address at the opening exercises of the University, Sept. 22, 1904, mentioned, **15**:491,n1

Address at the reception given by the Philadelphian Society to the Class of 1908, Murray-Dodge Hall, Sept. 24, 1904, news report, **15**:492-93

Religious talk before the Philadelphian Society, Murray Hall, Sept. 28, 1904, news report, **15**:495

Address of welcome to the 18th Annual Convention of the Association of Colleges and Preparatory Schools of the Middle States and Maryland, Murray Hall, Nov. 25, 1904, text, **15**:540-42; news notice, **15**:545

Address of welcome to the Association of Teachers of Mathematics, Chancellor Green Library, Nov. 29, 1904, mentioned, **15**:545

Annual report to the Board of Trustees, Dec. 8, 1904, text, **15**:554-69; mentioned, **15**:580,n1

Member of committee to raise funds for McCosh Hall, **15**:570; committee to choose site, **15**:572

Statement of the Tutorial System in *Princeton Alumni Weekly*, Feb. 25, 1905, **16**:6-7

Response to toast, Princeton, at annual banquet of the *Daily Princetonian*, Princeton Inn, March 22, 1905; news report, **16**:36-37

Practical Journalism in University Life, response to toast at Princeton Press Club banquet, Princeton Inn, April 15, 1905, news report, **16**:61-62

After dinner speech at retirement dinner for Professor Charles Augustus Young at Princeton Inn, May 17, 1905, mentioned, **16**:102

Baccalaureate Sermon, June 11, 1905, **16**:119-28

*Woodrow Wilson, President of Prince-*
*ton University, cont.*
Address at the alumni luncheon, June
13, 1905, news report, **16:**141
Commencement address delivered at Al-
exander Hall, June 14, 1905, news re-
port, **16:**137-41
Address at the Opening Exercises, Sept.
21, 1905, news report, **16:**187-88
Remarks at reception to the Class of
1909 by the Philadelphian Society,
Sept. 23, 1905, news report, **16:**188
Address at mass meeting in the interests
of Whig and Clio Halls, Oct. 26, 1905,
news report, **16:**205
Notes for undelivered speech to
Princeton Municipal Club, **16:**206
Princeton Ideals, talk before the Monday
Night Club, Nov. 13, 1905, notes,
**16:**222
Annual report to the Board of Trustees,
Dec. 14, 1905, **16:**245-65
Remarks at *Daily Princetonian* banquet,
Princeton Inn, March 28, 1906, news
report, **16:**345-46
The College Man in Journalism, re-
sponse to toast at Princeton Press Club
banquet, Princeton Inn, April 25,
1906, news report, **16:**374-75
Graduation message to the Class of
1906, **16:**420,n2
Remarks at the opening of the Faculty
Room in Nassau Hall, Nov. 2, 1906,
notes, **16:**479; news report, **16:**485
Address to Philadelphian Society on Col-
lege Men's Problems, Nov. 22, 1906,
news report, **16:**490-91
Annual Report to the Board of Trustees,
Dec. 13, 1906, text, **16:**506-19; supplementary report, **16:**519-25
Talk at banquet of the University Press
Club, Princeton Inn, April 22, 1907,
news report, **17:**115
The College Man in Public Life, address
to Philadelphian Society, May 9,
1907, notes, **17:**139; news report,

Report on the Social Coordination of the
University, text, **17:**176-86; mentioned, **18:**219, 404
Baccalaureate Sermon, June 9, 1907,
**17:**187-96, mentioned, **17:**211; published as *The Free Life* (1908),
**17:**457,n1
Remarks at the Alumni Luncheon, University Gymnasium, June 11, 1907,
notes, **17:**209, mentioned, **17:**395
Speech on City Government to the Municipal Club, Dodge Hall, Sept. 27,
1907, notes, **17:**403-404; news report,
**17:**404
The Importance of Singlemindedness,
talk before the Philadelphian Society
in Murray Hall, Oct. 24, 1907, notes,
**17:**454; news report, **17:**455-56,n1

*Woodrow Wilson, President of Prince-*
*ton University, cont.*
Annual Report to the Board of Trustees,
Dec. 13, 1907, **17:**555-59
Statement for Trustees on location of
Graduate College, **17:**590-94
Member of subcommittee of Trustees
Committee on the Graduate School,
**18:**9n2
Talk before Law Club, March 25, 1908,
news report, **18:**216
Member of subcommittee on Graduate
College site, **18:**247-48
Address at the tenth annual banquet of
the *Daily Princetonian*, April 10,
1908, news report, **18:**260
Address to Philadelphian Society, May
28, 1908, mentioned, **18:**310
Baccalaureate Sermon, June 7, 1908,
**18:**323-33
Baccalaureate Sermon, June 13, 1909,
scriptural text selected, **18:**358; text of
sermon, **19:**242-51
Address at the Alumni Luncheon, Gym-
nasium, June 10, 1908, news report,
**18:**334-35
Talk at opening exercises, Marquand
Chapel, Sept. 25, 1908, **18:**421-22
Meditation, talk before Philadelphian
Society, Nov. 19, 1908, news report,
**18:**518-19
City Government, address before the
Municipal Club, Dec. 2, 1908, news re-
port, **18:**530-32; mentioned, **18:**493
Address of welcome to the Modern Lan-
guage Association in Princeton, Dec.
28, 1908, notes, **18:**566
Annual Report to the Board of Trustees,
Jan. 1, 1909, **18:**569-87
Address to Monday Night Club, Jan. 25,
1909, notes, **19:**9-10
University Ideals, response to toast at
*Daily Princetonian* banquet, Princeton
Inn, April 30, 1909, news report,
**19:**178-79, mentioned, **19:**181
Address to the graduate students at
Merwick, May 12, 1909, notes, **19:**194
The Problems of the University, address
at a dinner given in his honor by the
Class of 1909, Princeton Inn, June 10,
1909, notes, **19:**241, mentioned, **19:**
261-62
Baccalaureate Sermon, June 13, 1909,
text, **19:**242-51; mentioned, **19:**255,
263, 269, 310; **21:**288, 297, 322, 323,
335n2, 337, 379
Remarks in accepting Campbell Hall as
gift of Class of 1877, June 12, 1909,
mentioned, **19:**242
Address at the Alumni Luncheon, June
15, 1909, news report, **19:**253-55
Address at opening exercises, Sept. 23,
1909, news report, **19:**389-90
Resignation considered, **19:**443, 446,
654, 660, 673, 701, 702, 748

*Woodrow Wilson, President of Prince-
ton University, cont.*

Address at the formal presentation of
Palmer Physical Laboratory, Oct. 22,
1909, news report, **19**:450-51

Address of welcome to the New Jersey
Library Association, Oct. 27, 1909,
notes, **19**:451-52

Talk at Whig Hall Smoker, Oct. 27,
1909, notes, **19**:452

Talk before the Graduate Students' Association, Nov. 9, 1909, news report,
**19**:491

Address of welcome to meeting of the
National Academy of Sciences, Faculty Room, Nassau Hall, Nov. 16,
1909, news report, **19**:506

Talk at Princeton Charter Club, Nov. 19,
1909, mentioned, **19**:529

Talk at Senior Council dinner, Dec. 8,
1909, notes, **19**:560-61, news report,
**19**:579-81

Jersey City Station letter to Pyne, Dec.
22, 1909, **19**:620, 628, 630; Pyne reply,
**19**:627

Annual Report to the Board of Trustees,
Jan. 1, 1910, **19**:674-95

The Choosing of a Law School, address to
Law Club, March 10, 1910, news report, **20**:228-29

The Power of Literary and Oratorical
Form, talk at Whig Hall graduation,
April 4, 1910, notes, **20**:315

Remarks at banquet of the Princeton
Press Club at Princeton Inn, April 5,
1910, news report, **20**:326-27; mentioned, **20**:383-84n4

After dinner speech at *Daily
Princetonian* Banquet, Princeton Inn,
April 29, 1910, news report, **20**:404-
407

lectures on constitutional law, mentioned, **20**:424

Remarks at dinner in his honor given by
the Class of 1910, June 9, 1910, notes,
**20**:511-12; mentioned, **20**:421,n2

Baccalaureate Sermon, June 12, 1910,
text, **20**:520-28; mentioned, **20**:492,
501,n3

Address at Alumni Luncheon, June 14,
1910, abstract, **20**:528-30

Resignation envisioned and discussed,
**20**:65, 90, 122, 189, 276, 291, 297, 317,
325, 359, 362, 501,n2, 545, 549-50,
567, 571, 576

Resignation as president, news announcement, **21**:101; mentioned, **21**:
122-23, 143, 160, 321; proposed resolution and letter by Pyne, **21**:353;
WW letter of resignation, **21**:362, 364;
mentioned, **21**:377-78; trustee action,
**21**:364-66; WW resigns McCormick
professorship, **21**:492; trustee resolutions on accepting resignation, LL.D.

*Woodrow Wilson, President of Prince-
ton University, cont.*

conferred, **21**:537-39; mentioned, **21**:
556

Remarks at the opening exercises in
Marquand Chapel, Sept. 22, 1910,
news report, **21**:151-52

Address to the Class of 1914 at Murray
Hall, Sept. 24, 1910, news report,
**21**:169-71

True University Spirit, address to Philadelphian Society, Murray Hall, Sept.
27, 1910, news report, **21**:176-78

Remarks to student demonstration, Oct.
10, 1910, news report, **21**:289-90

Jurisprudence lectures, **21**:381-82,
470-71

Talk to undergraduate demonstrators
after election as governor, **22**:3-4

Talk to football team, **22**:4-5

Address at a dinner in his honor given by
the Class of 1911, Princeton Inn, Dec.
7, 1910, news reports, **22**:149-52

Remarks at a meeting in celebration of
Princeton work in Peking, Alexander
Hall, Dec. 8, 1910, news report,
**22**:159-60

Requests salary be stopped on Oct. 20,
1910, **22**:165, 177, 186-87

Testimonial volume presented by classes
of 1911, 1912, 1913 and 1914, news report, **22**:322-23

Princeton Ideals, response to a toast at
the 13th annual banquet of the *Daily
Princetonian*, Princeton Inn, May 1,
1911, text, **22**:600-601

Graduate College controversy described
by W. B. Hale, **24**:28,n2

Editorial in New York *Globe and Commercial Advertiser* about graduate college controversy, **24**:585,n1; *see also*,
Princeton University: *Graduate College and the controversy over its location*; *preceptorial system*; and *Quadrangle plan and the upper class clubs*

POLITICAL CAREER

Proposed for the U.S. presidency by Col.
George Harvey at the Lotos Club, Feb.
3, 1906, text, **16**:299-301; WW thanks
Harvey, **16**:301

Colyer Meriwether offers support, **16**:302

B. W. Morris III trusts for Princeton's
sake there is nothing in Wilson boom
for 1908, **16**:305

Harvey prints speech supporting WW
candidacy in *Harper's Weekly*, March
10, 1906, **16**:307n1

University Club of Washington prefers
Taft, **16**:318

Disclaims interest in high political office
in letter to St. Clair McKelway,
**16**:329-31

*Woodrow Wilson, Political career, cont.*
R. H. Fitzhugh approves candidacy, **16**:334-35; WW replies not taking Harvey suggestion seriously, **16**:338
Letter of endorsement from W. C. Browning in Santiago de Chile, **16**:358
Refuses to be candidate for Senate from N. J., **16**:454-55,n1,3, 456-57, 482
John Cawley supports WW for senator, **16**:471
Meshes spread for me by wireless telegraphy before I landed [Oct. 14, 1906], **16**:482
Letter to Col. Harvey and reply, **16**:531-33
Plainly Disqualified (New York *Evening Sun*), **16**:533n5
Memorandum on men interested in his candidacy, **16**:534
J. R. Wilson, Jr. on presidential boom, **16**:537-38
Correspondence with E. A. Stevens on N. J. senatorial nomination, **16**:539-41, 545, 548-49, 561-62
Withdraws name from senate candidacy in letter to Col. Harvey, **16**:549-50; Col. Harvey's reply, **16**:554-55; WW response, **16**:560
E. H. Wright, Jr. to put WW in nomination for U. S. Senate, **16**:547; WW reply, **16**:551-52
Withdraws as candidate for nomination for U. S. Senate in letter to C. C. Black, **16**:560-61,n1
C. C. Black puts WW forward as nominee for presidency, **16**:563
N. J. senatorial contest of 1907, **17**:9-10,n1,2,3,4, 12n1, 23-25
Gamaliel Bradford urges WW for president, **17**:30-31,n1; WW reply, **17**:32-33
Suggested for Democratic nomination for president, **17**:121, 262, 490
Article in *North American Review* on WW as possible candidate for Democratic nomination in 1908, **18**:258-59, 271-72,n1
Republican banker at American Bankers Association convention in Denver enthusiastic to vote for WW, **18**:435
Reflections on political career, **18**:480
A. Ragan urges him to seek Democratic nomination for governor of N. J., **19**:272; WW reply, **19**:292
Running for governor of N. J. suggested, **19**:309-10
H. D. Thompson urges him to run for governor, **19**:328
The Democratic Opportunity, *National Monthly*, Jan. 1910, text, **19**:465-71; mentioned, **19**:464-65
Endorsed for president at Princeton alumni dinner at Chicago, Nov. 2, 1909, **19**:479

*Woodrow Wilson, Political career, cont.*
Talked of for governor in Plainfield, **19**:492, 493
H. E. Alexander of Trenton *True American* strong supporter, **19**:522n1
Unable to attend dinner of Democratic State Auxiliary Committee in Trenton, Jan. 11, 1910, **19**:554,n2
Colonel Harvey's Plan for Wilson's Entry into Politics, Editorial Note, **20**:146n-48n
Free to accept nomination for governor, **20**:189
Talk and plans for nomination for governor and president, **20**:289,n5, 297, 313, 325, 352-53,n1, 359, 371, 424,n1, 454, 455,n4, 459-60, 478-79, 519-20, 540-41, 541n1, 543-45, 545-47, 548-50, 556-57, 557, 558n2, 561-62; Lawyers' Club Conference, Editorial Note, **20**:565-66n, 567, 567-68, 569, 570, 571, 572, 572-73, 573, 576-77, 577-78, 578, 578-79, 580; **22**:181n1; WW statement, **20**:581
Draft of a platform for the Democratic party of Pennsylvania, **20**:315-17, 352,n1
Elected vice president of National League of Democratic Clubs, **20**:390
Candidacy and nomination for governor, **21**:3, 5, 6, 7, 8, 9, 10, 11, 12, 13, 14-29, 31, 33-38, 39-46, 49-50, 52-64, 81-91
Nomination for governor by the Democratic State Convention, Taylor Opera House, Trenton, Sept. 15, 1910, **21**:91n1
Platform of the New Jersey Democratic Party, Sept. 15, 1910, **21**:87-88,n3, 89, 91, 94-96, 99, 139; (proposed), **21**:43-46
Elected governor of New Jersey, Nov. 8, 1910, **21**:584n1
Mentioned for presidency (1910-1912), **21**:10, 18, 40,n1, 99, 108, 109, 115, 117, 129, 133, 138, 162, 168, 171-72, 298, 320n1,2, 328, 442, 479, 525, 539n2, 581, 584, 585, 588, 589, 592, 594, 596, 597, 598-99, 600, 602, 603, 605, 607, 609, 612, 613, 622; **22**:9, 14, 18, 20, 21, 22, 23, 27, 31, 32, 33, 38,n2, 43, 45, 52, 55, 78, 95, 96, 99, 117n1, 118, 123, 139, 143, 160, 161, 208, 213-14, 216-17, 237, 248, 254, 255n1, 258, 275, 292-93, 327, 334, 362, 375, 376, 393, 395, 410, 413, 437, 439, 454n1, 466n4, 466, 479, 483, 488, 489, 499n1, 500, 502, 509, 518-19,n4, 524, 533, 543n2, 545, 553, 554, 570, 573, 573n2, 576, 578, 587, 588, 592, 595, 598; **23**:5, 21, 22, 26, 30, 32n5, 40, 41, 43, 45, 52n3,4, 53, 54, 55, 56-57, 60, 61-62, 63, 80, 112,n2,3, 113, 114, 128-31, 133, 134, 138, 139, 152-53, 171, 172, 173, 177, 184, 199,n1, 200, 212, 213n2, 213, 214-15, 215-16, 221, 227, 228, 230, 231, 233-36, 243n3,

*Woodrow Wilson, Political career, cont.*
245n1, 252n1, 253, 256, 258, 262, 263,
272, 287n2, 288, 290-91, 291, 294, 298,
300, 310n3, 315, 325, 326, 330, 339,
341, 354, 359, 366, 372, 385, 386, 388-
89, 458, 478, 511-12, 519, 532, 539,
546, 549, 550, 552, 559, 564n2, 584,
589, 597-98, 601-602, 614-15
New Democratic Governors; biographical sketch by Fabian Franklin, 22:
32,n3
New York campaign headquarters and
information office, 42 Broadway,
23:135n3, 252n1,2, 614-15, 631
Wilson campaign fund, 23:437
Joline letter, 24:5,n1,2, 8-9, 28
Harvey-Watterson affair, 24:40-42,
45-47, 48-50, 59-64, 71, 72-74, 77-78,
79, 80-81,n1, 97n2, 118, 237
Pennsylvania primary vote, 24:330n3
Nebraska primary vote, 24:358n2
Georgia primary vote, 24:382n2
Florida primary vote, 24:382n1
California primary vote, 24:383n1
Maryland primary vote, 24:387n1
Statement on primary victory, May 29,
1912, 24:449
Platform plank on trusts, 24:470
Outline of Democratic platform, 24:474,
476-77
Platform planks, 24:477-81
Democratic National Convention, vote
on tenth ballot, 24:507n1; on thirtieth,
24:516n1; on forty-third, 24:521n5; re-
ceives Democratic nomination for
President, 24:522; *see also* Democratic
National Convention, 1912
Plans for preparing acceptance speech,
24:564, 572, 573
Meets W. F. McCombs to choose cam-
paign officers, 24:587
Believes in keeping campaign promises,
25:69
Made brave of Sioux Indians, 25:162-63
Meets President Taft in Boston, 25:269-
71
Record as governor, 25:336
Compares political atmosphere of 1910
with that of 1912, 25:355
Learned about American political and
economic life from experience with
New Jersey corporations, 25:358
Straw vote of American missionaries in
Japan, 25:390
Effect of assassination attempt on
T. Roosevelt, 25:418, 419, 421-22, 448
Sorry that he didn't enter politics at the
beginning of the progressive move-
ment, 25:429
Explains return of campaign contribu-
tions by McCormick and Dodge, 25:
459,n1,3
Resumes presidential campaigning, 25:
461
Cabinet suggestions and decisions, 25:

*Woodrow Wilson, Political career, cont.*
507, 590; Labor Department, 25:615;
by W. J. Bryan, 25:616-17, 622-23,
645-46; E. M. House, 25:448, 550-51,
557-59, 563-66, 610-11; A. J. McKelway, 25:544; O. W. Underwood,
25:593n1; G. F. Peabody, 25:609; T. B.
Love, 25:624
Popular and electoral vote for president,
25:520n1; Pennsylvania vote, 25:
527n1
Inaugural plans, 25:550, 571, 572, 620,
640,n1
Congratulatory messages upon nomination for governor, 1910, vol. 21:Ar-
chibald Stevens Alexander, 112-14;
Caroline Bayard Stevens Alexander,
150; Charles Dexter Allen, 168; Alfred
Brittin Baker, 117; Simeon Eben
Baldwin, 133; Clarence Hughson Bax-
ter, 158; Edward William Bok, 118;
Robert Gunn Bremner, 133; Robert
Bridges, 298; Herbert Bruce
Brougham, 97-98; Edward Capps,
166-67; Hunsdon Cary, 117-18; Edwin
Grant Conklin, 116-17; Richard Heath
Dabney, 138; Joseph Albert Dear, Jr.,
116; Arthur Granville Dewalt, 103;
Clinton Roy Dickinson, 169; Cleveland
Hoadley Dodge, 112; Joseph Dorsey,
156; James Fairman Fielder, 97;
Henry Burchard Fine, 112; Christian
Frederick Gauss, 111; William Cav-
anagh Gebhardt, 110-11; Otis Allan
Glazebrook, 98; Charles Henry
Grasty, 102; Samuel Allen Harlow,
110; Azel Washburn Hazen, 107;
Joseph Stanislaus Hoff, 97, 102-103;
William Hughes, 145; Melancthon
Williams Jacobus, 109, 142-43; Robert
Underwood Johnson, 109; David Ben-
ton Jones, 132; Harry Pratt Judson,
144-45; Edward Lawrence Katzen-
bach, 132; Frank Snowden Katzen-
bach, Jr., 96; Richard Vliet Lindabury,
140; Job Herbert Lippincott, 145-46;
Edgar Odell Lovett, 159; Abbott
Lawrence Lowell, 109; William Gibbs
McAdoo, 108; Robert Harris McCarter,
131-32; Thomas Nesbitt McCarter, Jr.,
139; William Frank McCombs, 108;
Walter Lee McCorkle, 105; Cyrus Hall
McCormick, 140; Norman Edward
Mack, 102; Isaac Wayne MacVeagh,
152; William Francis Magie, 406;
Erwin E. Marshall, 106; James Cow-
den Meyers, 107-108; John Alexander
Montgomery, 104; Franklin Murphy,
212; Joseph M. Noonan, 108; James
Richard Nugent, 106-107; William
Church Osborn, 155-56; Bliss Perry,
406; Dan Fellows Platt, 140-42; Henry
Smith Pritchett, 160; Charles Alexan-
der Richmond, 146; Edward Seiler
Salmon, 105-106; Charles Scribner,

*Woodrow Wilson, Political career, cont.*
104; Michael Welsh Scully, 131; Bayard Stockton, 131; Henry Burling Thompson, 104; Samuel Huston Thompson, Jr., 130; Walker Whiting Vick, 115-16; Williamson Updike Vreeland, 154-55; William Henry Welch, 129-30; William Royal Wilder, 129; Walter Maurice Wilkins and the Class of 1910, 98; Edgar Williamson, 115; John Adams Wilson, 161-62; Joseph R. Wilson, Jr., 114-15; Henry Otto Wittpenn, 155; Charles Albert Woods, 128; Lawrence Crane Woods, 157-58

Congratulatory messages on election as Governor, 1910, vol. **21**:Edwin Anderson Alderman, 595-96; Simeon Eben Baldwin, 590; Daniel Moreau Barringer, 603; Sylvester Woodbridge Beach, 597; Edward Webster Bemis, 617-18,n1; Robert Bridges, 591; William Jennings Bryan, 600-601; Richard Heath Dabney, 597-99; Josephus Daniels, 585,n1; Frank Miles Day, 618; William Henry Steele Demarest, 620,n1; Alfred Lewis Dennis, 592-93,n1; Bessie Louise Dickson, 587,n1; Cleveland Hoadley Dodge, 591-92; Charles Joel Fisk, 614,n1; Henry Jones Ford, 606-607; John Franklin Fort, 605-606; Eugene Noble Foss, 610; John Watson Foster, 600; Harry Augustus Garfield, 609; James Rudolph Garfield, 609-10,n1; Robert Garrett, 622; Lindley Miller Garrison, 587,n1; Franklin Potts Glass, 588; Henry Mayer Goldfogle, 618,n1; Edward Herrick Griffin, 586-87,n1; John Ralph Hardin, 610; George Brinton McClellan Harvey, 585; Robert Randolph Henderson, 599-600; Henry Lee Higginson, 612; James Alfred Hoyt, Jr., 588-89,n1; Robert Stephen Hudspeth, 607; William Hughes, 603; Theodore Whitefield Hunt, 602; William Burhans Isham, 602; Melancthon Williams Jacobus, 594; Caesar Augustus Rodney Janvier, 588; David Benton Jones, 593-94; Thomas Davies Jones, 599; Francis Fisher Kane, 604-605; John Worth Kern, 587; John Thompson Kerr, 592,n1; Darwin Pearl Kingsley, 621-22,n1; George Mason LaMonte, 610; Franklin Knight Lane, 586,n1; Robert Lansing, 607,n1; John Holladay Latané, 613,n1; David Lawrence, 608,n1; Vivian Murchison Lewis, 591; William C. Liller, 587-88; Thomas Bell Love, 584,n1; George Brinton McClellan, 599; William Frank McCombs, 607; Cyrus Hall McCormick, 594-95; John Bach McMaster, 609,n1; Theodore Marburg, 614-15,n1; Thomas Riley Marshall,

*Woodrow Wilson, Political career, cont.*
587, 603; Victor Louis Mason, 586,n1; William Hunter Maxwell, 617; Raleigh Colston Minor, 585,n1; Charles Wellman Mitchell, 599; Roland Sletor Morris, 584; Alexander Thomas Ormond, 603-604; Sir William Osler, M.D., 618,n1; Thomas Nelson Page, 602; Alexander Mitchell Palmer, 604,n1; Charles Henry Parkhurst, 621,n1; W. C. Payne, 616,n1; Magnus Fraser Peterson, 619-20,n1; Edgar Allan Poe, 600,n1; Henry Smith Pritchett, 596-97; Joseph Pulitzer, 595; George Lawrence Record, 596; Leo Stanton Rowe, 614,n1; Rudolph Edward Schirmer, 617; Jacob Gould Schurman, 611,n1; Ashton Cokayne Shallenberger, 622,n1; Edward Wright Sheldon, 594; George Sebastian Silzer, 585; James Smith, Jr., 590; Edwin Augustus Stevens, 601; Isidor Straus, 613,n1; Nathan Straus, 613; Roger Charles Sullivan, 584; William Sulzer, 616; Charles Andrew Talcott, 583; Henry Burling Thompson, 593; Joseph Patrick Tumulty, 589; Frederick Jackson Turner, 602; Walker Whiting Vick, 608; John Wanamaker, 601; John Wesley Wescott, 604; Brand Whitlock, 607,n1; Hiram Woods, 599; John Joseph Wynne, 612,n1; George Green Yeomans, 611-12,n1

Congratulatory messages upon election as President, 1912, vol. **25**:Louis Dembitz Brandeis, 528; William Jennings Bryan, 522; James Bryce, 531-32; Carter Glass, 530-31; John Grier Hibben, 522; Abbot Lawrence Lowell, 535-36; William Frank McCombs, 522; Thomas Riley Marshall, 521; Walter Hines Page, 515-17; Princeton University faculty, 575; Theodore Roosevelt, 521; William Howard Taft, 521; Felexiana Shepherd Baker Woodrow, 536

GOVERNOR OF NEW JERSEY

Statement on the senatorship, **22**:153-54
Proposed public statement on candidacy of James Smith, Jr., **22**:239,n1
Statement on James Smith, Jr., as candidate, **22**:248-52; mentioned, **22**:257
Form letter on senatorship, **22**:252
Patronage, **22**:262n2, 513, 514n2, 518
Inaugural address, Jan. 17, 1911, text, **22**:345-54; mentioned, **22**:53, 333, 363, 375, 521
Martinique Hotel Conference, Jan. 16, 1911, **22**:357-58
Appointments, **22**:413,n1, 414-15,n1, 510, 516, 532
Statement on a proposed increase in postal rates, **22**:427,n1
Remarks at the annual dinner of the

*Woodrow Wilson, Governor of New Jersey, cont.*

New Jersey Senate, Ritz-Carlton Hotel, New York, March 3, 1911, news report, **22**:474-76; mentioned, **22**:477, 582

Conferences with Democratic assemblymen, March 6, 1911, news report, **22**:481-82; March 13, 1911, news report, 504-505

Veto messages, **22**:508, 524-25, 526-27, 548; **24**:261-65, 266-67, 268-69, 276-84, 324-28

Message to the House of Assembly on public school administration and city government reform, April 11, 1911, text, **22**:549-52

Remarks about the commission government bill, **22**:574-75

Statement on the work of the New Jersey legislative session of 1911, **22**:578-79

Visit to the state penal and charitable institutions, **23**:290, 304-305

Informal report on his first year as governor, **23**:331f

Statement on election frauds, **23**:358-59

Statement on the New Jersey election of 1911, **23**:544

Thanksgiving Proclamation, 1911, **23**:545

Speech to New Jersey Mayors at Castle Point, Hoboken, Jan. 3, 1912, news report, **23**:634-36

Annual message to the New Jersey Legislature, **24**:18-25

Favors exposure of those who seek to influence appointments, **24**:76-77

Doesn't mind being likened to schoolmaster in governorship, **24**:95

Confers with Democratic senators on Fitzherbert scandal, **24**:244-47,n1

Characterizes 1912 legislature as "petty and barren," **24**:271

Would not bestow political job or make pledge to gain political advantage, **24**:300

Republican reaction to vetoes, **24**:324

Deplores time wasted with office-seekers, **24**:437-38

Approves investigation of Atlantic City graft cases, **24**:452-53; statement on, **24**:458-60

Not at liberty to intervene in Perth Amboy strike except as adviser, unless local authorities are unable to maintain order, **24**:475-76

Will not resign governorship at once, **24**:529, 555, 583-84; will remain until convening of legislature in January, **25**:511, 523

Still facing strain of writing and signing letters; has discarded rubber stamp used earlier, **24**:584

Jersey Day address at Sea Girt, **25**:43-44

*Woodrow Wilson, Governor of New Jersey, cont.*

Statement on senatorial candidacy of James Smith, Jr., **25**:116-18

Reflects on two years as Governor, **25**:181

Achievements of governorship, **25**:305-10

New Jersey Democratic platform, Oct. 1, 1912, principal author, **25**:305n1; text, **25**:306-10

Refers to failure of full train crew bill in New Jersey, **25**:336

Remembers exact moment when fellow Jerseymen accepted him as candidate, "Doc, you're all right!" **25**:348

Compares political atmosphere of 1910 with that of 1912, **25**:355

New Jersey as owned by Public Service Corporation, **25**:431

Wants to speak very frankly about situation in Essex County, **25**:467

New Jersey lacked representative government under Board of Guardians, **25**:474-75

New Jersey voters have seen promises fulfilled, **25**:482

New Jersey has emancipated herself, **25**:485-87

Looks forward to working with legislature in January, **25**:511

Casts vote in presidential election, **25**:517-18

Pledged to New Jersey legislative program until March 1913, **25**:574

Will use every proper power as President to continue support for progressive forces in New Jersey, **25**:591

Recalls reading of his *History of the American People* by New Jersey opponents, **25**:639

POLITICAL, RELIGIOUS, AND EDUCATIONAL ADDRESSES

Religion and Patriotism, delivered at the Northfield Student Conference, July 4, 1902, text, **12**:474-78; mentioned, **14**:8-9,n2, 26, news account, 102,n1

Princeton in the Nation's Service, Sesquicentennial oration at Princeton, Oct. 21, 1896, text, **10**:11-31; mentioned, **14**:40n1, 558, quoted, 22n2

The Ideals of America, text, **12**:208-27; mentioned, **14**:265,n1, 325

Sir Henry Maine, a Lawyer with a Style, Johns Hopkins University, Feb. 25, 1898, text, **10**:443-61; mentioned, **14**:463,n2; **15**:494

Before the Society of Alumni of the University of Virginia, Charlottesville, June 12, 1895, report in **9**:286-91; mentioned, **15**:16,n1

What It Means to Be an American, before the Peninsula Twentieth Century

*Woodrow Wilson, Political, Religious, and Educational Addresses, cont.*

Club, Fort Monroe, Va., Jan. 25, 1902, notice, **12:**265; mentioned, **15:** 160,n5,6, 165, 168

Six lectures on the Great Leaders of Political Thought, Philadelphia, Jan.-Feb. 1901, *see indexes to vols. 9 and 10*; mentioned, **15:**494,n4

Democracy, delivered at Vassar College, Dec. 9, 1892, text, **7:**345-68; mentioned, **19:**533,n1

To the New England Society in the City of New York, Dec. 22, 1900, text, **12:**52-58; mentioned, **19:**758,n1

Leaderless Government, to Virginia Bar Association, Hot Springs, Aug. 5, 1897, text, **10:**288-304; mentioned, **21:**117,n2

Nature of Democracy in the United States, before the Owl Club, Hartford, May 17, 1889, text, **6:**221-39; mentioned, **21:**168

The Real Idea of Democracy, Aug. 31, 1901, text, **12:**175-79; mentioned, **22:**395,n3

———

At vesper service, Marquand Chapel, Sept. 21, 1902, notes, **14:**133

To New York Society of Mayflower Decendants, Delmonico's New York, Nov. 21, 1902, notes, **14:**209-10, newspaper report, 210

The Future of the University, to the Chicago alumni of Princeton, University Club, Chicago, Nov. 28, 1902, notes, **14:**223, news report, 226-27, mentioned, 211, 274n3

The Relation of University Education to Commerce, to the Commercial Club of Chicago, Nov. 29, 1902, text, **14:**228-45, news report, 247-48, mentioned, 211, 226, 227

To the Presbyterian Union of New York, Hotel Savoy, Dec. 1, 1902, notes, **14:**252, news report, 253

At a banquet of the Presbyterian Union of Baltimore, Music Hall, Baltimore, Dec. 4, 1902, news report, **14:**260-61, mentioned, 277n1

The Meaning of a University Education, before the New Jersey High School Teachers' Association, Continental Hotel, Newark, Dec. 5, 1902, news report, **14:**261-65

The Significance of the Student Movement to the Nation, at the 25th anniversary exercises of the Student Christian Movement, Marquand Chapel, Dec. 6, 1902, news report, **14:**266-67

To the Princeton alumni of New York, Waldorf-Astoria Hotel, Dec. 9, 1902, text, **14:**268-76, news report, 287-91; mentioned, **20:**66,n3

*Woodrow Wilson, Political, Religious, and Educational Addresses, cont.*

The Function of the University in the United States, before the Brooklyn Institute of Arts and Sciences, Dec. 11, 1902, news report, **14:**283-85

The Relation of the University to Business, remarks at a dinner of the New York State Bankers Association, Waldorf-Astoria Hotel, Dec. 18, 1902, news report, **14:**298-99; mentioned, **14:**292; **17:**498

The University and Our Country, Forefathers' Day address at Lafayette Avenue Presbyterian Church, Brooklyn, Dec. 21, 1902, notes, **14:**299-300, news report, 300-301

At Forefathers' Day observance of the New England Society of Orange, Commonwealth Hall, East Orange, N. J., Dec. 22, 1902, news report, **14:** 301-303

A welcome to the Archaeological Institute of America at Princeton, Dec. 31, 1902, mentioned, **14:**382

What It Means to Be an American, to the Middlesex Women's Club, Lowell, Mass., Jan. 2, 1903, news report, **14:**314-16

State Education: Its Relation to Political Life and Development, to the Twentieth Century Club, Colonial Theatre, Boston, Jan. 3, 1903, notes, **14:**307-308, news report, 316-19, mentioned, 254

At a dinner of Princeton alumni at Baltimore, Feb. 6, 1903, news report, **14:**358-59, mentioned, 347,n1

God is Love, to the Trenton Y.M.C.A., Association Hall, Feb. 8, 1903, news report, **14:**354-55

The Meaning of a College Course, at Peddie Institute, Hightstown, N. J., Feb. 12, 1903, news report, **14:**356-57; also given at Bordentown (N. J.) Academy, March 14, 1903, mentioned, **14:**358n1

Princeton University: Great in the Past, Greater in the Future, response to toast at dinner of Princeton alumni, Harrisburg Club, Harrisburg, Pa., Feb. 19, 1903, news report, **14:**362-64

Patriotism, to the Washington Association of New Jersey, Ford House, Morristown, Feb. 23, 1903, stenographic report, **14:**365-78; mentioned, **14:**131,-n1, 142, 144, 222, 247, 348, 349, 353-54, 355-56, 394, 495, 496, 497, 501; **15:**32-33, 48, 49, 51,n1,2

To the Princeton alumni of Western Pennsylvania, Union Club, Frick Building, Pittsburgh, March 7, 1903, news report, **14:**383, 385-86, mentioned, 386

The Laws of the Lord, to the Philadel-

*Woodrow Wilson, Political, Religious, and Educational Addresses, cont.*
phian Society, Murray Hall, March 26, 1903, news report, **14**:399
To Princeton alumni of the District of Columbia, New Willard Hotel, Washington, March 27, 1903, news report, **14**:400-403
To the Princeton Club of Philadelphia, Horticultural Hall, April 14, 1903, news report, **14**:408-410, mentioned, 411
The National and University Life, at Association Hall, Philadelphia, under the auspices of the Princeton Club, April 17, 1903, news report, **14**:415-17
Patriotism, lecture before the University of Michigan in University Hall, Ann Arbor, April 21, 1903, news report, **14**:419-21, mentioned, 421
To the Princeton Alumni Association of the Northwest, Minnesota Club, St. Paul, April 24, 1903, news report, **14**:445-46, mentioned, 426,n1
What It Means to Be an American, lecture in the New Century course at Plymouth Church, Minneapolis, April 25, 1903, news report, **14**:427-28
The Expansion and Character of the United States, to the University Club of St. Louis, April 28, 1903, news report, **14**:433-34, mentioned, 431,n2, 434
To the Princeton Club of St. Louis, University Club, April 29, 1903, mentioned, **14**:436
What Can Be Done by the Western Association of Princeton Clubs for the Furtherance of the Interests of the University? delivered before the Association at Grand Hotel, Cincinnati, May 2, 1903, news report, **14**:448-49
To the Cincinnati Y.M.C.A., Sinton Hall, Cincinnati, May 3, 1903, news report, **14**:450-51, mentioned, 448
Patriotism, before the Twentieth Century Club, at the Fine Arts Building, Chicago, May 5, 1903, news report, **14**:454-55
To the Philadelphian Society of Princeton University on Romans viii, Murray Hall, May 14, 1903, news report, **14**:457-58
To Princeton alumni in New Auditorium, Newark, May 15, 1903, news report, **14**:459-62
What It Means to Be an American, at Keil Hall, Mercersburg Academy, June 3, 1903, news comment, **14**:471-72, mentioned, 464n1
At Lawrenceville School alumni reunion, June 5, 1903, news report, **14**:475
Patriotism, before the Rhode Island Alpha Chapter of Phi Beta Kappa in

*Woodrow Wilson, Political, Religious, and Educational Addresses, cont.*
Sayles Hall, Brown University, June 16, 1903, news report, **14**:491-94
Upon receiving the LL.D. degree at Brown University, First Baptist Church, Providence, June 17, 1903, news report, **14**:495
John Wesley's Place in History, at the Wesley Bicentennial celebration of Wesleyan University in the North Church, Middletown, Conn., June 30, 1903, text, **14**:502-15, news report, 515; mentioned, **12**:314,n1
At a 4th of July observance on the R.M.S. *Oceanic*, July 4, 1903, notes, **14**:520
Before the St. Paul's Society of Princeton University, Sept. 30, 1903, announcement, **15**:9, notes, 9-10, 11
Before the Philadelphian Society of Princeton University, Oct. 1, 1903, news report, **15**:10, mentioned, 9,n1
At a banquet following the inauguration of Francis Landey Patton as president of Princeton Theological Seminary, Stuart Hall, Oct. 14, 1903, mentioned, **15**:16
The Statesmanship of Letters, Founder's Day address at the Carnegie Institute of Pittsburgh, Carnegie Music Hall, Nov. 5, 1903, text, **15**:33-46, news report, 46-47; mentioned, 129,n2
The Land We Live In, before the St. Andrew's Society of the State of New York, Delmonico's, New York, Nov. 30, 1903, news report, **15**:58-60, mentioned, 50, 64,n1, 67
Civic Patriotism, at a banquet given by the Passaic Board of Trade, Acquackanonk Club, Passaic, N. J., Dec. 3, 1903, news report, **15**:61-64; mentioned, **21**:133,n3
The Southerner in the North, to the Southern Society, Waldorf-Astoria Hotel, New York City, Dec. 9, 1903, news report, **15**:68-69
The College Course and Methods of Instruction, to the Schoolmasters' Association of New York and Vicinity, Hotel St. Denis, New York City, Dec. 12, 1903, text, **15**:79-98
The Church and Society, at the Second Presbyterian Church, Philadelphia, Dec. 13, 1903, notes, **15**:78, news report, 98-99
Princeton, response to a toast at the annual dinner of the Princeton Club of Philadelphia, Horticultural Hall, Dec. 18, 1903, news report, **15**:101-103, news item, 79
Americanism, to the Outlook Club, Montclair, N. J., Jan. 22, 1904, news report, **15**:137-39, 142-43, mentioned, 137

*Woodrow Wilson, Political, Religious, and Educational Addresses*, cont.

At a banquet of The Pilgrims of the United States, Delmonico's, New York, Jan. 29, 1904, news report, **15**:147-49, 150, mentioned, 146

The University and the Church, to the Presbyterian Union of Albany, Ten Eyck Hotel, Feb. 15, 1904, news report, **15**:168-69

Princeton, response to a toast at a banquet of the Princeton Alumni Association of Albany, Fort Orange Club, Feb. 15, 1904, mentioned, **15**:169

Patriotism, to the University Club of Syracuse, N. Y., Feb. 16, 1904, news report, **15**:169-73, mentioned, 141,n4

At Phillips Exeter Academy, Feb. 17, 1904, news report, **15**:175, mentioned, 141

On George Washington to children of Princeton Public School, Feb. 19, 1904, notes, **15**:174, mentioned, 175n1

The Young People and the Church, to the Philadelphia County Sabbath School Association at Grace Baptist Temple, Philadelphia, Feb. 26, 1904, notes, **15**:177-78, news report, 179

University Men and the Country, to the University Club of Hudson County, Jersey City, N. J., March 15, 1904, news report, **15**:195-97

Before the Philadelphian Society of Princeton University, Murray Hall, March 17, 1904, news report, **15**:197-98

The Teaching of United States History in Grammar and High Schools, to the New York Educational Council, New York University, March 19, 1904, mentioned, **15**:201,n2; **16**:39,n2

Community Cooperation, to the Princeton Village Improvement Society, May 10, 1904, notes, **15**:316-17, news report, 330-32

Business and Politics, response to toast at banquet of the New York Chapter of the American Institute of Bank Clerks, Hotel St. Denis, Manhattan, May 12, 1904, notes, **15**:328, news report, 328-29, mentioned, 272, 326

The Universities and the Law, at banquet of the Pennsylvania State Bar Association, Cape May, N. J., June 30, 1904, notes, **15**:400, news report, 401, mentioned, 391, 401

The Variety and Unity of History, delivered before the Division of Historical Science of the Congress of Arts and Science of the Universal Exposition, St. Louis, Sept. 20, 1904, text, **15**:472-91, invitation, 105-106; mentioned, **14**:395,n1; **15**:433,n3

Before the Philadelphian Society of

*Woodrow Wilson, Political, Religious, and Educational Addresses*, cont.

Princeton University, Sept. 28, 1904, news report, **15**:495

At the centennial of the presidency of Eliphalet Nott at Union College, First Presbyterian Church, Schenectady, N. Y., Sept. 29, 1904, text, **15**:496-500, mentioned, 500

To the Schoolmasters' Association of New York and Vicinity, Oct. 8, 1904, Hotel St. Denis, Manhattan, notes, **15**:505-506,n1,2,3,4, mentioned, 468

The Young People and the Church, to the 40th annual convention of the Pennsylvania State Sabbath School Association at the Sixth United Presbyterian Church and the Emory Methodist Protestant Church, Pittsburgh, Oct. 13, 1904, text, **15**:510-19, news report, 519-20, mentioned, 126,n2, 461, 492, 521-22

Remarks at Princeton alumni Smoker, Hotel Astor, New York, Nov. 3, 1904, mentioned, **15**:536

Response to toast to Princeton University at dinner of the Princeton Alumni Association of the Oranges, Berkeley Hall, East Orange, N. J., Nov. 10, 1904, news report, **15**:542-44, mentioned, 503-504

Americanism, lecture under the auspices of the New York City Department of Education, delivered at Cooper Union, Nov. 19, 1904, news report, **15**:536-39

The South and the Democratic Party, to the Society of the Virginians, Waldorf-Astoria Hotel, New York City, Nov. 29, 1904, news report, **15**:545-49, mentioned, 550,n2,4

The University and the Nation, to the League for Political Education, New York City, Dec. 3, 1904, mentioned, **15**:501-502, 552

To a conference of leaders of Christian work among students, Murray-Dodge Hall, Princeton University, Feb. 19, 1905, mentioned, **16**:7,n1

Response to toast to George Washington at banquet of the Sons of the Revolution, Delmonico's, New York City, Feb. 22, 1905, news report, **16**:11-12

The Individual and the Organization, before the People's Forum, New Rochelle, N. Y., Feb. 26, 1905, notes, **16**:13-14, news report, **16**:14-15; mentioned, **15**:392, 417; **16**:30,n2, 35; **21**:322-23, 335n2, 337

Before the Princeton Club of Western Pennsylvania, Hotel Schenley, Pittsburgh, March 18, 1905, notes, **16**:31, news report, 32-35

At the University Club of Philadelphia, March 24, 1905, news report, **16**:38-39

At the University Club of Detroit, March

*Woodrow Wilson, Political, Religious, and Educational Addresses, cont.*
30, 1905, notes, **16**:42, news report, 42-43

To Detroit alumni at the Detroit Club, March 30, 1905, mentioned, **16**:43

The University and the Nation, at Ann Arbor under the auspices of the Michigan Schoolmasters' Club and the Michigan Student Lecture Association, March 31, 1905, news report, **16**:44-45

The University and the Nation, before the Presbyterian Union of Newark, in the Roseville Presbyterian Church, April 10, 1905, news report, **16**:48-50

The Memory of Franklin, response to toast at banquet of the American Philosophical Society, Bellevue-Stratford Hotel, Philadelphia, April 14, 1905, notes, **16**:53, news report, 56-57

The Profit of Belief, to Trenton Y.M.C.A. at Association Hall, April 16, 1905, news report, **16**:63-64

Government Day address before Judson College and the Marion, Alabama, Military Institute, April 20, 1905, news report, **16**:71-72, mentioned, 73

To students of Dallas Academy, Selma, Alabama, April 21, 1905, news account, **16**:72-73

The University and the Nation, to the Girls' High School, Montgomery, Alabama, April 21, 1905, news report, **16**:74-78

To the Philadelphian Society of Princeton University, May 4, 1905, news report, **16**:91

To Central High School, Manual Training High School and Westport High School, Kansas City, May 12, 1905, news report, **16**:98-100

To the Western Association of Princeton Clubs, University Club, Kansas City, May 13, 1905, mentioned, **16**:100-101

To the Pennsylvania Society, Sons of the Revolution, at their visit to the Princeton Battlefield, June 17, 1905, news report, **16**:143

University Spirit, to Philadelphian Society of Princeton University, Sept. 28, 1905, news report, **16**:189

At the dedication of Madison Hall, the Y.M.C.A. headquarters, University of Virginia, Oct. 19, 1905, notes, **16**:193-94, news report, 195-97

The University and the Schools, to Schoolmasters of Queens Borough, New York, Oct. 28, 1905, notes, **16**:207-208

At the opening exercises of the Institute of Musical Art, New York, Oct. 31, 1905, text, **16**:208-10, news report, 210-11

To the Princeton Alumni Association of

*Woodrow Wilson, Political, Religious, and Educational Addresses, cont.*
the Oranges, Berkeley Hall, East Orange, N. J., Nov. 9, 1905, notes, **16**:214, news report, 217-18

The University and the School, to the Barnard Club of Providence, Nov. 11, 1905, news report, **16**:219-22

At the University Club, Providence, Nov. 11, 1905, mentioned, **16**:222

At the Dedication of the Northeast Manual Training School, Philadelphia, Nov. 17, 1905, news report, **16**:225-26

Mediation of Youth in Christian Progress, to the Inter-Church Conference on Federation, Carnegie Hall, New York, Nov. 19, 1905, notes, **16**:227, news reports, 228-30, mentioned, 231, 233; **17**:621-22

To a prayer meeting of the Y.M.C.A. of Princeton Theological Seminary, Stuart Hall, Nov. 22, 1905, news report, **16**:232

To the Webb School, Bell Buckle, Tennessee, Nov. 27, 1905, mentioned, **16**:235,n3

To the Princeton Alumni Association of Tennessee, Maxwell House, Nashville, Nov. 28, 1905, news report, **16**:235-38

Liberal Education, to the Nashville Teachers' Association, Watkins Hall, Nov. 29, 1905, news report, **16**:240-42, mentioned, 235

University Ideals, before the Twentieth Century Club of Hartford at the Hartford Club, Dec. 11, 1905, news report, **16**:244, mentioned, 273-74

The University and the Nation, at Parrish Hall, Swarthmore College, Dec. 15, 1905, text, **16**:267-71

To the Association of History Teachers of the Middle States and Maryland, Trenton, Jan. 6, 1906, news report, **16**:279-80

Newness of Spirit, to the Philadelphian Society of Princeton University, Jan. 11, 1906, news report, **16**:280-81

Patriotism, at the State Normal School, West Chester, Pa., Jan. 13, 1906, mentioned, **16**:282

At a memorial service for William Rainey Harper at Teachers College, Columbia University, Jan. 14, 1906, news report, **16**:282-83

What it Means to be an American, Lyceum lecture at Hibernian Hall, Charleston, S. C., Jan. 18, 1906, news report, **16**:285-86

The University Man, to the University Club of Brooklyn, Jan. 27, 1906, mentioned, **16**:289-90

To the Lotos Club of New York, Feb. 3, 1906, text, **16**:292-99, mentioned, 307,n1

The Relation of the University to Com-

*Woodrow Wilson, Political, Religious, and Educational Addresses, cont.*
merce, to the Commercial Club of Providence, Narragansett Hotel, Feb. 9, 1906, news report, **16**:309-12, mentioned, 305,n1

To the Friends School, New York City, Feb. 17, 1906, mentioned, **16**:305n3

At a banquet of the University Club at Rauscher's, Washington, D. C., Feb. 22, 1906, news report, **16**:315-18

The Young Man's Burden, before the North Carolina Society of New York, Waldorf-Astoria Hotel, Feb. 27, 1906, notes, **16**:319, news report, 320

A Liberal Training, to the Private Secondary School Association in the chapel of the University of Pennsylvania, March 9, 1906, news report, **16**:327-28

What Does it Mean to be an American? in Undergraduate Lecture Association course at Oberlin College, March 13, 1906, news report, **16**:340-41

Patriotism, to the People's Institute of Youngstown, Ohio, in the First Presbyterian Church, March 14, 1906, news report, **16**:332-33

On the advantages of college athletics at a dinner of Alumni Association of Lawrenceville School in honor of General Horace Porter, Waldorf-Astoria Hotel, New York, March 24, 1906, news report, **16**:344

At a luncheon of Princeton alumni, Hartford Club, Hartford, Conn., March 30, 1906, news report, **16**:352-53, 356,n2

On Secondary Education at Rayen School, Youngstown, Ohio, March 14, 1906, news report, **16**:354-55

The Minister and the Community, to a Student Conference at Hosmer Hall, Hartford Theological Seminary, March 30, 1906, text, **16**:346-51, news report, **16**:352, 355-56; **19**:178n1

At the Class of 1909 prayer meeting, Dodge Hall, April 7, 1906, notice, **16**:357

On Thomas Jefferson delivered at the annual Jefferson Day Dinner of the National Democratic Club of New York at the Waldorf-Astoria Hotel, April 16, 1906, text, **16**:362-69, news release, 358-62, mentioned, 322, 330, 372, 372,n3, 373

To the Philadelphian Society of Princeton University, April 26, 1906, notes, **16**:377-78, news report, 378-79

Technical Education, to Princeton Alumni Association of New England, University Club, Boston, May 3, 1906, news report, **16**:384-85, mentioned, 357

At a dinner in his honor at the Univer-

*Woodrow Wilson, Political, Religious, and Educational Addresses, cont.*
sity Club, Cleveland, May 18, 1906, news report, **16**:396-97

Princeton University, response to toast at banquet of the Western Association of Princeton Clubs, Hotel Hollenden, Cleveland, May 19, 1906, text, **16**:406-11, mentioned, 383,n3, 386, 389, 396

Americanism and What It Means, at reception of the Princeton Alumni Association of Tennessee, Chattanooga, Oct. 27, 1906, news report, **16**:474-76

Ideals, at banquet of the Princeton Alumni Association of Tennessee, Read House, Chattanooga, Oct. 27, 1906, news report, **16**:476-77, mentioned, 481

To the Philadelphian Society of Princeton University, Nov. 22, 1906, news report, **16**:490-91

Patriotism, to the Southern Society of New York, Waldorf-Astoria Hotel, Dec. 14, 1906, news report, **16**:529-31, mentioned,**16**:533,n5, 557; **17**:449-50, 456,n4

At St. Andrew's Presbyterian Church, Hamilton, Bermuda, Jan. 27, 1907, notes, **17**:22-23, mentioned, 25

Sermon at Christ Church, Warwick, Bermuda, Feb. 3, 1907, notes, **17**:27-28

To Princeton Alumni of Philadelphia, Horticultural Hall, Feb. 14, 1907, notes, **17**:38, news reports, 38-40, mentioned, 36, 41, 43, 44, 48,n2

To Maryland alumni of Princeton, Arundel Club, Baltimore, Feb. 18, 1907, news report, **17**:43-45, mentioned, 46, 59,n1

Discretion, at Hill School, Pottstown, Pa., Feb. 22, 1907, notes, **17**:49, news report, 50

Constitutional Government in the United States: Blumenthal Foundation lectures delivered at Columbia University, March 1—April 26, 1907; mentioned, **16**:373-74,n1, 375-76, 383, 395, 396, 413, 495-96, 559,n1; **17**:3n2, 6,n12, 7, 11, 15, 26, 62,n1, 65,n1, 73,n1, 94, 121, 365-66, 427,n2, 605-606, 607,n5, 611-12, 616; schedule, **17**:45-46,n1; published as book (1908), text, **18**:69-216

To Rutgers College Alumni Association, Hotel Manhattan, New York, March 1, 1907, mentioned, **17**:31,n1

John C. Calhoun, reply to toast at a dinner of the South Carolina Society of New York, Waldorf-Astoria Hotel, March 18, 1907, text, **17**:78-83, mentioned, 85, 86

At the dedication of new chapel and Sunday school rooms of the First Presbyterian Church, Princeton, March 27,

*Woodrow Wilson, Political, Religious, and Educational Addresses, cont.*

1907, news report, **17**:98-99,n1,2, mentioned, 259,n2

The Hegemony of Princeton, response to toast at Princeton alumni banquet, Schenley Hotel, Pittsburgh, April 2, 1907, news report, **17**:100-101, mentioned, **16**:559; **17**:65,n1, 94, 97, 100, 107, 211,n1

At Memorial Hall, Harvard University, June 26, 1907, text, **17**:226-28, mentioned, 307n1, 334

The Author and Signers of the Declaration of Independence, at Jamestown Exposition, Norfolk, Va., July 4, 1907, text, **17**:248-59, news account, 247-48, mentioned, 261, 262, 456n5, 515-16,n1

To students of St. Mary's School in Memphis, Nov. 8, 1907, mentioned, **17**:474

Problems of the Future, at the University School, Memphis, Nov. 8, 1907, summarized, **17**:474-75

At Memphis High School, Nov. 8, 1907, quoted, **17**:475-76

Ideals of Public Life, at the Goodwyn Institute, Memphis, Nov. 8, 1907, news report, **17**:476-80

To the Princeton Alumni Association of Tennessee, Gayoso Hotel, Memphis, Nov. 9, 1907, text, **17**:480-87, mentioned, 377n1, 473

False and True Conservatism, at the Watauga Club, Nashville, Nov. 11, 1907, news report, **17**:491-95

The Ideals of Public Life, to the Cleveland Chamber of Commerce, Nov. 16, 1907, text, **17**:497-506, mentioned, **17**:507-509; **18**:217,n2, 262,n2; **19**:725-26,n1

Response to address of welcome at the Association of Colleges and Preparatory Schools of the Middle States and Maryland, Townsend Harris Hall, College of the City of New York, Nov. 29, 1907, text, **17**:528-29

School and College, presidential address to the Association of Colleges and Preparatory Schools of the Middle States and Maryland, Townsend Harris Hall, College of the City of New York, Nov. 29, 1907, text, **17**:529-45, mentioned, 560, 565-66

To the Indiana State Teachers' Association, Tomlinson Hall, Indianapolis, Dec. 27, 1907, text, **17**:569-82, mentioned, 568, 603

The Ideals of Public Life, to the Contemporary Club at the Propylaeum, Indianapolis, Dec. 28, 1907, news report, **17**:582-84

To the Princeton Alumni Association of Maryland, Arundel Club, Baltimore, March 6, 1908, news report, **18**:10-11

*Woodrow Wilson, Political, Religious, and Educational Addresses, cont.*

Talk on Good Citizenship to students of Chicago Latin School, March 12, 1908; repeated on same day before students of the University School for Boys, news report, **18**:16-17

To the Princeton Club of Chicago, University Club, March 12, 1908, text, **18**:17-34; mentioned, **17**:598,n1, 615,n2; **18**:16, 219

The Government and Business, to the Commercial Club of Chicago, Congress Hotel, March 14, 1908, text, **18**:35-51, mentioned, 17, 59, 60

The Training of Intellect, Phi Beta Kappa address at Yale University, March 18, 1908, text, **18**:53-59, mentioned, 10,n2, 60, 312

The Government and Business, to the Traffic Club of Pittsburgh, April 3, 1908, abstract, **18**:221-25, mentioned, 262-63

Law or Personal Power, at the Jefferson Day dinner of the National Democratic Club, Hotel Knickerbocker, New York, April 13, 1908, text, **18**:263-69, news report, 269-71, mentioned, 59-60, 219-20

The Contribution of the Young Men's Christian Association to the Life of the Nation, to the Chicago Y.M.C.A., at Congress Hotel, April 27, 1908, outline, **18**:276, news report, 276-77, mentioned, **17**:615,n3; **18**:60,n2, 272-73,n3, 274, 313, 545

To the Western Association of Princeton Clubs, Pittsburgh, May 2, 1908, **18**:51-52, 218n1; text, **18**:280-85, mentioned, **17**:459, 598,n1

To the Princeton Alumni Association of New England, Hotel Vendome, Boston, May 15, 1908, text, **18**:297-300, mentioned, 295,n1, 303

Mere Science, response to toast at retirement dinner to Cyrus Fogg Brackett, Princeton Inn, May 18, 1908, mentioned, **18**:301

College Work and College Administration, commencement address at the Woman's College of Baltimore (now Goucher College), Lyric Theatre, June 3, 1908, outline, **18**:318, news report, 318-20, mentioned, 278; **20**:16,n3

After dinner speech on S.S. *California*, June 27, 1908, outline, **18**:347

After dinner speech at entertainment on S.S. *Caledonia*, Sept. 11, 1908, notes, **18**:418

The Banker and the Nation, to the American Bankers' Association at Denver, Sept. 30, 1908, text, **18**:424-34, mentioned, 435, 436, 441, 469,n1,2, 470; **19**:95,n4

To the Wednesday Morning Club of

*Woodrow Wilson, Political, Religious, and Educational Addresses, cont.*
Pittsfield at the Berkshire Athenaeum, Oct. 6, 1908, mentioned, **18**:436

At the Inauguration of Harry Augustus Garfield as president of Williams College, Thompson Memorial Chapel, Oct. 7, 1908, text, **18**:437-39, mentioned, 436

Public Affairs and Private Responsibility, to the Men's League of the First Congregational Church, Pittsfield, Mass., Oct. 8, 1908, news report, **18**:440-44, announcement, 436, mentioned, 424,n2

At the Seventy-fifth anniversary of Haverford College, Oct. 16, 1908, text, **18**:459-65, invitation, 67, mentioned, 420

What Kind of Citizen Shall We Be? at Lawrenceville School, Nov. 4, 1908, notes, **18**:482-83, mentioned, 275-76, 278

To the University Club of Jersey City at Hasbrouck Hall, Nov. 5, 1908, news report, **18**:485-87

To the Jersey City High School, Nov. 6, 1908, news report, **18**:487-89, mentioned, 534-35

The Meaning of a College Education, at the Hotchkiss School, Lakeville, Conn., Nov. 12, 1908, text, **18**:495-507, mentioned, 509

To the City History Club of New York, Hotel Plaza, Nov. 13, 1908, news report, **18**:509-10, mentioned, 516

Success and How to Attain It, to the East Liberty Y.M.C.A., Pittsburgh, Nov. 22, 1908, news report, **18**:520-21, mentioned, 507-508,n4,5

The Contribution of the Young Men's Christian Association to the Life of the Nation, at the thirty-fourth anniversary services of the East Liberty Y.M.C.A., Pittsburgh, Sunday evening, Nov. 22, 1908, news report, **18**:521-22, mentioned, 507,n5

The Business Man and the Community, to the Toledo Chamber of Commerce, Valentine Theatre, Nov. 27, 1908, news announcement, **18**:524, news report, 526-28, mentioned, 530

Conservatism: True and False, to the New York Southern Society, Waldorf-Astoria Hotel, Dec. 9, 1908, text, **18**:535-40, mentioned, 532,n3, 563

The Business Man and the Nation, to the Wednesday Club of Newark, Continental Hotel, Dec. 16, 1908, news report, **18**:551-52, mentioned, 548,n3, 556

The Meaning of a Liberal Education, to the High School Teachers' Association of New York City, Jan. 9, 1909, text, **18**:593-606, mentioned, 533,n2

*Woodrow Wilson, Political, Religious, and Educational Addresses, cont.*
To the Alumni of Newark Academy, Jan. 15, 1909, news report, **18**: 628-29, mentioned, 547-48,n3

Robert E. Lee, at the University of North Carolina, Jan. 19, 1909, text, **18**:631-45, invitation, 561-62,n3, mentioned, **19**:4,n1, 4-5, 19n1

At a dinner of Williams College alumni, Delmonico's, New York, Feb. 5, 1909, news report, **19**:30-31

Abraham Lincoln: A Man of the People, centennial address delivered at the Auditorium, Chicago, Feb. 12, 1909, text, **19**:33-46, mentioned, **18**:545, 546-47, 553-54, 562, 564; **19**:11n3

To the Princeton Club of Chicago, University Club, Feb. 13, 1909, news report, **19**:47-48, mentioned, **18**:645-46; **19**:74, 76, 79

To the Presbyterian Union of Baltimore, Feb. 19, 1909, text, **19**:52-63, mentioned, 48-49,n1, 76,n5

In behalf of Hampton Normal and Agricultural Institute, Academy of Music, Philadelphia, Feb. 26, 1909, notes, **19**:69, mentioned, **18**:629-30; **19**:49

Civic Problems, to the Civic League of St. Louis, Hotel Jefferson, March 9, 1909, text, **19**:81-97, mentioned, **18**:516-17,n2, 532-33, 567, 568; **19**:101; **20**:43,n6

At Washington University, St. Louis, March 10, 1909, news report, **19**:101-102

To the Virginia Society of St. Louis, University Club, March 10, 1909, news report, **19**:97, mentioned, **18**: 567,n4, 568, 593; **19**:102

Academic Ideals and Public Service, to the American Society for the Extension of University Teaching, Witherspoon Hall, Philadelphia, March 12, 1909, news report, **19**:98-100, mentioned, **18**:525, 544,n3; **19**:108-109

At dinner of the Friendly Sons of St. Patrick, Delmonico's New York, March 17, 1909, text, **19**:102-108

Americanism, before the Culture Society of Temple Rodeph Sholom, New York, March 18, 1909, news report, **19**: 112, mentioned, **18**:523,n2, 550

Before the Princeton Club of Philadelphia, March 19, 1909, news report, **19**:112-13, mentioned, **18**:550, 564

What Ought a Man to Do? at Witherspoon Street Presbyterian Church, Princeton, March 31, 1909, news report, **19**:148-49

To the Philadelphian Society of Princeton University, April 1, 1909, news report, **19**:147-48

On Political Reform at the University

*Woodrow Wilson, Political, Religious, and Educational Addresses, cont.*
Club of Detroit, April 16, 1909, notes, **19**:164,n1
At a dinner of Princeton alumni honoring Mayor George Brinton McClellan (Princeton 1886) at the Waldorf-Astoria, New York, April 20, 1909, news report, **19**:175-77, mentioned, 169,n1
The Schoolmaster, at a dinner in honor of J. Albert Reinhart, Paterson, N. J., April 23, 1909, news report, **19**:171-72, mentioned, **18**:563-64,n2, 590-91, 612-13
The Claims and Character of the Christian Ministry, to the Ministerial Club of Princeton University, April 26, 1909, news report, **19**:173-74
The Ideals and Objects of the University, to Delaware alumni of Princeton at Wilmington, May 1, 1909, mentioned, **19**:152,n1
Problems of College Life, to Princeton alumni of Newark, May 5, 1909, news report, **19**:186-88, mentioned, 265
At the unveiling of a statue to John Witherspoon in Washington, May 20, 1909, text, **19**:202-10, mentioned, 201, 214
Princeton, to the Western Association of Princeton Clubs, Hotel Seelbach, Louisville, Ky., May 22, 1909, news report, **19**:212-14, mentioned, 201, 202, 211, 214
The Present Task of the Ministry, at 75th anniversary of Hartford Theological Seminary, May 26, 1909, text, **19**:215-22, mentioned, 214, 229,n2, 274, 310-11, 319, 441,n2, 473,n1, 487
Anniversary address at St. Paul's School, Concord, N. H., June 3, 1909, news report, **19**:226-28, mentioned, 201, 229, 230,n1, 238, 239, 347
At the inauguration of Charles Alexander Richmond as President of Union College, Schenectady, June 7, 1909, text, **19**:231-37, mentioned, **19**:20,n2
The Spirit of Learning, Phi Beta Kappa oration delivered at Harvard University, July 1, 1909, text, **19**:277-89, mentioned, **17**:488n2; **19**:11, 270, 290, 292-93, 293-94, 319, 407n1, 439, 441
At the inauguration of Ernest Fox Nichols as President of Dartmouth College, Hanover, N. H., Oct. 14, 1909, text, **19**:413-18, mentioned, 408,n1, 409, 410
The Democratic Opportunity, to the Democratic Club, Plainfield Theatre, Plainfield, N. J., Oct. 29, 1909, news report, **19**:461-64, mentioned, 384, 464; **20**:307,n2
The Ministry and the Individual, at McCormick Theological Seminary,

*Woodrow Wilson, Political, Religious, and Educational Addresses, cont.*
Nov. 2, 1909, text, **19**:471-79, mentioned, 398-99, 481, 485, 486-87; **20**:151,n1
Talk to Princeton alumni at the University Club, Chicago, Nov. 2, 1909, news report, **19**:479
To the Christian Fraternity of Phillips Exeter Academy, Exeter, N. H., Nov. 11, 1909, news report, **19**:498-99
Religion and Citizenship, at Harvard Church, Brookline, Mass., Nov. 12, 1909, notes, **19**:496, news report, 497, mentioned, 383
To Princeton Alumni at the University Club, Boston, Nov. 13, 1909, news report, **19**:497, mentioned, 383,n6
On political reform to the City Club of Philadelphia, Hotel Walton, Nov. 18, 1909, text, **19**:509-22; mentioned, **20**:43,n7, 534n2
To the Philadelphia Teachers' Association, William Penn High School, Dec. 4, 1909, news report, **19**:554-56
Our Country and Our Day, before the Athenaeum Club, Summit, N. J., Dec. 9, 1909, news report, **19**:599-601, mentioned, 533-34,n3
To Princeton alumni at Englewood, N. J., Dec. 17, 1909, notes, **19**:608
The State and the Citizen's Relation to It, to the New Jersey State Teachers' Association at Atlantic City, Dec. 28, 1909, text, **19**:635-48, mentioned, 387-88, 634, 738-39
At a dinner given by the faculty of the University of Wisconsin to representatives of the Association of American Universities, Jan. 1910, mentioned, **19**:635,n3
Position and Importance of the Arts Course as Distinct from the Professional and Semi-Professional Courses, to the Association of American Universities at the University of Wisconsin, Madison, Jan. 5, 1910, text, **19**:713-27, mentioned, 448,n1, 550,n4, 552, 620, 634, 635, 657, 698, 704, 705, 747
At the Inauguration of Henry Harbaugh Apple as President of Franklin and Marshall College, Lancaster, Pa., Jan. 7, 1910, text, **19**:740-47, mentioned, 552, 634, 698, 704
To Group 8 of the New York State Bankers' Association at Hotel Waldorf-Astoria, New York, Jan. 17, 1910, news reports, **20**:23-27; mentioned, **19**:604, 607, 609-10,n4; **20**:44-45
Before a dinner meeting of the Short Ballot Association at the Hotel Astor, New York, Jan. 21, 1910, text, **20**:32-43; mentioned, **19**:553, 579
To Maryland alumni of Princeton in Bal-

*Woodrow Wilson, Political, Religious, and Educational Addresses, cont.*
timore, March 11, 1910, text, **20**:229-35, mentioned, 27-28,n2, 50,n1, 247, 254, 265, 268, 269, 285, 311
The Opportunity for Young Men in Politics, to the Contemporary Club of Philadelphia, Bellevue-Stratford Hotel, March 14, 1910, news report, **20**:242-43; mentioned, **19**:529,n2, 531, 605-606; **20**:223,n1, 243
To the Philadelphian Society of Princeton University, March 17, 1910, news report, **20**:255-56
On Grover Cleveland at the National Democratic Club of New York, March 18, 1910, text, **20**:257-62, mentioned, 249,n1
To the Princeton Alumni Association of Long Island in Brooklyn, March 21, 1910, abstract, **20**:272-76, mentioned, 311, 320, 410
To the Princeton Alumni Association of Hudson County, N. J., Carteret Club, Jersey City, March 24, 1910, news report, **20**:290-91, mentioned, 311
To the Western Association of Princeton Clubs at St. Louis, March 26, 1910, abstract, **20**:291-96; mentioned, **19**:505-506; **20**:211, 212, 220, 237, 238, 243-44, 252, 252-53, 254, 256, 262, 271, 284, 303, 304,n2, 306-307,n1, 311, 312, 320, 321, 322, 387, 410
Living Principles of Democracy, address at Democratic Dollar Dinner, Elizabeth, N. J., March 29, 1910, text, **20**:297-303, mentioned, 215,n2, 288-89, 297, 306, 307, 349,n2, 350,n1
Lecture under the auspices of the Brotherhood of the First Presbyterian Church, Princeton, March 31, 1910, notice, **20**:312
At a Senior Prayer Meeting, April 3, 1910, notes, **20**:314
The Clergyman and the State, at the General Theological Seminary, New York City, April 6, 1910, text, **20**:328-35; mentioned, **21**:105,n2
To the Princeton Club of New York, April 7, 1910, text, **20**:337-48, mentioned, 64,n2, 263,n1, 328, 357, 382n4,5, 392
To the Princeton Alumni Association of Western Pennsylvania, Hotel Schenley, Pittsburgh, April 16, 1910, news reports, **20**:363-68, 373-76; mentioned, **19**:401; **20**:53, 81,n2, 85, 368-69, 370, 372, 376, 377, 378-79,n1,2, 379-80, 380, 381, 386-87,n2, 387, 389, 390, 397-98, 398-99, 424,n1, 444, 453, 458; **21**:31n1
At the Methodist Church, Ridgewood, N. J., April 22, 1910, news report, **20**:385
To the Associated Press and the Ameri-

*Woodrow Wilson, Political, Religious, and Educational Addresses, cont.*
can Newspaper Publishers' Association, Waldorf-Astoria Hotel, New York, April 28, 1910, abstract, **20**:399-401, mentioned, 58-59
To New Jersey Bankers' Association, Hotel Chelsea, Atlantic City, May 6, 1910, text, **20**:414-21
To the Princeton Club of Chicago, May 12, 1910, text, **20**:433-43, mentioned, 351,n1,3, 360, 403, 453, 520,n1
To the Essex County Lawyers' Club, Newark, May 20, 1910, news report, **20**:462-63; mentioned, **19**:709,n4
At the Centennial Celebration of the Lawrenceville School, June 11, 1910, text, **20**:514-18
The Function of the Country Church, at dedication of new meeting house of the First Congregational Church of Old Lyme, Conn., July 16, 1910, news report, **21**:4
The Lawyer and the Community, to the American Bar Association at Chattanooga, Aug. 31, 1910, **21**:64-81; mentioned, **20**:21-22, 66, 71, 86, 572; **21**:51, 85, 300n2, 386, 557, 609; **22**:68n4, 185, 315

———

*Gubernatorial campaign speeches (vol. 21, Sept. 15—Nov. 5, 1910)*
Accepting the Democratic Gubernatorial Nomination, Taylor Opera House, Trenton, Sept. 15, 91-94, 118-20
Jersey City, Die Wilde Gans Club, Sept. 20, news report, 147-48, mentioned, 128,n1
Opening the campaign, St. Peter's Hall, Jersey City, Sept. 28, text, 181-91, mentioned, 199,n1, 239, 265, 564
Jersey City, St. Patrick's Hall, Sept. 28, mentioned, 191n1
Jersey City, Grand View Hall, Sept. 28, mentioned, 191n1
Plainfield, Reform Club Hall, Sept. 29, text, 193-98
Newark, Krueger Auditorium, Sept. 30, text, 202-12
Red Bank, Frick Lyceum, Oct. 1, text, 213-18, mentioned, 227,n2
Long Branch, Ocean Park Casino, Oct. 1, news report, 227-28
Trenton, Taylor Opera House, Oct. 3, text, 229-38, mentioned, 243, 260, 267, 274
Woodbury, Green's Opera House, Oct. 5, text, 245-59, mentioned, 243
Burlington Auditorium, Oct. 6, news report, 269-74
Bridgeton, Criterion Theatre, Oct. 7, news report, 276-81, mentioned, 287-88, 322, 336

*Woodrow Wilson, Political, Religious, and Educational Addresses, cont.*

Cape May Court House, Oct. 8, news report, 281-87

Wildwood Hippodrome, Oct. 8, news report, 281-87

Paterson, Paterson Opera House, Oct. 11, news report, 301-306

Caldwell, birthplace of Grover Cleveland, Oct. 12, news report, 309-10, mentioned, 309n3

Caldwell, Monomonock Inn, Oct. 12, transcript, 306-309

Atlantic City, Steeple Chase Pier Theatre, Oct. 13, transcript, 310-20

Ocean County: Pleasantville, Tuckerton, Lakewood, Toms River, Oct. 14, news report, 325-27

Asbury Park, the Hippodrome, Oct. 15, transcript, 328-34, mentioned, 320, 338

Freehold, Armory Opera House, Oct. 15, mentioned, 320, 334n4

Remarks to Democratic leaders of Mercer County, Masonic Hall, Trenton, Oct. 18, news report, 349-51,n1

Bound Brook, Oct. 19, news report, 354-61

Somerville Armory, Oct. 19, news report, 354-61

Flemington, Opera House and Court House, Oct. 20, news reports, 369-77, 377n4, 381

Warren County, Oct. 21, news report, 382-85

Washington, Baker's Hotel, Oct. 21, news report, 383

Hackettstown, American House, Oct. 21, news report, 383-84

Blairstown, Blairstown Hotel, Oct. 21, news report, 384

Hope, Village Green, Oct. 20, news report, 384

Oxford, Allen's drugstore, Oct. 20, news report, 384

Belvidere Court House, Oct. 20, news report, 384-85

Phillipsburg, Ortygian Hall, Oct. 21, news report, 390-96

Newton, Newton Public School, Oct. 22, news report, 396-405

Camden, Temple Theatre, Broadway Theatre, Oct. 24, news report, 413-21

Salem, Grand Opera House, Oct. 25, transcript, 423-33, mentioned, 412, 463

New Brunswick, Opera House, Oct. 26, news report, 436-41, mentioned, 412

Bergen County: Rutherford, Englewood, and Hackensack, Oct. 27, news report, 446-49, mentioned, 412

Hackensack, Second Regiment Armory, Oct. 27, news report, 452-54, mentioned, 412

Elizabeth, Proctor's Theatre, Oct. 28, transcript, 454-62, mentioned, 412

*Woodrow Wilson, Political, Religious, and Educational Addresses, cont.*

Elizabethport, St. Patrick's Parish Hall, Oct. 28, news report, 465-70, mentioned, 454n1

Hudson County: West Hoboken, West New York, Hoboken, Oct. 29, news report, 471-76, mentioned, 412

Bayonne Democratic Club, Oct. 31, news report, 485-92, mentioned, 412

Jersey City, St. John's Hall, Oct. 31, mentioned, 492n1

Passaic, Passaic High School, Nov. 1, transcript, 493-502, mentioned, 507

Carlstadt, Nov. 1, news report, 507-508, mentioned, 502n3

Montclair, Hillside Grammar School, Nov. 3, transcript, 508-18, mentioned, 520

Orange, Columbus Hall, Nov. 2, news report, 520-21

Madison, Nov. 3, news report, 525-26

Dover, Baker Theatre, Nov. 3, news report, 526-27

Morristown, Lyceum Theatre, Nov. 3, transcript, 527-36

Perth Amboy, Donahoe Auditorium, Nov. 4, transcript, 543-55

Carteret, Nov. 5, news report, 560-61

East Orange, Commonwealth Hall, Nov. 5, news report, 563

Bloomfield, Nov. 5, mentioned, 563

Glen Ridge Town Hall, Nov. 5, news report, 563-64

Final address, Newark, Krueger Auditorium, Nov. 5, transcript, 564-76, mentioned, 412, 561

At a luncheon of the City Club of Milwaukee, Schlitz Palm Garden, Nov. 17, 1910, news report, **22**:57-61; mentioned, **21**:163,n1; **22**:56

Before the Milwaukee Lecture Service League, Pabst Theater, Nov. 17, 1910, text, **22**:61-71; mentioned, **21**:163,n1

Development of the Business Conscience, before the Business Service Lecture League, Y.M.C.A. Hall, Chicago, Nov. 18, 1910, news report, **22**:74-76; mentioned, **21**:163,n1, 593, 594; **22**:48,n2

The Spirit of America, Thanksgiving Day address at Har Sinai Temple, Trenton, Nov. 24, 1910, text, **22**:87-93

To the Conference of Governors, Frankfort, Ky., Nov. 29, 1910, text, **22**:102-13, mentioned, 185, 315,n3

To the Illinois Manufacturers' Association, Congress Hotel, Chicago, Dec. 12, 1910, advance text, **22**:178-80, news report, 180-81; mentioned, **21**:389,n1; **22**:71,n2

To the New York Southern Society, Hotel Waldorf-Astoria, Dec. 14, 1910,

*Woodrow Wilson, Political, Religious, and Educational Addresses,* cont.
text, **22:**188-96, mentioned, 51, 51n1, 202-203,n4, 223, 257, 288

Proposed public statement on candidacy of James Smith, Jr., **22:**239,n1

Statement on senatorial candidacy of James Smith, Jr., **22:**248-52, mentioned, 257

Form letter on the senatorship, **22:**252

The Law and the Facts, presidential address to the American Political Science Association, Southern Hotel, St. Louis, Dec. 27, 1910, text, **22:**263-72

To the City Club of St. Louis, Dec. 29, 1910, news report, **22:**276-77

To the Princeton Club of St. Louis, Dec. 29, 1910, news report, **22:**283-84, mentioned, 198,n1

On the senatorial situation in New Jersey, St. Patrick's Hall, Jersey City, Jan. 5, 1911, text, **22:**295-307, mentioned, 233,n1, 295, 309, 311, 311,n1

At the golden jubilee of the Hebrew Benevolent and Orphan Asylum Society of Newark, Temple B'nai Jeshurun, Jan. 8, 1911, text, **22:**316-21, mentioned, 183, 260

In New Auditorium, Newark, on United States senatorial contest, Jan. 14, 1911, news report, **22:**335-44, mentioned, 286n1, 333,n1, 335

Inaugural address as Governor of New Jersey, Taylor Opera House, Trenton, Jan. 17, 1911, text, **22:**345-54, mentioned, 53, 333, 363, 375, 521

At the annual dinner of the Jersey City Board of Trade, Jersey City Club Theatre, Jan. 19, 1911, news report, **22:**359-60, mentioned, 399

To the Newark Board of Trade, Jan. 25, 1911, text, **22:**367-74

In behalf of Know Your City Week, Y.M.C.A. auditorium, Trenton, Jan. 26, 1911, news report, **22:**379-82

To the Inter-Church Federation of New Jersey at the First Methodist Episcopal Church, Trenton, Jan. 27, 1911, news report, **22:**385-87

To the Kansas Society of New York, Waldorf-Astoria Hotel, Jan. 28, 1911, news report, **22:**389-91, mentioned, 392

To the National Press Club, Washington, Jan. 31, 1911, text, **22:**396-99, mentioned, 377,n1, 396, 404

Tribute to Mark Anthony Sullivan at a banquet in his honor, Columbian Club, Jersey City, given by alumni of St. Peter's College, Feb. 1, 1911, text, **22:**400-404

To a banquet of Stevens Institute alumni, Hotel Astor, New York, Feb. 8, 1911, news report, **22:**410-11

In behalf of Berea College, at Carnegie Hall, New York, Feb. 10, 1911, text,

*Woodrow Wilson, Political, Religious, and Educational Addresses,* cont.
**22:**417-21, mentioned, 49,n2, 172,n2, 214, 424, 425

To the Kentuckians of New York, Plaza Hotel, Feb. 10, 1911, news report, **22:**421-22, mentioned, 425

To the Democratic Club of Philadelphia, Hotel Bellevue-Stratford, Feb. 21, 1911, text, **22:**441-50, mentioned, 246-47, 435n1, 450, 451, 451,n1

At a meeting of the New Jersey Consumers' League, First Presbyterian Church, Trenton, Feb. 24, 1911, news report, **22:**452-53

To the New Jersey Editorial Association, Trenton, Feb. 27, 1911, news report, **22:**455

To the West Hudson Board of Trade, Harrison, N. J., Feb. 28, 1911, text, **22:**456-65, mentioned, 477

To the Hoboken Board of Trade, German Club, March 2, 1911, text, **22:**468-74, mentioned, 477

To the Trenton Chamber of Commerce, March 7, 1911, news report, **22:**482-86, mentioned, 499

At a dinner in his honor given by Hoke Smith, Piedmont Hotel, Atlanta, March 9, 1911, news report, **22:**489-91

The Citizen and the State, to the Southern Commercial Congress, Atlanta Auditorium, March 10, 1911, text, **22:**491-98, mentioned, 206,n2, 500, 507n2

To the New Jersey Conference of Charities and Correction, Alexander Hall, Princeton, April 2, 1911, text, **22:**528-31

At the Jefferson Day dinner of the Burlington County Democratic Club in the Auditorium, Burlington, April 5, 1911, text, **22:**535-42, mentioned, 502, 543-44

At a banquet of the National Democratic League of Clubs, Murat Temple, Indianapolis, April 13, 1911, text, **22:**557-68, mentioned, 466,n3, 569, 570, 570-71, 576, 578, 604

At a dinner in honor of the 4th anniversary of the founding of the Free Synagogue, Hotel Astor, New York, April 24, 1911, news report, **22:**585-86

At a dinner given in his honor by Ernest Robinson Ackerman, president of the New Jersey Senate, Hotel Astor, New York, April 26, 1911, news report, **22:**588-89

Before the Phillipsburg, N. J. Board of Trade, April 27, 1911, news report, **22:**590-91

To the Pewter Platter Club, Norfolk, Va., April 29, 1911, news reports, **22:**592-97

At a dinner of the National Democratic Club in honor of Senator James A.

*Woodrow Wilson, Political, Religious, and Educational Addresses, cont.*
O'Gorman, Hotel Astor, New York, May 2, 1911, news report, **22**:601-604
To the Knife and Fork Club, Coates House, Kansas City, Mo., May 5, 1911, news report, **23**:5-9
At Manual Training High School, Kansas City, May 5, 1911, mentioned, **23**:9
To the Commercial Club of Kansas City, May 5, 1911, news report, **23**:9-10
The Bible and Progress, address on the Tercentenary of the English translation of the Bible, Denver Auditorium, May 7, 1911, news report, **23**:12-20, mentioned, 11, 80
At a dinner of Bryn Mawr alumnae in Denver, May 7, 1911, news report, **23**:21-22
To the Denver Chamber of Commerce in El Jebel Temple, May 8, 1911, news report, **23**:23-26
At a luncheon of Princeton alumni, University Club, Denver, May 9, 1911, news report, **23**:27-28
The Relation of Business to Politics, to the Mile High Club of Denver, Adams Hotel, May 9, 1911, news report, **23**:28-29
To the Jefferson Club of Los Angeles, May 12, 1911, transcript, **23**:32-40
Luncheon speech at Hotel Maryland, Pasadena, Cal., May 13, 1911, news report, **23**:45-48
To the City Club of Los Angeles, Temple Auditorium, May 13, 1911, news report, **23**:50-51, mentioned, 41,n3
On the "Oregon System" to the Commercial Club of Portland, Ore., May 18, 1911, news report, **23**:65-68, mentioned, 68
To the Press Club of Portland, Ore., May 18, 1911, news report, **23**:68-69
At the Portland Armory, May 19, 1911, text, **23**:69-72, mentioned, 64, 76
At a dinner in his honor, University Club, Portland, Ore., May 19, 1911, mentioned, **23**:64, 76
On the Problems of Government, in Portland at the Y.M.C.A., May 19, 1911, news report, **23**:73-76
To Democratic Leaders of the State of Washington, Hotel Washington, Seattle, May 20, 1911, news report, **23**:78-79, mentioned, 79
On Commission Government, Dreamland Pavilion, Seattle, May 20, 1911, news report, **23**:79-80
To the working newspapermen of Seattle, Press Club, May 20, 1911, mentioned, **23**:80
On the relationship of business and politics to the Publicity Club of Minneapolis, West Hotel, May 24, 1911, news report, **23**:86-87

*Woodrow Wilson, Political, Religious, and Educational Addresses, cont.*
To the Association of Commerce of St. Paul, Hotel St. Paul, May 24, 1911, news report, **23**:87-92, mentioned, 93
At the University of Minnesota, University Chapel, May 25, 1911, news report, **23**:93-95
At a banquet of the Commercial Club, Lincoln Hotel, Lincoln, Neb., May 26, 1911, news report, **23**:100-102
Commencement address at the University of North Carolina, May 30, 1911, text, **23**:104-110; mentioned, **22**:406, 517; **23**:97
In Capitol Square, Raleigh, N. C., May 31, 1911, news report, **23**:110-11,n1, mentioned, 128
At the cornerstone laying of the Y.M.C.A. building in Columbia, S. C., delivered in the First Baptist Church, June 1, 1911, news report, **23**:113-14
To the South Carolina Press Association, Columbia Theatre, Columbia, S. C., June 2, 1911, news report, **23**:114-27
On government by commission under the auspices of the Government by Commission Association, High School, Bayonne, N. J., June 7, 1911, news report, **23**:136-38
On behalf of commission government in Trenton, June 13, 1911, text, **23**:140-52
To Reform Democrats in Harrisburg, Pa., June 15, 1911: at the Board of Trade Auditorium, news report, **23**:154-56; at the Casino Theatre, news report, **23**:156-57, mentioned, 243, 243n3, 246n1, 504
To the New Jersey State Bar Association at Atlantic City, June 16, 1911, news report, **23**:158-60
On behalf of commission government before the Commission Government League, St. Mary's Hall, Hoboken, N. J., June 21, 1911, news report, **23**:161-71
To the Woodrow Wilson Democratic League of Essex County, Krueger Auditorium, Newark, June 28, 1911, news reports, **23**:177-82
Fourth of July address in the Auditorium, Ocean Grove, N. J., July 4, 1911, news report, **23**:186-89, mentioned, 190
At the opening of the lift-bridge over Great Channel, Stone Harbor, N. J., July 5, 1911, news report, **23**:185-86, mentioned, 190
The Lawyer in Politics, to the Kentucky Bar Association in the Opera House, Lexington, July 12, 1911, text, **23**:194-99, mentioned, 190, 231
On behalf of commission government, High School auditorium, Jersey City, July 14, 1911, text, **23**:201-11

*Woodrow Wilson, Political, Religious, and Educational Addresses, cont.*

To Monmouth County Democrats at Asbury Park, July 18, 1911, news report, 23:219

On behalf of commission government in the High School auditorium, Passaic, N. J., July 21, 1911, news report, 23:222

Political talks on a visit to Cape May County, N. J., Aug. 14, 1911, news report, 23:272-75

To the Warren County farmers' picnic, Belvidere, N. J., Aug. 16, 1911, news report, 23:270-72

To farmers in Washington Park, near Gloucester City, N. J., Aug. 17, 1911, news report, 23:275-77

At the dedication of the synagogue of the Congregation Oheb Shalom, Newark, Sept. 7, 1911, transcript, 23:305-308

At a dinner of the Hotel Men's Association, Atlantic City, Sept. 12, 1911, news report, 23:315-16, mentioned, 313,n2

Welcoming remarks to the fourth annual conference of Governors of the States of the Union, Spring Lake, N. J., Sept. 12, 1911, news report, 23:317-19

———

*Primary campaign speeches (vol.* 23, *Sept. 18—Nov. 6, 1911)*

Opening the Democratic Primary Campaign, at Harburger's Hall and the First Troop Armory, Newark, Sept. 18, 1911, news report, 330-39, mentioned 341, 385, 388

In St. Patrick's Hall, Jersey City, Sept. 21, 1911, news report, 342-51

In Orange and Newark, Sept. 22, 1911, news report, 353-54

At the laying of the cornerstone of the Woodbury (N. J.) High School, Sept. 28, 1911, news report, 362-64

Three in Cape May County, N. J., Sept. 29, 1911, news report, 364-65

At Toms River and Lakewood, N. J., Sept. 30, 1911, news report, 380-81

Before a Sunday School rally in the Second Regiment Armory, Trenton, Oct. 1, 1911, news report, 372-80

In Salem County, N. J., Oct. 4, 1911, news report, 391-95

In Green's Opera House, Woodbury, N. J., Oct. 5, 1911, news report, 395-408.

Two in Camden, N. J., Oct. 6, 1911, news report, 409-11

In the Opera House, Flemington, N. J., Oct. 7, 1911, news report, 411-24

In Taylor Opera House, Trenton, Oct. 9, 1911, news report, 425-36

In New Brunswick and Perth Amboy, Oct. 10, 1911, news report, 437-42

*Woodrow Wilson, Political, Religious, and Educational Addresses, cont.*

Four in Monmouth County, N. J., Oct. 11, 1911, news report, 442-47

In Alexander Hall, Princeton University, Oct. 12, 1911, news report, 447-49

In Hackensack and Ridgewood, N. J., Oct. 13, 1911, news report, 449-51

In Morristown, Dover, and Madison, N. J., Oct. 14, 1911, news report, 451-53

In Paterson, N. J., Oct. 16, 1911, news report, 461-63

In Sussex County, N. J., Oct. 17, 1911, news report, 464-66

In Phillipsburg, N. J., Oct. 18, 1911, news report, 466-68

Eight in Union County, N. J., Oct. 19, 1911, news report, 468-69, mentioned, 476-78

In Somerset County, N. J., Oct. 20, 1911, news report, 470-76

On Community Centers delivered at the University of Wisconsin, Madison, Oct. 25, 1911, news report, 480-88

To the Democratic League of Wisconsin, at the University of Wisconsin, Oct. 26, 1911, news report, 488-94

Life and the Bible, at the First Baptist Church, Dallas, Texas, Oct. 28, 1911, news report, 494-99, mentioned, 506, 510-11

At the Texas State Fair, State Fair Coliseum, Dallas, Oct. 28, 1911, news report, 499-506, mentioned, 458, 515

At a luncheon at the Oriental Hotel, Dallas, Texas, Oct. 28, 1911, news report, 509-10

At the City Hall auditorium, Fort Worth, Texas, Oct. 28, 1911, news report, 511-12

At the railroad station, Little Rock, Ark., Oct. 30, 1911, news report, 517-18

At Glassboro, N. J. auditorium, Nov. 1, 1911, news report, 520-21

At Apollo Theatre, Atlantic City, N. J., Nov. 1, 1911, news report, 522-31

Four in South Jersey, Nov. 2, 1911, news report, 531-34

Three in Hudson County, Nov. 3, 1911, news report, 535-38

Three in Burlington County, N. J., Nov. 6, 1911, news report, 539-40

Two in Somerset County, N. J., Nov. 6, 1911, news report, 540-42

———

To University of Virginia Students, Woodrow Wilson Club and Jefferson Literary Society, Nov. 15, 1911, mentioned, 23:550

Memorial address at the Elks Lodge, Savoy Theatre, Asbury Park, Dec. 3, 1911, news report, 23:561-62

On the problems of Southern Develop-

*Woodrow Wilson, Political, Religious, and Educational Addresses, cont.*

ment, to the Maryland Week Celebration and Horticultural Exhibition, Regiment Armory, Baltimore, Dec. 5, 1911, news report, **23**:569-72

On behalf of commission government, under the auspices of the Women's Good Government Committee, Lyric Theatre, Baltimore, Dec. 5, 1911, news report, **23**:572-83

In protest of Russian discrimination against American Jews, delivered under the auspices of the National Citizen's Committee, Carnegie Hall, Manhattan, Dec. 6, 1911, ne⁻ ₃ report, **23**:583-87, mentioned, 588

On the tariff to the National Democratic Club of New York, Jan. 3, 1912, news report, **23**:637-50

Editors' method of correcting corrupt transcripts of WW speeches, **24**:xi

At a Jackson Day Dinner in Washington, Jan. 8, 1912, text, **24**:9-16, mentioned, 5-6, 43

To the National Press Club of Washington, Jan. 9, 1912, news report, **24**:16-17, mentioned, 7

Annual Message to the Legislature of New Jersey, Jan. 9, 1912, text, **24**:18-25, mentioned, 28

To the National League of Commission Merchants in New York, Jan. 11, 1912, text, **24**:32-40

To Businessmen in Detroit, Mich., Jan. 18, 1912, news report, **24**:47

Two in Detroit, Jan. 19, 1912, news reports, **24**:51-53

Two in Ann Arbor, Mich., Jan. 19, 1912, news report, **24**:53-58

To the Newark Board of Trade, Jan. 25, 1912, news report, **24**:67-68

To the Jersey City Board of Trade, Jan. 25, 1912, news report, **24**:68-70

To the Real Estate Men of Boston, Jan. 27, 1912, text, **24**:83-92, mentioned, 107, 126-27

To the General Assembly of Virginia and the City Council of Richmond, Feb. 1, 1912, text, **24**:101-17, mentioned, 133, 238n4, 339,n4

Three in Richmond, Feb. 2, 1912, news report, **24**:117-22

To the Periodical Publishers' Association of America in Philadelphia, Feb. 2, 1912, text, **24**:122-31; La Follette incident, 137,n2

In Allentown, Pa., Feb. 8, 1912, news report, **24**:138-40

Two in Frankfort, Ky., Feb. 9, 1912, news report, **24**:141-46, mentioned, 150-51

To Democrats on Lincoln's Birthday in Chicago, Feb. 12, 1912, text, **24**:151-62, mentioned, 151

*Woodrow Wilson, Political, Religious, and Educational Addresses, cont.*

Political speech in Concord, N. H., Feb. 16, 1912, news report, **24**:165-66

On Civil Service Reform in New Haven, Conn., Feb. 16, 1912, text, **24**:166-77

To the Sussex Society of New York, Feb. 19, 1912, news report, **24**:179-81

To the Universal Peace Union in Philadelphia, Feb. 19, 1912, news report, **24**:181-83

In Trenton, Feb. 20, 1912, news report, **24**:183-85

To the Kansas Democratic Club in Topeka, Feb. 23, 1912, news report, **24**:188-89, mentioned, 191

At a reception in Nashville, Feb. 24, 1912, news report, **24**:190-91

In Nashville, Feb. 24, 1912, text, **24**:191-205

On behalf of the Y.M.C.A. in Nashville, Feb. 24, 1912, text, **24**:206-16

Two in Des Moines, Iowa, March 2, 1912, news report, **24**:220-22

To the General Assembly of Maryland, March 7, 1912, text, **24**:227-36

To the Brooklyn League of Brooklyn, New York, March 10, 1912, news report, **24**:238

To the Friendly Sons of St. Patrick in Elizabeth, N. J., March 18, 1912, news report, **24**:251-52, mentioned, 250

To the Friendly Sons of St. Patrick of Montclair, New Jersey, March 18, 1912, news report, **24**:253, mentioned, 250

Three in Milwaukee, Wisc., March 24, 1912, news report, **24**:259-61

In Springfield, Ill., April 6, 1912, news report, **24**:292-98

To the University Club of Buffalo, N. Y., April 10, 1912, news report, **24**:309-10

In Buffalo, April 10, 1912, news report, **24**:311-14

In Pittsburgh, April 11, 1912, news report, **24**:316-20

In Atlanta, April 17, 1912, news report, **24**:335-44

In Georgia, April 18, 1912, news reports, **24**:344-47

In Jacksonville, Fla., April 19, 1912, news report, **24**:347-48

In Savannah, Ga., April 20, 1912, news report, **24**:349-51

To College Students in Macon, Ga., April 21, 1912, news report, **24**:354-55

In Macon, Ga., April 21, 1912, news report, **24**:355-56

In Paterson, N. J., April 24, 1912, news report, **24**:358-60

In Boston, April 27, 1912, news report, **24**:360-67

In Baltimore, April 30, 1912, news report, **24**:370-79, mentioned, 360n1

To the Methodist Social Union of New

*Woodrow Wilson, Political, Religious, and Educational Addresses, cont.*
York, May 2, 1912, news report, **24**:381
To New Jersey Wilson Men in Trenton, May 10, 1912, news report, **24**:389-90
To the Reform Club of New York, May 12, 1912, news report, **24**:394-95, mentioned, 391
To the Camden, N. J., Democratic Club, May 19, 1912, news report, **24**:407-408
In Burlington, N. J., May 21, 1912, news report, **24**:410-12
To the Economic Club of New York, May 23, 1912, text, **24**:413-28, mentioned, **24**:xi, xii-xiii, 439
In Jersey City, N. J., May 25, 1912, text, **24**:434-44
Welcome to the American Medical Association in Atlantic City, N. J., June 4, 1912, text, **24**:454-57
Editing WW's campaign speeches, **25**:viii-xiii; WW's manner of preparing and delivering speeches, **25**:111,n1, 493,n1
To Williams College Alumni at Delmonico's, New York City, Feb. 5, 1909, mentioned, **25**:50-51,n1

*Presidential campaign speeches (vol. 25, Aug. 7—Nov. 5, 1912)*
Accepting the Democratic nomination in Sea Girt, N. J., Aug. 7, 1912, text, 3-18, mentioned, ix, 50, 51
At a Farmers' Picnic at Washington Park, N. J., Aug. 15, 1912, text, 31-40
Jersey Day address at Sea Girt, N. J., Aug. 17, 1912, news report, 43-44
To Democratic Women at Sea Girt, Aug. 17, 1912, text, 44-45
At a German picnic at Schuetzen Park, Aug. 20, 1912, news report, 47-49
At a luncheon in Buffalo, N. Y., Sept. 2, 1912, text, 67-69
Labor Day address in Buffalo, N. Y., Sept. 2, 1912, text, 69-79, mentioned, 92, 114
Evening address in Buffalo, N. Y., Sept. 2, 1912, text, 80-92
To Editors of foreign-language newspapers in New York, Sept. 4, 1912, text, 94-97, mentioned, 108-109
At a Workingmen's Dinner in New York, Sept. 4, 1912, text, 98-106
To an Italian-American Delegation at Sea Girt, N. J., Sept. 5, 1912, text, 107-109
To the New York Press Club, Sept. 9, 1912, text, 118-28
To Spanish War Veterans in Atlantic City, Sept. 10, 1912, text, 129-32
To Democrats in Jersey City, Sept. 11, 1912, text, 136-37

*Woodrow Wilson, Political, Religious, and Educational Addresses, cont.*
On the tariff in Syracuse, N. Y., Sept. 12, 1912, text, 137-43
To New York State Democratic leaders in Syracuse, N. Y., Sept. 12, 1912, text, 143-46, mentioned, 146
To newspapermen on the train, Sept. 12, 1912, text, 146
From the rear platform in Union City, Ind., Sept. 16, 1912, text, 148
In Sioux City, Iowa, Sept. 17, 1912, text, 148-56, mentioned, 162, 282
From a rear platform in Elk Point, S. D., Sept. 17, 1912, text, 156-58
In Sioux Falls, S. D., Sept. 17, 1912, extracts, 158-61
From a rear platform in Hawarden, S. D., Sept. 17, 1912, text, 161
To the Commercial Club of Minneapolis, Sept. 18, 1912, text, 164-69
At the University of Minnesota, Sept. 18, 1912, text, 169-72
At the Parade Grounds in Minneapolis, Sept. 18, 1912, text, 173-84
In Michigan City, Ind., from a rear platform, Sept. 19, 1912, text, 184
Rear platform talk in Kalamazoo, Mich., Sept. 19, 1912, text, 185-86
In Detroit, Mich., Sept. 19, 1912, text, 186-98
To businessmen in Columbus, Ohio, Sept. 20, 1912, text, 198-203
Opening the Ohio campaign in Columbus, Sept. 20, 1912, text, 203-12
In Hoboken supporting William Hughes for Senator, Sept. 12, 1912, text, 213-20
In Scranton, Pa., Sept. 23, 1912, text, 221-31
On new issues in Hartford, Conn., Sept. 25, 1912, text, 234-45
Opening the Connecticut State Campaign in New Haven, Sept. 25, 1912, text, 245-57
To workingmen in Fall River, Mass., Sept. 26, 1912, text, 257-69
Tribute to William Frank McCombs at a dinner in New York given by the College Men's League, Sept. 28, 1912, text, 274-80, mentioned, 312
To the New Jersey Democratic Convention in Trenton, Oct. 1, 1912, text, 304-305
In Indianapolis on conservation, Oct. 3, 1912, text, 312-21
Proclaiming the New Freedom in Indianapolis, Oct. 3, 1912, text, 321-29
Portion of address in Kokomo, Ind., Oct. 4, 1912, text, 330-32
To workingmen in Peru, Ind., Oct. 4, 1912, text, 332-38
To the Women's Democratic Club in Omaha, Neb., Oct. 5, 1912, text, 339-40

*Woodrow Wilson, Political, Religious, and Educational Addresses, cont.*

Nonpartisan talk to the Commercial Club of Omaha, Oct. 5, 1912, text, 340-47

To Democratic Workers in Lincoln, Neb., Oct. 5, 1912, text, 347-49

In the Lincoln Auditorium, Neb., Oct. 5, 1912, text, 350-59

In the Opera House, Colorado Springs, Colo., Oct. 7, 1912, text, 362-68

Call in Denver for a "Second Emancipation," Denver Auditorium, Oct. 7, 1912, text, 369-77

In the Topeka Auditorium, Topeka, Kan., Oct. 8, 1912, text, 378-85

In Convention Hall, Kansas City, Mo., Oct. 8, 1912, text, 385-90

On the main issue of the campaign in Springfield, Ill., Oct. 9, 1912, text, 390-92

In the Coliseum in Springfield, Ill., Oct. 9, 1912, text, 393-95

To Democratic newspapermen in St. Louis, Oct. 9, 1912, text, 395-99

In Chicago, Oct. 10, 1912, text, 400-404

In Cleveland, Oct. 11, 1912, text, 404-13

Extract from speech in Georgetown, Del., Oct. 17, 1912, 424

Extract from speech in Dover, Del., Oct. 17, 1912, 424-25

In Wilmington, Del., Oct. 17, 1912, text, 425-32

Public letter to the voters, Oct. 19, 1912, text, 433-35

At Academy of Music in Brooklyn, Oct. 19, 1912, text, 435-40

In Carnegie Hall, Oct. 19, 1912, text, 441-47

Religious address at the Two Hundredth Anniversary of the First Presbyterian Church, Trenton, Oct. 23, 1912, text, 453-57

At West Chester, Pa., Oct. 28, 1912, text, 462-66

In Montclair, N. J., Oct. 29, 1912, text, 467-73

Two in Cape May County, N. J., Oct. 30, 1912, text, 474-85

In Burlington, N. J., Oct. 30, 1912, text, 485-92

In Madison Square Garden, Oct. 31, 1912, text, 493-501

Message to Democratic Rallies, Nov. 2, 1912, text, 501-504

Portion of speech in Long Branch, N. J., Nov. 2, 1912, 504-507

Statement to voters, Nov. 4, 1912, text, 511-12

Final speeches of campaign in Passaic and Paterson, Nov. 5, 1912, news report, 513-14

———

Remarks to Princeton students and

*Woodrow Wilson, Political, Religious, and Educational Addresses, cont.*

neighbors, Nov. 5, 1912, text, **25**:520-21

Statement after election, Nov. 6, 1912, news report, **25**:524

Remarks at the Dedication of Wilson Cottage at the N. J. State Home for Girls, Nov. 12, 1912, **25**:536-39

Remarks upon arriving in Bermuda, Nov. 18, 1912, **25**:551

Remarks to the Bermuda House of Assembly, Dec. 2, 1912, **25**:575

Statement to New Jersey Democrats, Dec. 17, 1912, text, **25**:590-91, news report, 591

To the New York Southern Society, Dec. 17, 1912, text, **25**:593-603, mentioned, 609

At Mary Baldwin Seminary, Dec. 28, 1912, **25**:626-32

At a Birthday Banquet in Staunton, Va., Dec. 28, 1912, text, **25**:632-40, mentioned, 647,n1

INTERVIEWS

**16**:113-19; **17**:444-45, 453, 472-73, 519,n3, 513-21, 524-27; **18**:3-5, 465-66, 467; **19**:110-11; **21**:6n2, 14-16, 17,n1, 31, 34, 35, 98-100, 120-28, 134-36, 179-81, 220-25, 477-85, 522-25; **22**:5-12, 216-23, 235-36, 312-16 (mentioned 186n1), 354-56, 554-56, 591-92; **23**:3-5, 60-63, 277-82, 292-300, 312-13, 366-72, 454-58, 607-29; **24**:74-78, 309-10, 368-70; **25**:451

WRITINGS

The College Course and Methods of Instruction (1903), text, **15**:79-98; mentioned, **16**:4n2

*Congressional Government* (1885), text, **4**:13-179; mentioned, **14**:125, 340; **16**:97, 374; **17**:262; **18**:477; **20**:313; **22**:138,n2; **23**:133

*Constitutional Government in the United States,* lectures delivered on the Blumenthal Foundation at Columbia University in March and April, 1907; published as book (1908), text, **18**:69-216; reviews: *Independent,* **18**:477-78; *Nation,* **18**:384; *Outlook,* **18**:446-48; mentioned, **22**:12n4; *see also* Woodrow Wilson, POLITICAL, RELIGIOUS, AND EDUCATIONAL ADDRESSES

The Country and the Colleges (earlier The Reorganization of our Colleges), unpublished essay written for *Scribner's Magazine,* outline, **19**:536-37,n1; text, **20**:157-72; mentioned, **19**:530; **20**:119,n1, 133,n6, 139, 148n, 177

A Credo, **17**:335-38

The Democratic Opportunity, article in

*Woodrow Wilson, Writings, cont.*
the *National Monthly*, Jan. 1910; text,
**19**:465-71; mentioned, **19**:464-65
*Division and Reunion, 1829-1889* (1893),
Editorial Note, **8**:141-48; mentioned,
**14**:281, 344, 352, 517
Education and Democracy (1907), an essay, text, **17**:131-36; mentioned, **16**:
281n1, 332n2, 337
*George Washington* (1897), *see* indexes of
volumes **9** and **10**; mentioned, **14**:
439n3, 445; **15**:213,n2; **17**:620,n3; **18**:
647; **19**:66; **21**:482
Grover Cleveland, Man of Integrity; article in *New York Times*, magazine
section, March 17, 1907; text, **17**:73-
78; mentioned, **17**:89
Hide-and-Seek Politics, article in *North
American Review*, May 1910; text,
**20**:192-207; mentioned, **20**:119,n1,
148n, 177, 180
*A History of the American People* (1902),
Editorial Note, **11**:360-65; mentioned,
**14**:3,n2, 42, 51,n1, 295, 328, 346-47,
364-65, 379-80, 387, 391, 551; **15**:56-
57, 155, 327-28, 345; **16**:94-95,n1, 144,
343, 387, 390, 405; **18**:638-39;
**19**:759,n2; **20**:558; **21**:228, 425, 541n2,
542; **23**:564-65, 650,n1; **24**:132,n3,
133-34, 134, 135, 136, 219, 223,n1,
226, 241-43, 260, 269,n1, 351n2,
383n1, 405; **25**:639; reviews: *American
Historical Review* (Frederick Jackson
Turner), **14**:516-19; *Annals of the
American Academy of Political and
Social Science* (Claude Halstead Van
Tyne), **14**:441-45; *Book Buyer* (George
McLean Harper), **14**:309-13; *Critic*
(George Louis Beer), **14**:338-46; *Dial*
(Francis Wayland Shepardson), **14**:
248-52; *Independent* (Charles McLean
Andrews), **14**:280-83,n1; *Nation* (Wil-
liam MacDonald), **14**:350-53; *New
York Times Saturday Review of Books
and Art* (Augustus C. Buell), **14**:286-
87; selling price, royalties, subscrip-
tion editions, etc., **14**:31,n2, 38, 141-
42, 439n3; illustrations, **14**:98, 108,
122, 231n3, 283, 312, 350, 352, 445,
516-17; *see also* the indexes for volumes **11** and **12**
Introduction to John Rogers Williams,
*The Handbook of Princeton* (1905),
text, **15**:427-31, mentioned, 436
A Lawyer with a Style [Sir Henry
Maine] (1898), text, **10**:443-61; mentioned, **17**:58,n1
Leaderless Government (1897), text,
**10**:288-304, mentioned, **14**:11,n4,5
Life and Education, *Nassau Literary
Magazine*, Oct. 1910, mentioned,
**21**:16,n3, 32-33
The Man Behind the Trusts, unpub-
lished article, **19**:324-27
*Mere Literature and Other Essays* (1896),

*Woodrow Wilson, Writings, cont.*
mentioned, **17**:488n2; **19**:356; *see* in-
dexes of volumes **9** and **10**
Message to a banquet of the Sons of
Delaware of Philadelphia at the
Bellevue-Stratford, Dec. 7, 1910, text,
**22**:148-49
Message to First Voters, text, **20**:502-
505, mentioned, 391,n3, 501,n5, 512
My Ideal of the True University, *The
Delineator*, Nov. 1909, text, **19**:295-
303
*The New Freedom* (1913), WW's
speeches during 1911 and 1912, cited,
**25**:609n1
The New Freedom, *World's Work* (1912),
mentioned, **25**:609n1, 640-41
New Plans for Princeton, article on the
Preceptorial System, *Harper's Weekly*,
June 24, 1905, text, **16**:146-49; mentioned, **17**:456,n3
An Old Master [Adam Smith] (1887),
text, **5**:444-55; mentioned, **14**:339n4
On the Writing of History (1895), later
published as The Truth of the Matter
(1896), text, **9**:293-305; mentioned,
**14**:444,n4; **17**:488n2
The Personal Factor in Education,
*Youth's Companion*, text, **17**:325-33;
mentioned, **16**:534,n1
The Philosophy of Politics (projected),
mentioned, **14**:190,n1
Politics (1857-1907), *Atlantic Monthly*,
text, **17**:309-25, mentioned, 122-23,n5,
334
The Princeton Preceptorial System,
*Independent*, Aug. 3, 1905, text, **16**:
107-109; mentioned, **17**:456,n1
Princeton's New Plan of Study, unpub-
lished reply to *Cosmopolitan* article of
Aug. 1904, text, **15**:450-60
Proposed Life of Thomas Jefferson, plans
accepted by Harper and Brothers,
**16**:343
Proposed volume of essays for Harper
and Brothers (1909), **19**:402; **21**:51,n1
The Reconstruction of the Southern
States (written 1900, published 1901),
text, **11**:459-79; mentioned, **14**:33,n3
Responsible Government under the
Constitution, *Atlantic Monthly*, April
1886, text, **5**:107-24; mentioned,
**23**:134,n1
The Southern Colonist, *Youth's Companion*, April 18, 1907, text, **17**:51-56;
mentioned, **16**:538,n1
*The State* (1889), mentioned, **15**:227,
426-27; revision of 1898 mentioned,
**14**:559,n2; **23**:440, 619
*The State* (1889); Spanish translation by
Adolfo Posada, *El estado: elementos de
politica histórea y practica . . .* with introduction by Oscar Browning, **14**:
356,n2,3
The Tariff Make-Believe, *North Ameri-*

*Woodrow Wilson, Writings, cont.*
can Review, Oct. 1909, text, **19**:359-80, mentioned, 191n2, 193, 358, 384
What Is a College For? *Scribner's Magazine*, Nov. 1909, text, **19**:334-47, mentioned, 348, 390,n2, 391, 503-504,n1,2; **20**:161,n1, 378,n1, 380
Tribute to Charles William Eliot, **18**: 528-29
When a Man Comes to Himself, *Century Magazine*, June 1901, text, **11**:263-73; mentioned, **14**:386; **16**:353-54,n2

PORTRAITS AND PHOTOGRAPHS

*illustrations appear in the center
section of each volume*

References to photographs, **14**:40,n2, 43, 56, 76
Two Purdy photographs, taken in August 1902, **14**; references, **14**:87-88, 93, 97, 101
On day of his inauguration, **14**
Speaking from steps of Nassau Hall after inaugural ceremony, **14**
Breaking ground for Seventy-Nine Hall, **14**
Drawing by George Timothy Tobin (1904), **15**; reference, **15**:223,n2
Oil portrait by Frederic Yates, **16**; references, **16**:437, 438, 441, 442, 449, 506, 541-42
Drawing by Frederic Yates (1906), **16**
In 1907, **17**
With James Bryce at the dedication of the Mather Sundial, **17**
With Mary Allen Peck at Shoreby, Paget West, Bermuda, **17**

*Woodrow Wilson, Portraits and Photographs, cont.*
Pastel portrait by Frederic Yates (1908), **18**; references, **18**:377, 378, 406,n2, 407, 410, 422, 448
In 1908, **19**
With family on terrace at Prospect, **19**
Walking on campus in academic garb, **20**
In 1910, **21**
With Vivian Murchison Lewis and John Franklin Fort, **21**
With Joseph Patrick Tumulty in the Inaugural Parade, **22**
At his desk in the New Jersey State House, **22**
Bust by Blanche Nevin (1911), **23**
With William Bayard Hale and Joseph Patrick Tumulty in the Governor's office, Trenton, **23**
With McKee Barclay and Frank Parker Stockbridge, **23**
In Denver hotel, **23**
With Rocky Mountain Princeton Club, Denver, **23**
In conference on porch at Sea Girt, **23**
Reviewing the New Jersey National Guard on horseback, **23**
Speaking at a political gathering, **23**
In Governor's office, Trenton, **24**
With William Frank McCombs, **24**
Greeting visitors at Sea Girt, N. J., **24**
Accepting the nomination at Sea Girt, **25**
With family on the porch at Sea Girt, **25**
Reception at Sea Girt, **25**
Talking to school children in Minneapolis, **25**
New Jersey Day at Sea Girt, **25**
On a carriage ride with Mrs. Wilson and Eleanor in Bermuda, **25**

*End of Woodrow Wilson entry*

Wilson and the Negro (*New York Age*), **24**:558n2
Wilson and the Preceptors (Root), **16**: 71n1
Wilson and Virginia's Bill of Rights (Richmond *Times-Dispatch*), **25**:647n1
Wilson Club proposed in Virginia, **23**: 138, 152
Wilson-Gorman tariff of 1894, **22**:113,n2, 173, 226n3, 282, 535n2
Wilson Honest and Truthful (Richmond *Times-Dispatch*), **24**:97,n2
Wilson Movement in Texas, 1910-1912 (Link), **22**:123n2; **23**:267n1; **24**:225n1
Wilson Mystery (*Boston Herald*), **24**: 559n1, 585,n1
*Wilson: The New Freedom* (Link), **25**: 566n1, 579n2, 587n3, 632n1
*Wilson: The Road to the White House* (Link), **16**:480n1; **17**:124n1; **20**:362n4, 564n3, 566n; **21**:91n1; **22**:262n2, 436n1, 447n5, 512n1, 575n2, 579n3,4;

**23**:262n3, 432n9, 544n1, 583n1, 591n1, 602n1, 603n1; **24**:5n2, 9n1, 42n2, 225n2, 248n1, 308n1, 400n2, 501n1, 524n3; **25**:23n2, 25n1, 96n2, 143n1, 284n4, 493n1, 520n1
Wilson whiskey, **21**:302,n1, 526,n1
Wilson's Nomination (New York *Evening Post*), **24**:538n1
Winans, Samuel Ross, **14**:34, 162-66, 258, 278-79, 326, 389-91, 394, 477-79, 486, 489; **15**:75; **16**:234, 301, 382; **17**:218-19, 408; **18**:582; **21**:30,n1, 151-52
Winans, Sarah E. Macdonald (Mrs. Samuel Ross), **16**:234; **21**:30, 31
Winchester, Caleb Thomas, **20**:184,n2; **22**:35,n1
Winchester, Hants, **15**:395, 396; Cathedral, **15**:396; Church of St. Cross, **15**:396; Winchester College, **15**:396
Windermere, Westmorland, **16**:444, 450; **18**:378, 381, 382, 383, 391, 416

Winnington-Ingram, Arthur Foley, **19:** 109

Winona, Minn., **21:**252,n7, 468; **25:** 380,n4, 409

Winslow, Erving, **20:**309,n1, 312; **24:** 224n3

Winslow, John Bradley, **22:**57

Winsor, Justin, **14:**342,n5, 443n3; **15:**482

Winsor, Robert, **21:**40n1

Winter, Anne McKinne (Mrs. George W.), **23:**556,n2

Winthrop, Alice Worthington (Mrs. William Woolsey), **14:**148,n2

Winthrop, Mary Jones Gelston (Mrs. Henry Rogers), **14:**290,n4

Winton, Henry D., **21:**142,n3, 446

Wisconsin, **22:**461, 485; **23:**320, 415; **24:**257-58, 258-59, 285,n1, 286, 488, 546; **25:**379, 429, 492; ballot system, **23:**455; Democratic League, **23:**254n3, 488; Democratic State Committee, **23:**259; Democrats, **23:**253-54, 259-60, 488f; political reforms, **23:**488, 493; public service commission, **21:**93; public-service corporations, **24:**427; **25:**431-32; railroad commission, **22:** 277; railroad law, **21:**141; Republicans, **23:**253, 540; **25:**247; WW addresses in Milwaukee, **24:**259-61

Wisconsin, University of, **14:**231; **15:** 100n3, 145, 375n2, 558; **16:**132, 161, 249, 252, 253, 465, 508, 539; **17:**208, 240,n2,3, 286, 551, 557; **18:**17, 577, 578; **19:**550, 676, 678, 706, 713; **24:**546,n1; **25:**276, 287, 546n1; *Bulletin*, **23:**488n; gymnasium, **23:**254, 480n1, 488n1

Wisconsin: The Utilitarian University (Corbin), **17:**240,n2

*Wisconsin Idea* (McCarthy), **24:**554n1

*Wisconsin State Journal* (Madison), **23:**494n

Wise, John Sergeant, **14:**298,n1; **16:** 292n1

Wise, Stephen Samuel, **22:**585,n1; **23:** 259,n5

Wishard, Luther Deloraine, **14:**265-66

Wissowa, Georg, **14:**245,n2

Wister, Owen, **14:**452,n3; **17:**130

witchcraft affair at Salem Village, **14:** 351

*With Congress and Cabinet* (Redfield), **23:**561n2

Witherspoon, John, **14:**185, 259, 307, 410, 411-12, 412, 414, 415, 416; **15:**111, 174, 429, 462n2; **16:**499, 500, 501; **17:**249, 352n2; **18:**633; **19:**202-10, 622; **21:**369; **23:**595; statue in Washington, **19:**64,n1,2,3

Witherspoon Memorial Association and Fund, **19:**64, 64n1, 239, 619, 622

*Witherspoon Memorial: Sketch of the Association and Unveiling of the Statue*, **19:**210n, 240,n3

Witte, Sergei Yulyevich, Count, **17:**159

Wittpenn, Henry Otto, **18:**487; **20:**576,n1,2; **21:**7, 8,n1, 16, 19, 37n1, 42, 42n1, 63, 90, 112, 155, 412, 434; **22:**173n1; **23:**201,n2, 536, 537; **24:**408, 436n5, 525; **25:**582, 584

Wooford College, **16:**255

Wohlgelernter, Maurice, **25:**105n5

Wolcott, Anna, **23:**21,n6

Wolfe, Albert Benedict, **16:**41,n5

Wolff, Frank J., **24:**257,n1

Wolsey, Thomas, **17:**87

woman suffrage, **18:**3-4; **22:**356; **23:**160; **24:**100, 140, 180, 307n4, 315; **25:**26, 29, 42,n1; **25:**438 Δ D. P. Buell, **23:**478n1; F.J.H. Harriman, **23:**261n1; W. F. McCombs, **23:**261; New Jersey Woman Suffrage Association, **22:**289-90; Oswald Garrison Villard, **25:**29

Woman Suffrage Party, **24:**100,n1

Woman's Christian Temperance Union of New Jersey, **23:**250

Woman's College of Baltimore, *see* Goucher College

Woman's Democratic Club of New York, **25:**617n3

woman's franchise, *see* woman suffrage

Woman's National Democratic Club, **25:**621,n1

*Woman's Hardy Garden* (Ely), **14:**520,n2

women, **22:**594, 596; **25:**44-45, 366, 339-40

Women's Wilson and Marshall League, **25:**527n2

Wood, Alicia Cox (Mrs. Charles), **20:** 29,n2

Wood, Charles, **14:**168n1, 409; **15:**99, 167, 437; **16:**225,n2, 277, 278; **17:**434, 441, 595, 596, 598; **19:**439, 711, 712, 729, 733, 753; **20:**4, 28-29, 245, 247, 357; **25:**544

Wood, Charles Erskine Scott, **23:**65,n1; **25:**645,n4

Wood, Dr. (physician for S. Axson), **14:**438

Wood, Leonard, **14:**381; **19:**552; **22:**396n1

Wood, Robert N., **24:**556,n2

Woodbridge, Jeanie Woodrow (Mrs. Samuel Isett), first cousin of WW, **14:**76,n3

Woodburn House, **24:**150,n1

Woodbury, N. J., **23:**409; Board of Education, **23:**364; City Council, **23:**364; Green's Opera House, **23:**395n1; High School, **23:**362-64, 396; Loyal Order of Moose band, **23:**364; WW speeches, **21:**245-59, 243; **23:**395-408

Woodhull, Alfred Alexander, M.D., **14:**99,n1, 349; **15:**156

Woodhull, Margaret Ellicott (Mrs. Alfred Alexander), **15:**156

Woodhull, Josiah Townsend, Jr., **21:**16-17,n1

Woodroe, Mrs. (of West Virginia), **21:**107

Woodrow, Felexiana Shepherd Baker (Mrs. James), **21:**581,n2; **22:**576,n2, 577; **23:**113,n1; **25:**536, 540-41

Woodrow, Fitz William McMaster, **25:** 519,n3, 540

Woodrow, Harriet ("Hattie") Augusta, (afterwards Mrs. Edward Freeman Welles), **25:**627n2,3

Woodrow, Helen Sill (Mrs. Thomas, Jr.), **14:**425; **15:**444n1; **23:**12,n2

Woodrow, Herbert Hollingsworth, cousin of WW, **14:**425; **15:**444,n1

Woodrow, James, maternal uncle of WW, **14:**335-36; **17:**17,n10; **18:**32-33,n8, 363; **21:**581, 581n1; **22:**507, 576n2; **23:**114

Woodrow, James II (Princeton 1909), **14:**336n; **25:**518, 519, 539

Woodrow, James Hamilton, first cousin of WW, **25:**519n2

Woodrow, James Wilson, **17:**5n11; **18:**520n3; **23:**12,n4

Woodrow, Jeanie Wilson, first cousin of WW, **25:**627n2

Woodrow, Katherine McGregor McMaster (Mrs. James Hamilton), **25:**519n2

Woodrow, Marion Woodville, **21:**581,n1; **25:**627n2

Woodrow, Nancy Mann Waddel (Mrs. James Wilson), **17:**5,n11; **18:**520,-n1,2,3; **23:**12n4

Woodrow, Thomas, Jr., maternal uncle of WW, **14:**29, 425; **15:**444n1

Woodrow, Thomas Robert, first cousin of WW, **14:**425; **23:**12n4, 28

Woodrow, Wilson, Mrs., *see* Woodrow, Nancy Mann Waddel

*Woodrow Wilson* (White), **20:**566n

*Woodrow Wilson, A Character Sketch* (Ford), **23:**10,n4

*Woodrow Wilson, A Character Study* (Annin), **15:**503n1

*Woodrow Wilson: Life and Letters* (Baker), **16:**304n1; **19:**475n3; **20:**566n; **22:**412n2; **23:**55n1

*Woodrow Wilson: Political Leader* (Hendrick), **22:**81n1, 142n1, 504n1; **23:**303n3

*Woodrow Wilson: Possible President* (Hale), **22:**414n3; **23:**200n1, 655

*Woodrow Wilson, Presidential Possibility* (MacCosson), **23:**366-72

*Woodrow Wilson, Reform Governor: A Documentary Narrative* (ed. Hirst), **20:**541n1

*Woodrow Wilson: Some Princeton Memories* (ed. Myers), **16:**37n, 71n1, 308,n1; **17:**437n1; **18:**294n1

*Woodrow Wilson: The Academic Years* (Bragdon), **15:**288n15; **16:**481n1; **17:**85n2

*Woodrow Wilson: The Story of His Life* (Hale), **20:**565n4; **22:**142n1, 414n1; **24:**380,n1

Woodrow Wilson and the New Jersey Governorship, *Review of Reviews*, Nov. 1910, **22:**139,n2

*Woodrow Wilson and New Jersey Made Over* (Hosford), **24:**523n2

Woodrow Wilson and Virginia (Richmond *Times-Dispatch*), **23:**601n1

*Woodrow Wilson as I Know Him* (Tumulty), **22:**81n1, 142n1; **24:**524n3

*Woodrow Wilson at Princeton* (Craig), **14:**46n2

Woodrow Wilson Club of Princeton University, **25:**273

Woodrow Wilson College Men's League, **25:**274n1

Woodrow Wilson Democratic Association, **22:**213

Woodrow Wilson Foundation, **16:**138

*Woodrow Wilson on Efficiency . . . January 27, 1912* (pamphlet), **24:**92n

*Woodrow Wilson Places Human Rights Above Property Rights* (campaign pamphlet), **25:**543n2

Woodrow Wilson Plan (*Chicago Evening Post*), **17:**496,n1

Woodrow Wilson—The Man (Malone), **25:**272,n4

Woodrow Wilson Working Men's League, **25:**98n1

Woodrow Wilson's Ideas of the Presidency (Garner), **25:**617n1

Woodrow Wilson's Neurological Illness (Weinstein), **16:**412n1

Woodrow Wilson's Weakness (New York *World*), **24:**96

Woodruff, Clinton Rogers, **19:**156,n2, 157, 307

Woodruff, Edward N., **24:**291,n2

Woodruff, John, Mrs., **22:**415n

Woodruff, Timothy Lester, **19:**500,n4; **22:**429

Woods, Charles Albert, **18:**345,n4, 350; **21:**128,n1

Woods, Edward Augustus, **15:**391-92, 461n1; **16:**404,n2; **17:**361,n2; **19:**66, 401,n1

Woods, Ellen Cornelia Crane (Mrs. George), **17:**211,n2

Woods, George Jedediah, **23:**95,n1, 96, 99

Woods, Gertrude Macrum (Mrs. Edward Augustus), **15:**461,n1; **19:**401,n1

Woods, Hiram, M.D., **15:**361; **19:**252; **20:**50, 247, 264-69, 285-86, 402,n3, 478-79, 482-83; **21:**555-56, 599; **22:**158, 175, 177; **23:**568; **25:**553

Woods, Laura Hall (Mrs. Hiram), **21:**556; **22:**177,n2

Woods, Lawrence Crane, **16:**404,n1; **17:** 211-12, 360-61, 378-79, 384-85, 452-53, 456-57, 603, 616-18; **19:**230, 239, 264, 266, 396, 401; **20:**50-51, 53, 81, 376, 387-89, 391-92, 404; **21:**157-58, 385n1, 444

Woods, Neander Montgomery, 17:154
Woods, Rebekah Campbell (Mrs. Lawrence Crane), 17:361
Woods, Sally Wannamaker (Mrs. Charles Albert), 18:350; 21:128,n2
Woods Hole, Mass., Marine Biological Laboratory, 16:249
Woodstown, N. J., Baptist Church, 23:394
Woodward, Comer Vann, 19:10n2
Woodward, Truman Stephen, 14:215,n5, 216, 217, 218, 221; 16:11,n2
wool schedule, see tariff, Schedule K
wollen industry, 25:243,n6, 335-36
Wooley, J. W., 22:39,n18
Woolley, Mary Emma, 14:191; 19:405n2
Woolley, Robert Wickliffe, 25:612,n2
Woolverton, Frederick Tappen, 20:27,n3
Woolverton, Mary Chichester (Mrs. Samuel), 20:27,n2
Woolverton, Maurice, 20:27,n3
Woolverton, Samuel, 20:27,n1
Woonsocket, R. I., 19:324
Worcester, Joseph Emerson, 16:510,n5
Worcester's Academic Dictionary, 16:510,n5
Wordsworth, Adelaide Troutbeck (Mrs. Henry Curwen), 16:431n1, 493; 18:366,n9, 368,n4,5, 376
Wordsworth, Dorothy, 18:369,n2
Wordsworth, Gordon Graham, 18:370,n4
Wordsworth, Henry Curwen, 16:431n1, 493
Wordsworth, John (d. 1805), 18:369
Wordsworth, John (1805-1839), 18:368, 369,n1
Wordsworth, John Fisher Jones, 16:493n1; 18:366n10, 369,n3
Wordsworth, Violet Wordsworth (Mrs. John Fisher Jones), 16:493,n1; 18:366,n10, 369,n3,4
Wordsworth, William (1770-1850), 14:224,n1, 503, 521,n2; 16:378,n2, 431n1, 493; 17:192-93; 18:368, 369, 370n4, 371, 371n6, 415,n4; 19:573; 22:117n1, 408; 24:524, 541
Wordsworth, William (son of John), 18:368, 369, 370n4
Workingmen, Read and Reflect!, 21:335n2
Working Men's League, see Woodrow Wilson Working Men's League
workmen's compensation, 22:347, 462f; 23:322-24,n1; see also New Jersey: employer's liability and working men's compensation act
Works of William H. Prescott, 14:134, 135,n1
World Missionary Conference, Edinburgh, 1910, 22:385,n2
World Peace Foundation, 22:131n3; 25:19n1,4
World Series (1912), 25:390,n3

World Today, 17:451
World's Columbian Exposition, Chicago, 16:508
World's Fair, see Louisiana Purchase Exposition, St. Louis, 1904
World's Student Christian Federation, 19:109, 152
World's Work, 14:62n1, 63-64, 65, 76, 83, 93; 17:449,n1, 450n1; 18:259, 469, 469n2, 576; 21:6n2; 22:414,n1,3, 439, 509, 520, 526; 23:234,n4, 655n3; 24:28,n2, 237n1; 25:448n1, 609n1, 640
Worrell, Shinn & Co., 16:185
Wraxall, Peter, 16:42n1
Wright, Carroll Davidson, 19:240,n3
Wright, Charles Baker, 14:125,n1
Wright, Chester Whitney, 16:372,n2, 376
Wright, Edward Henry (Princeton 1844), 16:547
Wright, Edward Henry, Jr. (Princeton 1894), 16:547, 551-52
Wright, Helen Kirk (Mrs. Henry Brooke Hagstromer), 20:150,n3, 151, 177, 179, 180, 181; 22:500,n2
Wright, Henry Brooke Hagstromer, 20:177, 179, 180, 181; 22:500,n2
Wright, Henry Collier, 19:155
Wright, Henry Parks, 17:587,n2
Wright, Jacob Ridgway, 15:471
Wright, John Henry, 17:588,n4
Wright, Julius Tutwiler, 15:395,n1, 402-403
Wright, Luke Edward, 17:474,n2
Wright, Thomas R., M.D., 23:553
Wrinch, Frank Sidney, 14:145,n8
Writings of Thomas Jefferson (ed. Lipscomb and Bugh), 14:360n1
Wu T'ing-fang, 19:23,n1,2, 31
Württemberg, Paul, Prince of, 16:144
Wyckoff, James Edwards, 18:300
Wyckoff, Leah Lucile Ehrich (Mrs. Walter Augustus), 14:488,n2
Wyckoff, Walter Augustus, 14:325, 394, 456-57,n1,3,4, 474, 488,n2; 16:197, 208; 17:284, 291, 408; 18:300,n2, 310, 311, 570, 577
Wyeth, Florence Nightingale Sims (Mrs. John Allan), 17:66,n1, 220, 347
Wyeth, John Allan, M.D., 17:40-41,n1, 65, 66, 93, 99, 215-16, 220, 335n1, 347; 18:532; 22:202
Wyeth, Marion Sims, 17:216,n2
Wylly, Albert, 23:558,n10
Wyllys, Rufus Kay, 22:291n2
Wyman, Isaac, 20:465-66
Wyman, Isaac Chauncey, 14:67,n1, 70; 19:225,n1; 20:464,n2, 465, 467, 469, 472, 476, 477, 480, 482, 484, 491, 494, 502, 507, 510, 512-13, 530, 532, 542, 561, 573; 21:12
Wymore City, Neb., 23:116,n3, 609; 25:333,n3

Wyncote, Pa., **23**:103
Wyndham, Sir Charles, **15**:396,n3
Wynne, John Joseph, **21**:612,n1
Wynne, Richard Moore, **23**:268,n5, 512
Wynne, Robert John, **16**:434,n1
Wynne, Thomas H., **17**:620,n2
Wyoming, University of, **19**:676
Wythburn, Cumberland, Wilsons at, **14**:522

Yacht Club, Bermuda, **17**:4,n9
*Yale*, S.S., **23**:41,n6
*Yale Alumni Weekly*, **18**:59n; **19**:728n1
*Yale College: An Educational History, 1871-1921* (Pierson), **15**:292n29; **19**: 728n1
*Yale Daily News*, **14**:388; **15**:200
Yale Lectures on the Responsibilities of Citizenship, **14**:135-37, 138
*Yale Review*, **18**:575
Yale University, **14**:135-37, 138, 157, 266; **15**:65, 100n3, 234; **16**:46, 71n1, 132, 250, 251, 253, 255, 256, 272n1, 306, 315, 488,n3, 509, 511; **17**:113, 114, 122, 127-28, 136, 230, 244, 245, 296, 412, 555, 556, 557, 587-88, 601; **18**:27, 68, 230, 246, 297n1, 298, 575, 578, 579; **19**:7n4, 71, 109, 122, 138, 152, 264n1, 266, 453, 480, 541, 556, 557, 603, 625n1, 627, 672, 699, 700, 704, 705, 728,n1; **20**:65,n2, 72, 75, 293, 294, 341, 436, 487, 488, 533, 539, 540; **21**:167, 259, 438; **23**:57n5; alumni dinner, **14**:295; architecture students, **17**:20; baseball games with Princeton, **14**:386, 489,n1; **15**:22,n4; **16**:419; **17**:216,n1; **18**:310,n2; **19**:195; **20**:519n; bicentennial, 1901, **14**:191; corporation, **19**:708; **20**:488; debates with Princeton University, **15**:164,n1, 207, 215; **17**:564,n1; Dept. of Education, **23**:103; Divinity School, **21**:4n2; faculty compared with Princeton's, **14**: 121, 154; football games with Princeton, **15**:102,n1, 508,n3; **17**:491,-n2; **18**:406; **20**:547; **21**:556,n4; **22**:3-4,n1; **23**:554,n7; Hillhouse property, **19**:728,n1; Phi Beta Kappa address by WW, 1908, **18**:53-59, 63, 68; Responsibility of Citizenship, lecture series, **22**:184, 187; School of Forestry, **22**:144,n3; Scroll and Key, **14**:480; Sheffield Scientific School, **16**:389; **17**:582n3; **19**:728n1; Skull and Bones, **14**:480; Storrs (William Lucius) Lectures, **21**:386,n2; Wolf's Head, **14**:480
Yancey (Univ. of Virginia coach), **23**:550
Yancey, William Lowndes, **19**:207
Yates, Emily Chapman Martin (Mrs. Frederic), **16**:437, 440, 441, 469-70, 481-82; **17**:242, 290, 365; **18**:312,n2, 361, 364, 365, 368, 369, 370, 374, 375,

377, 378, 379n8, 380, 385, 387, 389, 390, 391, 407, 411, 416, 422; **21**:59,n2, 619; **22**:235,n2
Yates, Frederic, **16**:437,n1, 438, 440, 441, 442, 449, 450, 451, 455, 469-70, 479-80, 481-82, 485-86, 506, 542; **17**:242-43, 290, 365; **18**:312-13, 361, 364, 365, 368, 369, 370, 374, 375, 377, 378, 382, 383, 385, 387, 389, 390, 393, 402, 404, 406, 406n2, 407, 410, 411, 413, 415, 416, 417, 422, 448; **19**: 465n2; **21**:59, 87, 619; **22**:187, 234-35; **24**:524,n5
Yates, Mary, **16**:437,n2,3, 438, 440, 441, 480, 486; **17**:242; **18**:365,n4, 370, 377, 378, 379, 389, 390, 391, 413, 422; **21**:59,n2; **25**:25n2; diary quoted, **18**:386-87
Yeomans, George Green, **14**:187; **21**: 611-12
Yereance, James, **14**:253
Yoakum, Benjamin Franklin, **22**:40,n27, 466,n5
York, England, Cathedral, **14**:551; **15**: 334; Harken's Hotel, **14**:525; Merchants Hall, **14**:525; St. Denis Church, **14**:525; York Minster, **14**:525; EAW in, **16**:438, 439; Wilsons in, **14**:525, 551
Yorkville Casino (NYC), **25**:98n1
Young, Charles Augustus, **14**:326, 395, 558; **15**:56, 73n3, 74, 553, 571-72; **16**:81, 102, 103, 194, 245-46, 419, 488, 489,n5, 518n6; **18**:570, 571; **19**:732
Young, Eugenia, **15**:347,n1
Young, George Washington, **22**:39,n19
Young, James Thomas, **17**:555,n1
Young, John Wesley, **16**:152, 160, 162, 179, 198, 259; **17**:408
Young, John Clarke, **15**:348n1, 356
Young, Lawrence, **15**:385,n2
Young, Mrs. Lawrence, **15**:385,n2
Young, Mr. and Mrs. (from Bermuda), **25**:556
Young, Sara Lee, **15**:347,n1
Young England party, **14**:555
Young Men's Christian Association, **14**:265-67, 354-55, 447, 448, 450-51, 452; **16**:193,n3, 195, 227, 228, 229; **18**:291, 313, 521, 545, 612; **23**:113-14; **24**:206-16; in China, **24**:208-209; intercollegiate, **19**:151,n1,2
Young Men's Woodrow Wilson Democratic Association, **22**:213
*Young People and the Church* (Wilson), **15**:519n
Youngstown, Ohio, First Presbyterian Church, **16**:332; People's Institute, **16**:332,n1; Rayen School, **16**:333,n3, 354; *Rayen Record*, **16**:355n; WW addresses, **16**:332-33, 354-55
*Youngstown Vindicator*, **16**:333n
*Youth's Companion*, **16**:496, 505, 538; **17**:56n, 333n; **22**:406,n1

Zangwill, Israel, **25:**105,n4,5
Zapf, William C. C., **17:**351n2, 352
Zeiger, Franklin, **18:**563-64,n1, 590-91, 612-13
Zeiss, Harold, **17:**233-34
Ziegler, Jesse Reinhart, **24:**141,n1

Zimmerman, Charles Fishburn, **15:**412-13,n1
Zionism, **25:**105,n5
Zornow, William Frank, **25:**621n2
Zürich, University of, **16:**507